CHINA AND JAPAN

CHINA AND JAPAN

Facing History

EZRA F. VOGEL

The Belknap Press of Harvard University Press

CAMBRIDGE, MASSACHUSETTS

LONDON, ENGLAND

2019

Library of Congress Cataloging-in-Publication Data
Names: Vogel, Ezra F., author.
Title: China and Japan : facing history / Ezra F. Vogel.
Description: Cambridge, Massachusetts : The Belknap Press of Harvard University
Press, 2019. | Includes bibliographical references and index.
Identifiers: LCCN 2018053335 | ISBN 9780674916579 (alk. paper)
Subjects: LCSH: China—Relations—Japan. | Japan—Relations—China. |
China—Foreign relations—Japan. | Japan—Foreign relations—China. |
China—Civilization—Japanese influences. | Japan—Civilization—
Chinese influences.
Classification: LCC DS740.5.J3 V59 2019 | DDC 327.51052—dc23
LC record available at https://lccn.loc.gov/2018053335

Contents

Preface

If the relationship between China and the United States, the world's two largest economies, is the most important relationship in the world, then arguably the second most important relationship is that between China, which is about to become the world's largest economy, and its neighbor, Japan, the third largest economy. China's biggest trading partner is the United States, and its second biggest trading partner is Japan. Japan's largest trading partner is China.

The relationship between China and Japan is tense, dangerous, deep, and complicated. Ships and planes from the two countries confront each other regularly over the Senkaku / Diaoyu Islands, which Japan administers but China claims as its territory, and the risk of dangerous incidents is high. After incidents that occurred in 2010 and 2012, fewer than 10 percent of the Chinese polled expressed positive feelings toward Japan and fewer than 10 percent of the Japanese expressed positive feelings toward China. In China, emotions about Japan run high enough that officials can easily mobilize the Chinese public to join anti-Japanese demonstrations and protests, as witnessed in recent years when protesters, roused by anti-Japanese sentiment in the media, have thrown rocks at the Japanese ambassador's residence and at Japanese stores in China. Fewer Japanese tourists travel to China now than some years ago, and Japanese citizens living and working in China have sometimes tried to disguise their nationality.

If the Sino-Japanese relationship is mishandled, it could lead to vast military spending by both nations, frustrate cooperation on bilateral, regional, and global issues, and even descend into conflict. If handled well, the two countries could cooperate in preserving the international order and supporting regional organizations that provide a framework for collaboration in trade, construction, scientific research, peacekeeping, and responding to natural disasters.

Leaders of both countries have said that for relations to improve, the other side must deal properly with history. No countries can compare with China and Japan in terms of the length of their historical contact: 1,500 years. Given the depth of emotion among the Chinese and Japanese people concerning their past, it would be impossible for them to gain a balanced perspective without discussing history.

Japanese and Chinese scholars have a much deeper understanding of their own history than we foreigners can match. Unfortunately, when scholars from China and Japan come together to try to resolve differences, the meetings result in renewed tensions and a lack of agreement on important issues. Outsiders can potentially contribute to their mutual understanding by examining the history with more objectivity and balance. The Chinese have a saying, "Bystanders can be clearer" (*pangguanzhe qing*), and the Japanese have made this expression into a Japanese saying as well.

I see myself as a friend of both China and Japan. I undertook this study as a bystander sympathetic to both countries, which I have been studying for more than half a century. I want both countries to succeed. Therefore, in this book I attempt to the best of my ability to provide an objective understanding of the history of relations between the two countries, in the hope that it will help them improve their relations with each other. I see my mission as seeking truth from facts, not slanting the truth toward the interests of any one country, including my own.

Throughout my career, I saw it as my responsibility to convey the results of my research on China and Japan to an audience of Americans and other Westerners who want to understand those two countries. While writing this book, however, I was thinking about how I might reach audiences not only in the West but also in China and Japan. I am aware that many Chinese and Japanese people who dislike the other country will not be interested in reading a book on Sino-Japanese relations written by a Westerner, no matter how accurate the book might be. However, I have written this book for those in China and Japan who do seek, as I do, to achieve an objective understanding of the other country. I feel a responsibility as a bystander who can potentially reach audiences in both countries. I have had the unique good fortune of having the Japanese translation of my book *Japan as Number One* become a bestseller in Japan, and my book *Deng Xiaoping and the Transformation of China*, in Chinese translation, become a bestseller in China. As a friend of both China and Japan, I fervently hope the two countries can improve their ability to work together for their common interests. I believe their cooperation is also in the interest of the rest of the world.

I have no training as a professional historian. I am a sociologist who until now has focused on the broad features of contemporary society. In this book, I write as a historical sociologist, following the perspective of my teacher (and later my senior colleague) Talcott Parsons. A leading specialist on Max Weber, Parsons analyzed societies in terms of their basic political, economic, and social structures and their underlying values. My interest in using a broad sociological framework to analyze the history of national societies dates back to my graduate-student days before I became an Asia specialist, when I benefited from the teaching of Parsons and from discussions in the circle of graduate students gathered around him, including Bob Bellah, Cliff Geertz, Chuck Tilly, Jesse Pitts, Norman Bell, Ed Tiryakian, and Bob LeVine. We were all passionately absorbed in an effort to understand the broad structural features and values of national societies.

I have organized this book sequentially, covering the 1,500 years of recorded contacts between China and Japan. Throughout, in addition to relating the most important events, I have endeavored to consider the larger social structures of China and Japan and the structure of their relationship.

The history of Sino-Japanese relations was shaped not only by broad forces but also by individual people. For recent centuries, when more biographical information is available, I also include brief biographies of some of the main individuals involved; these are found in the Biographies of Key Figures section. My purpose is to understand what drove them, how they related to the other country, and what impact they had on history.

I am unable to read original documents in classical Chinese or classical Japanese. The task of reading all the relevant original documents to cover such a vast period is beyond my ability, and perhaps beyond the ability of any single scholar or any small group of scholars. I do read modern Chinese and Japanese. In preparation for this book I spent years reading works on the history of relations between China and Japan by Western, Japanese, and Chinese scholars. There are many outstanding books by dedicated scholars of great ability from China, Japan, and the West who have studied the interactions between China and Japan throughout history. I also had the opportunity to speak with many of the authors. I am deeply indebted to all of the scholars who made it possible for me to attempt to write this historical overview. For each chapter, I include at the back of the book a section on "Sources and Further Reading."

To make this book accessible to general readers, I have minimized the use of notes. I have also simplified transliterations. I do not use macrons in Japanese terms, but for scholars seeking to use the sources, I use them in the notes. For Chinese names, I use the most widely accepted transliterations for the names of familiar figures, such as Chiang Kai-shek, Chiang Ching-kuo, and Sun Yat-sen; otherwise I use pinyin, following the current mainland usage. For Chinese cities, I use their current names throughout, with one exception. I refer to Beijing, the "Northern Capital," as Beiping when it was not the capital, to make it clear when it was and when it was not the capital city. I use the name Guangzhou even in the era when it was known as Canton, and I use Shenyang rather than Mukden (the city's Manchu name), Hoten (its Japanese name), or Fengtian. I present Chinese and Japanese personal names in their original order, surnames first.

Two chapters were written jointly with friends, Paula Harrell and Rick Dyck, who were extraordinarily generous with their time, expertise, and contributions. Harrell, who studies late nineteenth- and early twentieth-century Sino-Japanese relations using both Chinese and Japanese sources, has written outstanding books on exchanges between China and Japan after the Sino-Japanese War of 1894–1895. Dyck, who received his Ph.D. from Harvard, has spent more than four decades living in Japan, where he is an exceptional scholar as well as a successful businessman.

In this book, I pay special attention to the three periods when one country was engaged in deep learning from the other: from 600 to 838, when Japan was learning the basics of Chinese civilization, and two later periods, 1895 to 1937 and 1972 to 1992, when China was learning from Japan. I have arranged the chapters chronologically with the exception of Chapters 5 through 7, which address different aspects of the period from 1895 and 1937, when important developments—China's learning from Japan, Japanese colonialism, and the politics that led to war—were so diverse that I chose to cover them in three separate chapters. Since my goal is to understand contemporary East Asia, I have written about the past 200 years in more detail than earlier centuries. Chapters 1 and 2, however, trace the relations between the two countries across more than 1,200 years, from 600 to 1862. In those initial chapters I have tried to provide an overview while also focusing on issues that are particularly crucial for understanding current Sino-Japanese relations.

CHINA AND JAPAN

CHAPTER ONE

Chinese Contributions to Japanese Civilization, 600–838

AFTER EMPRESS SUIKO, at age thirty-nine, became sovereign of the Yamato clan in Japan in 593, to expand her control over a broader geographical area she sought to import features of the more advanced Chinese civilization that had enabled China's leaders to govern far larger areas than those that she controlled.[1] In 589, four years before Empress Suiko rose to power, Emperor Wen Di of China had united a substantial part of China for the first time in several centuries and had established the Sui dynasty. To maintain peaceful relations beyond the borders that he governed, Emperor Wen Di revived the practice of meeting with representatives of foreign groups and spreading Buddhism in territories that were part of what are today Korea and Japan. The Yamato clan sent its first mission to China in 600, and it continued studying and learning from China until 838, when it sent its last diplomatic mission. Japan's missions to China began because of the fortuitous timing and complementary perspectives of these two leaders, Empress Suiko, who sought to learn from China, and Emperor Wen Di, who welcomed the establishment of formal relations with territories that later would become part of Japan.

During this period, the Japanese mastered a written language, Chinese characters, that allowed officials to communicate over a broader geographical distance and to provide greater consistency in contacts among the highest officials in the capital and officials who served elsewhere. Japan developed standardized rules to clarify what local officials were expected to do and a specialized administrative staff to manage a larger and more complex organization. The Japanese learned how to write histories of former rulers to support the legitimacy of the current ones. They also learned about Buddhism, and strengthened the legitimacy of their rulers by linking them with the natural order. They learned how to plan large communities in a systematic way and how to build large Buddhist temples. Furthermore, they imported Confucianism, which reinforced the importance of the loyalty of the subjects to their leaders and emphasized the rules of propriety to maintain a stable organization. They developed new art techniques and poetry styles after studying Chinese culture, and they imported musical instruments. Of course, the Japanese adapted all that they learned to their own needs and tastes.

The Chinese were receptive to teaching others about their civilization, for they were fully confident of their superiority, both culturally and militarily, and they had no fear that ethnic groups outside China's borders might overtake them. Teaching other ethnic groups about their civilization was indeed a conscious part of China's political strategy.

The structure of Yamato that Empress Suiko had inherited was essentially a federation of clans, with one being first among others. Empress Suiko's mother was a member of the Soga clan (*uji*), which was attempting to provide overall leadership for the Yamato administration by controlling an unwieldy group of some thirty other clans, each of which had acquired official recognition in the form of a title (*kabane*) awarded by the leader of the dominant clan at the time.[2] When Suiko assumed office, one clan, the imperial clan—theoretically descended from the sun goddess, Amaterasu Omikami, and the first emperor on earth, Jimmu Tenno—was competing with the Soga clan for dominance among the others, for the emperor or empress was not necessarily chosen from the imperial clan. The Soga clan had risen to power because, as the clan responsible for imports and exports, it had earned more funds and thus had some leverage over the others. Other clans had received their titles because they had been able to supply one or more wives to the imperial males, thus making them in-laws of the imperial clan. In the fourth, fifth, and sixth centuries, titles were also given to individuals who performed special functions for the Yamato government, such as managing court rituals, building and storing armaments, taking care of irrigation, or raising horses. Such individuals were then allowed to pass their titles on to their descendants, who continued to perform those functions. Clans that had a specific responsibility were known as *be*, and their rankings, as reflected in their titles, were not as high as those of the Soga or imperial clan. One such *be* that was particularly difficult for the Soga clan to control was the Monono *be*, which, because it was responsible for producing and maintaining armaments, had access to weapons.

Empress Suiko appointed her nephew, posthumously known as Prince Shotoku, as regent.[3] Prince Shotoku, like his aunt, had taken an early interest in Buddhism, even before he became regent. Empress Suiko and Prince Shotoku worked together closely and were successful in using what they learned from China to strengthen their control over the other clans. Prince Shotoku also took an active role in promoting relations with the Sui dynasty in China and with the Paekche kingdom, which controlled the southwestern part of the Korean Peninsula.

When Suiko was enthroned as sovereign it was difficult for any clan to exercise complete control over all the other clans, some of which were large and spread-out geographically. The main issue for Empress Suiko and the Soga clan was to maintain control over the *be*, as well as other clans that had been given titles, while devising a new system of centralized administrative appointments to create a more effective overall structure.

The power of the Soga was contested by other clans, but in general Empress Suiko and the Soga clan were able to achieve more centralized control than their predecessors. The period during which Empress Suiko held power in Japan is known as the period of the Asuka enlightenment. The Asuka Temple was completed in 596.

In 618 the Sui dynasty was defeated and replaced by the Tang dynasty; in 645 the Soga clan also lost power in Japan. But the process of learning from China that had begun under the Soga, in cooperation with the Sui dynasty, not only continued but reached even greater heights.

China had developed a pattern of relations that some Western scholars call the "tribute system," designed to maintain stable, peaceful relations outside the territory it could control and rule directly. This was not a formal contractual system but a body of principles and rituals that China used to guide relationships with foreign states and various ethnic groups. Every several years, China's partners would bring a tribute, some animal species, plant, or product that was either rare or nonexistent in China, and China would reciprocate by presenting something, perhaps more valuable, that was rare in the partner's territory. Such rituals between foreign envoys and their Chinese hosts symbolized recognition by the outsiders of the superiority of Chinese civilization, both morally and militarily. In exchange, China, the great center of civilization that claimed a unique link between the Chinese emperor and Heaven, helped legitimate the reign of the leader of the tribute-bearing country by bestowing a title and the right to engage in trade with China. The tribute system was sufficiently flexible to consider changing economic and political situations. It was also well adapted for relations with the smaller groups of people who lived along the thousands of miles of China's northern and western borders—the Tungusic, Mongol, Turkic, and Tibetan people—and helped reduce the risk that they might invade China. However, the larger nations along the periphery, notably Korea, Vietnam, and especially Japan, after absorbing Chinese culture in the seventh and eighth centuries, sometimes expressed resistance to accepting the superiority of Chinese civilization.

The Japanese tribute missions sent to China under Empress Suiko were unusual because sending a large overseas mission from the more populated Japan was a much bigger undertaking than sending a small group across a land border. Shortly after she was enthroned, Empress Suiko began planning to send her first tribute mission to China in 600—ordering preparations for the ships, collecting the requisite supplies, and selecting those who would take part in the trip.

Contacts before Empress Suiko and the Base for Borrowing

Archaeological evidence from burial mounds in Japan reveals that Chinese pottery, bronze mirrors, swords, beads, and metal implements had spread from China to Japan by way of Korea during the Yayoi period (now dated as early as 1000 BC).[4] For example, it is believed that a gold seal discovered in Fukuoka prefecture was given to a Japanese envoy in the Later Han dynasty in AD 57. Rice agriculture was introduced into Japan during this period as well as metal and stone implements used for agriculture, arrowheads, and cutting.

A few Japanese writings before the seventh century have been discovered but they are not enough to confirm the nature of Japan's earlier contacts with Korea. The Japanese historical records, the *Kojiki* (A record of ancient matters) of 712, and the *Nihon shoki* (The chronicles of Japan) of 720, are considered by specialists to be reliable for the history in the decades immediately before 712 but little reliable information is available for the period before 500. Some scholars believe that the authors of the *Kojiki* and *Nihon shoki* had access to sixth-century written records in

Japan and in the Korean Paekche kingdom but they were subsequently lost.

Before the *Kojiki*, in the absence of a written history legends were passed down orally, the best known of which is the story of Xu Fu. According to the legend, Qin Shi Huangdi (who unified China and ruled from 221 to 210 BC) dispatched Xu Fu to a magical island to seek an elixir that would bring the emperor eternal life. It was said that he eventually reached Japan, but he never returned. Alas, there is no evidence to support this contact, even though statues of Xu Fu in several places in Japan celebrate the legend.

The Chinese had written records for many centuries before Japan adopted its written language from China, and during those centuries there are some references to Japan in Chinese records. Japan is mentioned in the *Hanshu* (Records of the Han dynasty) of 82, for example. The *Hanshu* does not go into detail, but it refers to the *woren* (in Japanese, *wajin*) people living in areas that correspond to present-day Korea and Japan.[5]

The *Records of the Wei Dynasty*, reportedly completed in 297, contain the first reliable written record about Japan in any language. The *Records*, and Chinese and Japanese scholarship analyzing them, recently introduced to English-language readers by Joshua Fogel's translation of the work by Saeki Arikiyo, include enough detailed information, such as the names of local places in Kyushu, that one can tell they were based on observations by travelers to Kyushu and possibly to Japan's main island, Honshu. The *Records* describe a visit by representatives of the Wei dynasty who brought gifts to Empress Himiko (ca. 170–248), and missions sent by Empress Himiko bringing tribute to the Wei ruler in 238 when the Wei granted her the title of "Ruler of the Wa" and she was friendly to the Wei. She again sent a mission in 243.

The *Records of the Wei Dynasty* report that there had been as many as one hundred different clan groups in the land of the Wa, varying in size from 1,000 to 70,000 households. It is noted that the Japanese were engaged in agriculture and fishing, and Japan had granaries and markets. The *Records* also report that Japan was sometimes ruled by men and sometimes by women. The *Wei Records* provide a positive view of Japan: "They have no theft and little in the way of arguments," the text reports. Those lower in the hierarchical rankings were reported to be obedient to those of higher ranks.

Less than two decades after the *Records of the Wei*, there are reports of people from China migrating to live in Japan to escape turmoil in their own country. According to Professor Wang Yong, one of China's leading historians of Japan, there were at least two sizable migrations from China to Japan, one soon after 313, when an estimated seven thousand families migrated, and another some decades later. According to Wang Yong, in the fifth and sixth centuries even more Koreans migrated to Japan. Among the Koreans, some were capable of writing Chinese characters, whereas no one in Japan at the time was literate in Chinese characters.

Valuables that may have come from China have been found in the third-century tombs of some Japanese leaders. Later discoveries of key-hole shaped tombs of Japanese chieftains provide evidence that Chinese mirrors, swords, and beads had reached Japan by the fourth and fifth centuries. Japan sent a mission to China in 478, but there is little information about what the envoys learned, and there is no evidence of formal contacts thereafter until the very last years of the sixth century, when the Sui dynasty rose to power. For the following two hundred years there are ample documents to provide a considerable historical record.

In the three centuries before Suiko of the Soga clan came to power, Japan had made some advances that provided a base for the effort to learn from China that Empress Suiko began in 600. Some Japanese people had moved from the southern island of Kyushu to the fertile area on the main island of Honshu, around Nara, which supported wet rice agriculture. Other people in this area had learned how to make pottery and were using bronze and iron implements that had been brought to Japan from Korea. Horses had been introduced by the sixth century, allowing Japanese officials to cover long distances relatively quickly. And although they had not yet mastered a written language, some clans had come together in an administrative structure under the Yamato.

The people living in the area around Nara, like people elsewhere in Japan, expressed respect for certain awe-inspiring natural sites, such as mountain peaks, cliffs, waterfalls, large trees, and rocks, by marking them with special signs. The practice of paying respect to these sites for their *kami*, the spiritual force they contained, opened the Japanese to learning about Buddhism, a religion that taught broad respect for spiritual forces. Some sources state that the Korean kingdom of Paekche began sending missions to Japan as early as 538 to promote the spread of Buddhism. Among the Koreans sent to Japan were specialists in monastic meditation, incantations, and architecture. Empress Suiko played a key role in Japan by introducing Buddhism and learning from China. Her nephew Shotoku is reported to have believed that Buddhism encouraged respect for social order and could restrain challenges to the political hierarchy. As soon as he took office, Shotoku lent his support to the introduction and expansion of Buddhism.

Many of the advances in the area of Nara came from the Korean immigrants to Japan. At its closest point, Japan was separated from China by some 500 miles, but Korea was adjacent to China. Therefore Koreans, being closer geographically with China, had incorporated elements of Chinese civilization that had not yet reached Japan. Kyushu, in turn, was less than 120 miles from Pusan in Korea, so the Japanese more easily learned elements of Chinese culture through the Koreans. At the time, the Korean Peninsula was divided into three kingdoms, Koguryo in the north, Paekche, with which Japan had the closest relations, in the southwest, and Silla in the southeast. There were struggles among the three kingdoms, and it is believed that some of the Korean immigrants to Japan were among those who had lost out in those struggles, while others fled from Korea after the invasion of Tang dynasty troops. Some scholars are convinced that the Soga clan, which in 600 decided to send tribute missions to China, may have had Korean members; regardless, the presence in Japan of Koreans, who were more familiar with developments in China, certainly played a role in Japan's decision to send missions to China.

How Japan Learned from China after 600

In 600, under Empress Suiko and Prince Shotoku, Japan sent its first mission to China since 478, and other missions followed quickly thereafter in 607, 608, and 614. The missions in 607 and 608 included tens of Buddhist monks who were to remain in Chang'an (Xi'an) to advance their study of Buddhism in order to bring it back to Japan. The Tang dynasty was established in 618, after defeating the Sui, but the Japanese monks remained in Chang'an and continued their studies. One monk, Somin, returned to Japan in 632. Another monk, Eon, remained in China until 639. Back in Japan these monks played not only a religious role but also a broader role as intellectuals and advisers to Japan's political leaders. Somin and Eon provided information about many aspects of Chinese culture and institutions, assisting the leaders who were beginning to transform Japan. The missions to Chang'an, which continued after 618, came to be known in Japan as *kentoshi* (envoys sent to the Tang).

Chang'an was then a cosmopolitan city, with an estimated population of more than one million. It attracted Koreans, Central Asians, and Middle Easterners, as well as Chinese. The nearby Yellow River was far larger than any river in Japan, and the plains around Chang'an were far broader than any in Japan, thus permitting a larger population and a larger scale of agricultural production than any that existed in Japan. The Sui and Tang dynasties thereby had achieved an organizational complexity that was far beyond what Japan knew at the time.

Prince Shotoku endeavored to establish a system that would break up the power of the clans. In 604 he inaugurated the "twelve-cap system" (sometimes also referred to as the "cap and rank" system), a system for selecting officials regardless of the rank of their clan. He appointed officials as individuals and then assigned the individual a rank. Following the Chinese pattern, he gave the person a cap, the color and shape of which conveyed the person's rank. In addition, Prince Shotoku introduced population registers that could be used to collect taxes and recruit men for labor projects and military service. He also brought priests into the governmental structure.

To underpin his efforts to reform the clan system and promote stability, Shotoku promulgated what is known as the Seventeen Article Constitution. Although there is disagreement among scholars as to its authenticity, the *Nihon shoki* reports that it was issued in 604 by Prince Shotoku. Not as detailed as a modern constitution, it was a preliminary set of guidelines drawn from the early lessons learned from China, and it reflected the efforts by Empress Suiko and Prince Shotoku to centralize authority and to weaken the power of the clans. Officials were not to assume their positions by birth; rather, they were to be appointed by the emperor. Land that had formerly belonged to the clans could be transferred by central officials, and land could be owned independently of the clans. At the time, Confucianism had not yet been introduced in an organized fashion. Nevertheless, Confucian concepts of morality and respect for officials, already introduced by Koreans, were incorporated in the constitution. People were to seek "harmony," officials were to follow the directions of the ruler, and children were to follow the directions of their parents. Rules of propriety were established to govern relations among officials of different ranks. (The Imperial Academy with a heavy Confucian content, designed to prepare young people for official examinations, would not be introduced until late in the seventh century.)

Prince Shotoku arranged for a small number of Chinese and Korean individuals to serve as advisers in Japan. The Paekche kingdom, following the example of China, had already introduced a bureaucratic system in Korea, with six government departments. Empress Suiko and, after her death in 628, her successor Emperor Jomei, did not go so far as to establish a bureaucratic structure. However, Emperor Jomei did introduce ceremonial protocols for welcoming foreign visitors that followed the examples of China and Paekche. Also, with the help of craftsmen from Paekche, Japan began the construction of monasteries and temples that symbolized the centralization of power.

Empress Suiko and Prince Shotoku wanted Japan to be treated with respect by China. At the time, Chinese officials believed that only the Chinese emperor should be called the "Child of Heaven" (in Chinese, *tianzi*; Japanese, *tenshi*) and that the top leader of Japan or any other tribute-bearing group could only be considered a *wang* (king), a position not as high as the Child of Heaven. In 607 Empress Suiko signed a memorial, passed on to Chinese emperor Yangdi by her envoy, that read, "The Child of Heaven in the land where the sun rises addresses the Child of Heaven in the land where the sun sets." The Chinese emperor was displeased with Empress Suiko for presuming to address him as an equal and is reported to have said to a subordinate, "If memorials from barbarian states are written by persons who lack propriety, do not accept them."[6] Japanese representatives, however, concerned that their country should receive proper respect, began referring to their country not as the land of *Wa* but as *Nihon*, which in Japanese literally means "the origin of the Sun."

As in Chinese cosmology, in Japan the emperor came to be seen as part of the natural order linked to Heaven. There is disagreement as to exactly when this change in Japanese cosmology took place. While Suiko reigned, she was referred to as the *okimi* (great king), and sometime after her reign the Japanese began to refer to her as *tenno* (emperor, or heavenly lord). The first character of the Japanese word for emperor, *ten* (Heaven), is the same character as *tian* (Heaven, in Chinese), used in reference to the Chinese emperor (*tianzi*). For the Japanese, the term *tenno* indicated equality with the Chinese emperor, and within Japan, it also elevated the emperor above the clan members who served the emperor. Officials under the Japanese emperor were thereafter known as vassals.

The Taika Reforms

In 645, after an internal struggle within the Yamato, the Soga clan lost power to the imperial clan, and Emperor Kotoku of the imperial clan came to power. Emperor Kotoku, like the Soga clan leaders before him, wanted to centralize power, but he had the advantage of being able to draw on a greater number of monks by this time who had returned from China and on the comprehensive legal codes that by then had been developed during the Tang dynasty. Soon after coming to power Emperor Kotoku undertook the Taika (Great Change) Reforms of 645. Modeled after changes made in China during the Tang dynasty, they went much further than changes made by the Soga to weaken the clans and to establish central administrative control.

On the first day of 646, Emperor Kotoku issued his Four Article Edict. Some Japanese scholars have compared the role of these Four Articles in laying out the aims of the new administration with the Five-Article Charter Oath issued when Emperor Meiji came to power in 1868. Article 1 eliminated the power of the clans and their ability to control the fate of clan members. Article 2 provided for the reorganization of geographical areas that, rather than the clans, would be the local administrative units responsible to the central leadership. The capital was divided into four districts, and the boundaries of more distant regions, to be under direct central control, were delineated. Article 3 provided for the rationalization of household registration for purposes of taxation, labor contributions, and military service. Article 4 outlined the taxes that were to be assessed, and the salaries that were to be set for administrative officials. The new administrative structure was extended to most of the main island of Honshu, in addition to Kyushu and Shikoku, and the prefecture system (then called *kuni*), with the subdivision of the prefectures into counties (*gun*), was made more explicit. With this new reform, following the Chinese model Japan ended the capacity of the clans to dominate the government and established an administrative state covering a broader geographical area.

Although the power of the clans had basically ended, Japan did not go as far as China in terms of abolishing the importance of inheritance. From the beginning of recorded history until the end of the Tokugawa period (1868), Japan used birth, much more than China did, as an important criterion for one's hierarchical position. And Japan did not rely as much as China on examinations to select its officials. However, Japan attached great importance to training. The new leadership under Emperor Kotoku devised a program for sending many more young officials to China for training than the Soga leadership had. Immediately after assuming office, Emperor Kotoku arranged for two groups to go to China. One group of 121 promising young men was sent by ship along the northern route and then across Korea. The other group, of similar size, was sent by the southern route, directly across the ocean to China. The ship taking the southern route encountered a storm and nearly all on board drowned. Those who had gone by the northern route reached their destination and studied government administration in China before returning home some years later.

Tang China was remarkably cosmopolitan. Not only did it allow Koreans and Japanese to study but some Koreans and one unusually talented Japanese official, Abe no Nakamaro, who went on the mission in 717, passed the Chinese examinations and became Chinese officials. Abe served as an official in several Chinese locations from 761 to 767, including in Annam (Vietnam), in the position of Chinese representative. He was also a poet, best known for a nostalgic poem about Nara, and he became friends with China's leading poets of the day. He tried several times to return to Japan, but the ships always encountered weather problems. He died in China in 770.

Japan's Military Lessons from Its Defeat by the Tang

Before 661, the Japanese had no experience fighting against military forces outside of Japan's four islands. The Tang dynasty had developed a very strong military to unify the country in 618, and it maintained a very strong military throughout the seventh century.

Because the Korean Peninsula is across a river (the Yalu) from China, Korea has always been more vulnerable than Japan to advancing Chinese armies, and it was therefore quicker to learn some military skills from China. By the fifth century, Korean military forces were therefore more advanced than Japan's. Japan had developed good relations with the Paekche, one of the three kingdoms (along with Silla and Koguryo) on the Korean Peninsula.

In 660 when Tang forces, with their Korean ally the Silla, invaded Paekche, the Paekche kingdom appealed to Japan for help. Although precise records are lacking and figures may be exaggerated, it was estimated that Japan sent 5,000 troops in 661, more troops in 662, and 27,000 troops in 663. But in 663, the Tang and Silla rulers sent in even more troops and decimated the Paekche and Japanese forces in a huge battle. The Japanese are said to have lost 400 ships and 10,000 men. The Japanese had already learned how to use horses from the Koguryo, and they were also reported to have lost 1,000 horses.[7] Most of the lessons that Japan had learned from the Tang came from peaceful visits to the capital of Chang'an, but military lessons were also learned from fighting the larger and more advanced Chinese forces. The *Kojiki* explains that the Japanese were defeated because the Chinese were more numerous, better armed, and engaged in mass infantry attacks for which the Japanese were unprepared. Thereafter, some Japanese people began wearing swords and daggers, and preparing shields and bows and arrows, to defend against a possible invasion. After battles in Korea, Japan cultivated horses, and during Japan's 672 Civil War, which began as a succession struggle and then expanded beyond the royal family, Japanese forces engaged in large-scale attacks on horseback. In 670, after its experience of losing to the superior Tang forces, Japan also began preparing a conscription system like that in China, to bring more able-bodied men into the military. The system was consolidated in the Taiho Code of 701.

The Taiho Code of 701

The Taiho Code further centralized the administrative structure in Japan, and a census enabled the drafting of peasants into the army or to work on construction projects. Under the code, the Japanese also expanded the teaching of Confucianism, stressing that lower-level officials should respect higher-level officials and children should respect their parents. The Taiho Code was written by some eighteen Japanese authors, with the cooperation of one specialist from China. The introduction of woodblock printing from China late in the eighth century made possible the wider distribution of these collections that began in the eleventh century.

By the time the Taiho Code was enacted, great advances had been made in the study of the Chinese system. Japan reduced the number of students it sent to China and established its own advanced training institute for officials. The focus of study at the institute, as in China, was Confucianism, but the curriculum also included mathematics and Chinese literature. And since all students were expected to be able to write in Chinese, training in Chinese language was central. Chinese literature was the most popular course, and poems by Bai Juyi, expressing feelings about everyday life in clear everyday language, were especially popular among the students.

In line with Japan's stress on family lineage, children of Japanese aristocrats could become high officials even if they did not study at the institute or pass examinations, so many did not bother attending the training institute. Most students at the institute were children of lower-ranking officials, especially children of regional officials. Those students who did well on the examinations had a chance of rising somewhat within the hierarchy, but lineage background remained more important than the examinations in determining one's position as an official.

At the time of the Taiho Code of 701 and then the Yoro Code of 718, officials were concerned about the collection of land taxes. As the model for rural organization, Japan introduced the Chinese "well-field" system, wherein eight families on their own private plots were settled to form a square around one field of common land. Japan's local government administrators were able to collect taxes from private landowners near the capital, but they had difficulty collecting taxes from lands that were at a great distance from the capital. Furthermore, Japan allowed some people who were well connected to high officials to set up their own estates without paying taxes. Buddhist monasteries were also not required to pay taxes. These exemptions and collection difficulties placed a heavy burden on the small landholders closer to the capital, who both paid taxes and supplied young men for construction projects and military service.

The Nara Period, 710–794

A new milestone in urban development was reached in 710 when, after two years of construction, the Japanese government occupied the newly built capital city of Nara. Nara was far larger than the previous capitals at Naniwa, Asuka, and Fujiwara. Nara was laid out in the same rectangular pattern as Chang'an, with the palace in the north, the main thoroughfare running north to south, and side streets running east to west, although the area of the Nara administrative center was smaller, just three miles by two and two-thirds miles, compared with Chang'an's six by five miles. Before the Nara period, each Japanese ruler had governed from his own location, so the location of the capital changed with each change of rule. In the two and a half centuries before the capital's relocation to Nara, there had been twenty-three rulers in the region of the Yamato plains and thirty-one different capitals. Nara, like Chang'an, was expected to remain the capital for a long time. Indeed, it was the capital for almost a century.

Kyoto, the Heian Capital, 794–1185

In 794 a strong emperor, Kammu, founded the Heian period and located the center of government in Kyoto. Some Japanese leaders had become concerned about the growing power of the Shinto shrines and Buddhist monasteries in Nara and wanted a new capital free of Buddhist pressures.

Kyoto, larger than Nara, covered an area measuring three by three and one-third miles. It proved to be an enduring capital, lasting more than one thousand years. Unlike the Chinese cities that were surrounded by walls to ward off horseback-riding warriors who might swoop down from outside, Kyoto, which then had no such worries, did not have city walls. The Heian period was relatively peaceful, although during its later years, because of turmoil in the surrounding areas, some cities built castles to defend themselves from outside attacks. Like Chang'an and Nara, Kyoto was laid out with the capital buildings in the north, the main street running north and south, and numbered cross streets. Even today Kyoto retains the same basic grid structure that was introduced in 794, based on what the city planners had learned from Chang'an.

Although monks during the Heian period did not go to China in such great numbers as they had in the last half of the seventh century, some continued to travel to China and to provide information about Tang China to Japanese government officials. Among those monks sent to China were some outstanding intellectuals of the day, such as Kukai (known posthumously as Kobo Daishi), who was in China from 804 to 806 and returned to Japan to establish the Shingon sect, and the monk Saicho (767–822), known by his posthumous name Dengyo Daishi, who introduced the Tendai sect in Japan. Ennin, who was in China from 838 to 846, left a detailed diary, translated by Edwin O. Reischauer and authenticated by others who, in recent decades, have retraced the routes of his travels. Ennin's diary provides the most reliable and complete account of a mission to China and of the situation in China at the time. It has even been used by Chinese scholars to describe China of the time. By the time Ennin returned to Japan, the Chinese had placed strict limits on Buddhist activities. During the following century, Japanese monks had difficulty traveling to China.

Language, Literature, and Music

Until the sixth century Japan had no written language, and before the seventh century even Japanese priests and political leaders were illiterate. But during the fifth and sixth centuries Chinese written characters began to appear in Japan on swords, mirrors, coins, and funeral objects coming from Korea. At the time, there were still no texts written in Japan. Because printing presses were not yet available, one of the main tasks of the first Buddhist monks going to China was to laboriously copy the Buddhist texts and bring them home for Japanese Buddhists to study. A document from 757 reports that the Japanese court had at its disposal some 1,500 Chinese works.

Texts were brought to Japan from various localities in Korea and China. Because of regional variations in pronunciation within China and Korea, there was initially no standardized way to match written Chinese texts with pronunciation. There was also widespread variation in writing style and content, reflecting the various purposes for which language was introduced: state building, enhancing legitimacy, communicating among those within a more complex administrative structure, writing poems to enrich the culture and support the state, and propagating religious faith.

After 600, as Japan was setting up a centralized political structure and beginning to use written documents for communication, Japanese officials began to standardize the language they used, and the number of written works grew rapidly. Buddhists establishing monasteries and interacting with monks from broader geographical areas also sought to standardize their written language.

Between 712 and 760, compilations of three major collections of writings were released to the public. These have become lasting cultural landmarks: the *Kojiki*, 712, the *Nihon shoki* (also called *Nihongi*), 720, and the *Manyoshu* (Collection of poetry), completed in 759. The first two, histories written in Chinese characters, were modeled after the Chinese dynastic histories. All three works represented efforts to provide legitimacy for the emperor and a common culture for the people living under his rule. All three also helped to extend the emperor's rule beyond the immediate area around Nara. Not tightly integrated, they contain materials diverse enough to reflect a variety of local perspectives. Many parts were from the oral tradition that had been passed down through the generations, before literacy began to spread in the seventh century. By writing down the ancient legends and including them with the newly written materials, the compilers created the core of a common culture that has persisted to the present day. The introduction of woodblock printing from China late in the eighth century and its wide use in the eleventh to the nineteenth centuries made possible the distribution of these collections of works to a broader audience.

The *Kojiki*, the first of the three to be published, was commissioned in 681. It was released two years after the capital was moved to Nara, with the goal of providing a stable cultural base for a long-lasting capital. The *Kojiki* is the oldest Japanese document in existence. It is likely that in writing the history of the most recent decades at the time, the compilers were able to draw on documents, perhaps written by Koreans, that were quite reliable. But the earlier periods are clearly mythical, and specialists who have examined the documents and studied archaeological sites are skeptical about the reliability of the sections of the *Kojiki* that concern the period before the sixth century.

The first part of the *Kojiki* is an account of how heavenly beings formed the Japanese islands and then, in 660 BC, sent Emperor Jimmu from the

Heaven to establish Japan. Scholars specializing in ancient Japan have conjectured that 660 BC was selected as the date Jimmu Tenno was said to have descended from Heaven because it was twenty-one sixty-year cycles, or 1,260 years, before Prince Shotoku ascended to his imperial position.

Although some of the accounts recorded in the *Kojiki* were based on oral legends, the *Kojiki* and the *Nihon shoki* remain the best available written sources for Japanese history prior to that time. In the later part of the twentieth century, wooden tablets (*mokkan*) discovered in grave sites provided credibility for some of the accounts in the *Kojiki*. Since then, scholars conducting research on pre-600 Japan have tried to combine archaeological evidence with the *Kojiki* in order to understand Japan's history before the early seventh century. Whether legend or history, the reports by Prince Shotoku and other parts of the *Kojiki* are still taught to Japanese schoolchildren and remain part of Japanese historical consciousness.

Unlike the Chinese dynastic histories that record a separate history for each dynasty, each written by historians of that dynasty who claimed that their dynasty had received the "Mandate of Heaven," the *Kojiki* presents an uninterrupted continuum since Japan's mythical beginning. The *Kojiki* provides accounts of succession struggles—tilted, of course, to stress the virtue of the winner, whose descendant was still ruling Japan. But each of Japan's emperors or empresses was assigned a place on a continuous line that theoretically extended from the beginning of Japan.

After their writing system was developed, the Japanese followed the Chinese pattern of keeping official dynastic records. The histories of events after 712 are much more detailed and reliable than earlier histories. In addition, following the Chinese model, gazetteers (*fudoki*) were compiled to provide detailed accounts of local developments.

The *Nihon shoki* provides even more details than the *Kojiki* about all the emperors and empresses, dating back to the fictitious Emperor Jimmu. It also includes reports of relations with China and Korea. Although it emphasizes the continuity of the imperial line, it discusses the strengths and weaknesses of various emperors, as well as some of the cosmology and mythology introduced from Chinese Daoist practices.

The *Manyoshu* is a massive collection of literature composed over the centuries, including 265 long poems, more than 4,200 short poems, essays, and stories. Most of the poems and essays in the *Manyoshu* were written at the time of Empress Suiko and Prince Shotoku or later. The work also includes 4 poems and 22 brief essays by Chinese writers. Compared with the two books of history, this collection of literature expresses a much broader range of human sentiment and is known for striking an emotional chord with readers. There are writings by peasants and laborers as well as by the literati of the day.

When Chinese written characters were first introduced in Japan, some written texts used Chinese language. Gradually, Chinese characters were matched with Japanese pronunciations that had the same meaning as the Chinese characters, but the characters were arranged according to Japanese sentence structure and some Japanese grammatical elements were added. This pattern of writing Japanese with Chinese characters (known as *kundoku*), used in compiling the *Kojiki*, became standard Japanese. By the time literary works were selected for the *Manyoshu*, some authors were using kana, a system of abbreviated Chinese characters that signify a syllable, making it possible for the *Manyoshu* to include many vernacular Japanese expressions with their original Japanese sounds.

The *Manyoshu* followed the tradition of the Tang dynasty's *Yiwen leiju*, a Chinese encyclopedia that brought together various kinds of knowledge for use by bureaucrats. Literary works that focus on the sovereigns and trace the evolution of the imperial leadership, such as the *Kojiki* and *Nihon shoki*, were used to support the legitimacy of the current national leadership. However, the compilers of the *Manyoshu* did not try to unify thinking, and many of the poems are simple, direct expressions describing a variety of observations and feelings about everyday life, thus enriching Japanese culture.

After the *Manyoshu* was compiled, the use of kana spread, allowing for the growth of Japanese literature that reflected the oral tradition, something that had not been possible with the use of standard Chinese characters, which imposed constraints on the variety of possible expressions. For centuries there were no efforts to rationalize and unify these two highly different writing systems (the syllabaries based on simplified Chinese characters to represent Japanese sounds, and the use of Chinese characters to signify their original meaning in Chinese), and the Japanese language that evolved is a complicated combination of both systems.

Like the Chinese, the Japanese turned calligraphy, the writing of Chinese characters with brush and ink, into an art form. They shared styles and schools of calligraphy as well as a common evaluation system for ranking calligraphers. Calligraphers in each country have long been aware of the work of calligraphers in the other country, and the Chinese have been quite complimentary of some of Japan's most distinguished calligraphers.

Musical instruments and court music were introduced from China during the time of Prince Shotoku. Instruments adopted by the Japanese included the koto (a large zither) and the biwa (a type of lute). These instruments and their music remain popular in Japanese culture and are still in use for formal occasions.

Japan has made great efforts to preserve historical treasures, and Chinese specialists visiting Japan have expressed appreciation for displays of ancient artifacts that make use of skills imported from China, some of which are no longer found in China. The Shosoin Treasure House on the grounds of the Todaiji Temple in Nara, for example, protected by the imperial household, is much appreciated by Chinese specialists. Although not ordinarily open to the public, some of the treasures are displayed each fall at the Nara National Museum. These include examples of fourth-century Chinese calligraphy, judged to be among the best in Chinese history; musical instruments, such as a five-stringed lute from the eighth century; and various Buddhist treasures.

Buddhism

The Chinese originally learned about Buddhism from travelers who went to India, and by the beginning of the fourth century Buddhism had developed deep roots in China. The Chinese court embraced Buddhism, Buddhist temples were erected in various localities, monasteries were established, and training programs were set up to educate monks. By the time Prince Shotoku began to introduce Buddhism in Japan, it was sufficiently developed in both China and Korea that virtually no one from Japan went to India to learn about Buddhism. The Japanese learned about Buddhism from the Koreans, who had learned from the Chinese, and through Japanese monks who traveled to China to study. For Japanese Buddhists, China was the holy land and well-known Chinese monks were their teachers. Chinese mountains, with their famous temples, became their mecca, where they went to receive enlightenment.

Before Buddhism was introduced in Japan, the Japanese expressed reverence toward awe-inspiring natural phenomena and took part in rituals designed to bring rich harvests, overcome natural disasters, and preserve a long life. Some Japanese writers described visits to wondrous natural spots as *shinto* (the way of the gods), and appreciation of these natural spots was later incorporated into the Shinto religion. But before the arrival of Buddhism, Shinto beliefs were not part of a complex religious organization. Shinto is not even mentioned in the *Kojiki*. Since there was no national religious institution in Japan before Buddhism was introduced at the time of Prince Shotoku, there was little organized resistance to it. And once Buddhism was introduced in Japan it spread rapidly.

For national rulers in both China and Japan, Buddhism provided legitimacy through the teaching that the ruler was linked to the heavens. Prince Shotoku had a Buddhist teacher, and thereafter Buddhist priests were invited by other Japanese rulers to assist in dealing with natural forces, particularly in obtaining appropriate weather to cultivate crops. There was a clear distinction between those who had a religious role as monks and those who had a secular role, and Buddhist priests could enhance their status by invoking prayers to deal with the forces of nature. However, there always was the risk that they would lose status if they could not control natural disasters.

Central to Buddhist philosophy as introduced in Korea and Japan was a belief in the overall harmony of the world and Heaven. Buddhism promoted meditation to reach enlightenment and to control worldly desires. Because it was a peaceful religion, it was attractive to Korean and Japanese political leaders, who were seeking not only a spiritual base to help preserve national health but also a social base for a political system that would bring peace and unity. When Buddhism first arrived in Japan, for example, it spread as a result of sponsorship by the court and the leading clans. But it gradually became popular among ordinary people, who believed that one could attain rebirth in peaceful surroundings if one performed the proper Buddhist rituals.

Some political leaders believed that the building of large Buddhist temples would provide heavenly protection for their rule. The monasteries trained and housed monks, who in turn recited sutras to help believers seek Nirvana and control their desires. Buddhist organizations could be used by political leaders for support against their opponents and factions, but monasteries that owned their own land could also cut into the potential tax base, creating difficult problems for the leadership. By the late Nara period, some rulers found that the Buddhists had strengthened their power so much that they could not be easily be controlled.

By the middle of the sixth century, Korean Buddhist craftsmen began going to Japan to join in the building of Buddhist statues and temples and to train Japanese craftsmen. With the help of Korean Buddhists, the Japanese acquired skills that enabled them to duplicate the art and architecture that they had seen in China and Korea.

Only a small number of Japanese monks could make the voyage to visit Chinese sites during the Sui and Tang dynasties. Such visits, which enabled the Japanese monks to enhance their learning of the sutras, were considered a special privilege. The Japanese visitors enjoyed good relations with the Chinese monasteries in which they lived while they studied with Chinese masters. Throughout the period when Japan was learning from China, Japanese monks treasured the opportunity to visit the respected Chinese temples and monasteries to strengthen their understanding of the Buddhist scriptures and sutras. Chinese monks, in turn, traveled to Japan to spread their doctrine, conveying the message that believers could relieve suffering and pave the way for rebirth in a Buddhist paradise. Once Buddhism began to prosper in Japan, various Buddhist sects, some headquartered in China or Korea, became popular in Japan. A number of Buddhist sects, such as the Pure Land Sect, had broad appeal among the masses.

Buddhism offered a more comprehensive system of belief than the traditional Japanese expressions of reverence toward awe-inspiring natural sites. After Buddhism arrived from China, the Japanese attempted to organize their beliefs and practices into a more comprehensive structure. Buddhism did not replace traditional Japanese practices, but it spurred those practices to become more systematic. Thereafter, Buddhism and Shintoism coexisted in Japan. Even in the Nara and early Heian periods when Buddhism became the state religion in Japan, Shinto shrines continued under the overall umbrella of Buddhism.

In China, after 845 there was a crackdown on Buddhist monasteries that continued for more than a century, because the monasteries were not paying taxes, but in Japan there was no such backlash. In addition to its growing number of monasteries, Japan witnessed a great expansion in Buddhist art, including Buddhist images, statues, and temples. Except for the period when China was cracking down on Buddhist monasteries, Buddhism was a cosmopolitan religion that provided a strong cultural link between Japan and China. Shinto, in contrast, was limited to Japan. When Japanese nationalism became strong, Japan's leaders would later call on Shinto rather than Buddhism to justify their behavior.

Architecture

The Chinese built large palaces before they began building Buddhist temples, but in Japan, large temples, made possible with new technologies from China, were erected first, before large palaces. Japan's architectural breakthrough for constructing large buildings came from temple architecture, and what Japanese craftsmen learned from their counterparts in Korea and China they later applied to their own large public buildings.

Scholars have carefully examined the surviving buildings and documents in Japan to reconstruct the process by which the skills needed to build temples reached Japan. Information is not complete, but evidence suggests that Japanese diplomats who went to China on tribute missions arranged to bring back skilled Chinese and Korean carpenters and artists. In any case, there is evidence that from the early sixth century, Korean designers, carpenters, craftsmen, and painters emigrated to Japan, where they transmitted Korean and Chinese temple-building technologies. In Japan, they raised their families and passed on construction skills to later generations of Korean-Japanese builders, who would continue to take part in temple construction.

Before the new Chinese technology for temple building was introduced in Japan, temples were constructed with a post-and-lintel frame topped by a thatched roof. The thatched roof and the unpainted wooden pillars, which were sunk into the ground, would rot relatively quickly, and such structures could not support a heavier roof. The new Chinese engineering practices introduced to Japan by Korean carpenters made it possible to enclose a much larger space in the main area of a building. With the new system, the weight of a heavy tiled roof could be distributed along an outer perimeter of columns, through bracket sets and spanning beams, allowing for a large unpartitioned area inside the building. The wooden framework of the building would last much longer because of the tiled roof, which provided much better protection from rain and snow than a thatched roof. And Japanese builders learned from the Chinese how to set pillars in a stone foundation instead of thrusting them directly into the ground, an advance that also greatly extended the life of a building.

The temples were huge buildings, and their construction required large numbers of workers. But by the time Japan began constructing large temples, a system for recruiting laborers had already been developed, so workers were available for the various tasks connected with temple construction.

The Great Shrine of Ise, the national Shinto shrine erected in Japan on the Shima Peninsula, had commonly been viewed as entirely derived from indigenous designs that existed prior to the introduction of Buddhist architecture from China. But Japanese scholars now acknowledge that some features of this national shrine were imported from China. The Inner Shrine (Naiku) on the large grounds of the Great Shrine had a traditional thatched roof and wooden poles for pillars; because of the structure's rapid decay, it had to be rebuilt every twenty years. However, recent analysis of features of the Great Shrine of Ise suggests that several other aspects of its construction did not exist in Japan before the time of Emperor Temmu (673–686). By the time the shrine was rebuilt in 690, skilled artisans had already started arriving in Japan from Korea and China. The buildings on the grounds of the shrine are located on a direct north-south axis, a common feature of Chinese temple building that had not previously existed in Japan. The use of doors within doors, a feature of Chinese architecture, also had not existed in Japan before it was introduced at Ise. To preserve tradition, Japan has chosen to continue rebuilding the Inner Shrine every twenty years in its old style, even with the thatched roof. The elaborate preparations for the reconstruction of the Ise Shrine every twenty years allow for the continuous involvement of new generations of Japanese builders with traditional construction techniques, thus reinforcing a commitment to old traditions, including some traditions that originally came from China.

The Horyuji Temple is the oldest standing wooden structure in the world. Its construction made use of timber-frame engineering and required an analysis of the stress levels that the timber would support. The Horyuji was originally built in 607 under the direction of Prince Shotoku at a time when he was busy learning from China. It burned down in 670, but the temple's Western Precinct, which was reconstructed over the next several decades, has been in continuous use since the seventh century. The Buddhist community attached to the Horyuji is the oldest Buddhist community in Japan. Through new research techniques for analyzing the age of structures, it has been determined that the central shaft of the Horyuji's five-story pagoda, completed in 711, was constructed of cypress wood from trees that had been cut down in 594. Therefore, some of the timber in the Horyuji was harvested a century before the temple was built and had first been used in earlier buildings. This is indicative of the hardiness of cypress beams, which when properly protected have an extraordinarily long life.

The Horyuji is far older than any temple still standing in China. Foguang Temple on Mount Wutai, for example, was built in 857. Thus, it is impossible to trace the Chinese origins of the Horyuji Temple. Instead, scholars in both China and Japan have used the Horyuji's structures to try to understand what buildings in China before that time might have been like.

After Japan's devastating smallpox epidemic of 735–737 and the ensuing serious famine, the Japanese emperor directed in 741 that Japanese provinces should build temples to protect the country from such disasters. In 743, to provide additional protection, he decreed that a Great Buddha statue should be erected in Kokomyoji (later Todaiji, the Great Eastern Temple), which would serve as an administrative center for all the provincial temples in the entire country. Dozens of carpenters from China and Korea helped guide local architects and builders in its construction, and large numbers of Japanese peasants were drafted to work on the project. Such construction required not only carpentry skills but also great advances in metallurgy.

The Todaiji, a far more advanced structure than anything previously attempted in Japan, was modeled after temples in China and Korea. In addition to smaller statues displayed in the Todaiji, a statue of Buddha in its Great Buddha Hall is nearly fifty feet tall and weighs about 500 metric tons. It is the largest bronze statue in the world, modeled after an even larger statue in China that no longer exists. The Great Buddha statue in the Todaiji has been damaged and repaired several times, but it still retains its original shape. The scale of the Great Buddha and the temple's construction (expansion) in general were a great drain on manpower, on bronze and other materials, and on court funding, but Japan's rulers considered it well worth the cost to protect against disaster and provide grandeur for the Japanese state.

A leading Chinese monk, Ganjin (Jianzhen in Chinese), arrived in Nara in 754, invited by the emperor to attend the dedication of the great statue of Buddha. He had been invited to Japan years earlier, in 742, by a Japanese visitor to China who wanted him to teach Japanese monks. He had tried on five different occasions to travel to Japan, but each attempt was unsuccessful because of the weather. It was only on his sixth try, aboard a ship that was part of a Japanese mission returning home, that he was finally able to reach Japan. By that time, Ganjin had become blind; nonetheless, he presided over the dedication of the great Todaiji Temple. Carpenters and monks accompanying him on his journey built another temple, the Toshodaiji (Tang Meditation Compound). There, he and the younger monks he had brought with him were able to serve as teachers, training new generations of Japanese monks. His disciples built a life-size statue of him, with portrait-like details including tendons beneath the jaw, closed eyes to reflect his vision problem, and hair in his ears. Although damaged, the statue remains today, treasured as one of the most important works in the history of East Asian art, and one that provides a cultural link when the two nations wish to emphasize their common heritage.

Currency and the Beginnings of a Commercial Economy

Although some Chinese coins from before the Nara period have been discovered in Japanese tombs, it was not until 708, on the eve of the Nara period, that Japan, following the Chinese example, began minting coins. The Japanese technology for minting coins was inferior to China's, and after some decades Japan gave up minting coins and instead imported large amounts of copper coins from China. In the eighth century, the Japanese monetary economy was mostly limited to the area near Nara. During the Nara period, there were two markets in Nara where rice, medicine, cloth, some simple handicrafts, and ceramics were sold. At the time, the monetary economy in China covered a much larger geographical area. Rice remained the main medium of exchange in Japan for several centuries thereafter, but in exchanges with Korea and China, bolts of silk were used as well as rice.

The Legacy of Japanese Borrowing from China

What Japan learned from China between 600 and 838—written language, Buddhism, Confucianism, literature, music, and architecture, or the basic building blocks of Japanese culture—survived even after the arrival of Western culture in the nineteenth and twentieth centuries. These elements of the culture came not through the advance of Chinese troops, nor from large-scale migration, but from a small number of Koreans in Japan who brought with them aspects of Chinese culture, from a still smaller number of Chinese migrants who came to Japan, and primarily from a small number of Japanese monks and officials who had been to Chang'an to study, some of whom had stayed in China for many years. Considering the scope of China's impact on Japan, it is remarkable that such comprehensive borrowing took place through such a small number of people.

After 838, when Japan sent its last formal mission to China, Japan's active learning from China tapered off. The critical learning from China took place as Japan's leaders were building a more centralized administration that would cover a broader geographical area. By the time Japan stopped sending missions to China, its regions had begun to gain strength compared with the center. In 792, two years before the Japanese capital was moved to Kyoto and the Heian period was founded, Japan ended its system of nationwide conscription and permitted local officials to develop their own militias. By then, relatives of the imperial family had begun to spread out to areas at a considerable distance from Kyoto and had begun to build up their own regional armies.

With decentralization, the cultural elements that Japan had adopted from China were spread more broadly throughout Japan's main islands. In their shared written language, although the Chinese characters would be abbreviated differently in the language reforms carried out in each country in the twentieth century, the basic concepts of many of the characters continued to provide a basis for communication between China and Japan. Even today, the Chinese and Japanese can still learn the written language of the other country far more rapidly than Westerners can, and they often catch nuances that Westerners do not.

Over the centuries, Confucian teachings have undergone many changes in both countries, but a common core of texts, beliefs, and practices remains. In Japan, people can still recite proverbs that were introduced from China. They play stringed instruments that were first brought from China, and they recite poems that originally came from China as if they were their own. With mass education, which began spreading in each country late in the nineteenth century, more youths in Japan and China received standardized training in their own culture. Both countries have now achieved almost universal literacy, which makes available to the entire population not only Western learning but also elements of their own traditional culture.

The popularity of Buddhism provides much of the population in both countries with a common foundation of overlapping beliefs and ceremonies. Even though Buddhist sects have been much stronger in Japan than they have been in China, the sects in Japan can still trace their ancestry not only to the Japanese monks who introduced them but also to the Chinese temples where the founders of the Japanese sects studied. During the early period when Buddhism was first introduced in Japan, many of the contacts came via Korea, but after the ninth century Japan had fewer contacts with Korea and Buddhist contacts came directly from China to Japan.

When nationalism becomes strong, the differences in historical memory between the Chinese and the Japanese can become the focus for mobilizing and expressing antagonism. But the two nations' broad cultural overlap also provides a basis for common understanding. Japanese and Chinese travelers who visit the other's country and see signs written in the local language feel a level of familiarity that is not possible for Westerners. Buddhists in the two countries share rituals, beliefs, and a common culture that provide a basis for working together and for offering compassion and assistance across national borders. Japanese Buddhists continue to visit their sacred historical sites in China. Devoted practitioners can recite their common sutras and enjoy their shared temples and art. In 1980, when the Chinese brought a statue of Ganjin back to Daming Temple, his native temple in

China, Japanese Buddhists sent a stone lantern, dating back to the eighth century, from the temple in Japan where Ganjin had taught. Ganjin remains a symbol of the shared culture that can be called upon when Chinese and Japanese leaders choose to reinforce goodwill between the people of their countries.

CHAPTER TWO

Trade without Transformative
Learning, 838–1862

By 838, Japanese leaders had succeeded in transforming their governing structure, which had originally rested on relationships among clans, into a centralized administrative state. Japan still had things it could learn from China, and Japanese leaders continued to gain knowledge from Japanese visitors to China, Chinese visitors to Japan, and Korean monks and artisans who brought to Japan the skills they had learned in China. But what the Japanese learned after 838 was minor in comparison with what they had learned earlier. By 838 the Japanese had learned from China how to set up a governmental bureaucracy and how to create basic rules to guide governmental operations. They had introduced Chinese Confucianism and Buddhism to provide legitimacy for their government. They had learned a written language that made it possible to keep records, to write histories that could further legitimate their rule, and to communicate more easily with far-flung officials. They had laid out cities, built temples, painted realistic portraits, learned how to play Chinese musical instruments, and upgraded their skills in making ceramics. Therefore, by this time Japanese leaders had reason to feel that Japan's governmental structure, philosophical underpinnings, religion, and art were all comparable to China's, and that it was no longer necessary to accept a formal tribute relationship in which they had to acknowledge that the Chinese leader was the "Son of Heaven," ranked far above the "King of Japan."

Furthermore, the Chinese state was no longer such a compelling model. After the An Lushan Rebellion of 755–763, the Tang dynasty had begun to decline. By 838, China no longer had the appeal as a model that the great Tang dynasty had earlier, at the peak of its dynamism. Many groups outside China's boundaries had stopped sending tribute missions to China, and in 838 Japan sent its last tribute mission. In the decades just before and after the collapse of the Tang dynasty in 907, there were continuing struggles for power, and the succeeding dynasties had difficulty gaining the necessary unity and leverage to control China's trading partners.

Six centuries later, from 1403 to 1547, when the Ming dynasty (1368–1644) was strong and the Japanese shogunate was weak, Japan agreed to return to the ritual subordination to China by resuming a tribute relationship. The founder of the Ming dynasty, Zhu Yuanzhang, confident that China had all the trade it needed, demanded that Japan resume its tributary relationship if it wanted to trade with China. The shogun at the time, Ashikaga Yoshimitsu, believed that trade would be beneficial to Japan and that China's recognition of the shogun as a partner would also strengthen the shogunate. The tribute relationship in 1403 continued for more than a century, until Japanese leaders again felt they were in a strong enough position to abandon it.

During the millennium from 838 to 1862, the basic relationship between China and Japan revolved around trade.[1] As Chinese shipbuilding progressed during the Song and Yuan dynasties China began to produce ships that were larger and stronger, and trade increased.[2] But compared with the scale of trade in the late nineteenth and twentieth centuries, the amount of trade between Japan and China at the time was still miniscule.

Chinese and Japanese leaders generally sought to maintain peaceful working relations with each other. The major exceptions were two wildly ambitious leaders who wanted to conquer overseas territories. One was a Mongol, Kublai Khan, who led Yuan dynasty troops to attack Japan in the late thirteenth century, and the other was Japanese, Toyotomi Hideyoshi, who invaded Korea on the way to a planned conquest of China in the late sixteenth century. However, both failed in their attempts to conquer the other country. Thereafter, in both cases trade resumed and officials promoted peaceful relations between the two countries.

The countries' images of each other underwent changes over the years. As Joshua Fogel observes, earlier Chinese images of the Japanese had largely been derived from Japan's "sagacious monks," who had studied in China during the Sui and Tang periods. However, during the Ming period the dominant Chinese image of the Japanese was formed by the "bloodthirsty pirates" who then ravaged the Chinese coast.

In Japan, images of China and its people were dominated by the respect that the Japanese had for learned Chinese officials and monks. The Japanese never lost sight of China's huge size, its wealth of resources, and the extraordinary objects its artisans produced, and Japanese traders never lost sight of China's high level of commercial activity. However, victories by Toyotomi Hideyoshi's troops in some battles with Chinese troops in Korea reduced Japan's awe for China because its military was not so overwhelming.

Until 1895, the Japanese took far more interest in Chinese matters than the Chinese took interest in Japan. Japanese scholars continued to read Chinese works, but few in China were interested in Japanese culture. In the middle of the nineteenth century, as Japan began to look outward, the Japanese, rather than Chinese, took the initiative to renew official contacts between the two countries.

In contrast to the transformation of Japanese civilization brought about by what Japan learned from China from 600 to 838, and the later transformation of China by what it would learn from Japan after 1895, during the millennium from 838 to 1862 neither country was fundamentally transformed by what it learned from the other. To trace the major changes in Sino-Japanese relations during this long period, it is useful to divide the millennium into the period from 838 to 1403, when there were no tributary relations; the period from 1403 to 1547, when China and Japan had a tributary relationship; and the period from 1547 to 1862, when there were no official contacts.

Local Supervisors, Merchants, and Monks, 838–1403

By the time Japan stopped sending tribute missions, the major economic center of China had shifted from China's northwest in the Wei River valley to the lower Yangtze River area along the Pacific coast. Advances in irrigation and planting in the lower Yangtze region enabled the development and expansion of rice paddy agriculture. The good harbors in the region made possible more rapid economic development, which led to an increase in the region's population.

Because the Japanese central government no longer controlled trade, Japanese merchants were free to transport goods from Japan to the lower Yangtze ports—Yangzhou, Hangzhou, Ningbo, and to Fujian and Guangzhou on the Pacific coast south of the Yangtze River—and to return with Chinese exports. Similarly, Chinese merchant ships could carry goods to sell in Japan and return with goods for the Chinese market. At the time, Japan's most active international port was Hakata (present-day Fukuoka, in Kyushu), where local officials appointed by the shogun were stationed to supervise the comings and goings of ships for international travel.

During the Song dynasty (960–1279) the Chinese economy became more commercialized, and copper coins were used as exchange. Song officials found it advantageous to carry on trade with Japan and to collect customs fees, so they did not insist on continuing the tribute relations. Sino-Japanese trade grew, and exchanges were relatively smooth. Because Chinese ships were generally sturdier than Japanese ships, more Chinese ships than Japanese ships made the voyage between Hakata and China's ports.

Before, when ships were smaller and less sturdy, traders from Japan generally took the northern route from Kyushu to Korea, and then along the western coast of Korea through the Gulf of Bohai to North China. However, as Richard Von Glahn explains, with larger ships travel increased via the more direct but more dangerous southern route, across the rougher seas between Hakata and Ningbo.

During much of its rule, the Song dynasty managed to coexist peacefully with the Liao dynasty (970–1125) to its north. Although most trade from Japan was conducted with the Song dynasty in the lower Yangtze area, Japan also carried on a small amount of trade with the Liao. Goods from the Liao dynasty, whose territory covered much of present-day China's Northeast, were transported across the Korean Peninsula to Japan.

In 1127, Jurchen invaders from the north conquered Kaifeng, capital of the Song dynasty. After the Song retreated southward and established a new capital in Hangzhou, the dynasty was called the Southern Song and the previous era when Kaifeng was the Song capital became known as the Northern Song. With the capital in Hangzhou, located on the southern bank of the Yangtze River where it could take advantage of the economic growth in the lower Yangtze region, Southern Song trade flourished between the ports in the Yangtze delta and Hakata, up until Hangzhou was overwhelmed by the Mongols in 1279.

Japanese recognized that the Song dynasty, with its large continental base and its massive public works projects, had a more advanced economy and more specialized markets than Japan, and it had attractive products

Japan could buy. As overseas trade grew, craftsmen along China's coastal areas expanded their businesses, making porcelain, ceramics, silk, and cotton textiles to sell to Japanese and other foreign buyers.

The Chinese had begun making copper coins (sometimes called bronze coins) even before the Han dynasty was established in 206 BC, and by the time of the Northern Song dynasty they were producing extensive quantities of such coins. Scholars have estimated that there may have been as many as two billion copper coins in circulation during Song China.[3] The coins could be used not only as a measure for collecting taxes but also for long-distance commercial exchanges. During the time of the Song dynasty, Japan made efforts to produce copper coins on its own, but Japan's coin-making technology was inferior to China's, and Japan soon abandoned its attempts and began using Chinese copper coins. The Japanese, eager for more coins, were willing to export cloth, pottery, and other goods to China in exchange for Chinese copper coins. At times, government supervisors in Chinese port cities endeavored to limit the amount of copper coins going to Japan. As an alternative, in the late ninth century the Japanese monk Ennin and others used gold dust to pay for Chinese goods, and there was a set conversion rate between rice and gold dust. By the tenth century less gold dust was available, and the Japanese resorted to using rice again to pay for Chinese goods. Papermaking skills in China had by then improved, and for a time the Song dynasty used paper currency, but after some decades it abandoned the use of paper currency and returned to using copper coins.

During the 838–1403 period, without tribute relations—and thus without diplomatic relations—the central governments of China and Japan did not play important roles in organizing trade. The key actors carrying out and regulating trade between China and Japan were government supervisors at the trading ports, merchants, and monks.

Port Supervisors

Although the successive Chinese and Japanese governments no longer organized trade missions after the end of tribute relations, they still set rules governing trade and established offices in port cities to supervise trade, examine the goods entering and leaving the ports, and collect customs fees.

The local port supervisors sought to make certain that the government got an appropriate share of the imports and that goods in short supply were not exported. Because China had more ships and exchanged more goods with more countries than Japan, it was easier for China's port supervisors to exercise some standardization and to exact set fees. In contrast, in Japan there were so few ships that it was difficult to set standard fees, leaving more leeway for local officials to set fees themselves. There were continuing tensions with the merchants over the fees that port officials extracted. The port supervisors also had the right to refuse to accept certain cargo. But demand for many goods was high and the distance from Chinese ports to the Song capital and from Japanese ports to the court in Kyoto made it difficult for both governments to maintain tight control over port supervisors. Local port supervisors often found opportunities to pass on some of the goods and some of the income from fees to family and friends. Corruption, by its nature, is impossible for scholars to measure, but there are documents from the time acknowledging that such problems existed and that violators were punished.

In some years, to prevent the outflow of certain goods, local supervisors in both China and Japan limited the frequency that ships could enter the ports and the amount of those goods that could be exported. For example, when Chinese officials grew concerned about the shortage of copper and the great demand for coins, they required that supervisors restrict the number of copper coins being exported to Japan.

The office supervising trade at the Hakata port was the Kyushu Headquarters in nearby Dazaifu. When the Kyushu Headquarters was first established in the seventh century, the Kyoto court assigned some officials from the nobility in Kyoto to serve there, to ensure central control over foreign trade, and to make sure the court in Kyoto had the first opportunity to purchase select goods from China. Because of the difficulty of supervising local port officials from a distance before modern communication and transport facilities were available, the local port supervisors assumed considerable independence in managing trade.

Some goods that arrived from China cleared customs in Hakata and could be transported by ship to other Japanese ports that were not allowed to engage in direct foreign trade. By 1469 the port of Sakai, located on the outskirts of Osaka, an independent city similar to the merchant cities of medieval Europe and famous for metalworking and textiles, was opened. Domestic ships traveling from Hakata up through the Inland Sea to Sakai could pass on foreign goods that had come into Japan at Hakata. Sakai provided opportunities for wealthy families in the prosperous Kansai region, including Osaka, Kobe, Kyoto, and Nara, to acquire imported goods. Only a very small number of localities could engage in direct foreign trade. One such port was Bungo Funai (in present-day Oita City, Oita prefecture, in northeastern Kyushu), and a regional trade headquarters was established there with supervisors to oversee the import and export of goods.

Hakata is not as well known in the Western world as Nagasaki, but as the only open port in Japan at the time, it followed many policies that were later adopted in Nagasaki when it was the only open port during the Tokugawa period (1603–1868). For example, local officials in Hakata were expected to inform the court in Kyoto about the foreign ships that arrived in Japan and about the goods that were imported and exported. In nearby Dazaifu there was a guest house, the Korokan, that provided the hotel services for foreign visitors, enabling local officials to have a measure of control over the activities of those foreigners who docked their ships nearby. After the middle of the eleventh century, when the guest house was no longer used, Chinese traders who stayed in Hakata were grouped together in a "Chinatown" district, similar to that in Nagasaki during the Tokugawa period. Some remains of the Korokan guest house were discovered in 1987, and they have been studied by archaeologists seeking to gather information about the types of goods exchanged.

In 971 the Chinese government established a Marine Trade Superintendence Office (Shibosi) in Guangzhou (in Guangdong province) to serve as the gatekeeper on the Chinese side. Later, as the lower Yangtze region began to prosper, government offices to supervise the trade were established in Hangzhou (989) and Ningbo (992). Merchants were required to obtain licenses to engage in foreign trade. In 1080 Ningbo was the only city allowed to issue licenses for Chinese ships to travel to Korea and Japan. All arriving ships had to undergo inspections, and their goods were taxed. Actual taxes varied greatly over time, ranging from as low as 5 percent at times to as high as 70 percent. When the taxes were very high, merchants had greater incentives to resort to smuggling. Because there were far more foreign ships in Chinese ports than there were in Japanese ports, China developed facilities and more standardized methods for taxing imported goods.

Prior to the Tang dynasty (618–907), Guangzhou was the key port in China for foreign trade. Until the eleventh century, Dengzhou, in Shandong province, a port for trade with Korea, was also used for trade with Japan. Guangzhou remained a lively port for foreign trade until the thirteenth century, when Fuzhou and Quanzhou, both in Fujian province, gradually became more important. Because porcelain from Fujian was then a key export to Japan and Southeast Asia, the production of porcelain increased in southern Fujian and as far south as Chaozhou, in northeastern Guangdong province.

Even though Chinese port supervisors allowed Japanese ships and others to unload goods in designated ports, there were frequent tensions with Japanese merchants because Chinese port officials would often impound Japanese goods. In 1309, Japanese traders in Ningbo were so upset when Chinese officials confiscated many of their goods that they used sulfur they had planned to sell to the Chinese for use in gunpowder to set fires, causing the destruction of many Ningbo buildings, including monasteries and government offices. A Chinese inscription later erected near the site does not blame the Japanese; instead, it describes the improper behavior of the Chinese who unfairly tried to take Japanese property.

In general, during this period Chinese skills in producing goods were more advanced than Japanese skills. As traced by Charlotte von Verschuer, China produced and exported porcelain, medicines, perfumes, and silk, while Japan exported gold dust, mercury, sulfur, woven silk, pearls, and pottery. Gold was discovered in a Japanese mine in 749, and as other gold mines were established, gold soon dominated Japanese exports. By the eleventh century less gold was available, but after new discoveries of gold in the thirteenth and fourteenth centuries it again became a key export. Japan also continued to upgrade its handicraft skills, and by the eleventh century it was exporting paper fans, swords, armor, silk, and some ceramics. In 1242, after a fire destroyed the Jingshan Monastery near Hangzhou, because of a shortage of lumber in China Japanese Buddhists sent lumber to China to repair the monastery and to build coffins.

Merchants

Merchants were of course interested in making profits and paying lower customs fees. Although supervisors in the port cities could examine goods on their arrival, it was difficult to control the activities of merchants as they prepared goods for export and distributed imported goods. Given the modest size of cargo ships during this period, it was difficult to transport large items, and because the voyages were expensive, they required considerable preparation. Merchants sometimes shipped lumber to be used for special building projects, and occasionally they shipped horses and other animals, but the goods exchanged were generally smaller items of lesser value that could be stored in chests on the ships. Owing to the small quantity of goods transported over these long distances, they were distributed to people in government offices, large estates, monasteries, and the rich elite, but not to ordinary farm families.

Since court officials in Kyoto and the well-to-do Japanese were eager to buy Chinese goods, Chinese merchants who went to Japan during the Song dynasty were often able to establish good working relationships with officials in various localities. After imported goods were taxed by officials in Dazaifu, the Chinese merchants could sometimes then proceed with their goods to other cities. Because of high demand, they were often able to reap substantial profits.

Monks

Monks, as men of faith, were regarded as more trustworthy than merchants who focused on profits, and Japanese Buddhist monks who visited China developed relations of trust with their Chinese counterparts. With the end of the tribute system, Japanese monks in China, in addition to their religious role and as the intellectuals of the day, could, in the absence of government officials, play a role as a trusted go-between, facilitating trade between the two countries.

Only about twenty Japanese Buddhist monks visited China during the Northern Song (960–1126), but during the Southern Song (1126–1279) as many as one hundred Japanese monks traveled to China, often on Chinese merchant ships. In their religious role, Japanese monks continued to spend time studying in Chinese monasteries and paying homage to famous religious sites. According to Li Yiwen, who has studied the role of monks in the six centuries between tribute missions, Japanese monks, in addition to making pilgrimages to places like Mount Wutai (in today's Shanxi province) and Mount Tiantai (in today's Zhejiang province), continued to study under famous Chinese monks to advance their knowledge of the Buddhist texts. Although Japanese monks made great advances in their understanding of the texts, they still looked up to the leading Chinese teachers. They were eager to bring back Buddhist texts and objects of art for display in Japan. Some Japanese Buddhists also believed that Chinese Buddhists had learned how to cure certain physical ailments, and they sought to understand such secrets.

At the time, Buddhist adherents, especially in Japan, identified with particular Buddhist sects. Some leading Japanese monks, on their return from study in China, established sects in their homeland that were linked to those in China. One prominent Chinese sect, the Chan, which emphasized meditation and the search for enlightenment more than the study of texts, was brought to Japan in the eighth century and introduced under its Japanese name, Zen. The Zen Buddhist sect grew rapidly and became very popular in Kamakura, where the shogunate was located from 1185 to 1333. The Japanese monk Eisai (1141–1215) introduced one sect of Zen Buddhism in Japan, and his disciple Dogen (1200–1253) introduced another. Zen's stress on developing a strong and determined personal spirit had great appeal to leading Japanese warriors, some of whom used Zen to train young soldiers.

In their broader nonreligious role, Japanese monks communicated with the Japanese court in Kyoto, with Chinese officialdom, with port supervisors in both Japan and China, and with merchants. Although the Chinese government cracked down on Buddhism in 845 and eliminated China's monasteries, which paid no taxes, within several decades the repression eased and monks could again openly practice their religion and work with Chinese government officials.

During the Northern Song period, three Japanese monks were even received by the Chinese emperor and brought him gifts, much like Japanese envoys had during the earlier tribute missions. In 983 Emperor Song Taizong, second emperor of the Song dynasty (976–997), welcomed a Japanese monk, Chonen, and accepted two Japanese scrolls containing information about Japan, including a list of the sixty-four emperors claimed by Japan to represent a continuous line since Jimmu Tenno. Song Taizong expressed interest in Chonen and met him again during the following two years. A second Japanese monk, Jakusho, was received by Emperor Zhenzhong in 1004, and a third, Jojin, was received by Emperor Shenzong in 1072.

Japanese monks were sometimes able to negotiate with the Chinese government and with the Japanese court in Kyoto. Many officials in the Kyoto court were practicing Buddhists, which facilitated dealings with Japanese monks. Some merchants were also Buddhists, which made them more willing to cooperate with the monks as they organized voyages to China.

Some of the Japanese monks who played a broad negotiating role had gained considerable administrative experience from leading Japanese monasteries. During most of this period, Japan's monasteries operated tax-free, and some occupied large estates. Often, monks who went to China were trying to raise money for their monasteries, and they insisted that a certain portion of the income from their voyages be used for the renovation or expansion of their monasteries. The chief priest of the Tenryuji Temple, for example, led delegations to China and used the income from the trips for construction of a temple that was completed in 1345. The large monasteries situated near ports had greater opportunities than smaller monasteries located farther away to take part in trade and to obtain credit. Several monks were reported to have been corrupted by opportunities to take part in trade.

Although the Japanese were reluctant to accept the subordinate position imposed by China's tribute system, they remained respectful of Chinese Buddhism and Chinese intellectual life. The great neo-Confucian scholar Zhu Xi (1130–1200), who created a new synthesis of Confucianism that emphasized the importance of human reason in forming a harmonious relationship with the universe, was widely respected in Japan, and the Japanese version of his philosophy later became the underlying philosophy of the Tokugawa period.

In short, during the Song period China was open to trade, and Buddhist monks helped to smooth Chinese-Japanese relations and facilitate trade between the two countries.

The Second Sino-Japanese Conflict: Yuan Dynasty Troops Invade Kyushu, 1274 and 1281

The first time that Chinese and Japanese forces clashed, in the 660s, it was in Korea. The second time, when the Mongol-led troops of the Yuan dynasty attacked, it was in Japan—the only time in history when Chinese and Japanese forces fought in Japan.

Although the Mongols are ethnically distinct from Han Chinese, after they defeated the Southern Song in the thirteenth century, they established China's Yuan dynasty (1271–1368) and ruled over China's territory, following Chinese patterns of rule. For several years before the Mongol-led troops invaded Japan in 1274, the Japanese had been warned that Mongol troops were advancing down the Korean Peninsula, preparing to invade Japan as part of their goal of conquering all the known world. Beginning in 1266, Kublai Khan, whose troops already dominated the Korean Peninsula, sent messages to Japan demanding that it become a vassal state under the Yuan dynasty. Kublai Khan began large-scale shipbuilding in Korea in preparation for an invasion; meanwhile, Japan not only did not respond to Kublai Khan's messages but even refused to receive his messengers. Kublai Khan hoped the Japanese would not resist his demand, but when a messenger sent to Japan was killed by the Japanese, Kublai Khan moved ahead with his plans to invade.

In 1274 an estimated 23,000 Mongol and Korean troops sailed from Korea, joined by Han Chinese troops from Zhejiang, to invade Japan. After taking over Tsushima Island (located between Korea and Japan) and several of the smaller islands off Kyushu, the invaders landed in Hakata Bay. Initially the Mongol forces had some success in defeating the Japanese, who had no experience in fighting an outside enemy. But a typhoon struck, wiping out many of the Mongol ships and stranding those troops that had already landed. After the typhoon, the invaders were overwhelmed by a large number of Japanese troops. The invaders tried to withdraw to their ships, but further typhoons destroyed most of their remaining forces, and the remnants of the Mongol invasion force withdrew to the Korean Peninsula.

Japanese officials concluded that they had been saved by the *kamikaze* (divine wind). This interpretation, that Japan was a special country protected by the heavens, would later be employed by ultranationalists to propagandize Japan's undefeatable nationalist spirit, and the term *kamikaze* itself would be used to describe Japanese pilots who flew suicide missions during World War II, diving into Allied naval ships in the Pacific. Although historians differ as to the seriousness of the storms' actual effect on the outcome, typhoons did destroy some Chinese ships and leave some Mongol-led troops stranded.

When the Japanese learned that the Mongols were planning a second attack, in preparation they built defensive structures, including a six-foot-high wall and ditches for flooding the area if the Mongol-led troops were to land. In 1281 an estimated 40,000 Mongol and Korean troops in Korea and some 20,000 Han Chinese forces from Zhejiang launched a second invasion. In the battle, parts of Hakata were burned down, including an area where Chinese sailors lived. By the time of this second invasion, however, the Japanese had amassed a large defensive force, and they were much better prepared because they had studied the tactics and equipment used by the invaders during the first attack. The Japanese warriors fought bravely, killing nearly all the Mongol and Korean troops who came ashore. They spared some Chinese troops who were skilled artisans and allowed them to remain and settle in Hakata to contribute to the Japanese economy.

After the Yuan soldiers retreated, trade between China and Japan resumed quickly. Several years later, the Yuan's Mongol leaders, in an effort to restore relations with Japan, sent as their envoy a Chinese Zen monk, who stayed in Kamakura, where the shogun was located, and played a role as trusted go-between, similar to the role that Japanese monks had played in China.

Reviving the Tribute Missions, 1403–1547

The founding emperor of the Ming dynasty, Zhu Yuanzhang (who ruled from 1368 to 1398), believed that China had all the goods it needed. Since the country had a solid income base from taxes on rice agriculture, the leaders did not see a need to gather further income from foreign trade. Furthermore, Emperor Zhu Yuanzhang wanted to maintain order along the seacoast. During his first year in office, he announced the prohibition of all trade with foreign countries and fortified the coast to clamp down on smuggling. He recognized that Japanese merchants wished to trade with China, but he would permit it only if Japan accepted the tribute system. Furthermore, all ships sailing between the two countries were required to obtain "tallies" (licenses) to transport certain goods. A ship that lacked a license was regarded as a pirate ship.

In 1369, during his second year of rule, Emperor Zhu Yuanzhang sent envoys to Japan and to Southeast Asian countries to promote the revival of the tribute system and the addition of the licensing system. He was convinced that Japan needed trade more than China did and that he had enough leverage to maintain firm control over trade. In 1371 Japan sent ten monks to China, carrying a letter from Prince Kaneyoshi, son of Emperor Godaigo. Emperor Zhu Yuanzhang sent a return delegation of eight Chinese monks bearing gifts for Prince Kaneyoshi. Negotiations between the two sides continued from 1370 to 1402. All the Japanese negotiating missions, as well as the Chinese missions, were led by monks.

Over the next several years, as the Japanese continued discussions with the Chinese, they gave no sign of accepting the reestablishment of the tributary relationship. In 1380, when a trade mission from Japan arrived in China, because Japan had not agreed to resume the tributary relationship China refused to accept the ship and its goods. Further efforts by Japanese traders to unload their ships in China were similarly rebuffed. The situation was also complicated by Zhu Yuanzhang's suspicion that his chief minister, Hu Weiyong, was cooperating with the Japanese to overthrow him. Chinese officials made their stance very clear: they would not allow trade with China unless the Japanese accepted the tribute system, which would give China ceremonial recognition of its superior position.

Ashikaga Yoshimitsu, who became Japan's minister of state in 1394, was acutely aware that the Ashikaga shoguns did not enjoy the widespread national support that the Kamakura shoguns (1185–1333) had enjoyed at their peak. Convinced that reviving trade with China would be good for Japan and would help legitimate the position of the Ashikaga shoguns within Japan, and aware that Japan had little leverage with China, Yoshimitsu finally relented and agreed to accept a tributary relationship that subordinated Japan to China.

By the time Yoshimitsu was ready to acknowledge that the Chinese emperor was the Son of Heaven and that Yoshimitsu was in effect his subordinate, Zhu Yuanzhang had died and there was a power struggle within China between Jianwen, Zhu's grandson (son of his first son), and Jianwen's uncle, a son of Zhu Yuanzhang. In 1403 Yoshimitsu sent a mission of some three hundred people to China to accept the inferior position of a tributary nation. The mission carried two different letters, one in case Jianwen was chosen to be emperor, and one in case Jianwen's uncle was chosen to be emperor. By the time the ship arrived, Jianwen's uncle had become the Yongle emperor, so the mission handed over the appropriate letter. An agreement to reestablish a tributary relationship, including trade, was reached in 1403. The Ming rulers would permit Japan to send two ships to China every ten years. They would be certified with tallies allowing them to engage in private trade. When Yoshimitsu's mission returned to Japan, the Yongle emperor allowed eighty Chinese passengers to return on the Japanese ship.

There is no record that the Japanese emperor or the imperial court had approved the decision by Ashikaga Yoshimitsu to resume the tribute relationship. Some Japanese scholars have speculated that since the imperial court never supported the decision, some members of the court must have disagreed with the decision. Later, the Japanese were very critical of Ashikaga Yoshimitsu for lacking more backbone and allowing Japan to accept an inferior status.

Between 1404 and 1410, in addition to allowing tribute missions to visit China, the Chinese also allowed six other Japanese ships to land. Thereafter, the Chinese allowed only three ships engaged in private trade to land every ten years. However, many Japanese ships went to China as part of a tribute mission. When a Japanese tribute mission arrived in Beijing, the tribute gifts were first exchanged. Then other goods brought in addition to the tribute were sold to the Chinese at negotiated prices. If Chinese officials did not purchase all the goods, the Japanese could sell the remaining goods on the market in China.

In 1451 a Japanese mission sailed to China with nine ships and an unusually large amount of cargo. The Chinese had trouble selling so much cargo at high prices. On one occasion, two warring families, the Ouchi and Hosokawa, could not reach agreement on a joint mission, and so they sent separate missions. Some Japanese officials remained unhappy with the subordination to China required by the tribute system, and by the middle of the sixteenth century Japan's domestic disputes made it increasingly difficult to organize the missions. Between 1403 and 1549, Japan sent a total of eleven tribute system missions to China, bringing with them gifts and additional goods to be sold. The last tribute mission was sent to China in 1549.

Japanese Pirates and Their Enduring Image in China

During the period of the tribute missions, the Ming dynasty prohibited private trade except when specifically permitted by tallies, so any Japanese merchant attempting to sell goods in China outside that framework was regarded as a *wokou* (pirate). For the Chinese, the term *wokou* included smugglers as well those who preyed on ships at sea. After the tribute missions ended, the Ming dynasty did not allow the Japanese to trade with China. At that point, any Japanese person trading with China was classified as a *wokou*. Those who smuggled goods and raided the Chinese coast were sometimes Japanese, sometimes Korean, and sometimes Chinese. Scholars, Chinese as well as non-Chinese, have estimated that the majority of *wokou* were actually Chinese, and sometimes a single pirate gang included members from different countries. Japanese pirates were reported by the Chinese as early as the fourth century, but they were small in number until the mid-fifteenth century. Piracy was fairly widespread throughout the sixteenth century.

The conditions that led to widespread smuggling and piracy included prohibitions on trade that were inherently difficult to enforce, domestic turmoil in both Japan and China that rendered policing difficult, and the existence of strong economic incentives for those who were successful smugglers.

Along the long Chinese coastline there are countless inlets where smugglers could enter. Neither Japan nor China had sufficient personnel to apprehend all smugglers or pirates who raided other ships. It was easy for foreign smugglers to find local Chinese partners along the coast, in Guangdong, Fujian, Zhejiang, and along the Yangtze River in Jiangsu province, who were eager to share in the rewards. Even though Chinese officials attempted to relocate those Chinese smuggling participants living near the coast, those who were relocated could easily sneak back.

There were excellent economic opportunities for smugglers. Within China, in the mid-sixteenth century there was great demand for silver, as a medium of exchange and for making tax payments. In 1530, the Japanese discovered silver and opened the Iwami silver mine, which began producing very large amounts of the precious metal. Compared with silver, gold was cheaper in China than it was in Japan, so it was possible for sea merchants to make quick profits by selling Japanese silver in China and then buying gold in China for resale in Japan. Chinese smugglers brought silk and other goods to Japanese ports from China to exchange for silver, and they employed Japanese crew members to work on their ships. When Japanese merchants and their Chinese collaborators had difficulties smuggling along the Chinese coast, some used force to obtain what they were unable to buy.

Japanese pirates came mostly from Kyushu, especially from the Satsuma domain in the south and from the Hosokawa domain near Kumamoto. The islands of Hirado, near Nagasaki, and Tsushima became smuggling centers. Within Japan, the ultimate destinations for most imports were Osaka and nearby cities served by the port of Sakai.

The Chinese did make some progress in controlling piracy. Two Chinese military leaders who gained a reputation for success in suppressing the pirates are still celebrated as heroes today: General Yu Dayou and Qi Jiguang, who achieved great success when he was a young military officer. There were an estimated one hundred military attacks on pirates during the reigns of the first three Ming emperors (1368–1424). Without consistently strong leadership, however, military men sometimes joined the pirates rather than fighting them. Some of the "Japanese pirates" were in fact Chinese military personnel with access to ships and military equipment.

Some Ming officials proposed liberalizing the trade rules to reduce the incentives for smuggling and piracy. In 1567 the governor of Fujian received permission to license private trade voyages to Southeast Asia. This partial liberalization provided incentives for both Chinese and Japanese traders, who might otherwise have continued to engage in piracy, to begin sailing to Southeast Asian ports where they could trade with each other and also acquire local goods for resale in their home ports.

Ming official Xu Guangqi (1562–1633) was in favor of liberalizing the rules for trading with Japan. After passing the *jinshi* examination for officialdom in 1604, Xu then studied with Matteo Ricci, the well-known Jesuit who was then in China, and became a Jesuit, perhaps the most famous Chinese convert to Christianity before the twentieth century. He developed a deep knowledge of agriculture and national defense, both of which he considered very central to national strength. As a Jesuit he had access to information gathered by Jesuits in other countries, and he then became an adviser to the emperor. Xu Guangqi argued that it would be impossible to stop the pirates, who had access to so many locations along the coast. In his view, piracy was prevalent not because the Japanese were avaricious but because they were not allowed to trade, and because some Chinese buyers who purchased goods from the Japanese did not honor their agreements to pay for those goods. The solution he proposed was to permit the Japanese to trade, so they could obtain the silk, ceramics, and medicines that they wanted.

Xu's arguments lost the day to those who argued that the Japanese were cunning, bloodthirsty pirates, and that the way to deal with them was to crack down. Chinese and occasionally European piracy remained widespread until after Xu's death.

The Japanese began clamping down on piracy in 1587, when Toyotomi Hideyoshi forced the lords of Kyushu to accept his authority and to suppress piracy. When Toyotomi Hideyoshi and his successor, Tokugawa Ieyasu, banned piracy, sea captains recognized that attacking settlements in other countries and on the seas would bring the wrath of the Japanese authorities. In 1592 Toyotomi Hideyoshi legalized trade by issuing nine licenses, each with his red seal. After becoming shogun in 1603, Tokugawa Ieyasu continued the antipiracy policies of his predecessor and the use of red seals to promote legal trade, thus reducing the need for merchants to resort to piracy. Pirates learned that if they attacked ships that carried the red seal, they would face active reprisals from Japanese officials. In 1635 Tokugawa Ieyasu's grandson gained further control over piracy by banning all overseas travel by Japanese citizens.

When piracy was at its peak, Europeans—first the Portuguese and then the Spanish, Dutch, and English—began to play a greater role in Asian trade. From the time the Portuguese established a base in Macao in 1557 until their expulsion from Japan in 1639, the Portuguese provided a legitimate channel for Japanese silver to be traded for Chinese silk and gold. The Portuguese profits from this trade cut into profitability for the *wokou* and, along with the Japanese crackdowns, contributed to the decline of piracy.

The combination of Japan's clamping down on piracy during the Tokugawa after 1603 and China's more open trade policy contributed to reducing piracy. Later, during the Qing dynasty, China permitted more open trade with Japan and, as Xu Guangqi had argued, this further reduced the need for piracy.

Even though Japanese piracy finally ended, stories of so-called cunning and bloodthirsty Japanese pirates remained popular in Chinese literature. Chinese children were warned to behave or else the Japanese pirates would get them. Stories abounded of Japanese pirates using tricks to plunder local people. Lurid tales described Japanese pirates stealing property, setting fires, robbing graves, killing men, and raping women. It was said they cruelly cut women open and boiled men in water. Such images of Japanese cruelty can be found in the popular novel *Shuihu houzhuan* (Sequel to Water Margin). Toward the end of this story, the heroes take revenge on the Japanese. In another novel, published shortly after Toyotomi Hideyoshi invaded Korea, Toyotomi Hideyoshi is described as an incarnation of an evil dragon and is finally slain by the heroes. The *Treatise on Japan* (*Riben zhuan*), which is part of the official Ming history (*Ming shi*), is somewhat less fanciful but still includes descriptions of the bloodthirsty Japanese. In this way, such horrifying images of the Japanese were passed on to future generations in China.

The Third Sino-Japanese Conflict: Toyotomi Hideyoshi's Invasion of Korea, 1592–1597

Just as the Chinese Warring States period ended when a strong leader emerged victorious and became Qin Shihuang, the first emperor of the Qin in 221 BC, so Japan's Warring States struggles ceased in 1590 when Toyotomi Hideyoshi, building on the successes of Oda Nobunaga, emerged victorious and unified Japan. Like such leaders as Qin Shihuang, Alexander the Great, and Genghis Khan, Toyotomi Hideyoshi had vaulting ambitions to conquer the world. He had massive numbers of battle-hardened soldiers on whom he could call, and he did not agonize over the suffering that resulted from conquering new worlds. Some historians have argued that one reason Toyotomi Hideyoshi pursued foreign conquests was to keep his own troops occupied, owing to his fear that if they returned to their homes, they would have trouble earning a decent living and might become unruly, causing domestic turmoil. Unlike the later Japanese who, in the late nineteenth century, would be preparing for the Sino-Japanese War of 1894–1895, Toyotomi Hideyoshi did not undertake detailed studies to understand either his enemy or the terrain where the fighting would take place.

Toyotomi Hideyoshi, who believed that he had been endowed by heaven with the capacity for conquest, succeeded in unifying Japan in 1590, but by 1585, after defeating several rivals in Japan, he had already conceived the idea of conquering China. He planned to go through Korea and then on to China, which he believed he could easily defeat. After he conquered China, he would visit Beijing, make it his capital, and then personally settle down in Ningbo, where he could govern China and remain in close contact with Japan. After conquering China, he would then conquer India and the Southeast Asian countries. He began adopting sons and preparing them to serve as the leaders of the countries he would conquer. But despite his vast ambitions, he also had vast ignorance about other countries and the problems he would encounter in trying to realize such ambitions.

Toyotomi Hideyoshi ordered the Koreans to allow his troops to pass through their country unobstructed on their way to conquer China. Korea firmly refused more than once, so in August 1590 Toyotomi Hideyoshi began preparations to invade Korea. In addition to the experienced swordsmen, gunmen, and horseback riders whom he called upon, he also required that all the daimyo, lords of the feudal domains, requisition foot soldiers from all over Japan. In April 1592 Toyotomi Hideyoshi, from his base in Nagoya, ordered the transport of 160,000 warriors to Pusan, with the intention of marching them through Korea into Manchuria, and then on to Beijing. He mobilized another 120,000 warriors as a reserve force.

Unlike the Mongol invasion of Kyushu when the invaders barely got ashore, the Japanese moved north rapidly into Korea after they landed in Pusan. The Koreans were poorly prepared, and the Japanese troops, with horsemen and guns and swords backed by cannons, marched 275 miles northward from Pusan to capture Pyongyang, the capital. Korean troops were ineffective in resisting the advances of Toyotomi Hideyoshi's troops. The Japanese troops terrorized the local population, and such behavior stimulated local Korean leaders to organize a guerrilla resistance that ultimately slowed down the Japanese advance. The Japanese could control their forts and the narrow roads between towns, but the Koreans controlled the countryside.

Within six weeks the Japanese troops had marched north from Seoul to P'yongyang and were preparing to move on to China. By the time the Japanese took P'yongyang, several thousand Chinese troops, dispatched by Ming dynasty Emperor Wanli, had crossed the Yalu River into Korea, but they were quickly defeated by the Japanese. Emperor Wanli, surprised by the failure of his troops, quickly dispatched some 43,000 soldiers, who crossed the Yalu River into the northern part of Korea. The Japanese were shocked by the entry of such large numbers of Ming troops, who succeeded in driving the Japanese, overstretched throughout the country, out of P'yongyang. The Chinese pursued the Japanese troops as they retreated southward. In a valley some ten miles north of Seoul, Japanese and Chinese troops fought once again, and the Japanese defeated the Ming troops. But when the Japanese attacked Chinese forces in Haengju, near Seoul, they were in turn defeated by the Chinese. The Japanese were able to use muskets, which they had learned how to make from Europeans, but the Chinese also had good technology, such as cannons that they had learned to make from the Portuguese.

The Koreans had by then become excellent shipbuilders. Before the invasion, Korean admiral Yi Sun-sin had been building up the Korean naval force with highly maneuverable armored "turtle ships" that had very strong firepower. Between May and September 1592, the naval force under Admiral Yi fought ten battles with the Japanese naval force along the coast of Korea. The Korean ships were superior to the Japanese ships, and Admiral Yi Sun-sin was clever in surprising and outmaneuvering the Japanese. In each encounter Admiral Yi was successful in defeating the Japanese. His control of the sea lanes around Korea made it impossible for Japan to reinforce its troops in Korea and to send in needed supplies. To feed their troops, the Japanese emptied out Korea's large granaries, but their food supplies still remained very tight.

During the first year of the war, an estimated one-third of the Japanese troops died—from fighting, cold weather, hunger, and disease.[4] By the end of the year, Japanese forces had settled into forts from where they could defend themselves, but they were unable to advance or to control the rural areas. In April 1593 the Chinese and Japanese, recognizing the stalemate, reached a truce in which the Japanese agreed to pull back their troops from Seoul to encampments in the Pusan area. In May 1593 Chinese negotiators traveled to Nagoya to engage in truce talks. Toyotomi Hideyoshi, who believed that Japan was the land of the gods and took a bold stance as if the Japanese had won the war, proposed that a portion of Korea be ceded to Japan, and that Korea send several high officials to Japan as hostages. The Ming demanded that the Japanese resume tributary relations to subordinate themselves to China. The truce talks continued for more than two years, but the positions of the two sides remained far apart.

Although some Japanese troops returned to Japan, other troops remained in camps not far from Pusan. From 1593 to 1597, some of these Japanese even engaged in farming in Korea to supply food to their men. They retained the capacity to defend themselves and when attacked they could successfully ward off their attackers.

In August 1597 Toyotomi Hideyoshi launched a second invasion to end the stalemate and enable his troops to march on to China. This time the Koreans and the Ming forces were better prepared and they quickly mobilized to stop the Japanese attack. Japanese forces advanced westward into Cholla in southwestern Korea and then marched northward toward Seoul, where they met great opposition.

Jealous Korean officials had replaced the hero Admiral Yi Sun-sin, and in this second invasion, Japanese naval forces initially defeated the Korean ships that tried to stop them, enabling the Japanese troops to get ashore. In desperation, the Koreans brought out of retirement Admiral Yi Sun-sin, who outmaneuvered Japan's naval forces in a number of battles, destroying Japanese ships and blocking them from reinforcing their troops. Early in 1598 the Ming sent in some 150,000 troops. The Japanese Army was stopped on both land and sea. In mid-1598, in the midst of these battles, Toyotomi Hideyoshi died of natural causes. His successors did not provoke the fear among the Japanese that he had, and therefore they could not force as many Japanese men to join their armies. Although the Japanese leaders initially tried to keep the death of Toyotomi Hideyoshi a secret, they realized that even if he had lived they had no hope of victory, so they began to withdraw. Chinese and Korean troops massed in large numbers to attack the Japanese, causing them heavy losses as they retreated. The great Korean hero Admiral Yi Sun-sin died during the naval battles.

The war was a lose-lose-lose situation, a disaster for Japan, for China, and for Korea. Although the Japanese won many battles and benefited from some of the Korean artisans who were taken to Japan as prisoners, Japan suffered great losses and earned long-lasting enmity from both China and Korea.

Even though Chinese casualties were high, Korean casualties were much higher. Many cultural treasures were destroyed, the economy suffered great losses, and wartime food shortages were difficult to overcome. The success of Admiral Yi Sun-sin, however, made him Korea's greatest national hero of all time. His statue still stands in Seoul, a symbol of the anti-Japanese struggle.

Although the Koreans and Chinese fought as allies, many Koreans were resentful of the Chinese troops who had ravaged the countryside as they fought and arrogantly ordered around the Korean troops. The Koreans were also upset with the Chinese leaders who, after the fighting, negotiated with the Japanese without including the Koreans in the talks.

For China, the fighting was a drain on Ming resources, including people, finances, and military equipment. This weakened the Ming's ability to resist the Jurchens, later known as the Manchus, who were strengthening their base in Manchuria in preparation for fighting the Ming and establishing their own Qing dynasty.

Local Development in the Tokugawa and the Qing

The Tokugawa period (1603–1868) and the Qing dynasty (1644–1911) were each able to achieve relative stability for more than two and a half centuries, but the number of contacts between them was limited. The system established by the Tokugawa led to local governance structures that strengthened local economic and educational development. The system established by the Qing enabled that large, diverse country to avoid strong local threats to the dynasty, but it put a damper on local economic development.

Struggles in Japan continued after the death of Toyotomi Hideyoshi in 1598. He had appointed a Council of Regents to support his young son as his successor, but the most powerful of the regents, Tokugawa Ieyasu, and his allies decisively defeated those supporting Toyotomi Hideyoshi's son in a huge battle at Sekigahara, west of today's Nagoya. The battle ended the period of Warring States, and in 1603 the emperor formally named Tokugawa

Ieyasu as shogun. Tokugawa Ieyasu then began the process of establishing a new order at home and a new pattern for dealing with foreign countries. Unlike Toyotomi Hideyoshi, Tokugawa had no ambition for foreign conquest; he first concentrated on building a stable domestic system and then on trying to overcome Korean and Chinese anger over Toyotomi Hideyoshi's invasion and to improve relations with those countries. Although some foreigners mistakenly later described the Tokugawa policy as exclusion (*sakoku*), in fact Tokugawa Ieyasu and his successors, like the founder of the Ming dynasty, Zhu Yuanzhang, sought to maintain foreign trade and relations with foreign countries but to keep them under tight control.

Tokugawa Ieyasu was remarkably successful in his efforts to establish a stable system that brought domestic peace. He passed on the position of shogun to his son in 1605, but in fact remained leader until his death in 1616, giving him time to eliminate all opposition and establish the new system. His son, in turn, passed the leadership on to his son in 1623. Ieyasu knew he did not have the power to eliminate the other daimyo, so he established a system of centralized feudalism whereby he kept family hostages from 270 daimyo in Edo (which after the Meiji Restoration was renamed Tokyo), where he erected the castle that, after the Meiji Restoration, would become the imperial palace. He acknowledged that he could not eliminate the daimyo who fought against him at Sekigahara (notably Choshu and Satsuma), so he gave them generous amounts of land and located them far away from Edo, where they posed less risk. His allies at Sekigahara were given land closer to Edo, and relatives of the Tokugawa directly ruled critical locations, such as Nagasaki, the only port on the four main islands that remained open for international trade.

In contrast to the Qing system, the Japanese system for maintaining control over local areas, by keeping hostages in Edo while permitting daimyo to build up their domains, allowed for strong local development. Each daimyo was deeply committed to the long-term development of his own domain, and therefore supported the economic development and education of everyone in the domain. Thus, the Japanese system of "centralized feudalism"— maintaining tight national control while allowing strong regional development by the daimyo—gave Japan a strong economic and educational base to face the Westerners who began arriving in the nineteenth century.

The Manchus, like the Tokugawa, proved successful in 1644 in establishing a stable new structure that lasted until the 1911 Revolution. By 1681, when the Manchus put down a revolt by the Three Feudatories (Fujian, Guangdong, and Yunnan), they were sufficiently unified that Japanese officials worried about the danger of a possible invasion. Qing officials were selected by examinations that tested their ability to devote themselves to years of rigorous study and their knowledge of the Confucian classics. They were not allowed to serve in their home area, so they could not link up with local people to resist the national leadership, and they were rotated among regions after two to three years to ensure they did not form deep roots in one area. Therefore, officials had little incentive to promote long-term development in the place where they were assigned. Inspectors were sent out to make sure officials did not form special relations with the people they governed, and officials were judged by their ability to maintain peace in their districts. This system had remarkable staying power, but it did not support strong local economic development.

Tokugawa Relations with China and Other Countries

When he came to power the Tokugawa shogun feared that Christianity, especially Catholicism, being promoted by Portuguese Jesuits, was causing disorder. In 1639, following a rebellion by Christian peasants in Kyushu, he banned trade with Portugal and Spain. Convinced that the Dutch, even if Protestant, were the European trading partners least likely to cause control problems, the shogun placed the Dutch on Dejima, an artificial island built near Nagasaki, where the Japanese could continue trading. Dutch traders thus became an important window on developments in the West. Through the Dutch, the Japanese learned about Western medicine and military technology.

The shogun allowed trade with China to continue, and even though Japanese residents were not allowed to travel abroad, Chinese could live in Nagasaki. In 1689, to control smuggling, the Chinese were required to move to a special compound within Nagasaki that eventually became a Chinatown. In effect, the Chinese residents of Nagasaki managed the trade with China.

From 1611 to 1625 a series of letters were exchanged between Chinese and Japanese officials concerning the possibility of reestablishing tribute relations. The Chinese were dissatisfied with Japan's apologies for the invasion of Korea and with Japanese efforts to apprehend "Japanese pirates." But the key issue was whether Japan would accept a subordinate status. The correspondence began with a Japanese letter to the governor of Fujian. It was signed by a foreign-policy adviser to Tokugawa rather than by Tokugawa or the emperor, and the Chinese did not accept it as a proper document since it did not come from the emperor. Additionally, in this letter the Japanese had used Japanese-era names for the calendar years rather than Chinese-era names. The Chinese were slow to respond, but in 1619 they hinted that there might be some progress toward resuming formal relations if Japan were to end all piracy. The Japanese discussed the proposal for some time, but in 1621 they made it clear that they would not accept use of Chinese-era names, which would indicate that the Chinese emperor had a higher status than the Japanese emperor. The Japanese thus chose not to be part of the Chinese world order. In 1635, when all Chinese trade in Japan was confined to Nagasaki, Chinese ships had to be certified to enter the harbor, and not all Chinese ships were granted such a certification. China's acceptance of this certification system gave the Japanese a sense of superiority over the Chinese, and the procedure allowed private trade to continue even though the two governments had no official relations until the 1870s.

To deal with others—the Koreans, the Russians, and the Ryukyus—Tokugawa delegated much of the responsibility to the daimyo whose domain was closest geographically to the people in question. The Tsushima daimyo, on the island closest to Korea, was assigned responsibility for managing relations with Korea. The Matsumae daimyo, the only Japanese daimyo on the northern island of Ezo (Hokkaido), was assigned responsibility for dealing with the Russians and the Ainu, a minority group living on Ezo. The Satsuma daimyo on the southern end of Kyushu managed relations with the Ryukyu Islands.

Ming Loyalists Flee to Taiwan and Japan

After the Manchus defeated the Ming in northern China and established the Qing dynasty in 1644, Ming loyalists who fled from the north to Fujian province in the south were able to join other Ming loyalists and continue their resistance for some decades. The leader of these Ming forces was Zheng Zhilong (1604–1661), who was originally from Quanzhou in Fujian. As a youth Zheng had gone to Macao, where he had learned Portuguese. He then went to Taiwan, and from there to Hirado, just north of Nagasaki, where he arrived at age twenty. As both a business entrepreneur and a pirate, he developed many contacts with the local Japanese. While in Hirado he married a Japanese woman, Tagawa Matsu, who gave birth to a son, Zheng Chenggong (Koxinga). After several years, Zheng Zhilong returned to Fujian, but Koxinga remained in Hirado with his mother until the age of seven when, with her, he moved to Fujian to join his father.

Some of the Ming loyalists hoped to use the relationships between Chinese and Japanese traders to win Japanese support for their efforts to defeat the Manchus and reestablish Ming rule in Beijing. Many Chinese migrants to Nagasaki had come from areas in Fujian that were controlled by Zheng Zhilong. According to historian Ronald Toby, the first contact by Ming loyalists seeking Japanese support was made in 1645 by Lin Gao, an associate of Zheng Zhilong then living in Fujian. Lin Gao was dispatched to Hirado where he, like Zheng Zhilong, had friends from earlier years, in the hope that they might help him line up support for the Ming loyalists.

When Lin Gao arrived in Nagasaki in 1645, he brought a letter from Admiral Cui Zhi, an assistant to Zheng Zhilong, with a request for Japanese support against the Manchus. The request was forwarded to Edo, where it was seriously discussed for some weeks. In the end, Japanese officials, cautious because of so many uncertainties about the situation in China, decided not to send aid at the time but to continue to study the situation. The Japanese dispatched a number of people to China to gather information about the efforts by Ming loyalists to overcome the Qing. The Japanese also gathered information about China from Chinese and Dutch merchants in Nagasaki; from Satsuma, which received reports of the struggle via the Ryukyu Islands; and from Tsushima, which received reports via Korea.

As Manchu forces advanced southward in 1645, to avoid large-scale fighting in Fujian they made an offer to Zheng Zhilong, hoping that he would abandon his anti-Manchu position. If he did, he would then be rewarded with a position in the new government in Beijing. After some negotiations, Zheng accepted the offer and moved to Beijing. His son Koxinga, however, remained a Ming loyalist and assumed command of those who had formerly served under his father. Koxinga, like his father, sought Japanese support through the Japanese authorities in Nagasaki. Although there is no record of the Japanese providing such support, Koxinga's junks continued to operate in Nagasaki and the loyalists even acquired some armaments through Nagasaki, despite the Tokugawa ban on exports that had existed since 1621.

One of the people the Japanese used to follow the developments of the Ming loyalists was the prominent Chan monk Yin Yuan (in Japanese, Ingen), who was from a rural area near Fuzhou in Fujian province, where he maintained contacts with the loyalists. At the time he was in power, Toyotomi Hideyoshi had been worried about the disruptive potential of the Christians converted by the Portuguese Jesuits who had come to Japan, and in 1587 he banned the practice of Christianity. In 1640 the shogun required that all the Chinese living in Nagasaki be registered under a Buddhist temple. The Buddhist temples had some monks, originally from Fujian, but there were not enough monks to serve all those registered, so the Buddhists appealed to Yin Yuan to come to Japan. He initially hesitated, but in 1654, after a fourth invitation, he went to Nagasaki.

Although the Japanese required all Chinese residents in Japan at that time to live in Nagasaki, they made an exception for Yin Yuan. After a year in Nagasaki, he went to a location near Kyoto where he was permitted to build a new temple, the Fumonji. In 1658, he was given an audience with the shogun, in much the same manner that the shogun welcomed diplomats from other countries. The shogun, Ietsuna, used the occasion to gain information about the Ming loyalists.

Koxinga's loyalist forces were strong enough to mount an attack on Nanjing in 1659, but they were defeated. The Qing dynasty pressured Zheng Zhilong to urge his son Koxinga to yield, but Koxinga refused and the Qing executed his father. Koxinga and some 25,000 troops fled to Taiwan, where they overwhelmed the Dutch fort of Zeelandia in southern Taiwan and established control over the island. However, in the following year, at the age of thirty-seven, Koxinga died of malaria. Koxinga's successors surrendered to the Qing dynasty in 1683 and the Qing incorporated Taiwan as part of Fujian province.

The Japanese government had provided no formal support to Koxinga, but in Japanese literature he became a legend and a celebrated hero. Chikamatsu Monzaemon's puppet play, the *Battles of Koxinga*, was a leading hit in Tokugawa theater from 1715 to 1717, and it remains one of Japan's most enduring popular plays. In Japanese minds, the play links the Manchus, along with the Mongols, as Tatars, that are outsider barbarians who took over China's great civilization. The stories about Koxinga, who was half Japanese and therefore, in Japanese minds, superior to the full-blooded Chinese, helped strengthen the popular Japanese view that Japanese leaders were superior to the Manchu barbarians in China.

While Koxinga and some Ming loyalists fled to Taiwan, another Ming loyalist, Zhu Shunshui, a former scholar-official who refused to remain in China during the Qing conquest, went to Japan and, as one loyal to the Ming emperor, played a role in discussions about strengthening Japanese loyalty to their emperor. Various currents of the Chinese intellectual tradition remained alive during the Tokugawa period. One of Tokugawa Ieyasu's grandsons, Tokugawa Mitsukuni, conceived the Chinese-style compilation *Dai Nihonshi* (A history of great Japan), and Zhu Shunshui was a key adviser to the project, which was not completed until 1720. Loyalty to the throne was central to the thinking of Zhu Shunshui and his compilers. By praising the continuity of the imperial line, Zhu helped reinforce the Japanese tradition of loyalty to the emperor.

Trade between Tokugawa Japan and Qing China

In the mid-seventeenth century, the Qing dynasty did not block the flourishing trade between Nagasaki and Fujian province, and the Tokugawa government actively encouraged it. During the peak trading years in the middle of the century, nearly forty Chinese junks called at Nagasaki each year. The Japanese had developed an appetite for Chinese silk, especially silk yarn that could be used by the weavers at Nishijin Textile Mills in Kyoto, which rapidly expanded its manufacturing of silk products that were then very popular among high Japanese officials. Japan also continued to import deerskins and medicinal herbs from China. Using a mining process developed by China in the fifteenth century that the Japanese had learned from the Koreans, Japan made great advances in silver mining. Several Japanese domains opened new mines, producing silver that could be exchanged for silk yarn.

The shogunate supported this trade because it earned income from taxing the mines and the silver mints (*ginza*) that refined the silver. The shogun also required officials in Nagasaki to sell some silk imports to his officials at lower prices, before the remainder would be sold to the yarn guild at a higher price. The import of silk also helped the Kyoto silk weavers, who were directly under the shogun's control.

At the height of the conflict between the Ming loyalists and the Qing, trade between China and Japan slowed down. From 1663 to 1673 approximately 36 Chinese junks called on Nagasaki per year, but from 1673 to 1683 the number dropped to 25 per year.[5] After the Ming loyalists on Taiwan surrendered in 1683, trade spurted ahead rapidly. In 1688 some 117 Chinese junks called on Nagasaki. By that time, however, Japan had largely exhausted its supply of silver. To stop the outflow of silver, Japanese officials placed controls on the trade. At the same time, because the Chinese wanted copper to mint coins, Japan rapidly increased the mining of copper, which by 1685 became its largest export item. Japan then placed stricter limits on imports and passed sumptuary laws to control the consumption of imported goods.

Japan also engaged in import substitution. It expanded its own sericulture in northern Japan to promote domestic production of silk. By the end of the eighteenth century, all the silk required by the Nishijin silk weavers in Kyoto was produced in Japan. The Japanese also learned from China how to grow a variety of medicinal plants. They expanded the planting of sugarcane in the southern areas where there was a suitable climate, especially in Satsuma and the Ryukyu Islands, which Satsuma had ruled since 1609. Satsuma was greatly enriched by the income from sugar production, which provided a financial base for its military strength at the end of the Tokugawa period.

By the end of the seventeenth century, with Japan's controls on the export of silver and copper and its import substitution, trade between China and Japan slowed down. For much of the eighteenth century an average of only twenty or thirty Chinese trading ships docked in Nagasaki per year. Japanese importers seeking to maintain their business diversified the goods they bought from China and began importing books, writing brushes, ink, and high-quality handicrafts.

From its beginning in 1603 to its end in 1868, Tokugawa Japan had no diplomatic relations with China, during either the Ming or the Qing dynasty. Tokugawa leaders were so strict about prohibiting the Japanese from going abroad that after 1635, Japanese fishermen who were shipwrecked and ended up in China were not even welcomed back home. As a result, it was the Chinese living in Nagasaki, and the Chinese abroad who visited Nagasaki, who carried on trade relations between the two countries.

Three Tokugawa Views of Qing China: Nationalists, Kangaku Scholars, and Traders

During the Qing dynasty, aside from the Chinese traders who traveled back and forth between Nagasaki and China, the Chinese people continued to show little interest in Japan. Some Buddhist texts and commentaries on the Chinese Confucian classics that were lost in China had been preserved in Japan, and when these works were "reimported" back into China, a small number of people took great interest in these documents—although some Chinese were doubtful of their authenticity. Occasionally a gazetteer in China published information about Japan, sometimes quite detailed, but generally books about Japan attracted little interest.

In contrast to China's lack of interest in Japanese culture, the Japanese in various circles retained a deep respect for traditional Chinese culture and continued to learn about China, despite the ban on travel. Japanese scholars studied under the small number of scholars from China who had fled to Japan after the fall of the Ming dynasty. The shogun followed developments in China through the information obtained in Nagasaki. Japanese Buddhists continued to learn from Chinese Buddhist texts coming in through Nagasaki and from Chinese monks who had come to Japan to teach Japanese monks. Japanese artists continued to learn from Chinese artists in Nagasaki; by the end of the Tokugawa, some one hundred Chinese artists and art dealers were living there, earning a living from the Japanese demand for Chinese art. Imported Chinese handicrafts continued to inspire Japanese artisans. Japanese medical practitioners studied the Chinese practice of medicine, and Japanese agriculture specialists studied the work of their counterparts in China in the hope of improving agricultural yields within Japan.

Japanese learning from China during the Tokugawa period did not have the transformative impact it had during the Nara and Heian periods, but three categories of people in Japan continued to take a deep interest in China: high officials under the shogun, teachers of Chinese studies in the domain schools and in Edo, and traders in Nagasaki, the Ryukyus, and Tsushima. Later, when Japan opened during the Meiji period (1868–1911), these three groups would play an important role in shaping Japanese relations with China.

Nationalist Officials and Scholars

Once Tokugawa officials had united Japan and the country became more stable, many Japanese officials began to take great pride in Japanese successes. Some in Japan who had looked up to Chinese civilization believed that the Manchus who led the Qing were barbarians, that Chinese civilization was deteriorating under barbarian rule, and that Japanese civilization, never subject to barbarian rule, was prospering.

By the 1660s Japanese officials were no longer using names like Chugoku (literally, "the central country") to refer to China, for they implied that China was the central kingdom. Japan, they believed, was also the center of its world. The notion that Japan was unique and special, that it was the "land of the gods," was reinforced by Japan's survival against the Mongol invasion thanks to the *kamikaze*. To some, the fact that their country had never lost any territory was a sign that Japan enjoyed special divine protection.

In the seventeenth century, some Japanese scholars began to promote "native studies" (*kokugaku*), which stressed the purity of Japanese tradition. They sought to replace *kangaku*, Chinese studies, with pure Japanese studies, and they promoted Shinto, the indigenous Japanese religion, rather than Buddhism, which was imported from China. Although native studies never gained the prominence of *kangaku*, it did attract significant numbers of supporters, and some Japanese began to assert that, with its version of neo-Confucianism, Japan, not China, represented the best of the Confucian tradition.

Having been overshadowed by China for so many centuries, the Japanese never matched the unquestioned self-confidence in the superiority of their civilization instinctively felt by many Chinese. Many who professed the belief that Japan would be protected by the gods nonetheless panicked at the thought that some outside power, whether China, Korea, or a Western power, might attack Japan. Yet they asserted pride in Japan, a pride that would grow during the Meiji period as Japan moved ahead of China in modernizing.

A small number of Japanese individuals expressed visions of how Japan might expand its power beyond its borders. Throughout the Tokugawa era they had continued to collect materials on military technology and strategy from Dutch sources. Hayashi Shihei (1738–1793), a military strategist in the Sendai domain of northeastern Japan, wrote that Japan should gain better control over Hokkaido and the Ryukyu Islands as a first step to becoming the leader of Asia. In 1791 he published the book *Kaikoku heidan* (Military defense of a maritime nation) in an attempt to alert others to the seriousness of the threat from Russia and China. From his passion about the urgency of defending Japan, he moved on to espouse a grandiose vision of how Japan could become the dominant power in the region. Japanese scholars today see Hayashi as representing one of many views, somewhat extremist, and certainly not the dominant view at the time. However, some Chinese scholars today pay great attention to Hayashi as a sign that the Japanese were already laying the foundation for their grand designs for Japanese aggression that began in the late nineteenth century and continued through World War II.

Kangaku (Chinese Learning) Scholars and Buddhists

While some Japanese elites exuded confidence in the superiority of Japan over barbarian-led China, teachers of *kangaku* and Buddhists, who represented the mainstream in Japan at the time, had a very different perspective on Chinese culture.

During the Tokugawa period the daimyo throughout the country continued to support the training of youths of the samurai class, and an important aspect of their education was *kangaku*. Although interest in native Japanese studies grew during the Tokugawa era, even those scholars who criticized Chinese learning were trained in the Chinese classics, which remained in the mainstream for Japanese students. The Tokugawa leadership sought loyalty because it contributed to the stability of society, and they strongly encouraged the study of the Confucian classics to provide proper mental training. Each domain had *kangaku* scholars, especially knowledgeable about the Chinese classics, who taught in the schools.

Whereas lower-level Japanese teachers used the Japanese rendering of the Chinese language, the leading scholars of Confucianism acquired full fluency in the original Chinese language of the texts. These scholars highly valued the wisdom of the ancient Chinese sages and also admired Japanese teachers who had mastered Chinese classical studies. *Kangaku* teachers in the domains typically learned to write poems in the classical Chinese style, and those skilled in writing Chinese poems took great pride in their achievements. Scholars have estimated that more poems were composed in Chinese than in Japanese during the Tokugawa period. Most *kangaku* scholars focused on reading and writing classical Chinese, but some Japanese, such as the leading scholar Ogyu Sorai (1666–1728), famous for applying Confucian learning to government, took pride in their ability to also speak colloquial Chinese.

With the growth of literacy during the Tokugawa era, an unprecedented proportion of Japanese people became familiar with the Chinese classics. During the last decades of the Tokugawa period, not only the samurai but also many nonsamurai were studying *kangaku* in the domain schools. Even many who believed in *kokugaku* displayed a reverence for the Confucian classics and for scholars in both China and Japan who preserved Chinese civilization.

Although Japanese people could not go abroad during the Tokugawa period, there was a continued demand for Chinese books in Japan, which arrived in the country through Nagasaki. Some were Buddhist books, and some were about Chinese history. In addition, Japanese scholars studied Chinese law to deepen their understanding of the role of regulations in governance.

Japanese monks continued to admire the high level of Buddhist scholarship in China. A decree issued in 1671, that all Japanese families were required to register at local Buddhist temples, remained in force throughout the Tokugawa period, and funeral ceremonies in Japan also remained Buddhist. Yin Yuan (Ingen), the Chinese monk who came to Nagasaki in 1654, founded the Manpukuji Temple near Kyoto in 1661 and recruited many Chinese monks to teach there, and Japanese monks went there to study under them. Buddhist monks in Japan continued to look to China as the respected homeland of their religion.

Nagasaki Traders

Nagasaki had been a small fishing village until 1571, when Portuguese ships began docking there, and after 1641, when it became the only port on Japan's four main islands open to international trade, it quickly grew into a cosmopolitan port city. Nagasaki's population was about 25,000 in 1609 but it reached 64,000 by 1696.[6] Although the city's population began to decline late in the eighteenth century as the shogun placed more restrictions on trade, it remained Japan's key port to the outside. The spirit of Nagasaki was commerce, an outlook that was shared by Tsushima and the Ryukyu Islands.

Nagasaki became a center for information about the world outside of Japan. After 1644, each ship's captain arriving in Nagasaki had to fill out a report that would be passed on to the shogun in Edo. Because the Netherlands was the only Western country allowed to trade with Japan, Nagasaki became the window in Japan to introduce "Dutch learning," which in turn enabled the Japanese to learn about scientific, military, and medical advances in the West.

Yet as the Japanese China specialist Oba Osamu said, Nagasaki trade was really China trade, because the overwhelming majority of trade at that time was with China. Even many of the goods that went through Tsushima and the Ryukyu Islands were merely on their way to or from China. Though Nagasaki officials sent detailed reports to the shogun in Edo, the marketplace for the daily exchange of information about China was on the front lines, in Nagasaki.

Only a handful of Chinese people lived in Nagasaki before the Tokugawa era, but by 1618, shortly after the other ports were closed to foreign traders, more than 2,000 Chinese were living there to service the trade with China. A small number of Chinese individuals did remain in other ports, some involved in the transfer of goods that had cleared customs in Nagasaki, others in various lines of work, but the Chinese community in Nagasaki continued to grow. By the end of the seventeenth century, nearly 5,000 lived in Nagasaki's Chinatown.[7] The Chinese residents in Nagasaki spoke a variety of dialects and kept in touch with Chinese merchants in their homeland. In the 1620s the key groups—from Fuzhou and Zhangzhou, both in the province of Fujian, and a group from the Yangtze delta area—had built their own Buddhist temples, which served as gathering spots for the different groups of Chinese living in Nagasaki. In 1678, as more Cantonese began arriving in Nagasaki, they built their own temple as well. And after Guangzhou was opened to trade in 1757, Nagasaki's trade with Guangzhou expanded. The British, after their victory in the Opium War in 1842, forced open the Chinese ports of Amoy, Fuzhou, Shanghai, Ningbo, and Hong Kong Island. The British and the French, after their victory in the Second Opium War (the Arrow War) in 1860, forced open eleven new treaty ports, providing further opportunities for the Chinese in Nagasaki. Toward the end of the Tokugawa period, as Japan stemmed the outflow of silver and promoted the domestic production of silk and medicinal herbs, trade through Nagasaki declined. Nonetheless, at the end of the Tokugawa period there were still some 1,000 ethnic Chinese living in Nagasaki's Chinatown.

The Chinese in Nagasaki, in addition to servicing China's trade with Japan, also facilitated trade with ethnic Chinese merchants in Southeast Asia. Thus the Nagasaki Chinese became a source of information for Japanese officials about developments in Southeast Asia as well as China. As Marius Jansen reports, the Nagasaki Chinese maintained generally good relations with the Japanese living in Nagasaki, many of whom were looking for opportunities to serve as brokers for selling imported goods from China elsewhere in Japan.

Despite the lively trade through Nagasaki, for more than two centuries there were no meetings between government officials from the two countries. In 1862, Japanese and Chinese officials finally met in Shanghai.

CHAPTER THREE

Responding to Western Challenges and Reopening Relations, 1839–1882

AFTER THE BRITISH defeated China in the First Opium War (1839–1842) and Commodore Perry opened Japan in 1853, Asia could no longer maintain a separate existence. It began the process of becoming part of the world. The immediate threat from the West to China and Japan was to their military security and to their economic resources, which Westerners were ready to exploit. To respond to these threats effectively, China and Japan had to find a method for conscripting more soldiers and training them, and they also had to create an industrial base and a communications and transport network. They needed a taxation system to raise more funds, a modern bureaucracy with new specializations to guide such efforts, an expanded educational system to train people in new skills, and a stronger centralized leadership structure to cope with the entrenched interests and to coordinate new developments. To those who sought to preserve their old ways, threats came not only from Westerners but also from those in their own country who were trying to initiate change. In 1882, when China and Japan clashed in Korea, China won the first round in their military confrontation. But by 1895 Japan had proved more successful in overcoming domestic resistance and implementing a comprehensive program to modernize the country. During the following century, Japan was in the stronger position in relations between the two countries.

Japan's Advantages in Responding to Western Challenges

Japan had some natural advantages over China that allowed it to respond more quickly to the massive challenges from the West. It was easier to get a unified national response in a compact territory of four small islands, and the sea transportation available at the time made it relatively easy to establish communications and transportation links among all parts of Japan. In China, until the 1880s when the first telegraph wires were laid, it took nearly a month for government communications to travel from one end of the country to the other. Living on a small group of islands, the Japanese had long felt more vulnerable to dangers from across the sea than the Chinese had. That sense of danger had made them eager to acquire more information from abroad. Chinese leaders had long worried about possible invaders by land, coming by horseback from the north, and they were less concerned about learning about the world across the seas. Early in the nineteenth century, even before the Meiji Restoration, the shogun in Edo began sending missions abroad to learn from other countries how to modernize, just as the Japanese had done by sending missions to China in the seventh and eighth centuries. Chinese leaders, confident of the greatness of their rich civilization, were never eager to learn from other countries.

Japan was a smaller and more homogeneous country and therefore easier to unify. China had a far larger population with more varied ethnic groups—Han, Mongols, Manchus, Uighurs, Tibetans, and many others with different languages and cultures—which made it difficult to unify national policy and maintain domestic harmony. The Qing rulers devised different policies for different ethnic areas. The Hakka ("guest people"), latecomer migrants to certain areas, and their descendants often had a sense of separateness from the descendants of long-established residents, and they were more open to becoming rebels. By the nineteenth century China was suffering from great population growth and massive food shortages. The shortages helped spark the Taiping Rebellion, the Nian Rebellion, and the Muslim Rebellion, devastating uprisings that took time and energy from the government that could have been used to respond to challenges from the West.

The Tokugawa system had encouraged more economic and educational development in local areas than the Qing system. Although individual Chinese had outstanding achievements in culture, science, and technology, when the two countries began to open to the West in the middle of the late nineteenth century, Japanese local areas, on average, had a higher educational and economic base than their Chinese counterparts.

By the late nineteenth century, an estimated half of all males in Japan were literate, a higher percentage than in China. Japanese youths from the various domains who spent time in the capital and would later become leaders of their domains tended to share a common language and culture and to develop friendships across fief lines. The small number of Japanese domains provided a broader base of a common culture among the top leaders than the common culture of Chinese youths, who were together only in Beijing while preparing for the examinations. Thus the Japanese young men who would later become leaders of their domains acquired a similar understanding of the issues facing the country.

Chinese leaders, much more confident than Japanese leaders about their own country's strength, were not as afraid of foreign countries as Japanese leaders, and they did not feel the same urgency about importing new systems and new technology from abroad. Perhaps nothing contributed more to Japan's rapid modernization than its organized search for information about the outside world, its analysis of that new information, and its readiness to make changes based on what had been learned and analyzed. During the Tokugawa period, Japan's listening post in Nagasaki had provided the Japanese with experience in dealing with foreigners, as well as knowledge about foreign affairs. Tokugawa Japan had proved more eager to acquire information than Qing China and far more systematic in analyzing that information to defend its national interest. Dutch officials working for the Japanese in Nagasaki were required to interview every ship's captain who arrived in Nagasaki for information about the outside world and to write a report for the shogun government in Edo. The Chinese living in Nagasaki provided a window through which to gain information about developments in China and, when Westerners began arriving in Japan, for learning about what Westerners were doing in China. Japan's Tsushima Island, situated between Kyushu and Korea, was a base for learning about Korea and, through Korea, China. The Matsumae clan, in the northern island, provided a base for learning about Russia, and the Satsuma clan provided a base for learning about the Ryukyu Islands.

In 1844 a Chinese writer, Wei Yuan, completed the book *Haiguo tuzhi* (An illustrated treatise on the maritime kingdoms), a collection of information about Western countries gathered at the time. It had many inaccuracies, such as in its descriptions of Western government systems, but it also contained much useful information. The response of the Japanese to the book reflected their worries about challenges from the West. Soon more

Japanese than Chinese were reading Wei Yuan's book. In 1853, when Commodore Perry arrived in Japan, the U.S. officers accompanying him were understandably surprised to find that the leaders of Japan, that "closed country," had a deep knowledge of world geography and of recent Western scientific and industrial developments, such as the steam engine.

Immediately after Commodore Perry and his armada forced Japan to open up in 1853, Japanese leaders realized they had to learn more about how to deal with the rest of the world than what could be provided through the window of Nagasaki.

The first American consul general assigned to Japan, Townsend Harris, arrived in Japan in August 1856. Though it had been centuries since Japan had sent missions abroad, three months after Harris's arrival a shogun official told him, "The time will soon come when we will build ships like yours, and then we can visit the United States in a proper manner."[1] In late 1857, a high shogun official, Hotta Masayoshi, wrote that Japan's policy should be "to conclude friendly alliances, to send ships to foreign countries everywhere and conduct trade, to copy the foreigners where they are at their best and so repair our own shortcomings, to foster our national strength. . . ."[2] Chinese leaders were not as convinced of their own shortcomings or as eager to learn from the West.

Turning Points in the 1860s

The 1860s was a decade of fundamental change that shaped the future of China and Japan as well as their relations. Both China and Japan gained new governing structures, and they resumed official contacts for the first time in two centuries.

When the Tongzhi Restoration took place in 1861, the Second Opium War was over and the Taiping were losing power; by 1864 they were thoroughly defeated. This gave China's new Tongzhi leadership an opportunity to arrest the dynastic decline and rebuild national strength. In Japan, the shogun was overthrown in 1868 and the Meiji Restoration gave Japan a new leadership structure to confront its problems. The leaders of the Tongzhi Restoration had a very different perspective than the leaders of the Meiji Restoration on their nation's problems and on their priorities in responding to the challenges from the West.

In 1862, after a two-century hiatus, officials from the two countries met. In the late 1860s they began discussions that enabled them to sign a formal treaty in the 1870s and to establish, for the first time in history, permanent embassies in each other's country.

Confucian Revival and Self-Strengthening under Emperor Tongzhi

In 1861 the child emperor Tongzhi, age five, ascended the throne following the death of his father, Xianfeng. Chinese leaders were eager to restore the social order that had been so damaged by the Taiping Rebellion and the Second Opium War (1856–1860). Xianfeng, who died at the age of thirty, was considered a failed emperor because he left the country in such a disastrous state, but the end of the Second Opium War and the defeat of the Taiping provided the leadership of the new Tongzhi Restoration an opportunity to move forward.

Emperor Tongzhi died in 1875 at the age of nineteen, so he never really held the reins of power during the Tongzhi era. Instead, his uncle Prince Gong, Xianfeng's brother, and his mother, Empress Dowager Cixi, who had been brought in as an imperial concubine for Xianfeng and became Xianfeng's favorite when she bore him his son Tongzhi, actually held power during the Tongzhi period. On the death of Tongzhi, the empress dowager appointed a three-year-old, her nephew Guangxu, as emperor so that she could continue to rule.

The empress dowager proved to be very skilled in managing court politics and was the dominant power not only during the Tongzhi but also during the Guangxu period. Prince Gong and a number of local officials realized that to cope with the foreigners, new skills and new technology, including new ships and weapons, would be required. Yet many Chinese officials remained focused on cultivating the moral qualities that they considered essential for national vitality.

Empress Dowager Cixi and many high officials believed that the essence of China's problems stemmed from the loss of a true Confucian spirit. To address this, they had to rebuild the moral base of traditional Confucian civilization, restore the importance of the examination system, and eliminate the buying and selling of offices. The empress dowager valued the importance of symbolism. She undertook the building of a grand palace that would help strengthen the dynasty, and later, during the Guangxu era after the Summer Palace had been destroyed, she sought to build a new, vast, and expensive Summer Palace.

In 1861 China launched the Self-Strengthening Movement, focused on training its own troops, building its own ships, and producing its own military weapons. With the support of Prince Gong, Li Hongzhang (see Biographies of Key Figures), Zeng Guofan, and others established factories to produce weapons. Initially they made use of foreign workers to help build the factories. They established the Jiangnan Arsenal in Shanghai, which by 1871 was already producing rifles. They also built naval dockyards in Fuzhou, Shanghai, and elsewhere. By the 1880s China had moved ahead of Japan in purchasing ships and then building them on its own. In the 1880s Li Hongzhang established the China Merchants Steam Navigation Company so that China would have its own commercial shipping to help Chinese merchants. Although the empress dowager had originally delayed the building of railways because she considered them too noisy, by the 1890s railways were being built to link the port cities with cities in eastern and central China. The Chinese also began creating public utilities.

The Chinese sent a mission abroad to learn about foreign developments, but the mission was not as large or as systematic as Japan's Iwakura Mission of 1871–1873, and after its return the members of the mission did not play the key role that their Japanese counterparts had played in designing and implementing new programs. However, because many foreigners had cooperated with Zeng Guofan, the great political and military leader who led the fight against the Taiping rebels, China was able to use its contacts with them to obtain information that would be useful for producing the technology and military equipment required during the Self-Strengthening Movement.

As Jenny Huangfu Day concludes from her study of Chinese missions sent abroad during this period, the Chinese who took part in the missions had a broad range of contacts, and some of them had a good understanding of the science and technology they observed. They made thoughtful individual efforts to come to terms with the differences between Western and Chinese cultures.

In May 1868, three years before Japan's Iwakura Mission set out, a Chinese delegation, the Burlingame Mission, arrived in the United States. This delegation went on to spend extended time in Britain, France, Prussia, and Russia, with briefer visits to other European countries, before it returned to China in October 1870. The purpose of the delegation was to better learn how Westerners conducted diplomacy and to attempt to bring about a revocation of the so-called unequal treaties. Anson Burlingame, a highly respected American who had recently retired after seven years as the second U.S. minister (in effect, the ambassador) to Beijing, was appointed by the Chinese to lead the delegation. On the mission, there were some thirty members, including two senior Chinese representatives. On behalf of China, Burlingame negotiated the Burlingame-Seward Treaty, considered China's first equal treaty.

Burlingame died of pneumonia in February 1870 while on the trip, and two Chinese delegates, Zhigang, a Manchu, and Sun Jiagu, a Han, both degree-holding officials well trained in the classics, took over as leaders of the delegation for the remainder of the trip. The mission met with heads of state, including the Russian czar, diplomats, businesspeople, missionaries, and Chinese citizens who were living abroad. In Europe, they visited industrial sites, mines, and shipyards. They observed steam engines and the use of electricity. In his diary, Zhigang revealed a good understanding of the machinery he saw during the trip and of the scientific principles that underlay such new technology. The delegates also engaged in broad-ranged discussions, and, as their diaries show, they asked discerning questions. For example, they asked missionaries why Christians, who had such high ideals and performed such good work in China, were bullying Chinese workers in the California mines and oppressing people in the colonies. On their return, the participants wrote reports and memorials, and Zhigang's more detailed diary of informal observations was later published as a book.

Some of the Chinese participants on the missions that China sent abroad, including Zeng Jize, eldest son of Zeng Guofan, had positive opinions of the things they had observed and got in trouble with the conservative officials at home for being too sympathetic toward foreign customs. Li Hongzhang and other officials, however, took a great interest in what the Chinese travelers reported about developments abroad and encouraged participants to provide broad descriptions of political and economic matters. Empress Dowager Cixi personally met with some of the mission participants to understand what was happening abroad. However, a group of conservative officials in high positions, well trained in the Confucian tradition, did not support the efforts to modernize and did not implement any of their suggestions. The result was that unlike the Iwakura Mission, which returned to lead Japan's rapid industrial and technological advances, the Burlingame Mission members were unable to make good use of what they observed.

While Japanese leaders were investing in industry and infrastructure, Korean and Chinese leaders were looking to restore a national spirit in their countries by displaying imperial grandeur through lavish new buildings. In the 1860s the Koreans undertook a massive rebuilding of their palace, with some 330 buildings and nearly 6,000 rooms. Similarly, the empress dowager enlarged and renovated the Summer Palace in Beijing, including its Marble Boat pavilion, using funds that could have been used to strengthen China's foundation for modern industry. In fact, she rebuilt the expensive Marble Boat in the palace garden with funds that were earmarked for modernizing the navy.

Some officials, such as Li Hongzhang, believed that in addition to new factories, arsenals, and shipyards, fundamental changes were needed in China's educational system. He advocated that, like Japan, China should send young people abroad to study, and that civil-service exams should be offered in technical areas as well as in cultural areas, but his proposals were not accepted. China made some progress in constructing a modern industrial base through its "self-strengthening," but after 1885 conservative officials in Beijing slowed down efforts to support new industries. China achieved some successes in building up industry and producing weapons, but it did not undertake the thoroughgoing institutional reform that Japan achieved.

The Meiji Leaders Promote Study Abroad and Modernization

In contrast to China's limited program for self-strengthening, Meiji Japan undertook comprehensive modernization in all fields, including political and social organization, the economy, education, and the military. The arrival of Commodore Perry in 1853 had immediately set off debates throughout Japan about how to respond, but by 1861 the shogunate had concluded that

Japan did not have sufficient military power to resist the West. Righteous young samurai from several of the large southern domains—Satsuma, Choshu, and Tosa—indignant about this humiliation, began holding meetings in the late 1850s. In 1868 hundreds of young samurai from these three domains marched from Kyoto to the shogun's palace in Edo, where the leaders of the Tokugawa shogunate, aware that they had lost the support of the domains around the country, agreed to transfer power to the emperor to avoid entering into a devastating, prolonged war.

On April 7, 1868, in a Shinto ceremony attended by leading officials, the fourteen-year-old Emperor Meiji, who had ascended to the throne fourteen months earlier, advanced to a Shinto altar, bowed in prayer, and made an offering. An official, in the name of the emperor, then read from the Charter Oath, proclaiming that all future matters would be decided by public discussion and that knowledge would be sought from throughout the world. Thereafter, fundamental changes were made in the name of the emperor, and in 1869 the emperor moved in a procession from Kyoto to Tokyo, which officially became the capital.

The samurai rebels agreed that for Japan to survive, it not only had to abolish the old domains and create prefectures under a new national administrative system, but it also had to abolish the formal class system that had given them their special status as samurai. In 1871 the feudal domains were abolished and replaced by a system of prefectures that were under much more centralized control by Tokyo. Also, the four social class designations—samurai, peasants, workers, merchants—were abolished, and former samurai were prohibited from wearing swords, the symbol of their class. Former samurai initially received stipends, but after several years they were paid off in cash or bonds and the stipends were terminated. The legitimacy that was derived from imperial proclamations led to fundamental changes without a revolution, and a rear-guard reaction, the Satsuma Rebellion of 1877, was put down relatively quickly. By 1869 the emperor was living in Tokyo, and by 1877 all branches of government, as well as all foreign legations, were also located in Tokyo.

The Japanese undertook learning from abroad on a much larger scale than China, and they used study tours abroad, especially the Iwakura Mission, to build a consensus among those who led Japan during the Meiji period. The shogun had already sent a mission to the United States in 1860.

But in 1868 the leaders of the new Meiji government began planning Japan's even grander study-abroad tour, the Iwakura Mission.

The mission was led by Count Iwakura Tomomi. Upon its return, he and the deputy heads of the mission (Okubo Toshimichi, Kido Takeyoshi, and Ito Hirobumi [see Biographies of Key Figures]) were expected to and later did in fact play major leadership roles in government. Advance parties were sent abroad to prepare for the trip, which included visits to the United States, most European countries, Southeast Asia, and then China. The Iwakura Mission set off in December 1871, visited fifteen countries, and returned to Japan in September 1873. In addition to meeting national political leaders and studying the different forms of government in the various countries the mission visited, the members of the mission split up into specialty groups to study developments at factories, mines, ports, railways, research centers, experimental agricultural stations, universities, schools, army bases, and military arsenals. Never before and never since has any country sent so many young officials on such a long study tour of other countries.

The last stop on the trip was Shanghai, which the mission reached toward the end of the Tongzhi period. The mission members spent less than three days in Shanghai, where they were given an elaborate welcome banquet by the top Shanghai official, Chen Fuxun. They were not entirely shocked by what they saw in the city because Japanese officials had been going to Shanghai since the 1862 *Senzaimaru* visit. However, after seeing the wonders that industrialization had brought to the United States and Europe, the travelers were struck by how much China had fallen behind. Kume Kunitake, the chief chronicler of the voyage, recorded his impressions of Shanghai: "There are no sewers, and urine flows along the streets. Amid all this, the inhabitants seem quite unconcerned." Believing that the Japanese were harboring illusions about Chinese sophistication based on the past, he tried to correct the view of his countrymen who "regarded every Chinese to be a refined gentleman well versed in literature and the arts. Thus [in Japan] the custom still persists of holding any curios, calligraphy, paintings, poetry or literature from China in high esteem. . . . Under the Qing dynasty," he wrote, "learning has been stagnant in China."

At the time of the Tang dynasty there had been so much to learn from China, but by 1873 the mission members felt that there was very little they could learn. Many of the travelers continued to nourish the hope that China,

Japan, and Korea could work together to resist the advances of Western imperialism, but some had already begun wondering whether that would be possible when China was so far behind, so disorganized, lacking a strategy that could be effective in responding to the West, and short of wise overall leadership. But, like Japanese officials on the *Senzaimaru's* visit to China, the Iwakura Mission officials expressed great compassion for the impoverished Chinese people, a sense of kinship with people whose culture they shared, a sense of sadness about what had happened to the great civilization, and hope that the situation in China would improve.

When the mission returned home, chronicler Kume Kunitake compiled his diary notes into five volumes reporting on what participants on the Iwakura Mission had learned. These volumes became part of a basic handbook guiding discussions of what changes were to be introduced in Japan, and the compilations of later volumes from the trip were used to guide industrial policy. Japan sent additional observers abroad to follow up with more specialized studies on certain topics.

Those who were sent abroad were convinced of the depth of the changes required to bring about modernization in Japan. During the trip they had opportunities to discuss what might be appropriate for Japan, and by the time they returned to Japan they were beginning to arrive at a consensus about the broad features of the programs that needed to be designed. After their return, the mission members were placed in key government positions from which they could begin to plan the institutions and programs necessary to build a modern country. Many disagreements on specific issues followed, but no other country undertaking modernization had such a deep and broad common understanding of the issues involved.

At the time of Emperor Meiji, China and Korea, like Japan, were also ruled by young emperors, but neither of them acquired the authority that Emperor Meiji would have when he reached maturity. In China, Emperor Tongzhi was five years old when he ascended the throne (and Guangxu was four years old), but when Tongzhi ascended the throne, power remained largely in the hands of his mother, Empress Dowager Cixi, and her advisers, who were resistant to a fundamental governmental reorganization. In Korea, Emperor Kojong ascended the throne at the age of twelve in 1864, but his father, the Taewongun, was still alive and held ultimate power. Even after 1873 when King Kojong and Queen Min and her family temporarily pushed aside the Taewongun, the conservative Taewongun remained influential. In Japan, in contrast, in the name of the emperor the young samurai, inspired by what they saw on the Iwakura Mission, moved boldly to bring about great changes. The senior advisers to Emperor Meiji began tutoring him in 1868, preparing him for those issues he would face when he reached maturity and became Japan's ultimate authority.

Japan's Military Modernization

Within two decades of the Meiji Restoration, Japan built a national army, with unified direction and organization. Unlike China, which sent talented young men abroad but did not always make good use of them, Japan put those people it had sent abroad to study fields such as public health, science, and technology in key positions where they could incorporate the new information in national institutions.

In 1870 a bright young student from the Satsuma domain, Oyama Iwao, was sent to France. After training in the language, he began studying the French military. He had arrived in France in time to observe the French Army in the Franco-Prussian War (July 1870–May 1871), and when he returned to Japan he played a role in shaping the development of the Japanese Army, rose in the ranks to become minister of war, and was able to incorporate what he had learned abroad as he guided the nation's military. Oyama not only advanced military training in Japan but also accepted the need for rules that placed limits on violence. He required that his military officers take a course on the laws of war, he supported Japan's decision to join the 1864 Geneva Convention on the proper treatment of the wounded, and he was later a founder of Japan's Red Cross.

Some months after Oyama's trip abroad, Katsura Taro, from the Choshu domain, was dispatched to France for advanced military training. When he arrived in England in 1871 on his way to France, he learned that France had just lost the Franco-Prussian War. Instead of going on to France to study, he went to the victor's military schools in Germany, where he remained a student and a military attaché until 1878. Shortly after he returned to Japan, he submitted a blueprint for modernizing the Japanese Army. Yamagata Aritomo, supreme military adviser to Emperor Meiji, was favorably impressed with Katsura's plans and used them as the basis for his broad-ranged plans to modernize the army. Katsura later served as war minister for three terms, and as prime minister during the period of the Russo-Japanese War.

Oyama, Katsura, and other military officers who led Japan's military modernization were from the samurai class and its culture of honor and discipline, and the bureaucrats who led Meiji civilian modernization were also overwhelmingly from the samurai class. Although the samurai in Japan had not fought for more than 200 years and had become bureaucrats in their respective domains, their spiritual training, discipline, and respect for the warrior who was prepared for sacrifice remained influential throughout the Tokugawa era and penetrated the officer corps in Meiji Japan's new army. The high levels of literacy in Japan enabled enlisted men as well as officers to read documents, and they were given strict disciplinary training by officers who promoted and maintained the samurai spirit.

Chinese and Japanese Management of Foreign Relations

In the centuries before the arrival of Westerners in the nineteenth century, neither China nor Japan had enough contacts with the outside to require a specialized bureaucracy knowledgeable about foreign affairs. Management of foreign affairs in East Asia largely consisted of overseeing the ritual aspects of the relations among countries and managing the activities of crews that arrived in ports where trade took place.

Prince Gong and Empress Dowager Cixi realized that new issues not easily handled within the traditional bureaucracy, such as dealing with foreigners, required new institutions. They therefore chose to build quasi-governmental institutions outside the regular bureaucracy that would hire their own officials, some of whom had passed the Chinese official examinations and some of whom had not. This provided some flexibility for China in adapting to the changing world, but it also resulted in a governmental structure at the top that was led by Manchu Confucian literati, most of whom lacked specialized training and were not eager to learn from those they considered barbarians.

In 1861, the Zongli Yamen (Zongli Geguo Shiwu Yamen, or Office of Affairs of All Nations) was created as a quasi-governmental institution to handle the demands of increased contacts with foreign nations. Officials were assigned to interact with foreigners and also to build up the arms necessary to resist pressures from foreign nations. It was designed to be a temporary institution, until the crisis in dealing with foreigners ended. Zongli Yamen officials were selected not according to their training in foreign affairs but through the traditional examinations used to select government officials. Although Li Hongzhang and others in the Zongli Yamen acquired some practical knowledge in dealing with foreigners, the decisions of the Zongli Yamen were subject to final approval by higher-level Manchu officials.

The Imperial Maritime Customs Service was established in 1854, before the Tongzhi Restoration. In 1863, after the restoration, it was placed under the direction of a British citizen named Robert Hart, who successfully guided the institution for several decades. Hart, who had studied the Chinese classics, had arrived in China in 1854 to work in the British consulate. He proved to be remarkably successful in building an institution that worked with the Chinese government as well as with the British and French, managing the growth of contacts that stemmed from the increased trade between China and other countries. The Imperial Maritime Customs Service was staffed by both foreigners and Chinese citizens, and over the years it established offices in all of China's ports. It not only collected customs, which grew to represent nearly half of the government's budget, but also managed the harbors, trained diplomats, and undertook studies of foreign affairs. In the absence of formal government institutions for international relations, it also served as a go-between for China and the outside world.

In 1862 a school for interpreters opened in Beijing, and soon thereafter foreign-language schools were opened in Shanghai, Guangzhou, and Fuzhou. Chinese leaders, who were much more confident than the Japanese about the ability of Confucian generalists to deal with outsiders (both Japanese and Westerners), did not give important positions to Chinese officials who had studied Western legal systems. Perhaps the Chinese individual most familiar with Western institutions and thinking at the time was Yan Fu. Yan Fu and Ito Hirobumi had been classmates in England from 1877 to 1879, and some scholars report that Yan Fu, who never achieved his goal of becoming a Chinese official, was a better student than Ito, who eventually became the leading statesman in Meiji Japan. It was not until China lost the war with Japan in 1895 that Yan Fu's writings about the West were even published in China. After 1895 neither Yan Fu nor anyone else with comparable knowledge was given a high position to negotiate with other countries. High-level Manchu officials in China did not spend a great deal of time on foreign affairs, and the key person who managed foreign affairs was Li Hongzhang.

Even in the 1870s the Chinese took little interest in Japan. The Zongli Yamen was responsible for training interpreters, but it did not train interpreters in Japanese, nor did it hire any Japan specialists or publish materials on Japan. There were a few Chinese individuals who had visited Japan, such as Luo Sen, who had served as an interpreter for Commodore Perry, and there were some Chinese traders who, during short stays in Nagasaki or Yokohama, had contacts with Japanese merchants. These individuals recorded superficial observations of what they had seen on the streets during their brief sojourns, but they had little understanding of Japanese politics, the Japanese economy, or Japanese society. When additional Japanese ports were opened under foreign pressure, Chinese merchants began branching out from Nagasaki to trade in Yokohama, Hakodate, and Kobe, but the Chinese government still showed little interest in gathering information about Japan.

The lack of Chinese interest in training foreign-affairs specialists in general, and Japan specialists in particular, was in striking contrast to Japanese efforts to learn about foreign affairs. In Japan, not only high-level political officials and foreign-policy specialists but even Emperor Meiji took an interest in learning about foreign affairs.

Japan hired many Western specialists in all aspects of governmental bureaucracy to help train the Japanese, including foreign-affairs specialists. At their peak, in 1875, there were more than five hundred foreign advisers in Japan, and their salaries accounted for approximately one-third of Japan's national budget. When Chinese officials went to Japan in 1877 to set up their legation, they were astonished to find that the Japanese bureaucracy for foreign affairs, unlike that in China, had already completely adopted European procedures and protocols.

In Japan, when young Emperor Meiji ascended the throne he was still being tutored, and decisions were made by senior officials under his name. Throughout his life, he continued his education through lectures on Japanese history, the Chinese Confucian classics, Chinese history, and the policies of European monarchs, as well as current issues. Count Iwakura, observing the emperor's intellectual growth, believed that when Emperor Meiji reached maturity he had acquired sufficient knowledge and sound judgment to make all decisions on his own. But Emperor Meiji chose to let others make daily decisions until 1880 when he turned twenty-six and announced that, after reviewing the evidence, Japan would no longer borrow money from abroad. He then established himself as the final arbiter when there were disagreements among high-level officials.

Emperor Meiji regularly received distinguished foreign guests as well as the foreign ambassadors serving in Japan. Although he focused on the big issues facing the country, throughout his reign, he attended high-level official meetings and he was diligent in carrying out his daily responsibilities. Although the emperor retained authority to make the final decisions about key appointments, including for prime minister and foreign minister, he came to rely on officials, such as Ito Hirobumi and Yamagata Aritomo, to manage both foreign and domestic policy. He favored diplomacy over the use of military force and was cautious about antagonizing the major Western powers. Nevertheless, he approved of decisions that expanded resources to build up the Japanese military.

Important documents issued in Emperor Meiji's name, such as the Constitution and the Educational Rescript that underpinned the nation's educational system, were drawn up by his staff but were approved by the emperor before they were issued. Once they were issued in his name, such documents took on a sacred "above the clouds" aura that reduced the danger that they would be subject to controversy. The Japanese took pride in the fact that their emperor was a direct descendant of the founding emperors of Japan, a continuity that they believed placed him above the rulers in many other countries. They considered Emperor Meiji to be superior in position to the Korean emperor and equal in position to the Chinese emperor. The Japanese were pleased when, in 1887, Emperor Guangxu of China sent a letter to Emperor Meiji referring to himself as the Great Emperor of the Great Qing Country and referring to Emperor Meiji as the Great Emperor of Great Japan, formally recognizing for the first time that the two leaders were equals.

As soon as the Meiji government was formed, it established a Foreign Office, which in 1869 was renamed the Foreign Ministry and began recruiting and training specialists on foreign relations. Major decisions about foreign affairs, though approved by Emperor Meiji, were made by five senior officials, three of whom (Ito Hirobumi, Okubo Toshimichi, and Kido Takeyoshi) had been deputy leaders of the Iwakura Mission. A fourth official, Mori Arinori, Japan's first ambassador to the United States and first ambassador to China, had studied in London from 1865 to 1868, and the fifth, Yamagata Aritomo, had participated in a study tour of European military systems from August 1869 to September 1870. These five leaders bonded with other Meiji officials, such as Iwakura Tomomi, and they had long discussions with former officials of the shogunate who had dealt with Commodore Perry and other foreigners, to prepare themselves for dealing with foreign officials. All five had been samurai, but they were not from high-ranking samurai families, and they had been selected based only on their individual ability. Ito Hirobumi had served in the Foreign Office before he traveled on the Iwakura Mission and had considerable experience in foreign affairs before he became prime minister in 1885. He had returned from study in England aware that Japan was far weaker than the Western countries and that it needed the cooperation of the Western countries to learn from them. With his ability to work in English, he was given major responsibility for negotiating with other countries. Ito was Li Hongzhang's partner in negotiating the Treaty of Tianjin in 1858 and in negotiating the Treaty of Shimonoseki at the end of the Sino-Japanese War in 1895.

Another influential official was Mutsu Munemitsu, the best-known professional diplomat during the Meiji period, who had studied in Europe in 1884. He played a key role in the strategic decisions in Japan's confrontation with China in 1894–1895, and he spent many years trying to end the unequal treaties with the Western powers. By 1899, when Mutsu achieved his goal of ending the unequal treaties, he had already earned a high reputation.

The Senzaimaru *Visit, 1862*

The first time Chinese and Japanese officials met in more than two centuries was when the *Senzaimaru* arrived in the port of Shanghai in 1862. During the Qing and Tokugawa periods, some goods had been traded and some books had been exchanged, but the Japanese were not allowed to go abroad and no Chinese official had visited Japan. The Chinese and Japanese officials who met when the *Senzaimaru* arrived in Shanghai were strangers and had no rules to follow. The visit of the *Senzaimaru*, introduced to the Western world by the research of Joshua Fogel, opened the door between officials of the two countries, but only a crack.

However, in the following decade the Chinese and Japanese governments followed Western patterns and developed normal diplomatic relations with each other. Some Japanese defense specialists, worried that Russia and Western European powers might establish bases in Korea and the nearby islands, began considering how Japan might use its new military force to reach out beyond its borders to control territories in the vicinity that its enemies might use to gain access to new resources and control markets. Individual Chinese leaders had similar ideas, but China did not develop such an institutional structure as quickly as Japan.

In 1859 the magistrate of Hakodate, one of Japan's two newly opened ports, had written to the shogun advising him on steamboats, which in the future would quite likely dominate travel to China. Since it would take some years before Japan could build a steamboat, he suggested that Japan should buy one in order to make profits from trade, train its own crews, learn what Japanese products might be sold in China, and become familiar with Chinese trade regulations. The shogun accepted this advice, shopped around, and then paid cash to purchase the *Armistice*, a 385-ton British ship that traveled by both steam and sail. The *Armistice*, built in 1855, was considered one of the best of its class, with considerable capacity for freight, and it had already made several successful voyages under the British flag between Nagasaki and Shanghai. The Japanese renamed the ship the *Senzaimaru* ("the ship to last a thousand years"). Soon after it was purchased and outfitted, it was sent on its mission to China. No Japanese ship's captain had experience guiding steamships, so Japan hired the previous owner and pilot of the *Armistice*, Henry Richardson, and his crew to operate the ship on its maiden voyage to China under the Japanese flag.

The members of this first *Senzaimaru* trip were very carefully selected for their ability not only to learn about potential markets for Japanese goods but also to report on the political situation, begin negotiations toward establishing formal relations with China, observe how foreigners were treated, and explore opportunities for future trade. Some fifty-one Japanese participants were part of the mission, including high-level shogun officials to carry out the negotiations, thirteen merchants, Chinese and Dutch interpreters, and some highly educated young staff members from various feudal domains. The 516-mile voyage from Nagasaki to Shanghai took seven days.

Since there were no official representatives of the Chinese government living in Japan, the Japanese had no direct way of contacting the Chinese about their plans to visit Shanghai. When they arrived in Shanghai, they relied on the Dutch, whom they knew through the trade in Nagasaki, to make introductions to the Chinese officials.

During the delegation's two months in Shanghai, the highest Chinese official in Shanghai, circuit attendant Wu Xu, met with the members several times. Wu Xu, perplexed as to how to receive the delegation, sent a report to his superiors in Beijing, and when the reply came without clear directions, Wu Xu decided to act with caution. The Dutch had assured him that the Japanese were reliable traders, and Wu Xu decided to be gracious and to help in selling their goods.

From goods that Chinese ships had previously carried from Nagasaki to Hong Kong and Shanghai, the Japanese merchants already had some idea of what Chinese markets might bear. For this trip, they had brought a variety of goods to test Chinese demand, including some sea products, lacquerware, and paper fans. Even with the help of the Dutch, sales in Shanghai went slowly, and many of the goods did not sell at all.

Wu Xu expressed appreciation to the Japanese officials for their willingness to go through customs procedures, for cooperating with local officials, and for not creating difficulties. But he was not prepared to accept responsibility for the foreigners' activities. He advised them to leave promptly and not to send another mission to China without first receiving prior official approval. Although high-level Japanese officials had already decided to promote trade and diplomacy with the Chinese, the Chinese had yet to accept it.

Conversations with Wu Xu were conducted through an interpreter, but the Japanese did not have enough interpreters for all of their meetings with the Chinese. Some used "brush conversations," writing down comments in Chinese characters and sharing them with their Chinese counterparts, to ask questions about local conditions and to learn Chinese views on trade, politics, and their relations with Western countries. Some of the Japanese, through their interpreters, were also able to converse with Western traders in Shanghai, especially those from the Netherlands and Great Britain. They kept diaries of their conversations and observations for distribution upon return.

The *Senzaimaru* returned from China without making profitable sales, without negotiating a treaty, and without a welcome to return. In a sense, however, the Japanese felt the trip had "paid their tuition" for learning about the port of Shanghai, trade on the China coast, and the procedures for dealing with China. Thus those on the ship judged the trip to have been a success.

When the *Senzaimaru* was in Shanghai, the city had not yet recovered from the damage caused by the Taiping Rebellion. The Japanese were appalled by the chaotic situation they observed—the poverty, the filth, and the lack of concern for hygiene. The Japanese travelers were deeply disappointed with the Chinese civilization they saw; it was a striking contrast to what they had expected and to what their counterparts had reported a millennium earlier after visiting Yangzhou and Chang'an. Japanese newspapers did not begin to flourish until several years after the visit, but after the ship's return, the observations of the *Senzaimaru* travelers were nevertheless passed on in reports, in books, and by word of mouth, and they began to have an impact on Japanese leaders' views of China.

Though they were disappointed that China had so many problems, the Japanese on the trip identified with Chinese attitudes toward foreigners. They were furious about the arrogant way in which Westerners treated the Chinese—like slaves—in their own country. Takasugi Shinsaku, the Japanese official on the trip whose reports had the greatest influence in Japan, expressed kinship with the Chinese and disgust at the Westerners, whom he referred to as "barbarians."

Japanese officials at home worried that the British and French who had attacked China during the Opium Wars of 1856–1860 might also attack Japan. Indeed, in 1863 the British attacked the Satsuma domain and in 1864 Western ships bombarded the Choshu domain. Japanese strategists were beginning to think about cooperating with China against the Western powers.

Although Chinese officials had advised officials on the *Senzaimaru* not to send other ships without first receiving permission, two years later when the Japanese ship *Kenjunmaru* docked in Shanghai without special permission, the Chinese did not turn it away. The following year, when a ship from the Choshu domain arrived in Shanghai, those Japanese merchants were allowed to engage in trade.

Treaty Negotiations, 1870–1873

In the early 1860s, even before Emperor Meiji came to power, the Japanese had been seeking to establish diplomatic relations with China. Japanese officials regarded China as a huge country that could provide markets for their merchants, but the main goal of Japanese officials at the time was to cooperate with China in the face of the Western challenges.

Following some discussions between officials of the two countries, a Japanese official, Date Munenari, was dispatched to Tianjin in October 1870 to meet with Li Hongzhang, who had just been given responsibility for the Chinese side of the negotiations, to discuss the possibility of a treaty to establish formal diplomatic relations. Li Hongzhang believed in the value of establishing relations with Japan and also in the importance of concluding an agreement fairly quickly, for he could see that, after the Meiji Restoration, Japan was strengthening its military more rapidly than China was, and he expected that as Japan grew stronger, it would demand more concessions. Li Hongzhang admired Japan for preventing Westerners from invading their country and for limiting the activities of Western missionaries in their country. The meeting was cordial, as both sides perceived a common interest in working together to resist Western pressures.

On September 13, 1871, a year after negotiations began, Li Hongzhang and Date Munenari met in Tianjin and signed the Friendship and Trade Treaty, the first formal diplomatic document between China and Japan in history. Li Hongzhang was able to negotiate an agreement that the two countries would not launch aggression against each other, and that if either nation were involved in a conflict with an outside power, the other would come to its assistance. Although the treaty documents were signed, some months later, before the treaty was ratified by the two countries, the Japanese tried to eliminate the clause in which each side agreed to provide assistance to the other and to add a most-favored-nation clause that would give Japan the same rights that the Western powers were accorded by China.

Li Hongzhang, annoyed by the change in Japanese demands, held firm, and ratification of the documents was delayed. Finally, in May 1873, the Japanese yielded, accepting the mutual-assistance clause and abandoning a most-favored-nation clause that would give Japan rights in China equal to those accorded to the Western powers. The leaders of both countries expressed the view that China and Japan, with a "common culture and common race" (*tongwen, tongzu* in Chinese; *dobun, doshu* in Japanese) shared an interest in working together to respond to threats from the Western countries.

Negotiations over Taiwan and Ryukyu, 1873

When the treaty was signed between China and Japan in 1873, the Iwakura Mission had not yet returned to Japan, but Emperor Meiji assigned Japan's foreign minister, Soejima Taneomi, to visit China to gain its understanding of Japan's position on the issue of the Ryukyus and Taiwan, where Japan was promoting a view that China was not prepared to accept. Not only was Soejima considered the finest calligrapher in the Japanese government, but he was also deeply knowledgeable about the Chinese classics and skilled in writing Chinese poems. Though his Chinese hosts tried to make it clear that Japan was the supplicant in its relationship with the great Chinese empire, Soejima used his deep knowledge of the Chinese classics to earn a special position for Japan. When he arrived at the port of Tianjin in China, he was received by Li Hongzhang. The Chinese did not approve of Japan's rush to replace traditional customs with those from the West; when Li, who was dressed in traditional clothes, met Soejima, he began by criticizing Soejima for wearing Western clothing.

From Tianjin, Soejima went on to Beijing where he was kept waiting for several days before he was received by high-level Chinese officials. The Chinese were clearly unhappy about Japan's new request for a most-favored-nation clause. Even though the two powers were equal, China was making it clear that in requesting the treaty, Japan was the supplicant. Soejima, upset at the condescension with which he was treated, quoted Confucian texts saying that visiting envoys should be regarded as friends and treated with sincerity and mutual respect. He quoted the Duke of Zhou: "If you treat [foreigners] as barbarians, they will be just that, but if you treat them as true gentlemen, they will indeed become true gentlemen."

Soejima was the first Japanese person in modern times to have an audience with the Chinese emperor. When Prince Gong finally received him, Soejima was told that since he was familiar with Chinese customs, of course he would not object to following the custom of kowtowing (kneeling and knocking one's head on the floor several times) when meeting the emperor. Western diplomats had already been complaining about being asked to kowtow, and Soejima helped make their case by declaring that foreign emissaries should not be asked to kowtow. The Chinese yielded, agreeing that foreigners would not be asked to kowtow; instead, they were only to bow five times. The Chinese showed respect for Soejima's knowledge of Chinese learning by receiving him ahead of the other foreign diplomats and allowing him to bow only three times. When Soejima stopped in Tianjin on the way home, Li Hongzhang, more cordial than during their earlier meeting, toasted to the eternal friendship between China and Japan. Soejima was pleased with the goodwill expressed by Li Hongzhang, and he returned to Japan proud that he had been recognized for his superior knowledge of the Chinese classics and treated with more dignity than other foreign representatives. He also returned confident that China would not stop Japan from expanding its trading activities in the Ryukyus and in China proper.

The Chinese Legation Opens in Tokyo, 1877

Soon after the Friendship and Trade Treaty was ratified in 1873, the Japanese began preparing to send their legation staff to China. Within months, Japan established a formal diplomatic office in Beijing, with Mori Arinori, who had already served as ambassador to Washington, as ambassador to China. Li Hongzhang advocated that Beijing establish a legation in Japan, arguing that if China had had a legation in Japan it could have prevented Japan's attack on Taiwan in 1874. However, China's legation staff of seventeen government officials did not arrive in Tokyo until December 1877. Although Li Hongzhang had by then grown suspicious of Japanese intentions, when Li Hongzhang and Mori Arinori met in November of 1876, they shared their concerns over Russian advances. Li Hongzhang suggested to Mori Arinori that the two countries should also cooperate on matters in Korea. Li Hongzhang still wanted peaceful relations with Japan, and in 1877, when Japan was attempting to put down the Satsuma Rebellion, Li

Hongzhang even supplied the Japanese government with 100,000 cartridges to use in its fight against the rebels.

According to directives they received, China's legation staff members were to report routine matters to the Zongli Yamen and to send memorials directly to the throne for important and urgent matters. The Tokyo legation was headed by He Ruzhang (Ho Ju-chang), then age thirty-nine, a Hakka from Guangdong who had been a scholar in the government-sponsored Hanlin Academy. He was a friend of Li Hongzhang, who had selected him. Also on the staff sent to Tokyo was a twenty-nine-year-old, Huang Zunxian (Huang Tsun-hsien), who would later write the most comprehensive and influential Chinese volume about Japan in the nineteenth century. Like He Ruzhang, his family members were Hakka from Guangdong. Huang's father had passed the second-level official examination (*juren*) and was a midlevel government official. Although Huang Zunxian had failed the imperial examinations several times, he was considered very bright and had the confidence to keep trying. He had spent time with his father, observing the life of an official, and his father eventually bought him a position. Both He Ruzhang and Huang Zunxian were selected for the legation because they had taken special interest in foreign affairs, even though they had no training in Japanese affairs. Li Hongzhang required ministers in each country to keep a daily journal detailing all important affairs in that country to provide an understanding of foreign developments.

In Japan, Huang Zunxian, whose career has been thoroughly studied by Noriko Kamachi, sought to understand the essence of Japan as it really was. He not only studied Japanese history but also its political system, economy, and foreign policy. The nature of the relationship between the Chinese staff in their Tokyo legation and the Japanese had less to do with economic and military issues and more to do with their common culture as men of learning. Huang did not speak Japanese, but he became friends with cultured Japanese individuals through extensive "brush conversations." Throughout the Meiji period, all well-educated Japanese, including those who would later fight against China, were trained in classical Chinese. Huang could write classical Japanese, so it was easy for him to grasp the meaning of Japanese documents and essays, particularly since nearly all of them were written in classical Chinese. He also kept lists of Japanese words to help facilitate communications. Huang believed that the Japanese and Chinese people shared a common culture, and he advocated that the two countries should work together. He respected the high quality of essays and poems written in Chinese by Japan's best intellectuals, with whom he enjoyed associating. He was delighted to find that copies of some ancient Chinese texts that had disappeared from China still existed in Japan and that some ancient Chinese customs and music no longer available in China could be found in Japan. His views of Japan were thus filtered through the eyes of Japanese intellectuals who were literate in Chinese and had great respect for traditional Chinese culture.

Huang had become an accomplished poet before he went to Japan, and while in Japan he was an active participant in poetry events. Well-educated Japanese familiar with the Chinese classics took great pleasure in meeting with both He and Huang, whom they greatly respected. At parties, Chinese diplomats and Japanese scholars would often drink together as they exchanged written notes, drawing heavily on poems by well-known Chinese poets. Both sides reported greatly enjoying these parties, which also became occasions for exchanging information. Japanese officials also used the occasions to improve their Chinese-language abilities. Among the Japanese who took part in such parties with the Chinese were Sone Toshitora, who later played a role in associations that managed exchanges of people between the two countries; Kawashima Naniwa, later an adventurer in China who played a central role in training the Chinese police; and Miyajima Seiichiro, who later became an important spy, gaining information for Japan during the Sino-Japanese War of 1894–1895. Huang Zunxian became friends with prominent scholars like Oka Senjin, who later spent a year in China from 1884 to 1885, and Okubo Toshimichi, the leading statesman of the early Meiji period who was assassinated in 1878 by disgruntled followers of Saigo Takamori, who had led the failed Satsuma Rebellion the previous year.

Through brush exchanges Huang learned a great deal about Japan and Japanese politics. He was shocked to find out how much the Japanese had learned about modern science and international behavior. However, he was not uncritical of Japan. He thought that Japan was wrong to distance itself from China and to rush headlong in the pursuit of Western customs. He also disliked the "excesses" of democracy that he saw in Japan and objected to the Japanese lust for foreign luxuries, which he believed wasted funds that could be used for national development. But he was impressed by Japanese achievements in government organization, public health, and education, and he felt China should make similar efforts. Huang completed a book of poetry about Japan in the spring of 1879, and the Zongli Yamen published it several months later. In 1887 he completed a detailed book about Japan, *Treatises on Japan*, the best-informed Chinese account of Japan from that era. He passed his manuscript on to Chinese publishers, but they chose not to publish it at the time. Only a decade later, after China lost the Sino-Japanese War and many Chinese were ready to learn about Japan, would it finally be published in China.

Before that time, the officials China sent to Japan were products of the Chinese examination system that stressed a classical Confucian education, and their contacts in Japan were largely with Japanese who admired classical Chinese studies. The shortage of information the Chinese had on current Japanese affairs, including politics, economics, and especially military affairs, would put China at a serious disadvantage during the war of 1894–1895.

Japan Begins Facing Outward, 1869–1879

After the Meiji Restoration, Japan's initial effort to enhance its homeland security was focused on strengthening its own northern island (then called Ezo) against threats from Russian activities to Japan's north and from Sakhalin, Manchuria, and Korea. During the Tokugawa period, Japan had effective control only of its one domain (the Matsumae domain), located on the southern tip of the island. The rest of the island was sparsely populated by some 15,000 aboriginal Ainu people. In 1869 the new Meiji government renamed the island Hokkaido (meaning "the circuit in the northern seas") and launched a plan to modernize the entire island, led directly by officials in Tokyo.

The development of Hokkaido would be a model for Japan's development of Taiwan after 1895, and some officials in Hokkaido were transferred to Taiwan. The officials Japan dispatched to Taiwan had been trained in Japanese universities when the dominant goal of education was to modernize Japan. Drawing on the Hokkaido model, they later prepared to help modernize Korea and Manchuria as well.

While Japan was worried about Russian encroachment on Hokkaido from the sea, China was worried about Russian encroachment on its Northeast region from the other side of the Sino-Russian land border. Although Russia did not start building the Trans-Siberian Railway until 1891, Russian efforts to settle more people in Siberia and its plans to build the railway already worried not only China, Japan, and Korea but also England, France, and Germany. Until that point, the Qing rulers had not allowed non-Manchu people to move into their homeland in Manchuria, now called China's Northeast. However, to strengthen resistance against the Russians, in 1878 the Qing rulers changed their immigration policy to allow and even encourage non-Manchus to cross over into Manchuria. Within years, many migrants from other parts of China, especially from Shandong and Hebei provinces, began settling in Manchuria. But in contrast to Japan's efforts to modernize Hokkaido, a region formerly occupied by the Ainu and relatively unsettled, the Chinese did not develop detailed plans to modernize Manchuria, the former royal reserve of the Manchu.

The Ryukyu Issue, 1871–1874

Soon after beginning their development of Hokkaido, the Japanese moved to gain control over the Ryukyu Islands to the south of Japan's four main islands, and this led to the first real tensions between China and Japan at the time. From 1862 until the mid-1870s, while Japan was concentrating on defense, most Chinese leaders were not worrying about actions that Japan might take outside of its four main islands. In their relatively few contacts during this period, the Japanese and Chinese approached each other with goodwill. After the mid-1870s, however, as Japan began to gain strength, its efforts to promote trade and expand its defense perimeters began to conflict with Chinese definitions of China's interests.

Since early in the seventeenth century, the Ryukyu (in Chinese, Liuqiu) kingdom, led by indigenous people, governed a group of small islands, totaling some 865 square miles, stretching between Japan's southern island, Kyushu, and Taiwan. The Ryukyu kingdom tried to maintain its independence but also to cultivate goodwill with China and Japan. Both the Qing dynasty and the Tokugawa *bakufu* (the shogun's government) maintained a presence in the Ryukyu kingdom. The Ryukyu kingdom provided housing for Japanese emissaries, who came regularly for part of the year, and for Chinese emissaries, who came at other times. The Ryukyu kingdom paid tribute to China, conducted trade with China, and, influenced by Chinese culture, used Chinese year names for its own calendar. But the Ryukyu language was closer to Japanese than to Chinese, and since 1609, when Japan's Satsuma domain sent troops to subdue the Ryukyu kingdom, Satsuma had been the dominant outside force in Ryukyu affairs.

From 1871 to 1874, Japan used an incident involving the shipwreck of Ryukyu fishermen off the coast of Taiwan, then a prefecture under China's Fujian province, to strengthen its rights to govern the Ryukyu Islands. In 1871, Ryukyu fishermen in four small ships near Taiwan encountered a typhoon, and one ship sank, two were shipwrecked, and one remained afloat. The surviving Ryukyu fishermen made their way to the Taiwan shore, where fifty-four of them were killed by Taiwan aborigines. Only twelve fishermen survived and managed to make use of the one boat still afloat to return to the Ryukyus. The Japanese government demanded that China pay compensation for the fishermen killed in Taiwan, since Taiwan was Chinese territory. With this demand, the Japanese government was thereby claiming that the Ryukyu Islands belonged to Japan. For more than two years, the issue of compensation was unresolved. In 1874 Japanese officials, irritated by the lack of response from China to their request for compensation for the lives of the Ryukyu fishermen, launched a punitive expedition led by Saigo Tsugumichi, brother of Saigo Takamori. Chinese officials, in response, explained that China did not have effective control over the aborigines in Taiwan and added that the Ryukyu Islands were actually under Chinese jurisdiction. Japanese forces remained on Taiwan, and the Chinese worried that further Japanese attacks might follow.

Okubo Toshimichi and Soejima Taneomi went to China to discuss the issue with Chinese officials and win the support of other embassies in Beijing. Under this pressure, Chinese officials agreed to pay compensation to Japan for the Ryukyu sailors, but they later said they were unaware that this payment provided support for Japan's claims to sovereignty over the islands. Li Hongzhang, angry at the Japanese for betraying the goodwill he had shown in agreeing to normalize relations with Japan, said that while Europeans were honest in their negotiations, the Japanese were duplicitous and unreliable.

By the mid-1870s Japan had more military forces in the vicinity of the Ryukyu Islands than China did and was gradually strengthening its presence. In 1879, as part of the process of abolishing the feudal domains and replacing them with prefectures, Japan incorporated the Ryukyu Islands as a Japanese prefecture and named it Okinawa. The Japanese government then ordered Okinawa prefecture to stop sending tribute missions to China. Li Hongzhang, who had supported relations with Japan in 1870–1871 and maintained relations despite the Japanese attack on Taiwan in 1874, was understandably furious. In 1880 China refused the proposals of the Japanese mission concerning the Ryukyus, but China did not forcibly resist the incorporation of the Ryukyus into Japanese territory.

Japan's Efforts to Open Korea, 1873–1879

Japan's interest in Korea had both a security and an economic dimension. Of all the territories in the proximity of Japan, the area that aroused the greatest security concerns for the early Meiji leaders was Korea, located at the vortex between Russia, China, and Japan. Korea had been the locus of two military clashes between China and Japan, in 661–663 and 1592–1598, and it had been the staging area for the Mongol invasion of Japan (1274–1281). Late in the nineteenth century, as reports reached Japan of Russian, German, and Chinese ships in the vicinity of Korea, Japanese strategists referred to Korea as a dagger thrust at the heart of Japan. Japan worried that other countries, particularly Russia, might use Korea as a base from which to attack Japan. Japan would be more secure if it could establish a military presence on the peninsula to prevent other countries from establishing a base there.

Japan's contacts with Korea took place through the Tsushima Islands and Pusan. Since the founding of the Choson dynasty in 1392, Korea had been even more closed than Japan had been under the Tokugawa, but just as Japan kept Nagasaki open, Korea also kept one port open, at Pusan. During the Tokugawa era the Tsushima domain, located on islands halfway between Kyushu and Korea, was given responsibility by Japan's rulers to deal with Korea. Until 1868, the Japanese official from Tsushima who resided in

Pusan represented the Japanese shogun in carrying on limited communications between Japan and Korea.

By 1873, Japanese leaders, who two decades earlier had been forced by Commodore Perry to allow foreign trade, not only accepted foreign trade but embraced it. They looked to the British example for how to build a strong economy. Japanese officials sought to import soybeans and wheat from Korea and looked forward to selling Korea its industrial products, just as England had exported manufactured products to its colonies to build up its own economy. At the time, Japan's largest export item was raw silk. The blight in France's silk industry and the destruction of much of China's silk-making capacity during the Taiping Rebellion had increased the demand abroad for Japanese silk. In 1872 a silk-reeling factory, the Tomioka Silk Mill, Japan's first modern industrial plant, was opened. Japanese businessmen were looking forward to exporting silk textiles.

In the early 1860s, Japanese leaders were already discussing how to get Korea to accept more traded goods. In late 1868, a few months after Emperor Meiji launched the new era, a Japanese representative from Tsushima was dispatched to Pusan to announce that Japan was replacing the former representative from the Tsushima domain with a new person representing the Japanese emperor. Korea, upset that the Japanese were using the term "emperor" and thus giving their ruler a status superior to that of the Korean king and equal to the Chinese emperor, refused to receive the new representative and his mission. The Japanese, determined to open up trade with Pusan, later sent two more missions, but the Koreans refused to receive them as well.

By the early 1870s some young samurai advocated that Japan should learn a lesson from Commodore Perry, who had used warships to open up Japan, and send warships to open Korea. Saigo Takamori, the charismatic Satsuma samurai who had played a major role in the restoration of the emperor, became the spokesman for this group of hot-blooded nationalists. Aware that public opinion in Japan did not support sending warships to Korea, Saigo offered to go to Korea as an emissary, expecting that he might be killed by the Koreans, an outcome that would strengthen support for subduing Korea. Saigo was becoming a symbol of the dedicated patriot ready to die for his country. In early 1873, taking advantage of the absence of more internationally minded leaders who were away on the Iwakura Mission to the West, Saigo tried to win government support for his plan. The Iwakura Mission returned before the issue was resolved, and on its return Count Iwakura Tomomi, Okubo Toshimichi, and others from the mission were able to block Saigo's plans. In the meantime, however, Japan's discussions of subduing Korea had alarmed both the Koreans and the Chinese, who began to fear that Japan had aggressive intentions.

In September 1875 Japan sent the ship *Unyo* to the western coast of Korea, where it provoked an attack by the Koreans and destroyed local cannons on the shore before it returned to Japan. The implicit threat was that if Korea refused to open, Japan would attack. Japanese military forces continued preparing for such an attack.

The primary concern for Saigo and his followers was not the opening of Korea but the impending abolition of the feudal domains, the end of the samurai class, and the end of the privileges of former samurai. In Saigo's view, a mission to Korea might strengthen the position of the samurai. The government had provided compensation for the samurai when the samurai class was abolished, but many former samurai were deeply upset when the stipends offered to ex-samurai were ended with lump-sum final payments. In 1877 Saigo and some 13,000 followers launched the Satsuma Rebellion. The new national conscript army, with some former samurai as officers and nonsamurai as ordinary troops, defeated Saigo's forces. Saigo, confronting defeat, followed the samurai ritual and, facing in the direction of the emperor, committed suicide by thrusting a sword into his stomach. The public realized that the era of the samurai had ended, but there was enormous public sympathy for Saigo and the glorious dedication he displayed in dying for a cause. After his suicide, support for Japanese military action in Korea increased.

At the time, most Japanese leaders, including Emperor Meiji and Ito Hirobumi, hoped to avoid conflict and to resolve the problems with China and Korea through diplomacy. Li Hongzhang, who was aware that a Japanese invasion of Korea might provoke a Russian response, also wanted to resolve the Korean issue through diplomacy. Officially, China still had suzerainty over Korea, with the right to approve Korea's foreign-policy decisions but not to interfere with its domestic affairs. However, for centuries China had not actively exercised its rights of suzerainty. In November 1875, when Japan dispatched Mori Arinori as its first minister (the equivalent of a present-day ambassador) to Beijing, Mori sought Chinese support for Japanese trade with Korea. When Mori Arinori met with Zongli Yamen officials for a series of discussions, the Chinese officials pointed out that Korea was a Chinese dependency, but they said they could not interfere in Korea's domestic affairs and therefore could not ask Korea to open up trade with Japan. In January 1876, when Mori Arinori and Li Hongzhang were negotiating over Korea, they both sought to reach a peaceful agreement. Mori, who saw Japan's interest as opening ports and carrying on trade, not in sending troops, advocated that Korea be treated under international law as a sovereign state.

The Kanghwa Treaty and the Opening of Wonsan and Inchon

Ito Hirobumi, who doubted that progress could be made in opening Korea by working with China, urged that Japan should work with Korea directly. Korea should make such decisions, he said, not China. In their discussions with Japan about Korea, the Chinese maintained that Korea made its decisions independently, but after 1872, in discussions with Japan over Korea, China took an increasingly proactive role. In 1873, when King Kojong reached the age of twenty-one and replaced his father, the Taewongun, as ruler of Korea, he proved to be more willing than his father to consider opening up and cooperating with Japan. In February 1876, just months after the Japanese ship the *Unyo* had entered Korean waters, Japan sent an emissary to Korea to conclude an agreement on opening up. King Kojong signed the Kanghwa Treaty, which allowed Japan to trade in three Korean ports. Pusan, the port at the southern tip of Korea that had long been open, was soon reopened, but the Koreans dragged their feet in opening the other two ports, Wonsan and Inchon. Some Koreans had begun to advocate following the example of Japan: opening and modernizing to resist the Western powers, but they lost out to conservatives. However, Japan continued to exert pressure. Wonsan, in northeast Korea, was opened by Japanese naval forces in 1880. At the time, the Koreans still refused to open Inchon, but with additional Japanese pressure they finally yielded and opened Inchon in 1883.

As China and Japan began to discuss the Korean issue, the Chinese started to suspect that Japan's desires for a presence on the peninsula did not accord with their own interests. Even Saigo Takamori, who in 1873 was ready to fight to open trade with Korea, had not expressed territorial ambitions, but by the mid-1870s some in Japan were considering the possibility that their country might someday be strong enough to occupy Korea. Li Hongzhang openly expressed the fear that Japan was developing territorial ambitions. The Chinese and Japanese continued to talk about cooperating against threats from the Western Europeans and the Russians, but by the mid-1870s they had become more wary of each other, and an uprising in Korea in 1882 precipitated a clash.

Japan's Military Ambitions: Coordinated Plan or Unpredictable Process?

After Japan moved ahead of China in the 1870s and the 1880s, with its developing industrial state, educated and patriotic citizenry, and growing military strength, did it already have a plan to conquer China?

Some Chinese scholars see a continuity in Japan's determination to conquer China, beginning with Hideyoshi's invasion of Korea in the late sixteenth century. In their view, Hideyoshi's aims were revived in the 1850s when Japan and China resumed contact and Japan expanded into the Ryukyus and Korea, and later by the attack on China that set off the Sino-Japanese War of 1894–1895—events that led to the occupation of Taiwan, the expansion into Manchuria after the end of the Russo-Japanese War in 1905, the invasion of Manchuria in 1931, and the invasion and occupation of much of the rest of China from 1937–1945. In the view of these scholars, the so-called friendship offered by the Japanese was a tactical strategy they employed as they gathered strength to carry out more invasions. Japan would temporarily accept a nearby buffer state, then move to take it over and make the next area beyond it a buffer state, and then move to take that state over as well. They believed that the Japanese, realizing that China was too big to absorb at once, aimed to divide China and then conquer it one part at a time. In their view, Japanese claims of friendship were not trustworthy; rather, they were deceitful expressions calculated to lull the Chinese into complacency as Japan gradually expanded its control.

These Chinese scholars also acknowledge that Chinese leaders prior to the Sino-Japanese War of 1894–1895 were too proud to take Japan seriously and lacked responsibility to their country to study, understand, and respond to the actions taken by the Japanese.

There is evidence that at each of these stages, from Hideyoshi to Ishiwara Kanji, who set off the Japanese takeover of Manchuria (see Biographies of Key Figures), there were those in Japan who did indeed intend to conquer China. When Toyotomi Hideyoshi invaded Korea in 1592, he clearly had the aim of advancing into China and conquering it. In 1597, Hideyoshi's troops were again on the march with the intention of invading China. In the eighteenth century, scholars like Hayashi Shihei advocated that Japan should plan to conquer China. When Yamagata Aritomo introduced universal military conscription in 1873, he announced that troops might be required to respond to China. In 1878, after Katsura Taro returned from spending six years studying the Germany military, Yamagata sought his help in building a modern military for Japan. After the Meiji Restoration, the Japanese government inherited a small number of ships and personnel who had served the Satsuma domain and formed a national navy, and in the mid-1880s the Japanese Navy undertook a large-scale expansion. Eto Shimpei, originally from the Hizen domain (present-day Saga prefecture), who became minister of justice in 1872, proposed at the time that Japan should secretly send monks to China to gather information in case a conflict with China were to break out.

However, other Chinese historians, along with Japanese and Western scholars who study Sino-Japanese relations, find no evidence that the early Meiji leaders constructed an integrated long-term plan for conquering the surrounding areas and moving on to conquer China. Japanese political leaders in the 1860s and the 1870s were primarily concerned with managing domestic political developments and defending Japan against threats from Russia and the Western powers, not with planning military ventures against China. At each stage of Japanese aggression there were many Japanese leaders who advocated maintaining peaceful relations with neighboring countries and avoiding military conflict. But at each stage there were also Japanese radicals who wanted to take more aggressive actions and over the years several political leaders, including prime ministers, were assassinated because they insisted on pursuing a more moderate course.

Mainstream scholars see the Japanese invasions as resulting from radical groups within Japan taking aggressive actions that some Japanese political leaders tried to stop and others passively accepted for fear of further assassinations or other radical actions. The decisions to carry out such aggressions, in this view, derived not from an integrated, clear, long-term plan but from a complex process involving Japanese politics, military leadership, intimidation, and radical activists.

Mainstream historians also believe that the outbreak of the Sino-Japanese War in 1894 could not have been predicted two decades earlier. Until several months before the outbreak of the war, many Chinese and Japanese diplomats and statesmen thought there was little chance that their rivalries would lead to open conflict. There is no clear evidence that Japan was planning a military conflict before 1894. And even in 1894, many leaders in both countries still hoped their people, who belonged to the same "race and culture" and shared the same anxieties about Western penetration into Asia, would cooperate against threats from the West. However, in the 1870s both the Chinese and the Japanese began to prepare for contingencies in case a conflict between them were to break out, and the clash in 1882 led Japan to expand its investment in the military.

CHAPTER FOUR

Rivalry in Korea and the Sino-Japanese War, 1882–1895

THE SOLDIERS' RIOT (Imo Uprising) in Korea in 1882 led both China and Japan to send troops into Korea. The two forces clashed and the Chinese won. As a result of China's victory, Japan increased the resources it was putting into its military. Tensions between China and Japan in Korea continued to rise until 1894, when Japan attacked China and set off the Sino-Japanese War.

In the 1880s China, Japan, and Korea were anxious about Western advances and the danger of colonization, and there were leaders in all three countries who wished to cooperate with one another to resist Western colonialism. At the time, however, Russia loomed as the biggest outside threat in the region. Russia did not start building its Trans-Siberian Railway until 1891, but the railway was already under discussion by 1880. Additional plans were in place in 1882 for Russia to start a steamship line from Ukraine to Priamur, on the coast of Siberia, within the next year to be followed by increased Russian efforts to upgrade the government of Priamur. The prospect of large numbers of Russians moving into East Asia worried the Koreans, Chinese, and Japanese who were concerned about long-term developments. But after their clash in Korea in 1882, tensions between Japan and China over Korea became stronger than their desire to cooperate against Russia.

Korea had the misfortune of being the "shrimp among the whales," located between China, Japan, and Russia. Chinese and Japanese troops had fought on the Korean Peninsula from 661 to 663, when Japan sent in troops to help the Paekche kingdom. Yuan dynasty troops had passed through Korea on the way to Japan in the 1190s, and Chinese and Japanese troops had clashed in Korea from 1592 to 1597, when Hideyoshi invaded Korea. Later, Korea would also be the locus of the Russo-Japanese War of 1904–1905 and the Korean War of 1950–1953.

In 1882 China still had official suzerainty over Korea, giving it the power to make decisions about Korea's foreign policy but not to interfere with domestic affairs. However, for centuries China had not exercised its suzerainty. When Japan began discussing possible moves into Korea in the 1870s, China began to consider taking a more active role. China had been alerted to Japanese ambitions in Korea in 1873, when Saigo Takamori declared that Japan should "pacify Korea" (*seikan*), and again in 1876 when Japan forced Korea to sign the Kanghwa Treaty that established diplomatic relations between Japan and Korea and opened two new Korean ports, Wonsan and Inchon. China, separated from Korea only by the Yalu River, had long had access to trade with Korea through the tribute system and markets along the border, so the opening of two new ports made little difference, but they allowed Japan to obtain more grain from Korea and to sell more industrial products.

In the latter part of the nineteenth century Korea's Choson dynasty, founded in 1392, was in a state of disorganization and decay. Unlike Japan, which had used its port in Nagasaki to remain informed about world affairs, Korea, the "hermit kingdom," had tried to defend itself from the surrounding powers by remaining closed off. Although individual Koreans learned about the outside world through China, the Korean government did not have Japan's eagerness to learn about the outside world. As the surrounding powers began to encroach on Korea in the nineteenth century, it was increasingly difficult for Korea to remain sealed, and members of the Korean royal family were divided as to how to respond to these challenges. King Kojong, who was born in 1852 and assumed office when he turned twenty-one in December 1873, was not a strong leader, but he was more willing to consider opening than his father, the Taewongun (Grand Premier). The Taewongun ruled from 1864 until Kojong reached maturity, but he never abandoned his political ambitions. King Kojong's wife, Queen Min, and her relatives were allied against the Taewongun. Both China and Japan were able to find allies within Korea's divided royal family.

The Soldiers' Riot and the Entry of Chinese and Japanese Troops

King Kojong and those more willing to open Korea had begun working with Japan to begin a Meiji-style modernization program in Korea. In 1880 a promising young Korean official, Kim Hong-jip, was sent to Japan to learn about Japanese modernization. When he returned to Korea, Kim Hong-jip called the king's attention to two essays that he said should guide Korean policy. One, an essay that King Kojong especially liked, was "A Strategy for Korea," written by Huang Zunxian, the official at the Chinese embassy in Tokyo who had been following Japanese developments. Huang argued that the Russian threat posed the greatest danger to Korea, and to deal with the Russian threat Korea should not only remain close to China but also strengthen its treaty ties with Japan, build new institutions to support modernization, and strengthen its alliance with the United States. The other essay, by Zheng Guanying, a Chinese merchant who had grown up in Guangdong but was very familiar with Japanese developments, advised that for Korea to acquire the necessary technology to produce modern industrial products, it had to create modern political institutions, and the place to learn how to do this was Japan. Within months of Kim Hong-jip's return to Korea, Korea expanded its discussions with Japan. It also sought to maintain good relations with China and, in line with Zheng Guanying's suggestions, to upgrade the management of foreign affairs. It established an Office for the Management of State Affairs, modeled after China's Zongli Yamen. Fifteen years later, Kim Hong-jip would become Korea's prime minister.

To follow up on Kim Hong-jip's suggestion about learning from Japan, in the next year, 1881, Korea sent what it called a Gentlemen's Sightseeing Group of twelve young Koreans to Japan to report in more detail on Japan's modernization efforts. The Gentlemen's Group was modeled after Japan's Iwakura Mission, but because the Korean government was short of funds, it visited only Japan and remained for only seventy days. Like members of the Iwakura Mission, the Koreans inspected administrative agencies, military facilities, schools, and industrial sites. Several members of the group remained in Japan after the mission and became the first Korean students to study in Japan. Although many Koreans at home still identified Japan with the Hideyoshi invasion and feared that Japan was planning to invade again, the members who toured Japan were impressed by what they saw, and when they returned to Korea, they sought ways for Korea to follow Japan's path to modernization.

Among the twelve young Korean leaders in the gentlemen's sightseeing group was Kim Ok-kyun, a talented and energetic official who served as the informal leader. After the tour of Japan ended, Fukuzawa Yukichi, perhaps Japan's leading liberal intellectual, who had been an interpreter on an 1860 mission to Washington, D.C., arranged for Kim Ok-kyun to remain in Japan and to study for six months at Keio University, which Fukuzawa had established in 1858 to promote Western studies. Kim Ok-kyun became convinced that modernization, following the path of Japan's Meiji Restoration, was essential to strengthen Korea and to help it adapt to the modern world. After he returned to Korea the next year, Kim Ok-kyun formed the Independence Party to promote modernization. His proposals encountered serious resistance from more conservative Korean officials, some of whom enjoyed good relations with Chinese officials.

In 1881 Korea expanded relations with all three major countries it believed could help it resist Russia: China, Japan, and the United States. Within China, responsibility for managing Korean policy was transferred from the Ministry of Rites, which had managed traditional tribute relations, to Li Hongzhang. Whereas Japan had developed a systematic program of training its Foreign Ministry officials, Chinese management of foreign policy rested heavily on that one person, Li Hongzhang. Li supported Korea's efforts to avoid conflict and promote stability by having good relations with both Japan and China. He did not object to Korean students studying in Japan, but he also invited a Korean mission to visit Tianjin to see the Tianjin Arsenal, which he had supported as part of China's Self-Strengthening Movement. Those who visited the Tianjin Arsenal later helped establish the first modern arsenal in Korea, in 1883. Li Hongzhang also believed that a U.S. presence in Korea would help promote stability because the United States did not have territorial ambitions and could provide a counterweight to Japan and Russia. Li supervised the signing of a treaty between China and Korea, and he personally mediated discussions between Korea and the United States over the drafting of a treaty that was completed in 1882. This marked a turning point in relations between Korea and the outside world—and the end of the old East Asian order based on tribute relations among Asian countries and its replacement by Western-style treaties built on legal specifications. Many high officials in the key countries involved nurtured the hope that Korea would modernize while maintaining peaceful relations with both China and Japan.

As part of their modernization efforts, in 1880 Korean military officials had invited Japanese military officials to help train eighty elite Korean cadets who were to form the nucleus of a modern Korean army. Korea had a very limited budget and chose to reduce the number of its old-style troops. In July 1882, like the Japanese samurai who had revolted against the ending of their stipends, some older Korean soldiers who had been retired against their will protested that they had been waiting more than a year for their pay. When they were given payment in the form of grain, they found that the grain had been mixed with chaff and was not edible. Infuriated by their treatment, they seized weapons from the government's arsenal and took to the streets, attacking Korean reformers as well as Japanese. The Japanese officer who had been training the Koreans to build a modern army and three of his aides were killed, other Japanese individuals were killed in the streets, and the Japanese legation was burned down. The minister at the Japanese legation barely escaped. The rioters attempted to kill Queen Min as well, but she escaped by being carried on the back of a servant. Rioters did, however, kill one official from the Min family. This event became known as the Soldiers' Riot of 1882, or the Imo Uprising.

The Taewongun supported the rioters but King Kojong did not. After the uprising, the Taewongun forced King Kojong to step aside and the Taewongun returned to power. He removed from office all officials from the Min family and executed his own brother, who had allied with the queen's family. In response to the killing of the Japanese officials, Japan sent several hundred Japanese soldiers to Korea to protect its citizens and to support Japan's allies in the government. Although China had not supported the Imo Uprising, it was alarmed by the Japanese troops, and in response it initiated the first Chinese military intervention in Korea since the Manchus attacked in 1636 by sending some 3,000 soldiers to Korea. The Chinese troops quickly overwhelmed the much smaller number of Japanese soldiers and lent their support to the conservatives in the Korean government. China thus abandoned its policy of suzerainty and began to take an active role in Korean domestic affairs for the first time in 250 years.

Li Hongzhang, who managed the Chinese response, was confident that in Korea the Chinese were stronger than the Japanese, but he could see that the Japanese were gaining strength and he sought to maintain a stable peaceful relationship with Japan. He was furious with the Taewongun, who had upset Chinese-Japanese relations by overthrowing the lawful Korean government, thus causing the Japanese to send in troops and setting off a confrontation between China and Japan. Li seized the Taewongun and took him to China, where he was placed under house arrest for three years, and he returned King Kojong to power. China invited former officials from the Min family, relatives of the queen, to return to office. Li Hongzhang also had the Koreans apologize to Japan for the killing of its citizens and pay Japan a small indemnity. Kong Kojong did not believe that he had to choose between the Chinese and the Japanese and he was ready to work with both nations. However, Li was criticized by some nationalists in China for being too generous to Japan, and Chinese military forces remained in Korea, in effect becoming an occupation army. Some Koreans saw China as their protector. Others saw China as an arrogant imperialist power interfering with Korean independence.

When the 3,000 Chinese soldiers were sent to Korea, Li Hongzhang had been away from his post, mourning his mother's death, but he soon returned to office to formulate Chinese policy and give directives to the officials dispatched to Seoul. To take charge of Seoul's new Capital Guard Command and oversee China's activities in Korea, Li Hongzhang sent an able twenty-three-year-old leader from his Anhui Army, Yuan Shikai. Yuan, who in 1912 would become president of the Republic of China, was to take charge of training the local Korean forces. China also signed a trade agreement with Korea that enabled the Chinese to dominate trade between Korea and the outside world. Thus, the Chinese acquired greater influence in Korea than the Japanese had.

King Kojong abandoned his earlier progressive policies following the Imo Uprising, and some Japanese and progressive Koreans were deeply disappointed that Korea would not undertake Meiji-style reforms. In Japanese eyes, such reforms not only would have led to a government reorganization but also would have made Korea a good trading partner that would export grain to Japan and import products from Japan's growing textile industry. But because the Chinese now had far more influence in Korea, Japan was not in a position to take bold steps there. King Kojong still favored Japanese-style modernization, but he wanted to work with the Chinese and he was also cautious about moving too quickly.

For the Japanese, the defeat of their small force in Korea by the Chinese in 1882 and the constraints the Chinese placed on their trade with Korea were deeply disturbing. Should there be another confrontation with the Chinese in Korea, they wanted to be better prepared. In 1873, following the advice of German Chancellor Otto von Bismarck, the Iwakura Mission had championed a policy known by the slogan the Chinese had used during their Warring States period: *Fuguo qiangbing* (in Japanese, *Fukoku kyouhei*, meaning "Enrich the country, strengthen military power"). In the 1870s, the Japanese budget had been under great constraints, but in December 1882, with a stronger economic base, Japan issued an imperial edict authorizing the expansion of military preparedness. Thereafter, the military budget quickly grew to represent more than 20 percent of the entire Japanese government's budget. So that the navy could increase the production of ships without overly taxing the budget, the government also issued bonds to help meet the costs.

Kim Ok-kyun's Disastrous Kapsin Coup, 1884

On December 4, 1884, Kim Ok-kyun, who had been a strong voice for reform since his visit to Japan as part of the gentlemen's sightseeing group of 1881 and was frustrated by the Korean government's continued unwillingness to take steps toward modernization, led a poorly planned coup in which six high-level ministers were killed, many more were injured, and a temporary government was installed. The bloody attack on Korea's leaders, which was overturned within three days, had disastrous consequences. It discredited reform efforts, set back the cause of modernization, and poisoned Japan's relations with both China and Korea. It is known as the Kapsin Coup because it occurred in the year Kapsin, in the East Asian sixty-year cycle.

Kim Ok-kyun had been encouraged by Fukuzawa Yukichi, as well as by other Japanese intellectuals, for his ideas about promoting Meiji-style modernization and had received popular approval in the Japanese press for his modernization goals, but Japan's leaders did not support his plans for the coup. Count Iwakura, who had led the Iwakura Mission, and Foreign Minister Inoue Kaoru both refused to support the coup because they believed it was important to retain the goodwill of China. Shibusawa Eiichi, the most prominent business leader in promoting Japanese business in various parts of Asia, also refused to support Kim Ok-kyun's plans for the coup.

By 1884 Kim Ok-kyun had grown frustrated with the Korean leaders' resistance to undertaking reforms. He admired the young Japanese samurai who had overthrown the shogun's government and initiated the Meiji Restoration, but before 1884, with 3,000 Chinese troops still in Korea, he knew he had no chance of overthrowing the Korean government. However, when the Sino-French War broke out in August 1884 and China sent forces to Vietnam to preserve Chinese interests there, Kim Ok-kyun saw an opportunity to carry out his coup. Although he did not have the support of leaders in Tokyo, he did have the support of some members of the Japanese embassy staff in Korea and the small number of Japanese troops in Seoul.

At a banquet celebrating the opening of Korea's new post office on December 4, 1884, when many high officials opposing reform were present, Kim's supporters set fire to a nearby building, creating noise and confusion. They seized King Kojong and took him to his palace. They then summoned the various Korean barracks commanders who might have mobilized Korean military forces, and as they arrived at the palace, one by one, they were killed by Kim's supporters. Kim immediately promulgated a fourteen-point reform program that called for the termination of China's suzerainty over Korea, the abolition of the *yangban* class (the large aristocratic class consisting of blood descendants of those who had passed Korea's official examinations). Until then only descendants of this class had been allowed to take the examinations. The program allowed anyone to take the exams and officials would be selected by individual merit. It also sought to introduce a state council and undertake other reforms.

Although Kim Ok-kyun had prepared a detailed list of reforms, he was astonishingly unprepared to implement them. His hope that he could maintain power when there were only about 200 Japanese troops in Korea who might support him against the 1,500 Chinese troops still stationed there was totally unrealistic. After three days, General Yuan Shikai, who had remained in Seoul after 1882, brought in his Chinese troops. In the fighting that followed, more than 180 people were killed, including some 38 Japanese troops and 10 Chinese. The officials who had been put in place by Kim Ok-kyun were all dismissed. Japanese citizens living in Seoul, who were viewed by many in Korea as exploiting capitalists, became targets for possible attack, and their homes were looted and burned. Kim Ok-kyun and eight of his followers managed to escape to Japan on a Japanese ship that had been docked in Inchon harbor.

Before the attempted coup, King Kojong had met with Kim Ok-Kyun and was ready to offer some support for his reform goals. But after the coup, all those who had been supportive of reform were discredited, and Kim Ok-kyun was regarded as villainous for his bloody attack on high officials. Many Koreans felt he should be shot. Although he had escaped to Japan, where he remained in hiding, Kim was still fearful of assassination. The Japanese press, however, presented a much more positive view of Kim Ok-kyun and his efforts to bring modernization to Korea.

Ito Hirobumi and Li Hongzhang, representing the Japanese and Chinese governments, respectively, made statesmanlike efforts to preserve the peace and maintain workable Sino-Japanese relations. In April 1885, they signed the Tianjin Convention, in which they agreed to pull all Japanese and Chinese troops out of Korea within four months. They also agreed that in the future, if one country were to send troops into Korea, it would immediately notify the other country, which could then also send in troops.

Li Hongzhang appointed Yuan Shikai, commander of the Chinese troops in Korea and only twenty-six years old at the time, as the "Director-General Resident in Korea of Diplomatic and Commercial Relations," to look after Chinese interests in a civilian capacity. Officially, in line with the Tianjin Convention, Yuan was no longer a military leader, but China and Japan both understood that he could call on Chinese troops if he judged it necessary. Li Hongzhang assigned Yuan Shikai responsibility for preventing Japan's commercial dominance in Korea, and indeed Chinese trade with Korea increased rapidly in the next several years. Although Japanese merchants continued to dominate commercial activities in Pusan, Chinese held the dominant position in Inchon, Wonsan, and along the Chinese border.

After Chinese and Japanese troops left Korea, in line with the Tianjin Convention, many Chinese troops remained in areas near the Korean border, and the Japanese had no choice but to accept China's greater influence in Korea. The telegraph lines in Korea, for example, were completely under Chinese control. Although Japan had telegraph lines from Japan to Pusan, it did not receive permission to link its lines from Pusan to Seoul. The Japanese could communicate with Seoul only by going through the Chinese telegraph system. Yuan Shikai, despite his youth, exercised strong leadership. Although the Koreans were happy to be rid of Kim Ok-kyun and his Japanese friends, some complained about Yuan Shikai's arrogance in giving directions to the Korean government. And to the Japanese, the shutdown of Korea's Meiji-style reform efforts and the dominance of Yuan Shikai represented yet another humiliating defeat. Some in Japan became determined that, in the future, Japan would be strong enough in Korea that it would no longer have to submit to China.

Fukuzawa Yukichi Advocates Turning Away from Chinese Culture

Despite the tensions over Korea, substantial numbers of Japanese trained in classical Chinese studies continued to travel to China and to write for Japanese audiences admiring accounts of Chinese culture. Takezoe Shin-ichiro, for example, who served under Mori Arinori in the Japanese lega-tion in Beijing, wrote in Chinese for a Japanese audience a report of his 111 days of travels in China. Reflecting his affection for Chinese culture, he de-scribed the beauty of the places he visited and provided accounts of some of the heroes described in Chinese literature as well as of contemporary Chinese food and agricultural practices. Many other Japanese scholars wrote poems describing their visits to important historical Chinese sites.

After the failure of the Kapsin Coup, however, a growing number of Japanese intellectuals became critical of Chinese culture because it was slow in adapting to the needs of modern society. Earlier, Japanese participants on the *Senzaimaru* trip and the Iwakura Mission had been disappointed by what they saw in China. Now, in 1885, a few months after the resounding defeat of his former student Kim Ok-kyun, Fukuzawa Yukichi, perhaps the most influential Japanese intellectual of the Meiji period, wrote an article stating that Japan should "*datsu a*" (leave Asia). Japan should no longer look to China as a model, he said, but should look to the West, which in his view was more advanced. At the time, Fukuzawa's essay did not attract much at-tention, but after World War II it would become the focus of China's criti-cism of Japan for allying with the West instead of with China.

For Fukuzawa, the decision to turn from China represented a tortuous change in his core beliefs. Fukuzawa's father, in naming him Yukichi, had taken the name "Yu" from a Chinese book to celebrate his respect for the

Chinese classics. Fukuzawa had received a basic Confucian education, and as a youth he liked the Chinese classics so much that he voluntarily memorized long passages of Confucian texts. However, after the triumph of Korean and Chinese conservatives following the failure of the Kapsin Coup, he began to write articles extolling European civilization as being far above that of China. Although many Japanese scholars trained in the Chinese classics still derived joy from their studies, Fukuzawa's sad farewell to Chinese culture as a source of inspiration represented a new evaluation of China among many Japanese intellectuals.

Oka Senjin, a well-known specialist in the Chinese classics who could communicate with leading Chinese intellectuals as an equal, traveled in China from May 29, 1884, to April 18, 1885. When he returned to Japan, he wrote that China was beset by two poisons: opium and the classics. The writer Wang Tao, with whom Oka had had wonderful conversations during Wang's earlier four-month visit to Japan, had been unable to meet with Oka in China because of his opium addiction. Oka was also deeply disappointed that so many Chinese elite were wallowing in luxury while doing nothing for other Chinese people who were starving. Those who aspired to officialdom wasted their time studying "eight-legged essays," he wrote, obstinately refusing to take the steps needed to adapt to modern times. Oka was also disappointed to find that although Japanese intellectuals had a deep knowledge of Chinese culture, Chinese intellectuals had very little knowledge of the changes taking place in Japan. Oka's criticisms of Chinese culture were strikingly similar to the critiques of traditional Chinese culture that would be voiced by Chinese intellectuals during the 1919 May Fourth Movement.

Growing Japanese Support for Overseas Expansion

The failure of the Kapsin Coup did not end Japan's efforts to cooperate with China and Korea against the West, but it strengthened public support in Japan for defending Japanese interests abroad. The expression "survival of the fittest," first coined by Herbert Spencer in 1864, spread quickly in Japan and was used to justify, without any moral compunction, a belief in the dominance of the strong over the weak. The members of the Iwakura Mission had learned that the European powers assumed that "civilized" countries would establish colonies in the "less civilized part of the world" and that the resources of the colonies would be used to benefit the economies of the home countries. The British had moved into Shanghai after the first Opium War, and in 1862 the British and Americans formally established the International Settlement in Shanghai. King Leopold of Belgium established the Congo Free State in 1862, during the same period that the French and British were setting up their colonies in Africa. The Dutch, already in Java before the Meiji period, invaded Aceh in Sumatra in 1873 and then began expanding into other parts of Indonesia. In 1884, the Russians established the region of Priamur along the coast north of Korea, including the cities of Vladivostok and Khabarovsk, opposite the island of Sakhalin, and installed a governor-general of Priamur, granting him power over the area. Priamur thus attained a regional identity and attracted immigrants from overcrowded areas in Ukraine, who came through the Suez and Indian Ocean by the steamship service that began in 1883. In Japanese eyes, Japan was a step behind and had to begin catching up with the other civilized societies.

Once the ports of Wonsan and Inchon were opened, Japanese manufacturing exports, taking advantage of Japan's early industrialization, grew rapidly. By 1893, 91 percent of imports into Korea were from Japan and 8 percent were from China. Of Korea's exports, 49 percent went to China and 50 percent went to Japan.[1] But in the eyes of Koreans, even though Korea was not formally colonized, the Japanese were behaving like imperialists and pursuing their own commercial interests, looking down on and exploiting Korean people without moral compunction.

When the Japanese public read of Japan's weak response to the killing of Japanese citizens after Kim Ok-kyun's failed coup, they were outraged that their government had not responded more firmly. Japanese leaders, however, were prudent enough to realize that at that point they lacked the necessary military power to respond. Nevertheless, public support for sending more troops to Korea, and even to China, began to grow. By 1884, the military's plans to modernize the army, which Katsura Taro and Yamagata Aritomo had introduced in 1878, had been completed, and the army, making use of the stepped-up military budget of 1882, was beginning to grow. A revision of the conscription law in 1883 expanded the number of recruits into the army and extended reserve service to nine years. Although in 1884 it was still judged premature to challenge the Chinese in Korea, military officials were beginning to imagine the day would come when the Japanese Army would be better prepared.

In 1886 the Beiyang Fleet, responsible for protecting China's northern coastline, made a port call in Nagasaki and displayed four modern battleships, including the *Dingyuan*, purchased from Germany, far larger than any Japanese battleship and then one of the most modern naval ships in the world. The Chinese were showing Japan the great power of the Chinese Navy, with the implicit message that Japan would be foolish to become involved in a conflict with China. During the port call, scuffles broke out between Chinese sailors and Japanese locals in Nagasaki's red-light district and resulted in the deaths of four Chinese sailors and two Mitsui police, and many injuries on both sides. The visit impressed Japan, but not in the way that China had intended. After seeing the *Dingyuan*, the Japanese government decided to construct three large cruisers, each with firepower comparable to that of the *Dingyuan*. After 1889, although China continued to invest in the Summer Palace, including the reconstruction of its large Marble Boat pavilion, there were no significant new investments in navy ships. In contrast, in Japan after 1893, in addition to imperial contributions to the navy, one-tenth of the salaries of civil officials and military officers was deducted and added to the funding allocated for the construction of naval ships and the purchase of arms.

Japanese Information and Intelligence about China, 1880s to 1894

Among the factors responsible for Japan's victory in the Sino-Japanese War of 1894–1895, one of the most critical was the high level of Japanese information about China and the lack of Chinese information about Japan.

Despite the tensions in Sino-Japanese relations around Korea, trade between the two countries was growing in the 1880s, and Japanese businessmen expected that trade with China would continue to expand. In preparation for this expansion, they had been collecting information about Chinese market opportunities. Before the establishment of diplomatic relations in 1871, there were no Japanese businesses in China, but by 1877 there were some twenty-five Japanese businesses in Shanghai alone, including the trading company Mitsui Bussan and the shipping company Nippon Yusen Kaisha (NYK).

There are no records showing that prior to 1894 Japan had plans to attack China, but Japan had been gathering information on Chinese military
installations and ships in case any conflict were to break out. As early as
1879 Katsura Taro, who would become a division commander during the
Sino-Japanese War, took a trip to China with ten other Japanese observers
to survey Chinese military facilities. The results of Katsura's survey were
published the following year in a book with a foreword by Yamagata
Aritomo, describing China's military bases, weapons, and military organization. The book was later revised in 1882 and 1889. By the time war broke
out between the two nations in 1894, the Japanese military had access to
detailed information about China's geography, the Chinese economy, ports,
ships, roads, and installations that had been collected by Japanese writers,
reporters, and businesspeople. From the records that are available, there is
no easy way to determine which writers were actually spies and which were
not. Even those from Japan who wanted good relations with China, who
wanted to help China develop economically and opposed military actions,
had provided information to Japanese officials that could be used either directly or indirectly by the military in the case of conflict.

One person who was well informed about China and had a broad range
of Chinese friends was Sone Toshitora. A strong advocate of Sino-Japanese
friendship, Sone traveled several times to China, where he made good
friends with Chinese reformers. He had kept detailed accounts of the places
he visited, including information on ports, ship cargos, and military installations, and his reports had been passed on to high-level Japanese officials
and military leaders. Whether or not Sone was a spy, his information was
certainly useful to the Japanese military.

Arao Sei, a businessman who founded a trading company in China, did
more than any other Japanese citizen to train people to gather information
about China. In 1892 he and his assistants produced the three-volume *Commercial Handbook*, which was filled with the kind of information needed
by those trying to set up a business in China. In 1890, with the help of
Japanese businessmen he had established the Nisshin Boeki Kenkyujo
(Japan-China Trading Research Center), a school in Shanghai that offered
a three-year training program for Japanese businessmen. The curriculum
focused on language training in Chinese and English, commercial geography, accounting, and bookkeeping. When the first class graduated in

1893, many of the graduates found business jobs in Shanghai. Arao believed that war with China was not in Japan's interest and that Japan should help China economically to counter Western advances. He personally opposed the Sino-Japanese War and sat out the war in a monastery. After the war ended, he advocated more favorable terms for China to promote Sino-Japanese trade. Yet despite Arao's personal stance against the conflict, military officials had helped finance his research center, and when the Sino-Japanese War broke out a year after the first class had graduated, more than seventy of the eighty-nine graduates were recruited to serve as interpreters or spies in the Japanese war effort.

The information that Japanese visitors to China collected was distributed to Japanese troops as well as businesspeople and the interested public. A Chinese writer describing the fighting in Manchuria during the Sino-Japanese War wrote that Japanese troops were much more aware of the Manchurian topography than the Chinese troops were and that maps of the local topography were found in the pockets of Japanese soldiers fighting in the area.

Information about China made its way to the very highest levels in Japan. In 1893, to control government expenses, Japan's House of Representatives voted to cut warship construction. Because of disagreements over budget issues, Emperor Meiji was asked to resolve the issue. He decided that because other nations, including China, were then increasing their military preparations, Japan should also increase its military preparedness. He agreed to cut palace expenses to increase the budget for building warships.

There were some Chinese reports from Japan on the Japanese economic situation. China's consul general in Nagasaki, who took up the post in 1878, wrote reports on the ships coming and going in Nagasaki harbor. The second Chinese ambassador to Tokyo, Li Shuchang, who served there from 1881 to 1884 and 1887 to 1890, did make a serious effort to report on Japanese matters. His warnings about developments in Korea played a key role in China's readiness to send troops to Korea in 1882 and 1884. But other reporting from Japan attracted virtually no interest in Beijing and was sometimes surprisingly out of touch with reality. Early in 1894, the year the Sino-Japanese War broke out, China's ambassador in Tokyo, Wang Fengcao, reported to Beijing that the Japanese were so beset with internal squabbling that they were unlikely to be active externally.

After the war broke out, even though Li Hongzhang followed the events, most other high officials in Beijing initially displayed little interest. The historian Samuel Chu, who has read through the memorials sent to the Imperial Court at the time, reports that high officials in Beijing were far more occupied with plans for the empress dowager's sixtieth-birthday celebration than with plans to pursue the war. Even after the war began, many officials were mostly concerned about whether the Western powers would enter the war and they did not consider Japan to be important enough to worry about.

Antecedents of the Sino-Japanese War, 1894

Yamagata Aritomo, who had led the development of the Japanese Army and was head of Japan's Privy Council, publicly stated in 1893 that Japan should cooperate with China and that Japan's main enemies were Russia, France, and England. Despite the tensions in Korea, many Japanese and Chinese scholars who have studied the outbreak of the war believe that without the timing of two key events, the assassination of Kim Ok-kyun, which inflamed the Japanese public, and the Tonghak Rebellion, which brought Chinese troops into Korea, the Sino-Japanese War might have been avoided, or at least postponed.

In early 1894 Kim Ok-kyun, who had led the coup in Korea in 1884, was invited to visit Li Hongzhang in Shanghai. For more than a decade he had lived in fear of assassination, but he accepted the invitation of a Korean acquaintance to travel with him to Shanghai. On March 27, on the ship to Shanghai, Kim Ok-kyun was shot by that acquaintance, who had in fact been tasked with assassinating him. Kim Ok-kyun's body was mutilated, cut up, and displayed in various Korean cities to show what would happen to people who committed treason by working with the Japanese enemies. From the Korean perspective, Kim had committed the villainous act of killing top Korean officials during the 1884 coup. But the Japanese press considered him a Korean patriot who was trying to modernize Korea. Stories in the Japanese papers of his assassination and the display of his body parts became a sensation and inflamed the Japanese public. A funeral ceremony was held in Tokyo at the Aoyama Cemetery, where Fukuzawa Yukichi, the highly respected intellectual leader who had taught Kim, spoke in his honor, reflecting Japanese respect for his efforts to modernize Korea and Japanese indignation at his assassination. The Japanese press was filled with public calls for a strong national response.

Shortly after Kim Ok-kyun was assassinated, the Tonghak Rebellion broke out in Korea. Much like the Taiping Rebellion in China, which had been initiated by a sect deeply upset with national policy, the Tonghak Rebellion began with a religious sect, Tonghak (Eastern Learning), that combined elements of local and foreign religions. Founded in 1860 by a poor member of the *yangban* class whose father had been a local village scholar, the Tonghak beliefs provided hope for poor people. Tonghak had originally encountered opposition in the Korean press, not because it had political goals but because its beliefs were considered a challenge to Confucian orthodoxy. The Tonghak influence was especially strong in Cholla province, Korea's breadbasket. Members of the sect were angry that corrupt officials in Seoul imposed high taxes on local areas. The group's rank and file were poor peasants who, because of their inability to pay their taxes, had either lost, or feared losing, their land.

The Tonghak sect was also anti-Japanese. Since the 1870s, rice agriculture in Korea had become increasingly commercialized as Japanese merchants in Korea bought up more and more Korean rice to ship to Japan, which was not producing enough to meet the needs of its population. Japanese rice merchants in Korea would lend money to the local peasants, and when the peasants could not repay the funds, the rice merchants confiscated their land. Korean farmers regarded the Japanese moneylenders as dishonest and exploitative. In 1894, a sudden increase in the support for Tonghak was triggered by the actions of a particularly oppressive county magistrate in northern Cholla who had forced young men to work on a water reservoir and then charged them and their families for use of the water. A rebellion started and spread quickly to the surrounding counties. King Kojong sent in a force of about 800 soldiers to clamp down on the Tonghak base in Cholla. But some of the troops deserted and others were overcome by the Tonghak rebels. As the Tonghak Rebellion spread northward, estimates varied as to the seriousness of the Tonghak threat, but King Kojong panicked because so many of his own troops were sympathetic to the Tonghak cause. Worried that Korea did not have a military force that could be counted on to put down the rebellion, King Kojong called on the Chinese to help by sending in troops.

The Chinese responded quickly. On June 7 China, following the 1885 Tianjin Treaty's requirement that if one country sent troops into Korea the other was to be notified, informed Japan that it was sending 2,000 troops to Inchon. Japanese leaders recalled what had happened in Korea in 1884, when the Chinese overwhelmed Japan's smaller force and cracked down on Japanese businesses in Korea and Japanese friends in the Korean government. In 1894, they were ready for the Chinese forces. Within hours of receiving notification from China, Japan notified China that it would be sending in 8,000 troops.

Based on the available evidence, scholars have not been able to agree on when Japan made the decision to launch the war with China. For some years both China and Japan had been preparing for such a contingency, determining how they would respond if a war were to break out between them. Some Chinese scholars believe Japan was simply waiting for an excuse to start a war, and that Japan decided to go to war as soon as China sent its troops to stop the Tonghak Rebellion. Although Japan officially declared war on China on August 1, it really began the war on July 25 with a surprise naval attack.

A decade later, in 1904, Japan would begin the Russo-Japanese War with a surprise attack, and on December 7, 1941, it would start the war with the United States with a surprise attack. Indeed, this strategy was reflected in the thinking of twentieth-century military leader Ishiwara Kanji, who advocated that if Japan went to war, it should start with a sudden decisive blow (*kessen*).

The Chinese public, Chinese officials, and Western observers overwhelmingly believed that if war were to break out, China could easily defeat Japan. Sir Robert Hart, inspector-general of China's Imperial Maritime Customs Service since 1863 and one of the most knowledgeable Westerners about China at the time, stated that "999 out of every 1,000 Chinese are sure big China can thrash little Japan." But Li Hongzhang had much better information about the readiness of Japan to carry out a war and was not so certain. He knew that Japan had political unity, training, organization, and much better intelligence, and he harbored doubts as to whether China could prevail. Even General Yuan Shikai, who had been responsible for China's troops in Korea since 1882 and had been China's leader in Korea since 1885, had doubts as to whether China could win. Shortly after Japanese forces began arriving in Korea, Yuan Shikai put on a disguise and, traveling with a Russian military attaché, returned to China.

Ever since he had been given responsibility for China's foreign policy in 1870, Li Hongzhang had tried to avoid war and to maintain stable relations with Japan. That objective had been behind his decision in 1882 to bring the Taewongun to China. It also underlay his decision to conclude the Tianjin Convention in 1885 as well as his efforts to convince the Western powers to take a more active role in Korea so that Japan would be less likely to undertake military action. In 1894, and even during the war, Li continued to try to involve other powers in ending the war, but without success. When King Kojong requested help to put down the Tonghak Rebellion, Li sent troops not to Seoul, which would have most upset the Japanese, but to Asan, on the western coast some forty miles south of Seoul, to head off the Tonghak rebels as they marched northward from Cholla toward Seoul, hoping that the Japanese would choose not to become involved in a conflict. After Japan sent in its own troops, Li proposed to the Japanese that both countries should agree to withdraw. On June 16, Japan responded with a counterproposal, that China and Japan should cooperate in assisting Korea to undertake major steps to promote modernization. But Chinese and Korean observers were convinced that Japan was driven not by a desire to promote Korea's economic development but by its own economic interests—to obtain Korean grain at cheap prices. In June 1894 when China refused Japan's proposal, Japan was ready to go to war.

The Sino-Japanese War, 1894–1895

On July 23, 1894, at 4:00 a.m., two days after China refused Japan's proposal to work together to modernize Korea, the Japanese broke into the Korean royal palace, captured the queen and the one surviving prince, and held them for "safekeeping" but they did not apprehend King Kojong.

On July 25, when three Chinese ships were passing near Feng (Pung) Island and Inchon, the open port city on the western coast that served Seoul, Japanese patrol ships fired on them. Within an hour, the Japanese had captured one of the ships, forced another to flee, and the third was grounded on a shoal. That same day a large Chinese ship, the *Kowshing*, which had been leased from England and was carrying 1,100 Chinese troops and some

Europeans on its way to Korea, was surrounded by three Japanese warships that ordered the *Kowshing* to follow them into port. After some hours of negotiation, the Chinese refused. The Japanese naval commander, Togo Heihachiro, then ordered an attack on the *Kowshing*, quickly sinking it and drowning some of the ablest soldiers in the Chinese military.

In the naval clashes that ensued, Japan drew on the advantages from its great progress in shipbuilding and the navy's unified strategy and training since the 1880s. By the mid-1880s Japan's navy had ended the use of sailing ships and was constructing only steam-driven warships. In 1894 it had brought its two fleets together into a single group, the Combined Fleet. Ever since the tensions in Korea in the mid-1880s, the battle plans formulated by the Japanese Navy had assumed that its opponent would be China. It followed the strategy it had developed under the guidance of John Ingles, a British Royal Navy captain and adviser to the Japanese Naval Staff College from 1887 to 1893: build ships with high speed and superior firepower and send them to battle in a straight line. The Japanese had determined that in battle, all ten of its ships would move together.

China, in contrast, had four fleets and twice as many ships as Japan. The Beiyang Fleet, under the direction of Li Hongzhang, China's largest fleet, took part in the war with Japan, but China was so lacking in unity that its other three fleets never joined in. Although China's ships were not as fast as Japanese ships, they included two large armored battleships purchased from Germany, for which Japan had no counterparts. However, its other ships were old and obsolete. Nevertheless, Chinese ships had the advantage of having two bases in the vicinity—Port Arthur (Lushun) on the Liaodong Peninsula and nearby Weihaiwei, on the tip of the Shandong Peninsula.

On July 29, four days after the sinking of the *Kowshing*, some 3,000 Japanese troops attacked a camp of Chinese soldiers just south of Seoul. On August 1, the Japanese declared war and landed additional troops at Pusan. China responded and declared war on the same day. Japan quickly gained dominance in the areas just south of Seoul, but it took some weeks for Japanese troops to advance beyond Seoul and prepare for battle at P'yongyang, where most of the Chinese troops were located.

Knowing that P'yongyang was well defended, the Japanese first focused on Moktan-tei, the Chinese fortress north of P'yongyang. Moktan-tei was at a higher elevation than P'yongyang, and from there the Japanese fired their artillery down into P'yongyang, which led the Chinese to surrender the city on September 15. The Chinese troops offered some resistance, but they ran out of ammunition. Some have estimated that as many as 2,000 Chinese and 700 Japanese troops perished at P'yongyang.[2] The battle for P'yongyang represented a major victory for the Japanese. The remaining Chinese troops quickly retreated northward, crossing the Yalu River back into China and ending the Chinese presence in Korea.

On September 17, the day after the end of the P'yongyang battle, a naval battle later known as the Battle of the Yalu, took place in the Yellow Sea near the mouth of the Yalu River. The Beiyang Fleet, built to protect China's coastline, had difficulties operating on the open ocean, where Japanese ships moved easily. China was able to use its two armored German battleships, but the ships could move at a maximum speed of only fifteen to sixteen knots, whereas the Japanese ships could move at speeds of more than twenty knots. The Beiyang Fleet's ten ships, arranged in a V formation, were outmaneuvered by the faster Japanese ships, which attacked from the side and the rear. The armor on the Chinese ships was not pierced, but with their firepower the Japanese were able to kill many of the Chinese sailors on deck. Five of the Chinese ships were sunk, and China suffered an estimated one thousand casualties. Other Chinese ships that had been damaged retreated to Port Arthur to undergo repairs. Only one Japanese ship was damaged, and it was able to get away. Evans and Peattie, in their monumental study of the Imperial Japanese Navy, *Kaigun*, attribute the Japanese victory in the Battle of the Yalu to the superior speed of their ships, the homogeneity of their ships in the battle line, the superiority of their firepower, and their strategy of waiting to fire until close, then maneuvering to the side and behind to continue the attack. The reputation of the Beiyang Fleet was seriously damaged by its loss; the Japanese Navy's victory gave it command of the seas, enabling Japan to move its troops around at will.

On September 25, a week after the naval defeat at the Battle of the Yalu, the Guangxu emperor announced that because of the suffering of Chinese soldiers and civilians, the empress dowager would not hold her sixtieth birthday party.

During the night on October 24, the Japanese secretly erected a pontoon bridge across the Yalu River, enabling Japanese troops coming from Korea to cross. They arrived in Manchuria by 4:00 a.m. the following morning. After crossing the Yalu, Japan's main targets were Dalian and Port Arthur, the ports on the Liaodong Peninsula. By the time Japan's troops reached the Liaodong Peninsula it was winter, and the soldiers marching through heavy snow made easy targets, enabling the Chinese to push them back. Nevertheless, by December 9 the Japanese had taken control of Port Arthur.

Until the capture of Port Arthur, foreign correspondents covering the war had reported favorably on the battlefield conduct of Japan's soldiers. But Japanese troops, following savage combat with Chinese forces in the preceding weeks, were in a vengeful mood as they approached Port Arthur. On entering the nearly empty city, out-of-control soldiers brutalized the remaining inhabitants, killing a reported 2,000 residents, 1,500 of whom were noncombatants. Chinese and Western newspapers carried stories of Japanese troops engaged in drinking and sex orgies and committing atrocities on the local populace—a preview of the violence that would take place in Nanjing four decades later.

An investigation that was immediately ordered by the commanding general, Oyama Iwao—the same Oyama who had supported the establishment of the Japanese Red Cross Society—found reasonable cause in the actions of the Japanese troops, a finding disputed by Oyama's legal adviser, Ariga Nagao, who had witnessed the events at Port Arthur firsthand and concluded that under international law Japan bore ultimate responsibility. Ariga wrote his own account, in French, which was published in French for a foreign audience and then immediately translated into Japanese for instructional use at Japan's military academy. But the news reaching the Japanese public was only about Japan's great success, which was celebrated by huge victory parades in Tokyo.

Having captured Port Arthur, the Japanese moved on to capture the other major port for the Beiyang Fleet, Weihaiwei, at the tip of the Shandong Peninsula, which was accessible by ship from Port Arthur. In January 1895 Japanese forces landed not far from Weihaiwei, and by coordinating its land and naval forces, Japan took control of the naval base and destroyed much of the Chinese fleet that was there. Now Japanese troops were in a strong position to attack Beijing.

On February 12, when it became clear that the Beiyang Fleet had suffered a strategic defeat, Admiral Ding Ruchang, a respected officer who as a cavalry officer had helped suppress the Taiping and Nian Rebellions and who had led the Beiyang Fleet since 1886, and his deputy, taking responsibility for the defeat, committed suicide. The Japanese, who knew of the admiral's reputation, admired him for taking responsibility in the manner of a proper defeated samurai. The Japanese allowed his body to be carried away on a Chinese ship, and as the ship passed, the Japanese lowered their flags in an expression of respect.

Sarah Paine, in her study of the Sino-Japanese War, concludes that Japan's remarkable military successes, winning every important battle without losing a single ship, did not result from the superiority of its ships or its weapons. The Chinese had purchased a number of excellent warships and had a large supply of rifles. One major factor in Japan's victory was that China was not sufficiently unified to bring all its forces to bear in the key battles. China's southern fleet did not even take part in the fighting. Also, regional dialects and loyalties rendered coordination among China's various units difficult. Japan, with its standardized weaponry, could manage weapon replacements better than China and could ensure the availability of appropriate ammunition. Japan's superior information about the enemy also gave it an advantage as it devised strategies for attack. And Japanese troops were better trained, more disciplined, and better organized. New rural recruits to the military during the Meiji period might not have understood the routines for hygiene, punctuality, and orderliness required by the military, but such military discipline was instilled in them through basic training. Some of China's leading military officers had been chosen because of their skills in the traditional essay examinations for selecting government officials, not for their military skills. And although some Chinese troops fought valiantly, others, less imbued with patriotism, quickly abandoned their posts when they were attacked. Thus, the forces of the smaller nation surprised, outmaneuvered, and decisively defeated the forces of the larger nation.

In 1894, on the eve of the war, Japan had signed a commercial treaty with Great Britain that ended the unequal treaties. For years Japan had been building up its court system, enacting laws, and training lawyers to meet international standards. Foreign Minister Mutsu Munemitsu and Prime Minister Ito Hirobumi, widely respected by foreign diplomats, had been actively involved in the negotiations with Great Britain. According to the new treaty, which was to go into effect five years later, Japan would have the right to try foreigners in Japanese courts. In contrast, while the Chinese had also long complained about the unequal treaties, the foreign powers, not yet confident of the professionalism of Chinese courts, would not abandon them until 1946. Among the unequal treaties that were finally ended in 1946 was the one unequal treaty that had been forced on China by a non-Western country, the Treaty of Shimonoseki, which Japan had imposed on China at the end of the Sino-Japanese War.

The Treaty of Shimonoseki, 1895

By January 1895, the devastating Chinese defeat and the continued presence of Japanese troops in China where they could easily attack Beijing gave the Japanese victors the power to impose a treaty that brought great pain to China. Within China, a small number of officials realized how little bargaining power they had, but some Chinese officials and citizens harbored illusions of Chinese leverage that was out of keeping with what the Japanese, confident of their position on the battlefield, would accept. Within Japan, there was a triumphant mood, a sense that Japan had arrived as a world power, that the Japanese could humiliate the Chinese, who had acted so arrogantly in the previous centuries, and that they could impose a victor's justice. They took as a model the conditions that Prussia had imposed on France in the Treaty of Frankfurt following its victory in the 1871 Franco-Prussian War, a treaty that included large grants of territory and imposed heavy costs on France.

While the fighting continued during the Sino-Japanese War, the Chinese had sought on several occasions to negotiate a peace treaty. On November 26, 1894, just after the Japanese took Port Arthur, Li Hongzhang gave a letter to Gustav Detring, commissioner of customs in Tianjin, to pass on to Prime Minister Ito. Japanese officials, aware that China was not yet prepared to make what they considered an acceptable agreement, replied that Detring was not properly accredited. On January 10, 1895, as Japanese troops in Manchuria marched toward Dalian, the Chinese government requested a ceasefire, but the Japanese did not grant it. On February 1, two Chinese officials arrived in Hiroshima for discussions with Prime Minister Ito. One of the men had recently served in Taiwan, where he had offered bounties to those who delivered the heads of slain Japanese citizens. The two, as midlevel officials, were not empowered to make decisions, and yet shortly after their arrival they asked when they would meet the emperor. In Japanese eyes, this showed that the Chinese were still not treating Japan with the proper respect and were still unprepared to make concessions. Prime Minister Ito reminded the two officials that in the past, Chinese representatives had made agreements and then later refused to affix their seals. He explained that Emperor Meiji was prepared to carry on negotiations only with Chinese negotiators who had the power to conclude agreements and affix their seals. The two Chinese representatives were sent back to China empty-handed.

Six weeks later, after the Japanese had destroyed China's fleet at Weihaiwei and were poised to attack Beijing, the Chinese, in some haste, offered to send an envoy who had the power to affix seals to an agreement. The Japanese responded that they would accept as negotiators only Prince Gong or Li Hongzhang, both of whom could affix a seal. The top officials in Beijing, all Manchus, worried that if a Manchu, such as Prince Gong, were to sign a treaty that was certain to require unpopular concessions, it would strengthen the already widespread anti-Manchu sentiment in China. Better to have a Han Chinese representative, Li Hongzhang, make the unpleasant concessions and then be blamed for the difficulties.

The concessions Japan demanded were indeed onerous. The Imperial Japanese Army, concerned about the growing Russian presence in northeast Asia from the newly built Trans-Siberian Railway, demanded that it be given control over the Liaodong Peninsula, including Port Arthur and Dalian, which would deny the Russians a warm-water port in northeast Asia. Japan's Imperial Navy wanted control over Taiwan to strengthen its position in the western Pacific. And Japan's financial leaders sought a large indemnity to finance the costs of heavy industrialization. The Japanese were confident that they could impose all of these demands, even though they knew that the Western powers would not accept Japan's control over large amounts of territory on the Chinese mainland.

On March 19, Li Hongzhang and 100 other officials arrived in Shimonoseki, a port at the southwest corner of Honshu, Japan's main island. Shimonoseki was in Yamaguchi prefecture, which had formerly belonged to the Choshu domain where Ito Hirobumi had grown up. Prime Minister Ito, who spoke quite good English, spoke with Li Hongzhang in English. Although Li Hongzhang was able to speak some English, he spoke in Chinese and negotiated through a Chinese-English interpreter. At the time of the meeting, Japanese forces were within marching distance of Beijing. Ito started with a proposal that China would certainly refuse. He proposed Japanese occupation of Tianjin, Dagu (the military base guarding Beijing), and Shanhaiguan, the pass separating Manchuria from the rest of China; Japanese control over China's major railway; and Chinese funds to support the Japanese occupation. As expected, Li said he could not accept those conditions, so the negotiations continued. Li Hongzhang had negotiated with Ito before, and the two understood that their problems were not personal, that they were representing their countries. Li made a personal appeal, however, describing—very accurately, it turned out—how he would be seen within China for accepting such conditions.

On March 24, when Li Hongzhang was on his way back to his lodging from the building where the negotiations were being conducted, a young Japanese firebrand attempted to assassinate him. Before the police could apprehend him, the youth fired one shot that lodged in Li Hongzhang's cheek, just below his eye. Though it was painful, Li chose not to have the bullet removed.

Japanese officials and the Japanese press, thoroughly embarrassed and aware how this would damage Japan's international reputation, were full of apologies both at home and abroad. Japanese public spokesmen were very solicitous of Li Hongzhang's welfare, and the Japanese government sought to atone for what was considered a hideous act. Emperor Meiji issued an apology to the Chinese nation and offered to have his own physician treat Li. Li received a large number of letters of apology from the Japanese public, and the emperor offered China a three-week armistice.

Meanwhile, Li Hongzhang's blood nephew whom he had adopted as his son, Lord Li Jingfang, continued the negotiations with Prime Minister Ito. Following the shooting, the Japanese slightly lessened their demands, but their conditions remained harsh. Six days after the assassination attempt, an armistice agreement was signed. The treaty handed over Taiwan and the Pescadores Islands to Japan; a large indemnity, equivalent to three-fourths of China's annual budget, was to be paid to Japan over four and a half years; and Chinese suzerainty over Korea and China's tributary relationship with Korea were to be terminated. Korea was to be completely independent; a large portion of mainland territory that included the Liaodong Peninsula was to be handed over to Japan; Japan was to enjoy the same commercial privileges in China that the European powers enjoyed; Japanese traders would no longer pay the *lijin* (transit tax) on goods passing through toll gates as they were transported within China; Chinese offensive military operations were to end; seven key Chinese cities were to be opened to Japanese residents and businesses; and more inland markets were to be opened.

As expected, once the terms of the treaty were made known in China, the Chinese people were furious. Li Hongzhang was denounced for accepting the imposition of such conditions. Thousands of Chinese officials wrote memorials to their emperor denouncing the treaty. But the Chinese emperor knew that if China did not sign the treaty, Beijing and Shenyang would soon be devastated and the Ming tombs might be destroyed. On May 8, in Yantai (Chefu), Shandong, near where Confucius was born on the Bohai coast, the treaty was signed in the presence of warships from Russia, the United States, England, France, Germany, and Italy.

Having no choice but to sign the treaty, the Manchu court did what it could to pass down blame for accepting the harsh conditions. Empress Cixi passed responsibility on to the Guangxu emperor. By selecting Li Hongzhang to carry out the negotiations, the Manchu rulers could blame a Han Chinese for agreeing to the terms. In fact, although Li Hongzhang had been trying to strengthen China for several decades, his efforts had not been fully supported by conservative officials. As he told Ito Hirobumi when the treaty negotiations began, he had been attempting to do in China what Ito had accomplished in Japan. The assassination attempt slightly softened the Chinese reaction to Li Hongzhang, as it had slightly softened the Japanese demands, but on his return Li was stripped of all his titles except that of grand secretary. For generations, among Chinese patriots Li Hongzhang would be the scapegoat for agreeing to the Treaty of Shimonoseki, signed following China's defeat because of weaknesses he had dedicated his life to overcoming.

In earlier times the Japanese had felt humiliated by the way the Chinese had treated them, as if they were supplicants facing their superiors. Elaborate protocols, or "rites," for meetings had made clear their status. The Chinese were at the top and the Japanese were subordinate. Even in 1895 when Japan had won on the battlefield, the Chinese initially treated the

Japanese as inferiors, and only when their capital was in grave danger did they yield. Now the Japanese had an opportunity to return the humiliation. One territory that Japan had demanded was the area around Shenyang, which had no great strategic significance, but it was the location of the original Manchu capital and of the imperial tombs. Thus the Manchu, rulers of China for three centuries, were thoroughly humiliated. Anti-Manchu sentiment became widespread, and sixteen years later the dynasty was overthrown.

In their meetings, Ito Hirobumi had reminded Li Hongzhang that when they had met in 1886, Li had threatened Ito that if he did not agree to China's proposal to quiet things down in Korea, China might be forced to fight Japan. At the time, Li could not have imagined that one day Japan would be the victor. In 1886 Ito had said that China should do more to modernize. Li admitted that this assessment by Ito had been correct and that he had personally tried to pursue modernization, but those who believed in modernization could not overcome the resistance against it. Li asked Ito what he would have done differently if he were in Li's place. Ito admitted that he could not have done as well as Li. Although Li Hongzhang was impressed with Japanese achievements, it was reported that Li was so upset by the harsh conditions of the Treaty of Shimonoseki that he vowed never again to set foot on Japanese soil. The next year a ship on which he was traveling docked at Yokohama, but he refused to go ashore.

The Triple Intervention

Throughout the war the Japanese had made great efforts to reduce the chance that the Western nations might assist the Chinese in their war against Japan. Japan refrained from attacking Chinese ships in the Shanghai area to avoid disturbing the foreign settlements and took pains to assure the Western countries that it would not invade their settlements. Japan told Japanese residents in the United States to avoid displays of patriotism that could upset the Americans, who might then urge their government to act against Japan.

Before the war, key Western leaders had developed positive feelings toward Japan. They saw Japan as a modern country and found China to be a country that was not only poor, dirty, and chaotic, but also one that did less to abide by the legal practices of "civilized countries." But as the Japanese victories overwhelmed China, other countries, especially Russia, began to show concern about Japan's future territorial ambitions.

Six days after the signing of the Treaty of Shimonoseki, the ministers of Russia, Germany, and France who were stationed in Japan called on the Japanese Ministry of Foreign Affairs to offer "friendly advice." They told the Japanese that the Liaodong Peninsula (where Port Arthur and Dalian were located), which, according to the Treaty of Shimonoseki, was to be handed over to Japan, should remain in Chinese hands. They pointed out that if Japan were to occupy the Liaodong Peninsula, not far from Beijing, it would cause the Chinese undo worry, it would be considered a threat by Korea, and it would be an obstacle to peace in East Asia. It was clear to the Japanese that if they did not follow this friendly advice, the foreign powers were prepared to use force to intervene, and they knew that the Japanese military was no match for the combined Western forces. On November 7, 1895, six months after ratification of the treaty that gave Liaodong to Japan, a new treaty was signed that returned Liaodong to China.

Japanese government officials, fully aware that the Japanese public would regard this new concession as outrageous, withheld any public announcement in Japan until May of the following year. When they announced it, they did not refer to the pressure of foreign governments but explained that they were returning the Liaodong Peninsula as a magnanimous Japanese gesture to the Chinese. As expected, when the announcement was finally made the Japanese press exploded. Why did Japan, which had won the war and was finally ending its unequal treaties, still have to bow down to the demands of the Western powers? Japan, as the Japanese press announced, was not yet fully welcomed as a world power. Adding to the affront, three years later the Russians would take over the Liaodong Peninsula and begin to use Port Arthur as a warm-water port.

Just as the Chinese used Li Hongzhang as a scapegoat after he had bowed to pressures he could not control, the Japanese press was full of accounts that scapegoated the Japanese diplomats who had bowed to foreign pressures, when in fact they had lacked power to resist. Some Japanese patriots were already beginning to calculate how Japan could continue to gain strength and eventually overturn the concessions to the Western powers. A decade later, when Japan defeated Russia in the Russo-Japanese War, it would be able to do just that and reacquire rights to the Liaodong Peninsula.

The Impact of the Japanese Victory

China did not yet have a large public that followed national and international events. Some in inner China scarcely knew there had been a war in China's Northeast. But the elites, the bureaucrats, and the growing number of educated youth were devastated by China's defeat. Not only did China lose a war, it also lost its instinctive pride in the superiority of the Chinese civilization that had thrived for more than two millennia. The defeat was a heart-rending disaster, a humiliation that led many of the educated elites to question some of their most fundamental beliefs. Although many in China recognized that, realistically, they had no choice but to submit to Japan's dominance, the outcome brought not only economic disaster but also a spiritual void: they had no clear moral compass for navigating the new era.

The foreign powers, observing China's weakness after losing to Japan, took advantage of new opportunities to encroach on Chinese territory. In 1897 Russia forced China to allow it to build the Chinese Eastern Railway, linking Vladivostok and Manchuria and cutting 350 miles off the route of the Trans-Siberian Railway from Moscow to Vladivostok. In March 1898 Russia received a twenty-five-year lease for the use of Port Arthur, the port that Japan had been denied despite its military victory. Russia's expanding influence in China created threats not only for China but also for Japan, threats that would later spark the Russo-Japanese War in 1904.

In 1897 Germany took over Qingdao in Shandong. England took out a ninety-nine-year lease on the New Territories just north of Hong Kong. France opened a railway from Hanoi to Kunming in Yunnan and acquired a ninety-nine-year lease to use the port of Zhanjiang in western Guangdong. France, England, and the United States expanded their presence in the foreign concessions in Shanghai and Tianjin. Throughout China, the foreign powers used their bases along the coast and inland to expand their economic and cultural activities.

Even the Japanese had been surprised by the speed of their victory. Japanese statesmen were convinced that their country had now risen to become one of the handful of modern countries in the world. On the eve of the Sino-Japanese War, England had already signed a treaty to end extraterritoriality. In the settlement with China after the war, Japan became a colonial power like the advanced nations of Europe by acquiring Taiwan, and it was preparing to show the world that the Japanese could be model colonialists. The Triple Intervention, however, forcing Japan to withdraw from the Liaodong Peninsula, was an infuriating sign that Japan was still not fully accepted by the West. The Japanese became even more determined to play a new role, as the leader of East Asia, in standing up to the challenges of the West.

Paradoxically, Japan's military had defeated China's military because Japan had focused not only on its military strength but also on overall modernization. Japan's victory did not derive from the size of its military or from its modern ships and weapons. China had highly talented military officers and officials who had passed difficult examinations on the Confucian classics, but Japan had more officials trained in science, technology, public education, industry, commerce, transportation, communication, law, local administration, public health, and foreign affairs. Through nearly universal public education and basic military training, Japan had turned its peasants, warrior-administrators, and town and city dwellers into a relatively unified body of citizens who took pride in their nation. Nevertheless, Japan was still a relatively poor developing country. It was experiencing serious domestic difficulties and internal conflicts as a result of the forced march to modernization. But its 1895 victory strengthened national pride and the determination to continue modernizing. It also strengthened the drive for continued Japanese expansion in Asia.

China's "self-strengthening" policies had concentrated more narrowly on upgrading its military and technology. China had acquired ships, cannons, and rifles. It had built arsenals and established institutes to teach foreign languages. It also had many talented individuals who had learned a great deal about the outside world, but China lacked a governing system that could make good use of these individuals. It lacked an organization of bureaucrats with both a broad perspective and the specialized knowledge required to administer a complex and changing society. It lacked citizens who had a civic education and a common culture. The shocking defeat by Japan caused many in China to believe that the Chinese imperial system and the leadership by the Manchus were obstacles to progress, and that urgent changes were needed. When such opportunities arose several years later, many ambitious young people would travel abroad to gain the knowledge necessary to help build a system that would make China rich and powerful and that would restore the glory of its ancient civilization. The country where most of those Chinese young people would go to study was China's recent adversary, Japan.

CHAPTER FIVE

Japanese Lessons for a Modernizing China, 1895–1937

· with Paula S. Harrell ·

JAPAN'S UNEXPECTED VICTORY in the Sino-Japanese War rattled the geopolitical landscape in East Asia. With the signing of the Shimonoseki Treaty in 1895 and a commercial treaty with China the following year, Japan in effect became a treaty-port power, joining the ranks of the Europeans who had controlled the terms of trade with China—and with Japan until 1894—for the past fifty years. Practices once exclusive to Europe's China playbook were now Japan's to employ: most-favored-nation rules, exemptions from local laws, tariff controls, and the threat of force. Long used to arranging trade-offs among themselves, members of the old club responded unevenly to the fact that they had a new competitor, forcing Japan to return Liaodong, for example, yet acquiescing to China's cession of Taiwan. Japan also got a thumbs-up for its newly acquired inland navigation and manufacturing rights in China, benefits extended to all powers under most-favored-nation status. Apart from Liaodong, the focus of the Europeans was not on curbing Japan but on getting whatever concessions they could as soon as they could—rights to develop railways, ports, and mines— breaches of sovereignty that Western cartoonists at the time portrayed as "carving up the Chinese melon."

The Japanese public was treated to similar images of a weak China, fallen in global rankings below Japan. Widely distributed wartime prints showed Chinese soldiers in plain tunics, poorly armed, surrendering to Japanese troops that were as well equipped and outfitted as any European fighting force. Informed about the war not only visually but also through extensive press coverage, many Japanese readers were publicly critical of their government for caving in on Liaodong. Tokyo stood fast on this point, but it was clear that views mediated in an active press had to be considered in making foreign policy. Politicians calling for a Japan-led "Asia for the Asians" policy several years later were both leading and following a newly nationalistic public, confident of Japan's place in the world.

Public opinion, in the sense of people informed, engaged, and voicing views in newsprint, barely existed in China before 1895. The vast majority of China's 400 million people, rural and illiterate, were totally unaware of the short but devastating war that had been confined to China's faraway Northeast. Urban educated Chinese were eager followers of the news, but reporting on the conflict was limited to a few limited-circulation newspapers published in Shanghai. Only the senior bureaucrats running the war and a younger cohort just entering government service were fully apprised of China's mounting losses at the front and the tough negotiations that followed. Announcement of the terms of the treaty drew angry protests from younger bureaucrats, but this was short lived, effective only in highlighting the painful reality that Japan had taken the lead in Asia, leaving China behind. China's crushing defeat had exposed the shortcomings of its provincially based military upgrading projects that gave priority to self-reliance over outside assistance, while validating Japan's centrally directed modernization program, with its unabashed commitment to cultural borrowing from the West. Those at the highest levels of government made two pragmatic calculations: first, that a tilt to Japan could be a useful counterweight to the growing demands from the Western powers, and, second, that taking lessons from a modernizing Japan could be a shortcut to China's rejuvenation. Japanese leaders agreed on both counts.

The early decades of the twentieth century saw a remarkable turnabout. For the first time in their shared history there was a reversal in the one-way flow of culture from China to Japan. The *laihua,* or come-and-be-transformed-by-China assumption behind the Tang-Nara encounter thirteen centuries earlier, was replaced by the notion of Japan as a mediator of modern global culture. China engaged in a purposeful series of programs to learn from the Meiji development experience. Not only was there a reversal in the roles of teacher and student, there was also a vast difference from earlier centuries in the frequency of contacts and the number of people involved. For all the critical input from China as a model civilization, Japanese travelers to China from the seventh to the seventeenth centuries were few and far between, and thereafter the numbers dwindled to next to nothing under Japan's centuries-long ban on foreign travel. In contrast, as the twentieth century opened, hundreds of Chinese officials visited Japan, hundreds of Japanese teachers and advisers worked in China, and thousands of Chinese students—a conservative estimate suggests 50,000 up until 1937—studied in Japanese institutions. The scale of cultural contacts was unprecedented and the impact was far-reaching.

Assessing Japan's Victory

Li Hongzhang, aging, disgraced after Shimonoseki, was out of the limelight in the immediate aftermath of the 1895 war, having been dispatched on a trip around the world. Taking up the baton on questions of domestic reform and relations with Japan were provincial heavyweights Zhang Zhidong, Liu Kunyi, and Yuan Shikai. Like Li Hongzhang, they were Han Chinese loyal to the throne, builders of the private regional forces that had saved the Manchu-Qing dynasty from certain collapse after the midcentury rebellions. Although nine months of war had discredited thirty years of self-strengthening, these were capable, talented leaders who had engaged in a rational, ambitious strategy of building regional arsenals, dockyards, and supporting industries, and using Western advisory help for the production and procurement of advanced weaponry. Yet when it came to the test, Japan's fast-track modernization strategy, of which military upgrading was a part, but only a part, of the total package, had succeeded where China's single-sector approach had failed. If the 1895 conflict demonstrated anything, reported a leading Japanese politician, it was the essential link between public education and national strength. The reason China lost, he argued, was that its illiterate, demoralized troops were no match for Japan's highly motivated, well-trained Imperial Army.

The need for a serious course correction was on the minds of China's postwar governing class, from senior officials like Zhang Zhidong to aspiring bureaucrats like Kang Youwei and local community leaders making their way in business and other new professions. Within a few years, images hardened: Zhang was labeled a Han sellout to the Manchu establishment; Kang, an out-of-touch constitutional monarchist; and local leaders, too self-serving. But in the gloom of the immediate aftermath of China's defeat, things were more fluid, and what to do about China was the subject of debate in numerous reform clubs that sprouted up after the war. Should China simply develop new talent to manage the old bureaucracy or fundamentally restructure the basic governing institutions? On such issues, Zhang and his senior colleagues, though conservative to the core, were willing to lend a sympathetic ear to younger politicians such as Kang Youwei. Kang, who had talked reform with Zhang as early as 1886, regarded Zhang as an inspiring model of the innovative governor vigorously implementing development projects in the provinces under his jurisdiction. Zhang also found Kang interesting. When Kang organized his own reform club several months after the signing of the Treaty of Shimonoseki in April 1895, Zhang's name was on the roster of the forty-three members, along with Liu Kunyi and Yuan Shikai.

Suddenly Japan, unexpected victor in the recent war, was on the minds of China's reform advocates. However, what Japan had to offer in the way of development lessons was not clear. Japanese expertise was virtually non-existent. China had posted diplomats in Tokyo beginning in the late 1870s, but most worked in a cultural bubble, publishing collections of poetry admired by their Japanese literary friends, rather than reporting on current events in Japan's modernizing society. There were exceptions. In 1887, after years of effort and references to some 200 Japanese sources, Huang Zunxian, legation counselor in Tokyo, completed a multivolume study covering Meiji Japan from A to Z—from popular rights to universal education and the acquisition of advanced technology from abroad. The Chinese were foolish, he told his readers, to sneer at all foreigners as barbarians, a bit of criticism that contradicted the prevailing Chinese opinion, somewhere between confidence and condescension, that if a second-rate country like Japan could achieve success in thirty years, China could do it in three.

Kang Youwei, agreeing with Huang in substance and likely aware of Huang's work in progress, became more vocal about the need to study the Meiji experience. His words had carried little weight in the 1880s, in part because he was an unknown minor official, in part because Japan was just beginning to upgrade its military capabilities. In 1896, with the war over and Kang in a senior post in Beijing, things were different. He was able to procure funding to establish a translation bureau with the grand aim of translating 7,750 Japanese titles into Chinese. How many of these books were eventually translated is unclear; we know only that Kang contracted with a young Japanese freelancer to translate Japanese legal codes. But even compiling a list of the codes was good publicity. It brought home Kang's point that Chinese reformers had a long way to go to understand the mechanics of the reform process in Japan and elsewhere.

Kang may have been the best-known postwar advocate of thoroughgoing reform, but "concerned scholars" of lesser fame—those still competing for jobs within the civil-service system but wishing to change it—also began to contribute their views through a new venue, journalism. Like the reform clubs, periodicals aimed at shaping and reflecting public opinion were a postwar phenomenon. In 1896, as Kang busied himself with translation, his leading disciple, Liang Qichao, became editor of the newspaper *Shiwubao*, one of several fledgling ventures started in Shanghai, often with foreign financial backing. In the case of *Shiwubao*, one of the backers was Zhang Zhidong, whose moves to censor antigovernment content in the paper led to Liang's resignation. Liang immediately resurfaced as writer-publisher of several magazines in Japan. In this case, the Chinese government did not ban sales of the magazines in Shanghai and Beijing, apparently judging Liang's message moderate enough: after all, a well-informed, responsible citizenry (a "new people") was the necessary underpinning for a modern society.

The Hundred Days' Reform and the Japan Model

In early 1898 Kang Youwei petitioned Emperor Guangxu to assert his power and set up a Bureau of Government Reorganization, to be staffed by reform advisers who would remove all the powers of government from the current power holders and start the process of government restructuring. To buttress his arguments on the wisdom of such a move, Kang attached his just-completed work on Meiji Japan and on the reforms carried out in Russia under Peter the Great. While these documents were making their way to the top—and perhaps to preempt them—Zhang Zhidong presented the court with a series of essays, titled *Exhortation to Study*, which won immediate court approval for distribution to provincial officials.

The appeal of Zhang's work lay in its attempt to strike a balance between social and political conservatism—it strongly endorsed strengthening the established order—and a more liberal approach to designing a school system for the twentieth century. For years, Zhang had supported the idea of combining Chinese humanities and Western science to modernize China's school curriculum. What was new in his *Exhortation to Study* was the emphasis on revising the civil-service exam, centralizing education planning, and promoting a study-abroad program that specifically mentioned Japan. Arguing the advantages of firsthand observation over mere book learning, Zhang cited the examples of Japan's leaders Ito Hirobumi and Yamagata Aritomo, whose overseas experiences provided critical input to their subsequent service in government. His reasons for proposing study in Japan over Western countries, in China's case, were eminently pragmatic: geographical proximity, cost, ease of supervision, language similarities, and the relative compatibility of their social systems. In short, by Zhang's calculation, study in Japan would amount to twice the gain in half the time.

Kang's proposals were more drastic and certain to roil politics at the top. Whether the emperor was genuinely convinced by Kang's presentations or simply tired of playing understudy to his powerful, nominally retired aunt, the empress dowager, he took unilateral action in Kang's favor, issuing a stream of edicts from June 11 until September 21, 1898, in what became known as the Hundred Days' Reform. Everything from the tax system to military training to the civil-service examination was up for overhaul. Japan was the reference point for the reforms in education. Only the announcement of a constitutional monarchy was delayed, but as this was a signature Kang goal, it was clearly on the agenda. How the emperor and Kang could not have anticipated a reaction to this fundamental challenge to the dowager's conservative faction is difficult to fathom, even allowing for their political inexperience. Predictably, the reform movement failed. In a sudden counter-coup on September 21, the dowager and her supporters rescinded the reforms, ousted the reformers, executed those they could lay their hands on, and put Emperor Guangxu, who had backed the reformers, under virtual house arrest. Reform leader Kang and his junior colleague, Liang Qichao, escaped to Japan, where they hoped to gain permanent asylum.

Kang and Liang's presence in Japan posed a dilemma for the Tokyo government. On the one hand, providing safe haven for political dissidents was an international norm Japan wanted to abide by in its new role as the up-and-coming power in Asia. Thus Tokyo, like London, had countenanced the comings and goings of Sun Yat-sen (see Biographies of Key Figures), a man on the Qing hit list in 1895 for his part in an insurrection gone awry in South China. Sun was an anomaly, a political outsider, Hawaii-educated (at a time when American sugar planters were pressing for a U.S. takeover of Hawaii), unschooled in the Confucian classics, and a Christian with a Hong Kong medical degree. As something of a foreigner himself, he had come to believe that overthrowing the Manchus was the essential first step in China's rejuvenation. For Sun, Japan was a second home, a place where he found Japanese friends who shared his vision of pan-Asianism and revolution as the route to salvation for the Chinese people, and who were willing to join him in his relentless fund-raising efforts to achieve his goals.

At the same time, Japan was eager to establish closer ties with the Chinese regime in power. Today, Sun Yat-sen has pride of place as "the father of the nation." It is easy to forget that in 1898 he was on the political fringes, a minor irritant to the government in Beijing. Kang was a bigger problem. He was a political insider, a power player within the bureaucratic ranks and therefore more dangerous. Tokyo was well aware that granting Kang asylum after his 1898 coup attempt would anger the Qing authorities, possibly jeopardizing Japan's China interests, which centered on competing with the Western powers for influence over China's progressive leaders. Settling Kang's and Liang's asylum requests without alienating senior figures such as Zhang Zhidong and Liu Kunyi required someone highly placed who was comfortable in a negotiating role. The man Tokyo assigned to the job was Konoe Atsumaro, head of Japan's upper house of parliament.

Konoe Atsumaro and "Asia for the Asians" Diplomacy

Given his background, personality, and China interests, Konoe was the most obvious choice. He was truly a child of the new Meiji state, a melding of the traditional and modern. He was an imperial prince, head of Japan's most prominent regent family, the very standard bearer of the old traditions. He had been tutored in the Chinese classics by his grandfather, tutor to the previous emperor. At the same time, Konoe represented what was new about late nineteenth-century Japan: receptivity to outside ideas and institutional models. He had insisted on going abroad to study, a typical goal of his generation, but in his case a matter of state. Prime Minister Ito Hirobumi, a member of the original, groundbreaking Iwakura Mission, had interceded on his behalf, and as a result, he was off to Austria and Germany for five years of study. Also typical of those of his generation, Konoe had a high-minded view of public service, the kind of spirit his contemporary, Theodore Roosevelt, so valued and exhorted young people to follow. When Konoe returned to Japan in the fall of 1890, age twenty-seven and with a law degree from Leipzig University, he took the opportunity afforded by his rank to play a role in Japan's new constitutional government, serving as interim head, then head of Japan's upper house, the House of Peers.

Konoe was no figurehead. He was an activist politician who threw himself into the debates roiling the Diet in 1893 over foreign-controlled tariffs, and dared to clash with his mentor Ito Hirobumi in the process. In 1895, he accepted a position as head of the prestigious Peers School (forerunner of present-day Gakushuin University), shifting the school's mission from training military officers to producing diplomats—people schooled in "peaceful national defense," as he described them. He championed public education, including women's education, not simply with high-minded pronouncements but as an active participant in meetings with educators who were often at odds with one another over how to build a world-class school system. Konoe increasingly earned a reputation as a congenial, fair-minded consensus builder. It was in the context of working with one of Japan's teachers' associations that Konoe met the high-energy president of Tokyo Teachers College, Kano Jigoro.

Kano is known today as the founder of the Kodokan school of judo, the man who single-handedly secured a place for his sport and for Japan in the 1912 Olympics. In the 1890s he was known as a leading figure in education policy, head of the institution that set the standard for future teachers of Japan. This was an important job, with scope for input into all aspects of general public education, including physical education and schooling for women. Late in 1896, when he was meeting regularly with Konoe on policy matters, Kano was in the early stages of an entirely new project. The Chinese and Japanese governments, only a year after signing the Treaty of Shimonoseki, had agreed to launch the first-ever study-in-Japan program for Chinese students. Kano Jigoro was put in charge. In April he welcomed the first contingent of thirteen Chinese students—as foreign-looking a group, with their queues and long gowns, as any Westerners in Tokyo—into a special three-year course at the Teachers College. Only seven of them stuck it out. But within ten years and with continued input on Kano's part, the numbers of Chinese students who studied in Japan would swell to the thousands. It was the first large-scale study abroad program anywhere in the world.

As Konoe saw it, hosting Chinese students was a welcome first step, but it had to be placed in an entirely new framework of thinking about China and the rest of Asia. He staked out his position on Asia policy, and his intention to help shape it, in the January 1898 issue of the widely circulated magazine *The Sun*. Considering the many personal friends from his five-year stay in Germany, his core argument was startling. He questioned the extent of Western goodwill toward Japan and the Japanese. He felt that Japan's policy makers were naïve in failing to appreciate the reality that East and West were on a collision course, with race at the heart of it. "East Asia is ultimately destined to face a racial struggle between the yellow and white races, in the course of which both the Chinese and the Japanese will be regarded as the bitter enemies of the white race."[1] To prepare for this eventuality, Konoe called on his government to disengage from its current Eurocentric foreign policy and to focus instead on forging a strategic relationship with its natural ally, China. Sooner would be better than later, before the Western nations joined forces to try to colonize East Asia and while many in the Chinese leadership were in a pro-reform, pro-Japan mood. He recognized that some in China's central government remained stubbornly wedded to an isolationist view, but he insisted that reform-minded governors such as Zhang Zhidong saw it as in their best interests to strengthen ties with Japan. What Japan had to guard against, he warned, was becoming as arrogant toward the Chinese as the Westerners were.

For someone who wanted to expand the scope of his influence, Konoe had the best of both worlds. He could claim the outsider's freedom of action while retaining the advantage of the ultimate insider: easy access to anyone at any level of government and elite society. He was increasingly mentioned in the press as incorruptible and an ideal candidate for prime minister. He might have assumed the position, as his son Fumimaro did later, had he not died unexpectedly in 1904 at the age of forty.

But in 1898, energetic and committed, Konoe was a natural at bringing together Japan's various Asia-first groups, a mix of politicians, journalist-intellectuals, business promoters, and hotheaded youths concerned first and foremost with countering "Western powers advancing eastward" (*seiryoku tozen*). Konoe had previously headed the Oriental Association, whose members had numbered nearly one thousand on the eve of the Sino-Japanese War, and included Komura Jutaro, a Harvard Law School graduate, later foreign minister; Liberal Party leader and prime minister Okuma Shigenobu; Inukai Tsuyoshi, a supporter of Sun Yat-sen and a future prime minister; and Arao Sei, army officer and promoter of expanded trade with China.

In June 1898, just as Kang Youwei's Hundred Days' Reform was plunging China into political uncertainty, Konoe and his colleagues founded the Common Culture Society (Dobunkai) to strengthen bilateral ties, inform the Japanese public about Chinese affairs, and coordinate Japanese businesses, newspapers, and education projects in China. The very name of the new organization indicated a shift in thinking. Previous Asia-first groups had emphasized location—Asia, the Orient. *Dobun*, or "common culture," in contrast, was qualitative and evocative. Shorthand for "same culture, same race" (*dobun doshu*), Dobunkai gave voice to an idea, increasingly appealing in postwar Japan, that a China-Japan partnership had something unique to justify it beyond the usual realpolitik. Konoe's emphasis on "same culture" put history, language, and race at the forefront of what it took to create a successful alliance. It implied reaching out to the Chinese people more broadly, not only to the Chinese political leadership. The Japanese, Konoe said, should not ascribe to the Chinese people the faults of their corrupt politicians.

In early November 1898, the Common Culture Association merged with another Asia lobby group to form the East Asia Common Culture Association, with Korea now added to the agenda. The group's membership was broad and diverse enough to merit a grant from a Foreign Ministry discretionary fund, though the bulk of its funding was provided privately by the organization's new president, Konoe Atsumaro. The group's intention was to remain nonpartisan. Some members favored the go-slow pace of China's senior officials, others advocated the Kang-Liang version of constitutional monarchy, and still others—notably Miyazaki Torazo—advocated Sun

Yat-sen's more drastic solution of completely eradicating the imperial structure. Konoe urged consensus around the very general goal of improving conditions in China—which is what appeared in the association's official platform, along with commitments to maintain China's territorial integrity (*Shina hozen*) and not to interfere in China's domestic politics.

This was the state of play when Konoe and Kang met for the first time on the evening of November 12 at Konoe's residence. By Konoe's account, they became engaged in a verbal tug-of-war. Konoe opened with a bold statement: "Asians alone should have the right to solve Asia's problems, . . . presumably it is this very notion that is the principle behind America's Monroe Doctrine. And, as a matter of fact, the task of developing a Monroe Doctrine for Asia is the responsibility of your country and mine."[2] Kang would have none of an Asian Monroe Doctrine discussion. Instead, he turned the conversation to China's domestic politics and tried to persuade his host that Japan stood to gain politically if it helped engineer the emperor's return to power. Konoe countered that such an action could be taken only in concert with the international community. Not only that, he suggested that China appeared to be moving too fast with structural reforms that had taken years in the Meiji case. Konoe then raised a more provocative question: if the dowager were to be ousted from power, would local leaders necessarily place their support behind the emperor? In other words, as Konoe explained in his write-up of the meeting, would a republic be a possible alternative? If Kang understood the intended meaning of Konoe's question, he chose to ignore it.

Two weeks later, Konoe was willing to listen to a plea on Kang Youwei's behalf from Liang Qichao. But the decision had already been made. Kang had to go. Over the next several months, Konoe worked with the Foreign Ministry to arrange political asylum for Kang in Canada. Liang was warned to tone down his anti-Qing rhetoric but he was allowed to remain in Japan. In February, Konoe arranged for Kang and Liang to sit in on a session of the House of Peers. By mid-March Kang's departure date had been set, the Japanese legation in Vancouver had been alerted to his arrival, and funds from the Foreign Ministry to cover the cost of the trip were passed on to him by Konoe. On March 21, Kang paid a courtesy call on Konoe to thank him for efforts on his behalf. The next day, as Kang boarded a ship bound for Canada, Konoe got word that Zhang Zhidong had enrolled his grandson at Konoe's Peers School for the spring semester.

Laying the Groundwork for a China-Japan Partnership

Konoe had good personal reasons for wanting to settle the Kang Youwei matter to Zhang's satisfaction. He was anticipating face-to-face meetings with Zhang and other Chinese provincial leaders on their own turf, to discuss the specifics of building closer China-Japan ties. Planned for the fall of 1899, Konoe's China visit was to be part of an eight-month trip around the world, his first trip abroad since his student days, a kind of mini–Iwakura Mission that would give him a chance to update his knowledge and burnish his foreign-policy credentials. He went first to the United States, then on to England, Germany, Russia, and countries in between, with China as his final destination.

When Konoe's ship sailed into Hong Kong harbor on October 13, 1899, still seaworthy after a stormy passage from Colombo, he was met by an assorted group of representatives from Japan who had interests in South China, from diplomats to bankers to the head of the Guangdong office of the East Asia Common Culture Association to Miyazaki Torazo, Sun Yat-sen's faithful backer and companion in planning for revolution. One question that had to be resolved immediately was how Konoe should respond to requests from representatives of Sun Yat-sen and Kang Youwei for a meeting with them during his five-week China stay. Both groups had organizers posted in the two safe havens in territorial China, British-controlled Hong Kong and the Shanghai International Settlement. Konoe turned down both requests for a meeting. He did not trust the Kang people, and although he liked what he had heard about Sun, he felt he could not, as head of the nonpartisan East Asia Common Culture Association, meet with one and not the other.

But these were minor concerns. Of major political significance were Konoe's scheduled meetings with Liu Kunyi and Zhang Zhidong. (Plans to travel north, presumably to see Yuan Shikai, had to be scrapped because of travel delays.) These were the men with power in China, and they were key to constructing a new path forward in China-Japan relations. Liu Kunyi was governor-general of China's lower Yangtze provinces and concurrently commissioner for the southern ports, positions that gave him particular clout in determining China's commercial relations with foreign businesses. Zhang, governor-general of Hubei and Hunan provinces, was based in Wuhan, which had an estimated two million inhabitants. In his job for eight years at this point, Zhang was working to transform Wuhan into the industrial center of the middle Yangtze region, with iron works, coal mines, cotton mills, and water and rail links to the rest of the country. He was eager for advanced technology, both machines and systems that trained people to produce them. To Zhang, an old self-strengthener pushing for broad-scale modernization, Japan, as a source of technology and gradual reform, looked increasingly attractive in the late 1890s, just as it would in the late 1970s to Deng Xiaoping (see Biographies of Key Figures) as he searched for a way out of economic stagnation.

Visually and symbolically, the encounters between Konoe and these titans of power presented a study in contrasts: Konoe, age thirty-six, in Western attire, his cropped hair and moustache making him a Theodore Roosevelt look-alike, versus the old Mandarins Liu and Zhang, both in their sixties, dressed in the same silk jackets, long gowns, and domed hats that their grandfathers would have worn. Konoe was cosmopolitan, at home in London and Bonn. Liu and Zhang were of the same look-to-the-West generation of the Meiji founders, but they had never traveled to Europe or America. Nor, from Konoe's account, did they appear interested in what Konoe had to say about his just-completed, multination fact-finding tour. However, when it came to the substance of the talks, the prospects for a China-Japan partnership, the results were encouraging. Liu happily agreed that bilateral cooperation made sense. He made a point of mentioning that his Japan tilt was no passing phenomenon. In the great debate of the 1870s over whether to confront Russia in Xinjiang or Japan in the Ryukyus, he said he had argued against "offending our near neighbor, Japan, over insignificant islands like the Ryukyus."[3] When Konoe proposed establishing a Common Culture Association language and area studies institute in Nanjing, Liu offered his immediate support.

Konoe's talk with Zhang was one part success, one part disappointment. Zhang expressed delighted approval when Konoe proposed expanding Japanese assistance in education through study tours for Chinese educators, hiring Japanese teachers to teach in China, and scaling up the existing study-in-Japan program for Chinese youth. But when the conversation stumbled into politics, the mood turned sour. You ought to expel Liang Qichao from Japan, Zhang complained, citing the corrupting influence of Liang's magazine, *Public Opinion*, on Chinese students in Tokyo. To his later regret, fearing he had offended his host, Konoe came back with a sharp response: "If you think that by getting rid of Liang you will get rid of *Public Opinion*, you are greatly mistaken. There are more than one or two people in Liang's group in Japan; even if he goes, I want you to know that things will not change one iota."[4] Trying to distract Zhang, Konoe asked about Sun Yat-sen. "A small-time thug, not worth bothering about," was Zhang's dismissive reply.

Still, Konoe was in high spirits when he returned to Japan in November 1899 after his tour of the world from Victorian England to Qing China. Most concretely, the China-Japan project that was dear to his heart seemed to be getting off the ground. Although he subsequently failed to get the 100 percent increase in Common Culture Association funding that he requested from the Foreign Ministry, this was balanced by a personal note from Liu Kunyi in January 1900, approving final plans for their agreed school project in Nanjing, praising the association's efforts to promote closer ties among China, Japan, and Korea, and enclosing a photo from Konoe's recent visit. Konoe gave an enthusiastic report on China's activities to the press, including an update on the progress of Zhang's grandson in math.

From Antiforeign Extremism to New Policies Favoring Japan

There seemed to be reason for optimism. But as spring turned to summer, ominous reports began coming out of North China. The Boxers, as Westerners called them, impoverished peasants, at first only anti-Christian, then indiscriminately antiforeign, were filtering in from the countryside to the Tianjin-Beijing area, spreading violence along the way. Faced with new disorder just as it was recovering from the Hundred Days' Reform, the court in Beijing was once again thrown into political chaos over how to respond. Foreign residents wondered whether China's central government would deploy its troops to protect them or if they would have to call in their own troops to stop the violence. By June, it appeared that the foreigners in China could expect no help; the dominant view among court officials favored using populist antiforeignism as a weapon to push back against increasing foreign infringements on China's sovereignty. On June 21 the court issued a blanket declaration of war against the foreign powers. Attacks were launched on the diplomatic compounds in Beijing, where 500 foreign civilians (including Japanese) were trapped, virtual hostages of the Chinese government. As unclear as the fate of the foreign community was the long-term thinking of China's southeastern provincial authorities, Liu Kunyi, Zhang Zhidong, and Li Hongzhang. All opposed the court's decision to declare war.

Watching as conditions deteriorated, Konoe cautioned his government against overreaction, even after Chinese troops brutally murdered Japan's chief diplomat in Beijing, Sugiyama Akira. Konoe feared that severing diplomatic relations would disrupt Japanese trade and the entire network of official and private relationships that the Common Culture Association had been working to construct in South China. Order was restored in Beijing in mid-August by a coalition force (American, Austro-Hungarian, British, French, German, Italian, Japanese, Russian) of about 20,000, more than a third of them Japanese. Yet again thinking long term, Konoe was out in front, urging his government to be the first to withdraw its troops. He saw withdrawal as a gesture of goodwill toward influential officials, such as Zhang Zhidong, Liu Kunyi, and Li Hongzhang, and a challenge to the other powers, Russia in particular, to follow suit.

For Konoe and the Japanese public, the big worry was Russia's growing presence in China's Northeast. Even with Beijing secure, Russian troops in the thousands continued to move south along the Trans-Siberian Railway to take up positions in Manchuria, the ancestral home of China's ruling Qing dynasty. However, some in the Chinese leadership were equally worried about the intentions of Japan and the other powers. Li Hongzhang, reportedly in the pro-Russian camp, had his doubts that, despite all the talk about *Shina hozen*, Japan could be relied upon in a crisis.

But Zhang Zhidong and Liu Kunyi were convinced of the benefits of a partnership with Japan. Thus began a months-long, two-track process, endorsed by the imperial court waiting fearfully in its place of exile in Xi'an. Li Hongzhang assumed the role of lead negotiator with the foreign powers over damages incurred during the Boxer siege. Zhang and Liu took on the task of drafting a package of reforms focused on revamping the content and purpose of education in China. On record for their opposition to the war with the foreign powers, these three mainstays of the Qing regime were the most credible figures to set things right in its aftermath. Li's Boxer Protocol, signed in September 1901, was highly punitive in terms of indemnity payments to be made by China, but aside from the execution of a few princes, it left the regime intact. Zhang and Liu's reform agenda—the New Policies (*Xinzheng*)—was likewise designed to retrofit the old Han-Manchu dyarchy with modernizing elements but not to replace it. The way to do that, as Zhang and Liu saw it, was to build a national system of schools on the Japanese model, while rapidly phasing out the civil-service exam system.

It is difficult to overstate the significance of these developments, both the admission that Japan, not China, was becoming a competitor on the international stage, and the realization that the centuries-old system for selecting civil servants, embedded in the very fabric of life of China's elite, had to be scrapped. The New Policies got to the specifics of the phase-out process. New exam questions were quickly introduced. For example, "When Japan renovated her style of government, what things were of prime importance and what things have proved to be of good effect?"[5] was a question included on a 1902 exam. Three years later, the exam system was abolished entirely and responsibility for educating the public for jobs in the bureaucracy shifted to a system of modern schools that was barely off the ground.

When reform-minded pragmatists such as Zhang and Liu chose to promote study in Japan, cost was a primary consideration. It was cheaper to send study missions and students to Japan to observe and to be trained in its modern schools than to ship them off to Europe or America. Likewise, Japanese teachers and advisers in China, while highly paid relative to those at home, would be expected to command lower salaries than their Western counterparts. Cultural factors likely played a role in Zhang's thinking as well. The similarity of written Chinese and written Japanese, the latter having been adapted from the former, would mean that Chinese students could learn more in less time than if they had to master the totally unfamiliar European languages. Japanese advisers working in China, all with basic schooling in written Chinese, presumably could pick up spoken Chinese rather easily, again an efficiency consideration. No doubt this was in contrast to the Germans Zhang had hired for his staff in Wuhan.

Choosing Japan as an outside source of expertise was also politically smart. It made educational restructuring more palatable to the lingering anti-Western elements in the Chinese leadership, those officials who had encouraged the Boxers and now feared European and American retribution and dominance of the reform process. Japan got good press in the Boxer aftermath. Western journalists praised the Japanese for their discipline and restraint in occupied Beijing, contrasting it with the looting and destruction carried out by the other coalition troops. This was not lost on Chinese officials, who for a time also liked what the Japanese had to say about China and Japan's joint interests and actions in defiance of the Western powers. Even the United States, still a junior power, had just taken over Hawaii and the Philippines, while making its position on Chinese immigration unmistakably clear in its series of Chinese Exclusion Acts. Aside from saving money and mollifying hardliners, there was a fundamental ideological reason for turning to Japan in the vital matter of education reform. Japan's educational philosophy fit the Chinese mindset, particularly its emphasis on moral education and on creating national standards to unite the citizenry behind the state. Finally, in the larger political context in which Zhang Zhidong and Liu Kunyi operated with skill, it made sense to give official sanction to experiments in popular education already being carried out in local communities in China.

Study Tours for Chinese Officials

China sponsored no single mission to study foreign developments that can compare with Japan's Iwakura Mission of 1871–1873. In the Iwakura case, mission members were already highly influential politicians, young men acting on a national mandate (the Charter Oath) "to seek knowledge throughout the world." The mission was methodically organized, carried out on a broad scale, and long—it visited fourteen Western countries in eighteen months. Goals were clearly defined: first, to make the case for treaty revision and, second, to study best practices in a range of fields—from naval science to medicine, manufacturing, school administration, law, and methods of governance—and then return to Japan and adapt the lessons learned to the Japanese cultural setting. The men with firsthand experience abroad were the ones charged with enacting change in Japan. They launched a process that moved forward experimentally, with multiple outside models considered and hundreds of foreign advisers hired to work within the Japanese bureaucracy. There were missteps and disagreements. Yet the leaders were solidly committed to a national wealth and strength strategy that had at its core building a world-class system of education. Japan's decision in 1872, at the opening bell of the Meiji era, to fund universal education had a profound ripple effect, spreading new know-how to the next generation, the most talented of whom were selected for further training abroad or simply worked to promote the spirit of innovation at home.

It was this study-tour mentality, an openness to "what works" elsewhere, that Zhang, Liu, and their Japanese counterparts saw as key to promoting modernization in China. Zhang had talked about this with Konoe Atsumaro, and it was part of the New Policies thinking. But unlike Japan thirty years earlier, China lacked a unified central leadership to fully back the idea. On the contrary, in the post-Boxer years China's center was increasingly paralyzed by dueling political factions, Han-Manchu and conservative-progressive, with each defining reform differently. There was also the ever-present problem of financing, which was particularly burdensome owing to the drain from Boxer indemnity payments. As a result, the study tours China dispatched to Japan tended to be organized locally, mostly by provincial officials in accordance with their own, not necessarily national, development priorities. This scattershot approach, in a country of 400 million, twelve times the population of Japan, run by only 40,000 bureaucrats whose jobs were being undermined by changes in the recruitment system, is hardly to be wondered at. What is surprising is the sudden change in attitude toward Japan, long disparaged as culturally second rate but now admired for its innovative capacity and regarded as a possible model for China's development.

Evidence from a collection of trip reports from 1901 to 1906 suggests that 500 to 1,000 Chinese officials participated in study tours to Japan during those years alone. The total for the entire 1901–1911 period is likely to be at least twice that number, especially considering that in many cases no formal reports were published and distributed. For example, according to newspaper accounts, in May 1901, the vice president of China's Board of Revenue and Population went to Japan to study Japan's financial institutions and policing system. Six months later, he was the imperial court's choice to head a delegation to Japan to apologize for the murder of the diplomat Sugiyama and other Boxer crimes against Japanese citizens in Beijing. Ad hoc visits triggered by crises multiplied after Chinese students in Japan became impatient with clampdowns by the authorities beginning in 1902. So too did study tours focusing on specialized subject areas. Particularly noteworthy were Chinese delegations sent to Japan in 1905 and 1908 for briefings on the Meiji Constitution, the model the Qing court was using as it slowly transitioned from absolutist rule to a constitutional monarchy.

Study-tour participants typically spent two to three months in Japan. Some were highly placed educators and businessmen, others ordinary teachers and agricultural specialists. Their overall goal was to get a firsthand look at a successfully modernizing society, in particular, to study the pivotal role of universal public education in preparing a workforce capable of driving rapid economic growth. Programming for the visits was done from the Japan side. Each official visitor was put in contact with essentially the same people: government officials, especially those from the Foreign Office, educators and school principals from the Ministry of Education, China-Japan friendship groups, and bankers and businessmen. The typical program focused on visits to schools at all levels and of all specializations, with additional time spent on tours of prisons, police stations, factories, banks, and, in 1903, the Osaka Exhibition, a miniature version of the then popular international events known as world's fairs. The tours were conducted in Chinese.

Orchestrating it all was Kano Jigoro, president of Tokyo Teachers College, host of the first Chinese students to arrive in Japan in 1896. Educating Chinese students was high on his personal agenda. By 1901 when the New Policies were announced, he had already guided the first batch of Chinese students to graduation, had enrolled another group in a special Teachers College course, and was finalizing plans to open the Kobun Institute, a new school exclusively for Chinese students and designed specifically to get them up to speed in math and science. In the summer of 1902, Kano received a four-month grant from the Foreign Ministry to visit China, where he lectured dozens of officials, including Zhang Zhidong, on the basics of pedagogy and how to motivate students. Study-tour participants traveling to Tokyo were given the same set of Kano briefings, with the additional feature of actual site visits to schools. What Kano sought to impress on them was the urgency of making elementary education universal in China, the need to expand teacher training, and the importance of developing a curriculum emphasizing practical knowledge, not simply the humanities.

Another prominent educator on everyone's study-tour list was Kano's colleague Shimoda Utako, head of the Peeresses School, proponent of a modern Asian / Japanese style of women's education centered on "good wives, wise mothers," a concept that had grown out of the home economics training Shimoda had received in England during the two years she was there before the 1894–1895 Sino-Japanese War. Shimoda was a high-profile figure, much talked about in the press. She was the founder, chief fundraiser, and spokesperson for the Imperial Women's Association, a lobbying group calling for not only a new, Asian, modern curriculum but also job training for low-income women entering new twentieth-century jobs. Her books were being translated into Chinese. In the summer of 1900 she had a meeting with Sun Yat-sen, who reportedly used the occasion to make an appeal for funds for his revolutionary campaign.

The typical study tour started with a briefing at the Education Ministry, where one can imagine Kano Jigoro giving a summary of Japan's thirty years of experience with educational development, starting with the government's bold decision in 1872 to build from the ground up a nationwide system of schools for both boys and girls. By 1893, 75 percent of school-age boys and 40 percent of school-age girls were enrolled in four years of compulsory schooling, figures that were comparable to those in Europe and the United States at the time. Data of this sort did not generally make it into the study-tour reports, nor did the report writers elaborate on Japan's debates over educational policy, its sequence of experiments with different Western models, the process of building a new university, the use of foreign advisers, and the like that had worked together to produce the school system as it looked in the early 1900s. Emphasis was more on the results than on the difficult road to reaching them. Appended to most reports were detailed organizational charts of the present school system, sample curricula, and descriptions of the planning and management functions of the Ministry of Education.

But the study-tour reports were by no means all about charts and diagrams. They also conveyed the sense of excitement participants felt on first seeing a modern school system in operation. "Primary education is national, universal education without distinction between rich and poor, clever and simple," one official wrote. "Everyone is required to attend school; no one lacks this daily necessity of life."[6] They were impressed that "universal" meant extending schooling even to the disabled. Virtually all visitors were given a tour of the Tokyo School for the Blind and Deaf, where they saw children reading using a system of modified Braille. "The nation wastes no talent," one visitor remarked. "With this approach how can education not but 'raise the country.'"[7]

"Raising the country," or, in Meiji terms, creating wealth and power, was an explicit goal of education, visitors were told. And integral to this was the fostering of patriotism, love of country, and loyalty to the emperor from the earliest grades in school. Japan began promoting patriotism in the 1880s, and the loyalty doctrine was finalized in the Imperial Rescript of Education issued in 1890. For the Chinese, whose terms of reference centered on understanding ways to preserve the imperial regime, witnessing pupils behaving in a disciplined, orderly way, cheerfully bowing to the portrait of Emperor Meiji displayed on classroom walls, gladdened their hearts. They were quick to point out to readers that this nationalism, nurtured through the school system, was meant to preserve Japanese values, not to supplant them with European alternatives, as some Chinese educators were inclined to do. Other than their admiring comments on Japanese nationalism, Chinese visitors had little to say about Meiji politics, the role of political parties, debates in the Diet, or the function of an active press.

Study-tour reports devoted as much space to describing educational practices as educational purposes—such things as curriculum choice, teaching methods, and school equipment. Whereas schools in China were set up solely for instruction in classical subjects, in Japan "what is taught has been extended to military subjects and trade to the arts, agriculture, music, sewing, teaching the blind to read, the deaf to speak, dance, and physical education," one official wrote.[8] Visitors were impressed with the emphasis placed on educating the young for the future world of work, and how this played into methods of content delivery through applied rather than rote learning. They described spacious, well-lit classrooms and the use of modern equipment. Science labs caught the attention of groups touring Tokyo University, as did the size of the library, with its 170,000 volumes in Chinese and Japanese plus 140,000 volumes in English and other European languages. Apart from classroom equipment, other new technology on view in "modern" Tokyo—trolleys, streetlights, and telephones—received little mention in the trip reports. More space was given to enthusiastic descriptions of the Ueno Zoo; there was nothing like it in China.

The development of new schools was not the exclusive focus of the Chinese study trips, though some element of education and training was always included on the tour agendas. At their request, some Chinese officials were taken to farming areas to talk with specialists about purchases of farm implements, to compare notes on scientific sericulture, and to get a firsthand look at Japan's agricultural extension system and how rural schools handled funding shortages. Chinese businessmen were given another variant of the standard tour. Well-known industrialist Zhou Xuexi received his entrepreneurial start on a Yuan Shikai–sponsored 1903 mission to Japan, where he was given a fast-paced tour of financial agencies, the Mitsui Bussan company, printing presses, schools, a copper-smelting factory, and a glassmaking plant. "Schools and factories, managed by the people themselves, have suddenly multiplied more than tenfold within the last ten-odd years," he wrote. "The speed of progress surpasses anything yet seen in the world.... Nearly every foreign product in daily use is now also manufactured in Japan. What's more, Japan is now shipping these manufactured commodities to Europe and America as part of its struggle for economic rights."[9] Cultural borrowing was the secret to success, Zhou was told by his Japanese hosts. If China could get its financial house in order, they said, it would be the strongest nation in the world.

Chinese visitors were optimists when it came to the potential benefits of "opening up" to the outside world through Japan. For most of them, a rung or two below Zhang Zhidong in rank, the development challenges they faced—institutional reform, economic growth, social betterment—were not only of academic interest but were urgent local issues demanding attention. What they found in Japan were workable models in diverse fields, but especially in education and training—the cornerstone of all programs of change, anywhere, anytime. They were wholeheartedly positive about what they saw, notwithstanding a tinge of "anything you can do, we can do better." Their reporting on Japan's best practices was precise and detailed, undoubtedly providing a boost to fellow officials already engaged in promoting the development of new schools at home.

Japanese in China as Advisers and Teachers

As study tours to Japan multiplied, a counterpart program of hiring Japanese advisers and teachers to work in China got under way. This, too, was jointly agreed to by the Japanese government and Chinese provincial leaders. Starting with about 20 teachers and advisers in 1901, the number jumped to 150 the following year. By 1909, according to a Japanese Foreign Ministry survey, some 550 Japanese advisers and teachers were working in China, more than from any other nation. The group also included women; the records for 1902–1912 show there were about 50 Japanese women in teaching posts in China during the decade. Though few in number, these Japanese hires, male and female, had the potential to make a significant contribution. For one thing, they were operating in a receptive policy environment that, for reasons of cost, communication, and pushback against the West, favored Japan as a source of technical assistance. For another, advisers serving in senior posts were hired precisely to lend their prestige, knowledge, and management skills to effect broad change. Even ordinary teachers in local areas often had influence beyond their numbers, and their new teaching methodologies, which were regarded as superior, were quickly copied.

Both sides participated in decisions to hire Japanese experts. Tokyo vetted the candidates and proposed their names to Chinese officials, central and local, who then made the decisions and issued the invitations. The two sides negotiated contract terms, including travel costs, housing allowances, and salaries, which were paid by the Chinese. While a measure of idealism and even excitement played into decisions to work in China, it was in plain terms a job that a candidate was applying for, a source of income, so salary was a key consideration. Just as the Japanese paid high wages to the foreign advisers they hired to work in Japan, so, too, did the Chinese pay Japanese teachers and advisers well, although less than their European and American counterparts. The standard contract was short term, with renewal subject to a performance review, a clause that enabled Chinese employers to maintain control over the people they hired. In a word, the Chinese were pragmatic; they chose their Japanese candidates carefully and managed them closely. There is no evidence that the Chinese were disadvantaged in the matter of contracts or ever felt themselves to be so.

A mix of personal motives led Japanese professionals to seek out or to respond to recruitment offers to work in China. And relative to their Western counterparts, they knew what they were getting into, both culturally and politically. For one thing, they were products of a school system that still included China studies in the curriculum, however downgraded its place, so they had a reading knowledge of Chinese and were familiar with the Chinese classics. For another, they were already involved with China professionally. They were part of a network of public intellectuals who followed the activities of Kano Jigoro, debated the merits of "Asia for the Asians," read about Common Culture Association projects, and even taught Chinese students who were studying in Japan. They were well aware, too, of the turmoil in Qing politics, the crisis of the Hundred Days' Reform, the summer of Boxer madness, and who among Han and Manchu politicians was up and who was down in the aftermath. This was all reported in detail in the Japanese press. China may have had a smattering of independent journals that were read by coastal elites at this time, but Japan had 375 newspapers, published across the country, with an estimated readership of 200,000 in Tokyo alone.

Above all else, what made Japanese advisers attractive to their Chinese employers was that, either directly or indirectly, they were a source of Western expertise. They were graduates of Japan's top schools, including Tokyo University, where they had been taught "modern" subjects by Japan's own foreign hires, English, French, German, and American. Not only that, many had studied overseas. Watanabe Ryusei, hired by Yuan Shikai in 1902, had a Ph.D. from Cornell University; Ariga Nagao, on Yuan Shikai's foreign advisory staff in 1913, had studied law in Germany and Austria; Haraguchi Kaname, adviser to Zhang Zhidong on railway development, graduated from Rensselaer Polytechnic in upstate New York in 1878; and Hattori Unokichi, hired by China's Education Ministry in 1902, was recruited directly from Germany where he was studying at the University of Berlin. The Chinese were getting Meiji Japan's best and brightest.

Teacher Education and University Development

When Hattori Unokichi arrived in Beijing in September 1902, he was fresh from Germany. His stay there had been interrupted midway by a request from Japan's Foreign Ministry that he accept a job as adviser to China's new minister of education. At the insistence of the Chinese, who wanted only top-notch candidates, he was made a full professor at Tokyo University just before his departure. Hattori had much to recommend him. He had studied China throughout his entire school career. He had a thorough knowledge of Chinese philosophy, history, and traditional institutions. His father-in-law was a noted China scholar who believed, along with many of his generation, that the field of China studies should be modernized, and that the Japanese needed to improve their skills in spoken Chinese so they could talk with the big names in Qing scholarship in person, in their own language. This line of argument had won Hattori a government grant in 1899 to study abroad, a year in China to be followed by a government grant intended to fund one year of study in China followed by three years in Germany.

In other words, Hattori had been to China before his advisory stint. But his first trip was badly timed. He had arrived in Beijing in October 1899. By spring, the Boxers were on the rampage. The big names in Qing scholarship were not only unavailable but in fear of their lives, caught up in the court's political infighting. Hattori learned one quick lesson: Japanese visitors were as vulnerable to Boxer antiforeign violence as Westerners. A summer of planned research turned into a summer under siege in the legation quarter. Hattori, a bespectacled university professor with notably weak eyesight, was handed a rifle and put on sentry duty.

In October 1902, Hattori signed a contract with the Ministry of Education to head the teacher-training division at the newly reconstructed Peking University. A Japanese colleague shared the honors with his appointment as head professor of the university's public administration division. The respectful welcome the new Japanese faculty received must have been especially gratifying to Hattori. Vivid in his mind was the university in shambles two years earlier, when one of its top administrators was executed as a foreign sympathizer and its buildings and equipment were vandalized by Russian and German forces in the aftermath of the siege. The scene in China had now shifted, and foreigners were once again being asked to play an advisory role in China's higher education.

Hattori's contract spelled out payments and remedies in case of termination but included no job description or scope of work. He was on his own to come up with a program, based on his three years of experience teaching at Kano Jigoro's Teachers College. Though hard-pressed to organize the curriculum; equip classrooms, laboratories, and dormitories; purchase books and lab specimens; and devise a school entrance exam in a matter of weeks, he somehow managed to sign up 130 students by mid-October as the first enrollees in Peking University's new teacher-training division. By the following year, enrollment topped 300. Thirteen Japanese teachers were on the education-division faculty, seven full-time. Hattori had an able staff of teaching assistants, chosen from Chinese students who had returned from Japan. Zhang Zhidong even attended one of Hattori's psychology lectures, appearing quite baffled by the subject matter. Hattori and his wife, a close friend of Shimoda Utako, felt confident enough to approach high-level Chinese contacts about making women's education a national priority, an area where they felt Japan had a comparative advantage.

Years later, in 1924, Fan Yuanlian, Hattori's former teaching assistant who was now president of Beijing Normal University, welcomed Hattori back to the campus in a speech citing his dedicated service and pioneering role in developing teacher education in China. Only the two of them knew the extent to which Hattori's "dedicated service" had been a matter of dealing with constant bureaucratic headaches. As an outsider, Hattori believed all along that he—and Japan—had more to offer in the field than he was being asked to provide. He had wanted to be a university-wide planner, not simply the man in charge of teacher training.

Hattori sought to move quickly to expand the teacher-training program and replace Japanese hires with Chinese educators. "Teachers responsible for at least the fundamental courses must be Chinese or the institution has no value as a Chinese university," Hattori said.[10] With this goal in mind, he started a program to send the best Chinese students for further training in Japan, but it ran into mismanagement on both sides. Hattori was apologetic about Japan's shortcomings, though he also complained about China's overall reform approach, in particular, that students returned from Japan were not being hired in sufficient numbers because hardliners in the central government saw the newly trained young people as a potential political threat.

More to the point as far as Hattori's own future in China was concerned, politics after 1905 took a conservative turn. The minister of education, receptive to Japanese assistance, was sacked; Fan Yuanlian, who shared his view, quit; and Hattori and six of his teachers returned to Japan in January 1909. The teacher-training program at Peking University continued, but with only Chinese administrators and faculty and with more teaching hours devoted to moral education. Regulations were issued to prohibit students from engaging in politics.

For all of China's interest in Japan's innovative capacity in educational development, politics typically intruded when it came down to dealing with the realities of institution building. Zhang Zhidong, identified as part of the pro-Japan group, may have supported Hattori's efforts (he had even come around to funding girls' kindergartens), but conservative Manchus did not. Japanese newspapers speculated that the real reason for the departure of Hattori and his colleagues was that they had lost out to the Europeans and Americans in the competition for influence over the Chinese government. Hattori as much as agreed, faulting the Japanese government for failing to make the necessary financial commitment to establish a first-class Japanese-staffed college in the Beijing area. As he saw it, Western efforts to win the hearts and minds of the Chinese had the advantage of multiple sources of funding and aggressive tactics to promote the sale of educational materials and equipment. He complained about the Chinese as well. He criticized them for what he identified as their historically begrudging attitude toward anything foreign and their failure to realize that, if updated, Confucian values were entirely compatible with modernization.

The experiences of Japanese advisers working in China were many and varied, but they essentially encountered the same sorts of problems again and again: competition from other foreigners trying to exert influence, uncertain signals from their own government, a slow-acting, technically inexperienced Chinese bureaucracy, and the messiness of late-Qing politics. The latter complication worsened in the post-Boxer years, as various groups, Han and Manchu, liberal and conservative, struggled for power in an increasingly unstable China.

Building a Public Security Force

The Japanese adviser who navigated these late-Qing hazards with the greatest success was Kawashima Naniwa. Kawashima was the epitome of an old China hand, so fluent in Chinese that he could pass as Chinese.

China was not only in his life, it was his life. Although the West was a constant reference point for him, as it was for the rest of his generation, it was so in an entirely negative sense. Whereas his schoolmates flocked to European language classes, he insisted on majoring in Chinese, and he happily recited the classics to all who would listen. He was consistently anti-Western, racially, culturally, and viscerally, and he took on Japan's humiliation at the hands of the foreign powers as his personal burden. His viewpoint was an early expression of the emotionally charged "liberation of Asia from white domination" version of Asia for the Asians that would inflame Japanese thinking in the 1930s and 1940s. Ironically, Kawashima's obsession with China shared something essential with Konoe's more sophisticated, reasoned, soft-power arguments for a redirection of Japan's foreign policy: the belief that prioritizing engagement with China as a counterweight to the West was both culturally feasible and in the best interests of both countries.

When it came to career choice, Kawashima rejected both military school and business. Yet he was also not drawn to China scholarship. He wanted real-life involvement in China, and in that respect—that is, in becoming a new-style China expert, a practitioner with an academic background—he resembled Hattori, who was unlike him in almost every other way. Kawashima spent years in China beginning in the 1880s, first as a freelance intelligence agent for the military and then under contract as an army interpreter during the Sino-Japanese War, directly followed by a brief stint as supervisor of a drug-suppression unit in occupied Taiwan. Ever restless, Kawashima returned to Tokyo in the late 1890s to teach Chinese language and literature at Japan's Military Academy and at Kano Jigoro's Tokyo Teachers College.

The Boxer Uprising was a turning point for Kawashima. As Japan put together an 8,000-man contingent to join the British-led coalition marching on Beijing, Kawashima's unique language skills were again sought out by the Japanese army, and he signed on as an interpreter in late June. Once coalition troops secured Beijing, they divided it into sectors, each run by a different national force and each force charged with ridding the city of suspected Boxers and restoring order. For Japan, the role of occupier meant proving its administrative capabilities for the first time before an international audience, a role made all the more prominent by the fact that, as the biggest contributor to the allied effort, Japan was given the largest area to govern. This was Kawashima's big break. Fluent in Chinese and with an insider's view of Chinese culture and politics, he was a natural to work with Japan's peacekeepers to train the old Beijing gendarmerie in modern police methods. Upgrading local security was a logical first step in bringing the city that had run riot back to normal. But there were long-term implications that Kawashima was well aware of: working within a Chinese government agency on the vital task of creating a modern public security system had the potential to give Japan the kind of commanding influence that the British had enjoyed for fifty years through their control of the Chinese Maritime Customs Service.

Pursuit of national interest worked both ways. As the streets became safer, Kawashima's reputation for getting things done attracted the attention of Li Hongzhang and senior Manchus in the transition government who were concerned about keeping the city clear of terrorist elements after the withdrawal of the international troops. When they established the Beijing Police Academy in June 1901 to replace the Japanese army's training unit, they asked Kawashima to stay on as director. The former army interpreter now had the job of directing the Police Academy, the title of adviser to the Chinese government, a precedent-setting (for a foreigner) second rank within the Chinese bureaucracy, and a handsome salary, probably twice what he had made at Tokyo Teachers College. Kawashima worked fast. One year later, he had put in place at the academy a staff of thirty-five, including fourteen Japanese teachers, and 300 students enrolled annually in the academy's three- to nine-month programs in city ordinances, street patrol methods, firefighting, and prison management. Promising students were already being selected for yearlong training programs in Japan. During its first five years, the Police Academy graduated 3,000 students, the elite core of Beijing's new police force. Governor Yuan Shikai contacted Kawashima about setting up a similar police training unit in Baoding, and he quickly had a program under way. During the 1903–1910 period, about twenty Japanese teachers and advisers worked in seven provinces to replicate the original Kawashima model.

Kawashima's career break at the academy gave him entrée to an even greater role. In 1902, China's Grand Council authorized the creation of a new Ministry of Public Works and Police, which was placed under the stewardship of a young Manchu, Prince Su. Kawashima, the most knowledgeable person around, was given the job of assisting Prince Su in getting the police-reform agenda moving forward rapidly. This was the start of a twenty-year friendship between Prince Su and Kawashima that ultimately saw the reversal of Qing fortunes as well as their own. Congenial and politically astute, Prince Su was not only receptive to power-sharing overtures from the exiled constitutional monarchists Kang Youwei and Liang Qichao, but he also kept channels open to anti-Qing activists like Wang Jingwei (see Biographies of Key Figures), an early associate of Sun Yat-sen in Japan, later head of the wartime collaborationist government in Nanjing. In fact, in a strange twist of fate, it was Prince Su who would save Wang from execution in 1909 when he was brought to trial for attempting to assassinate the prince regent. This same inclination to keep all options open characterized Prince Su's approach to managing foreign relations. Upon returning to Beijing in 1901 to find his villa destroyed by rocket attacks during the Boxer siege and his future precarious, he decided that teaming up with the Japanese as partners in reform made good political sense.

Japan was on the rise. In January 1902 Japan and Britain signed the Anglo-Japanese Treaty, the first-ever treaty between an Asian and a Western nation on equal treaty terms. The alliance was intended to counter the influence of Russia, which was moving troops over its northern rail route into Manchuria, the Manchu homeland. Prince Su and his fellow Manchu princes owned large tracts of land in Manchuria that were certain to be lost in the event of a Russian takeover.

The Prince Su–Kawashima connection was a marriage of convenience, with Kawashima the junior partner. Prince Su was out to capture leadership of the Manchu reform faction. Kawashima saw a chance to further expand Japan's interests in China while boosting his own career. A rare photo of the two of them, seated in identical poses and dressed alike in official Chinese garb, says it all. Kawashima was at his influential best until 1911. But as antiregime and anti-Manchu sentiment mounted, and revolution broke out in 1911, the dynamics of their relationship changed. Prince Su, as part of an ousted regime, became dependent on Kawashima to help the dynasty make a comeback in North China. The institution-building motif dominant in Kawashima's life from 1900 to 1911 gave way to the politics of ethnic separatism, which occupied his career for the next decade. Kawashima's timing was off, however. Facing the political minefield in China after 1911, Tokyo was inclined to back the international community's choice of

Yuan Shikai—and his successors—to rule China, so there was only tepid interest in armed intervention on behalf of Kawashima's Manchu and Mongol friends. In an ultimate twist of fate, the multiethnic monarchy in North China that Kawashima supported in vain after 1912 took shape in the Japanese-administered puppet state of Manchukuo in 1934.

Constructing a New Legal Framework for a New Republic

The same events that dimmed Kawashima's prospects—the end of Manchu rule in 1911 and Yuan Shikai's accession to the presidency of China's first republic—presented an exciting new opportunity for Professor Ariga Nagao of Waseda University at the peak of his distinguished career. Ariga was one of the creators of the field of international law in Japan. He was a law teacher, practitioner, and advocate. He deeply believed that through the application of international law, the world could become a more orderly place. Typical of his generation, Ariga was well versed in China studies, but he was a Europeanist by inclination and scholarship. A graduate of Tokyo University and a recipient of a grant to study in Germany, he was fluent in German, French, and English, and he was a capable translator of works in diverse fields, from pedagogy to political science. He taught "just war" theory at Japan's military colleges, and law and comparative politics at Waseda University, where his students included Chinese youths and visiting officials.

Beyond academia, Ariga was founder, editor, and managing director of *Gaiko jiho* (*Revue diplomatique*), Japan's first journal of foreign affairs. He was an active member of the Japanese Red Cross Society board and a delegate in 1899 to the international peace conference in The Hague, where landmark agreements were signed on the laws of war and dispute resolution. He served on the front lines in both the Sino-Japanese and the Russo-Japanese Wars as a legal adviser to the Japanese Army, a position new to both Japan and Europe, meant to ensure that war was conducted "justly," according to agreed-upon rules. In this spirit, Ariga took his own independent look at Japanese atrocities at Port Arthur in 1895, unafraid to contradict the conclusions of the fact-finding commission authorized by the general in charge. Japan, Ariga wrote, had signed on to the Geneva Conventions absolutely, not selectively, and therefore should accept responsibility.

The Russo-Japanese War was of a different order of magnitude from the short, contained conflict between China and Japan in 1895. The first war between an Asian nation and a major Western power, it involved the deployment of massive armies, the use of machine guns and trench warfare, and an estimated half a million casualties—a precursor to the brutality of World War I. In terms of conduct-of-war issues from the battlefield perspective, Japan came off well in the eyes of Western journalists tracking this "well-watched war." At the front lines himself, Ariga, as patriotic as anyone, was sobered by the enormous loss of life and ever more convinced that, however difficult it was to justify legally, Japan should establish a mandate over Manchuria to forestall a future threat from Russia.

Ariga was a man of international reputation. His French colleagues in international law recognized him—and Japan—as exceptional in their commitment to international norms. The Chinese were getting someone with an impressive résumé when, in 1913, they hired Ariga to serve as constitutional adviser to Yuan Shikai, president of China's first republic. Ariga had high hopes as he boarded the Tokyo-Kobe train, China-bound, armed with a suitcase full of sample constitutions and briefed by Sun Yat-sen along the way. Working with a team of foreign advisers to write a constitution for a new nation was a once-in-a-lifetime professional opportunity. He was assigned to the president's office, which was staffed by many of his former Chinese students at Waseda.

But drafting a constitution for a Chinese republic was no easy task in a world in which republics were few and far between, his employer was a military strongman, and the foreign advisory group was skeptical of China's readiness for representative institutions. Ariga's own belief was that the document should reflect China's Confucian core values and limit voting power to the well educated, while at the same time ensuring access to education as a national right. The constitution that emerged from Ariga's long hours of work was a kind of guided democracy under one-man rule, satisfactory to his colleagues, and even more so to Yuan Shikai, who took it as a green light to further consolidate his power. For all his knowledge and intellectual sophistication, Ariga was in over his head in trying to read the political mind of Yuan Shikai, who was soon embarked on a bid to become emperor. Nor would Ariga come out a clear winner in his 1915 clash with his own

Foreign Ministry over the Twenty-One Demands, an interventionist policy he argued against with characteristic vigor, returning to Japan as Yuan Shikai's emissary to make the case before Japan's elder statesmen. In the end, the demands were moderated, but Ariga was pegged as a politically naïve academic, Japan's standing suffered internationally, and rising anti-Japanese sentiment drove thousands of Chinese students then studying in Japan to return to China in protest.

Chinese Students, Japanese Teachers

When Konoe Atsumaro and Zhang Zhidong met in Wuhan in 1899, they agreed in principle to a three-part program of study tours, technical assistance, and overseas training. Remarkably, within several years and despite the turmoil in Qing politics, all three programs were established and growing. Although neither centralized nor well coordinated, these activities were mutually reinforcing and involved a supportive network of like-minded people. Study-tour officials checked up on Chinese students in Japan, Japanese advisers organized new programs with Japanese training built in, and Chinese students returned from abroad provided living proof of what an eye-opening experience study in Japan could be. In their New Policies, Zhang Zhidong and Liu Kunyi urged all provinces to send students abroad on scholarships to study military science, liberal arts, and technical specialties. On the Japan side, schools were built for Chinese students and special programs were expanded. What started out as a trickle of students quickly became a flood. This appeared to signal a mutually beneficial relationship.

The early 1900s were uncertain times for China's youth. The civil-service exam, the traditional path to career success, was being phased out, and by 1905 it had been ended entirely. More problematic—and clear to all in contemporaneous photos of occupied Beijing—was the very survival of a weakened China facing stronger foreign militaries readily deployed to preserve their array of China interests north to south. Now the foreign powers also included Japan, its China policy hard to read but, for the moment, a useful example of fast-track modernization. For China's leaders and young people alike, studying the Japan model seemed the best way to prepare for the future. By 1902, as part of a "New Policies effect," there were already 400 to 500 Chinese students in Japan; by 1903 there were 1,000, and by 1906, in a burst of enthusiasm after Japan's victory over Russia, the numbers rose to perhaps as many as 10,000. These were small numbers in an absolute sense but a huge percentage of those between the ages of seventeen and twenty-five who were then receiving a modern education. How to manage this group of scholarship and privately funded students, some of whom had radical leanings on arrival and others who were swept into protest politics on the scene, ultimately became a challenge for authorities on both sides.

Students were enrolled in a whole potpourri of programs and specialties, the more so as time went on and they began to go to Japan on their own funds and to demand short-term, intensive programs. According to the records of 660 students from 1903, about 40 percent were in liberal arts and teacher-training programs, notably at Kano Jigoro's Kobun Institute or Waseda and Hosei Universities. Another 30 percent were taking a mix of primary, vocational, and college-level specialized courses. The remaining 30 percent were enrolled in a police studies course at Kobun or were cadets at the military preparatory school Seijo Gakko, which had admitted its first Chinese students in 1898. In 1904 China's Bureau of Military Training announced a new joint central-government– and province-financed program to send 100 students a year to Japan for a four-year course of military studies. In 1932, half of the members of the Nationalist government's military commission were graduates of Japanese military schools.

Meiji Japan was a law-and-order society, but compared with Qing China it was open and vibrant, with discussion of new ideas to balance off debates and public protests in the streets. Openness to new ideas was what had brought Chinese students to Japan in the first place, and in 1900, even before the New Policies were announced, a handful of Chinese students had started a small journal to translate and publish Western and Japanese works. Ariga Nagao's *Contemporary Political History* was included among them, along with school lectures and articles from foreign-affairs magazines. With even more students going to Japan, these types of small ventures multiplied. The students began to organize, first an all-student union, and then provincial clubs, spaces where they not only could socialize but also compare notes on what they were learning, talk about the challenges China faced, vent about the state of politics, and criticize the Qing government. It was a natural next step to publish these discussions, and easy to do in Meiji Japan, as Liang Qichao had discovered. In 1906 there were six student provincial magazines; the next year, twenty. Total circulation figures were small (around 7,000), but they compared well with those for Liang's magazines and, similarly, they were distributed in Shanghai and widely shared. They helped supply an increasingly politically aware readership with new information—on Western political thought, legal systems, current events—along with critical commentary, increasingly scathing, on Manchu rule. Overall, the student publications contributed substantially to a new phenomenon in China: an opposition press.

Students were drawn to the diversity of ideas they encountered in Japan and the novelty of bringing them to the attention of the Chinese reading public. Articles in the provincial journals covered a mix of topics; an essay on the Russian anarchist movement might be followed by an article on the Meiji banking system and another on the functioning of the brain, all of them sounding like school reports. However, when it came to politics there was a single-minded focus on one vexing issue—the source of national power. What accounted for Western strength? Why had Japan made it in the world and China had not? How could the Chinese develop a stronger spirit of nationalism? By fixating on national power, the Chinese students were following, not leading, a trend. Discussions of social Darwinism and imperialism as applied to Japan were hot topics in the Meiji press at the time. In the view of some Japanese academics, not only were survival-of-the-fittest struggles inevitable but becoming imperialist, as Western nations had done, was an indicator of success and good policy. In fact, in the context of the times, it was axiomatic that if a nation could expand, it would expand. As Theodore Roosevelt said in 1899: "Every expansion of a great civilized power means a victory for law, order, and righteousness."[11] For Chinese students, imperialism became something both to resist and to strive for, while social Darwinist talk of the fittest races gave them a framework in which to cast the Manchus as not only incompetent but also racially inferior.

These were big issues for China's youth, worried about both China's future and their own, and increasingly frustrated that their government appeared unable to do anything about either. In the freer atmosphere in Japan they had a chance to make their complaints public, not only in writing but in person, at the Chinese legation or at their schools, in small representations or in larger protests. Very quickly after 1902, as more students arrived in Japan, some on scholarships, others privately funded, Zhang

Zhidong's study-in-Japan program essentially got away from him, with students becoming increasingly critical and accusing him of being a Manchu apologist in cahoots with Japanese imperialists. That it became difficult to supervise and control the students is hardly surprising, given the fact that this was the first large-scale study-abroad program anywhere. There were no available models to emulate for counseling students either before they went to Japan or while they studied there.

Students saw political slights everywhere. When they read news reports that the exhibit on Chinese culture at the Osaka Exhibition would feature Chinese women who had bound feet and smoked opium, they drafted angry letters to the Japanese organizers and to China's representatives in Tokyo, prompting an investigation. When the Chinese government announced that only carefully screened scholarship students, not privately funded students, would be eligible for admission to Seijo Gakko, Japan's premier military academy, they protested publicly that anyone patriotic enough to undertake the course should be allowed to enter. What seemed a minor matter escalated into an angry confrontation between several hundred students and the Chinese minister to Japan, a sit-in at the legation, and a call to the Japanese police to oust the protesters. This was clearly less about admissions and more about who should determine the intent of overseas study—the authorities, both Chinese and Japanese, or the students themselves.

In the spring of 1903 it was an international crisis that put the Chinese students in Tokyo at odds with their government in Beijing: Russia's refusal to finalize the withdrawal of its 100,000 troops from Manchuria, as agreed to with Britain, Japan, and China the previous year. As avid readers of Japanese newspapers, Chinese students in Tokyo were well informed, fully aware of Russia's new demands for concessions from China as well as familiar with arguments from some prominent Japanese that going to war was the only way to curb Russian ambitions. In their view, the silence from Beijing made China look weak and indecisive, inviting yet another round of humiliation at the hands of the foreign powers. Whatever their particular politics, virtually all the students saw themselves as Chinese patriots, responsible for a forceful response. Five hundred turned out in Tokyo at a "resist Russia" rally, and dozens wrote articles lambasting Qing officials for their incompetence. They also organized sympathy protests in Shanghai and Beijing, and even offered to volunteer for military service against the

Russians. It was all for naught in terms of pressuring Beijing, however. Japan broke off its yearlong negotiations with Russia on February 6, 1904, and two days later launched a surprise attack on the Russian Navy at Port Arthur. China claimed neutrality in the war that followed.

By far the largest student protest occurred in the fall of 1905 when, in the excitement of Japan's victory over Russia, the number of Chinese students in Japan shot up to nearly 10,000. As in the Seijo Gakko incident regarding admissions to Japan's premier military academy, student anger was triggered by a change in the rules—the announcement by Japanese authorities, with Chinese agreement, of new guidelines both for students and the schools catering to them. But the students caught political undertones in this new attempt to define what the overseas study experience was meant to be. Their objections were less about stricter controls per se and more about the motives of the authorities issuing them. Was the Japanese government treating Chinese students fairly and on a par with its own students? Was the Chinese government standing up for its students or colluding with Japan to curtail their personal freedoms? Were China's leaders patriotic enough, or even competent enough, to push back against foreign intervention? These were the basic issues—the behavior of Japan as the new imperialist, the capabilities and loyalties of Han Chinese versus Manchus—driving what started small, then grew into larger circles of protest. In 1905, an estimated 4,000 students were involved in clashes with the authorities; 2,000 left Japan in protest, though most quickly returned. Still, by 1909 student numbers had dropped to 5,000. In the ultimate irony, nearly all Chinese students left Japan in 1911 as the forces for change engulfed China's 2,000-year-old imperial system. Meant to infuse the system with new talent and moderate reform thinking, China's Japan-trained youth ultimately contributed to its demise.

Japan-Trained Students and the End of Imperial China

What Sun Yat-sen wanted from Japan was not lessons in Meiji-style state building but financial backing for his project to overthrow the Qing regime. His friends were primarily in the Japanese and overseas Chinese business communities, not in Japanese mainstream official circles, though he did try to make inroads there as well and he shared their vision of a pan-Asian future. He was on the margins of politics in the years around 1900, seeking an interview with Konoe, support from Shimoda Utako, and to exploit Inukai-Miyazaki-Konoe connections. Official China was not overly worried. Zhang Zhidong had expressed it best when he responded to Konoe's perceptive question about whether Sun was a threat to the regime by dismissing him as a "small-time thug."

With some notable exceptions, such as Ji Yihui, an 1899 graduate of the Kobun Institute, Chinese students regarded Sun Yat-sen as something of a curiosity in his efforts to market revolution, a person worth meeting but unconnected to their lives. Sun was completely out of touch with students between 1903 and 1905, as he was off on a Europe-U.S. fundraising tour. However, luck was in his favor. His return to Japan in July 1905 could not have been better timed. Japan's defeat of Russia, a huge European power, excited Asian nationalists and sparked a surge in the number of Chinese students making their way to Japan, either to attend school or to organize antiregime activities. Even so, it was not a sure thing that Sun could seize the moment and get this restive group, with its multiple viewpoints on reform and revolution, to join the new revolutionary organization he had established in Tokyo. His backer, Miyazaki Torazo, had to make the initial contacts. There was not great enthusiasm. The several hundred students who did appear at the inaugural meeting of the Revolutionary Alliance (Tongmenghui) represented but a small percentage of the thousands of students Sun had hoped to attract.

Even among the most vocal anti-Qing students in Tokyo, Sun's initial bid to capture a leadership role was a hard sell, despite the appeal of his clearly articulated vision for national revival. Huang Xing and many others were not willing to immediately disband their own radical groups from different regions of China to join the Sun-led organization. There were also clashes within the student group between Sun's people and the constitutional reformers who backed Liang Qichao. The Tokyo government was not happy either, particularly about harboring an organization calling for regime change in China, when that regime was recognized as legitimate by the rest of the international community. In 1907 Japan acceded to a request from Beijing to expel Sun Yat-sen, a move that propelled him over the next several years into a new round of resistance activities in South China and fundraising efforts targeting overseas Chinese in Southeast Asia, Europe, and America.

After 1905, students trained in Japan were the dominant element in the Revolutionary Alliance. Slipping into Shanghai and beyond from Tokyo, they were prominent in the mounting number of terrorist attacks and small uprisings that spelled danger to the Qing state. In their everyday lives, many held teaching posts in China's new schools or were officers in the new army. Others were employed as clerks in businesses along China's coast. All were well placed to sign up new revolutionary recruits and to pass on anti-Qing literature that originated among the Chinese students still in Japan. Ferreting out those involved in revolutionary plots was an impossible task.

But what left the Qing regime most vulnerable was an even more insidious phenomenon. Although most members of the revolutionary groups were students returned from Japan, the majority of the returned students were not revolutionaries but law-abiding ordinary folk with liberal leanings, whether they were educators, businessmen, bureaucrats, or in the military. Many found jobs in the new technical and financial agencies that the Chinese government had established after 1901. Of the 1,388 foreign-trained students hired by the government between 1906 and 1911, 90 percent were graduates of Japanese schools. Another highly influential segment of the Japan-educated group served in the provincial assemblies that were elected in 1909 as part of the late-in-the-game government-sanctioned move toward constitutional rule. Provincial membership lists suggest that the numbers here were substantial, accounting for as many as 20 percent of the total in some cases. Whatever their brand of politics, the returned students brought a new, pragmatic, and professional perspective to a country producing few graduates from China's homegrown, nominally modern public schools (which had roughly 80,000 graduates at all levels over the entire 1902–1909 period). They were open-minded, patriotic, and confident that China could bootstrap itself into a global position of power in the future. They also felt alienated from Qing rule and impatient with the slow pace of reform. With its support eroded, the Qing dynasty simply crumbled in 1911 under the weight of its incapacity to govern. Yet destabilizing and decentralizing forces remained strong, jeopardizing the new republic from the start.

After 1911, Chinese youths seeking the benefits of a modern education had options other than going to Japan. For one thing, they could stay at home and enroll in one of the new schools staffed by teachers trained in Japan. Opportunities were also opening up for Chinese students to study in Western countries, particularly the United States and France. Some took advantage of the 1908 decision in the United States to apply its Boxer indemnity funds (awarded to the United States in the Boxer Protocol) to a scholarship program for Chinese students. By 1911, 650 Chinese students were studying in the United States under such auspices, and by 1918 the number reached 1,124. After World War I, the Chinese government established a work-study program in France that drew some 6,000 students, though the formal study part of the program was of questionable value.

Still, for reasons of politics, proximity, and the pocketbook, Chinese students continued to enroll in Japanese schools up to the outbreak of the Second Sino-Japanese War in 1937. Although nearly all students returned to China in the heady days after the 1911 Revolution that ended the Qing dynasty, there was soon a reverse flow as Yuan Shikai's clampdown on opposition politicians signaled a turn toward autocratic rule and an uncertain future for China's youth. In 1914 about 4,000 Chinese citizens were officially listed as students in Japan. The figure remained steady at 3,000 to 4,000 over the next several years, dropping only when politically active elements within the group left Japan to protest Japan's deal making for concessions in China, notably after the Twenty-One Demands in 1915 and the award of Shandong province to Japan in the Versailles Treaty of 1919. Still, in 1936–1937, on the eve of the Second Sino-Japanese War, there would be between 5,000 and 6,000 Chinese students in Japan, the highest number since 1914. In part this reflected the Japanese government's continued efforts to attract Chinese students and, in practical terms, the impact of a favorable exchange rate. Altogether, the draw of Japan for Chinese youth would remain the same as it had been from the beginning: it offered the possibility of a low-cost, modern education and greater freedom of action.

Lessons Learned, Partnership Deferred

Study in Japan changed Chinese minds. As Ji Yihui said in his valedictory speech at the Kobun Institute in 1899, "If we compare our thinking with three years ago, we are really different people."[12] Arriving in Japan as young men from Sichuan, Hunan, or Guangdong, Chinese students began to see themselves as the Japanese public saw them: Chinese, pure and simple, foreigners from a neighboring country once great but that had fallen behind in the eyes of the rest of the world. If proof were needed of China's diminished stature and Japan's rise, daily life in Tokyo confirmed it. Tokyo was visibly modern, well run, and more open than China politically, with multiple outlets for the expression of public opinion. Students were drawn to this new openness and admired the Japanese power on display in the war against Russia, even as they resented Japanese restrictions on their own freedom of action and feared Japan's alignment with Western imperialism. The Qing government was increasingly in the students' crosshairs, too, attacked for its incompetence, corruption, and inability to confront Japan and the other powers. Study in Japan turned Chinese students into nationalists and taught them the powers of protest, the press, and public opinion in effecting change. Zhang Zhidong's idea of controlled reform in a controlled society was swamped by the thousands of students he had sent to Japan on his own initiative, now arguing in print or in person for an immediate end to Qing imperial rule.

Chinese officials on study tours to Japan were more measured in approach, but they too were impatient with the pace of change at home. What they witnessed firsthand in Japan was an experiment that seemed to be succeeding, a possible model to follow in getting China's modernization process moving forward, fast. Their Japanese hosts, well schooled in China studies, were properly respectful of China's past culture, but when it came to the mechanics of modern development, they felt they were the ones with lessons to offer. Chinese visitors agreed, took careful notes, and published and distributed trip reports. Totally pragmatic in their outlook, eager to work within and not against the bureaucracy, their reports on what they learned in Japan provided an added spark to get new schools started in China and new agencies upgraded in the interest of more efficient government.

In the same way, mirroring Japan's own experience in learning best practices from the rest of the world, China's policy of hiring Japanese advisers to work in China seemed a potential win-win situation, with Japan increasing its influence and China its institutional know-how. China's Japanese hires, many of them Western-trained, made significant contributions in a range of key sectors, from law to education to railways. Prominent Japanese legal scholars spent years in China coaching their Chinese counterparts in constitutional law and helping to write modern civil and criminal codes. Experienced administrators worked with China's reform-minded bureaucrats on public security, putting in place a police academy and a centralized structure of police agencies. Japanese military officers trained staff in Zhang Zhidong's and Yuan Shikai's provincial administrations, coordinating these efforts with instruction provided to Chinese students enrolled in military schools in Japan. Top executives with Japan's Imperial Railway advised their Chinese employers on modern railway development. And, as the capstone of advisory services, Japanese educators introduced elements of a Japanese-style national school system, from teacher-training institutions at the top to kindergarten education below. Most Japanese hires went to China with high hopes, believing that their unique knowledge of China made them a better fit than other foreign contractors to work with their Chinese counterparts. Most came away disappointed that they could not achieve more. Bureaucratic obstacles and unpredictable politics on the China side, plus Japan's opportunistic policies and World War I, intervened to limit the extent of official bilateral cooperation.

The late-Qing pivot to Japan had its greatest long-term impact in determining the career paths of thousands of Chinese youths who represented the next generation of Chinese leaders. Some of the most important figures in twentieth-century China got their start in Japanese schools. Lu Xun and Guo Moruo, literary giants of international reputation, attended secondary school in Japan, Lu Xun before 1911 and Guo Moruo just after. Both were headed toward careers in medicine but detoured to literature and the mission of diagnosing China's national condition through the written word, in all genres and in a new vernacular style. For Lu Xun's brother, noted essayist Zhou Zuoren, study in Japan cemented a lifelong devotion to foreign literature, translation, and the Japanese aesthetic. As public intellectuals, all three had to navigate the sometimes-perilous shoals of Chinese politics. This was equally true of the many Chinese graduates of Japanese university law programs, prominent in public life as the very creators of the legal profession in Republican China but always politically vulnerable, in part because of their Japanese connections. Cao Rulin, attacked as a Japanese sympathizer for his failure to press China's case at Versailles, is a prime example. Other Chinese graduates of Japanese universities rose quickly in China's academic hierarchy, notably Chen Duxiu and Li Dazhao. Products of Waseda University's law and politics program, Chen became dean at Peking University, Li head librarian, and both became celebrated co-founders of the Chinese Communist Party in 1921.

The list goes on. It is well known that Zhou Enlai, Chiang Kai-shek, and Wang Jingwei, three of the main protagonists in China's wartime drama, studied in Japan. It is less known that Zhang Zongxiang, a Tokyo University law graduate, later China's minister to Japan, assisted a Japanese legal adviser in writing a new criminal code for China, or that Hattori Unokichi's Japan-trained teaching assistant, Fan Yuanlian, became president of Beijing Normal University and minister of education, or that Shen Junru, appointed president of the Supreme People's Court of China in 1949, studied at Hosei University from 1905 to 1908. As indicated in these few cases and the hundreds more that have been documented, "learn from Japan" policies produced a variety of outcomes; much more research needs to be done to arrive at a full and balanced assessment. But it is safe to say at this stage that the young Chinese students who were sent or decided to go to Japan were primed to absorb what was modern and useful for their own future and China's, that their subsequent careers had a kind of ripple effect in changing Chinese social and political structures in significant ways, and that over the long term they established professional networks with Japanese counterparts that endured remarkably, even in the period of post–World War II reconstruction. Their attitudes toward Japan, their host country, were on balance ambivalent and ever shifting, not an unusual aftereffect of study-abroad programs in any part of the world.

For all the plans and projects launched by China's newly trained elite, many of whom were Japan-educated, the story of China after 1915 was one of unceasing disorder, a sad narrative of fractured politics, military conflict among contending warlords, and ultimately all-out war with Japan. Even after 1949 when political unity was achieved, the sheer size, complexity, and poverty of Chinese society made it difficult to catch up economically without foreign help. It was not until 1978, after the failures of the Great Leap Forward and the Cultural Revolution, that Chinese leaders turned once again to "reform and opening to the outside world," including Japan, the policy that Zhang Zhidong had endorsed with mixed success after 1895. In a conversation with Japan's Prime Minister Fukuda in 1978, China's Deng Xiaoping, reflecting on the wide scope of Japanese learning from China during the Tang dynasty, commented that "now the roles of teacher and student are reversed." This had been the unspoken assumption and the hope of the Zhangs and Konoes of the world in the early twentieth century.

CHAPTER SIX

The Colonization of Taiwan and Manchuria, 1895–1945

WHEN JAPAN ACQUIRED TAIWAN in 1895 after the Sino-Japanese War, the Japanese believed that just as the Western powers had used their colonies to strengthen their own economies, so Taiwan could help strengthen the Japanese economy. Taiwan had fewer than three million residents compared with Japan's nearly forty million, but nonetheless Taiwan represented a significant increase in the potential market for Japanese manufactured goods. Japan could also import from Taiwan tropical agricultural products, such as sugar, that it could not produce on its own four islands. But for the Japanese, acquiring a colony had more than economic benefits. It was another important sign that their nation had joined the ranks of the advanced Western countries. Japan wanted to show the Western powers that it could be a model colonial power. It also expected in the future to acquire other colonies, such as Korea, and it wanted to demonstrate that there were advantages to becoming a Japanese colony.

In 1905, after the Russo-Japanese War, Japan also acquired the South Manchurian Railway and rights to the Liaodong Peninsula. In Manchuria it faced a much larger and more complex situation than in Taiwan. Manchuria had a population of fifteen million people in 1905 and covered 380,000 square miles, more than twice the area of the Japanese islands. Furthermore, the population of Manchuria was still growing rapidly—it would reach fifty million by 1945. In Manchuria the Japanese also faced a security threat from Russia, growing popular protests from Chinese nationalists, and, after 1931, criticism from Western countries for their occupation of Chinese territory. From 1905 to 1931, Japanese leaders tried to operate the South Manchurian Railway as a successful business while using it as a quasi-government institution through which it gathered information about Manchuria and North China, fostered relations with the political leaders in those areas, and developed businesses on both sides of the railway. The Japanese brought in troops to provide defense against Russian security threats and to protect the region's Japanese residents. In 1931, after they had set off the Manchurian Incident, they installed a puppet government and took over formal control of all of Manchuria. Unlike the countries colonized by the West, Manchuria was industrialized and it attracted hundreds of thousands of settlers from the Japanese homeland.

The Japanese brought colonial modernity to Taiwan and Manchuria. The two colonies grew economically with the introduction of modern technology and infrastructure, and the average standard of living improved. However, local people in both colonies were acutely aware that the Japanese held the important positions in government and business, enjoyed higher incomes and better living conditions, and did not treat them as equals. In local schools, Japanese history was taught in ways that reflected positively on Japan. Classical Chinese culture was also taught, but on issues where China and Japan disagreed, the Japanese perspective prevailed.

Taiwan under Japanese Rule, 1895–1945

Qing dynasty officials in Beijing had taken little interest in Taiwan until the late nineteenth century, when some key officials became worried about threats from both Japan and France. The Japanese attacks on aborigines in Taiwan in 1874 to punish them for killing the shipwrecked Ryukyu fishermen, and the dangers of French attacks during the Sino-French War of 1883–1885, worried Li Hongzhang, Zuo Zongtang, and other officials. Li encountered resistance to his efforts to strengthen the defense of Taiwan, but in 1885 he received approval to raise Taiwan from prefectural-level to provincial-level status, which warranted sending a higher official to serve as its first governor and increasing its budget. In 1885 Li assigned as the first governor-general Liu Mingchuan, an able official from Li's Huai Army in Anhui who had helped put down the Taiping Rebellion. After he arrived in Taiwan, Liu Mingchuan brought in naval forces to build up coastal defenses. He laid a telegraph line from Taiwan to Fujian in the mainland and built a seventeen-mile railway from Keelung (Jilong) to Taipei. He undertook a cadastral survey to establish the basis for agricultural taxes that would pay for these developments. However, local landlords rioted, angry over the higher taxes, and in 1890 Liu was recalled and work ended on the projects he had initiated. It thus fell to the Japanese, when they gained control of the island in 1895, to build on Liu's development plans.

When they took over Taiwan, the Japanese encountered less resistance than they would face in Korea in 1910. In Korea the local people had a much stronger sense of national identity, a more distinct culture, and a long history of independent rule. As a prefectural-level island Taiwan had never, even under Liu Mingchuan, developed a sense of identity like that of the Koreans, who had their own language and culture, and earlier had an independent government that resisted outside invaders. When the Japanese took control of Taiwan in 1895, the population was about two-thirds Fujianese, descended from Qing-period migrants, including those who had come with Koxinga (Zheng Chenggong), and one-third Hakka, whose ancestors had escaped from the advancing Qing troops in the seventeenth century. By the time the Japanese arrived, an estimated 14,000 aborigines were left on the island, but they did not pose a serious problem for the Japanese. The Fujianese living on Taiwan also offered little resistance to the Japanese, but the Hakka, a significant minority who mostly lived in the hilly areas in central Taiwan, did put up armed resistance.

In 1895, Japan's priority was to pacify the island. General Nogi Maresuke, a Japanese hero in the Sino-Japanese War, was sent in to establish order. He and his troops were considered very tough. Over several weeks, Nogi's troops marched the entire length of the island, from Hualien in the northeast to Kaohsiung in the southwest. They encountered great resistance in mountainous Hakka areas in northern Taiwan. In January 1896, when some Japanese soldiers staying in a temple were killed during the night, Japanese officers ordered that all people found within a five-mile radius of the temple should be killed. General Nogi Maresuke, who served as the third governor-general from 1896 to 1898, was greatly feared by the local population.

After their march from northeastern to southwestern Taiwan, the Japanese signed amnesty agreements with local leaders and set about to establish a *baojia* system, wherein neighbors were held responsible for one another's behavior. By 1898 when General Nogi returned to Japan, the island was pacified. Nogi was replaced by General Kodama Gentaro, who had a reputation for being less savage and repressive.

Several times during Japanese colonial rule, local people revolted against the heavy repression imposed by the administration. In October 1907, in the coal-mining town of Beipu, in Hsinchu county, local Hakkas, upset by the behavior of the Japanese rulers, took part in an uprising that killed an estimated 57 Japanese people. In retaliation, the Japanese killed more than 100 locals. In 1915, members of a religious group in the city of Tainan, protesting against tight Japanese controls, attacked Japanese police stations and killed a number of officers in what came to be known as the Tapani Incident. Again Japanese officials clamped down, killing the leaders of the religious group. In 1930, in the Wushe Incident (Musha, in Japanese), led largely by indigenous people in Nantou county who were upset about forced-labor requirements and police brutality, some 130 Japanese residents were killed. Again the Japanese retaliated.

From 1898 to 1912 the colonial government spent twice as much on policing as it spent on civil servants. In 1912 there was roughly one Japanese police officer for every 580 locals in Taiwan, almost twice the number of police per capita as then employed in Japan. Despite the early violent incidents, once Taiwan was pacified in 1898 there were relatively few clashes, and relations between Japanese officials and local people were not as tense as those in Korea after it was colonized.

Until 1919 the top Japanese official in Taiwan was a military leader, but in 1898 the Japanese brought in a civilian, Goto Shimpei, previously the chief of Japan's National Bureau of Hygiene, to serve as head of the Civil Administration Bureau, with responsibility for governing Taiwan. Goto, a medical doctor who had been sent to Germany to study Bismarck's modern public health program, had already proved to be an able and highly respected public health administrator in Japan. At the time, the field of epidemiology was just developing, and in tropical climates progress was being made in managing yellow fever and malaria. In selecting Goto, the Japanese expected that they would make progress in gaining control over those diseases in Taiwan and this would help win popular support and respect. Goto led the construction of water projects to ensure the quality of the water supply, built regional hospitals and antimalaria centers, and carried out rodent-control projects, thereby making great progress in Taiwan's fight against malaria. Goto was prepared to cooperate with the Japanese police to maintain order, but he also won the cooperation and appreciation of the local people, as well as the respect of Western leaders, for his enlightened leadership.

Goto replaced the military police with civilian police, and prohibited the military from wearing uniforms or carrying swords. He believed that government policies should be adapted to local customs, and he established a center to carry out research on local customs. In Korea, serious tensions between the Koreans and Japanese continued throughout the occupation there. But in Taiwan, because order was established during the early years of rule, relations between the Taiwanese and their Japanese colonizers was relatively relaxed and comfortable.

To lead economic development work in Taiwan, Goto Shimpei brought in Nitobe Inazo, an agricultural economist who had studied at the University of Hokkaido. After Hokkaido, Nitobe spent a year at Tokyo Imperial University, three years studying economics at Johns Hopkins University in the United States, and three years in Germany, where he received a Ph.D. in agricultural economics. He arrived in Taiwan in 1901, and during his three years on the island he established Taiwan's economic priorities and worked to develop an economy that was complementary to Japan's. Generally, while Japan concentrated on industry, Taiwan was to concentrate on agriculture. Because tea production in Japan was ample, tea production in Taiwan was reduced and instead sugar production was expanded because Taiwan's warmer climate was more suitable for it than the climate in Japan. Taiwan was divided into fifty districts, each with a sugar mill. Chemical fertilizer was applied and irrigation networks were built. By the 1930s the Japanese sugar factories in Taiwan were the most modern sugar factories in the world. Sugar consumption in Japan rose throughout the 1920s and 1930s, and by the 1930s 90 percent of Taiwan's sugar was exported to Japan. After the riots in Japan in 1918 because of the shortage of rice, Nitobe also concentrated on improving rice yields in Taiwan, which enabled Taiwan to increase rice exports to Japan.

By the time Goto left Taiwan to take up new responsibilities with the Manchurian Railway in 1906, Taiwan had established telegraph and telephone lines and could generate electric power. The colony no longer required subsidies from Japan and operated within its own budget.

The Japanese sent far more midlevel administrators and settlers to Taiwan than the European countries sent to their colonies. The Japanese administration was more like the British administration of nearby Ireland than like the European administration of distant colonies in Africa or Asia. By 1924 there were 183,000 Japanese living in Taiwan, and by 1945, at the time of the Japanese surrender in World War II, there were roughly 200,000 Japanese citizens living there, amid a local population of six million. Since there were so many Japanese settlers working in different capacities, many Taiwanese people knew Japanese individuals personally, as their teachers, storekeepers, neighbors, and even friends.

If a British administrator in India was influenced by the lifestyle of an English country gentleman, or a Spanish administrator in the Philippines was influenced by the lifestyle of a hacienda owner, the higher-level Japanese administrators in Taiwan adopted the lifestyle of a Meiji bureaucrat. In Japan it was widely understood that a bureaucrat occupied a position of respect and remained somewhat aloof from the common people (*kanson minpi*). But the Japanese officials were also a disciplined group who took their work seriously and performed their work conscientiously. In addition to the high-level bureaucrats, who had been trained at Japan's best middle schools and universities, there were also large numbers of Japanese settlers in Taiwan who had been trained at various specialized technical schools.

All major businesses in Taiwan were owned by the Japanese, though some business owners had Taiwanese partners, and all the major Japanese zaibatsu (Mitsubishi, Mitsui, Sumitomo, and Yasuda) were active in Taiwan. Japanese companies had monopolies in salt, camphor, and tobacco. To encourage more trade with Japan, Taiwan's trade with mainland China was taxed but its trade with Japan was not. In response to peasants' complaints about cruel absentee landlords, Japan forced the landlords to sell their land and to buy government bonds with the income they received from the sale. To eliminate opium use in Taiwan, the Japanese first made opium production into a national monopoly so as to control the supply, and after they had control over opium cultivation and sales, they closed down both operations. In 1900 an estimated 165,000 opium addicts lived in Taiwan, but by the time Japan had completed its program, opium had essentially been wiped out.

The standard of living in Taiwan rose rapidly under Japanese rule, and by 1945 it was, on average, much higher than that on the Chinese mainland. The Japanese in Taiwan set up stores and businesses similar to those on their home islands; most businesses in Taiwan were operated by Japanese settlers. Western visitors to Taiwan in the 1930s praised its economic successes. Goto Shimpei and Nitobe Inazo, with their fluency in both German and English, became welcome participants in international organizations and were respected for their achievements in Taiwan.

The Japanese greatly expanded public education in Taiwan, far more than the Europeans expanded education in their colonies. Study of the Confucian classics, which had been part of an elite education for a small group of Taiwanese youths before the arrival of the Japanese, was largely replaced by a "scientific education." Isawa Shuji, a Ministry of Education official who had been sent for advanced training to Bridgewater Normal School in Massachusetts in 1875, was charged with establishing a modern educational system in Taiwan that would produce good Japanese citizens. The teaching of Japanese language began immediately, so that elementary schools could quickly change to the use of Japanese throughout the curriculum. In early 1896 the first group of thirty-six young Japanese-language teachers, all graduates of Japanese normal schools, arrived in Taiwan, and their numbers would expand rapidly. Local Taiwanese teachers, after intensive training in Japanese language, taught in Japanese and used Japanese textbooks. By 1944, 71 percent of Taiwan's elementary-school-age children would be in school, a far higher attendance rate than the rate in mainland China at the time. All classes were taught in Japanese.

In 1915 Japan opened middle schools in Taiwan, and in 1928 it opened Taihoku Imperial University (today's Taiwan University) in Taipei. The Japanese living in Taiwan attended these middle schools and the university, as did able local students. The best local students, especially in fields such as medicine, went on to study at Japanese universities, including Tokyo Imperial University, after completing university in Taiwan. In the 1930s, some 2,000 Taiwanese students were attending universities in Japan.

After Goto Shimpei was transferred from Taiwan to Manchuria to direct the Manchurian Railway, a number of Taiwanese administrators were also sent to Manchuria as bureaucrats to help jump-start government administration there. Migration from Taiwan to Manchuria increased after 1931, when Manchuria became a Japanese puppet state. After Japan invaded China in 1937, some Taiwanese who knew the Chinese language were assigned to mainland China to work as administrators under the Japanese occupation.

In general, throughout their occupation of Taiwan the Japanese held the higher positions in government and business and the Taiwanese occupied the lower positions. However, after the start of World War II many Japanese men who had been working in Taiwan's government or business offices were recruited into the military, so a considerable number of Taiwanese bureaucrats and administrators were promoted to higher positions in government and in Japanese-led businesses. Some, such as Li Denghui (Lee Teng-hui), later president of Taiwan under the Guomindang, who had studied agricultural economics at Kyoto Imperial University, even became officers in the Japanese Army. The Japanese had intended to transform Taiwan's youth into Japanese citizens, and to a remarkable extent, the better-educated Taiwanese young people, even after the war, worked and spoke to each other in Japanese.

Manchuria under Japanese Rule, 1905–1945

In 1904 when Japan attacked Russian ships and launched the Russo-Japanese War, many Japanese strategists did not plan to make Manchuria the center of Japan's expansion plans. Rather, they wanted to focus on Fujian. Fujian at the time had a much larger economy than Manchuria; it had long carried out trade with Nagasaki; it was close to Taiwan, which the Japanese had just colonized; its dialects were spoken in Taiwan; and it could be a useful stepping-stone from Taiwan to expand business elsewhere along the China coast. But at the end of the Russo-Japanese War, when Japan obtained rights to the South Manchurian Railway and the Liaodong Peninsula (an acquisition Japan had been denied by the Western powers in the previous decade), Japanese leaders began to make the most of their new possessions. They were soon putting far more resources into Manchuria than into Fujian, and Fujian was already losing out as a dynamic economic base to Ningbo, Shanghai, and other areas along the Yangtze River. Manchuria was a vast and relatively undeveloped area. It also had a relatively small population during the Qing dynasty, as the Manchus until late in the nineteenth century prohibited non-Manchus from settling in their homeland.

Once the Japanese acquired rights to the South Manchurian Railway, they took advantage of opportunities to clear the land and to open up the mines. The railway the Russians had just built provided access to the sparsely settled areas. Just as Americans going West in the nineteenth century were pioneers in the new open spaces, the Japanese went into Manchuria for the great development opportunities the new territory could provide.

The Japanese started the Russo-Japanese War because of concerns about their security. They feared that Russia, after completing the Trans-Siberian Railway, expanding settlements in Siberia, constructing a railway in Manchuria, and building a port on the Liaodong Peninsula, would soon dominate the region, creating unending security threats. With its far larger population and greater resources, Russia also threatened Japan's economic interests not only in China but also in Korea, across the border from Manchuria. Work on the Trans-Siberian Railway, the world's longest railway, had begun in 1891 and by 1903 passengers could, with a boat ride across Lake Baikal, travel from St. Petersburg to Chita, then south to Vladivostok, all without leaving Russian territory. With Chinese approval, in 1903 the Russians also completed and then managed the Chinese Eastern Railway—creating a shortcut from Chita through Manchuria, passing through Harbin to Vladivostok, a route several hundred miles shorter than the one going from Chita to Vladivostok on the Russian side of the border.

Some leading Japanese strategists had hoped that Manchuria, following the U.S. open-door policy for China, would not be colonized by any one foreign country but would be opened to all countries, including Japan. The thinking was that if companies from all countries, including Western nations, acquired a stake in the area, the combined efforts of those countries could contain Russian advances.

But other countries did not make major investments in Manchuria. The Japanese sent in large numbers of troops, and within a decade Japan was building on the territorial rights it had acquired on both sides of the Manchurian Railway and on the rights to the Kwantung Leased Territory in the southern part of the Liaodong Peninsula, including Dalian and Port Arthur (Lushun). Its overseas investments were centered not in Fujian or Shanghai but in Manchuria.

Like nineteenth-century Americans who saw a chance to create their own future in the wide-open American West, many Japanese settlers—poor second and third sons in rural Japan who would not inherit farmland and did not face good economic prospects at home—were attracted to the opportunity to open up the relatively unsettled areas in Manchuria. Much of

Manchuria was comparatively sparsely populated when the Japanese began arriving. The Japanese appropriated land for their army bases, for their administrative offices, for their businesses, and for their farms. There are no precise figures available for how much they paid for the land, but to the local Chinese, the Japanese were invaders who either took their land without paying for it or "bought" it at below-market prices. It is estimated that by the time of the Second Sino-Japanese War in 1937, some 270,000 Japanese migrants had settled in Manchuria as farmers.

After 1931, when Japan took control of all of Manchuria, it expanded its investments in the region's mines and machinery factories. Unique among the colonies around the world, Manchuria became an industrialized colony, run by bureaucrats trained in Japan, where the dominant issue discussed at universities was how to modernize a country. Some in Japan, such as the wise essayist Ishibashi Tanzan (see Biographies of Key Figures), suspected that Japan's great industrial progress in Manchuria ultimately would fall victim to the rising tide of Chinese nationalism. However, Japanese officials in Manchuria responded to growing Chinese nationalism not by leaving the area but by calling for more troops to defend their businesses and the local settlers. The Japanese regarded the industrial development of Manchuria as a glorious symbol of Japan's position as a modern nation. However, by World War II Manchuria would become a quagmire, requiring more troops and more police to keep it under control. Japanese residents who hoped to return from Manchuria were unable to do so until Japan was defeated in the war.

The Russo-Japanese War, 1904–1905

The possibility of war had begun to concern the Japanese by 1898, when the Russians took over Port Arthur on the Liaodong Peninsula. In the Russian port of Vladivostok, ships were frozen in the sea for two to three months each winter, but in Port Arthur they gained a year-round warm-water port. The Chinese Eastern Railway, completed in 1903, created a link to Port Arthur that, with the Trans-Siberian Railway, gave Russia direct rail transportation from Moscow all the way to Port Arthur and then, by boat, to the Pacific. The Russians, like the Japanese, were intent on modernizing to catch up with Western Europe. They began building Port Arthur into a modern port as well as a European-style Western city, with new architecture based on up-to-date European models.

When the Russians completed the 550-mile southern spur of the Chinese Eastern Railway, linking Port Arthur and Harbin and passing through Changchun, Shenyang, and Anshan, the Japanese worried that nothing would stop Russia—which had a population of 130 million, compared with Japan's 46 million—from expanding into Korea, where Japanese investments were growing. During the Boxer Rebellion of 1900, the Russians had moved some 100,000 troops into Manchuria, and after the rebellion was quelled, Russian troops remained in Manchuria's three provinces, Heilongjiang, Jilin, and Liaoning. Japanese officials proposed to their Russian counterparts that Japan would recognize Russian interests in Manchuria if Russia would recognize Japanese interests in Korea, but the Russians initially refused. In April 1902, in line with discussions among Western countries to cease the carving up of China into different foreign-dominated territories, Russia changed its policy and agreed to remove its troops from Manchuria by the end of 1903. However, on May 15, 1903, Czar Nicholas ordered that other foreign interests should also be removed from Manchuria. He then began a rapid buildup of Russian troops, quickly moving them into the area along the Yalu River, the border between Manchuria and Korea. Japanese saw this as a threat to their interests in Korea.

In response to reports that Russia intended to keep other foreign interests out of Manchuria, high Japanese officials met in June 1903 to hear a report on the new military situation and to decide on a response. Major General Iguchi Shogo presented his analysis of what Japan faced: Russia's military resources were far larger than their own, and with the use of the Trans-Siberian Railway, it could gradually bring in far more people and resources. Given these advantages, time was on Russia's side; if Japan did not move quickly, it would be too late to protect Japanese interests in Korea. Major General Iguchi said Japan could not be certain it would win a war with Russia, but he argued that they had no choice but to launch a surprise attack. If Japan won, Manchuria would be neutral territory and Japan would maintain its rights in Korea. While officials debated their response, Japan continued to strengthen its military and began to expand its spying activities in Russia and on Russians in Asia. Most Russians, like the Chinese earlier, believed that Japan, as a small island country, could easily be defeated, and they had scarcely bothered to collect information on the Japanese military. Few Russians had any idea of Japan's strength.

Japanese Troops Invade Manchuria

On February 8, 1904, knowing that Russian troops would be celebrating a holiday, Japan launched a surprise attack on their ships at Port Arthur and at Inchon, Korea. The Russians were completely unprepared, and damage was extensive. For the Japanese, the first six months of fighting after that went better than expected, largely because the initial blow to the Russian Navy had inflicted such heavy damage. But the Russians then sent in a large number of troops and ships, and the battles continued for more than one year, on sea and on land, in Korea and in Manchuria. The Japanese had repeated difficulties in their effort to bottle up the Russian fleet in Port Arthur. Losses were heavy on both sides. Ariga Nagao estimated that some 80,000 Japanese were killed in battle or later died of their wounds in hospitals. But in the end, Japan's superior information, the high level of literacy and discipline among Japanese troops compared with Russian troops, and Japan's short supply lines, especially compared with the months it took for Russian Navy ships to reach East Asia, proved decisive in the Japanese victory.

The Japanese captured Port Arthur by the end of 1904. When the Russian Revolution broke out in January 1905, it sapped the energy of the Russian Army. Nonetheless, in May 1905 Russia's Baltic Fleet was on its way to fight the Japanese. By the time the fleet reached Indonesia, Japanese ships were observing its movements very carefully. After the Japanese discovered that the Russians would pass through the narrow strait near Tsushima, Japanese ships were deployed to lie in wait. When the Russians, who had not taken great care in following Japanese troop movements, passed through the Tsushima Strait, the Japanese caught them in another surprise attack. After a two-day battle, the Japanese had destroyed two-thirds of the Russian fleet and incurred very few losses themselves. By the end of the battle, Russia, preoccupied by the 1905 revolution at home, had lost the will to continue the war. In fact the Japanese were also exhausted by the end of the Russo-Japanese War, and had Russia continued the fight, it is doubtful Japan would have won. Once Russia sought an end to the war, Minister of Foreign Affairs Komura Jutaro went to his classmate from Harvard Law School, Theodore Roosevelt, to seek his cooperation in concluding a peace treaty.

Peace discussions, mediated by President Theodore Roosevelt, who was awarded the Nobel Peace Prize for his role, were held in Portsmouth, New Hampshire, in August 1905 and an agreement was signed on September 5. In the treaty, the Russians acknowledged that Japan had paramount interests in Korea and agreed that they would not interfere with Japan's activities there. Japan gained full sovereignty over the southern half of the island of Sakhalin. Russia also transferred its Port Arthur lease and nearby territorial waters to Japan. Russia did retain control of the railway from Harbin to Changchun and thus could continue to dominate northern Manchuria, but it transferred to Japan the lease, then good for twenty-five more years, to a 420-mile portion of the southern spur of the China Eastern Railway, from Changchun to Dalian, and other branches of the southern spur, such as the link from the city of Jilin to Changchun, a total of approximately 700 miles of railway. The Japanese renamed the railways that they received the South Manchurian Railway Company. Japan was also given rights to the land adjacent to the railway, extending out for ten kilometers on each side, and rights to the coal mines that supported the railway. In 1915, impressed by the ninety-nine-year lease Great Britain had received for Hong Kong in 1898, Japan pressured China to grant it an additional ninety-nine-year lease.

Rule by the South Manchurian Railway and the Kwantung Army, 1905–1931

After the Russo-Japanese War, Japanese political leaders remained anxious that Russia might launch a war of revenge. They were frightened by the growing number of Russian settlers in Siberia and by Russia's increasing ability to send troops and goods from Moscow to Vladivostok as a result of its double-tracking of the Trans-Siberian Railway and its completion of a new railway around Lake Baikal in 1905 that enabled the Russians to go by rail directly to East Asia without stopping to transfer goods to and from a boat to cross the lake. Japanese political leaders began planning for how to respond to Russian attacks if Russia were to launch such a war of revenge. But Russia was facing domestic turmoil, especially after the Russian Revolution of 1917, and though relations between Japan and Russia remained tense and Russians dominated the area north of Changchun where the railway remained in their hands, in the end Russia did not interfere with Japanese interests south of Changchun.

At the time, Japanese leaders realized that the United States and the European powers would not tolerate Japan's turning Manchuria into a Japanese colony, and after the Russo-Japanese War, China retained political sovereignty over Manchuria. But Japanese organization along the railway was far better than the regional organization of Manchurian warlord Zhang Zuolin, and Japan began to extend its influence beyond the leased territory. Although not part of Japan's formal empire, Manchuria in effect became part of its informal empire. Western businesses kept operating in Manchuria, but after 1905 Japanese businesses began to dominate the economy.

Japanese interests in other parts of China, especially in Shanghai and Fujian, continued to grow, but after 1905 its investments centered around the South Manchurian Railway Company (Minami Manshu Tetsudo Kabushiki Gaisha; abbreviated as Mantetsu in Japanese, Mantie in Chinese), and Japanese-owned companies in Manchuria grew faster than Japanese companies elsewhere in China. By 1914 an estimated 69 percent of Japanese direct investments in China were in Manchuria, and most Japanese activity in China remained in Manchuria until the Second Sino-Japanese War broke out in 1937. Manchuria remained an agricultural area, where soybeans and soybean products (including soy sauce and soybean pulp for fertilizer) were the major export items (to Japan, Europe, and to China proper, south of Manchuria). Since land in Manchuria was basically dry, little rice could be produced there, and sorghum (*gaoliang*) was the main grain. New Japanese investments were mainly focused on the railway and the construction projects near the rail lines.

The Japanese assassinated Manchurian warlord Zhang Zuolin in 1928 (see Chapter 7) and tightened Japan's control in Manchuria, and in 1931 Japan turned Manchuria into a Japanese-controlled puppet state. Army strategist Ishiwara Kanji began considering how to expand the industrial base in Manchuria so as to equip a modern army. In the mid-1930s his efforts were unsuccessful because he refused to make investments in Manchuria attractive to private companies. He wanted such investments to be controlled by the state, not by private capitalists. In 1935, a bright young bureaucrat from the Ministry of Commerce and Industry, Kishi Nobusuke, who believed in Soviet-style economic planning, was appointed deputy minister of Manchurian industrial development. Kishi made enough concessions to attract Nissan (Japan Industries), after World War II a car company, led by Ayukawa Yoshisuke, who was willing to cooperate with the government to develop heavy industry so as to strengthen the military-industrial base. Though Manchuria later suffered from U.S. attacks on its shipping fleet that made it difficult to transport the necessary machine tools from Japan and impossible to achieve its ambitious targets, Manchuria developed coal, iron, and copper mines. By 1942, it was producing more than three million tons of iron and steel per year.

Given the shortage of laborers in Manchuria, some of the physical labor during Japanese colonization—clearing the fields and growing the soybeans, working in the mines and on construction projects—was supplied by migrants from other Chinese provinces, particularly Shandong and Hebei. Once the Manchu rulers, concerned about Japanese and Russian pressures, had begun allowing non-Manchus to migrate to Manchuria in the late nineteenth century, Chinese migrants began to move into sparsely populated Manchuria from nearby Shandong and Hebei, which were heavily populated. From the 1890s until the beginning of World War II, approximately twenty-five million people migrated to Manchuria from Shandong and Hebei, and of them, approximately eight million remained there.[1] After 1942 the number of Chinese migrants declined as the economy slowed down in the chaos of the war.

About two-thirds of the Chinese migrants to Manchuria from 1905 to 1942 were seasonal workers, mostly young men who performed physical labor. In the early years, they worked in agriculture and construction, but later, as industry developed, they worked in factories and mines. The seasonal workers came from spring through fall and then they returned to their homes during the winter months when much of Manchuria was very cold. During the period Manchuria was under Japanese control, on average more than 500,000 migrants arrived in Manchuria each year. Most of them went to Manchuria only once and then returned home with earnings for their families. The migrant workers, unlike the young intellectuals, generally did not take part in political activities.

From 1905 until 1931 when the Japanese made Manchuria a puppet state, the two major centers of Japanese authority in Manchuria were the South

Manchurian Railway Company (Mantetsu) and the Kwantung Army of the Imperial Japanese Army. After 1931, although the highest Japanese official in Manchuria was the governor-general, in fact Mantetsu and its management retained considerable independence and had a far larger staff than the governor-general had.

Mantetsu (The South Manchurian Railway)

Beginning in 1905, the South Manchurian Railway Company became the administrative headquarters for the Japanese in Manchuria. As a model for how to manage Japan's role in Manchuria, some Japanese researchers were assigned to study how the Dutch East India Company conducted its business while representing Dutch broad national interests. As Mantetsu became a quasi-government institution, Japanese industrial, financial, and agricultural ministries assigned officials to serve under Mantetsu's leadership in Manchuria. Within Japan, Manchurian development was considered of sufficient importance that not only the ministries but the very highest levels of the political leadership were involved in development planning that went far beyond the operation of the railway.

The importance of Mantetsu's broader mission was reflected in the November 1906 transfer of Goto Shimpei from Taiwan to become the head of Mantetsu. Although officially Goto was only administering the railway and the land along the railway, in fact he had a mandate to strengthen Japan's overall interests in Manchuria. For this task, he drew on his broad experience as head of all civilian work in Taiwan.

Despite his wide-ranging mandate, Goto realized that Mantetsu was at its core a business, responsible for running a railway efficiently and profitably. Railways were then at the cutting edge of modern infrastructure around the world. Mantetsu purchased the world's best railway cars from the United States and quickly developed a reputation for providing high-class service for passengers, on-time arrivals, and reliable transport for freight traffic. The Japanese also quickly began double-tracking railways that originally had been single track and building wider-gauge tracks. The telephone and telegraph, which the Japanese were already using during the Russo-Japanese War, were linked with the transportation and communications advances built up around the railway.

After the damage from the Russo-Japanese War, considerable funds were required for reconstruction in Manchuria, but the Japanese government had exhausted its financial reserves during the war. To supplement the funding from the Japanese government, Mantetsu raised money from the financial community in London. As a business operation, the railway quickly became financially independent, and within years it was bringing in a large profit. During its early years, its major source of income was the transport of soybeans and soybean products that were being exported from the ports on the Liaodong Peninsula to Japan and Europe. In transporting soybeans, Mantetsu was competing with Chinese companies that used trucks and horse-drawn carts that could transport soybeans at a lower cost than Mantetsu.

Goto Shimpei was well known for his commitment to science and for the research he had organized in Taiwan to study local social customs. By April 1907, shortly after his arrival, he established Mantetsu's Research Department (Chosabu). The Research Department provided information and analysis to guide the operation of the railway and overall Japanese policies for the political, economic, and social development of Manchuria. It also became the center for Japanese government research on the economy, politics, and society of North China. Even the Kwantung Army drew on research conducted by Mantetsu's Research Department, which grew to be one of the largest research centers anywhere in the world. At its height in the early 1940s, the Research Department had more than 2,300 researchers. Its scale and scope reflected the Japanese belief in the importance of knowledge and in the role of enlightenment in guiding national policy. At the time, no research institution anywhere in China conducted work of such breadth and depth. As a result, the Mantetsu Research Department had a far deeper knowledge of Manchuria than the Chinese government did.

Goto was willing to work with the Kwantung Army, but he considered establishing rules and laws to be central to the development of an administrative infrastructure in China. He selected Okamatsu Santaro, a professor of Chinese law at Kyoto Imperial University, as the first head of the Research Department. Although Goto sent Okamatsu to Europe to study the role of the Western powers' colonial research centers, he hoped to surpass what those research centers were doing with respect to their colonies. Okamatsu and his staff believed that rules for Manchuria should grow out of existing law. While Americans guiding the development of local laws might have used American laws as a framework for teaching local people around the world, the Japanese realized that in some cases Western laws did not fit Asian traditions, and therefore they were more willing to create laws that accorded with local customs. A central task for Okamatsu after arriving in Manchuria was to organize research on Manchurian law and then to adopt appropriate policies that would prove effective.

Goto recruited young graduates from Japan's best universities to join the staff of the Mantetsu Research Department. Since they had been trained in Japan in an intellectual atmosphere that focused on how to promote development and modernization, they knew how to conduct research that would help the administrators in Manchuria build a modern economy, society, and governance structure. Like the faculty under whom they had studied in Japan, many came from modest social backgrounds, had risen because of their academic records, and held liberal or even leftist views.

Just as he had in Taiwan, Goto Shimpei attached a high priority to education in Manchuria. Teacher-training programs were established, and the number of elementary schools rapidly increased. In addition to Japanese language, the subjects taught included basic mathematics and science. In the better schools in towns and cities, where some Chinese students were admitted along with the more privileged Japanese students, the schools had some teachers from Japan and some Chinese teachers who had studied in Japan. Most of the educated Chinese in Manchuria who were of school age between 1931 and 1945 learned Japanese language.

In the 1930s nearly three-fourths of the employees of Mantetsu were Chinese. Although many did not hold positions as high as those of Japanese employees of comparable ability and length of service, they did have better working conditions and received more stable salaries than most people in Manchuria. Other Chinese workers in Manchuria served as household servants for Japanese families or operated small retail establishments that catered to Japanese customers. Some were upset that they were treated poorly by the Japanese for whom they worked, but others appreciated the higher wages they received from Japanese employers. For higher positions in Mantetsu and for teachers, the Japanese drew from the small group of Chinese who had studied in Japan and then had returned to Manchuria. In addition to working for the South Manchurian Railway and for the government, those educated in Japan could also teach Japanese language in schools.

Goto left Manchuria in 1908 to become minister of communications and director of the National Railway Bureau in Tokyo, where he could oversee the policies he had established in Manchuria. He remained influential in Japan, where he later became mayor of Tokyo and then the first director of Tokyo Broadcasting System Corporation (currently NHK, the Japan Broadcasting Corporation).

Goto Shimpei's successors generally shared his liberal vision. After the Russian Revolution of 1917 some Japanese intellectuals in Japan accepted many of the premises of the Russian revolutionaries—that officials should struggle to improve the lot of the working classes and, like some of the Chinese leftists with whom they had come in contact, they should use national planning to promote economic development. As leftist intellectuals within Japan felt pressure to conform to the increasing constraints imposed by Japan's ultranationalists, some migrated to Manchuria, where Goto's successors were more supportive of left-wing intellectuals than the government was at home in Tokyo.

The Russians had opened coal mines shortly before passing control of the railway over to the Japanese, and Mantetsu also invested in coal mines in Fushun, which became one of the largest open-pit coal mines in the world. The railway began shipping coal to nearby Anshan, the site of iron-ore mines, where it expanded the production of pig iron. As coal production increased, the transport of coal became a major source of revenue for Mantetsu.

During World War I, when the embattled European countries had little energy for activities in Asia, the Japanese had more opportunities to expand their commercial role in Manchuria and elsewhere in China. Japan's growing power during World War I, and in particular the publication in 1915 of the its Twenty-One Demands, presented as an ultimatum to China for increased Japanese influence and control, led to anti-Japanese demonstrations by many young intellectuals and labor unions in Manchuria.

The Kwantung Army

After 1905, the danger that Russia would start a war of revenge was used by the Imperial Japanese Army as a pretext for undertaking a sizable military buildup of Japanese troops on the Liaodong Peninsula. In accordance with the Portsmouth Treaty signed at the end of the Russo-Japanese War, which required Japanese and Russian troops to clear out of Manchuria within eighteen months, most demobilized Russian and Japanese troops had left Manchuria by 1907. However, the Japanese were allowed to retain guards posted every fifteen kilometers along the railway and to station troops in Port Arthur and Dalian (Dairen) on the Liaodong Peninsula. Initially totaling 10,000, the number of Japanese troops in the Kwantung Army expanded in 1931.

Since Manchuria was the main overseas location for Japanese troops and an assignment in Manchuria was considered challenging, the Kwantung Army attracted some of the brightest, most patriotic, and most ambitious graduates of Japan's military academies. The Kwantung Army was responsible for defending the area in case Russian troops should seek revenge for their defeat in 1905 and for protecting Japanese citizens from attacks by local patriots. The Imperial Japanese Army took deep pride in its successes during the Sino-Japanese War and its dedication to the nation, giving soldiers a sense of moral superiority over businessmen and politicians who pursued only selfish, personal interests. Many of Japan's military officers believed they had a glorious national mission to protect Asia from Westerners.

When they saw that the Chinese government was not taking a strong stand against the Twenty-One Demands, patriotic young Chinese protesters responded with boycotts and occasional personal attacks on the Japanese. Japanese citizens living in Manchuria sought the protection of the Kwantung Army. Some Japanese settlers in Manchuria, as well as some in the home islands, resented the haughtiness of Japanese soldiers and were more sympathetic to the Chinese people than they were to the military, just as some Mantetsu bureaucrats were sympathetic to the Chinese because of the harshness with which Kwantung Army officials dealt with local people. In 1934, when several top positions at Mantetsu went to Kwantung Army officers, a number of Mantetsu officials resigned and tensions between the two institutions grew. However, ordinary Japanese residents in Manchuria welcomed the protection the Kwantung Army provided against Chinese nationalists.

In responding to anti-Japanese attacks in Manchuria, Kwantung Army officers often moved quickly and forcefully, without waiting for directions from Tokyo. It was difficult for Imperial Army officials in Japan to restrain the Kwantung troops, and political leaders in Tokyo, intimidated by the readiness of impetuous soldiers to assassinate government officials, were cautious about restraining them.

Zhang Zuolin, Zhang Xueliang, and the Japanese

From the time Mantetsu was established, Mantetsu and the Kwantung Army were allowed to direct Japan's activities in the Liaodong Peninsula, but before 1931, aside from those along the strip of railway territory belonging to Mantetsu, the Japanese did not officially control developments at the local level in the rest of Manchuria. However, the Japanese gradually used their military power and funding to form relations with local leaders so that they could extend their informal power beyond the official strip next to the railway.

After 1911 Zhang Zuolin, a shrewd, ambitious local warlord with little formal education, formed linkages with other local strongmen and lent his support to Yuan Shikai, who dominated Chinese national politics until his death in 1916. By the time of Yuan Shikai's death, Zhang Zuolin had established himself as the dominant warlord in Manchuria, and in 1920 China's central government appointed Zhang governor-general of the three provinces in Manchuria.

Zhang hoped to get rid of the Japanese in the region, but he realized the limits of his power against Japan's greater economic and military strength. He therefore made efforts to accommodate his rule to the realities of Japanese power. The Japanese, while trying to extend their power, also made some accommodations to Zhang Zuolin. In 1925, when Zhang Zuolin faced a revolt led by Guo Songling, an officer under him, the Japanese assisted Zhang by refusing to allow Guo's forces to travel on the railway and by resisting efforts by his troops to travel across territory under their control.

After 1926, as Zhang Zuolin was trying to build up his own railways and horse carriages to compete with the Japanese in transporting soybeans and other supplies, and as Zhang's ambitions were growing beyond Manchuria, relations between Zhang and the Japanese became strained. Zhang was cooperating with Wu Peifu and other warlords in Beiping to resist the

Northern Expedition of Chiang Kai-shek (see Biographies of Key Figures), who sought to unite all of China. Japanese leaders in Tokyo did not support the warlords against Chiang Kai-shek, and Zhang was upset that the Japanese did not cooperate with him. Zhang's efforts to secure supplies within Manchuria for his activities beyond his provinces created shortages, which in turn led to runaway inflation in the region. The resultant social instability made it more difficult for Mantetsu and the Kwantung Army to maintain order and heightened tensions between Japan and Zhang Zuolin.

By 1927 Zhang Zuolin had become the dominant leader in Beiping, but in June 1928 his allies lost ground and he was forced out of the city. As he was returning to his home in Manchuria, he was assassinated by the Japanese. After his assassination, the Kwantung Army had to contend with Zhang Zuolin's son, Zhang Xueliang, who inherited his father's troops and followers. Zhang Xueliang, knowing Japan's great military power, did not publicly criticize the Japanese, but he saw them as his adversaries. He not only tried to maintain his military forces but also sought to strengthen the economic base that his father had built. He had his own port facilities for exporting soybeans and he worked to build up his own small railway network. Tensions between the Japanese and Zhang Xueliang were exacerbated by the economic depression that broke out in 1929, and in 1930, for the first time in its history, Mantetsu lost money.

The Manchurian Incident, 1931

At 10:20 p.m. on the night of September 18, 1931, a dynamite explosion on a track near Shenyang derailed a train transporting Zhang Xueliang, who was unharmed. The explosion caused only minor damage, and within minutes another train was able to pass over the spot where the train had been derailed. The next morning Japan, claiming it was responding to the sabotage, sent in troops, and before the end of the day they had destroyed Zhang Xueliang's small air force and taken over his small garrison in Shenyang. This event, the Manchurian Incident, quickly reverberated around the world with implications that rippled out far beyond China and Japan.

Within two weeks it became clear that a group of right-wing radicals within Japan's Kwantung Army, following the plans of their strategist Ishiwara Kanji, had set off the explosion and used the incident to enable Japanese troops to come in and gain control of all of Manchuria. Within days after the explosion, more Japanese troops arrived directly from Korea and then from Japan. Chiang Kai-shek, who believed that Chinese forces were not yet ready to fight the Japanese, sent word that the Chinese troops should not resist the Japanese and should preserve their strength. The largest city in Manchuria, Shenyang, was under Japanese control within one day, and within a week the city was back to work and Japan had gained control over Changchun. Zhang Xueliang's troops offered some resistance in Jinzhou, a smaller city located not far from the pass separating Manchuria from the rest of China. Emperor Hirohito said that the Japanese troops should not attack Jinzhou, but the troops carried out an attack nonetheless, and several hundred people were killed. Five months after the Manchurian Incident, armed resistance to the Japanese had basically ceased. At the time of the Manchurian Incident, there were roughly 10,000 Japanese troops in Manchuria, approximately the same number of troops that had been there since 1906. But within a year that number had increased to over 100,000 and the Japanese military was able to occupy the civilian government offices throughout Manchuria.

After the Manchurian Incident, the Japanese began building a new capital city in Manchuria. They named it Xinjing (Shinkyo in Japanese, or "New Capital") and located it at Changchun, which had been the northern terminus of the South Manchurian Railway and until that point had been dominated by the Russians, making it clear that Xinjing would be used to strengthen Japan's position in northern Manchuria. The Japanese had worried about possible resistance by the Russians to the placement of their Manchurian capital so far north, but the Russian military had been greatly weakened by Stalin's purges and Russia did not offer any organized resistance. At the time, Changchun, with 311,000 people, was smaller than Shenyang, which had a population of 527,000. Drawing on their experience in establishing a modern capital for Taiwan in Taipei, the Japanese built a modern city, with all the buildings patterned after the new government centers they had built in Tokyo and Taipei, which in turn were based on their careful study of the most modern buildings in Europe and the United States. Architects flocked in to take advantage of the design opportunities, and project managers directed tens of thousands of local workers, who strained to carry in large rocks and put them in place in an era before mechanized construction equipment was available. Dozens of buildings were constructed, including those for administrators and one for the Manchurian parliament that the Japanese had established. To create a new medical center, a large modern hospital was built, doctors were brought in, and medical training programs were established. A large public square and parks were laid out. A grand new train station was built and the world's most modern railway cars were imported. Xinjing became one of the grand modern capitals of the world.

Some Japanese leaders in Tokyo were deeply troubled by the Kwantung Army, referring to its actions in fomenting the Manchurian Incident and then using the incident to establish military control in Manchuria as an insurrection. By the 1920s the government of Japan had lost the strong central direction it had had when the *genro*, the senior leaders who had taken part in the Meiji Restoration, passed from the scene, and many Japanese political leaders feared assassination by extremists on the right. In 1931, with the Japanese government divided, Prime Minister Wakatsuki Reijiro was unable to control the military. Inukai Tsuyoshi, who became prime minister in December 1931, tried to stop the Kwantung Army from occupying Jinzhou. He was preparing to send a representative to improve relations with China when he was assassinated by right-wing naval officers on May 15, 1932. His assassination further intimidated Japanese government officials. To the Chinese and Koreans, Japan's emperor, Hirohito, was the symbol of Japan and a justification for Japanese aggression. The emperor had the right to approve the appointment of the prime minister, but he saw his role as being a symbol of national unity, above any political struggles, and he made no effort to restrain the activities of the Kwantung Army in Manchuria.

The Independent Kingdom of Manchuria, 1931–1945

Immediately after the Manchurian Incident, Japanese officials in Tokyo, aware that direct colonization of Manchuria would be strongly opposed by the Western powers, began preparing a puppet government to give the appearance that Manchuria was ruled by a Manchurian government, not by Japan. Pu Yi, China's last emperor, who was five years old when the Manchu dynasty was overthrown in 1911, was installed as chief executive of Manchuria in March 1932, when the new government was officially announced.

In 1934 the Japanese made him emperor of the "Independent Kingdom of Manchuria." He accepted the position but later complained that he was forced to take orders from the Japanese.

Even before the Manchurian Incident, officials from the Kwantung Army and the South Manchurian Railway had made contacts with local officials and small-scale warlords throughout Manchuria, beyond the areas they governed directly. Some local officials had received financial assistance from the Japanese. In Manchurian cities, the Japanese worked with local elites who shared their interest in stability and established committees to maintain public order. After the Manchurian Incident in 1931, when the Japanese were choosing local officials for the new government, they selected some whom they had already been paying as advisers and other local officials with whom they were familiar. Most local officials and small warlords were allowed to remain in their positions.

By the time the so-called Independent Kingdom of Manchuria was established in 1934, the Manchus represented only a small percentage of the population of Manchuria. According to estimates by the Mantetsu Research Department, of the 34.4 million people living in Manchuria in 1930, approximately 3 percent were Manchu, whereas 90 percent were Chinese, 6 percent were Mongolian, and scarcely 1 percent were Korean, Russian, or Japanese. In the 1940 census there were 850,000 Japanese and 1,450,000 Koreans living in Manchuria.

Within Japan, the establishment of the Independent Kingdom of Manchuria was celebrated. At the time of the Manchurian Incident, Japanese newspapers had a circulation of some 650,000, but several months after the incident readership had increased to more than one million. Most Japanese families by then owned radios, and radio broadcasts and newspaper reports helped fan the flames of excitement over Japanese advances in Manchuria. Even many liberal-minded Japanese in both Manchuria and Japan who felt kindly toward China and the Chinese people did not oppose the Japanese-led Manchurian government, for they thought that Japan would not only protect the Japanese living there but also provide enlightened leadership that would in turn create stability, develop the Manchurian economy, and enhance the welfare of the Chinese people. Seiji Ozawa, for example, who was born in Shenyang in 1935, lived in Manchuria until 1944, and later became the longest-serving director of the Boston Symphony Orchestra (from 1973 to 2002), was named Seiji by his father, a dental school professor, in honor of Itagaki *Seishiro* and Ishiwara *Kanji*, who four years before Seiji was born were the main conspirators behind the Manchurian Incident.

Through the 1930s Japan tightened its control over those who questioned Japanese aggression. In 1931 Ishibashi Tanzan wrote in the journal he edited that Japan should abandon its special rights in Manchuria, as it was not worth turning China and the Western nations into enemies. But by the late 1930s, as the Japanese right wing was killing political leaders who opposed them and the Japanese military was establishing firm control over the national government, the vast majority of Japanese intellectuals chose not to publicly criticize the Japanese government.

There was a huge gap between public opinion in Japan and public opinion about Japan in China and the Western countries. Most of the Western media by this time had become critical of the Japanese government. In October 1932 when the Japanese government recognized Manchuria as an independent country, only Japan's future World War II allies Germany and Italy joined in recognizing it. Western officials criticized the military occupation of Manchuria and worried that Japan had further territorial ambitions. From the 1880s until 1905, the interested public in England, Germany, France, and the United States generally held favorable impressions of Japan, which they regarded as the most modern civilized country in Asia, and they appreciated Japan's contribution in putting down the Boxer Rebellion in 1900. However, after Japan's victory over the Russians in 1905, its issuance of the Twenty-One Demands in 1915, the continued presence of Japanese troops in Manchuria after troops from other countries left in 1918, and the growth of the Japanese Navy, the Western powers grew watchful and more worried. Japan's activities in Manchuria further heightened their concern.

Within months after the Manchurian Incident, members of the League of Nations organized a commission, headed by Lord Bulwer-Lytton of England, to investigate Japanese activities in Manchuria. The Lytton Commission, after spending six weeks in China, Japan, and Manchuria, wrote a report clearly stating that the Japanese had invaded Manchuria and that there was no international legal basis for Japan's territorial claims. The report was released in late 1932 and the League of Nations named Japan an aggressor nation. In early 1933 Japan withdrew from the League of Nations, maintaining its control over Manchuria.

Manchuria and Chinese Nationalism

As Thomas Gottschang and Diana Lary conclude from their research, there was no large-scale anti-Japanese resistance in Manchuria, even among migrant laborers.[1] Compared with areas the Japanese Army invaded during World War II, there was almost no fighting in Manchuria during its Japanese occupation. Even during the Manchurian Incident of 1931, only a small number of people were directly involved. In many parts of China, university students played a major role in leading demonstrations against Japanese aggression, but there were few university students in Manchuria and there were no labor unions. On December 9, 1935, when students in Beiping took to the streets advocating that China's Communists and Nationalists should unite to oppose Japan, and students in many other cities took part in similar demonstrations, there were no demonstrations in Manchuria.

There was some resistance to the Japanese in Manchuria from Ma Zhanshan, a local warlord in Heilongjiang, and from other local warlords, but as Rana Mitter concludes, despite the great publicity given to Ma's heroism in resisting the Japanese, his resistance was not carried out on a large scale and it did not last long. Ma Zhanshan behaved more like a local warlord defending his own turf than an anti-Japanese patriot promoting a national revolution, and in early 1932 he even cooperated with the Japanese. A small group of Manchurian residents moved south, out of Manchuria, and formed the Northeast National Salvation Society in an effort to link Manchurian resistance to national goals, but they had little influence in either Manchuria or the nationalist movement.

However, the Manchurian Incident became well known in other parts of China, especially among young intellectuals, in whom it stirred up anti-Japanese sentiment. As Parks Coble concludes, the negative sentiment generated by Japanese aggression was also turned into criticism of those officials' failure to resist the Japanese. The failure of Zhang Xueliang to stand up to Japan after his father's assassination gave his opponents an opportunity to criticize him for being weak in the face of the Japanese. Chiang Kaishek, long cautious about speaking out against the Japanese because of their military strength, was constantly criticized by the Communists for his failure to stand up to Japan.

The Legacy of Colonization in Taiwan and Manchuria

The Chinese in Taiwan and Manchuria who lived under Japanese rule had learned how to live in what was then a modern society. They had become familiar with electric lighting, the radio, and the telephone, and they knew how to use banks. They had become familiar with trains and motor vehicles. Many had become literate under Japanese teachers.

People in Taiwan were introduced to a modern lifestyle through Japanese culture. A generation of people in Taiwan knew how to operate in Japanese culture, and a group of Japanese people had become comfortable working in Taiwan. These connections would prove useful in carrying out rapid economic development in Taiwan after the Chinese Civil War and in establishing political, economic, and personal relationships between Taiwan and Japan that would continue long after China's Civil War between the Communists and Nationalists ended in 1949. These ties would also create difficulties in the relationship between Beijing and Tokyo.

In Manchuria, many of the buildings erected by the Japanese, such as those in the new capital of Xinjing (Changchun) and in the city of Dalian, remain today. The Kwantung Army headquarters is now the headquarters of the Jilin Provincial Committee of the Chinese Communist Party. Because many youths in Manchuria were educated in Japanese schools between 1931 and 1945, many of China's Japan specialists after 1949—in business, government, and academic life—came from China's Northeast. They had experienced Japanese colonial rule, but unlike people in many other parts of China, they had not directly fought against the Japanese. Because there were so many Japanese people in Manchuria at the time, many of the Chinese living there under Japanese rule had become familiar with the Japanese through local businesses, schools, and workplaces, and therefore they had a more nuanced view of the Japanese than those who had known them only as enemy soldiers. After the reform and opening of China in 1978, people in Manchuria were therefore more welcoming to the Japanese than people in other parts of China, and many Japanese also felt more comfortable in China's Northeast than elsewhere.

CHAPTER SEVEN

Political Disorder and the
Road to War, 1911–1937

· with Richard Dyck ·

JAPAN INVADED CHINA in 1937 not because of a well-organized long-term plan but because of a failure of military and political leadership. Japanese leaders made serious miscalculations, the greatest of which was the failure to recognize Chinese determination and persistence.

The systems that had held each country together started changing fundamentally at the same time, around 1911–1912, with the downfall of the Qing dynasty in China and the death of Emperor Meiji in Japan. Disorder followed and continued in both countries because the new systems inaugurated in 1912, the Chinese Republic and the reign of Emperor Taisho, both failed to reestablish effective and stable systems of political rule. In the quarter of a century from 1912 to 1937, the growth of Japanese investment and settlement in China, in addition to the increase in communication, travel, and trade, enabled relations between China and Japan to grow closer and more intertwined than ever before. Unfortunately, the disorder in both countries created forces that also made their relations more tense and adversarial, ultimately exceeding the capacity of their leaders to manage them peacefully.

Disorder in China and the 1911 Revolution

In 1911 the Qing dynasty fell because of its inability to cope with challenges at home and abroad and because of the growing opposition to the Manchus as an outside group of rulers. However, the immediate events that led to the Qing's downfall happened by accident. On October 9, 1911, in the Russian concession of Hankou, now part of the city of Wuhan, a group of rebels accidentally exploded a bomb. When the Russian police came to arrest them, the rebels resisted. The rebels took the local Manchu authorities by surprise and prevailed, sparking the 1911 Revolution. October 10 thus became the official date of the beginning of the Republic of China. Although some revolutionaries had been planning to overthrow the Qing dynasty, the 1911 Revolution was not a coordinated effort by a strong rebel organization able to establish a new order; rather, it was a spark that set off the collapse of an old system that had already lost its base of support.

Sun Yat-sen, who at the time of the revolution was in Denver raising money, promptly headed back to China. On the way, he stopped in Japan to consult with supporters he hoped would help finance his efforts to form a new government. Thus the "father of the revolution" arrived in Shanghai in December, two months after the so-called revolution occurred. Yuan Shikai, who would eventually lead the new republic, was summoned from retirement not by the rebel side but by the Qing officials to prepare the Beiyang Army in hopes of putting down the rebellion. There was no unified group ready to take leadership of the revolt and transform an accidental skirmish into a movement, much less to create a new republic to replace the Qing. The main goal uniting the rebels was a desire to oust the Manchus, and once they succeeded they had neither political order nor a well-developed vision for the future.

Britain and Japan were the two countries with the most commercial interests in China, and the events of October 1911 were communicated instantly to Tokyo and London by way of undersea telegraph lines. Wuhan was an important inland treaty port on the Yangtze River. It had a large British population, and it was one of the ports through which coal and iron ore were transported to the Yawata Steel Works in Japan. The British and Japanese, through the Anglo-Japanese Treaty, had pledged to cooperate in protecting their interests in China, so diplomats urgently launched a series of meetings in London, Tokyo, and Beijing to ensure that traffic on the Yangtze would not be interrupted by the Wuhan disturbance.

As the drama unfolded, the two top contenders for China's leadership were Yuan Shikai, the recently retired Qing general, and Sun Yat-sen, the publicist who had spent years overseas drumming up support to topple the Qing dynasty. Initially it was not clear if Yuan would align with the rebels or align with his former Manchu masters and try to craft a constitutional monarchy similar to that in Meiji Japan. Yuan had an advantage over Sun because he had commanded the Imperial Beiyang Army, and he also knew how to manipulate the British and the Japanese by telling them what they wanted to hear. Yuan tried to win over the British with his plan to restore order along the Yangtze and maintain peace in Wuhan, Shanghai, and the other treaty ports. To the Japanese ambassador in Beijing, he spoke of his loyalty to the emperor. And yet at the same time that Yuan was extolling the virtues of the monarchy to the Japanese ambassador, he was negotiating with the Qing household for the child emperor's abdication. Yuan was clever, and in his lust for power he covered all his bases.

The loosely organized Revolutionary Alliance met in Shanghai and named Sun as provisional president of the new republic, but Sun quickly realized that Yuan Shikai had the military's support and in February 1912, after the Qing dynasty abdicated, he yielded the presidency to Yuan. Later, in 1913, Sun became dissatisfied and obtained the support of some troops to challenge Yuan, but his force was defeated and Sun sought asylum in Japan.

Disorder in Japan Following the Death of Emperor Meiji

Emperor Meiji died in July 1912, at age sixty, ending an incredibly consequential forty-four year reign. In the last six months of his life, Meiji had received daily briefings on the revolution in China. In November 1911, in his last address to open the Diet, he expressed his deep concern about the disturbances in China and his hope that order would be restored and peace would prevail. When the Qing emperor abdicated in February 1912, ending 2,000 years of imperial rule, it could not but have had an impact on a Japanese emperor whose ancestors for centuries had sent embassies to the emperors of China. Knowing that he was nearing the end of his own life and having witnessed the passing of several of his advisers, it must have been disturbing to him in his final days as he was briefed on what was transpiring after the end of the imperial line in China.

The changes that occurred with the death of Meiji were less dramatic than the fall of the Qing dynasty, and they came when Japan was already much further along in its modernization process than China. Despite the political chaos at the top during the Taisho era (1912–1926), the changes introduced under Emperor Meiji—Western-style bureaucracy, a capitalist economy, Western-style factories, and a professional military—all survived him. By the beginning of the Taisho period, not only were universities and technical schools functioning but nearly 100 percent of Japanese elementary-school-age children were in school.

While the Meiji system had the appearance of a British-style constitutional monarchy, with a cabinet, prime minister, and parliament, strategic decisions during the Meiji period had actually been made by an oligarchy consisting of Meiji himself and the founding fathers, the *genro*. After much debate, the model that the *genro* had favored for the 1889 Constitution was not Britain's constitution but the Prussian constitution, which limited participation in decision making and placed the emperor at the center. Under the Meiji Constitution, the emperor had the authority to appoint and dismiss ministers, determine the structure of the administration, convene and dismiss the Diet, appoint officers in the army and navy, declare war, make peace, and conclude treaties. In practice, the emperor was careful never to publicly display his powers, but always to work through the *genro*. Thus, the *genro* shielded the emperor from blame when policies failed, and the institutionalized charisma of the emperor provided legitimacy for the *genro*. The system depended on the team of talented individuals serving at a specific time in Japan's institutional development, and after those team members left the scene, Japan struggled with central authority.

The center of Japan's political system faltered at a time of important historical transitions in other countries. The fall of the Qing dynasty was at the top of the list. Japan had important interests in China that had been negotiated with the Qing, particularly in the Northeast. The Western imperialist powers stood ready to take advantage of the collapse of the Qing, and although the Anglo-Japanese Treaty provided the framework for cooperation between Japan and Britain, Russia, Germany, France, and, potentially, the United States, could also try to expand their respective interests, to the detriment of Japan. The political structure in the Pacific was also beginning to change. The United States had become a Pacific power with its colonization of the Philippines, its annexation of Hawaii and Guam, and the scheduled completion of the Panama Canal in 1916. The state governments on the West Coast, most prominently in California, passed racially tainted laws limiting Japanese and Chinese immigration and land ownership. For the Japanese, the United States was increasingly taking on the appearance of an adversary. Then, in 1914, the catastrophic war broke out in Europe, followed by the Bolshevik Revolution in Japan's other neighbor, Russia. Most of Japan's leaders—the remaining *genro* and their successors—were realists, meaning they understood the limitations of Japan's resources and military power in relation to those of the Western powers, and therefore they preferred to maintain a low posture while securing Japan's position in northeast Asia. But Japan also had its share of aggressive ultranationalists who believed in Japan's exceptionalism and its superiority over its Asian neighbors and the West.

The myth and sanctity of Emperor Meiji was further enhanced by the ritual suicide of General Nogi, the Japanese hero of the Russo-Japanese War, and his wife, in the sacred Japanese tradition of *junshi* (i.e., following their leader in death). The entire country mobilized to build the Meiji Shrine, a huge Shinto shrine in the middle of Tokyo. Ishibashi Tanzan, the liberal journalist and a great admirer of Meiji, objected to the shrine, not only because of the expense but also because he felt that it conveyed the wrong image of the emperor who had led the modernization of Japan. Ishibashi thought Meiji's legacy would be better served by building universities and research centers. For the next several decades, Ishibashi frequently wrote of the dangers of the cultish reverence with which many Japanese, particularly extreme nationalists, viewed the monarchy. Many of the assassinations, coups, and terrorist acts of the 1920s and 1930s were carried out for the cause of "restoring the absolute authority" of the emperor. The terrorists believed the myth and misunderstood the imperial system.

Meiji's son, Yoshihito, the Taisho emperor, suffered from a neurological disorder and could not perform his duties at the same level his father had. This had been recognized long before Meiji's death, and the efforts by the palace had been focused on grooming the grandson, Hirohito, the Showa emperor, who was only eleven years old at the time of Meiji's death.

From Disorder to Military Dominance, 1911–1937

In both China and Japan, the history from 1911 to the outbreak of war in 1937 is the story of political leaders struggling to maintain domestic order and good relations with other countries but losing out to their militaries. By the end of the period, amid the domestic disorder in Japan and China the militaries had gained control, and public opinion in both countries increasingly supported stronger assertions of patriotism against the other. But the Chinese military was not unified in a single national force, and the Japanese Army and Japanese Navy were not united in a single command structure and they were quite competitive with each other.

After 1911, amid China's disintegration into regions, any attempt to gain political control inevitably required military force. In the struggle between Sun Yat-sen and Yuan Shikai, power ended in the hands of the soldier, Yuan Shikai. Similarly in the regions, political power accrued to those with military power, the warlords. In the struggle within the Guomindang after Sun's death, power went not to Wang Jingwei, Sun's political deputy, but to the commandant of the military academy, Chiang Kai-shek. The militarists, not the politicians, became the arbiters of Chinese policy.

In Japan, too, power gravitated to the hands of the military at a time when China itself and Japanese policies toward China were both in disarray. Skilled political leaders, such as Hara Takashi, and seasoned diplomats, such as Shidehara Kijuro, voiced policies that, in the spirit of the Washington framework, were intended to respect Chinese sovereignty and allow China the opportunity to develop a stable government. But Hara was assassinated, Shidehara was replaced, and in Tokyo the power of the military grew stronger. In contrast to China, within Japan the army and the navy were both centrally organized national military services, and they gradually gained power, but it was unclear who was in charge at the top as the generals and admirals struggled with one another the control and direction of their China policy. In Manchuria, as in Tokyo, Japanese civilian officials at Mantetsu and in Changchun attempted to maintain control, but amid tensions with the Chinese and local Manchurian warlords, power accrued to the military, the Kwantung Army.

In the late 1920s, as the Guomindang became more organized and Chinese nationalism grew stronger, insubordination by Japanese military units in Manchuria became more of a problem. This started a tragic cycle. Military command in Tokyo too often turned a blind eye to the insubordination that destroyed discipline. The Chinese public became increasingly anti-Japanese, particularly when Chinese blood was shed. And the growing population of Japanese citizens living in China began to fear for their safety, causing an anti-Chinese backlash in Japan.

The anti-China fervor in Japan was so strong by late 1931 that the Japanese public welcomed the takeover of Manchuria, even though it was an obvious act of military insubordination. Insubordination continued after the Manchurian Incident, and the public continued to show support. Not only had the political parties and civil authorities lost control of the military, but the higher military command in Tokyo had also lost control. It was not until the failed uprising of February 26, 1936, that the central military finally took the required steps to regain control and purge the ultranationalists from the military. The assassinations, attempted coups, and acts of obvious insubordination ended after February 1936 under tighter military control. Japanese military leaders who gained control of the government completely underestimated the resolve of the Chinese. Because most of their military encounters with the Chinese up through 1936 had been short, the Japanese did not have a plan for a larger invasion of China, nor did any of Japan's leaders expect a long war.

China's Weak Government and Strong Voices, 1915–1937

After 1911, the weaknesses of the Chinese government strengthened the voices in Japan calling for their country to take advantage of its greater power, and strengthened the voices of Chinese youth demanding that their government take stronger action against Japan.

Once Yuan Shikai prevailed in the power struggle in China, the most important priority for Japanese leaders was to secure the rights that they believed they had won in the Russo-Japanese War, namely the leasehold rights in the Liaodong Peninsula, including the lease on the land along the Mantetsu rail line. Some of these leases were due to expire in 1923. The British had been prescient and strong enough to obtain a ninety-nine-year lease on the New Territories near Hong Kong before the collapse of the Qing. The Japanese were intent on getting a similar lease for Liaodong. The Japanese had a strong belief, not shared by other countries, that their rights in Manchuria were vital to Japan's well-being. This mindset had solidified by 1895, when the European powers prevented Japan from taking over the

Liaodong Peninsula, Dalian, and Port Arthur after the Sino-Japanese War. In the minds of the Japanese, the blood of 100,000 Japanese soldiers had been shed in battles with the Russians that had "won" Manchuria for Japan. The Japanese also believed that their population was too large for the home islands, and they needed the sparsely populated expanse of Manchuria for their excess population, as a place to relocate and prosper. During the forty-four years of Meiji rule, the population of Japan grew from thirty-five million to fifty million, and with improvements in public health and hygiene it was adding half a million people to the population every year. Emigration to the United States was becoming more difficult because of anti-Japanese U.S. immigration policies, including the Gentlemen's Agreement that limited emigration during the administration of Theodore Roosevelt. The wide-open spaces of Manchuria, more than two times the size of Japan, seemed to offer unlimited possibilities.

The most articulate and prominent critic of the dominant mindset about Manchuria was Ishibashi Tanzan (see Biographies of Key Figures). A columnist, and later the publisher of *Toyo keizai*, an influential business magazine, Ishibashi argued against the Manchuria dream on practical grounds. Manchuria shared a border of thousands of kilometers with Japan's main adversary, Russia, so defending the border and pacifying the wide expanse of Manchuria would require enormous military expenditures. It would be cheaper to buy the agricultural products, as well as the coal and iron ore from Manchuria's mines, on the open market at standard world prices. Ishibashi also argued that Japan should think of its educated population as an asset, not a liability. To deal with the problem of excess population Ishibashi advocated birth control. He began promoting the articles of Margaret Sanger, the American birth-control activist, as early as 1915. Along with the small minority of anti-imperialists in Japan, Ishibashi felt that Japan's colonial policy in China and Korea was creating populations that for generations would be "anti-Japanese, despise the Japanese, and hold an eternal resentment against Japan."

The cabinet that was to take on the negotiations to gain control over the Liaodong Peninsula was that of Okuma Shigenobu, who took office in early 1914. Okuma, a prominent political leader who had not been a *genro* insider and who had long advocated British-style cabinets, became prime minister, for the second time, at the advanced age of seventy-six. He was enormously popular and well known for founding Waseda University, a private institution that produced journalists and members of the political parties. As foreign minister he appointed Kato Takaaki, a seasoned but arrogant diplomat, devoted Anglophile, and former executive of Mitsubishi, who would later become prime minister. Okuma was known as a friend of China, but like other Japanese who were supportive of China, he viewed Manchuria as a separate issue and, with the chaotic changes after 1911, was determined to secure Japan's "rights."

Then, just as Foreign Minister Kato was preparing for negotiations, World War I broke out in Europe. Japan had an official alliance with Britain, and Kato had served as ambassador in Britain. He sided with the British against the Germans in attacking Germany's holdings on the Shandong Peninsula, including the fortified port at Qingdao in Jiaozhou Bay, a strategic naval station. In August 1914 a force of 23,000 Japanese soldiers, combined with the token support of 1,500 British troops, attacked 5,000 German soldiers at Qingdao in what was expected to be a quick battle. The Japanese prevailed, but the battle turned out to be more difficult than expected, with more casualties and deaths. Much to the shock of the army's leaders, Japan's military technology had fallen behind. They were expecting a traditional battle of infantry soldiers with rifles and bayonets, similar to battles during the Russo-Japanese War, but they were confronted with modern artillery and, for the first time, air power. Articles in the Japanese press glossed over the difficulties and celebrated Japan's glorious victory, its first since 1905. However, the battle set off a debate about the need to reassess Japan's military policy. The debate began quietly, but it continued for decades because Japan had no central authority that could resolve the issue.

Twenty-One Demands, Versailles, and the Burst of Chinese Nationalism

After the "victory" at Qingdao, Japanese leaders had the political momentum and confidence not only to negotiate with the Yuan Shikai regime to secure Japan's rights in China's Northeast but also to demand rights to the newly won German territory in Shandong. The document the Japanese government produced was known as the "Twenty-One Demands," which soon became notorious as an aggressive, ham-fisted diplomatic blunder that further aroused Chinese hostility to Japan. The demands were patterned after the six demands the Russians had delivered to the Qing twenty years earlier, but the Japanese government carried them much further with demands for territory, exclusive rights to ports, and the placement of advisers in the Yuan government.

The Twenty-One Demands, 1915

The Twenty-One Demands, presented by the Japanese government led by Prime Minister Okuma Shigenobu, represented the first test of a post-Meiji cabinet's ability to deal with a totally new regime in China. Whereas the Meiji approach would have been for the palace and the *genro* to set the strategy and then delegate implementation of the negotiations to the cabinet and the bureaucrats, Prime Minister Okuma and Foreign Minister Kato Takaaki intentionally did not consult with the *genro*. Also, there is no record that they consulted with the emperor, even though the Taisho emperor, according to the Constitution, had sole authority to make treaties. Okuma waited until the close of the Diet session in December so his proposed draft of the demands was not subject to a chaotic debate in the Diet. The majority party in the Diet at the time was led by Okuma's political adversary Hara Takashi (prime minister from 1918 to 1921).

In January 1915 Kato directed Japan's top diplomat in Beijing, Minister to China Eki Hioki, to present the Twenty-One Demands to Yuan Shikai, with instructions to tell Yuan to keep the negotiations confidential. Kato wanted them secret not only from foreign powers but also from other power centers in Japan.

Yuan was in a weak position, but he was clever and he knew how to get the most out of a weak hand. He put together a skilled negotiating team. For the negotiations with the Japanese minister, he brought in Cao Rulin, a graduate of Waseda University who was fluent in Japanese, and he also made good use of the Japanese academic Ariga Nagao (see Chapter 5). To buy time, Cao set up the negotiations so that he and Minister Hioki held their sessions once a week, on Saturdays, and took on one demand at a time. Having begun in January, the sessions were still ongoing in May, when finally Yuan could no longer resist and yielded to all but the fifth set of demands, which would have given Japan the right to establish schools and religious institutions anywhere in China.

Yuan had no intention of keeping the negotiations confidential and he began using a weapon of the weak—global public opinion. He enlisted an able young graduate of Columbia University, Wellington Koo (Gu Weijun), to communicate with the foreign diplomats and the press corps in Beijing to generate sympathy for China. Koo, very effective in this assignment, met frequently with the Westerners, and as the weeks passed, the image spread of a cunning and aggressive Japan taking advantage of a weak China. Once the news had gotten out, Yuan started sending groups of Chinese spokesmen to New York, Chicago, Washington, London, and elsewhere to speak at foreign-affairs gatherings, chambers of commerce, and political gatherings. This model of public diplomacy was followed by Yuan's successors and evolved into what became known as the "China lobby."

The U.S. ambassador to Beijing at the time, Paul Reinsch, an academic and a devout Christian appointed by Woodrow Wilson, took up the cause for China with a passion and became an equally impassioned critic of Japan. But the United States was not prepared to do anything except make moralistic pronouncements. The best efforts by Reinsch resulted in nothing more than an official statement: "The United States cannot recognize any agreement or undertaking which has been entered into or which may be entered into between the government of Japan and China impairing the rights of the United States and its citizens in China." From this time through the 1930s, the world came to understand that American criticism would not be backed up by action.

The Chinese publicity campaign was effective, even in Japan, where it gave ammunition to Kato's numerous adversaries, including Hara Takashi. Kato's critics, many of whom learned about the negotiations from the embarrassing articles in the foreign press, tended to focus on the bungled tactics rather than the substance of the demands. Many shared the view that Japan should solidify its interests in areas such as Liaodong, particularly since Yuan seemed so unpredictable. Even some foreign observers noted that the demands were conventional within the context of the diplomacy of the time. However, all factions, including the *genro* and political leaders like Hara, recognized that Kato had unnecessarily provoked the Chinese and, in turn, the United States, thereby isolating Japan in international affairs.

Versailles, 1919

Many in the Chinese government pinned their hopes on the Versailles peace conference to block Japan's expansion into China. Woodrow Wilson's speeches about national self-determination and his opposition to colonialism had raised the hopes of China's leaders.

The first issue for China was determining who would go to Paris, and the second issue was how to fund the trip. In all, China sent fifty delegates, including several non-Chinese advisers. Some of the key Chinese delegates would become familiar faces as they represented various Chinese governments and factions over the years. They included Wellington Koo, who was then ambassador to Washington from the Beijing government of warlord Duan Qirui; Alfred Sze, who had been educated at Cornell and was serving as minister to London; and C. T. Wang, a graduate of Yale, originally from Shanghai, who was in Washington representing a rival faction from Guangzhou. The funding came from a loan taken out by Duan Qirui. Although the group was highly fragmented, the Chinese were united in their goal to recover the German territories from the Japanese.

In the end, the Chinese failed. No Asia issue was a high priority at the peace conference, particularly for the Americans. The Japanese delegation was defeated in its efforts to incorporate a clause into the Covenant of the League of Nations prohibiting racial discrimination, although the Chinese delegate Wellington Koo supported Japan on this issue. Then, when some members of Japan's delegation threatened to bolt from the conference if they were not allowed to take over German rights in Shandong, the American delegation supported the Japanese for fear their most important achievement, the League of Nations, would come unraveled without Japan. Because China lost its rights in Shandong, it was the only country that did not sign the Treaty of Versailles that concluded World War I. After China's efforts failed, Ambassador Reinsch, Wilson's appointee in China, resigned from his position, declaring, "The Chinese trusted America, they trusted the frequent declarations of principle uttered by President Wilson, whose words had reached China in its remotest parts. . . . It sickened and disheartened me to think how the Chinese people would receive this blow which meant the blasting of their hopes and the destruction of their confidence in the equity of nations."

When word reached Beijing and Shanghai that China had lost its rights in Shandong, Chinese youths demonstrated in protest, sparking a movement of young intellectuals that many saw as the birth of a new China. The demonstrations in Beijing continued for weeks and spread to other cities. The eruption of public gatherings and the writings that followed after May 4 flourished in an environment of new institutional developments, especially the establishment of new universities, that had taken place in China in the years before 1919. The modern universities that were opened in China as the old examination system was eliminated had attracted large numbers of students, who lived together, interacted, and, as in other countries with large universities, developed a sense of camaraderie and a youth culture. Assembled together and studying new ideas, it was easy for students to organize and take to the streets. China's defeat at Versailles led to a breakthrough, as young Chinese intellectuals began expanding their public involvement in national issues.

The Washington Conference, Hara Takashi, and Shidehara Kijuro

After the Versailles Treaty brought an end to World War I but failed to address China's issues or Asia generally, the United States organized the Washington Conference, the brainchild of Charles Evans Hughes, U.S. secretary of state under the Harding administration. The goals of the conference were to rein in the expensive race among the world's naval powers to build new ships and "to address misunderstandings which could lead to military conflict, particularly in China."

Washington Conference, 1921–1922

It was a huge conference, with 100 to 150 delegates taking part from each of the participating countries: Belgium, Britain (with representatives from Australia, Canada, India, and New Zealand), China, France, Italy, Japan, the Netherlands, Portugal, and the United States. The conference lasted from November 12, 1921, to February 6, 1922. Germany and Russia were not participants, and some criticized the conference as an Anglo-Saxon–led venture.

The Chinese participants welcomed the conference as an opportunity to right the wrongs of the Versailles Treaty. As at Versailles, the decision about who should represent China was complex. In May 1921 a rump parliament in Guangzhou had elected Sun Yat-sen as president of China, and when Secretary of State Hughes suggested that Beijing and Sun Yat-sen's government should both send representatives, Sun refused, claiming that his government was the only true government of China. More than 100 Chinese representatives from the Beijing government attended the conference, including, once again, Wellington Koo and Alfred Sze. But it was not clear how much of China the Beijing government controlled, nor was it clear who was in charge in Beijing. When the delegation departed China, the government was headed by the warlord Duan Qirui, but midway through the conference Duan was deposed by the Manchurian warlord Zhang Zuolin. Although the Chinese delegates were accorded the respect and dignity of diplomats, it was known that they could not lay claim to representing a unified China.

Many in the Japanese government initially viewed the Washington Conference with suspicion. Some had criticized President Woodrow Wilson's style as "moralistic aggressiveness," and they had not yet figured out the new Republican administration under Warren Harding. But Prime Minister Hara endorsed the goals of the conference and saw it as an opportunity to soften the blow of the Twenty-One Demands by returning the German territories to China and also to improve Japan's standing with the United States. Hara welcomed the chance to cut military expenditures as well. He appointed Admiral Kato Tomosaburo to serve as head of Japan's delegation. Kato was a hero of the Russo-Japanese War and a person with enough clout to get military support for arms limitations. A key participant was Shidehara Kijuro, who was serving at the time as ambassador to the United States.

According to agreed-upon conference procedures, any agreement by the conference required the consent of all; for the China portion of the conference, nine nations had to agree. Elihu Root, a former U.S. secretary of state and senator, drafted a resolution regarding China that was sufficiently abstract that all nine nations agreed. The nations resolved that they would: respect the sovereignty, territorial, and administrative integrity of China; provide the fullest opportunity for China to develop and maintain itself as an effective stable government; aim to maintain equal opportunity for commerce and industry for all nations throughout the territory of China; and refrain from taking advantage of the present conditions in China to seek special rights or privileges that would abridge the rights of the subjects or citizens of friendly states, or countenance actions inimical to the security of the states.

At the conference, Wellington Koo and Alfred Sze established good working relationships with Shidehara Kijuro and his assistant, Saburi Sadao. They had originally become acquainted at the Paris Peace Conference, and the intense four months they spent together in Washington helped solidify their relationship. Saburi observed that in contrast to Paris, where participants were looking out for their respective national interests, in Washington they were more of a cross-national team trying to resolve mutual problems. Like Shidehara, Saburi was a well-trained young diplomat who had held several postings in China. He was married to the daughter of diplomat Komura Jutaro, a former classmate of Theodore Roosevelt at Harvard who had negotiated the Portsmouth Treaty to end the Russo-Japanese War. During the conference, Shidehara became ill, so Saburi covered for him in many of the meetings with Koo and Sze.

Prior to the Washington Conference, under Prime Minister Hara's guidance Shidehara made plans to negotiate the return of the Shandong Peninsula and Qingdao to China. Together with the Chinese team, the two sides agreed on a six-month timetable, with compensation to come from the Chinese for Japan's infrastructure improvements. The British announced that if Japan gave up its rights in Qingdao, Britain would give up its rights in nearby Weihaiwei. The conference participants did not succeed in completely dismantling the complex system of unequal treaties but they made progress, and the discussions at the conference served to set the agenda for the remainder of the 1920s on issues such as tariff autonomy. Shidehara put together a team, including Saburi and also Yada Shichitaro, that continued to work on China-related issues after the conference. Yada, who had served in several positions in China, is quoted as saying that the problems of Japan and China could not be solved until the unequal treaties, an affront to Chinese sovereignty, were removed. The one issue that the Japanese were not willing to put on the agenda was Manchuria, including Japan's rights in the Liaodong Peninsula.

The Washington Conference was a success, with some qualifications. The large naval powers agreed to stop their race to build huge, expensive battleships, but they continued to build lighter destroyers, frigates, and submarines. Aircraft carriers were also still being developed. The powers with interests in China came to some agreement on basic issues, such as tariff structures, postal services, and contested areas like the Shandong Peninsula. Issues that were important for Chinese sovereignty, such as legal jurisdiction and the presence of foreign military and foreign police, were documented but not solved. The common caveat used by Japan and the Western powers was that the unequal treaties could not be fully rescinded until China regained unity and control of its territory and could guarantee the safety of foreigners living within its borders. The assertion that China was not unified was both the cause and the excuse for treating China as less than a fully sovereign nation.

Hara's Uncompleted Agenda

Tragically, Prime Minister Hara was shot and killed by an assassin in November 1921, just when the delegation was departing Japan to attend the Washington Conference. Japan, a country that does not produce many strong charismatic politicians, was robbed of one of its best at a crucial moment. Prior to becoming prime minister in 1918 at the age of sixty-two, Hara had been a diplomat, had served in several cabinet-level posts, and had chaired Japan's first major political party. After years of "transcendental cabinets" in which the prime minister was chosen by the emperor and the *genro*, not by the Diet, Hara's was the first "normal cabinet," meaning a cabinet in which the prime minister and most of the cabinet members were members of the majority party, in this case the Seiyukai Party. Hara had said he could have done much more to improve the governance system established by the Meiji Constitution if he had become prime minister ten years earlier.

Hara had several objectives during his administration that were reflected in the way he managed preparations for the Washington Conference. First, immediately prior to becoming prime minister Hara took a private study tour to the United States and China. He was surprised by the dynamism of the United States and shocked by the strong anti-Japanese sentiment in China. He decided that Japan should try to develop good relations with the

United States and ameliorate its bad relations with China. Second, he wanted to establish civilian control of the military and break the ability of the army or the navy to topple a cabinet by withdrawing its minister. For this reason, when he appointed Admiral Kato as chief delegate to the Washington Conference, Hara appointed himself as interim minister of the navy. It was a significant move in the context of the Meiji Constitution, and Hara made sure that he had Yamagata Aritomo's full support for the decision. As another step toward civilian control, Hara changed the governor-generalship in Taiwan from a military to a civilian position.

In 1922, the year after Hara was assassinated, Yamagata Aritomo, the father of Japan's modern military, died. These two deaths left a hole in Japan's governing structure nearly as large as that left by the death of the Meiji emperor. Even though the two men were very different in personality and ideology, they had developed a solid working relationship, and Hara was skilled at convincing Yamagata, the stubborn field marshal, to cooperate in addressing some of the weaknesses of the Meiji system, such as the need to strengthen civilian control and the military chain of command. Unfortunately, their reforms were still incomplete when they died, and the weaknesses that they left behind became problems, particularly for Japan's China policy.

From Shidehara Diplomacy to Preparations for War

After Hara's assassination, Finance Minister Takahashi Korekiyo was appointed interim prime minister. Takahashi had served with distinction in several key positions in which he had resolved complicated problems in the economy and government finance, but he had neither the skill nor the interest in political bargaining. Whereas Hara had known the strengths, weaknesses, and the needs of all the members of his party in the Diet, Takahashi could not even remember their names.

On September 1, 1923, Tokyo and Yokohama were struck by a major earthquake that in terms of death and destruction ranks as one of the worst natural disasters in human history. More than 100,000 died and 500,000 homes were destroyed. Recovery efforts occupied Japan for years. The nation's economy, already suffering from a postwar depression, fell into a further slump, requiring further economic retrenchment and resulting in debts that weighed on the government budget for the remainder of the decade.

In dramatic contrast to the aftermath of the earthquake and tsunami of 2011, when the Japanese people amazed the world with their self-control and discipline, after the 1923 earthquake panicked gangs of young Japanese vigilantes attacked and murdered thousands of Korean residents. The massacre seems to have been sparked by false rumors of a Korean revolt, and the rampage forced the government to declare martial law. The event stands as another black mark on Japan's relations with its Asian neighbors.

Finally, after three years of coping with economic and natural disasters, in 1924 a "Grand Coalition" of three major political parties in the Diet joined forces to support the appointment of Kato Takaaki as prime minister. Partly in an effort to overcome his reputation as the author of the Twenty-One Demands, Kato appointed Shidehara Kijuro as his foreign minister. Shidehara, after his role at the Washington Conference and his tenure as ambassador to the United States, was to continue the foreign policies started in the Hara administration—an approach that became known as "Shidehara diplomacy." In his first speech in the Diet, Shidehara declared: "Japan will not interfere with China's domestic politics. Japan will not take any action that ignores the legitimate positions of China. At the same time, we in Japan believe China will not take any action that ignores the legitimate positions of Japan." After taking office, Shidehara immediately contacted Wellington Koo, who was guiding foreign policy in Beijing. He explained his policy of noninterference, to which Koo replied, in English: "In the spirit of Sino-Japanese friendship, the Chinese government will do its best to protect Japan's interests."

Shidehara was the first career diplomat to be appointed foreign minister. He was not a politician, and in the prewar period he had never run for political office. Later, immediately after World War II, he would serve briefly as prime minister and would have a key influence on Article 9, denouncing the use of war, in Japan's postwar Constitution. Both Shidehara and Prime Minister Kato were married to daughters of Iwasaki Yataro, the founder of the Mitsubishi Zaibatsu, so they were brothers-in-law and were well connected in the business community. Perhaps for this reason, Shidehara usually couched his China policy in terms of business interests, stating that Japan sought markets in China, not territory.

For military policy, the important member of the Kato cabinet was the minister of the army, General Ugaki Kazushige. Just as Shidehara represented a new era of diplomacy, Ugaki came to represent a new era of military policy. His view of military strategy was heavily affected by World War I. Ugaki, who had served two terms as military attaché in Germany and was an expert on German military principles, had been shocked to see Germany's defeat. He also observed that Japan had missed a full generation of military technology. The lesson Ugaki took away from World War I was the concept of "total war," meaning the military and civilian industries should both be mobilized on a nationwide scale.

Because Ugaki knew that money was tight, his first move as army minister was to decrease the army by four divisions. This policy, the *Ugaki gunshuku* (Ugaki disarmament), led to a reduction of 34,000 soldiers. The idea was to use the savings from this troop reduction to begin investing in modern military equipment. The reduction in the number of posts was extremely unpopular within the army, and over time it helped fuel the growth of radical, insubordinate factions.

Ugaki called Shidehara's policy of noninterference naïve, mainly because he knew that in northern China the local Japanese military units were heavily involved with the Chinese warlords, mainly to protect Japan's interests in Manchuria. For Ugaki, Manchuria was vital to his total-war strategy, which required Japan to be self-sufficient in iron ore and coal. Over time, he saw Manchuria as important to the build-up of heavy industry, such as the Anshan steel mills and, eventually, factories for manufacturing trucks and army vehicles with the steel from Anshan. Ugaki's position is clearly stated in an entry in his diary at the time: "Regardless of what anyone may say, we absolutely cannot concede our existing position in Manchuria . . . [and] there is no chance that we will consider such matters as a revision of the Twenty-One Demands, the retrocession of the Leased Territories, or the return of the Mantetsu."

No foreign policy was more important to Japan than its policy toward China. But after the deaths of Yamagata and Hara, the divisions between the China policies of the Foreign Ministry and the military became increasingly pronounced. Shidehara's policy of noninterference, which was in line with the Washington Conference framework, was easily ignored by the military. At the same time, a split occurred in the army. From the time of Meiji, the responsibility for supervising army affairs had been divided between the Ministry of the Army and the General Staff Headquarters.

Technically, the heads of both of these departments reported separately to the emperor. When Yamagata was alive, he and his disciples had bridged this division, but now that he was gone the only link in the army's divided chain of command was the emperor. Army troops stationed in China, such as the Kwantung Army and the garrison forces, reported to the General Staff Headquarters, not to the Ministry of the Army, and their orders came from a chain of command that was not linked to the cabinet. The inability of the Ministry of the Army to control developments in Manchuria would soon bring problems.

Disorder in the Yangtze Delta and Growing Chinese Nationalism

Even though China was deeply fragmented in the early 1920s, Sun Yat-sen, much to the surprise of many, and with the backing of Soviet strongmen, was beginning to build a following. In November 1921, after exile in Japan and two years spent hiding out in Shanghai, Sun returned to Guangzhou, where he linked up with a local warlord in an effort to establish a power base. This alliance proved to be unstable, so Sun, using Guangzhou as his base, struck an alliance with Stalin and the Soviet Comintern. Stalin saw more hope in Sun than in the fledgling Chinese Communist Party, so he sent Mikhail Borodin to help organize the Guomindang and also to help set up the Huangpu (Whampoa) Military Academy to train officers who would form the core of a national army that might unify China. The commandant of the military academy was Chiang Kai-shek, who would later become Sun Yat-sen's successor, and one of the political commissars at the academy was Zhou Enlai (see Biographies of Key Figures), who, as a Communist, would become Chiang's political enemy. Sun's alliance with the Soviets was anathema to most of his Japanese supporters, and in November 1924 Sun made a desperate trip to Japan where, in a famous speech in Kobe, he tried to make a claim for pan-Asianism, a theme that had always resonated with his Japanese friends in the past, but this time he tried to make the case that the Soviets were really Asians and stood with China and Japan against the Western imperialists. Sun's Japanese supporters were mainly entrepreneurs and Asian nationalists who tended to be anti-

Bolshevik, so this new policy had no appeal. More important, most of Japan's top military leaders were strongly anti-Communist, and they began to see the Guomindang, then allied with the Communists, as a potential threat.

In 1925 Sun went to Beijing, where he hoped to forge an alliance with the northern warlords, but on the trip he fell ill. He was diagnosed with cancer and he died shortly thereafter. The Guomindang splintered into several factions. Chiang Kai-shek became the leader of one of the strongest factions because of his control of the army.

Labor unrest began to become an issue in the factories of Shanghai. The first major strike took place in a Japanese-owned mill in February 1925 as a protest against the firing of forty Chinese workers who were suspected of being union organizers. Within weeks, the movement spread and more than 50,000 workers in Shanghai were on strike. Some of the strikes were reported to have been organized by the Communist Party, a rumor that confirmed the fear held by both Japanese and British employers that proletarian movements would come to China. In 1925 at least three Japanese managers were killed by strikers, and on May 15, a Chinese striker named Gu Zhenghong was shot by a police officer at a Japanese mill.

On May 30, a group of demonstrators, including many students, gathered at a police station on the main shopping street, Nanjing Road, in Shanghai's International Settlement to protest the killing of Gu Zhenghong and also the arrest of some of the Chinese strikers. The British captain of the station, who should have been on duty, was at the nearby racetrack. A skeleton crew of British, Sikh, and Chinese police officers confronted the crowd of demonstrators, and at one point one of them fired his pistol directly into the crowd. With that, the other officers started firing, resulting in four deaths and many injuries. The shooting set off rioting all over Shanghai, mainly directed against the British.

In the anti-imperialism movement, the date of this confrontation, May 30, became a symbol inspiring Chinese patriotism. Mikhail Borodin, the Soviet adviser to the Guomindang, regarded the May Thirtieth Incident as a "gift" from the gods. Even today, a May Thirtieth monument stands in People's Park in Shanghai, not far from the police station where the incident occurred.

Two years later, in April 1927, Chiang Kai-shek suddenly started to purge the Communists from the Guomindang, and he embarked on what became known as the Northern Expedition—a military campaign to take over Nanjing and, eventually, Beijing. Knowing that there might be trouble, the British sent a fleet of heavy cruisers and destroyers to Nanjing. When Chiang's troops entered the city, retreating members of the Beiyang Army started attacking the ships and foreign consulates in the city. This sparked riots, mainly aimed at foreigners. The British panicked and requested that Shidehara commit more Japanese troops to the fighting. Normally Shidehara would have tried to cooperate with the British, but in this case he felt that an increase in the Japanese military force would only make the situation worse, and he suspected the incidents were being carried out by Communist agents who were trying to damage Chiang Kai-shek's image with the foreign community. He thus committed only a bare minimum of 300 soldiers to protect Japanese citizens in Nanjing and encouraged the British to use restraint.

Even though the violence was directed mostly at the British, a few Japanese citizens were injured. Photojournalism had become popular in Japan, and full-page photos of Japanese women and children being menaced by the Chinese were common in the Japanese press. Thus, just as the May 1925 incidents aroused Chinese passions when the British shot into the crowd in Shanghai, the 1927 riots in Nanjing aroused anti-Chinese passions in Japan. Shidehara diplomacy became another name for being "weak on China."

Tanaka Giichi, a retired general and chairman of the Seiyukai, the opposition party, was appointed prime minister of Japan in April 1927. Tanaka dissolved the Diet in January 1928 and called for the first election under the new universal manhood suffrage law. Tanaka ran a vigorous campaign opposing Shidehara's weak China policy. Voter turnout was high, and Tanaka's party won a majority of the seats in the Diet, partly because of Tanaka's talk of "getting tough on China." Although Tanaka was from a different political party than the Kato cabinet, he had worked closely with General Ugaki on the strategy to modernize the military, and his army minister, General Shirakawa, was Ugaki's classmate and close friend. So when Tanaka became prime minister, the basic military policy toward China, particularly the policy to defend Japan's rights in the north, did not change.

Tanaka Giichi, Chiang Kai-shek, and the Failure in Ji'nan

In December 1927 Chiang Kai-shek went to Japan and met with Tanaka Giichi. He was about to restart his Northern Expedition to occupy Beijing in his effort to unify a large portion of China for the first time since 1911. He wanted Japan's cooperation for the expedition, and since it would take him through Shandong, he particularly wanted to avoid a conflict with the Japanese troops there. At the time, Beijing was under the control of Zhang Zuolin, the warlord from Manchuria who was working with the Japanese, and Chiang hoped the Japanese would help get Zhang to go back to Manchuria. Another purpose of Chiang's trip to Japan was to meet Soong Meiling, then in Japan with her mother, and propose marriage.

Chiang Kai-shek was accompanied on his trip to Japan by his longtime ally Zhang Qun. The two had been close friends since they were students together in Japan in 1908, and they had worked closely ever since. Zhang Qun had served as mayor of Shanghai, foreign minister, and premier. Later, when Chiang fled to Taiwan, Zhang would serve as his secretary in the office of the president. Chiang Kai-shek could speak some Japanese, but Zhang Qun was fluent and was particularly helpful in matters that involved the Japanese. During their visit to Japan, they met with an impressive list of influential friends, including Inukai Tsuyoshi, later prime minister; Shibusawa Eiichi, an influential business leader; Yamamoto Jotaro, a Mitsui executive and later president of Mantetsu; Uchida Ryohei, a right-wing pan-Asianist; and Nagaoka Gaishi, author of the 1909 classic military manual and division commander of the Thirteenth Division, in which Chiang Kai-shek had served in 1910.

The meeting between Chiang and Tanaka took place at Tanaka's home and lasted for two hours. Only four people were present: Chiang, Zhang, Tanaka, and Major General Sato Yasunosuke, a China specialist who had already been giving Tanaka daily briefings on Chinese affairs. Tanaka was pleased to hear of the progress toward unification and the purge of the Communists. However, he encouraged Chiang to consolidate his position in the south before moving toward the north, advice that Chiang did not heed.

Chiang was aware that Japanese troops were located in Shandong province (in Qingdao and Ji'nan), and he wanted to avoid a repeat of the massive conflict between China and the foreign community that took place in

Nanjing in April 1927. Chiang assured Tanaka that his troops would do more to protect Japanese lives and property when they passed through Shandong than they had done in Nanjing.

At the time, there were some 2,000 Japanese residents living in Ji'nan. Tanaka Giichi sought to avoid conflict, but he was under pressure to keep his promise to protect Japanese lives and property, so he sent General Fukuda Hikosuke and 4,000 troops to Ji'nan. Chiang Kai-shek was camped nearby, and on the evening of May 3 it looked as if the situation was under control so that the Guomindang troops would move on peacefully and Japanese troops could exit the city. To this day, it is not clear why the efforts to avoid conflict failed and ended in a deadly clash. An incident at the residence of a Japanese citizen caused either the Japanese or the Chinese to open fire. The fighting escalated and got out of control. Fukuda's troops, with prior orders from General Staff Headquarters in Tokyo to protect the lives of Japanese residents, started an all-out assault against the Chinese troops, with the result that 6,000 Chinese soldiers were killed or injured.

A maneuver that could have enhanced the trust between Chiang Kai-shek and Tanaka had gone seriously wrong. Perhaps as the two sides went into Ji'nan tensions were already so high and the level of trust so low that a slight accident sparked the fierce fighting. Perhaps a soldier from the Japanese side intentionally provoked an incident to slow down the Northern Expedition. The Japanese newspapers published reports of the incident along with a photograph of the body of a mutilated Japanese civilian, placing the blame squarely on the Chinese. The massacre provoked an emotional reaction in both countries, and monuments commemorating the massacre are still visited by Chinese tourists and schoolchildren. The documents recording who at General Staff Headquarters gave the orders to General Fukuda's troops were burned, along with thousands of other files, after the Japanese surrender in 1945. What is known is that the general in charge of operations at General Staff Headquarters was Araki Sadao, who would soon become the charismatic leader of the army's ultranationalist Imperial Way faction.

While most of the daily newspaper reports in Japan were about Chinese attacks on the Japanese, Ishibashi Tanzan wrote articles about the disproportionate number of Chinese deaths in the conflict, and pointed out the absurdity of having sent 4,000 troops to protect 2,000 Japanese residents; by his calculations, it would have been much cheaper to simply evacuate the Japanese residents to get them out of harm's way.

The Assassination of Zhang Zuolin

In the spring of 1928 it appeared to the Japanese military officers in Beijing that Chiang Kai-shek's Northern Expedition, then poised to take over Beijing, had the military power to defeat Zhang Zuolin, who had become the top warlord in Beijing. Tanaka Giichi and the Japanese diplomats believed it would be better for Zhang Zuolin's troops to return to Manchuria in an orderly, face-saving retreat than to fight losing battles and make a disorderly retreat. The Japanese military did not want Chiang Kai-shek's troops chasing Zhang north of the Great Wall, so the Japanese successfully persuaded Zhang Zuolin that it was in his own interest to return to Manchuria, and he boarded a train for Shenyang. Beginning with General Ugaki, the top military leaders in Japan felt that Zhang Zuolin could best serve the needs of Japan as a collaborator in managing Manchuria. Zhang had never been a docile puppet of the Japanese, but Ugaki felt that he was the best choice for managing the vast expanse of Manchuria and keeping it out of the hands of the Guomindang.

Komoto Daisaku of the Kwantung Army had a different idea. He and his troops wanted to create an accident in Manchuria that would lead to chaos and serve as an excuse for the Japanese to expand their control. The train carrying Zhang Zuolin left Beijing on June 3, 1928. Komoto and a group of conspiring subordinates planted a bomb on a bridge over the railroad, and when it exploded it brought the bridge crashing down on Zhang's private train car as it was passing into Shenyang, killing Zhang. Although they tried to make it appear that the explosion was caused by the Chinese, within a few weeks it became obvious that Komoto and his group had committed the assassination. General Ugaki, for one, was furious and accused Komoto of being a spoiled, traitorous child.

The truth about the explosion gradually made its way to the Japanese cabinet and the Imperial Palace. Army Minister Shirakawa, like General Ugaki, was furious about traitorous insubordination, but he also strongly felt that the truth should be concealed to protect the reputation of the army and Japan's position in dealing with China. Prime Minister Tanaka thought the perpetrators should be tried and punished. Prime Minister Tanaka and War Minister Shirakawa held several separate meetings with Hirohito. Finally, Tanaka changed his mind and decided to conceal the truth. In the process, however, he felt that he had lost the confidence of the twenty-seven-year-old Hirohito and he therefore resigned. Tanaka died shortly thereafter, and there is some suspicion that he took his own life.

These two incidents—the slaughter at Ji'nan and the assassination of Zhang Zuolin—became fatal turning points. Both acts exposed weaknesses in the Japanese Army's chain of command. If the incidents had been avoided, relations between China and Japan might have improved. Instead, they cleared the path to war.

The Hamaguchi Cabinet, More Assassinations

After the resignation of Tanaka Giichi, the president of the rival Minseito Party, veteran politician Hamaguchi Osachi, formed a cabinet in July 1929. Shidehara returned as foreign minister and Ugaki returned as army minister. Shidehara started once again to work with the British and the Guomindang on a plan to give China tariff autonomy and to dismantle other elements of the unequal treaties. Ugaki tried to continue his project to modernize the army, which for him meant further downsizing the troops and investing in modern artillery, but the economic situation was even worse than it had been before, and within several months the collapse of the U.S. stock market plunged the entire world into an economic depression.

Shidehara, facing problems left over from the Tanaka cabinet, needed an experienced China hand, and he named as minister to China one of Japan's best diplomats, his long-time protégé Saburi Sadao. Shortly after taking up his post in China, Saburi returned to Japan to take a rest at the Fujiya Hotel in Hakone, and on November 29 he was found dead in his room, with a bullet wound to his head. The death was reported as a suicide, but the mystery of Saburi's death has never been solved. Like many in Japan at the time, he carried a revolver, but the gun that shot him was not his own.

This was a heavy blow to Shidehara and his China strategy. He immediately appointed Shigemitsu Mamoru, another seasoned diplomat, to take Saburi's place. Shigemitsu moved to Shanghai and took up residence in a house in the French section, next to that of his long-time friend T. V. Soong, a Harvard graduate and the influential brother-in-law of Chiang Kai-shek.

The finance minister was Inoue Junnosuke, a conservative economist and the former president of the Central Bank of Japan. Hamaguchi's Minseito Party had made a campaign promise to return the yen to the gold standard, and in preparation, Inoue had tried to deflate prices and lower wages. Even government employees took salary cuts. Inoue returned the yen to the gold standard in January 1930, which, because of the U.S. stock market crash, was the worst possible time. The value of the yen went up, forcing Japanese exporters to lower their prices. Many smaller companies went out of business. Rural areas were particularly hard hit, partly because of a drop in the demand for Japanese silk. Desperate families began practicing infanticide because they could not afford to feed another child, or selling their daughters into prostitution. Two years later, in February 1932, a member of an ultranationalist group, influenced by a deranged Nichiren Buddhist priest, murdered Inoue. At the same time, another member of the group murdered the president of Mitsui Corporation, Dan Takuma. In both cases, the criminals were arrested and sentenced to death, but their sentences were later commuted. The influential Nichiren priest later served as an adviser to Konoe Fumimaro when he became prime minister.

In April 1930 Japan took part in the London Naval Conference, an extension of the Washington Conference of 1921. The negotiating team was headed by former prime minister Wakatsuki Reijiro (prime minister from April to December 1931) and included a team of civilians. The main focus of the conference was on heavy cruisers, and Japan was able to strike a compromise that provided a ratio that the Imperial Navy could tolerate. But the results of the negotiations on submarines were unfavorable to Japan. In fact, perhaps owing to blunders by the Japanese negotiating team, the agreement forced Japan to give up building submarines all together, which for a time caused Japan to lose its technical edge.

Of the many issues faced by the Hamaguchi administration, the outcome of the London Naval Conference was the least popular with Japan's military. The navy protested that the negotiations infringed on the emperor's right of supreme command. Some members of the Diet, including longtime politicians such as Inukai Tsuyoshi, made the same claim.

Hamaguchi was a capable politician with a long, distinguished career. But with the collapse of the worldwide economy, he came into office at the wrong time. Many Japanese people, particularly those in the military, had lost confidence in politicians because of scandals and incompetence. Soldiers had been trained to revere the emperor, but no one had been trained to respect the political process or political leaders. The extreme reverence for the emperor evolved into what came to be known as the Showa Restoration, as Showa was the reign name for Emperor Hirohito.

The following year, in November 1930, Prime Minister Hamaguchi was shot in the stomach at Tokyo Station by an ultranationalist terrorist, a member of the right-wing Aikoku Society named Sagoya Tomeo, who had spent time in China as a so-called China ronin (a samurai adventurer). Hamaguchi survived the attack and struggled to recover for nine months until finally succumbing in August 1931; he was actually reelected from his hospital bed in March 1931. Shidehara assumed many of Hamaguchi's duties until the cabinet resigned in April 1931. Like many of the assassins captured during this period, Sagoya was sentenced to death, but his sentence was commuted to life, and he was released from prison in 1940. He would continue to be a right-wing activist until his death in 1972, at the age of sixty-four.

Assassinations, beginning with the murder in 1921 of Prime Minister Hara, had become common in Japanese politics. The system for addressing them was also commonplace, with a public trial providing a platform from which a sympathetic defense attorney extolled the "pure" ultranationalistic ideals of the accused. The criminals were usually convicted, followed sometime later by a commuted sentence and their release from prison. Even the assassin of Prime Minister Hara was released; he went on to work as a bureaucrat in Manchuria.

Insubordination in Manchuria

On September 18, 1931, a group of Japanese soldiers, thinly disguised as Chinese, planted explosive material near the tracks of the Mantetsu. The explosion caused minor damage, but the ensuing uproar gave the group of conspirators, led by Lieutenant Colonel Ishiwara Kanji and Colonel Itagaki

Seishiro, an excuse to commence an attack on Zhang Xueliang's forces and thus begin the Japanese invasion of Manchuria.

In Tokyo the cabinet gathered at 10:00 a.m. on September 19 for the first of many urgent meetings. Army Minister Minami Jiro stated that the fighting by the Japanese had begun in self-defense, but this was challenged by Foreign Minister Shidehara. The Army's General Staff office in Tokyo issued an order to avoid expansion of the conflict. When Ishiwara and his team received this order, they were temporarily dismayed. Over the next few days, they staged further provocations that gave them cover to expand their attacks. For example, a staged uprising in Jilin allowed the army to invade and take over the province. On September 21, the minister of the army requested permission at a cabinet meeting to deploy the Japanese Army divisions stationed in Korea, but his request was refused. Later, when it was learned that the Korea divisions were already deployed, Prime Minister Wakatsuki gave his permission post facto. Similar excuses were used to occupy Harbin, which was in the far north and totally out of the range of the Mantetsu or Japan's span of control. Piece by piece, provocation by provocation, the Kwantung Army expanded its reach across Manchuria.

Prime Minister Wakatsuki could not build a consensus in his cabinet about the invasion, nor could he gain a consensus about how to keep from losing control over the military. He began discussions with the opposition party, the Seiyukai, to form a joint cabinet in an effort to overcome the military with political force, but the invasion of Manchuria was so popular with the public that nearly all the Diet members had already succumbed to the momentum. Wakatsuki was forced to resign, and a new cabinet, under veteran politician Inukai Tsuyoshi, was formed.

Inukai had been a member of the lower house since the first election in 1890. He was a popular politician and good friend of China. He was one of two Japanese dignitaries invited to China for the entombment of Sun Yat-sen at Purple Mountain in 1927. However, despite his pro-China stance, Inukai was a strong advocate claiming Japan's rights in Manchuria.

Inukai named Takahashi Korekiyo to replace Inoue Junnosuke as finance minister. Unlike Inoue, Takahashi Korekiyo used Keynes's approach. He allowed prices to increase, thereby giving relief to farmers, and he allowed wages to rise, which increased domestic demand. He also devalued the yen, making Japanese products more competitive overseas. Japan was quickly on the way to recovering from the depression.

The second important and surprising appointment was Araki Sadao as army minister. Araki had been first in his class at both the military academy and the war college, but he was a hard-core nationalist and he was viewed as the leader of the army's Imperial Way faction. Araki was popular among young nationalistic officers, and one reason for his appointment was to placate the radical elements in the army.

The domestic reaction to the expansion of the Manchurian conflict was strongly favorable. In December 1931, all political parties in the Diet supported a bill to thank the military for protecting Japan's rights in China. Even though the Kwantung Army had been insubordinate, on January 8, 1932, Emperor Hirohito issued an imperial rescript that praised the Kwantung Army for having fought courageously in "self-defense" against Chinese "bandits" and for having "strengthened the authority of the emperor's army."

The most vocal overseas critic of the events in Manchuria was Secretary of State Stimson of the United States. After the invasion of Manchuria on September 18, he restrained his staff from putting too much pressure on Japan in the hope that his longtime colleague Shidehara could keep the matter under control. He warned Shidehara not to let the army attack Jinzhou, which was the headquarters of Zhang Xueliang's army north of the Great Wall. Japan's ambassador to the United States, Debuchi Katsuji, met with Stimson daily to provide updates, usually accompanied by assurances that the matter would soon be under control. On October 4, when the Japanese started bombing Jinzhou, Stimson knew that Shidehara was unable to control the situation, so he arranged to have President Hoover write letters to both Japan and the Republic of China, stating that the United States would not recognize any changes in Manchuria.

In contrast to Stimson, Undersecretary of State for Asian Affairs William R. Castle stated that although he was cautious about Japan's move, the Japanese approach was not unlike that of America in the Western Hemisphere—for example, in its control over Nicaragua. He was convinced that in the long run America's interests in the Far East would be best served by a strong Japan as a guarantor of order.

Except for Stimson, most world leaders were not critical of Japan's move into Manchuria, and many were actually in favor of it. The British government, headed by Labourite Ramsay MacDonald, saw more danger from a chaotic China than from a rightist Japan. The British press also tended to favor Japan. The *Daily Telegraph* stated in an editorial that "the right of a government to protect its interests against barbarism and anarchy is a well-recognized one."

What is remarkable about Japan's invasion is the total absence of resistance from Zhang Xueliang's troops. Of his total army of 200,000 soldiers, fewer than 50,000 were north of the Great Wall in Manchuria; the rest were south of the wall, mainly in Hebei province, securing territory for Chiang Kai-shek. Chiang Kai-shek's forces, in turn, were preoccupied in Jiangxi province in a prolonged battle with Communist troops. In 1931 Chiang had failed three times in his efforts to rout the Communist forces from Jiangxi, incurring nearly 100,000 casualties. If Zhang Xueliang were to deploy his troops north of the Great Wall to fight the Japanese, Chiang would have had to take some of his troops away from the fight with the Communists and send them to the north. An effective fight against the Japanese would require 300,000 to 400,000 soldiers, which would mean totally abandoning the fight against the Communists in Jiangxi. The alternative was to wage a token battle against the Japanese with 50,000 to 100,000 troops, which would have been a suicide mission. Using Chiang's math, it was better not to resist at all.

This logic, in various forms, continued through 1936. Because his troops were limited, Chiang Kai-shek figured he had to choose between fighting the Communists or fighting the Japanese. He chose the Communists, saying that they were a "disease of the heart," whereas the Japanese were a "disease of the skin."

China and Japan Become Enemies

One of the few times that Chinese troops resisted Japanese aggression was during the Shanghai Incident of 1932. This rare case of resistance probably occurred because Chiang Kai-shek was temporarily out of power and a rival faction from Guangzhou, under the leadership of Sun Fo, the son of Sun

Yat-sen, had come to Nanjing to form a coalition cabinet. For protection against possible reprisals from Chiang Kai-shek, Sun Fo ordered 30,000 soldiers from the Nineteenth Route Army to move to Shanghai from their home base in Guangdong. Sun Fo also named his own ally, Wu Tiecheng, to replace Zhang Qun as mayor of Shanghai. Wu had studied law at Meiji University in Tokyo and was fluent in both Japanese and English.

After the invasion of Manchuria, anti-Japanese sentiment in Shanghai reached a new height. Major boycotts of Japanese products were organized. The impact was particularly severe on Japanese textile manufacturers and Japanese owners of small retail shops, many of which went out of business. On January 18, according to a Japanese news release at the time, a group of five Japanese Nichiren Buddhist priests and laymen were chanting sutras and beating on ceremonial drums near a Chinese towel factory when they were attacked by a group of sixty Chinese young men. The Buddhists were seriously injured, and later one of them died. On January 19, thirty members of the Japanese Youth Corps, a quasi-military reserve group, mounted a retaliatory attack and set fire to two Chinese towel factories and, in the process, killed a Chinese police officer.

Japan Consul General Murai Kuramatsu demanded that Mayor Wu arrest the Chinese group responsible for the attack on the priests and clamp down on all anti-Japanese activities. He gave Mayor Wu a deadline of midnight on January 28 to meet his demands. Mayor Wu Tiecheng, eager to keep the incident from escalating, agreed to the demands, including a commitment to close the offices of the Shanghai Anti-Japanese National Salvation Association and to post guards to make sure that no one entered the building.

The Imperial Navy, under the command of Rear Admiral Shiozawa Koichi, was responsible for protecting the safety of Japanese citizens in Shanghai with a permanent force of several thousand marines billeted in barracks in Hongkou, the Japanese section of the city. Shiozawa sent for reinforcements from Japan, and within ten days an armada of twenty-three ships arrived in the port of Shanghai and another thirteen ships were moored in waiting at the mouth of the Yangtze. This was an incredibly large force to send in response to the death of a single Buddhist priest. One explanation for the overreaction by the Japanese Navy is that it desired to compete with the popularity of the army after Manchuria. Araki Sadao, the nationalistic army minister in the Inukai cabinet, boasted that the Japanese military could occupy Shanghai within four hours and occupy all of China within three months.

It was not until twenty-five years later, at the Tokyo War Crimes Trials in the 1950s, that Major General Tanaka Ryukichi, a defendant who turned "state's witness" at the trials, revealed that he had staged the attack on the Buddhist priests that set off the Shanghai Incident to deflect attention from Manchuria. Tanaka's coconspirator, the famous Manchurian princess Kawashima Yoshiko (Eastern Jewel), had bribed the Chinese youths to attack the priests. Tanaka, then a major, was serving as the army attaché in Shanghai at the time. Earlier in January he had gone to Manchuria to work out the plan for the Shanghai Incident with Itagaki Seishiro, Ishiwara Kanji's co-conspirator in the September 18 Manchurian Incident. As attaché, Tanaka had command of the local reserve units and also of the youth corps, which numbered in the thousands, and he armed both forces with rifles and swords. Many of those local Japanese soldiers and youths became eager vigilantes, seeking revenge on the Chinese for their anti-Japanese activities.

The Japanese may have missed the fact that Chiang Kai-shek had been displaced at the time, and that in his absence Shanghai was protected by the Nineteenth Route Army, a seasoned, motivated force that had been fighting Communist guerillas in Jiangxi. The Nineteenth Route Army was under the command of two violently anti-Japanese generals, Jiang Guangnai and the charismatic Cai Tingkai. On January 29, the two generals sent out a notice to the Chinese community that they would not allow Japanese citizens to place "one foot on Chinese soil or trample one blade of Chinese grass." Jiang Baili, a brilliant military leader and analyst, was highly respected by the two generals and served as their adviser (see Biographies of Key Figures). In 1931, before the invasion of Manchuria, Jiang had visited Tokyo and met with Araki Sadao, among others, and he had a sense of the jingoistic mood in Japan.

Hongkou was adjacent to a densely populated Chinese section of Shanghai called Zhabei, which was outside the boundary of the treaty port and under the jurisdiction of Mayor Wu. Normally, Japanese police or military could not enter the Chinese part of the city, but on January 28 Admiral Shiozawa decided to send several thousand Japanese soldiers into Zhabei to check on the well-being of the Japanese residents. The incursion into Zhabei began with armored vehicles driving down the narrow streets shooting out the streetlamps. The Nineteenth Route Army held its fire until the Japanese soldiers were deep in the narrow streets of Zhabei, and then it opened fire from all sides. The result was confusion and panic among the Japanese troops, who had not been trained for urban battles. Shiozawa reported the response from the Nineteenth Route Army as an "unwarranted attack" on Japanese reconnaissance troops; he did not explain why a reconnaissance group had entered a Chinese section of the city in armored vehicles and had begun shooting out the streetlights.

Immediately, the Japanese called for reinforcements from Japan. The navy sent 17 additional ships, including a seaplane carrier and the *Kaga*, Japan's first aircraft carrier. Over the course of the next three weeks, the Japanese sent a total of 100 planes, 90 tanks, 160 heavy cannons, 5,000 packhorses, and 2 army divisions, and a total of 40,000 soldiers. The logistics were complex, but because of the prolonged boycott of Japanese products, the military had access to idle merchant ships. During his 1931 trip, Jiang Baili had noticed that the Japanese had not made progress toward mechanizing their army. In contrast to what he had observed in Europe, the Japanese were still using horses and humans to transport outmoded field artillery. The Japanese troops' lack of mobility was one reason Jiang thought a strategy of resistance would serve China in the case of a full-scale invasion.

On the Chinese side, the battle helped forge a rare moment of unity. Chiang Kai-shek returned to active duty in mid-February and committed the Guomindang's Fifth Route Army to join the Nineteenth Route Army. T. V. Soong returned as finance minister to raise money for the campaign. Huge numbers of people in Shanghai volunteered, including members of the Communist Party. In keeping with Jiang Baili's strategy of retreating to the "three yangs" (Luoyang, Xianyang, and Hengyang), the Guomindang moved its capital to Luoyang, far out of the reach of both Japan's navy and its army.

Because they were failing at infantry combat in the narrow streets of Zhabei, the Japanese took to dropping bombs from planes and to lobbing shells into the city from cannons on the navy ships. This was the first aerial bombing of a civilian population in Asia. The Japanese claimed they aimed only at military targets, but in the densely populated neighborhoods of Zhabei, they destroyed thousands of houses, the North Shanghai Railway

Station, and the headquarters of the Commercial Press Company, owned by the Soong family, as well as the adjacent library of rare books. Japanese bombs also hit a camp on the outskirts of Shanghai that housed refugees from the 1931 flood of the Yangtze, even though a large Red Cross symbol was displayed on the roof of the camp dormitory. This seems not to have been an accident, because the bombing of the dormitory continued for four days.

The losses on the Japanese side were kept secret, but a *New York Times* reporter, Hallett Abend, made it a practice to attend Japanese funeral services and count the urns of ashes and to tour hospitals and count the beds. Abend estimated that in the first month of fighting, the Japanese suffered about 4,000 casualties and 700 deaths. There were many more losses on the Chinese side, including civilians.

The Japanese newspapers reported the battles as a glorious victory for Japan. The large dailies published extras filled with photos every week, and for the first time the Chinese adversaries were called "enemy soldiers." Heretofore, Chinese soldiers were referred to simply as Chinese, or southern or northern warlord troops; now, Chinese soldiers became the "enemy."

After a disastrous first month, the emperor asked General Shirakawa Yoshinori, the former army minister under Prime Minister Tanaka Giichi, to take command in Shanghai. Admiral Nomura Kichisaburo was sent to Shanghai to take charge of the naval forces. What had begun with the alleged murder of one Japanese Buddhist priest thus became a major battle commanded by Japan's most senior officers.

Ishibashi Tanzan and Finance Minister Takahashi both strongly criticized the expense of the Shanghai battle. Takahashi, who had raised money for the Russo-Japanese War in 1905 by selling bonds to an American financier, Jacob Schiff, head of the investment bank Kuhn and Loeb, pointed out that Japan could not afford this battle and said he could not think of a compelling explanation for the battle that would convince investors to loan money to Japan or to buy its bonds.

The Japanese eventually occupied Shanghai, but at enormous cost. The battle gave the Chinese a badly needed sense of confidence. General Cai became a national hero, and his photo appeared all over the country, even on packages of cigarettes and containers of salt. Statues of Cai can still be found in China today. The battle showed the Chinese that the Japanese were willing to commit a disproportionate amount of firepower to what could have been a minor scuffle.

With mediation by ambassadors from Britain, the United States, and Italy, the two sides agreed on a ceasefire in late April 1932. The battle had continued for three months, including during the week of February 6, when the Chinese New Year was celebrated. The Japanese ceremony to commemorate the ceasefire was scheduled for April 29, 1932, which was also Emperor Hirohito's birthday. The Japanese built a temporary stage on an athletic field in Hongkou. As the ceremony began, General Shirakawa, Ambassador Shigemitsu, Admiral Nomura, Consul General Murai, and Chairman Kawabata Teiji of the Japan Residents' Association climbed onto the stage. Just at the moment when the band started playing the Japanese national anthem, *Kimigayo*, a Korean man ran to the stage and threw a bomb. The explosion killed General Shirakawa and Chairman Kawabata. Shigemitsu was injured and had to have his right leg amputated below the knee.

Because of the explosion, the signing of the official armistice agreement was postponed to May 5. On behalf of Japan, the agreement was signed by Shigemitsu Mamoru from his hospital bed, where surgeons were preparing his leg for amputation. Shigemitsu, barely able to speak, told Samuel Chang, the official who was carrying the armistice document, "Tell your people I dearly wish that we shall be at peace." Samuel Chang was moved by Shigemitsu's statement and attempted to shake his hand, but since his right hand was completely bandaged, Shigemitsu extended his left hand and patted Chang with his bandaged right hand. Samuel Chang then took the agreement to the bedside of Vice Foreign Minister Guo Taiqi, who had been designated to sign on behalf of the Guomindang government. Guo Taiqi was also hospitalized, after having been beaten by a mob of angry students who were protesting the ceasefire. To prevent further attacks by angry students, Guo's hospital room was guarded by five police officers. In Tokyo, General Araki issued a statement saying he hoped that with this agreement the Chinese would abandon their "provocative policies." Prime Minister Inukai's statement was more conciliatory: "The armistice benefits both parties, though restoration of complete harmony is impossible unless the suspicions that have poisoned the relations of China and Japan have been cleared away." He added: "History has shown that the Chinese can unite when they are determined." This was May 5, 1932. Prime Minister Inukai was assassinated by a group of young navy officers ten days later.

The bomb thrown by the Korean on April 29 had been made in laboratories at Fudan University. Thereafter, compact bombs became a common weapon for terrorists in places like Shanghai. As a result, in the Japanese section of Shanghai, before the start of gatherings such as meetings or movies, the audience was always instructed to stand and look under their seats for possible bombs.

After the ceasefire the Nineteenth Route Army was deployed to Fujian, where it split from the Guomindang. The Sun Fo cabinet fell and was replaced by a cabinet led by Wang Jingwei. Chiang Kai-shek returned to his post as the head of the army and continued the fight against the Communists in Jiangxi. Whatever unity had arisen in China during the Shanghai battle was gone, and although all the factions espoused nationalism, each seemed to turn the fight against the Japanese to their own personal gain. This aerial bombing by the Japanese was one of the first bombings of a civilian population in history. The bombing of the Basque town of Guernica in Spain, commemorated by Picasso's famous painting, took place five years later in 1937 and had a death toll of 400 to 1,600. By comparison, the Japanese bombing of densely populated Shanghai in 1932 killed 5,000 or more. Japan had never planned to invade all of China. With the possible exception of Araki Sadao, most military leaders sought to avoid a full-scale invasion of China.

Chiang Kai-shek's Final Attempt to Appease Japan

In December 1932 the Saito cabinet approved the invasion of Rehe (Jehol), a province north of the Great Wall, covering an area of 114,000 square kilometers. Chiang Kai-shek, who was preoccupied with the battles in Jiangxi, pledged to join Zhang Xueliang to defend Rehe, but he was only paying lip service. Chiang assigned his weakest troops to the battle. Japan's Kwantung Army was eager to take the province before the spring thaw. It struck in February with 20,000 troops. The local warlord, Tang Yulin, gave up without a fight and mounted a retreat; he used 200 trucks to carry away his household goods. As his soldiers began to pull back, they tried to sell their rifles to the

Japanese. Zhang Xueliang brought his troops to the border not to fight the Japanese but to disarm Tang's soldiers before they could carry their weapons south of the Great Wall.

Zhang Xueliang, who was forced to take responsibility for the defeat, went into exile in Europe. This was convenient for Chiang Kai-shek because it allowed him to avoid responsibility for the defeat, and it also eliminated a potential rival.

The Kwantung Army then joined with the garrison forces in Tianjin and started invading local areas south of the Great Wall, in defiance of an order from Emperor Hirohito. Ironically, after Japan, represented by Matsuoka Yosuke, walked out of the League of Nations in March 1933, the Kwantung Army was no longer constrained by the pretense of international rules of cooperation. Japan had become a rogue country, and the Kwantung Army was a rogue army.

Chiang Kai-shek's greatest concern was not to lose Tianjin or Beijing; short of that, he was willing to compromise. So that his Nationalist government in Nanjing would not be held responsible for making concessions, Chiang formed a political affairs council in Beijing to negotiate with the Japanese. Chiang called Huang Fu, who was fluent in Japanese and well connected in Japan, out of retirement and made him head of the council. The two sides worked out an agreement that established a disarmament zone from the Great Wall to Beijing. The agreement, known as the Tangku Truce of May 31, 1933, was a scandal to any patriotic Chinese person. Surprisingly, Hu Shi wrote an article in favor of the Tangku Truce because he saw it as the only immediate way to save Beijing and Tianjin, but for many Nationalists, Hu Shi's article put him on the enemies list. Huang Fu was held responsible and branded a traitor for making the agreement. As a sign of things to come, Chiang Kai-shek, acutely aware of Japan's growing ambitions, gave the order to start packing the treasures of the Imperial Palace and getting them ready to be stored in the south.

Because of the Tangku Truce, Chiang Kai-shek was confronted with an even stronger anti-Japanese movement that was highly critical of his appeasement policies. The Chinese Communist Party became a vocal anti-Japanese force, but at the time it did not have sufficient troops in place to make a difference against Japan. The Guomindang's failure to respond boldly to the Japanese problem created a huge gap between the Nationalist Party and the population.

From Tokyo's perspective, the Tangku Truce was another in a long list of arrangements made by its local military in China and then communicated to Tokyo as a fait accompli. Tokyo had no plans and no strategies for dealing with its troops in China that were popular with the Japanese public. The Manchurian Army not only had its own strategy but also its own funds from the sale of opium from Rehe to Manchuria and other parts of China.

With the Tangku Truce and the establishment of the demilitarized zone, the period from 1933 through 1935 was relatively quiet for the Japanese military in North China. After transforming the puppet state of Manchuria into Manchukuo, the military and a group of "reform bureaucrats" in the Ministry of Commerce and Industry began investigating in earnest the potential for natural resources extraction, industrialization, and hydroelectric power generation in Manchuria. In 1935 Japan succeeded in purchasing the Chinese Eastern Railroad from the Russians, which helped expand its rail network in Manchuria.

Jiang Baili and China's Strategy for Defeating Japan

When Liang Qichao, the great publicist, traveled to Europe in 1919, one of five disciples who accompanied him was Jiang Baili. Because their funds were modest, the Chinese visitors lived like students although they were all prominent intellectuals in their respective fields, and they all wrote articles for audiences back in China. During the trip, Jiang Baili wrote one of his best-selling books on the Italian renaissance.

Jiang had studied military science in both Japan and Germany, and he was particularly shocked by the deadly scale of the battles and the changes in military strategy in the Great War of 1914–1918. In Europe Jiang saw the aftermath of trench warfare firsthand, along with the massive casualties inflicted by such technologically advanced weapons as tanks, howitzers, warplanes, and poisonous gas. When he started out on the trip, Jiang Baili had said that he was in search of the "light of dawn." At the end of the journey, he said that he had found it, because as he looked at the destruction in

Europe, he saw the possibility of China prevailing in a war of resistance against Japan.

Jiang Baili had graduated first in his class from Japan's military academy in 1906, after which he went to Germany to study military science. Many Japanese students at the academy had also gone to Europe. When Jiang was in Germany, Ugaki Kazushige was Japan's military attaché, and Jiang was invited to gatherings at the embassy with the Japanese students. The cornerstone of military science in Germany at that time was the strategy of attacking with massive numbers of troops in order to win in short battles. This was similar to what Jiang had learned in Japan, and it was the tactic Japan had used in the Russo-Japanese War.

For Jiang Baili, his epiphany, the "light of dawn" he found in Europe, was that the German tactics had failed. The strategy had failed, first, because the Germans took a long route through Belgium to reach France that extended their supply lines and forced them to leave troops behind to occupy Belgian towns. Most important, though, was the fact that Germany was fighting an offensive war, whereas the French were defending. Jiang concluded that it is easier to motivate troops to resist than to attack as the aggressor.

Since the days of his studies in Japan, Jiang Baili had been thinking that someday Japan would again invade China. In his studies with Liang Qichao in Yokohama, he read Fukuzawa Yukichi and, in Japanese translation, Herbert Spencer. There he learned an application of Darwin's theory of survival of the fittest, that societal development often ended in territorial expansion. He could thus envision a strategy by which the Chinese might resist a Japanese invasion. With remarkable foresight about Japanese strategy in the Sino-Japanese War, Jiang wrote that the Japanese would naturally come in via the coast, and they would capture the railroad network. If the Chinese were to retreat inland and the Japanese were to try to follow, their supply lines would become long, and they would have to assign troops to occupy Chinese towns, where they would be vulnerable to guerrilla-type attacks. Jiang kept working on this plan until the Japanese invaded in 1937.

Up until the trip to Europe with Liang Qichao, Jiang Baili had thought of China's problem in terms of a leadership crisis. Since the fall of the Qing, Jiang Baili had been searching for the right leader for China, but all of them, from Yuan Shikai through the warlords, were corrupt and self-serving. In the classical Confucian sense, they lacked moral leadership, which made it impossible to motivate their troops.

After analyzing Germany's defeat in World War I, Jiang changed his conclusions about China. He decided that it was hopeless to depend on the right leadership for China; no one on the political horizon was of the caliber to acquire the "mandate of heaven." But even without strong leadership, the Chinese people could be awakened to resist and defend their country. They could be more effective in resisting aggression than in attacking. The problem, therefore, was not leadership but how to overcome the apathy and ignorance of the Chinese public.

In a speech after he returned home, Jiang said, "In the past twenty years, what we have seen and learned about strategy and tactics was all imported from the jingoistic, aggressive countries, which contaminated us." He went on to say that self-defense was the wisdom the Chinese had inherited from history, but in the short span of the first two decades of the twentieth century, this had been forgotten with the importing of offensive military tactics that were not appropriate for China.[1] Using his knowledge of the strengths and weaknesses of the Japanese military, Jiang Baili planned the strategy for the 1932 battle in Shanghai, including temporarily moving the capital from Nanjing to Luoyang. Thereafter, he and Chiang Kai-shek patched up what had been a difficult relationship. Although Jiang died suddenly in 1938, by then he had already played a key role in devising China's strategy to respond to a Japanese invasion.

From Appeasement to the United Front

In a June 1934 speech to his troops, Chiang Kai-shek stated that the time was not right to do battle with Japan. According to his figures, Japan had 3.3 million soldiers, its navy had 1.2 million tons of ships, and the air force had 3,000 planes. Japan's preparations for war with China were complete, but Chiang realized that China was not prepared psychologically or materially to take on Japan. In October Chiang, thinly disguised under a pseudonym, wrote an article in which he asked whether Japan was China's friend or enemy. He noted that China had made a mistake by not negotiating with Japan after the invasion of Manchuria, when there were still moderate voices in Japan. As an example of proper timing, he noted that Lenin's signing of the armistice with Germany in World War I had saved the Bolshevik Revolution.

Many in China criticized Chiang's article, including Hu Shi, who objected to the use of the word "friend" in any article related to Japan. Hu Shi said the issue was how to make Japan less of an enemy, but talking about Japan as a friend was out of the question.

At about the same time that Chiang Kai-shek wrote his article, Jiang Baili was writing a series of essays, later compiled into a best-selling book entitled *One Foreigner's Study of the Japanese.* He countered Chiang Kai-shek's argument by noting that it was impossible to negotiate with the Japanese because no one in Japan controlled both the army and the other parts of the government.

Jiang Baili concluded that war between Japan and China was unavoidable, even though his friend and confidante, General Nagata Tetsuzan of the Imperial Japanese Army, maintained that China was not Japan's enemy. Jiang knew that for China it would be a war of resistance, entailing heavy casualties and requiring the strength to endure humiliation. But with a careful strategy, Jiang believed China could resist Japan and emerge as a victorious unified country. He was less clear about how China could defeat Japan, because the Japanese had an apocalyptic, suicidal view of war. But he was confident that Japan could not defeat China.

In 1935, just as Jiang's articles began to appear, General Nagata Tetsuzan was assassinated by Lieutenant Colonel Aizawa Saburō. Aizawa slashed Nagata to death with a military sword similar to the one that Jiang and Nagata had each received from Emperor Meiji for being valedictorians of their respective classes at the Imperial Japanese Army Academy—the class of 1904 for Nagata and the class of 1906 for Jiang. Japan had had many brutal assassinations, but this one struck particularly close to home for Jiang. Nagata was a leader of the conservative Toseiha, or Control Faction, in the military, and along with Ugaki, he had focused on modernizing the army. His death was another sign of the resistance to modernization among midlevel Japanese officers and the broken chain of command in the Japanese Army.

In the following year, on February 26, 1936, more than 1,400 soldiers led an elaborate uprising in central Tokyo, attacking government offices and the *Asahi* newspaper building. The rebels succeeded in assassinating five government officials, including Finance Minister Takahashi. As a coup, their audacious act did not succeed, but it came perilously close. Moreover, it was obvious that the group had been rehearsing maneuvers in downtown Tokyo for several days, which meant that members of the Tokyo police had been involved. This incident finally awakened Japan's military leadership and the emperor to the dangers of the radical elements in the army. For the first time, punishments were handed down: seventeen of the ringleaders were tried and hanged. In July 1936 Aizawa Saburō, who had killed Nagata Tetsuzan the previous year, was also hanged. Ishiwara Kanji, the bold planner behind the Manchurian Incident, believed that the February 26 attack on the government was fundamentally wrong and played a key role in getting the soldiers who had plotted the coup to turn themselves in. The leadership in Japan that emerged after the February 26 attempted coup did not come from among civilian politicians or bureaucrats but from the Toseiha.

In December 1936 Chiang Kai-shek went to Xi'an to meet with a group of Guomindang leaders. Subordinates of Zhang Xueliang kidnapped Chiang in an effort to make him commit to join with the Communists in a combined campaign to defeat Japan. After two weeks, Chiang finally capitulated and agreed to join forces with the Communists to fight the Japanese. Jiang Baili had been immediately summoned to Xi'an when word came of Chiang's kidnapping. He went as a member of Chiang Kai-shek's staff, but unlike Chiang, he strongly supported combining forces to resist the Japanese. In his strategy, this was a first, necessary step.

Chiang Kai-shek was a realist. He knew that he could not confront the Japanese north of the Yellow River; he would have to open a second front, probably in Shanghai, as in 1932. The Japanese would probably react with an armada of ships and massive troops, as they had in 1932. Eventually the Guomindang could retreat as far as Sichuan province, beyond the reach of the Japanese, but also far from the industrial infrastructure. The Chinese could resist the Japanese, but defeating them was another issue. Surrender required negotiation, and the Chinese had learned long ago that Japanese ambassadors and diplomats were not authorized to negotiate, nor were generals and admirals. In the Japanese system, the only person who could possibly negotiate or surrender for Japan was the emperor, and he had chosen not to exercise that power.

The Eve of War

During the Meiji period, a small Japanese oligarchy working with the emperor had a broad perspective and the power to make decisions. The Japanese leaders who had traveled on the Iwakura Mission from December 1871 until September 1873 had been able to visit different countries and study their national systems as a whole, without worrying about the details of daily political management. When the mission returned to Japan, it brought home a core group of leaders who had gained a broad understanding of what it took to make national systems work. They shared a consensus about overall national policy, and after their return they provided long-term, stable leadership. In 1894–1895 Japanese leaders had started planning for peace negotiations even before going to war with China; because they understood their own limitations, they planned their exit before they entered into the First Sino-Japanese War.

In contrast, by the 1930s the Japanese government had grown much larger, its power centers were widely dispersed, and different groups were struggling for control. During the 1930s the Japanese collected massive amounts of information on regional geography, on the names of Chinese military leaders and their backgrounds, and on supply-line logistics. But no single group had the authority to make decisions for the country as a whole. Leaders changed so rapidly, with so many assassinations, that those in power were unable to carry out comprehensive long-term analysis or to provide stable leadership. Based on Japan's past military victories, military officers had dreams of glory that exceeded what the nation was now capable of realizing. Japan was drifting toward war; it was not planning for war, and even less was it planning for peace after the end of war.

Before the Sino-Japanese War of 1894–1895, Chinese leaders had taken so little interest in Japan that they had scant information about the country and lacked an understanding of the enemy they faced. By the 1930s there were tens of thousands of people in China who had studied in Japan. Some had close Japanese friends and knew Japan extremely well. Not only did the Chinese have detailed information about Japan but they also had a deep understanding of Japanese psychology. They could undertake excellent analyses of what to expect from the Japanese. But the Chinese did not have the unified national structure to build on what they knew.

Japan's tragedy was that it had the ability to mobilize military forces without a clear strategy or mission, without a central authority capable of creating and implementing a strategy. China's tragedy was that while it could brilliantly analyze the overall strategic picture, it lacked the unified government, the industrial base, the weapons, and the disciplined soldiers to stop the advancing Japanese troops. The result was a war that not only brought devastation to both China and Japan but also created difficulties for coming generations that hoped to build a peaceful future.

CHAPTER EIGHT

The Sino-Japanese War, 1937–1945

LATE AT NIGHT on July 7, 1937, a Japanese soldier stationed near the Marco Polo Bridge on the outskirts of Beiping became separated from his unit.[1] A small group of Japanese soldiers, assuming the missing soldier had been taken into the nearby walled village of Wanping, crossed the bridge and demanded entry into the village to carry out a search. Ordinarily, when Japanese garrison forces in the region made such demands, local people would yield to their requests rather than starting a fight with well-armed Japanese troops. This time, however, Chinese troops guarding the village refused to allow the Japanese soldiers to enter, and before dawn a small skirmish broke out between the Chinese and Japanese soldiers. Who fired first was a matter of dispute among those on the scene and others who later tried to piece together the story. As tensions grew over the next several days, troops on the two sides engaged in several other small skirmishes near Beiping.

To the Chinese, the action at Marco Polo Bridge was clearly a planned aggression, the first step in Japan's plan to launch a total war with China. The speed with which the Japanese sent in more troops revealed that the Japanese were prepared for a large-scale war. When the confrontation, which became known as the Marco Polo Bridge Incident, broke out, there were 5,600 Japanese soldiers in the Beiping and Tianjin area and an additional 16,400 soldiers in North China. By July 18 the Japanese had brought in two brigades from their Kwantung Army in Manchuria, plus a division from Korea, to reinforce their garrison near Beiping. When fighting expanded in late July, the Japanese quickly sent in three more divisions. By then, some 210,000 Japanese soldiers were in North China, south of the Great Wall. Japanese military leaders expected that a decisive display of force in Beiping and Tianjin would lead to a quick victory (*sokusen sokketsu*). But they had underestimated the growing willingness of the Chinese to resist, and they were not prepared for a conflict to last more than three months. The Japanese had to call up their reserves and strain their resources. During the next two years, they would win all the battles and occupy eastern and central China, but their victories would exhaust them and lead to a stalemate. In 1944, in desperation, the Japanese would launch another offensive in a determined but unsuccessful effort to avoid defeat.

Initially, following the Marco Polo Bridge Incident, some of Chiang Kai-shek's leading officers advised him that China was not sufficiently prepared to fight Japan. Such a war would devastate China, they said, and therefore China had no choice but to continue pursuing the path of peace. Chiang did not accept this advice. On July 16, in a meeting with some 150 Chinese officials at his summer resort in Lushan (in Jiangxi province), Chiang proclaimed that it was the duty of all Chinese to defend their country. Four days later, his announcement was publicized in the press.

Japanese troops marched to Tianjin, where Chinese troops offered some resistance, but on July 31 the Japanese succeeded in taking over the city. By July 29, Chinese troops had already left Beiping, and on August 8, when Japanese troops marched into Beiping, they met with little resistance. Chiang was convinced that losing the two great northern cities to Japan would arouse such anger among the Chinese people that he would lose their support if he did not respond militarily. He was aware that China's military strength did not match that of Japan and that China would face many problems in trying to fight a war. Nonetheless, he hoped that if he mobilized the nation, the Chinese could, as Jiang Baili had predicted, outlast the Japanese. On August 7, when Chiang met with his National Defense Council, the council agreed that China would resist the Japanese. Although Japanese and Chinese forces had exchanged some gunfire in North China, Chiang Kai-shek decided that conditions were more favorable to his forces if the fighting were centered around Shanghai, where more of his trained officers were stationed. On August 14 Chiang decided to clear the Japanese out of the city, thus making Shanghai the first major battleground.

When the war broke out in 1937, Japan, as an industrialized nation, was producing planes, ships, and artillery, as well as enough weapons to arm every individual in Japan. The entire population was literate, and soldiers throughout the country also had basic mechanical skills. All Japanese adults shared a common culture, for they had all received Japan's standardized education; soldiers, too, were educated before they received their military training. There was a national system for recruiting soldiers, and all young men at the age of twenty were given a physical examination. Military veterans, organized into reservist organizations in their local communities, helped provide support for patriotic education and for patriotic organizations of women and youth in the villages. John Embree, an anthropologist who studied a Japanese village in the 1930s, reports that when a young man went off to military service, the patriotic association in the village gave him a special send-off ceremony, showing that the community was proud of him. In addition to having been taught respect for the emperor in their early schooling, soldiers felt a responsibility to uphold the honor of their family and their community. They took pride in their country, which had defeated China and Russia in earlier wars.

China was still an impoverished rural country, without enough weapons even for every soldier. Compared with Japan, China was also short of planes, ships, and artillery. Many soldiers had not received a patriotic education, and many were still illiterate. They spoke local dialects that were unintelligible to those soldiers who spoke other dialects. There was no standard system for recruiting all able-bodied men, and some soldiers had been forced into service. Only a small number of officers had been trained at military academies. Many soldiers had originally been recruited into warlord armies and had not received any additional training. Chiang Kai-shek could not count on the loyalty of all the different warlords, and he sometimes had to make concessions to various warlords so their troops would fight for the nation. And because China, lacking an effective national tax system, could not afford to equip all its troops, some soldiers had to requisition food and supplies from local people, who were not necessarily receptive to such demands.

The Military Balance on the Eve of the War

Since 1911, Japanese Army headquarters had made contingency plans in case conflict should break out between Japan and China. The plans called for Japanese troops to remain stationed in Japan. When needed, they would go to China, quickly quell any disturbances, and then return to Japan. In 1932 the Japanese had serious concerns about the threat from the Soviet

Union, so they developed contingency plans in case of a conflict with the Soviet Union. To reduce expenses Japan kept down the size of its standing army but maintained large numbers of trained reservists. In January 1937 there were approximately 247,000 officers and men in the Imperial Japanese Army, in seventeen infantry divisions, four mixed brigades, and four tank divisions, and the army had some 549 planes. Two divisions were stationed in Korea, four in Manchuria, and the remainder were in Japan.[2] Japanese Army troops had modern light and heavy artillery. The Japanese Navy was the third largest in the world; by the time of the outbreak of the Pacific War in 1941, Japan would have more aircraft carriers than the United States. Japan also had a sizable air force, and its fighter plane, the "Zero," could outmaneuver any U.S. warplane. Since the Manchurian Incident of 1931, the heavy industrial base in Manchuria had been expanding its production of military equipment. Although there were rivalries between the navy and the army, each service had high-quality training programs.

As Japanese military activities in and around China were increasing in 1936, more Chinese were calling on Chiang Kai-shek to change the target of his attacks from the Communists to the Japanese. After the Xi'an Incident of December 1936, Chiang Kai-shek agreed that the Nationalists would join the Communists in forming a new United Front to fight against their common enemy. Although both sides began focusing on resisting the Japanese, they remained aware that they might again fight each other after the end of the Sino-Japanese War.

Chiang Kai-shek had at his disposal a small number of well-trained officers who had graduated from Huangpu, Baoding, and other military academies. He also had a small Nationalist Army, but for larger battles he had to draw on the troops of the various warlords, some of whom were loyal to Chiang and some of whom were not eager to send their troops to risk their lives fighting under Chiang. From his days leading the Northern Expedition, Chiang was known as a micromanager who did not have confidence in the skill of his lower-level commanders, and he was prepared to give detailed directions to his local field commanders. He had a knack for selecting able commanders and visiting his armies to show his appreciation for their service. But when he was not present, he would make key decisions during battles without having good knowledge of the changing situation on the battlefield.

Chiang's naval forces were negligible compared with Japan's. At the beginning of the fighting, China had only about 100 serviceable planes, purchased from abroad. China's advantages were its vast size and its huge population of 500 million, seven times that of Japan. But Japan had more firepower and more well-trained troops. Japanese forces could occupy cities and railways, but they did not have enough troops to control all the surrounding countryside. Even in provinces where they could control the cities and towns, their number of troops was insufficient to penetrate into the mountainous areas.

Chiang, who had great respect for German military discipline and strategy, had been inviting German advisers to train his core troops since 1928. He had only thirty-nine German advisers when the war broke out in 1937, and even fewer thereafter, but they had played an important role in setting up the military system for Chiang's core troops and advising on military strategy.

The Campaigns in North China and Shanghai, July–November 1937

The Japanese strategy was to move troops quickly, encircle the enemy's soldiers, and then annihilate them. Rather than aiming to occupy territory, they sought to destroy the enemy. Because they depended on surprise and speed, Japanese troops carried light weapons. They relied on bombing and heavy artillery to weaken their targets before and sometimes during their attacks.

Japanese troops moved along the railways to get behind the Chinese troops, blocking off their retreat. At the outbreak of the war, large numbers of Chinese troops were in Baoding, the capital of Hebei province, southwest of Beijing, which had again become the national capital. Baoding, a small city, was also the site of a leading Chinese military academy. The Japanese concentrated aerial bombing and artillery attacks on Baoding, but the Chinese defenders, by camouflaging their military equipment, misled the bombers. On the ground, they managed to offer resistance and escape, eluding the Japanese troops who tried to surround and destroy them.

As Japanese forces moved west from Beijing toward Chahar in eastern Mongolia, they encountered resistance near Pingxingguan, a small town in a pass through the Taihang Mountains, across the border from Hebei province in Shanxi province. Just as they had done in the Sino-Japanese War of 1894–1895 when they attacked P'yongyang, the Japanese first seized the high ground, just west of Pingxingguan. At Pingxingguan, a division of Chiang's Central Army launched several counterattacks. The Chinese Communist 115th Division, commanded by Lin Biao, then age twenty-nine, maneuvered south of the Japanese forces and then moved north toward the east end of the pass, hiding close to the road in a location between the Japanese troops at Pingxingguan and their supply lines coming from the east. When the Japanese supply column, with some 170 soldiers, approached the east end of the pass with its seventy horse-drawn wagons and eighty trucks carrying rations and ammunition, it was completely unprepared for the surprise attack by Lin Biao and his Chinese troops. Lin Biao's force virtually wiped out the Japanese supply column and seized some of the supplies. Although it was a small-scale battle, the victory provided great publicity for the Chinese Communist forces as they struggled against Japan's powerful military. Farther south in Shanxi province, at Xinkou, there was a much larger battle. Although nearly 5,000 Japanese troops were killed, the Japanese prevailed and took over the northern half of Shanxi and Chahar. They then began selecting local officials to maintain order and to serve in their puppet regime.

Chiang Kai-shek quickly shifted the main battlefront from north China to Shanghai, where he could make use of the able, well-trained Guomindang military officers and their troops, who were near Shanghai. Other troops were dispatched from Xi'an and Nanjing before the fighting in Shanghai began. To overcome Chiang's forces in the Shanghai area, the Japanese were forced to dispatch some of their troops south to the Shanghai area, thus relieving pressure on the Guomindang forces in the north. Chiang, aware that there were more foreigners in Shanghai than anywhere else in China, hoped that fighting in the area would encourage the foreigners to back the Chinese against Japan. Over the years, Japanese businesspeople in Shanghai had found ways to work with the Chinese, but tensions between Japanese citizens living in the Japanese Settlement in Shanghai and the local Chinese had been high ever since the Twenty-One Demands of 1915. As soon as fighting broke out after the Marco Polo Bridge Incident, Shanghai residents began to fear that clashes would again break out in their city, as they had in both 1925 and 1932.

On August 1, 1937, as Japanese Navy troops started arriving in Shanghai, clashes broke out when the Chinese tried to prevent 1,200 Japanese naval infantrymen from landing to join the small number of Japanese troops in the Shanghai area. On August 2, Chinese planes attacked the Japanese troops that were already in Shanghai to protect Japanese people and property. On the next day, Japanese warplanes began bombing Shanghai as well as Nanjing and Nanchang, a day away by train, to wipe out China's small air force.

Both sides called for reinforcements. Chiang appealed to the warlords to send in troops, and he quickly had 190,000 soldiers at his disposal. The Japanese naval infantrymen who had arrived in Shanghai could not fend off the larger numbers of Chinese, so on August 18 and 19 three more Japanese battalions of naval infantrymen arrived.

By August 23, troops from three Japanese Army infantry divisions also began coming ashore, but they met more resistance than they had anticipated. On September 11 the Japanese mobilized three more divisions, and on the following day, the army received imperial approval to mobilize four more divisions. The Japanese still hoped for a quick, decisive victory, but that goal was beginning to seem elusive.

The Japanese believed that with a quick and decisive war they could avoid the participation of the Western nations. To avoid further alienating the Western powers and thus increase the risk that they might join the Chinese in a war against Japan, Japanese troops did not enter the foreign concessions in Shanghai. The fighting took place in the Chinese sections of the city and in the surrounding areas. Many Chinese civilians, trying to find a safe haven, flooded into the foreign concessions.

The Japanese made use of their superior firepower and much larger air force, but the Chinese brought in more troops. Chiang's forces fought well and troop morale was high. The two sides engaged in hand-to-hand fighting in Shanghai. With superior firepower from its naval air support and newly arrived artillery, Japan, after more than two months of heavy fighting, finally began to overwhelm Chinese defenses and to prevent the Chinese from bringing in reinforcements. On October 25 Chiang Kai-shek, unable to stop the Japanese assaults, began pulling his troops out of Shanghai, although his men made a last stand at a large warehouse, the Sihang Warehouse, where they held off the Japanese until November 1.

The three months of fighting over Shanghai constituted one of the largest confrontations of the Second Sino-Japanese War. Except for the foreign concessions, which the Japanese did not invade, the city of Shanghai lay in ruins. An estimated 330,000 Chinese were killed or injured in the fighting, including more than 10,000 of Chiang's officers, many of whom were his best officers. More than 11,000 Japanese were killed and in excess of 31,000 were injured.

The Japanese won the battle at Shanghai, but they failed to achieve their goal of ending the war with a quick attack. Chiang Kai-shek knew that the Japanese were too strong for him to be able win a fight to defend his capital city of Nanjing, the next likely target, some 160 miles west of Shanghai. He therefore began to move his military headquarters to Wuhan, where his troops would offer a forceful resistance. He also began to move his government officials from Nanjing to Chongqing, beyond the mountains. Chiang thus began to follow the strategy that Jiang Baili, many years earlier, had conceived to achieve ultimate victory against a Japanese invasion: the Chinese forces, moved beyond the mountains, would pursue a long war of attrition until the Japanese were exhausted and ultimately defeated. A small number of Chiang's officials remained behind, but most of his officers and troops began the process of moving toward Chongqing.

As the Japanese troops marched toward Nanjing, there were a few days when some believed it was possible to reach an agreement to end the war. The Japanese entrusted the German ambassador to China, Oskar Trautmann, to represent them in a meeting with Chiang Kai-shek. In the discussions with Trautmann, Chiang at first seemed willing to consider Japan's proposals for ending the war, but by December 7 Chiang had decided that he had no choice but to continue the war. In contrast, Wang Jingwei, who was then working under Chiang but remained his rival, felt that it would save lives if the Chinese and Japanese could reach an agreement to stop the fighting. After Chiang rejected Trautmann's efforts, Wang Jingwei continued to explore the possibility of working with the Japanese to end the war on terms the Japanese might accept.

Before the Shanghai campaign, the Japanese had still been confident that their quick attacks in North China and Shanghai would cause the Chinese to accept Japanese domination, but after Shanghai, they started making preparations for a longer war. They called into service a higher proportion of young men and began to activate more reserve forces. They also expanded the production of planes, ships, tanks, artillery, and other weapons.

The Massacre at Nanjing, December 1937

At the end of the three months of heavy fighting in Shanghai, the troops on both sides, deprived of sleep and food, were exhausted. Both sides had suffered heavy losses, including some of their best young officers. To the Chinese, the Japanese were the hated enemy. After seeing their comrades killed in action, the Japanese marching to Nanjing were already battle-hardened. The Chinese in the Nanjing area were terrified.

Because the Japanese had not anticipated that heavy fighting would move from northern China to Shanghai so quickly, when they met with formidable resistance in Shanghai, Japan's military planners rushed to get more men and armaments into position to fight. They did not have time to make adequate logistical preparations. As a result, their troops had to find their own food, which inevitably meant taking it from local storehouses, shops, and families, thus further alienating the local people.

Nanjing was not a great economic or military center, but since it was the capital, Japanese leaders hoped that by capturing it they could control the country and end the war quickly. Nanjing had symbolic value, not only as the capital that Chiang Kai-shek had been building up since 1927 but as the historic site where Chinese kingdoms had been located in antiquity and where there were remains from the Ming dynasty when the capital was located there between 1368 and 1421.

With little pause after the Shanghai battles, Japanese troops quickly began marching toward Nanjing. As they marched through small cities along the way—Kunshan, Suzhou, Wuxi—they had to remain alert for Chinese soldiers who could be hiding and be prepared to shoot them. To reduce such a risk, they carried out a massive campaign of burning trees, and even entire villages, along their path to prepare for the troops that were to follow. By December it was already getting colder, and Japanese troops lacked enough warm clothing for the winter. Reports that reached Nanjing of the approaching Japanese troops described them as a terrifying enemy, with unruly soldiers who stole food and goods and shot people along their route. Even before they arrived in Nanjing, there were reports of Japanese soldiers raping women and stealing their jewelry. Many Japanese commanders, aware of the suffering of their troops, the unexpected death of so many comrades, the risks they were taking, and their deep disappointment that the anticipated short war was turning into a war with no end in sight, were lenient when they heard the reports of stealing, raping, and killing.

As the Japanese approached Nanjing, the Chinese established three defensive rings of soldiers around the city, but the Japanese easily broke through them. Rather than have his government officials under siege, Chiang had decided that the officials should move, with all their records and documents, to Chongqing before the arrival of the Japanese. On November 20, Nanjing newspapers reported that government officials had already packed up and set out for Chongqing. Local people panicked when they heard this news, and they hurried out of the city and tried to hide in the nearby countryside. Radio reports, however, stated that the army would remain and that Nanjing would be defended to the last drop of blood. Chiang Kai-shek had already decided that he and his crack troops would move on to Wuhan, where his forces would reassemble and prepare to fight. Chiang appointed General Tang Shengzhi and his troops, not part of Chiang's top force, to stay and defend Nanjing.

On November 22, a group of foreigners from Germany, Denmark, Great Britain, and the United States who had decided to remain in Nanjing despite the Japanese attack, met to form the International Committee for Establishing a Neutral Zone for Noncombatants in Nanjing. They hoped that the zone, like the foreign settlements in Shanghai, would be a safe haven from the fighting. The committee included a small group of medical doctors, missionaries, professors, and businessmen. At the time, Germany and Japan were on good terms following their signing of the Anti-Comintern Pact in November 1936, and the group selected a respected German, John Rabe, a Siemens company representative, to be their chairman. Rabe had a large swastika placed in his yard in hopes that it would escape Japanese bombing. With the support of ambassadors from several countries who were still in their embassies in the city, the committee sent a telegram to the Japanese ambassador to China, asking the Japanese, for humanitarian reasons, to allow the formation of a neutral zone to protect noncombatants.

The zone would be located in the western part of the city, in an area that included Nanjing University, several hospitals, several of the embassies, and some government buildings and elementary schools, as well as the homes of John Rabe and other foreigners.

For days the committee received no response from the Japanese. Deeply worried about whether their zone would be recognized by the Japanese, committee members tried contacting the Japanese through intermediaries. Finally, on December 1, a telegram arrived reporting the Japanese response: "The Japanese authorities responsible for Nanjing cannot grant a safety zone for fear that the Chinese forces might use it for military purposes." However, they also stated that they would "endeavor to respect the district as consistent with military necessity." The committee understood this as it was intended, that the Japanese authorities would try to cooperate with the establishment of a safety zone if it were not used to harbor Chinese troops and it did not cause problems for the Japanese military. Rabe approached General Tang to request that no soldiers be allowed in the proposed zone, to reassure Japanese officials and protect civilians. General Tang responded that that would be impossible.

Before Chiang Kai-shek and Mayor Ma Chaochun left Nanjing on December 7, 1937, they passed administrative leadership of the city over to John Rabe, who in effect became the acting mayor as well as the chairman of the neutral zone. At the time, Chinese troops were burning many of the buildings in Nanjing so that they could not be used by the Japanese. By the beginning of December, most government officials and other residents of Nanjing had already moved out, headed toward Chongqing or the countryside. Before the exodus began, Nanjing is estimated to have had a population of about one million people, but by December 7 only about 200,000 remained, and nearly all of them, except for soldiers and an estimated 10,000 civilians, were in the safety zone.

By December 9, the Japanese were at the city gates. Japanese representatives demanded that the Chinese surrender to avoid a fight. They announced that if the city did not surrender within twenty-four hours, attacks would begin. John Rabe and his Safety Committee, hoping that Chinese officials would want to avoid further damage to the city, had already asked General Tang to agree to surrender, and after the ultimatum they urgently pleaded with the general to agree. General Tang, who until that point had been refusing, said that if Chiang Kai-shek would agree, then he would also agree. But Chiang felt that if they did not try to defend Nanjing, it would send the wrong signal to the Chinese public. He refused to surrender. On December 10, 11, and 12 Japanese artillery subjected the city to a massive bombardment, leaving it in flames. In the bombing attacks on December 12, they sank an American ship, the *Panay*, which was docked on the Yangtze, just west of the safety zone. The Japanese, still hoping to avoid war with the Americans, two weeks later apologized to the United States and agreed to pay compensation for the ship's bombing. On the evening of December 12, General Tang left the city with most of his troops. The departure of the forces under Chiang and Tang preserved large numbers of troops for later battles. But Chiang's officer corps was badly depleted. In the battles in Shanghai and Nanjing, Chiang lost about 70 percent of the officers directly under his command.

On December 13 Japanese troops marched into the city, and it is estimated that, by the end of the day, some 70,000 Japanese troops had arrived. By the evening of December 13, when the bombardment stopped, Japanese soldiers had broken the glass on many shopfronts and begun looting, sometimes carrying away their booty in crates, sometimes in rickshaws. Foreign reporters wrote that uncontrolled Japanese troops outside the zone were wildly slaughtering local people and raping women.

Over the next several weeks, the Japanese rounded up thousands of Chinese soldiers who had remained in the city and machine-gunned them to death. Many Chinese soldiers disguised themselves by putting on civilian clothes, sometimes obtained by raiding clothing shops. Some of these former soldiers in civilian dress moved into the safety zone, and Japanese soldiers followed to search for them, herding up suspects by the hundreds, and then shooting or burning them. The presence of Chinese soldiers disguised in civilian clothes in the safety zone made the zone much less safe for the international residents and other civilians. The death toll among Chinese men rose not so much from combat as from the rounding up of local young men suspected of being soldiers in civilian clothes. Foreign residents of the safety zone took walks outside and reported daily on the massive numbers of corpses they saw, sometimes piled high in ditches, sometimes left lying in the streets for weeks. The Japanese then began burning the city's remaining buildings. Some leaders of the safety zone believed that this was done to disguise their looting in the commercial area of the city.

On December 24, to stabilize Nanjing, the Japanese began registering the local population. Those registered and given armbands theoretically would no longer be at risk of being shot. The Japanese quickly registered some 160,000 local people who were not considered risks to public order— in addition to children under the age of ten, older women were not registered. Thus, at the time, the number of Chinese remaining in Nanjing is estimated to have been between 200,000 and 250,000.[3] Many Chinese continued living in the safety zone because of the fear of assault by Japanese soldiers in other parts of the city and also because much of the original housing in Nanjing had been destroyed by fires—both the fires set earlier by the Chinese and those set later by the Japanese. However, the zone became overcrowded and by February many Chinese who were not originally housed in the safety zone were forced out and relocated to other parts of the city.

In late December and early January, through negotiations between the leaders of the safety zone and the Japanese Foreign Ministry, the administrative functions that committee members in the safety zone had assumed since Mayor Ma Chaochun had left Nanjing on December 7 were gradually transferred to committees under the direction of the Japanese. The role of the international committee in the safety zone was transformed into that of a relief organization trying to provide food and services to the Chinese population.

The leaders of the neutral zone had appealed for help to Japanese diplomats, some of whom made efforts to protect the people in the zone and to stop the looting, raping, and shooting. The Japanese military, however, was often unsympathetic to the zone leaders' complaints. Rabe and others wrote daily reports on the killings and looting that they observed. Day by day, they reported on the hundreds, sometimes thousands, of people being killed, and the rapes of students, housewives, and other young women. These daily reports and Rabe's diary are considered by scholars to be the most reliable materials for understanding the extent of the atrocities in Nanjing.

All scholars who have examined the evidence, including Japanese scholars, acknowledge that Japanese did commit atrocities in Nanjing and that tens of thousands of people were killed. However, there remains great controversy over how many Chinese men and women were killed and raped in Nanjing and its surrounding areas during the six weeks of fighting. The Chinese police chief at the time, Wang Kepang, estimated there were 200,000 people left in the city. Lewis Smythe, a sociologist with a Ph.D. from the University of Chicago who was then in Nanjing, reported in his survey that there was a population of 212,600 in Nanjing at the time of the Japanese attacks, although he noted that there could have been another 10,000 people who were not reached in the survey. Foreigners in Nanjing at the time reported estimates of 12,000 to 40,000 Chinese killed by Japanese soldiers in the city. The Red Swastika Society, a Chinese charitable organization that buried the corpses, estimated that 43,071 bodies were buried.[4] In his reports to Germany, Rabe estimated that in Nanjing and its surroundings, between 50,000 and 60,000 Chinese were killed in the six weeks during and after the attack on Nanjing. At the Tokyo War Crimes Trials (the International Military Tribunal for the Far East) in 1946, representatives of the two burial associations in Nanjing at the time of the atrocities estimated that they had buried 155,000 bodies. The justices at the War Crimes Trials, based on the testimony and the information provided by Lewis Smythe, estimated that between 260,000 and 300,000 people had been killed. In the 1950s, when the atrocities in Nanjing became the center of Chinese discussions about Japanese cruelties in China, the Chinese authorities said 300,000 or more were killed, and since then Chinese scholars have used the figure of 300,000 or more.

Hata Ikuhiko, a scholar who worked briefly as a historian in Japan's Finance Ministry, recorded his conclusions in a small book, *Nankin Jiken* (The Nanjing Incident), published in 1986. He acknowledges that Japanese troops went wild in committing cruelties. After examining reporters' accounts from the Nanjing area at the time, the population registers, and the estimates of people who had already fled the Nanjing area before the arrival of the Japanese troops, Hata concludes that there were fewer people left in the Nanjing area at the time Japanese troops entered the city than had been claimed. He also examined the testimony of the four witnesses who spoke about Nanjing at the War Crimes Trials, information from the later Nanjing trials conducted by the Chinese, and the movements of the Japanese forces in Nanjing at the time. In addition, he looked at the data used by the Chinese, who claimed that 300,000 or more were killed. Based on the sources he investigated, Hata estimates that about 42,000 people were killed. A handful of those on the right in Japan claim there was no massacre, but the majority of Japanese people acknowledge that atrocities were indeed committed in Nanjing by Japanese soldiers. During the war there was no way of determining precise numbers, but all scholars who have examined the evidence conclude that what happened in Nanjing was a tragedy of immense proportions. The Nanjing Massacre left a legacy of bitterness that remains to this day, and it has become a symbol of Japanese wartime cruelty, a focus of Chinese complaints that the Japanese do not acknowledge the extent of the Sino-Japanese War atrocities.

Fighting in Xuzhou and Wuhan, 1938

The Japanese planned that after taking Nanjing, they would dispatch their victorious troops to gain control of a major railway junction, Xuzhou, 200 miles north of Nanjing, where a north-south railway (the Jin-Pu) crossed an east-west railway (the Long-Hai). Near Xuzhou, the Japanese forces would join other troops coming west from the Beiping area. After taking Xuzhou, the combined Japanese forces would then go west to Zhengzhou and then south to Wuhan, the major city in Central China, some 300 miles south of Xuzhou. They were optimistic that they could take Wuhan by the end of March 1938. Victory in Wuhan, they believed, would enable them to control Central China and break the Chinese resistance. They could then put military and political pressure on China to end the war and establish a government under Japanese leadership.

Chiang Kai-shek, realizing the crucial role of Xuzhou in Japan's plans, decided to make a strong stand there to stop or at least slow down the Japanese advance. Before Chiang moved his forces out of Nanjing he had 80,000 troops in Xuzhou. He decided to reinforce the troops in Xuzhou not only with soldiers coming from Nanjing but also with troops from various smaller cities along the two rail lines that crossed in Xuzhou. In all, he brought in some 300,000 soldiers who arrived in Xuzhou ready to fight. The Communists at this point still had a relatively small force in Shaanxi. For the battle at Xuzhou, Chiang drew heavily on the Guangxi warlords Bai Chongxi and Li Zongren and their well-trained men.

Japanese troops approached Xuzhou from the north, south, and east. In early February 1938, fighting broke out roughly 100 miles north of Xuzhou and 100 miles south of Xuzhou, as Chinese troops resisted the approaching Japanese forces. Chinese troops also fought the advancing Japanese east of the city. The biggest battle of the campaign took place at Taierzhuang, about 13 miles northeast of Xuzhou. Fighting broke out near Taierzhuang on March 22 and continued for two weeks, until the Japanese ran low on ammunition. At that point the Chinese were able to drive the three Japanese divisions out of Taierzhuang. The Japanese estimate that they suffered 5,000 casualties, either dead or wounded. Chinese casualties are estimated to be as high as 20,000. By late April, with new arrivals, Japan massed 400,000 troops near Xuzhou and with their massive firepower drove the Chinese out of Taierzhuang. The town of Taierzhuang was devastated by the fighting. The Japanese regarded the battle at Taierzhuang as a costly success. The Chinese, proud of their initial ability to push the Japanese out of Taierzhuang, were even more buoyed by what they considered to be their own success.

The battles for Xuzhou and Taierzhuang lasted five months and were costly to both sides. It was not until late May, after the arrival of more Japanese reinforcements, that Japanese commanders felt ready to march into the city of Xuzhou. Japanese generals planned to surround the Chinese in Xuzhou, some 200,000 soldiers, and crush them. On May 17, in preparation for the entry of Japanese troops, Japanese artillery began pounding areas within the city, and on May 19 the Japanese marched into the city to surround the Chinese troops. The Chinese, however, had performed a clever maneuver: they had been sending small groups of soldiers out of Xuzhou at night to blend into the countryside and disperse in different directions, so that when the Japanese troops massed into the city to surround and destroy them, the Chinese troops had already escaped.

The Chinese considered their fight in Xuzhou a great victory, for they had killed or wounded many Japanese troops, exhausted the Japanese survivors, frustrated Japan's plans to quickly conquer China, and enabled most of the Chinese soldiers to escape. Chinese politicians and historians disagree about which Chinese commanders deserve the most credit for the victory: Chiang Kai-shek, who managed many of the decisions, the

Guangxi generals Li Zongren and Bai Chongxi, who led their own troops, or the midlevel officers on the ground.

On June 5, 1938, after abandoning Xuzhou and as Chinese troops were moving south, Chiang Kai-shek made the most controversial decision in the entire war—the decision to destroy the dikes on the Yellow River. The Japanese had just moved into Kaifeng, the ancient capital and cosmopolitan cultural and economic center of the Northern Song dynasty (960–1127). Chiang, fearing that Japanese troops were about to cross the Yellow River and threaten Zhengzhou in Henan province, decided to flood the area to block their advance. On June 9, on Chiang's orders, the dikes at Hua-yuankou, just north of Zhengzhou, were blown up, causing the river to change its course and water to flow into the surrounding areas. Although there are widely different estimates of the damage, Diana Lary, after examining various reports, estimates that several hundred thousand people were drowned, several million became homeless, and between two and three million died as a result of the subsequent floods and famine that followed the dikes' destruction. Problems in the area continued until 1946 and 1947, when the dikes were finally repaired and restored to their pre-1938 condition. The flooding did prevent the Japanese troops from moving into Zhengzhou and delayed for several weeks the arrival of Japanese troops in Wuhan. Debates continue today about the wisdom of destroying the dikes, but the weight of opinion is largely critical of Chiang for sacrificing the lives of so many Chinese people for what proved to be only a minor delay in the battle for Wuhan. The flooding also forced the Japanese to approach Wuhan by attacking from the east along the Yangtze, with the Japanese Navy playing a major role, rather than the Japanese troops who were marching south.

The Japanese hoped that a victory in Wuhan would give them access to the central portion of the Yangtze, which was the great east-west transport route, and end the Chinese resistance. Chiang decided to concentrate large numbers of troops in the areas east of Wuhan as the Japanese approached, in the hope of destroying the Japanese threat. On the eve of the battle, the Chinese had amassed approximately 1.1 million troops to defend Wuhan. By June, the Japanese had amassed some 400,000 troops. As elsewhere, the Japanese were very mobile, and they used their navy and air force, relying on planes and heavy artillery to provide support for the soldiers, whereas the Chinese relied on small arms, machine guns, and hand grenades.

As in other battles, the Chinese troops came from different regions and were under different commanders, some of whom were not particularly loyal to Chiang Kai-shek. Many Western military specialists at the time thought that the Chinese would be able to hold off the Japanese for only about one month. In the end, however, the Chinese were able to hold them off for ten months, and they inflicted far heavier casualties than the Japanese had anticipated.

The Japanese military and foreign military specialists had greatly underestimated China's capacity to resist the Japanese in fighting over Xuzhou and Wuhan in 1938. Stephen MacKinnon concludes that the key to China's success in the fighting for Xuzhou and Wuhan was the military skill, the camaraderie, and fighting spirit of the field commanders, who had graduated from Baoding Military Academy. The senior Chinese generals, who had graduated from Huangpu Military Academy, were not nearly as effective in guiding strategy and leading troops in battle as the younger generation of field commanders trained at Baoding. The graduates of Huangpu were better trained in politics, but the Baoding graduates were trained in military strategy and operations. Although they commanded troops who came from different localities and had varying backgrounds, the common training of the officers from Baoding Academy enabled them to work together to slow down the Japanese military, which had much greater firepower. Chiang Kai-shek was also personally present for the battles at Xuzhou and Wuhan and was considered effective in providing overall leadership.

Some of the heaviest fighting during the war took place during the approach to Wuhan in the summer of 1938, and fighting continued in Wuhan until October 25. In mid-June, as the Japanese began advancing toward Wuhan, initial clashes occurred in Anqing (southern Anhui) and Jiujiang (northern Jiangxi, on the Yangtze River), more than 100 miles east of Wuhan. In both areas, Japanese troops outmaneuvered the Chinese and quickly broke through their defenses, enabling them to take Jiujiang on July 28. However, once the Japanese occupied Jiujiang, they met well-organized resistance and suffered heavy losses. It took two months of heavy fighting for the Japanese to advance from Jiujiang to Wuhan. As the Japanese troops entered Wuhan on October 25, Japanese officers, aware of the worldwide anti-Japanese sentiment created by their unruly soldiers in Nanjing, made a greater effort to enforce discipline and prevent looting and rape.

After the heavy fighting during the Chinese defense of Wuhan, both Japanese and Chinese troops were exhausted. After Wuhan, the two sides paused for several months to recoup their strength. Then, in early 1939 the Japanese launched offensives in the central Chinese cities of Nanchang (Jiangxi province), Changsha (Hunan province), and Yichang (Hubei province). In the battles for each of these cities, the Chinese forces put up stubborn resistance, and in some cases they surprised Japanese commanders with their skill and commitment. Chiang Kai-shek had personally stayed in Wuhan until the very end of the battle there. Chinese troops even initiated attacks on places that the Japanese had earlier occupied. The Japanese eventually occupied Nanchang and Yichang, but they suffered heavy losses and failed to annihilate the Chinese forces. After Wuhan, Japanese military commanders worried about a decline in the quality of their own forces, as the Japanese Army had to lower its recruitment standards to meet the demand for more soldiers.

Some months later, in February 1940, at a conference with his high-level strategists, Chiang Kai-shek analyzed the strengths and weaknesses of the Japanese military. Among its strong points, he acknowledged, was its ability to make surprise attacks on poorly defended areas by disguising its intentions. The battles of Xuzhou and Wuhan were the turning point in the Second Sino-Japanese War, for after those battles, the exhausted Japanese slowed down their effort to subdue China. The decision to do so was also based on Japan's need to set aside troops and personnel to deal with the Soviet threat. In May 1939 Soviet and Japanese troops clashed in the village of Nomonhan on the border between Manchuria and Mongolia. The clash led to a large battle, the Nomonhan Incident, in which Japanese troops were badly defeated. Thereafter, Japan saw that it needed to set aside more resources for a possible clash with the Soviet Union. In 1938, even before the Nomonhan Incident, the Japanese Ministry of the Army, concerned about a conflict with the Soviet Union, had decided to reduce troop levels in China from the 850,000 there in 1938 to 700,000 by the end of 1939 and 500,000 by the end of 1940.

In the spring of 1940, when Germany occupied France and the Netherlands, Japan saw new opportunities to attack the European colonies in Southeast Asia and bring them into the Greater East Asia Co-Prosperity Sphere, of which Japan was the leader.

After leaving Wuhan, Chiang and his supporters moved through the mountains to Chongqing, in southwestern China, which became Chiang's capital for the remainder of the war. Some Japanese military leaders wanted to inflict an all-out attack on Chongqing, but after 1940 they lost out in arguments with those who wanted to pursue the fighting in Southeast Asia instead, and after December 1941 they lost out to those pursuing the conflict with the United States. From December 1941 until 1944, while Japan was preoccupied with fighting the United States, it maintained control over its occupied areas in China, but it did not undertake any large new campaigns. The Second Sino-Japanese War had reached a stalemate.

The National Puppet Government

On March 30, 1940, the Japanese set up a "national" Chinese puppet government in Nanjing, led by Wang Jingwei, similar to the so-called national government they had established in Manchuria with Emperor Pu Yi as the titular head. The Japanese had been slow to set up a separate national puppet government because they had continued to hope that Chiang Kai-shek, who had engaged in some informal peace initiatives with Japan, might come to some accommodation with the Japanese military occupation. On March 20, after it became clear that Chiang would not make such accommodations, Japan recruited Wang Jingwei, who had been Chiang Kai-shek's leading rival to succeed Sun Yat-sen, to serve as the head of a puppet regime, the Reorganized National Government of Nanjing. Chiang, who never completely trusted Wang, had sometimes removed Wang from his positions and sometimes reinstated him in other positions. When Chiang first went to Chongqing, Wang initially joined him. However, as the Japanese advanced, Wang expressed the view that China was unable to defeat Japan and that continued efforts to fight Japan would be devastating to China and the Chinese people. He advocated finding a way to make peace with Japan.

When the Japanese set up its puppet government in 1940, Wang and the Japanese who supported him claimed that Wang's administration, with ministers and a government structure like the one that Sun Yat-sen had established in 1925, represented a restoration of the true Nationalist government. In inaugurating his government, Wang visited the tomb of Sun Yat-sen at Purple Mountain in Nanjing to show that his government was the true successor of Sun's government. Similar to the Nationalist government that had been formed by Sun Yat-sen and continued by Chiang, Wang established an Executive Yuan and a Legislative Yuan. Although Wang claimed it was a national government and he amassed a sizable administrative staff in Nanjing, his government in fact had limited control only over several northern Chinese provinces.

As in Manchuria, the real power behind Wang's puppet government was the Japanese military. When Wang Jingwei's government appealed for international recognition, it was recognized only by Japan, Germany, and Italy, whereas the other major Western powers continued to recognize Chiang Kai-shek's government. The Japanese controlled the propaganda issued by Wang's government that was designed to win support for Japan's efforts in China. Japanese propaganda attempted to rally support in China and Southeast Asia for Japan's resistance to communism and Western imperialism.

Both the Guomindang and the Communists considered Wang a traitor for collaborating with Japan. Wang and his Japanese supporters established a network of spies who reported about possible resistance, and those suspected of being spies against Japan were killed. In cooperation with his Japanese superiors, Wang resorted to a reign of terror to subdue the opposition. Although he died during the war, after the end of World War II some 2,700 of his former subordinates were executed and 2,300 were sentenced to life imprisonment.[5] Since his death, the Chinese have continued to regard him as one of China's most infamous traitors, despised by both the Nationalists and the Communists.

Local Administration in the Japanese Occupied Areas

In areas such as Nanjing and Wuhan, where there was massive damage and loss of life, it was difficult under wartime conditions to engage in rebuilding; other places were affected by the dislocation of supply lines. Most higher-level Chinese officials and elites fled to the southwest with Chiang Kai-shek. The populations of cities such as Beiping, Tianjin, and Shanghai grew slightly between 1937 and 1945 as refugees poured in to escape the fighting. Japanese commanders were given responsibility for administering the occupied areas.

Japanese troops were able to dominate the cities and larger towns and to control the rail lines, the main means of transport between cities. The Japanese had access to the 4,000 miles of railways in North and Central China.[6] However, because China was so large the Japanese could not dominate the countryside, even though in 1939 they tried to pacify rural areas. The Japanese could control the commercial activities in the larger cities, but even the peddlers in the cities, to say nothing of the small-scale Chinese businesses in the countryside, were largely beyond Japanese control. Because the Japanese could not control the countryside, local people in areas near the cities and along rail lines could engage in resistance and occasional small-scale guerrilla attacks. In some cases, they could even carry out somewhat larger attacks. The Japanese troops, like U.S. troops during the Vietnam War who were unable to track down those who had launched the attacks against them, resorted to the brutal destruction of areas that they believed the attackers had come from. When guerrillas attacked Japanese forces along the railways, the Japanese often retaliated by destroying entire villages, in a policy the Chinese publicized as "kill all, burn all, loot all." The "three all's" became a rallying cry for strengthening anti-Japanese sentiment and promoting patriotism.

The Japanese military made virtually no specific plans for administering each city or town that it took over. Although many places were devastated by Japanese attacks during the takeover, once the Japanese were the occupying power, the Japanese officers responsible for pacifying the local areas tried to achieve stability. Even when some Japanese troops continued looting, raping local women, and shooting local people who resisted, their leaders knew that stability required having working relationships with the local people. To succeed, they had to get municipal services up and running again.

Japanese military officials led the reorganization of the local governments they took over, although in such a huge country they had no choice but to rely on Chinese bureaucrats to fill the majority of administrative positions. A small number of Chinese individuals who had studied in Japan were willing to accept leadership positions under Japanese administration, generally at the national or provincial levels or in the large cities. In addition, a small number of people from Taiwan and Manchuria, who could speak some Japanese and had worked with the Japanese in the colonies, were brought to the occupied areas to fill higher-level positions or to serve as liaisons between the Japanese and the locals. In some cases, to establish order in local communities under the Japanese military, the Japanese would hire the local militia that had served in the local warlord's army. But the majority of those on the administrative staff in the occupied areas were local people who did not speak Japanese. The few who could serve as translators had an opportunity to use their special access to the Japanese to shape the information going to and from the Japanese, and they would sometimes use it for their own personal gain. Without interpreters, the Japanese had little communication with local people and had to resort to "brush conversations" in which they and the literate locals wrote notes to each other using Chinese characters.

When the Japanese took over a city or town, one of the most urgent tasks was to find enough food to feed the local population and the Japanese troops. In addition, they had to arrange for medical attention for injured survivors and homes for orphans. In many localities, local members of the Red Swastika Society buried the corpses without expecting any compensation. People had to be recruited to help clean up damage from the fighting and the burning of buildings. Others arranged temporary shelters and then longer-term housing for refugees and for local people whose homes had been destroyed.

While the war continued, it was not possible for local leaders, either Japanese or Chinese, to make long-term plans, but as the invaders brought the chaos under control, those in local administration had to arrange for collecting taxes and providing local services such as policing, supplying electricity and water, and making road repairs.

Some well-known schools moved farther inland, to Yunnan and Sichuan provinces, to escape the Japanese invaders. Some factories also moved inland, along with hospitals and medical facilities, which had to be rebuilt in their new locations. Roads and railways had to be repaired as well. Even if the Japanese sometimes played a role in guiding such reconstruction, the labor was Chinese, and because little construction machinery was available, most of the construction was done manually, using shovels, picks, and buckets.

In some cities and towns, the Japanese were able to hire local administrators shortly after their arrival, but sometimes it took several months of hiring and firing before the local government staff was stabilized. The Japanese tried to develop a group of Chinese informants who would supply confidential intelligence on local people, especially those who might be organizing anti-Japanese resistance. In larger communities, as soon as the Japanese took over, those responsible for organizing the community commonly set up temporary committees to organize the local government. Then, after a few weeks or a few months, with some replacements of personnel who had proved unreliable or ineffective, they established regular organizations.

Chiang was able to produce a limited supply of weapons in Sichuan, using machinery that had been transported from factories east of the mountains. To survive in areas occupied by the Japanese, local businessmen had to work under Japanese leadership and, in some cases, with Japanese partners. In general, businesses did not do well under the wartime conditions, not only because of the destruction of the physical plants but also because of the disruption of markets and transportation.

Local Chinese administrators had no choice but to obey their Japanese superiors, although some also felt a responsibility to provide for the needs of the local people. However, their work made many Chinese people suspicious or resentful of them. Some of their tasks, such as collecting taxes, or recruiting people to work as laborers or construction workers for minimal pay, inevitably incurred the enmity of the local people. The Japanese assigned many of these unpleasant tasks to Chinese administrators, who were then regarded as detestable collaborators by other Chinese. Those suspected of passing on information to the Japanese that resulted in the arrests or executions of Chinese individuals were despised as traitors. Those who used their positions for their own benefit, or for the benefit of their family or friends, rather than for the good of the community, were despised for their lack of morality. In many communities, any Chinese person who worked closely with the Japanese was suspect. But in others, local Chinese administrators did make some efforts to provide police protection, keep the streets clean, procure daily-life necessities such as food and supplies, ensure the availability of water and electricity, and repair buildings.

Some of the Japanese responsible for local administration—in particular, soldiers who originally had fought their way into the area—were generally hated for their arrogance and cruelty. And some Japanese administrators whose job it was to provide stability were accepted by the local people, owing to their pragmatic efforts to improve local living conditions and to restrain other Japanese from attacking people in the community, stealing property, and violating Chinese women. As they did in Taiwan and Manchuria, some of the Japanese made efforts in China proper to improve public health and to provide some medical care. But Japanese troops also used their positions of power to rape local women and girls, to help themselves to local property, and to respond viciously to those who did not follow their orders—actions that have been kept alive in Chinese memories through movies about World War II.

When the war ended, the Chinese had a chance to settle accounts with other Chinese whom they considered collaborators. The Chinese who had served under the Japanese often destroyed the records they had kept, for fear that some people would want to seek revenge for the things they had done. Many of those who had worked under the Japanese escaped to other communities and changed their names to escape retribution at the hands of local people who were ready to attack them as traitors.

In the southwest, areas that remained under Chinese rule during the war were called on by the Nationalists to supply soldiers to help Chiang's troops fight the Japanese, draining the region of local able-bodied men. The province tasked with supplying more troops than any other was Guangxi. The warlords Bai Chongxi and Li Zongren, who moved their troops from Guangxi to fight in other parts of China, proved to have some of the most effective soldiers among the Nationalist forces, and they earned special praise for their contributions to the battles of Xuzhou and Taierzhuang.

Japanese Civilians in Wartime China

Once war broke out in 1937, Japanese civilians who remained in China during the war felt the enmity of the Chinese people, and in many localities the Chinese carried out attacks on Japanese residents. Some Japanese companies sent employees and their families back to Japan. The Japanese who remained in China turned to the Japanese military for protection. Except in Taiwan and Manchuria, relations between the Japanese and Chinese became tense and the cooperative and even friendly contacts between them in business, religion, education, and culture largely ended. Japanese residents who felt unsafe in smaller communities moved to larger cities, to Harbin, Shenyang, Changchun, Tianjin, Qingdao, Beiping, Hankou, and especially Shanghai, where they sought protection in larger Japanese communities.

Shanghai had the largest Japanese community in China, with about 20,000 Japanese residents at the outbreak of the war, mostly in the International Settlement. As Japanese refugees from smaller towns began flowing into Shanghai, the Japanese population increased to about 90,000. The Japanese in Shanghai felt protected by their troops, and the Japanese Residence Association, described by Joshua Fogel, looked after their needs. However, relations with the local Chinese in Shanghai had been tense ever since the 1932 air raids and fighting.

In smaller Japanese communities, such as that in Tianjin, the Japanese residents had been more integrated into the local community than they were in Shanghai, but when war broke out they became more separated from the Chinese living in the same city because they had their own military protection and their own stores and other facilities. Just as the Chinese became more nationalistic and anti-Japanese in wartime, so the Japanese residents who remained in China worked more closely with fellow Japanese residents and tended to become suspicious of the Chinese and insulated from the surrounding Chinese community.

The Unoccupied Areas

Japanese troops, worn out after taking Wuhan and stretched thin across northern, central, and southeastern China, never penetrated into the southwest where the Nationalists were located, or into northern Shaanxi and other mountainous areas where the Communists were based. They also never penetrated the border areas (including Gansu, Suiyuan, Qinghai, Xinjiang, and Tibet) that were peripheral to the Sino-Japanese War and the Civil War that followed. The Japanese did carry out massive air raids on Chongqing, where Chiang and the Nationalist government and army were located, as well as a few air raids on Yan'an, in Shaanxi province, where Communist headquarters was located, but they never sent troops to attack either the Communist or Nationalist base areas.

The Communists

For Communists, resisting the hated Japanese was far more popular than their earlier struggle against Nationalist landlords and businessmen, and they made good use of the opportunity to publicize their patriotism. The core group in Yan'an were the 8,000 soldiers who had arrived in late 1935 after the Long March, having escaped the Nationalist Army's Fifth Encirclement Campaign. There, in northern Shaanxi province, a very poor area, they lived simple lives but their movement thrived. An estimated 100,000 newcomers arrived in Yan'an during the war. Some were refugees fleeing the Japanese and others were young intellectuals moved by a desire to serve their country, attracted by the idealism of the Communists and disillusioned with the Nationalists. In Yan'an, with no immediate pressure from the outside, the Communists had time to develop their underlying ideology, their organization, and their military, and to devise strategies for taking over the country. They expanded the Communist Party, regularized rules about membership, and carried out a rectification campaign to establish party unity and achieve a clear chain of command. They organized the Anti-Japanese University, where they trained military and political officers. They also developed art and literature to use for propaganda among the broader Chinese public. In 1937 there were roughly 40,000 members of the Chinese Communist Party, but by the end of the war in 1945 there were 1.2 million. The Eighth Route Army, the Communists' main force, had grown from 80,000 to more than 1 million, and its New Fourth Army had grown from 12,000 to 269,000.[7]

The Communists made one major thrust to fight the Japanese—the Hundred Regiments Campaign, led by General Peng Dehuai, the commander of the Eighth Route Army. From August to December 1940, Peng Dehuai led more than 100 regiments in attacking Japanese troops and destroying railway tracks and bridges in Hebei and Shanxi provinces. When the Japanese realized the effectiveness of the Hundred Regiments Campaign and expanded their forces dedicated to fighting it, Peng Dehuai pulled back. The Communist forces suffered some losses, and leader Mao Zedong decided that from then on, large-scale Communist units would preserve their strength for fighting the Nationalists. The Communists did not engage in any more major attacks on Japanese forces; instead they used their guerrilla forces in various places to harass the Japanese and damage their facilities.

After the Hundred Regiments Campaign, Peng Dehuai and other military leaders, including Liu Bocheng and Deng Xiaoping, moved east to the Taihang Mountains in eastern Shanxi province, where they formed another base in the border area between Hebei, Shanxi, Shandong, and Henan (Jin-Ji-Lu-Yu). There they could get enough food in the fertile areas of Shanxi province and the troops lived in the mountains, making it difficult for the Japanese to reach them. Yet they were close enough to Japanese troops that they could use their guerrilla forces to attack them and disrupt their railways.

In addition to the Eighth Route Army in northern China, the Communists had a large military presence, the New Fourth Army, in Central China, in Jiangsu and Anhui provinces, and there were smaller groups of guerrillas based in other areas. According to Communist publications, by the end of the war there were fifteen Communist bases located throughout the country, most of them relatively small and situated primarily in mountainous areas.

As Lucian Bianco has shown, Chinese peasants on the eve of the fighting between the Communists and Nationalists did not have a class consciousness. They were concerned about taxes, rents, and the collection of special fees. Ever since Chiang Kai-shek established his Nanjing government, he had raised taxes to cover the cost of his government and army. In contrast, the Communists' publicity stressed that they did not support a large bureaucracy, and that their armies were basically self-sufficient. They appealed to the peasants by forcing landlords to reduce their rents. The Communists also publicized their efforts to train their troops to treat peasants with respect, to pay for what they took, and to clean up the places where they stayed.

The Nationalists in Sichuan and Yunnan Provinces

When the Nationalists settled in Chongqing, which quickly became the largest city in Sichuan, they brought with them a large bureaucracy and a sizable military, which turned out to be a burden on the local economy. Large numbers of refugees followed. It has been estimated that the population of Chongqing at the end of the war was five times what it had been prior to the war. Chiang had to collect substantial taxes to support his large bureaucracy and his military forces, and the troops, like the other refugees who fled to Chongqing, had to rely on local people to supply their food and other goods. The local people found it hard to be welcoming to the outsiders because of the burdens they created. The incoming population also occupied some areas formerly used for growing rice. With the massive number of refugees, Chongqing was chronically short of goods. The shortages led to runaway inflation that all residents, already burdened by high taxes and overcrowding, found frightening. None of the measures designed to control inflation succeeded.

The high tax burden on the local populace made it difficult to provide adequate salaries for the many officials and soldiers so that they could live comfortably. Many civil servants who tried to find ways to increase their income were accused of corruption. The Japanese troops were far away, and it was difficult for those in Chongqing to feel that they were performing useful work. Those who had come from the cities in the east found the living conditions, with limited housing, inflation, a shortage of supplies, and sweltering summertime heat, difficult to bear, and as a result, morale suffered. Some of the Chinese, along with the Americans in Chongqing, criticized Chiang's authoritarian style and his readiness to torture and kill his opponents. Westerners found Chiang's American-educated wife, Soong Meiling, charming, but many saw the taciturn, reserved generalissimo as lacking in moral as well as political leadership. Military commanders considered Chiang too detail oriented and excessively controlling. Yet no one questioned his commitment to China's future, and his diary shows that he was thoughtful and even self-critical in assessing his own judgments and his ability to solve the problems he faced.

The territory ruled by the Nationalists extended beyond Chongqing to all of Sichuan and much of Yunnan. Refugees fled to various places in these two provinces from all parts of China. Some industries were relocated to Yunnan as well Sichuan, making use of workers from Shanghai and elsewhere. Faculty and students escaping Peking University, Tsinghua University, and Nankai University united to set up Southwest Associated University (Xi'nan Lianda) in the Yunnan capital of Kunming.

One of the most popular foreigners in Chongqing was Major General Claire Lee Chennault, who, after retiring from the U.S. Air Force in 1937, went to China to help train Chinese pilots. He led the Flying Tigers, a volunteer squadron of American military pilots, in attacking Japanese planes, and he and Chiang Kai-shek hit it off well. To bring supplies to the Nationalists from the outside, the British and the Chinese cooperated in building the Burma Road, which was completed to Kunming in 1938. In 1942, after the Japanese succeeded in closing the road, the United States helped by flying in goods from India over "the hump," the mountainous areas of Burma, to the Nationalist forces in Yunnan and Sichuan.

In February 1942 President Franklin Roosevelt, considering how to help the Chinese war effort, sent a Chinese-speaking general, Joseph Stilwell, to work with Chiang Kai-shek. Within a week, Stilwell, known as "Vinegar Joe" for his sharp personal style, was publicly referring to Chiang as "peanut," and Chiang reciprocated with disdain for Stilwell. They had a stormy relationship that continued until October 1944, when Roosevelt finally recalled Stilwell at Chiang's insistence. Stilwell tried to get Chiang to send his troops to fight Japan aggressively, but Chiang resisted. Underlying their personal bitterness were their different approaches to fighting the war. Chiang was worn down by two years of fighting the Japanese without success and by the years in Chongqing. He requested that the Americans supply more goods and planes to assist China, and he expressed disappointment that the United States was doing so little to help him. Roosevelt, preoccupied with fighting the war in Europe as well as in the Pacific, did not consider the China theater his highest priority until the end of the war in Europe. Later, as the United States began producing more bombers, Roosevelt, to Chiang's disappointment, placed a higher priority on directly bombing the Japanese islands than on bombing Japanese troops and facilities in China. For a brief time, at the Cairo Conference in November 1943, Chiang was elevated to the position of a partner, meeting with Roosevelt and Churchill, but Stilwell's view of Chiang strengthened Roosevelt's perception that Chiang was refusing to fight the Japanese and saving his strength in case he later had to fight the Communists.

The American officials and analysts sent to work with Chiang during World War II, including John Fairbank, Theodore White, and early postwar writers such as Barbara Tuchman, generally sided with Stilwell and had a low opinion of Chiang Kai-shek and the Nationalists in Chongqing, whom they saw as corrupt and decadent. Later scholars, including Yang Tianshi, Jay

Taylor, and Hans van de Ven, while acknowledging the corruption and decadence in Chongqing, have a more sympathetic perspective, recognizing the difficulties Chiang confronted and his persistence in trying to deal with them.

By 1944, some of the Americans assigned to Chongqing, disappointed with the discouraging scene there, expressed hope in the Chinese Communist forces, though they allowed that they really knew very little about them. In 1937 the Chinese Communists had been a small band struggling to survive, while the Nationalists, after a decade of bringing improvements to the country, were a large national party leading the government. But from 1937 to 1944 the Communists had gained on their Nationalist rivals. Though they had limited military power, they had a message. They were carrying out guerrilla attacks on the Japanese, they were living simply, and they advocated reducing rents, all of which had considerable appeal to those in Yan'an and to patriotic youths in the occupied areas. They had a spirit of optimism that was lacking among the Nationalists. In 1944 the Japanese launched a huge military campaign that tipped the scales even more in the direction of the Communists.

The Ichigo Campaign

By 1944, U.S. air and submarine attacks had put Japan on the defensive in the Pacific War. In response, Japan launched the Ichigo Campaign to wipe out U.S. air bases in China that could be used to launch bombing raids on Japan and to provide an unimpeded transport route for bringing supplies to Chongqing from India and Southeast Asia that could replace the sea route then controlled by U.S. submarines. The campaign lasted from April 1944 to January 1945. It was the largest campaign of the Sino-Japanese War, carried out on a scale comparable to the Normandy invasion in Europe and the German invasion of the Soviet Union. Of the 820,000 Japanese troops then in China, some 510,000 took part in the campaign. They had at their disposal 100,000 horses and 240 planes. Chiang Kai-shek, under pressure from his own supporters and from the United States to do more to stop the Japanese, mobilized more than one million men to respond to the Japanese attacks. Japanese troops in this campaign adopted a scorched-earth policy; as they moved southward, they destroyed granaries and farmland to weaken China's capacity to resist.

In Hengyang (Hunan province), in one of the largest battles of the war, even larger than the battles around Wuhan in 1938, Nationalist troops fought valiantly for three months. In the early stages of the Ichigo Campaign, the Chinese lacked good intelligence. Believing signs of Japanese movements toward Hengyang were a feint, they initially failed to send adequate numbers of troops to the battle. General Stilwell's view was that the Chinese soldiers fought bravely, but the officers were not well trained. Chiang Kai-shek would sometimes call on his commanders directly, giving orders that they could not disobey even if they thought that local conditions warranted a different response. Chiang also did not always notify his high-level officials of the directions he was giving to local commanders, a practice that sometimes created confusion among commanders at different levels. In addition, the Chinese lacked supplies and often were not adequately nourished. As during earlier phases of the war, Japan's soldiers were better trained, better equipped, and more disciplined. Chiang Kai-shek acknowledged that the battles of 1944 were the most disappointing and discouraging of all the campaigns of the war.

By January 1945 the Japanese had accomplished most of their goals for the campaign. They had wiped out several airfields the United States could have used for bombing Japan. They had opened the transport route from Nanning into Southeast Asia and defeated all the Chinese troops that stood in their way. But in their strategic goal of defending Japan from air raids, they failed, for two months after the Ichigo Campaign began, U.S. forces advanced into the Mariana Islands, including Saipan, where they built several airfields that were close enough to Japan to be used for massive bombing attacks. In the Ichigo Campaign the Japanese sacrificed great numbers of men. However, in the end, it was the Allied forces, led by the Americans, conducting air raids and then dropping two atomic bombs, that caused the Japanese to surrender.

The Ichigo Campaign had a far larger impact on China's Nationalists than it had on the Communists because it focused on areas where there were many Nationalist forces and few Communists. The Nationalist forces suffered such heavy losses during these battles that they were in a much weaker position when the Civil War broke out in China in the middle of 1946.

The Japanese Homefront

The war-making capacity of Japan was extraordinary. The Japanese people, living on four islands with a total area that is smaller than Montana, had taken on China, Southeast Asia, and the United States and held them at bay until August 1945. When Japan first put its Zero airplanes into battle over Chongqing, no American warplane was its equal, and U.S. pilots were instructed not to take them on in one-to-one encounters. Not until the Grumman fighter planes became available in September 1943 did the United States have a plane that could outmaneuver the Zero.

Japan had loyal citizens who were willing to sacrifice and do what they were told. Soldiers and citizens at home did not revolt, even when faced with the deaths of family members and crackdowns on free expression of opinion. The government controlled all information in Japan, so the public learned only of the military's glorious successes and did not learn of the horrible deeds committed by Japanese troops, or of their failures. When the Japanese were defeated in the Battle of Midway in 1942, in the midst of the Pacific War, those who had survived the battle were kept isolated and treated in separate hospitals so that the public would not learn of the defeat. In 1945, as air raids were destroying Japan's cities, Japanese propaganda, claiming that Japan's strategy was to draw the enemy closer to its shores so as to defeat it, began to ring hollow. Yet people continued with their daily lives and their daily work.

Some Japanese officials were smart enough to see that Japan would lose the war, but they could not say so publicly. In 1943 and 1944 Japan was still heavily dependent on Manchuria for supplies of coal, iron ore, and bauxite, but in February 1945, when Japanese planners had to adjust to the destruction of their ships bringing supplies from mainland China, they decided that importing soybeans and salt had priority because they would be needed to feed the Japanese population after the war ended. In July 1945, a small group began meeting to begin economic planning for the period after defeat. Under wartime politics, they could not refer to their work as postwar economic reconstruction, so they called themselves the Study Group for Japanese Self-Sufficiency. The day after Japan's surrender, the group held its first publicized meeting and changed the name of the organization to the Committee for Research into Postwar Problems.

On the eve of the Sino-Japanese War, top leaders in Japan did not have the empathy to think through how the Chinese people, with their growing sense of nationalism, would respond to Japan's ambitions for conquest. They did not have the wisdom to see the long-term hostility that would be created by their aggression in China. Nor did they have the understanding needed to properly evaluate how the Americans would respond to the attack on Pearl Harbor. Once Japan began losing the war, Japanese people remained loyal to their country, but their leaders did not have the courage to surrender and thereby stop the massive loss of Japanese lives and the devastation of their cities.

The Legacy

Atrocities committed by Japanese troops during the war became better known to the outside world after the conflict. The atrocities in Nanjing, which had been reported briefly in the West by journalists in 1937 as they occurred, were recounted more fully during the Tokyo War Crimes Trials, and they received even fuller attention after the 1990s. The destruction by the Japanese of entire Chinese villages suspected of harboring guerrillas had been reported during the war and continued to receive attention afterward. Lethal chemical and biological experiments on human subjects, largely Chinese and Korean prisoners, carried out by Japan's Unit 731 in Harbin were publicized by the Chinese, but they were not publicly acknowledged by the Japanese until 1993, when Japan finally admitted the existence of Unit 731 facilities. In 2018 the Japanese government released the names of 3,607 Japanese individuals who had worked in such facilities in Harbin, and the NHK television network aired a program giving a full picture of the experiments and acknowledging their existence.

The Japanese policy of forcing women ("comfort women") from East Asian countries, primarily China and Korea, to go to "comfort stations" where they were required to provide sexual services for Japanese soldiers began to receive wide attention in 1991, and former comfort women who were still alive at the time demanded compensation for their suffering. At the time, some Japanese officers believed it was better for sexual activities to be confined at comfort stations rather than having troops stir up local opposition by raping women in the countryside. After the war, Japanese officials initially denied that the government had played a role, but by 1993 Japanese officials were acknowledging the existence of this program and they had begun to offer compensation to the victims. The Chinese who have collected information about the program have estimated that between 50,000 and 200,000 young women were forced to leave their homes to work in brothels to service Japanese troops. The impact of the publicity about these brutalities put the Japanese people living decades after the war on the defensive for the cruelties committed by Japanese troops during the war.

Impact of the War on China

Chinese losses in the war were immeasurable. Some have estimated that as many as 3 million soldiers and 18 million civilians died and that as many as 100 million people were left homeless.[8] Cities and industries were devastated and yet, because of the subsequent Chinese Civil War, serious rebuilding could not begin until after 1949.

The Japanese invasion had led Chinese people in each region to recognize that to resist the invader it was necessary to cooperate with people in other regions. The invasion and occupation by Japan led to the spread of a strident nationalism, which had blossomed among the urban educated elite in major cities during World War I and then spread to residents of smaller inland cities and peasants in the countryside. Resisting the Japanese required local groups to subordinate themselves to those who represented broader national interests. The war thus strengthened the Nationalists compared with the warlords. The war enabled the Communists to transform themselves from a small group of rebels into a large group of patriots poised to compete for the right to govern China. It gave them the time and space to develop plans for fighting the Civil War and the outlines of the programs they would use for governing China. It provided an opportunity for the Communists to expand their key organizations, the army and the party, which would later serve as a basis for unifying all of China.

In the end, it was the United States that won the war and caused the Japanese to surrender but the Nationalists proclaimed victory over Japan. They could point to their endurance in tying down more than four million Japanese troops. But it was difficult to find other areas of national achievement during the war to which they, as the responsible ruling party, could point with pride. It was difficult to take pride in an army that had been defeated in virtually all major battles. The defeats had taken a toll on Nationalist morale. At the end of the China War, the Nationalists still had far more officials and troops than the Communists, including some who were very dedicated and capable. But even as the party in power, they could not easily match the appeal of the Communists, who advocated lowering rents in order to win the support of ordinary peasants and make them willing to let their sons serve in the Communist army. Nor could the Nationalists easily counter the Communists' demand that taxes be lowered.

When the Communists took power on October 1, 1949, they made use of the visions and organizational structure they had created in Yan'an during the war. After 1949, they placed in important positions those whom they had trained in Yan'an. Yan'an had been, in effect, a training and building ground for the people and the programs that brought to China the first truly national government since the fall of the Qing dynasty. And after being defeated and settling in Taiwan in 1949, the Nationalists similarly drew on the structure they had built and the people who had worked together in Chongqing. Although the Communists killed or discarded in political campaigns many of the remaining high-level Nationalists, China was so large, and the Communists needed so many people, that they put in lower-level positions many individuals who had been trained by the Nationalists before and during the war.

Impact of the War on Japan

In 1945, the dream that began in the later part of the nineteenth century, that Japan could play a leading role in bringing enlightenment and modernization to the countries of Asia, came crashing down and turned into a nightmare. Japan's extraordinary successes, beginning in the 1860s with the building of a modern administrative structure, a modern educational system, and a modern economy, ultimately did not lead to glory but to tragedy, for both Japan and its neighbors. Millions of Japanese died, not only in China but also in Japan. Japanese cities were destroyed and its industries lay in ruin. The occupation of Manchuria had brought earlier economic benefits to Japan, but the 1937–1945 Sino-Japanese War was for Japan an unmitigated disaster. Japan had poured resources into its effort in China, but in the end, it had nothing to bring home but defeated soldiers and settlers looking for work and help.

Ordinary Japanese citizens wanted to believe that their family members who had gone to China to serve their nation were doing their duty and were not doing evil things, and the government's wartime control of the media in Japan had spared families from learning about the horrors their soldiers committed in China. When Japan was forced to surrender, and the emperor told them to endure the unendurable, they blamed the militarists and politicians who had brought on and sustained the war. In the years after the war, they were dejected not only because of the destruction of their country, the poverty, the malnutrition, and the lack of employment opportunities, but also because they believed that the path Japan had been pursuing and to which they had dedicated their lives had failed and was morally wrong. The Japanese people were determined that their country should give up its militarism and follow a path of peace.

Japanese habits of hard work did not end with defeat. The Japanese, who had worked hard before and during the war, began cleaning up the rubble and rebuilding their country. With help from the United States, they turned their swords into plowshares and they built a civilian economy, using the skills that had been nurtured during wartime. Companies that had made lenses for weapons began making cameras for the consumer market. Nissan and Toyota, which had made trucks for the troops, learned how to make commercially viable automobiles. Shipbuilders who had produced warships began building tankers and transport ships. Government institutions that had been building for the war effort worked on building a domestic infrastructure.

The Japanese accepted the need to give up the authoritarian political structure that had supported the military leaders; they were ready to pursue democracy. They accepted the view that the emperor was not sacred. As a country that had been the target of atomic weapons, they were determined not to pursue atomic weapons. They decided that they would undertake political modernization, following the Western democratic countries, and would cooperate with other countries to create and sustain a peaceful world.

The Japanese who survived World War II wanted to take pride in their friends and relatives who had been willing to make sacrifices for what they thought would bring good results for other people as well as for themselves.

They wanted to think of themselves as good people, doing good things not only for themselves and their families and friends but also for the cause of world peace, and they were willing to make sacrifices to do those good things.

~:~

The Second Sino-Japanese War ended the Japanese vision that they were an enlightened, advanced nation helping the Chinese to modernize and resist Western imperialism. The vision turned into a nightmare as the Japanese came to be viewed by other nations as well as by the Chinese as ruthless, inhumane aggressors who had brought devastation to China.

Within China, hatred of the Japanese for the cruelties committed by their troops has helped to underpin patriotism and national unity. During the Civil War in 1945–1949, the content of many of the complaints about the cruelties committed by Nationalist soldiers overlapped with complaints about cruelties enacted by Japanese soldiers during the Sino-Japanese War. But later, after Taiwan and the mainland reestablished contacts, mainland publicity about Nationalist cruelties decreased. Publicity about Japanese cruelties during World War II in fact increased, beginning in the 1990s. The Sino-Japanese War from 1937 to 1945 inflicted enormous tragedies on the Japanese but even more tragedies on the Chinese, tragedies that have continued to shape Chinese attitudes toward Japan.

CHAPTER NINE

The Collapse of the Japanese Empire and the Cold War, 1945–1972

IN 1945 JAPAN lost not only the war but also its colonial empire, and it began to shrink back to the size it was in 1894, prior to the Sino-Japanese War. Manchuria became part of China, Korea became independent, and Taiwan became Chinese. More than 100 million people were relocated, mostly to their ancestral homes. Japanese people returned from China and elsewhere in Asia to their four home islands. Many of the Chinese who, during World War II, had escaped the Japanese and found refuge in China's southwestern and northwestern regions, and overseas, returned to the regions in China where their parents had lived. The new national governments began to rule within their respective geographical boundaries, and adjustments in national identity began to follow.

In 1950, as these massive relocations were tapering off, the Korean War broke out, reorienting Asian international relations to boundaries drawn by the Cold War, binding China with the Soviet Union and Japan with the United States, and splitting the governance of Taiwan from that of mainland China.

In the three decades after World War II both China and Japan underwent some of the most dramatic changes in their histories. The governments formed in China after 1949 when the Chinese Civil War ended and in Japan after 1952 when the Allied Occupation was over not only had different boundaries than those before the world war but also different governmental structures and national goals.

In 1949 the victorious Communists reunified China for the first time since the end of the imperial era in 1911 and established a national structure different from both that of imperial China and that of the Guomindang. China underwent many domestic changes when it established communist structures following its 1949 alliance with the Soviet Union. In 1953 it introduced economic planning and then undertook wrenching mobilization of its people during the Great Leap Forward program and the Cultural Revolution, both of which devastated the country and were ultimately abandoned. In 1969 China fought a border war with the Soviet Union and initiated a comprehensive opening to the West for the first time in its history.

The Allied Occupation that ruled Japan from 1945 to 1952 guided the most comprehensive reorganization and reorientation of a nation ever undertaken by an occupying force. Japan abandoned militarism, empowered democratic institutions, reoriented its economy, and revised its educational system. Beginning in the 1950s Japan strengthened its links to the global economy and launched the world's first rapid industrialization, setting the pattern for the spread of rapid industrialization to Korea, Taiwan, and mainland China, that brought dramatic improvements in the standard of living.

During the Cold War, between 1949 and 1972, China and Japan had few contacts. However, Chinese and Japanese merchants and leaders representing their changing governments managed to keep channels open between their two countries, channels that after 1972 provided a means for the two countries to develop the closest relations in their history.

The Collapse of Japanese Imperialism

The Japanese defeat not only ended Japanese imperialism but also its imperial ambitions. World War II saw the end of many colonial empires, but Japan had had far more colonial servants, soldiers, and settlers than any other country. During the war, some 6.9 million of Japan's 72 million people—3.7 million soldiers and 3.2 million civilians—were living abroad. Nor had any other imperial power penetrated so deeply into its colonies, with such thorough involvement in all aspects of life, as Japan had in Taiwan, Korea, and Manchuria. In the two-thirds of China that Japan occupied during World War II, it exercised far tighter control than the Western powers exercised in the distant colonies that they occupied.

Similar to the Chinese public's reaction in 1895 following the First Sino-Japanese War, the Japanese public in 1945 was stunned that their country had suffered such a stunning defeat. Just as the Chinese before 1895 had had no doubts about the superiority of Chinese civilization, the Japanese public, proud of their nation's victories over China and Russia and informed by a controlled press, was supremely confident of Japan's role as the leader of Asia—until the air raids and bombs began devastating their country in 1945. China's defeat in 1895 had forced the Chinese to recognize that their imperial system was no longer viable, and Japan's defeat in 1945 forced the Japanese to recognize that their military-dominated imperialism was no longer viable. The Japanese, like the Chinese, underwent a jarring readjustment as their proud self-image disintegrated. And as China after 1895 had learned about the new world from Japan, the country that had defeated it, Japan after 1945 learned about the new world from the United States, the country that had defeated it.

By August 1945 the imperialist Japanese, who only shortly before had dominated top positions of power in China, Korea, and Taiwan, were suddenly being told what to do. They had been the victimizers, proud soldiers and settlers, but now, defeated, they became the victims, refugees and supplicants. In China the currency that had been used by Japanese residents was no longer valid and the Japanese living there were almost immediately impoverished, many reduced to selling their clothing in an effort to get enough to eat.

Resettlement and the Narrowing of Japanese Identity

The end of Japanese imperialism brought a narrower definition of what it meant to be Japanese. By the 1920s after their incorporation into the Japanese empire, the people in Taiwan and Korea came to be regarded as Japanese citizens, and in Manchuria, if they were not regarded as Japanese citizens, at least they were Japanese subjects, part of the Japanese empire. Educated youths in Taiwan, Korea, and Manchuria attended Japanese-led schools, used the Japanese language, studied Japanese history; in Taiwan and Korea, they were given Japanese names. The Japanese had come to accept a broader, more cosmopolitan definition of what it meant to be "Japanese," a definition that included both Taiwanese and Korean people. Some members of these groups felt that they were treated as second-class citizens; nonetheless they were regarded as second-class Japanese citizens.

After Japan's defeat in 1945, in accordance with the Potsdam Agreement signed by three of the Allied powers, Great Britain, the United States, and the Soviet Union, Koreans, Taiwanese, and residents of Manchuria were no longer considered Japanese. The classification "Japanese" was narrowed to include only those whose ancestors had been Japanese and who had lived on one of Japan's four main islands or on one of its smaller islands before the Sino-Japanese War of 1894–1895. People living in Korea became Koreans and people living in Manchuria and Taiwan became Chinese. The Korean-Japanese and Taiwanese-Japanese people living in Japan became foreign residents of Japan.

Most of the Japanese in the three provinces of Manchuria (Heilongjiang, Liaoning, and Jilin) had been living in the northern province of Heilongjiang next to the Russian border, and at the end of the war they surrendered to the Russians. Some tried to run away and others committed suicide. Approximately 600,000 Japanese prisoners were taken across the border into Siberia, where many of them performed manual labor on construction projects. Russian officials estimated that during the next several years 60,000 Japanese prisoners died, but Japan estimated that a far higher number died or were missing. Between 1947 and 1949 some 450,000 Japanese prisoners in the Soviet Union were allowed to return to Japan. Survivors returning from Russia recalled not only the freezing climate but also the inhumane living conditions and the cruelty of their captors.

Because soldiers were given priority for space on ships returning to Japan, few Japanese civilians, most of whom had been living in Manchuria, had an opportunity to leave China before May 1946, when the United States began supplying ships to bring Japanese civilians back to their homeland. Amid food shortages and without any income after Japan's surrender, the Japanese civilians awaiting an opportunity to board a ship and return home had to struggle to survive. It has been estimated that as many as 200,000 Japanese civilians in China died while waiting to return to Japan. When Nationalist troops gained control over most of southern Manchuria in late 1946, Chiang Kai-shek cooperated with U.S. troops in assisting Japanese civilians to return to Japan. By the end of 1946 approximately 1,492,000 Japanese had returned to Japan, and by the end of the following year 3,758 more had returned. Repatriation continued until August 1948, but an estimated 60,000 Japanese, mostly children of mixed marriages, remained in China after 1949. Between 1949 and 1953 few returned to Japan, but in 1953 an estimated 26,000 returned.[1] Between August 1945 and December 1946, 6.7 million Japanese soldiers and civilians, mostly from China, but also from Southeast Asia, Korea, and Taiwan, returned to Japan.[2]

Some compassionate Chinese families supplied food and shelter to the needy Japanese in Manchuria, and some adopted Japanese children who either had been separated from their parents or whose parents had died. Thousands of Japanese widows, widowers, and single men and women married Chinese partners. Some Japanese children remained with their Chinese families even after the end of 1946, by which time most of the Japanese survivors in Manchuria had been repatriated.

When the once-stranded Japanese settlers finally found a place on a ship and returned to their country, the situation they faced at home was similar to the situation that Chinese refugees faced on returning to their home areas. The Japanese economy was depressed, the food supply was inadequate, and returnees struggled to find a place to live and a way to earn a living. Like the Chinese Hakka in earlier centuries, who after defeat had escaped to the south and settled in hilly, less-fertile land that was not already occupied by local farmers, many of the repatriated Japanese seeking to grow food to survive settled initially in hilly or mountainous areas of marginal productivity. Most settled on the southern island of Kyushu or in the southern part of the main island of Honshu, where their families had lived before setting off for Manchuria. Some returnees crowded into the homes of relatives and friends. Many Japanese relatives of the refugees, while struggling amid the postwar shortages to find food and housing for themselves, nonetheless tried to help the returnees. But others were less enthusiastic about sharing what little they had with relatives, acquaintances, and former coworkers, some of whom they had not seen and had rarely heard from for years or even decades.

Even after 1947 when, with wheat imported from the United States, food shortages in Japan began to ease, psychological strains between returnees and locals who had not traveled abroad did not disappear. Japan is sufficiently homogeneous that small differences sometimes loom large. To many local people, the returnees did not fully share their homogeneous culture, and they were regarded as outsiders. As Japan began expanding its global contacts, some of the talented, more cosmopolitan returnees connected easily with foreigners, but others suffered from being treated as outsiders.

The experiences of Japanese returnees, both while they had lived abroad and as they tried to adjust to local society in Japan, became popular topics for novels, short stories, television dramas, and movies.

When the Communists came to power in China in 1949, an estimated 34,000 Japanese still remained in China, mostly in the Northeast. Some Japanese settlers who had developed deep local roots in Chinese society chose to remain in China and work with the Chinese. Others who had technical skills and knowledge judged important for keeping former Japanese factories operating at least for some years were not given exit permits.[3] The Communist Chinese Air Force, for example, which later fought in Korea, was established by Japanese Army Air Corps officers who had surrendered to the Chinese.

At the end of the war, about two million people originally from Taiwan and Korea were still living and working in Japan. Some of them had gone to Japan of their own free will, but many were men who had been forced into manual labor on construction projects or in mines, replacing those who had been drafted into the military. Chinese, Korean, and some Western laborers referred to this work as "slave labor" and later wrote of their experiences toiling long hours under difficult conditions. But because of the unsettled situation in their homelands, some Taiwanese and Korean workers chose not to return home, and some Koreans who went back to Korea later returned to Japan. Eventually, roughly half of the forced laborers returned to Taiwan or Korea, where they faced the same problems as the Japanese who returned to the land of their ancestors.

In the heyday of Japanese imperialism, foreign workers had been regarded as Japanese, but after Japan's defeat, when employment opportunities were limited and the definition of what it meant to be Japanese changed, they faced difficulties being accepted as Japanese. Most of the foreign workers who were in Japan were not granted Japanese citizenship until decades later, when the economy had been revived and Japanese policy became more generous.

After 1945, the Koreans and Taiwanese who had remained in their own countries also faced problems of identity as they ceased being Japanese subjects. Because Taiwan had been a Japanese colony for half a century, all those under the age of sixty had received a Japanese education, and all Koreans under the age of forty-five had also received a Japanese education.

Many had become accustomed to Japanese banking and commercial practices. Because Japanese rule had penetrated so deeply, culturally the young Koreans and Taiwanese had become Japanese. Many had improved their standard of living, and some had worked closely with Japanese settlers and had Japanese friends. In Taiwan, the Japanese military had not been a prominent presence for more than four decades, and in Korea the Japanese military did not play as large a role as it did in Manchuria. Many Koreans and Taiwanese maintained contacts with their Japanese friends after 1945.

Before Japan took over Taiwan in 1895, Taiwan had been a Chinese prefecture and, for a few years, a province, but not a separate nation, and there was no nationalist rallying point against the Japanese occupation in Taiwan as there was in Korea. When Chinese mainlanders fled to Taiwan to escape the Civil War and the rise of communism, they renamed the streets and localities that had Japanese names, giving them new Chinese names instead. After February 1946, Japanese-language movies were no longer allowed; only Chinese-language movies could be shown, even though many local people could not understand them. After the Chinese Nationalist troops arrived in Taiwan, the Taiwanese, who had absorbed Japanese culture, were ruled by Chinese troops and government officials who introduced Chinese culture in the schools. In Taiwan—and in Korea—life was especially difficult for those who had worked with the Japanese during the war, for they were regarded as unpatriotic collaborators, and in some cases they were publicly criticized or even killed.

Some of the Japanese people who stayed in China after 1949 later expressed a wish to return home. After 1946 when the Civil War broke out in China, repatriating Japanese citizens was not a high priority for the Chinese. But after 1952, when contacts between the Chinese and Japanese governments began to increase, a key issue for the Japanese government was the return of its citizens still living in China. Liao Chengzhi, the leading Japan specialist among high-level Chinese officials, led talks with Japan on this issue in February and March 1953 (see Biographies of Key Figures). In the six months following the talks, approximately 20,000 Japanese were repatriated. In July 1955, when relations between the two countries improved, Japan asked China for information about 40,000 Japanese individuals believed to be missing in China. Information was provided about some of them, and many were allowed to return to Japan.

Most of the Japanese who returned from China after 1949 had learned the Chinese language and had found some way to earn a living in China. By the time they returned to Japan, there were better economic opportunities in their home country than there had been in 1945 and 1946, when Japanese returnees first began to arrive back home. However, culturally they were more Chinese than Japanese, and they often had even more difficult adjustment problems than those who had returned right after the war. Some found work in Japanese companies that wanted to carry on trade with China, where they could make use of their language skills, their knowledge of Chinese business practices, and their personal contacts in China.

Clusters of administrators from Mantetsu settled in Kyushu where they worked in regional planning. Scholars from Toa Dobun Shoin in Shanghai built up Chinese studies programs at Aichi University. Many who had been administrators became the backbone of Sino-Japanese friendship associations.

After Japan's surrender, the Chinese who, in the late 1930s, had escaped from the advancing Japanese troops and sought refuge in the countryside and in the Southwest, beyond the reach of the Japanese imperialists, began to move back to their original home regions. Most had become refugees during the first years of the war, but others had fled later, when the Japanese began bombing Shanghai and Chongqing and during the 1944 Ichigo Campaign, when Japanese troops marched into Henan, Hunan, and Guangxi. Most of the refugees were desperately poor, and many died of starvation. Many of the refugees had lived in areas with very different cultures in which they never felt at home.

There are no reliable figures on how many Chinese relocated after the end of the war, but the number was in the tens of millions. Some have estimated that it was as high as 100 million. Because few could make use of the trains, and highways were not yet built, most refugees walked, either carrying their few belongings by hand or pulling them on small carts.

The Race to Take Over Japanese Facilities in Manchuria

In the weeks after Japan's formal surrender on September 3, 1945, Japanese commanders throughout China surrendered to nearby Chinese officials and turned over Japanese facilities to the Chinese. In a few cases, high-level

Japanese commanders had known their Chinese counterparts when they were fellow students at military academies in Japan, and such former schoolmates found it easy to work with one another. In general, Japanese soldiers remained disciplined after their surrender. In some communities, because there were no Chinese troops in the area, they were asked to stay on for some weeks, or even some months, to maintain order. In Shanxi, former warlord Yan Xishan hired more than a thousand Japanese troops to serve on his staff, in the hope that the Japanese could help him resist the growing power of the Chinese Communist forces.

After the end of World War II, the Nationalists and Communists were unable to maintain the United Front they had formed against their common enemy during the war. Both sides began maneuvering to take over Japanese facilities and to position themselves for a possible civil war, which others still hoped could be avoided. In December 1945 the United States sent General George Marshall to Chongqing, where he hosted negotiations between Mao Zedong and Chiang Kai-shek in an effort to facilitate the formation of a coalition government and avoid a civil war. It quickly became clear that the two sides could not work together.

Within weeks after the end of the war, the victorious troops— Communist, Nationalist, and Russian—raced into Manchuria, where they vied to gain control of the facilities that the Japanese had built in the four decades since 1905. Manchuria was China's largest industrial base and the location with the largest assemblage of modern military weapons anywhere in China. As soon as World War II ended, Mao Zedong, acutely aware of his army's shortage of modern military equipment, directed Communist troops in northern and northwestern China to march at top speed to the Northeast, to take control of stockpiles of Japanese weapons and industrial equipment that they could use if war were to break out with the Nationalists. In addition to larger machinery, it has been estimated that the Nationalists acquired between 350,000 and 750,000 rifles in Manchuria.[4]

Although the Nationalist troops, centered in southwestern China, were far from the Northeast, the United States helped transport them to the Northeast and to China's east coast by air, by ship, and by rail. Officials in Washington specifically directed that U.S. forces were not to take part in military clashes or to provide military assistance to either side. However,

Chiang Kai-shek was the official ruler of China, and some American leaders, worried about the threat of communism, found ways to assist him.

Both Chinese Communists and Nationalists accused Russian troops of stripping Japanese factories to take industrial equipment across the border into Russia. The Russian troops recognized the Nationalists as the official government of China and allowed them to occupy key locations and to acquire some Japanese equipment. The Chinese Communists hoped that Soviet troops, as fellow Communists, would side with them. Some Soviet troops did provide assistance to the Chinese Communist troops that were establishing their bases in the rural areas. But the Russians had worked with the Nationalists since the early 1920s, beginning with Sun Yat-sen, and Stalin still thought the Nationalists might win the war in China, so he continued to work with the Nationalists until the Russian troops withdrew from the Northeast in the spring of 1946.

Although Japanese military equipment was taken by the various armies, enough of the former Japanese industrial base and infrastructure remained that for many years after 1949 the Northeast was the industrial base for the Chinese Communists. After 1949 the factories were operated by Chinese workers who had learned their skills under Japanese leadership as well as by some Japanese technicians and managers who stayed on in China until Chinese replacements could be trained. Even Mao Zedong expressed admiration for the Japanese state ownership of and planning for the industrial development of Manchuria. In 1949 Liao Chengzhi asked Takasaki Tatsunosuke (see Biographies of Key Figures), former chairman of the Manchurian Industrial Development Company, for a list of Japanese firms that could supply materials that could be used in the former Japanese factories in Manchuria, along with a price list for such materials. In 1952 China's Northeast accounted for about half of China's total industrial production. During the First Five-year Plan, 1953–1957, a high proportion of China's key industrial projects, including those that received Soviet help, were in China's Northeast, building on the original Japanese industrial base. The area remained China's main heavy industrial center until some years after reform and opening began in 1978, when industry in the Shanghai and Guangdong areas began to grow rapidly, soon achieving a much larger production scale than that of the factories in the Northeast.

The Chinese Civil War and Reunification, 1945–1949

Had it not been for the Japanese invasion, the Nationalists might have defeated the Communists in the mid-1930s. After Chiang Kai-shek was forced to form the United Front with the Communists to resist Japan in December 1936, the Nationalists could no longer attack the Communists. Once the Nationalists retreated to the Southwest, it was difficult for them to sustain national support, as they could do nothing to protect people in other parts of China. The Communists, based in China's northwest, used this opportunity when they were not under attack by the Nationalists, to build a tight organization, gain experience in carrying out land reform, hone a clear message to win public support, train an army that would be prepared to fight the Nationalists, and forge a general agreement among their followers about what policies should be pursued after their conquest of all of China.

During some of the early battles of the Chinese Civil War in Northeast China, the Nationalists fought well. They began with more weapons and had some well-trained troops. Gradually, however, the Communists gained in strength as their troops won key battles in the Northeast and took over Japanese weapons, supplies, and their industrial base. Chiang chose to fight rather than to concentrate on bringing the economy under control. But the resultant wild inflation, shortage of goods, and corruption among the Nationalist troops trying to provide for themselves and their families in this chaotic period alienated the general public. Because they promised land reform, the Communists had greater appeal to peasants, who hoped their families might acquire land if the Communists won the Civil War. By recruiting youths who were alienated by the corruption of the Nationalists and hopeful of gaining land, the Communists gained many soldiers who were more dedicated to the fight than the Nationalist soldiers, some of whom had been recruited by force.

After capturing the bases in the Northeast, Communist forces captured Beiping and then moved southward toward the Yangtze. By the time they crossed the Yangtze, they had gained sufficient strength that the Nationalist forces could no longer stop their advance. On October 1, 1949, even before their troops reached the Southwest, the Communists declared the founding of the People's Republic. Thereafter, they consolidated their power, and through campaigns to wipe out counterrevolutionaries, they eliminated the landlord class and distributed land to poor peasants. By building up party and youth-league organizations of loyal followers, they were able to unify the country for the first time since the collapse of the imperial order in 1911.

Japan's Reorientation from Allied Occupation, 1945–1952

American leaders, who dominated the Allied Occupation of Japan, believed that to prevent another world war, they had to help other countries make deep changes to remove the causes of war and create a basis for pursuing peace. From September 1945, when General Douglas MacArthur arrived to lead the Occupation, until April 1952, the Allied Occupation forces introduced changes in Japan's political, economic, and education systems and controlled Japan's foreign policy.

At the end of World War II, leaders in the United States, by far the strongest nation in the world at the time, believed that a prosperous country would not need to attack other countries. In 1945 many Americans wanted to punish Japan for its sneak attack on Pearl Harbor, for its cruelty to American soldiers during the Bataan Death March in the Philippines, and for its aggressive behavior in Asia and the western Pacific. But unlike the Chinese, who had suffered during eight years of Japanese occupation, Americans had not directly experienced Japanese occupation and the U.S. civilian population had had few personal contacts with Japanese soldiers. America's hatred of the Japanese enemy was not as deep, long lasting, or personal as China's.

After considering the issue, Occupation officials concluded that for the Japanese public to accept the decision to surrender and follow the Allied forces' guidelines, they needed the support of the emperor. Therefore, Occupation officials did not dwell on the question of the emperor's responsibility for the war. The emperor renounced his divinity, announced the surrender, and publicly appeared with General MacArthur, showing the Japanese public that he supported the Occupation.

American leaders had concluded that Germany had been punished too severely for war-making after World War I, resulting in a powerful German drive for revenge that resulted in its initiation of World War II. Hence, after

World War II they felt that they should be less vengeful in their occupation of Germany and Japan. In Japan, the Allied powers gave directions, but the government was administered by the Japanese. This required close collaboration. As a whole, the Japanese were orderly, accepted the directives of the Allied Occupation, and worked to carry them out. When U.S. soldiers began arriving in Japan, the Japanese found that they were a surprisingly friendly group that gave out candy and chewing gum to children.

Allied Occupation leaders believed that to prevent Japan from ever again pursuing militarism, a thorough attack on the root causes of war was necessary. They believed that democracies did not make war, so Japan was "forced to be free" to develop democratic institutions, including a democratically elected Diet, a free press, enterprises free of government control, and labor unions, as well as parent-teacher associations and textbooks that promoted democracy. To reduce the power of landlords and build up a rural base for democracy, the Occupation carried out land reform, dividing up the land formerly owned by large landlords. To strengthen democracy, the Occupation worked with Japanese leftists, labor unions, and liberal academics who supported the goals of the Occupation forces. The small number of Communists in Japan had been some of the boldest opponents of Japanese militarism in the 1930s, and they were welcomed as a legal party.

The Allied Occupation was successful in its attack on militarism not only because the Japanese knew it was necessary in order to bring an end to the Occupation but also because Japanese officials and the majority of the Japanese public firmly believed that militarism had brought disaster to Japan, to other countries, and to Japan's relations with other countries. The Occupation thus abolished Japan's military forces, making them illegal. It destroyed factories and closed large companies that produced military equipment. Some Japanese historians joined in criticizing the high concentration of power during the Meiji period, calling it "Meiji absolutism" because it had paved the way for the growth of the militarism that had resulted in suffering for all Asians and had alienated other Asians from Japan.

During the first two years of the Occupation, tens of thousands of Japanese died from starvation. Having lost the colonies that supplied food for Japan, Japanese leaders realized they had to increase exports to earn money to buy food from abroad. To a large extent, the United States replaced Manchuria as the main source of raw materials and soybeans for Japan. In 1951, for example, the United States supplied 34 percent of Japan's iron ore, 71 percent of its coal, and 97 percent of its soybean imports.[5]

The Japanese drew on their wartime experience in guiding the economy, but they chose to introduce indicative planning—setting targets but allowing companies the freedom to decide how to reach their targets— rather than imposing socialist-style government-administered planning. Japanese leaders realized that Japan's reputation for producing low-quality goods would negatively affect their exports, so they paid great attention to what was needed to improve quality, bringing in U.S. specialists and dedicating themselves to experimenting with new techniques. Within several years, Japan had gained a reputation for producing high-quality goods.

In the early years after 1945, Japanese scholars specializing in the study of China criticized some of Japan's leading prewar China specialists, including Naito Konan, who died in 1934, for not having done enough to oppose Japanese aggression in China. After the Occupation ended with a security pact with the United States, many intellectuals and students joined in criticizing the pact because it gave too much support to the military. Although support for Marxism and leftist views gradually weakened as Japan modernized, opposition to militarism, which in the eyes of the public had brought disaster, has remained deep and strong.

The War Crimes Trials

The International Military Tribunal of the Far East, presided over by judges from seven Allied countries, including China, met regularly from May 3, 1946, until sentences were announced on November 12, 1948, on the indictment of twenty-eight class-A war criminals—leaders who had played a role in guiding Japan into committing war crimes and crimes against humanity. One civilian (Prime Minister Hirota Koki) and six generals were hanged, sixteen class-A criminals were sentenced to life imprisonment and two were given shorter sentences, three were found not guilty, and no one was acquitted. In addition, class-B and class-C criminals who had committed conventional war crimes and crimes against humanity were also tried. Eighteen generals accused of being class-B criminals because they had command responsibilities when their troops committed atrocities were tried and found guilty. Some 4,200 class-C officers in lower positions were tried for other atrocities, about 700 of whom were sentenced to death; others were committed to prison for various terms.

Detailed evidence in the trials was presented by witnesses such as Lewis Smythe, a missionary and sociologist in Nanjing at the time of the massacre. Smythe had worked with John Rabe and others in Nanjing to follow closely the atrocities committed by the Japanese at the time. The court also collected evidence on the biological and chemical warfare carried out by Unit 731 on the outskirts of Harbin, where live experiments were conducted on human subjects, some of whom died.

No legal basis existed before World War II for war-crimes trials such as the Nuremberg trials in Germany and the International Military Tribunal in Tokyo, although legal procedures were used for judging who had initiated a war and who had committed atrocities. Volumes of information were collected and carefully analyzed for the Tokyo trials, but the number of cases tried was miniscule compared with the number of atrocities that had been committed during the war. Evidence was collected from more than 400 witnesses, and in excess of 700 affidavits were filed. Major cases were defended by a Western lawyer as well as a Japanese lawyer. Chinese lawyers at the trials strongly criticized the Japanese, but some judges from other countries believed that the Chinese presentations at trial were not well prepared and lacked careful analysis or descriptions of the evidence.

In addition to the trials of major war criminals in Tokyo, other criminals were tried in China and elsewhere. In China, some 883 Japanese individuals were brought to court, 149 were executed, and 350 were found not guilty.[6] At the higher levels of the Chinese government, Chiang Kai-shek and others wished to show that China was living up to high international professional standards. Unlike Chinese presentation at the War Crimes Trials in Tokyo, the evidence used in China was more carefully presented. Some of the Japanese who were brought to trial in China were acquitted. At the local levels in China, however, there were many cases of extralegal retribution carried out against Japanese and local collaborators.

Many Japanese people agreed that the attacks in Nanjing and the experiments on human subjects by Unit 731 were atrocities, but they also believed that the trials were based not on universal standards but on "victor's justice," for only Japanese defendants were tried. Westerners who, in the view of the Japanese, had also committed crimes, such as ordering the firebombing of civilians in Japanese cities and the dropping of two atom bombs, were not tried. Furthermore, the Japanese who examined the proceedings felt that a disproportionate percentage of the most serious punishments were handed down for crimes against Western victims, not Asian victims. After the trials had dragged on for more than two years, stories began to appear in the Japanese media of the hardships suffered by the Japanese who were being tried. In 1953, the year after the Occupation ended, prison letters from war criminals began to be published. Some of the Japanese public sympathized with those officials whom they claimed had been caught in difficult circumstances over which they had little control. One of the seven justices, the Indian judge Radhabinod Pal, considered the entire war crimes trial invalid because there had been no rules set for wartime behavior prior to the trials and there was no universal standard of justice. In general, the Japanese public did not try to hide or belittle the crimes, or to justify the atrocities, but Justice Radhabinod Pal's judgment received great attention from the Japanese, who resented the imposition of victor's justice that punished only Japanese and not others who committed war crimes.

In 1969, the Ministry of Health and Welfare sent the names of the class-A war criminals to the Yasukuni Shrine in Tokyo. In October 1978 the new chief priest at the shrine, Matsudaira Nagayashi, decided that they should be enshrined. Emperor Hirohito was so upset about this decision that he never again visited the shrine. In 1978, China and Japan were working to establish formal diplomatic relations, and three years later the Chinese began protesting about the enshrinement. From 1946 to 1948, at the time of the War Crimes Trials, the Chinese people were so preoccupied with their own Civil War that they had not paid much attention to the trials. Later, when the Chinese publicized information about the Nanjing Massacre and Unit 731 biological experiments, they drew on evidence presented at the trials. In 2006, when Chinese films on World War II were popular in China, one widely viewed Chinese film, *Tokyo Trial* (*Dongjing shenpan*), called attention to the evidence presented during the trials.

The Cold War and the "Reverse Course," 1947

Occupation officials wanted to destroy the Japanese military and its centralized military-industrial complex, which could support another war effort.

Until 1947, the Allied Occupation concentrated on breaking up large companies, especially those that might have been able to support war making and did little to aid Japan's economic recovery. In 1947, however, when the Cold War divisions had become sharper, Occupation officials began to regard Japan as a potential partner against the Soviet Union. After 1947, conservative Japanese officials who had taken part in World War II but supported the new U.S.-Japan alliance were allowed to return to office. After the Korean War broke out in 1950, a National Police Reserve was established in Japan to free up the U.S. Occupation forces to fight in Korea. And in 1954 Japan's Self-Defense Force was established—in effect, an army that could be used only to defend Japan, not to attack other countries—and within a decade it had 200,000 troops.

The strategic rationale for this "reverse course" in Occupation policy was spelled out by George Kennan, America's leading Cold War strategist, who was dispatched to Japan in March 1948 to evaluate U.S. policy on Japan. Kennan wrote a forty-two-page report based on his investigation, and his policy proposals for Japan were approved by President Truman in October 1948. Kennan believed that if the people of Western Europe and Japan continued to suffer from poverty, they could become prey to Communist advances. By the time his proposals were approved, the Communists had already taken over Czechoslovakia and blockaded Berlin, and the Chinese Communists were poised to win the Civil War in China.

The central goal of Kennan's Japan policy was to create a strong stable economy. He concluded that the Occupation policy of destroying large Japanese businesses should be reversed. With strong economies, he believed, Japan and Europe would become pillars in a global free-market economy. When Kennan was later asked to reflect on his career years, he said that along with his part in launching the Marshall Plan for Europe's recovery, his role in supporting the reverse course in Japan was the "most significant contribution" he had made in his service to the U.S. government.

By 1947 the United States was sending some of its excess grain to Japan to ease the food shortage there, and to address Japan's shortage of cotton for making clothing, the United States, which had just made advances in the production of synthetic fibers, supplied Japan with synthetic fiber technology. By manufacturing more goods, Japan was beginning to generate income to pay for the food and other supplies that the United States was exporting to Japan. U.S. industrial firms began transferring manufacturing skills to Japan, just as U.S. and Japanese firms would do in China three decades later. Japanese industry had been decimated by the massive bombing during the war, but the business and technology skills that it had developed since the Meiji period survived, and Japanese businesses began to grow quickly.

Although the Occupation authorities had discouraged Japan from greatly increasing trade with China for fear that it might pull Japan into the Communist economic order, Kennan did not believe it was necessary to oppose trade with China. In Kennan's view, China was a very poor and divided country, and at the time China was not considered a threat to the United States. Kennan, a Russia specialist, was convinced that even if China were to join with the Soviet Union, the forces of Chinese nationalism were so strong that an alliance with the Soviet Union would not last. John Foster Dulles, who was directing U.S. policy, did not agree. He believed that Communist China was already allied with the Soviets and that the United States should not assist China's economic growth.

The Korean War and the Freeze in Sino-Japanese Relations, 1948–1972

Just as Korea had been at the vortex of the struggles between Japan and China during the 1870s and 1880s, during the Sino-Japanese War of 1894–1895, and during the Russo-Japanese War of 1904–1905, it was at the center of the power struggles in Asia after World War II. But this time the conflict was not just between Japan and China or Japan and Russia. Now Korea was the focus in a struggle between the entire Communist world and the entire capitalist world.

At the end of World War II the United States firmly refused Stalin's request to divide Japan, as Germany was divided, into separate occupation zones. But on August 10, 1945, as the war's end approached, U.S. officials agreed that Soviet forces in Korea could occupy the area north of the 38th parallel, and the United States would occupy the area below the 38th parallel. The establishment of South Korea as a separate nation with its own government was officially declared on August 15, 1948, three years after the Japanese surrender, and the government of North Korea was officially declared on September 9, 1948. Shortly thereafter the Soviet Army left Korea and returned home, and in June 1949 the U.S. Army pulled out as well and returned either to the United States or to its bases in Japan.

Under Soviet guidance, Kim Il Sung became the leader of North Korea, and under U.S. guidance Syngman Rhee became the leader of South Korea. Kim Il Sung had been in Manchuria with the Chinese guerrilla forces fighting the Japanese, but after 1941, as pressures from the Japanese Army in Manchuria grew stronger, Kim had retreated with the Chinese guerillas to the Soviet Union, where he spent the rest of World War II. Syngman Rhee was a Christian who had studied under Woodrow Wilson at Princeton and married an Austrian woman. Before assuming the leadership of South Korea, he had spent only a few years of his life living in Korea. U.S. officials considered him their ally. In the absence of foreign troops, Kim Il Sung and Syngman Rhee each began to strengthen his military in the hope of reuniting Korea under his leadership. The United States was reluctant to send tanks and other heavy equipment to Syngman Rhee for fear that he might invade the North.

At the time, North Korea had a much larger industrial base than South Korea because of the electric power stations on the Yalu River and the chemical and related industries built by the Japanese during their occupation, whereas South Korea was primarily agricultural. Since educated Koreans had learned the Japanese language and been taught about Japanese culture, some had good relations with the Japanese. Koreans such as Park Chong-Hee, who had served in the Japanese military in Manchuria, had been deeply influenced by Japan. But because the Koreans, unlike the Taiwanese, had had their own national identity prior to being colonized and occupied by Japan, many had been far more resistant to Japan than the Taiwanese and they remained deeply ambivalent, respecting Japanese successes, enjoying Japanese culture and Japanese friendships, while hating Japanese domination.

In a speech on January 12, 1950, U.S. Secretary of State Dean Acheson did not include South Korea among the nations within the U.S. defense perimeter. It is likely that, owing to this, China and Russia assumed that the United States would not support South Korea if the North were to invade. By the spring of 1950 Kim Il Sung, who had received Stalin's permission to invade South Korea, was preparing his troops to cross the 38th parallel.

By April 1950, with Mao Zedong's approval, more than 47,700 ethnic Korean-Chinese in the Chinese Army, many of whom had fought the Japanese during World War II, had been transferred to North Korea to support Kim Il Sung.[7] Mao had already assured Kim Il Sung that by early 1950, once the Communists had basically subdued all of China, Chinese troops would be available to provide assistance if it were needed.

When Mao Zedong met Kim Il Sung in May 1950 to discuss a possible military conflict on the Korean Peninsula, Mao raised the possibility that the United States might make use of some 70,000 Japanese "mercenary" troops to defend South Korea, but he did not expect that U.S. troops would become involved. Mao was more worried about the revival of Japanese militarism. The Sino-Soviet Treaty of February 1950 had addressed the concern that Japanese troops might again invade China, but a conflict with U.S. troops in Korea was not anticipated.

On June 25, 1950, troops from the North crossed the 38th parallel with heavy military equipment. They advanced rapidly to Seoul, which they took on June 27, destroying tens of thousands of southern troops along the way. President Truman, who feared that, if he did not act, the Soviet Union would take all of Korea and then move on to an ever-broadening war, realized that U.S. intervention would require a major commitment of troops. In what he described as the most difficult decision of his life, even more difficult than whether to use the atomic bomb on Japan, Truman decided to seek the support of the United Nations for an immediate deployment of troops in Korea. He and his advisers believed the failure of the League of Nations to respond strongly to the Japanese invasion of Manchuria in the 1930s had allowed Japan to continue to expand and eventually to start the Pacific War. In addition to seeking a UN response in Korea, Truman also sent the U.S. Navy's Seventh Fleet to the Taiwan Strait, thus preventing the Chinese Communists from attacking Taiwan. On July 7, the UN agreed that United Nations command forces would be sent to Korea and U.S. troops began arriving in Korea.

That same day, Mao Zedong announced the creation of a Northeast China Border Defense Army, in case Chinese troops were needed for the war. In August, Mao decided that if he sent troops into Korea he would send them as "volunteers," rather than as Chinese troops, to reduce the risk that the United States would declare war on China. China expected that the war would quickly come to an end.

By September 15, UN forces began arriving in Inchon, and two weeks later they recaptured Seoul. On October 3 Zhou Enlai asked the Indian ambassador to China, K. M. Panikkar, to announce to the world that if UN forces moved north across the 38th parallel, China would enter the war. George Kennan and other officials advised against allowing the UN troops to cross the 38th parallel because the risk of China's or the Soviets' entry into the war was too great. General Douglas MacArthur and other American leaders, overly confident, believed that Zhou was bluffing, and UN troops immediately proceeded to cross the 38th parallel. Beginning on October 19, some 200,000 Chinese troops crossed the Yalu River into North Korea. Within months, the UN troops were pushed back below the 38th parallel and Seoul fell to North Korean and Chinese troops. The UN troops advanced again, and a stalemate was reached. Each side still hoped to push the enemy out of the Korean Peninsula. It was more than two years later, on July 27, 1953, when the two sides signed an armistice agreement and officially ended the fighting. It is estimated that 900,000 Chinese, 520,000 North Korean, and 400,000 UN soldiers, mostly South Koreans, died or were wounded in the war.[8]

Before the United States decided to seek UN support to fight in Korea, China had been preparing to invade Taiwan, but after the Korean War broke out and the United States dispatched the Seventh Fleet to the coast of Taiwan, it became impossible for the Chinese Communists to take Taiwan. Thus, as a result of the Korean War, Taiwan was able to remain separate from China.

Although Japanese soldiers did not take part in the war, as China had feared, Japan's ports served as a staging area for the UN troops. The revival of the Japanese economy was greatly strengthened by the UN's procurement of Japanese products for use by its troops in Korea, the military equipment repairs carried out in Japan, and the "relief and rehabilitation" of UN soldiers granted time off in Japan. Even more important, the Korean War strengthened the willingness of the United States to support the Japanese economy. Japanese businesspeople were welcomed in the United States to study U.S. technology and management skills. In contrast, the Korean War was a severe drain on China's resources. It also led the U.S. government to ban trade with China, freeze Chinese assets in the United States, and block other countries from helping Chinese industry.

Taiwan's Transformation from Colony to Business Partner, 1947–1972

Once the Japanese refugees had returned from China, pragmatic Japanese leaders tried to keep trade relations open with the mainland, but U.S. officials, firmly opposed to the Communist bloc, placed stringent limits on Japanese trade with Communist China. Japanese continued their close relationship with Taiwan, however, especially with the local people with whom they had had contacts since Taiwan's colonization in 1895. Japanese leaders also established relations with the "mainlanders" (*waishengren*)—those born outside Taiwan—as members of the Nationalist Army, the Nationalist government, and their allies began arriving in Taiwan in large numbers in 1947, when they were retreating from Communist advances.

After 1949, the mainlanders who had accompanied Chiang Kai-shek to Taiwan made up less than one-third of the island's population. The "locals" (*benshengren*)—those born in Taiwan—were mostly descended from immigrants from Fujian, some of whom had been Ming loyalists, who had arrived during the Qing dynasty. Taiwan's population also included aborigines descended from those who had lived in Taiwan before the arrival of Koxinga; they constituted about 2 percent of the population. The average standard of living and educational standards in Taiwan during the Japanese occupation had risen far above those on the mainland.

Once the mainlanders arrived in Taiwan, they controlled not only the military but also the government. Tensions between the mainlanders and the locals rose quickly. Riots broke out, first in Taipei and then in other cities. On February 28, 1947, after more troops arrived from the mainland to support the Nationalist military already stationed in Taiwan, the Japanese-speaking Nationalist general Chen Yi, who had been sent by Chiang Kai-shek to bring order to Taiwan, imposed a firm crackdown. According to a report by the Executive Yuan in 1992, it is estimated that mainland Nationalist troops killed between 18,000 and 28,000 locals, including most of the individuals capable of providing leadership to resist the new arrivals from the mainland. For decades, the date of the crackdown, "February 28" (Ererba), was a powerful symbol of the locals' hatred of the mainlanders. Even when the Nationalists later executed General Chen Yi, on charges of cooperating with the Communists, it did little to end the deep resentment.

Though some Taiwanese had complained about the Japanese when they occupied Taiwan, after the February 28 Incident, the local population preferred their former Japanese rulers to the recently arrived mainlanders. Showing an appreciation for Japanese culture became a way of indirectly protesting against mainland rule.

Even after the mainlanders arrived in Taiwan, it remained easy for Japanese businesses that had been established in Taiwan before World War II to work with Taiwan's companies. As wages for industrial workers in Japan rose in the 1960s, Japan passed on some of its textile and footwear manufacturing to Taiwan, where wages were lower. Thus Taiwan's industrialization followed soon after the postwar revival of Japanese industry. Some of the Japanese who had lived in Taiwan before the end of World War II remained there and took part in the continuing Taiwan-Japan business network.

The key positions in the Republic of China government on Taiwan and in the military were held by mainlanders. Most mainlanders, both soldiers and officials, looked down on what they saw as "lowly" business careers. Therefore the businesses in Taiwan in the 1950s were virtually all small-scale companies dominated by locals. During the first several years after 1949 and the end of the Chinese Civil War, the standard of living for local businesspeople was generally lower than that of the mainlanders, but as the economy grew, many locals began to succeed in business and to enjoy a standard of living that was higher than that of the mainlanders who were living on officials' salaries.

Japanese businesspeople enjoyed good relations with the Taiwanese in business, and some Japanese political leaders who had worked on the mainland before 1945 were able to establish good contacts with mainlander officials, some of whom they had known on the mainland. Even though their countries had been at war, the Japanese and Chinese who had gone to Taiwan were not necessarily personal enemies. Some Japanese individuals who had served in China shared an appreciation of the same regional mainland cuisine and culture (Zhejiang, Shanghai, or Beijing) as their Taiwan counterparts. The Japanese prime ministers Kishi Nobusuke and Sato Eisaku were among those who had worked on the mainland before 1945 and who maintained relations with political leaders on Taiwan.

Mainland Chinese officials in the 1950s and 1960s were furious with Japan for maintaining close relations with their enemies in Taiwan. Until 1971 the People's Republic of China could not take part in the United Nations because the Republic of China (on Taiwan) held the China seat. Because Japan did not support replacing Taiwan with the mainland for the UN China seat, in the view of mainland officials Japan was helping their enemy, the Nationalists.

Mainland leaders who remembered Japan's industrial strength and ambition before 1945 feared that, if given the opportunity, Japanese businesspeople would again dominate economic life on the mainland. Some in China expressed the fear that Japan was trying to reestablish the Greater East Asia Co-Prosperity Sphere, in which China, Japan, and the Southeast Asian nations would enjoy shared trade and prosperity under Japan's leadership. Therefore the Chinese were cautious about giving Japanese businessmen opportunities on the Chinese mainland.

Taiwan did not allow Japanese companies that were engaged in business in Taiwan to conduct business on the mainland. If they did, they were warned that they would be expelled from Taiwan. Similarly, the mainland did not allow Japanese firms doing business on the mainland to conduct business with Taiwan. Until the mid-1960s many Japanese businesspeople felt that, despite its small size, Taiwan offered greater business opportunities than the mainland. Despite the small population of Taiwan compared with that of the mainland (in 1970 mainland China had 825 million people, whereas Taiwan had only 15 million), until 1964 Japan sold more products in Taiwan than on the mainland.

Just as Japanese businesses hoped to operate both on Taiwan and on the mainland, so they hoped to have government relations with both Taiwan and the mainland. Even after Henry Kissinger visited China in the summer of 1971 and signaled a new relationship between the United States and Communist China, Japanese officials, hoping to retain official relations with the Republic of China on Taiwan, advocated a two-China policy. Once mainland China entered the United Nations in 1971 and President Nixon visited

China in February 1972, China was in a strong position to require Japan to cut off diplomatic relations with the Republic of China on Taiwan if it wanted to normalize relations with the mainland. Having no choice when he normalized relations with China in 1972, Tanaka Kakuei (see Biographies of Key Figures) cut formal diplomatic relations with the Republic of China on Taiwan, but Japan still maintained strong unofficial connections with the Taiwanese government.

Sino-Japanese Channels without Diplomatic Relations, 1949–1972

From 1949 to 1972, as during most of the period from 868 to 1873, China and Japan had no formal government-to-government relations, but trade between them continued. China was allied with the Communist bloc, had a planned economy, and stressed class struggle. In contrast, Japan was allied with the Western countries, had a market economy, and stressed cooperation among different social layers.

During the Song dynasty, in the absence of formal relations, monks had provided trustworthy connections that enabled trade to continue between Japan and China. During the period from 1949 to 1972, Japanese officials who were "friends of China" and Chinese officials who were "friends of Japan" served as go-betweens for conservative Japanese leaders and Chinese Communist Party leaders, thus enabling a modest amount of trade to take place between their two countries.

On the Chinese side, Liao Chengzhi (see Biographies of Key Figures) and Guo Moruo, a famous writer who had lived in Japan for twenty years and had spent many years in a Japanese-style home with a Japanese wife, were available to meet with Japanese visitors. On the Japanese side, Utsunomiya Tokuma (1906–2000) was a friend of China and an advocate of better relations with China. Utsunomiya had been a brilliant elite student of economics at Kyoto Imperial University, and he was elected to the lower house of the National Diet for ten terms, beginning in 1952. His father, Utsunomiya Taro (1861–1922), had been a Japanese Army intelligence officer and had served for five years in London as well as in China, where he enjoyed good relations with Chinese reformers, including Sun Yat-sen. Utsunomiya Taro was known as an advocate of pan-Asian cooperation. When his son Tokuma was studying at Kyoto Imperial University, the university had many leftist economics professors and Utsunomiya became a disciple of the great leftist faculty member Kawakami Hajime, who introduced Marxism to Japan. While still a student, Tokuma was arrested in the roundup of Communists on April 16, 1929. In the 1930s, after his release, Tokuma became president of a pharmaceutical company. Following World War II Tokuma joined the Liberal Party, which in 1955 was incorporated into the Liberal Democratic Party. Even though he was an avowed leftist, he was reelected so many times not only because he was respected but also because he looked after his local constituency. He remained an important channel for contacts with China.

Among other members of the Liberal Democratic Party considered friendly to China were Matsumura Kenzo, Oyama Ikuo, Kono Ichiro (father of Kono Yohei, who was later also considered friendly to China and was the grandfather of Foreign Minister Kono Taro, also friendly to China), and Takasaki Tatsunosuke (see Biographies of Key Figures). Takasaki was also a channel to Japanese "friendly firms" that did not trade with Taiwan. When China's relations with Japan improved, these individuals provided links to the mainstream Liberal Democratic Party. But before normalization of Sino-Japanese relations in 1972, China's Communist Party, which retained contacts with Japan's Socialist and Communist Parties, could use those parties as outlets for voicing complaints about Japanese policies and trying to win support for China within the International Communist Movement.

In the 1950s and early 1960s, on behalf of the Chinese Communist Party, Deng Xiaoping and Peng Zhen, who was then mayor of Beijing, frequently met with Japanese Communists and Socialists, and also with local Japanese officials from various other parties. Among China's leaders, these political channels before 1960 were key because politics was then considered more important than economics. After China split with the Soviets in 1960, Chinese Communist Party officials tried to convince the Japanese Communist Party to criticize the Soviet Communists, but the Japanese refused and in 1965 the Chinese Communist Party broke off relations with the Japanese Communists. Thereafter, the Chinese worked through the Japan Socialist Party and the Komeito Party. Just as Buddhist monks had played an important role in Sino-Japanese relations in earlier centuries, so Komeito, the political party in Japan affiliated with a Buddhist sect, Soka Gakkai, played a key go-between role. In 1968 the head of Soka Gakkai, Ikeda Daisaku, spoke out in favor of normalizing relations with China even before China began opening to the West in 1969. These Japanese political groups also provided channels through which the Chinese could gather information about their common enemy, the Liberal Democratic Party. Some of the criticisms China made of Japan's mainstream politics were essentially derived from criticisms by Japan's leftist parties.

Between 1953, when the armistice in Korea was signed, and 1972 there were many ups and downs in relations between the two countries. Between 1953 and 1957, Zhou Enlai and Japanese leaders Yoshida Shigeru (see Biographies of Key Figures) and Hatoyama Ichiro tried to improve relations. Between 1957 and 1961 relations worsened as China turned to the left and Japan turned to the right. But between 1961 and 1966, during China's retrenchment from the Great Leap Forward and Prime Minister Ikeda's efforts to avoid provocations, relations improved somewhat, allowing for the establishment of Liao-Takasaki trade. During the early years of the Cultural Revolution, 1966–1971, relations would once again deteriorate.

The Zhou-Hatoyama Effort to Improve Relations, 1953–1956

In 1953 when China was inaugurating its First Five-Year Plan for the economy, its leaders sought to detach Japan from the control of "U.S. imperialism" and gain access to Japanese technology. To influence the political process in Japan, China established links with Japanese citizens' groups, especially left-wing organizations and youth groups, and encouraged "Japanese friends" to criticize in the Japanese media U.S. domination and the U.S.-Japan Security Treaty.

Most Japanese, including conservative leaders like Prime Minister Yoshida Shigeru, were convinced that, as during the prewar period, Japan still needed imported food from China and that Japan had to sell manufactured goods to China to earn money to pay for its imports. As early as 1949 Japanese businesses seeking to trade with China had begun forming business associations to promote trade, and China was ready to work with them.

The United States restrained Yoshida from carrying on extensive trade with China. In 1952, in return for agreeing to end the Allied Occupation and allow Japan to govern itself, John Foster Dulles required Yoshida to agree that once Japan could make its own decisions, it would establish relations with Taiwan. Yoshida was also required to write what has become known as the "Yoshida Letter," declaring that Japan had no intention of signing a bilateral agreement with Communist China. On April 28, 1952, the day the peace treaty ending the Occupation went into effect, Japan and the United States signed a security pact that continues to this day. Yoshida agreed to continue the embargo on goods to China that had been put in place during the Korean War. However, in the Yoshida Letter he was able to get the United States to accept a statement that read: "The Japanese government desires ultimately to have a full measure of political peace and commercial intercourse with China."[9] In his treaty with Taiwan, Yoshida received permission from the Occupation authorities to avoid saying Chiang Kai-shek had power over the mainland. He said the treaty applied to "all the territory under the control of Taiwan." In his memoirs, published in 1957, Yoshida wrote that the United States did not understand China as well as Great Britain did, for Great Britain had normalized relations with China in 1950. He added that U.S. policies in China had been a failure.[10] Yoshida died in 1967, four years before Henry Kissinger's visit to China opened up a new era that would allow Yoshida's successors to do what he had been blocked from doing by the United States—expand economic relations with China.

In 1953, after the Korean armistice was signed, China had achieved sufficient stability to inaugurate its First Five-year Plan. Mobilization for the Korean War had ended, inflation sparked by wartime shortages was under control, the massive relocation of people after the Chinese Civil War was ending, local order had been restored through the campaign against counterrevolutionaries and the land-reform campaign, and newly chosen leaders were in place in the provinces. Chinese leaders began taking steps to improve relations with other countries, to provide a peaceful external climate for the advancement of trade and technology that would support economic growth. They knew that Japanese companies had both the capacity and the desire to carry on trade with China. Although Mao Zedong was the ultimate leader and made the final decisions, implementation of the policy to improve relations with other countries was generally in the hands of Premier Zhou Enlai. Having lived in Japan for a year and a half during his youth and having met many of Japan's leaders over the years, Zhou was comfortable dealing with the Japanese.

There were still an estimated 20,000 Japanese citizens remaining in China in 1953. However, there were almost no travelers between the two countries. From 1949 to 1953, only slightly more than 200 visas were issued to Japanese individuals to visit China, and there were no Chinese visitors to Japan.[11] Diplomats from China and Japan could meet in a third country, but they did not negotiate any significant agreements. The dominant conservative policies in Japan had been so subordinated to U.S. policy during the Occupation that Zhou Enlai had few opportunities to improve relations with Japan.

In September 1953, Premier Zhou told Oyama Ikuo, a visiting Japanese Diet member, that China was willing to restore normal relations with Japan and expand trade. Oyama, an upper house member who had been elected in 1950, supported international peace movements. He had taken part in leftist activities in the 1920s and early 1930s as a faculty member at Waseda University. By 1933 his opposition to Japanese imperialism had gotten him in trouble with the Japanese government, and he went to the United States, where he had studied earlier. He remained in the United States throughout World War II, working as a librarian and researcher at Northwestern University. He returned to Japan in 1947. When Zhou Enlai broke the news to Oyama that China was willing to restore relations, there were still many issues to settle. One month later, in a follow-up visit by Japanese Diet members to Beijing in October 1953, Guo Moruo told the visitors that China was ready to sign a nonaggression pact, but no agreements were reached at that time.

At the Geneva Conference on Indochina (April 26–July 20, 1954), Zhou Enlai laid out five principles of coexistence that spelled out China's desire to have good relations with other countries. While at the conference, Zhou had side meetings with the Japanese, as part of an effort to loosen ties between Japan and the United States, expand trade relations with Japan, weaken ties between Taiwan and the United States, and reduce the chance that Japan would once again become a military power. Japanese officials were concerned about U.S. reactions, because the United States still hoped to limit Japan's contacts with China. The Japanese government responded cautiously but began to explore ways to expand Sino-Japanese relations.

In 1952, as the Occupation was coming to an end, various Japanese political groups began jockeying to win political power. By late 1955, after many negotiations as different groups tried to aggregate their interests, relatively stable alliances among various political groups had been forged. Early that year several small progressive political groups united to form the Socialist Party of Japan, and then, to prevent the Socialists from taking power, conservative groups united to form the Liberal Democratic Party. The leading business federation, Keidanren, acquired a strong leader, Ishizaka Taizo, who could represent the business community in support of the Liberal Democratic Party. Businesses in various sectors strengthened their sectoral associations, enabling the business community to work with the bureaucracy and the politicians. Also in 1955, the government's Economic Planning Agency (Keizai kikakucho) was formed to guide Japan's long-term planning. These developments provided a stable political and economic structure for Japan, known as the 1955 system, that enabled politicians, bureaucrats, and business leaders to work together to achieve rapid economic growth. The system also provided a relatively well-coordinated base for conducting relations with China and other countries.

The mainland economy was still very small in 1955, but most Japanese, while unable to imagine how much China would grow in the next several decades, nonetheless expected that trade with the mainland would increase. In December 1954, Hatoyama Ichiro, a second-generation political leader who had spent most of World War II on his country estate because of disagreements with the military leaders, replaced Yoshida as prime minister. His minister of trade and industry, Ishibashi Tanzan, had just written articles in *The Oriental Economist* criticizing the United States for blocking closer economic relations between Japan and China. Hatoyama and Ishibashi took a bold approach toward improving relations with China just at the time when Zhou Enlai was ready to reach out to Japan.

Zhou Enlai followed up the Geneva Conference with the Bandung Conference in Indonesia (April 18–24, 1955) to promote peaceful coexistence. Despite the objections of the United States, Prime Minister Hatoyama sent a Japanese delegation, led by Takasaki Tatsunosuke, to the Bandung Conference. Both Zhou Enlai and Takasaki hoped to use the meeting to find a way to break through the impasse in Sino-Japanese relations. An intermediary had arranged for the two to exchange greetings several minutes before the meeting opened, whereupon they arranged to hold a secret meeting. Zhou assigned Liao Chengzhi to pick up Takasaki and take him to the secret meeting with Zhou Enlai and Vice Premier Chen Yi (not the same person as General Chen Yi, who served as chief executive and garrison commander of Taiwan). Liao and Takasaki had met in 1949 when Takasaki had been approached by Liao in an effort to arrange for Japan to supply spare parts and other industrial machinery so China could continue operating the Japanese-built factories in Manchuria. Although Zhou Enlai and Takasaki were not able to achieve a breakthrough in 1955, their meeting helped keep open the channels that seven years later resulted in the Liao-Takasaki trade agreement.[12]

Although Prime Minister Hatoyama wanted to improve relations with China, he put a greater priority on improving relations with the Soviet Union. He was also cautious about alienating Taiwan, which as a member of the UN Security Council could block Japan from entering the UN. Japan finally succeeded in doing in December 1956. In his effort to expand trade with China, Hatoyama faced considerable opposition in the Diet as well as from the United States. In the end, he and Zhou Enlai were able to make modest progress in improving relations between their countries. Ishibashi Tanzan, who succeeded Hatoyama as prime minister in December 1956, continued to work toward better relations with China, but two months after taking office Ishibashi developed a severe case of pneumonia and resigned from office.

The fortunate timing of Zhou's initiative and Japanese receptivity under Hatoyama and Ishibashi brought some progress, though on a much smaller scale than after normalization in 1972. In 1955 seventy-eight Diet members visited China, more than in any year since the end of World War II. Also in 1955, China had its first trade fair in Tokyo and Osaka and Japan had its first trade fair in Shanghai and Beijing. Trade increased from a very small base. The total value of trade between China and Japan in 1954 was $60 million, in 1955 it was $110 million, and in 1956 it was $151 million, which was the largest annual amount until 1964. In 1955 China and Japan also signed agreements on fisheries and cultural exchanges. In 1955 and 1956 some 2,000 Japanese visited China, and a number of Chinese delegations visited Japan.

In the first decades after 1945 there were many Chinese and Japanese individuals who, from their own experience, had a deep understanding of the other country and could be called upon, when policy permitted, to manage relations. Many of the tens of thousands of Chinese who had studied in Japan held important positions in China's military, government, businesses, and universities. Many Japanese who had previously lived in Manchuria, Shanghai, and other Chinese cities were familiar with Chinese culture and had Chinese acquaintances with whom they could work. But because there was so little contact between the two countries from 1945 until 1978, when the Treaty of Peace and Friendship finally enabled them to work together closely, there was virtually no one at the working level in either country who had a deep personal understanding of the other country.

China's Political Tightening and Prime Minister Kishi, 1957–1960

China's more open policies from 1953 to 1957 coincided with the more China-friendly policies of Hatoyama Ichiro and Ishibashi Tanzan. Similarly, China's tightening from 1957 to 1960 coincided with the rule of a conservative, pro-Taiwan leader in Japan, Prime Minister Kishi Nobusuke, thus halting the progress the two countries had made up to 1957. China's political tightening began in the summer of 1957 with the first phase of the "anti-rightist campaign," an attack on some 550,000 people who had criticized the government in the spring of 1957, after Mao said, "Let a hundred flowers bloom and a hundred schools of thought contend," to encourage intellectuals to speak out.

In 1957 Egyptian president Gamal Abdel Nasser's seizure of the Suez Canal, the Russians' successful launch of the first satellite, and China's economic growth during the First Five-Year Plan gave Mao confidence that the "East wind was prevailing over the West wind." In 1958 he launched the Great Leap Forward, and in the summer of 1958 China began shelling Quemoy and Matsu, two islands off the coast of Fujian that were governed by Taiwan, in preparation for a possible invasion of Taiwan.

In Japan, Prime Minister Ishibashi was succeeded in February 1957 by Kishi Nobusuke, who during the Sino-Japanese War had served as minister of commerce and later as minister of munitions in Tojo Hideki's cabinet. As minister of munitions, Kishi had been arrested after World War II on suspicion of being a class-A war criminal and imprisoned in Sugamo Prison from 1945 to 1948, but he was not indicted. The Chinese Communists were outraged that someone suspected of being a class-A war criminal would be selected as prime minister. In June 1957 Kishi became the first postwar prime minister to visit Taiwan, further infuriating the mainland.

At the Chinese trade mission in Tokyo in early 1958, the Chinese government displayed the Chinese flag. The Japanese government did not publicly express approval but it raised no objection, thus implicitly accepting it. Shortly thereafter, at an exhibition of mainland Chinese products at a Nagasaki department store, the Chinese again flew the flag. On May 2, 1958, a Japanese youth tore down the flag, and the Chinese responded by cutting off all economic and social relations with Japan, declaring that politics could not be separated from economics. Although the Japanese economy had begun to grow, China, with its much broader economic base had also made great progress during the 1953–1957 First Five-Year Plan. As he launched the Great Leap Forward, Mao was brimming with confidence, and he expected China would vault far ahead of Japan. Some in Japan believed that Mao was so confident that Japan needed China, as Japanese leaders had indeed said in the 1930s, that he thought Japanese voters might vote against Kishi in the May 22 election because of Kishi's failure to maintain economic relations with China. In fact, on May 22 Kishi was reelected by a wide margin. Sino-Japanese trade in 1957 was valued at $141 million; after Mao cut off economic relations with Japan, trade in 1959 and 1960 amounted to only $23 million in each year.

Improved Trade Relations and the Liao-Takasaki Office, 1960s

By the summer of 1959 Chinese officials recognized that while the Japanese economy was continuing its healthy growth, the first year of the Great Leap had been an economic disaster for China. In September 1959 Zhou Enlai invited "friends of China" Ishibashi Tanzan and Utsunomiya Tokuma to China to consider the possibility of increasing economic aid and trade. But by the time of their meeting, Mao had just criticized Peng Dehuai at the Lushan Plenum and was returning to the excesses of the Great Leap Forward. Zhou's efforts to expand trade were not successful.

By 1960, as the Japanese economy was steadily moving ahead, the Chinese economy was in a disastrous state. China urgently needed to expand food production to alleviate a famine that had already caused tens of millions of deaths. China needed chemical fertilizer for crops as well as iron and steel to make agricultural machinery. To decrease the acreage devoted to growing cotton and increase the acreage devoted to food production, China also needed help in manufacturing chemical fibers to replace cotton for the production of cloth. Furthermore, after the Sino-Soviet split in 1960, the Soviet Union withdrew 1,400 scientists from China and also scrapped more than 200 joint development projects and departed China without leaving any of the blueprints behind. China, in desperate need of help in advanced science and technology, looked to Japan as the most promising source of aid. But Chinese leaders did not feel they could work with Prime Minister Kishi, who supported Taiwan.

In July 1960, just ten days after Ikeda Hayato replaced Kishi as prime minister, a high-level Chinese delegation arrived in Japan, the first trade delegation to go to Japan since trade had been disrupted in 1958. Ikeda Hayato had not been a so-called friend of China, but he was not an enemy and he believed that trade between the two countries could help achieve his economic goals for Japan. In August, a month after Ikeda became prime minister, Zhou Enlai introduced the concept of "friendly firms."

During the Ming period, only those ships that had received licenses (tallies) approved by the Chinese government had been allowed to transport goods between China and Japan. In 1960, the friendly-firms policy operated in a similar way: Japanese firms that did not trade with Taiwan could be certified and allowed to trade with China. Eleven firms were classified as friendly firms in 1960, and by 1962 there were 190 such companies.

Private Japanese firms responded quickly to the new opportunities for trade and sales to China. In October 1960 Takasaki Tatsunosuke, representing private Japanese businesses but with the approval of the Japanese government, led a delegation to China where he met with Liao Chengzhi, with whom he had established good relations in 1955. In December 1962 Liao and Takasaki signed a five-year agreement, the Memorandum on Sino-Japanese Long-Term Comprehensive Trade, also known as the Liao-Takasaki (or L-T) trade agreement, whereby the governments made trade and finance arrangements for specific items, despite not having formal diplomatic relations. The agreement also permitted "friendly trade" by private companies outside the formal L-T trade agreement. The Liao-Takasaki trade offices became quasi-governmental agencies promoting exchanges between the two countries, just as the Manchurian Railway had been a quasi-governmental structure after the Russo-Japanese War. Several Japanese officials who served in the Liao-Takasaki office in Beijing had been officials in Japan's Ministry of Trade and Industry (MITI) prior to their assignment in Beijing.

The Chinese government would not then accept loans from Japan to build plants in China, but it did agree that it would make "deferred payments" when funds from the Export-Import Bank of Japan financed a vinylon plant in China built by Kurashiki Rayon. The vinylon plant became a model for synthetic fiber plants in China. Japan also sold China chemical fertilizer, iron, and steel.

The L-T trade agreement was strongly criticized by the pro-Taiwan groups in Japan and by the U.S. government, which was influenced by a powerful Taiwan lobby. After 1964, because of pressure from Taiwan, the Japanese government stopped funding the export of industrial plants to China. Although formal government trade did not increase dramatically, friendly trade by private companies approved by the Liao-Takasaki trade offices continued to grow rapidly. Two-way trade between China and Japan grew steadily from $48 million in 1961 to $621 million in 1966, whereupon the outbreak of the Cultural Revolution stopped any further increase.

China and Japan also expanded other contacts. In 1963 Liao became chairman of the China-Japan Friendship Association. To deepen Sino-Japanese relations, the two sides celebrated the 1,200th anniversary of the death in 763 of the famous blind Chinese monk Ganjin, who reached Japan in 753, after many failed efforts, and contributed to the development of Buddhism in Japan. China also celebrated the arrival of Abe no Nakamaro, the brilliant Japanese scholar and poet who passed the Chinese examination for officials and served in China as a governor-general. In 1963 the Chinese formed the Sino-Japan Friendship Association of the Chinese People's Association for Friendship with Foreign Countries, with Liao Chengzhi as president and Guo Moruo as honorary chairman.

Chinese officials who went on study tours to Japan to learn how it had advanced its economy while China suffered from the Great Leap Forward observed how Ikeda's goal of "income doubling" in the 1960s had provided a framework for Japanese planning. In 1980 Deng Xiaoping, impressed by Ikeda's income-doubling program, announced that China would "double its income twice" (i.e., quadruple it) by the end of the century.

Chinese officials, aware by the mid-1960s that Japan's trade with China was about to surpass its trade with Taiwan and that China's economy was growing faster than Taiwan's, announced that they would not permit trade with Japanese firms that traded with Taiwan. Japanese firms cut their ties with Taiwan but then set up dummy companies to trade with Taiwan, or opted for trade with Taiwan but then set up dummy companies to trade with the mainland. China tried to punish Japanese companies that set up such dummy firms, but it was difficult to keep track of all the new companies, and the policy did little to force Japanese companies to end their trade with Taiwan.

The scale of Sino-Japanese trade in the 1960s was miniscule compared with what it would be two decades later, but at the time, it gave China crucial support to recover from the disaster of the Great Leap Forward, and it allowed a key group of Japanese officials and private Japanese firms to keep up their knowledge of how to operate in China, making it easier to expand operations after the two countries normalized relations in 1972.

China's Turn Inward and the Cultural Revolution, 1966–1969

During the peak years of the Cultural Revolution, when so many top leaders were attacked, Liao Chengzhi also became a victim. Red Guards attacked the Liao-Takasaki office for helping Japan. Japanese trade representatives in Beijing were required to conduct "self-criticisms," to attend study sessions on Mao's political thought, to sing Red Guard songs, and to take part in Red Guard demonstrations. As a result, the number of Japanese businessmen working in Beijing declined.

However, owing to a 1964 agreement to exchange journalists, as arranged by the Liao-Takasaki office, a dozen Japanese journalists were working in Beijing when the Cultural Revolution broke out. Reporters from many other countries could not read the posters in Chinese characters, but the Japanese journalists could. They informally divided Beijing into districts, with different reporters covering different districts, and by pooling their findings, they were able to give far more detailed reports on the Red Guard posters and activities than news agencies from any other country. Eto Shinkichi, a leading Japanese China scholar at Tokyo University, and other Japanese academics later criticized the Japanese journalists who, they said, yielded to Chinese pressures and reported sympathetically on Red Guard activities.

Red Guard attacks had declined by early 1968, when Zhou Enlai was able to tell Japanese representatives that Liao and Takasaki could forge a new agreement. The L-T trade agreement, which had been criticized earlier during the Cultural Revolution, was replaced in 1968 by the Memorandum Trade Agreement, which had a similar function, and although their names were not used for the office, Liao Chengzhi and Takasaki Tatsunosuke resumed their important roles. Trade had declined in 1966 and 1967 because of the Cultural Revolution, but it increased in 1969 and 1970. In 1970 China had more trade with Japan than with any other country, although their two-way trade still amounted to less than $1 billion per year—less than 1 percent of what it would be thirty years later.

Asakai's Nightmare and the Turn to Tanaka, 1970–1972

When China started reaching out to other countries after the 1969 border clashes with the Soviet Union, Japanese businessmen and politicians who had long been hoping to restore and expand relations with mainland China began to feel that the opportunity had finally arrived. Since 1945 Japan had reluctantly followed U.S. requests to limit its trade with China. It had followed the U.S. lead in maintaining diplomatic relations with Taiwan and voting to keep Beijing out of the United Nations. But in 1969 and 1970, with signs that other countries were beginning to respond to Beijing's efforts to reach out and the prospect that within a year or two Beijing would have enough votes to replace Taiwan in the United Nations, Japan's business community wanted the government to respond more positively to China's overtures. They were dissatisfied with Prime Minister Sato Eisaku, then the longest-serving prime minister in postwar history, who was not taking sufficient steps to improve relations with China.

Japanese leaders had expected that when China began to open up, Japan and the United States would cooperate in managing the process. By early 1970 some Japanese diplomats began to worry that U.S. officials were changing their perspective on China and were not fully open in sharing the changes with Japan. U.S.-China talks had resumed in Warsaw in January and February 1970, and the United States had made some small trade concessions to China. On October 24, 1970, when Prime Minister Sato asked National Security Advisor Henry Kissinger if the United States was contemplating changes in its relationship with China, Kissinger assured Sato that he was not contemplating any change and that he would see that Prime Minister Sato was fully informed if there were to be any changes in China policy. In April 1971, at an international Ping-Pong tournament in Nagoya, Japan, the world-champion Chinese team, knowing that the U.S. team wanted to visit China, invited them to come; the U.S. team accepted, and the U.S. government approved. Amid headlines and cameras, the Ping-Pong teams eased U.S.-China tensions. Japanese diplomats had good reason to fear that the United States might be contemplating changes in its relations with China. Nevertheless, Melvin Laird, U.S. Secretary of Defense, again reassured Prime Minister Sato that the United States was not considering any basic change in its China policy.

Then suddenly, one week after Laird's reassurance, "Asakai's nightmare" became a reality. Asakai Koichiro, ambassador to the United States from 1957 to 1963, had over the years reported having trouble sleeping because of his fear that the United States might move suddenly to establish relations with China without consulting Japan. Thirty minutes before President Richard Nixon gave a speech on July 15, 1971, announcing that Kissinger had been in Beijing and that he himself would travel to China early the following year, Ambassador Ushiba Nobuhiko in Washington was informed by telephone, by Secretary of State William P. Rogers, that Nixon was about to announce his plan. Ushiba called the prime minister's office, and three minutes before Nixon began speaking, Prime Minister Sato learned of the speech. Prime Minister Sato and all in Japan were shocked and furious that the United States, their ally who had told them to defer establishing relations with China, had suddenly, and without consultation, moved ahead of Japan in opening up to China.

Henry Kissinger's visit to China, July 9–11, 1971, and President Nixon's public announcement that he would visit China in early 1972 were a terrible embarrassment to Prime Minister Sato, who had been yielding to U.S. pressure not to expand relations with China. But for Nixon and Kissinger, absolute secrecy had been necessary. If word had gotten out, Taiwan certainly would have pressured Congress to block the Nixon-Kissinger plan. Not only Japan but also the U.S. State Department and Congress had not been informed of Kissinger's plans to fly to Beijing.

Kissinger and Nixon had begun planning this move more than a year earlier. For years, the Americans had been continuing ambassador-level talks with China in Warsaw, and at their 134th meeting, which took place on January 20, 1970, Walter Stoessel Jr., the U.S. ambassador to Poland, told his Chinese counterpart, Lei Yang, that the United States was willing to back away from its exclusive relationship with Taiwan and send a representative to Beijing for discussions. One month later, Lei Yang conveyed Beijing's reply to Ambassador Stoessel. Chinese leaders would welcome a representative of the U.S. government to Beijing to prepare for a visit by President Nixon. At a dinner in Pakistan in July 1971, following carefully laid-out plans with both Pakistan and Beijing, Henry Kissinger feigned stomach trouble, excused himself from the dinner, and flew secretly from Pakistan to Beijing, where he met with Zhou Enlai and Mao Zedong for broad-ranging discussions in preparation for a visit to Beijing by President Nixon.

Prime Minister Sato expected that he would soon be out of office for not better managing relations with the United States and for having such poor relations with Beijing that he was unable to normalize them. Nixon and Kissinger had indeed been unhappy with Prime Minister Sato for his failure to implement a secret agreement he had made earlier with the Americans—that he would cut back textile exports to the United States, an issue of great political importance to President Richard Nixon. In his election campaign in 1968 Nixon had promised the textile-producing southern states that he would limit textile imports from Japan. Nixon needed support from the southern states to win reelection in November 1972, and because Sato had failed to deliver on his promise, he was understandably upset.

Prime Minister Sato Eisaku, like his blood brother Prime Minister Kishi (who had changed his name to Kishi to continue the line of his maternal uncle, who did not have a male heir), had close relations with Taiwan. Now, with the opening of relations between the United States and China, Japanese public opinion strongly supported taking immediate steps to improve relations with China. Diet members began discussing who might replace Sato as prime minister so that Japan could move boldly to improve relations with China. They naturally thought of Tanaka Kakuei, who had been appointed minister of trade and industry in the Sato cabinet just before Nixon's shocking announcement and who was very popular for standing up to U.S. pressures to curb Japanese exports to the United States.

A second shock from the United States came on August 15, 1971, one month after Nixon's speech. The United States, again without warning Japan, announced that it would place a 10 percent surcharge on imports from Japan and that the exchange rate, which had been fixed since early during the Occupation at 360 yen to the dollar, would thereafter be allowed to float. The markets immediately raised the value of the yen in relation to the dollar, thus raising the price of Japanese textiles going to the United States.

Growing tensions between Japan and the United States were derived from an underlying economic change, the spread of industrial skills from the United States to Japan, and the increase in industrial exports from Japan, where labor costs were lower, to the United States—a problem that would affect the relationship between the United States and China three decades later. From 1945 to the 1970s the United States was the world's greatest industrial power, but by the early 1970s, as other countries were gaining in industrial technology and paying low wages to their workers, U.S. industrial goods began to lose out, even in the United States, to foreign products. The rapidly declining costs of global shipping and the openness of U.S. markets contributed to this process. In the 1960s no country had expanded its industrial exports to the United States more rapidly than Japan. U.S. industrial workers were losing jobs and the trade imbalance was growing, creating a drain on the U.S. Treasury.

MITI was in charge of managing the Japanese side in trade negotiations with the United States. On July 5, 1971, Prime Minister Sato Eisaku had appointed Tanaka Kakuei minister of trade and industry to resolve the trade dispute with the United States. Tanaka, a rustic politician known for his ingenuity and his use of bundles of money to resolve problems, publicly criticized the United States to maintain popular support while laying the groundwork for yielding to U.S. demands. He carried on detailed discussions with key leaders on all sides, including U.S. officials, to learn what had to be done to reach an agreement. He resolved the surcharge problem by arranging payments to Japanese textile companies and textile workers to compensate them for limiting exports to meet the minimum the United

States required. Prime Minister Sato's failure to maintain good relations with the United States and his inability to normalize relations with China helped propel Tanaka, the popular problem solver, into position to succeed him as prime minister.

Tanaka took up office as the new prime minister on July 7, 1972, with the highest level of public support ever given to any incoming prime minister. It was widely expected that he would make rapid progress in improving relations with China. By September 29, scarcely two months after taking office, Prime Minister Tanaka was in Beijing.

CHAPTER TEN

Working Together, 1972–1992

ON SEPTEMBER 27, 1972, Tanaka Kakuei and Zhou Enlai met in Beijing. They were a strange pair. Tanaka, who came from a poor rural family and became a petit bourgeois entrepreneur and then a political deal maker, had little foreign experience. Zhou Enlai, by contrast, was one of the world's most sophisticated foreign-policy strategists, with unrivaled diplomatic experience. Yet they worked well together, for they were both bright, imaginative problem solvers who wanted to find a way to establish formal relations and who knew how to get the necessary political support in their own country. Zhou Enlai had stipulated some general principles that had to be met before the two countries could expand their relations, and on the basis of those principles, Zhou and Tanaka were able, with the support of other officials who helped prepare for their meeting, to resolve the related political issues in their own countries.

The preparations for the meeting had moved quickly after July 7, 1972, when Tanaka became prime minister. Tanaka Kakuei's announcement of his intention to normalize relations with China had helped him win the election for party president over Fukuda Takeo, and even before becoming prime minister he began to explore how he might achieve that goal. The day he took office, Tanaka announced that he would move ahead with normalization. Two days later Zhou Enlai announced that China welcomed Tanaka's speech and expressed a desire to work for early normalization of Sino-Japanese relations. Immediately, the Japan Socialist Party and Komeito, the political party affiliated with Soka Gakkai, said that they would cooperate in this effort.

The groundwork for normalization had begun by April 1972, when Okita Saburo, a cosmopolitan economic planner who grew up in Manchuria, was dispatched to Beijing, where he met with Zhou Enlai to explore the possibilities for normalization. In the course of their wide-ranging conversation Zhou Enlai said that he had heard that Tokyo was seriously polluted because there were so many automobiles in the Japanese capital. He told Okita that Beijing had been able to avoid air pollution because its main mode of transportation was the city's 1.5 million bicycles. Forty years later, when Tokyo had overcome its air pollution problem and Beijing, where cars had basically replaced bicycles, was one of the world's most polluted cities, Japan was giving assistance to China to resolve its pollution problems.

When Tanaka became prime minister, he made Foreign Minister Ohira Masayoshi responsible for working out the details of the normalization agreement. Ohira, from a small town on the island of Shikoku, was a shy person of modest background, completely sincere and impeccably honest, who wanted to improve relations with China. Like many of Japan's first generation of top postwar political leaders, Ohira had risen in the ranks by passing exams and becoming an elite-track bureaucrat in the Ministry of Finance before being recruited into politics by Yoshida Shigeru. Because of his personal philosophical convictions, he believed deeply in a vision of a peaceful world in which nations cooperated. Edwin O. Reischauer, the son of American missionaries and the U.S. ambassador to Japan at the time, developed immense respect for Ohira and later said that Ohira's premature death in 1980 was a tremendous loss to Japan and the world. Beneath his rumpled, comfortable exterior, Ohira was a thoughtful statesman ready to exert enormous effort to reach a political consensus for normalizing relations with China. Chinese political leaders regarded him as a special friend, the Japanese leader whom they most trusted at the time.

On July 10, three days after Tanaka became prime minister, Sun Pinghua, who had studied at Tokyo Engineering College and had been secretary-general of the China-Japan Friendship Association, arrived in Tokyo as an official envoy. He brought a message from Zhou Enlai stating that it was the right time to act. Foreign Minister Ohira, rather than leaving things to his Foreign Ministry officials, sought a personal meeting with Zhou. Several days later, on July 16, Ohira was in Beijing meeting with Zhou Enlai, who told him China would welcome a visit by Prime Minister Tanaka. When Ohira met with Sun Pinghua on July 22, he told him that Prime Minister Tanaka supported the normalization of diplomatic relations. However, Ohira explained, Japan wanted to be sure that it could retain the

U.S.-Japan Security Alliance and that it could maintain economic and cultural relations with Taiwan, a formula that would be used by the United States when it normalized relations with China six years later. Tanaka immediately set up a fifteen-member China Policy Council within the Ministry of Foreign Affairs to consider the details necessary for achieving normalization.

China had made it clear that three basic principles had to be met for normalization: Japan had to recognize that there is only one China, that the People's Republic is the sole government of China, and that Japan had to abrogate its treaty with the Nationalists.

Many Japanese business and government officials had hoped for a two-state solution that would allow Japan to have formal relations with both China and Taiwan, but mainland China was in a strong enough position to insist that it would not accept such a solution. Japanese businessmen urgently wanted to normalize relations with China for fear that the United States and the European countries would enter the China market first and leave Japan far behind. With this pressure, those who wanted to normalize relations with China had enough support to break diplomatic relations with Taiwan. Still, Japan wanted to find a way to continue economic and cultural relations with Taiwan.

On July 25, Takeiri Yoshikatsu, chairman of the Komeito Party, returned from Beijing, where he had held ten hours of talks with Zhou Enlai. Zhou had told Takeiri that maintaining the U.S.-Japan Security Alliance and the status of the Senkaku / Diaoyu Islands would not be obstacles to normalization and that China intended to abandon its claim for war reparations, but he repeated that Japan had to abrogate its treaty with the Nationalists. Takeiri assured Zhou that Japan would agree. On August 10, the Liberal Democratic Party approved a visit to China by Prime Minister Tanaka. The next day, this was conveyed to Sun Pinghua, and on August 15, Sun reported to Tanaka that China would welcome him to Beijing.

Tanaka requested a meeting with Nixon to discuss his plans for normalizing relations with China. At a meeting held in Hawaii from August 31 to September 1, President Nixon accepted Tanaka's effort to resolve the trade dispute with the United States. Tanaka offered approximately $710 million in special purchases from the United States and agreed to reduce textile exports. Nixon, in return for Tanaka's assistance in helping him firm up his southern political base, where the U.S. textile industry was located, raised no objection to Japan's move to normalize relations with China before the United States did.

In mid-September, scarcely a week before Tanaka visited Beijing, Diet member Kosaka Zentaro led a delegation of Diet members to Beijing, where they held talks with Zhou Enlai. The participation of the other Diet members helped consolidate support among Japanese political leaders for taking the required steps to normalize relations.

On September 18 and 19, former foreign minister Shiina Etsusaburo, one of Japan's political leaders with the closest relations to Taiwan, was sent to Taiwan with the unpleasant task of telling its leaders of Japan's plans to normalize relations with Beijing, and he was also to discuss plans for continuing trade and cultural relations. The leaders on Taiwan were so angry about the news that Chiang Kai-shek refused to meet with him, but Shiina did meet Chiang Ching-kuo, Chiang Kai-shek's son, to discuss how to continue unofficial relations without formal diplomatic relations.

Prime Minister Tanaka and Foreign Minister Ohira were in Beijing from September 25 to 30 to negotiate normalization of relations between the two countries. Ohira and Tanaka had made careful preparations for their visit by winning the support of Diet members, receiving approval from the United States, arranging to continue to work with Taiwan, and reaching a basic agreement with Zhou Enlai on the major issues.

Despite all the careful preparations, the atmosphere in Beijing during the first two days of Tanaka's visit to Beijing was tense, and the Japanese were uncertain that they would be successful in achieving normalization during the trip. The "Gang of Four," the radical faction led by Mao's wife, was still strong, and Chinese officials expressed dissatisfaction with Japan's lingering ties to Taiwan and its refusal to specify a date when it would cut off those relations. Chinese officials also expressed displeasure with Prime Minister Tanaka's formal remarks at the banquet on the first evening. Tanaka said that Japan wished to express its profound regret for the "great trouble" (*tadai no gomeiwaku*) it had caused during its military aggression. The phrase *tadai no gomeiwaku*, however, was translated into Chinese as *mafan*, which can be used in an apology for a minor inconvenience and was thus seen as downgrading the suffering Japan had caused and undercutting the seriousness of Tanaka's apology. Zhou Enlai criticized the apology, saying that it belittled the enormous suffering Japan had caused. Beginning on the second evening of the meeting, Ji Pengfei replaced Zhou Enlai as the Chinese negotiator, but Ohira remained the negotiator on the Japanese side. In his meeting with Ohira, Ji Pengfei wrote out messages that were taken to another room, and written answers would then come back. The Japanese assumed that Ji was communicating with Zhou Enlai, who was sending back the Chinese responses.

On the third evening, the Chinese surprised the Japanese by announcing that Chairman Mao would meet Prime Minister Tanaka and Foreign Minister Ohira. Mao told Tanaka that the expression "inconvenience" (*mafan*) had been too casual, that it was to be used when, for example, one spilled water on a woman's skirt. However, the hour-long meeting with Chairman Mao took the negotiations over the hump, for Mao basically approved the conclusions reached thus far. On the third day, Tanaka asked Zhou his views on the Senkaku / Diaoyu Islands. Zhou replied that it was better not to discuss the issue at that point. In fact, the islands became a problem only later, after oil was discovered in the area. Although Zhou had originally insisted that Japan announce a date when it would break off relations with Taiwan, Ohira told Zhou that he was not able to set a specific date; however, he did promise that Japan would end diplomatic relations and Zhou accepted his promise. On September 29, as flags from both countries were flying amid flashing cameras, Prime Minister Tanaka, Premier Zhou Enlai, Foreign Minister Ohira, and Foreign Minister Ji Pengfei signed the normalization agreement. The next day, September 30, Zhou and Ji accompanied the Japanese delegation to Shanghai as planned, and on the following day Zhou Enlai, Liao Chengzhi, and a crowd of other Chinese officials saw off the Japanese delegation at the Shanghai airport.

In a joint communiqué released on September 29, 1972, Japan agreed to issue a clear and strong statement about the damages it had caused: "The Japanese side is keenly conscious of the responsibility for the serious damage that Japan caused in the past to the Chinese people through war and deeply reproaches itself." China had initially demanded that Japan recognize that Taiwan was part of China, but in the end the two sides accepted a formula whereby Japan understood China's point of view but stopped short of saying it accepted it. The document reads: "The government of the People's Republic of China reiterates that Taiwan is an inalienable part of the territory of the

People's Republic of China. The government of Japan fully understands and respects this stand of the People's Republic of China."

Within Japan, the new friends of China, mainstream politicians and business hopefuls, replaced the old friends of China, the leftists, including the Socialists and Communists who had previously objected to Japanese mainstream opinion that did not recognize China. Some in Japan who had been friends of China before 1972 even felt betrayed by China, which was now dealing with their domestic enemies, the mainstream politicians and businessmen. As Robert Hoppens notes, the old friends of China had often been leery of patriotism, for it was tied too closely to Japan's aggressive past. After 1972 some new "friends of China" hoped that by improving relations with China, the primary victim of Japanese aggression, Japan could regain a positive view of patriotism and end the negative self-criticism that had been so prominent in the country during the early years after the war.

To many in Japan, wherever they stood on the political spectrum, normalization gave rise to the hope that the people of China and Japan could become friends, bound together by their common culture. Many thoughtful Japanese who had reached maturity after World War II, too young to feel responsible for Japan's actions during the war, believed that to show their sincerity they should focus not on apologizing for events that took place before they reached adulthood but on finding ways to help China modernize and to cooperate with other countries to maintain global peace.

For many older Japanese who had been in China before 1945, the opening to China stirred memories of the war in China, and they experienced an outpouring of guilt for the damage that they or their relatives and friends had caused. Some hoped that Chinese would forgive Japan for the atrocities that had occurred. Others wanted to forget what Japan had done and reframe the events of World War II so that the Japanese would be regarded as good people who had been forced to go to war to defend themselves from Western imperialists.

In China, the decision to normalize relations with Japan was made by a small group of leaders. For the wider Chinese public, the media did not provide a comprehensive explanation of Japanese politics and society. Without an understanding of the complexities of Japanese politics and the sentiments of the Japanese people, it was difficult for the Chinese to empathize with the Japanese and understand their perspective. In meetings between sister cities, religious groups, and youth groups following normalization, representatives on both sides would offer polite expressions of goodwill, but they rarely examined the troubled history between the two countries, which would again rise to the fore when relations between the two countries began to deteriorate.

The Limited Opening

From 1972, when relations were normalized, until 1978, when the Treaty of Peace and Friendship was signed, the number of Japanese visitors to China and the number of meetings between Zhou Enlai, Deng Xiaoping, and Japanese visitors increased rapidly, but business relations between China and Japan developed slowly. The two sides had rushed through normalization in 1972, but China did not reach a consensus to boldly promote reform and opening until 1978. In 1972 Mao had welcomed a number of foreign guests to Beijing, but he was not yet prepared to allow them to travel freely within the country. A Japanese diplomat, Sugimoto Nobuyuki, who had the rare opportunity at the time to attend a Chinese-language school and share a room with a Chinese student, reported that his roommate told him his surname but never revealed his given name. He would say *ni hao* (hello), but they never engaged in any further conversation.

Once China and Japan normalized relations in 1972, Japanese individuals in many different circles—business, local government, the media, religious groups, and former residents of China—sought to visit China. They hoped that China and Japan could enter a new era of friendship, and they wanted to make friends with their Chinese counterparts to help usher in the new age. Businessmen had visions of trade opportunities and were prepared to be patient and to postpone making profits. The number of visitors between the two countries increased from fewer than 3,000 in 1969 to 10,000 in 1973, although this was still less than 1 percent of the number of visitors who would travel between the two countries three decades later. Overwhelmingly, the visitors were Japanese travelers going to China.

In his last years before his death in 1976, Mao did not give a clear green light for moving ahead rapidly to improve relations with Japan. Mao continued to allow his wife, Jiang Qing, and the other members of the Gang of Four, to criticize those who wanted to promote reform and opening, but he also allowed Zhou Enlai and Deng Xiaoping to greet many foreign visitors, including those from Japan. After 1973, Zhou began to slow down his activities because he had been diagnosed with cancer, but he continued to meet with visiting Japanese dignitaries for two more years, and he supported Deng Xiaoping in meetings with foreign visitors. Deng personally met with more than forty Japanese delegations between 1972 and 1976, far more delegations than from any other country, for in the years immediately following normalization many Japanese wanted to visit China.

Through the discussions among Zhou Enlai, Deng Xiaoping, and their Japanese counterparts, Chinese leaders began to develop a more positive view of both Japanese and U.S. policies. Zhou Enlai acknowledged, as Henry Kissinger had told him, that Japan required a security treaty with the United States to provide for its defense. In a talk with Miyazawa Kiichi, who was later to become Japan's prime minister, Zhou even acknowledged that he understood the need for Japan to have a self-defense force. Chinese officials continued to worry, however, that as the Japanese economy grew, Japan might use its formidable economic power to develop a strong military.

Many Japanese were prepared to be generous to China, not because they feared Chinese power but because they felt guilty about Japan's aggression and the suffering that it had brought upon the Chinese people, and they believed they owed the Chinese extra favors before they would be able to make profits in the Chinese market. At the time, most Japanese people could never have imagined the speed with which China's economic power would take off over the next several decades, and they were not then seriously worried about competition. Japanese businesses entering the China market sought to develop long-term relationships. They were prepared to be generous in helping their Chinese counterparts even if they lost money for several years, because their goal was to establish lasting relationships.

Trade developed at a fairly fast pace, increasing from $1.1 billion per year in 1972 to almost $4 billion per year in 1975, by which time China had more trade and other contacts with Japan than it had with any other country. In 1974, 24 percent of Chinese trade was with Japan, although only 3 percent of Japanese trade was with China. China bought chemical fertilizer from Japan to help increase its crop yields, and Japan helped China build chemical fiber factories for producing cloth, so the acreage devoted to growing cotton could be reduced to make way for increased grain production. Japan also sent machine tools to China to help set up other factories. At the time, China did not yet have any manufactured goods to sell abroad but it did have petroleum, and with virtually no automobiles, China had little demand for petroleum at home. In 1973 China exported some 1 million tons of petroleum to Japan; by 1975, that figure had increased to 8 million tons, and both Chinese and Japanese specialists were optimistic that petroleum exports would increase rapidly, providing Japan with energy security, reducing its oil dependency on the Soviet Union, and allowing China to increase imports of machinery from Japan. It was entirely unexpected that, two decades later, China would have a growing need for petroleum and would be working with other countries to establish a stable supply of petroleum imports.

Chinese leaders continued to pressure Japan to cut ties with Taiwan in hopes of making progress in their goal of reuniting Taiwan with the mainland. But the Japanese and Taiwanese resisted giving up the deep ties they had established between 1895 and 1945. In 1973, when 10,000 Japanese visitors traveled to China, some 400,000 Japanese visitors traveled to Taiwan. In the mid-1970s, the amount of Japan's trade with Taiwan continued to rival the amount of its trade with mainland China. By using "dummy companies," Japanese companies managed to keep trading with the mainland and Taiwan, but by the late 1970s large Japanese companies were conducting more business with China and allowing smaller dummy companies to trade with Taiwan. Japanese businessmen and politicians who had close relations with Taiwan still found it much easier to deal with Taiwanese businesspeople, many of whom had learned Japanese during colonial days and were more comfortable with the Japanese than they were with the mainlander Chinese—few of whom, with the exception of some in the Northeast, could speak Japanese. Japanese companies preparing to expand their role in China hired Japanese employees who understood China from their days living there before 1945, as well as younger Japanese employees who had studied Chinese language in Japan or in Taiwan.

One of the most difficult issues between China and Japan was how to handle airline flights between the two countries. To keep pressure on Taiwan and ensure that the growing air travel market focused on flights from Japan to the mainland rather than from Japan to Taiwan, Beijing decided not to let Japanese airlines land in China if the company flew planes to Taiwan. In 1974 China and Japan finally reached an agreement that Japan Airlines (JAL) would end its cooperation with Taiwan's China Airlines. Flights from Taiwan to Japan would be allowed, but they would have to be on private carriers, not JAL, and the planes could not fly the Taiwan flag. Planes from China could land at Narita International Airport in Japan, but flights from Taiwan could land only at Haneda Airport, a smaller airport used primarily for domestic flights. Taiwan's officials were so angry about this arrangement that initially they cancelled all flights to and from Japan. It was more than a year before Taiwan backed down and "private airlines," not national carriers, could finally fly between Taiwan and Japan's Haneda Airport. Japan's largest private airline, Zennikku, All Nippon Airways (ANA), did not receive permission from the Japanese government to schedule flights abroad until 1986. But because flights to China were so central to ANA's expansion plans, ANA leaders began cultivating friendships with mainland officials in preparation for playing a key role in what they expected to be a growing number of flights between Japan and China in the future.

Negotiations over fishing rights, which began in 1974, also posed serious problems because China placed many restrictions on fishing near its coastlines. Japan eventually accepted many of China's restrictions. The United States had passed the administration of the Senkaku / Diaoyu Islands to Japan when Okinawa was transferred back to Japan in 1971. China claimed the islands for the first time in December 1971, but Japanese specialists believed that China did not have a strong legal basis for ownership. However, in 1978, when the two countries signed their Treaty of Peace and Friendship, Deng Xiaoping told the Japanese that the question of ownership could be put aside, to be decided by future generations. Thereafter, while Deng was in power, ownership of the islands was not an issue of serious dispute, but by the time of Hu Jintao it became a highly contested issue.

Relations between Japan and China did not blossom immediately after 1972 because they still needed to deal with a host of practical problems in managing their relations. A new treaty, to be known as the Treaty of Peace and Friendship, would provide a framework for making trade agreements, issuing visas, collecting customs fees, setting up consulates, and establishing airline rights. During the treaty discussions, China, in an attempt to strengthen the anti-Soviet stance of the Japanese government, insisted that the treaty should include an "antihegemony clause" directed at the Soviet Union. The Japanese were anti-Soviet, but they refused to agree to such a clause for they feared it would unduly provoke the Soviets. They feared, after the oil shock of 1973 had threatened them with a cutoff of oil from the Middle East, that the Soviets might send military ships and planes to harass Hokkaido and also cut off oil exports to Japan. It was difficult for relations between the two countries to move forward until they reached agreement on the new treaty.

The Treaty of Peace and Friendship and Deng Xiaoping's Visit to Japan

In the summer of 1977 Deng Xiaoping was allowed to return to work, after having been attacked and rusticated in Jiangxi during the Cultural Revolution, and he was given responsibility for guiding foreign policy. He realized that for China to grow, more than anything else it would need the cooperation and assistance of two countries that could provide funds and guidance to help it build a modern industrial economy—Japan and the United States. To begin the process of cooperating with Japan, Deng first had to resolve those issues that were blocking the signing of the Treaty of Peace and Friendship. Japanese diplomats suggested that they might accept an antihegemony clause if the treaty also stated that the clause was not aimed at a third country. The Japanese calculated that with this additional statement, the Soviet Union would not be so upset as to refuse to sell oil to Japan or to take aggressive military action. On July 21, 1978, China and Japan began their negotiations on the treaty. On August 10, after fifteen rounds of negotiations, the Chinese accepted the Japanese proposal to include the statement that the antihegemony clause was not aimed at a third party. At the negotiating table, one Japanese diplomat, the deputy head of the Treaties Division of the Ministry of Foreign Affairs, Togo Kazuhiko, was so happy at hearing that the Chinese had finally agreed that he shook hands with his superior under the table. Japanese diplomats understood that the Chinese decision had come directly from Deng Xiaoping.

Although Prime Minister Tanaka had gone to Beijing in 1972 to sign the normalization agreement, until 1978 no high-level Chinese leader had made a reciprocal visit to Tokyo. After the signing of the Treaty of Peace and Friendship, it was understood that a top Chinese leader should make a return visit to Japan. Yet never before in history had a top Chinese leader in office visited Japan, and never before in the 2,200 years of their history had a leader of China met the Japanese emperor. At Deng's side on his trip to Japan in October 1978 was Liao Chengzhi, ready to advise, translate, and greet his old friends.

On arriving in Japan, Deng announced that he had come for three reasons: to exchange the formal Treaty of Peace and Friendship documents, to thank Japanese friends who had worked to improve relations between the two countries, and to find the "magic drug" that Xu Fu had been looking for. The Xu Fu legend, still well known in China and Japan, tells of a Chinese man who went to Japan some 2,200 years ago in search of a drug that would bring eternal life. Deng explained that the magic drug he was looking for was the secret for how to modernize.

Deng Xiaoping's visit to Japan, October 19–29, 1978, was extraordinary not only because it was unique historically but also because it ushered in the closest relationship between China and Japan in their history. At Deng's press conference at the Foreign Press Center in Tokyo, there were more than 400 reporters in attendance—more than had been present when Queen Elizabeth visited Japan (and the Japanese take a great interest in royalty). In explaining China's situation, Deng said that China would not be like an ugly person trying to appear beautiful by putting on nice clothes. "We are a backward country and we need to learn from Japan." He said that although his visit would be brief, he wanted good relations between Japan and China to continue forever. When asked about China's view on the dispute over the Senkaku / Diaoyu Islands, he said that China and Japan had not reached any agreement on the islands and pointed out that each country even called the islands by different names. But he said that China and Japan should put aside their differences about the islands and work together to find ways to cooperate. After his press conference, Japanese reporters stood and clapped for several minutes.

The Japanese public viewed the Deng visit on television, and though few Chinese then had access to television, they could view the filmed visit in Chinese movie theaters. On his visit to Japan, he greeted as "old friends" many members of the forty delegations he had met with in Beijing. Never before had ordinary Chinese and Japanese people been able to view the leaders of their two countries meeting each other. Never before in history had Chinese and Japanese publics of this size been linked by viewing an event that was bringing the two countries together. When Deng visited Nijo Castle in Kyoto, his Japanese host explained that all of the culture Deng was seeing in Kyoto had been introduced by their Japanese ancestors, who had learned it from China.

The factories that Deng visited in Japan were well selected. They were all excellent models for the plants that Deng wanted to duplicate in China. Although Chiang Kai-shek, and later Mao Zedong, accepted that Japan would not be required to pay war reparations, Deng had reason to hope that Japan would provide far more financial and technical help than any other country to assist China's modernization. Most Japanese viewed the assistance they were giving China as voluntary contributions carried out in the spirit of reparations, without paying formal reparations.

Inayama Yoshihiro, chairman of New Japan Steel and president of the Japan-China Economic Association of business leaders that was supporting the assistance to China, personally accompanied Deng across Tokyo Bay in a hovercraft, something that until then was unknown in China, to the Kimitsu Steel Factory, the most state-of-the-art steel factory in the world. At Kimitsu, for his tour of the factory Deng donned a steel helmet like the one the workers wore. Inayama had already contributed to the modernization of Wuhan Steel, enabling it to become the most modern steel plant in China. Kimitsu was the model for Baoshan, a comprehensive, completely new facility that was being built on the outskirts of Shanghai to allow China, which scarcely a decade earlier was promoting "backyard steel factories," to leapfrog to state-of-the-art steelmaking. In 1977 all of China produced 24 million tons of steel, barely three times as much as Kimitsu alone was producing. There had been contacts between Baoshan and Kimitsu before Deng's visit, but shortly after Deng's visit, on December 22, 1978, the Chinese signed a contract with New Japan Steel to begin construction of the Baoshan Steel plant. The two huge construction projects, the Baoshan factory and a facility for joint petroleum exploration in the Gulf of Bohai, required extensive daily cooperation among Chinese and Japanese planners, managers, financiers, technicians, workers, lawyers, and government administrators.

Deng also visited the Nissan auto plant at Zama. The factory had just introduced robots on the assembly line, arguably making it the most modern auto factory in the world. At the time, the key mode of transportation in Chinese cities was still the bicycle. When Deng was told that the factory produced 94 cars a year per worker, he responded that that was 93 cars a year more than workers were producing at China's best auto factory, the First Automobile Works in Changchun. The industrial base that China was using in Changchun had originally been built by the Japanese when Manchuria was the heartland of Japanese industry, prior to World War II.

By 2015 China would have more than 12,000 miles of high-speed railways, more than all of the rest of the world combined. But in 1978, when Deng visited Japan, China had not yet even started to build its first high-speed railway. The first time a Chinese leader traveled on a high-speed train was in 1978, when Deng rode on the Shinkansen (the "bullet train"), which was completed in 1964 for travel between Tokyo and Kyoto. After Japan's initial success with high-speed trains, European countries also began to develop high-speed railways. In the past, some in China had tried to belittle Japan's industrial accomplishments, whereas others had fawned over Japan's modern industry. Before his trip to Japan, Deng was determined to show appreciation for Japan's accomplishments without groveling. When asked to comment on the ride on the Shinkansen, he said, "It is very fast." Before long, Japanese and European railway engineers and managers were in China teaching engineers the technology. It would take decades for China to acquire the basic technology and management know-how to implement what they began learning from Japan. It was not until 2008, for example, that the first high-speed railway from Beijing to Tianjin was completed. Thereafter, however, the Chinese high-speed railway system expanded very rapidly. The Japanese have had an extraordinary record of quality control and safety; even today, with more than one billion riders, there has never been a death in an accident on the high-speed system. In 2011, two high-speed Chinese trains collided in Wenzhou, China, but since then the Chinese have worked hard to improve safety and have maintained an excellent safety record.

In addition to visiting cultural sites in Kyoto that drew on what the Japanese had learned from the Sui and Tang dynasties, Deng visited the Panasonic factory in Osaka and met Matsushita Konosuke, who, some sixty-one years earlier, had founded the company. Matsushita had begun by making battery-operated bicycle lights, but he had developed his company into what had become at the time the world's dominant maker of consumer electronic products. When meeting with Matsushita in 1978, Deng called him by the nickname given to him by the popular press—the "god of management." Matsushita had a vision of making inexpensive TV sets and other electrical appliances for all of China's relatively poor people, and he responded immediately to Deng's suggestion that he set up factories in China. However, when Deng requested that Matsushita pass on his most recent technology, Matsushita explained that private businesses spend a great deal of resources inventing and developing new products, that this requires considerable time, trouble, and money, and that companies depend on using that technology to produce income to continue inventing new technology. Matsushita wanted to help China develop low-cost consumer electronics to supply to Chinese consumers, he said, but like entrepreneurs elsewhere, he understood that his company's survival in the marketplace depended on its keeping its advanced technology to itself.

Nevertheless, Deng and Matsushita hit it off, and Matsushita responded by moving quickly to establish consumer-electronics factories in China and to pass on some technology—though not the company's latest crown jewels—and management know-how. Matsushita established factories in many different regions of China, following his strategy of giving people in many localities an extra incentive to buy his products since the regional factories provided local people with employment.

While in Japan, Deng also asked broader questions, such as how Japan had moved from a government-led economic system during World War II to a more open market economy thereafter. It was clear that Deng was considering how he could provide leadership for a similar transition.

When Deng visited Japan, Tanaka Kakuei was under house arrest for his role in the Lockheed scandal—giving bribes to Lockheed so that ANA would buy its planes—but Deng persisted in asking to visit Tanaka to express his appreciation for what Tanaka had done to improve relations between the two countries. When a visit was finally approved, Deng told Tanaka what he had said to the families of those who had contributed to good Sino-Japanese relations in the 1950s, and what he had just told the daughter of the late Takasaki Tatsunosuke in Osaka, "When we drink water, we cannot forget those who dug the well." At Tanaka Kakuei's home, Deng explained that when Tanaka had visited China, he had not been able to welcome him because he had been in the "peach garden" (a euphemism for rusticating during the Cultural Revolution as punishment for his political errors). He told Tanaka, "We cannot forget what you did for our relationship," and he invited Tanaka to visit China as a guest of the government. After their meeting, Tanaka told reporters that the signing of the Treaty of Peace and Friendship with China was the best thing that had happened to Japan since the Meiji Restoration. He added that of all the foreign leaders he had previously met, Zhou Enlai had been the most impressive, and that he had similar feelings when he met Deng Xiaoping.

While in Tokyo, Deng had a two-hour lunch with Emperor Hirohito at the Imperial Palace. To allow the emperor to speak freely when greeting visitors, no records are kept of his private conversations. But Foreign Minister Huang Hua, who attended the luncheon, noted that the emperor had spoken of the "unfortunate happening," which Huang had taken as an apology to the Chinese people for war damages.

After the luncheon the two foreign ministers, Huang Hua and Sonoda Sunao, signed the formal papers for the Treaty of Peace and Friendship, and Deng gave Prime Minister Fukuda a hug. Prime Minister Fukuda appeared nonplussed by the hug but quickly recovered and accepted it as a sign of goodwill. In their conversation, Deng said, "Friendly relations and cooperation are the common wish of the billion Chinese and Japanese people. . . . Let us on behalf of the people in both countries continue the friendship generation after generation."[1] In a public opinion poll conducted in Japan not long after Deng's visit, some 78 percent of the Japanese public reported positive feelings toward China.

Shortly after Deng returned to Beijing, a delegation of leading economic officials from China visited Japan. In a report of their visit, they concluded that Japanese business leaders had made important adaptations to capitalism since the days of Marx. Japanese capitalists had learned how to make money by providing good conditions for their workers, who then worked harder than the exploited workers described by Marx. It was a brilliant interpretation, recognizing the value and accuracy of Marx's observations while also pointing out that the practices that China was introducing would be good for Chinese workers. The delegation also understood the key point in Japan's approach to quality control: make the product properly the first time rather than relying on inspection. During the following years, Chinese factories displayed big banners encouraging workers to study Japanese management practices.

Many Japanese businesspeople believed that the best way for their generation to respond to the suffering that Japanese aggression had caused was not to keep apologizing but to help China develop its industry and raise its living standards so that China could live peacefully with its neighbors. The Japan External Trade Organization (JETRO), under the Ministry of Trade and Industry, responded to Chinese requests for technology assistance by sending in specialists in sector after sector, to help the Chinese with their industrial development.

During 1981 the number of Chinese visitors to Japan surpassed 17,000 and the number of Japanese visitors to China reached 110,000. The total number of visitors was almost five times the number in 1978.[2] In 1981, roughly 250 scientific and technical delegations from China, with a total of 1,100 members, visited Japan to acquaint themselves with developments in Japan in their respective specializations. Between 1979 and 1982, approximately 480 Japanese students entered Chinese institutions of higher learning and some 960 Chinese students entered Japanese universities and research institutes for advanced study. Furthermore, the number of Chinese students in Japan continued to grow rapidly. During this time, Japan gave some 261 billion yen in grants or loans to Chinese applicants.[3]

China's Budget Tightening, 1979–1981

Chairman Hua Guofeng, who succeeded Mao after his death in September 1976, stopped using slogans from the Cultural Revolution and started importing new technology from abroad to provide a solid basis for economic growth. Local governments and various ministries, given the green light to move ahead, rushed to arrange for the import of machinery to set up model factories. Chinese officials eagerly began discussions with foreign companies and encouraged them to submit bids for projects. A group of officials known as the "petroleum faction," because of their experience in organizing huge undertakings to expand oil exploration and extraction, was given responsibility for supervising many of the new factory projects. The leaders of the petroleum faction had proved themselves to be dedicated, creative, and even heroic in overcoming shortages of transport, fuel, and materials while training inexperienced managers to complete projects such as the Daqing oil field. Japanese firms, taking advantage of the improved relationships since normalization in 1972, were especially active in signing contracts to build Chinese infrastructure and industrial facilities. They were also active in helping to construct electric power stations and petrochemical plants. A groundbreaking ceremony for the huge Baoshan Steelworks, involving many different Japanese companies, was held on December 24, 1978, just two months after Deng's visit to Japan.

Chinese local officials were all so eager, so hungry, for new factories that it was not easy for higher-level officials to restrain them from rushing to sign contracts to import factories before they had completed adequate preparations for the necessary land, labor, and technical skills, or had found resources to make their payments. Some Chinese officials, especially in the Ministry of Finance, the Planning Commission, and the banks—still chastened by the devastating errors made by rushing ahead during the Great Leap Forward—were concerned that Chinese officials were moving ahead too quickly without sufficient capital and preparation. Chen Yun, who had seen his First Five-Year Plan destroyed by the Great Leap Forward, became the spokesman for the cautious budget balancers.

In February 1979, after China invaded Vietnam, it became clear that the war required substantial funding and China could no longer afford all the contracts that Chinese officials had signed to build new factories. On the last day of February 1979, the budget balancers froze some $2.6 billion in contracts with Japanese companies, including the contracts for Baoshan. The project managers and Japanese companies still tried to find ways to move ahead. In most cases, Japanese firms and banks arranged to provide deferred payments and loans. In one case, however, the project came to a halt.

In late 1980, in the struggles between the builders and the budget balancers, the balancers under the leadership of Chen Yun won the day. Some projects were to be stopped. In 1978, Chinese planners had expected that oil production would continue to grow, but from 1979 to 1981 oil production stagnated. With a growing domestic demand for oil, China began restricting oil exports to Japan, which made it difficult for China to buy Japanese goods and to pay for Japanese investments in China. As Chen Yun and the budget balancers were prevailing, Hua Guofeng was being forced to accept responsibility for signing contracts that were beyond the government's means. Deng joined Chen Yun in criticizing Hua, who had expected a 20 percent annual increase in oil production until 1985, for his excessive optimism and his neglect of economic realities. The collapse of an oil rig in November 1979 became the reason for criticizing project managers who had tried to move ahead too quickly with oil exploration and steel production. Hua Guofeng became the scapegoat for poor management, and in late 1980 Chen Yun and Deng promoted a major readjustment policy that helped consolidate their power and remove Hua Guofeng from office. Many project managers were removed from their positions as well. The readjustment policy of late 1980 required the cancellation or postponement of projects that previously had been agreed to by foreign countries. More than half of all the foreign contracts that required readjustment were Japanese. In January 1981, telegrams were sent to Japanese firms announcing that the first phase of the Baoshan construction work, which had already begun, was cancelled.

The cancellation of work on the Baoshan project was particularly troublesome to the Japanese because its scale was so large, so many Japanese companies were involved, and many Japanese companies had already made huge investments in the project. Japanese officials, whose hopes were dashed, were upset about the money they would lose and about the disregard of the Chinese for international contracts. Some Japanese wondered whether the Chinese would resume all the projects for which they had signed contracts. The Chinese expressed frustration with the Japanese for their arrogance in lecturing them on the importance of respecting contracts, which seemed to them a minor issue, considering all the horrible things the Japanese had done to the Chinese during the Sino-Japanese War.

China's early hope that the expansion of oil production would earn foreign exchange for trade also ran into problems. Beginning in 1978, the Chinese were optimistic about oil exploration in many areas off the Chinese coast, and they had sought help from foreign firms for the expertise and technology they lacked. The Chinese chose to cooperate with French firms off the coast of Vietnam and with Japanese firms in the Gulf of Bohai.

Hoping to convince the Japanese of their need for the cancellations, Yao Yilin, one of Chen Yun's balancers, was sent to Japan to provide an explanation. He acknowledged that China had not been able to develop new oil fields as quickly as the Chinese had hoped. When Deng Xiaoping received Japanese leaders who were upset at the failure of the Chinese to fulfill their commitments, he explained the Chinese situation. Deng personally met Doko Toshio, then age eighty-five and chairman of Keidanren, a former engineer with tremendous moral authority owing to his integrity and humble lifestyle, and Ohira Masayoshi, the statesman who had negotiated normalization of relations. Both sought ways to keep the relationship moving forward. Deng was not a budget balancer by nature, nor was he the kind of person who would bow deeply in apology as many Japanese might have done, but he was straightforward in admitting China's errors and in acknowledging that the Chinese lacked experience. He forthrightly said that the Chinese had made some mistakes, they lacked foreign capital, and they could not afford to pay for all the factories for which they had signed contracts. He also made it clear that China intended to move forward on the projects as soon as it could afford them.

Japan's Economic Advice, Assistance, and Cooperation

Okita Saburo, a respected, cosmopolitan economic planner who had lived in Dalian from his birth in 1914 until he completed elementary school and had worked in the Ministry of Communications in Beijing from June 1939 to February 1942, was sent to China in January 1979 to impress on Chinese leaders how upset Japanese businesspeople were about the cancellations. He met with Deputy Prime Minister Gu Mu, the senior official guiding economic development. Okita warned him that Beijing's cancellation of the contracts could affect China's reputation in international business. When he returned to Japan, Okita explained to Japanese political and business leaders that China had not been able to exercise proper oversight when planning to import foreign plants because so many experienced officials had been pushed aside during the Cultural Revolution and they had not returned to their positions in time to provide due diligence.

While in China, Okita sought to understand what China and Japan could do to resume work on the contracted projects. He suggested a program of Japanese aid to relieve China's shortages of foreign exchange, and when he returned to Tokyo, he made the rounds to political leaders and bureaucrats to win their support for the aid program. He became Japan's foreign minister in November 1979, and in the next month he returned to Beijing with Prime Minister Ohira for the official launch of Japan's Overseas Development Assistance program for China.

Over the following two decades, from 1979 to 1999, Japan provided some 56 percent of all bilateral aid given to China, consisting of three kinds of aid: grant aid, primarily for health, education, and other social infrastructure; technical aid; and yen loans, primarily for the development of infrastructure. When China requested technical advice, JETRO identified appropriate Japanese technicians; it dispatched a total of 4,158 technicians to China, and China sent some 9,712 technicians to Japan for training programs. From 1979 to 2001 Japan supplied a total of $15.9 billion worth of aid to China.[4]

Japan did not give direct aid only to China. It also gave grants to Australia to support the mining of coal and iron ore that would be supplied to China at low prices so that the Baoshan steel project, by far the largest single project with Japanese funding, could soon be resumed.

Gu Mu invited Okita Saburo to organize a group of high-level Japanese advisers who could introduce their experiences in guiding Japanese economic development. By 1979 it was clear that China had made disastrous errors during the Great Leap Forward and the Cultural Revolution just as Japan was achieving its rapid industrialization. In early 1978 Gu Mu led a five-week, high-level study mission to Europe to learn about different approaches for guiding economic development. The governments of the European countries and the United States had guided their economies mainly by providing regulations to ensure fair market operations, but the Japanese government had promoted economic development by providing coordination and guidance, and assuring that funds were available for the development of key sectors. Gu Mu and his staff regarded Japan's experience as more appropriate for China than that of the Western countries. Okita himself had been head of research on Japan's Economic Stabilization Board, guiding economic activities in Japan immediately after World War II when the country was especially concerned about controlling inflation in a time of shortages. In 1955, when the Economic Planning Agency was established to provide long-range coordination for economic development, Okita was director-general of the agency's Planning Bureau. He thus had experience in both stabilization and planning for growth.

After initial discussions, an advisory group was formalized as the China-Japan Working Group for Exchange of Economic Information, and its first meeting was held in Hakone in May 1981. Gu Mu brought in Ma Hong, a well-known economist who would later be chiefly responsible for overseeing the introduction of a market economy, to head the Chinese side of the discussions. Okita brought in imaginative senior Japanese officials who since 1955 had played important roles in guiding Japan's economic development. Shimokobe Atsushi had played a key part in conceptualizing how to delineate regions and how to plan and coordinate the various components required for regional growth. Miyazaki Isamu was a leading scholar and official responsible for economic planning. Nagai Michio, the son of a leading Diet member and Japan's only academic specialist in higher education to serve as minister of education, was brought in for a discussion on higher education.

The China-Japan Working Group, with appropriate replacements over time, has continued to meet every year, with the exception of 2013 and 2014 when relations between the two countries were especially tense due to the dispute over the Senkaku / Diaoyu Islands. Over the years, the group took up such issues as macroeconomic policy in the two countries, Sino-Japanese relations, the Chinese economic reforms, and global changes. Japanese members spoke of their past experiences, including Japan's emphasis on the civilian economy rather than on military affairs, the stress on high-quality labor, the nature of cooperation between government and the private sector, the importance of allowing foreign companies to bring in ideas and technology, and the desirability of first investing in sectors that could produce quick payoffs. The group remained informal and did not publicize the results of its talks, but Chinese participants expressed appreciation for the frank discussions and advice as China was beginning to open its markets and link up with the international economy. The World Bank also played a large role by bringing in economic advisers from socialist as well as market economies. The economic advisers from the socialist countries had led economies where the government directly supplied inputs. Western economists had worked in countries where the role of the government was to provide regulations but not to lead the modernization of the economy. But in working with Japanese economic planners, the Chinese did not need to go through the World Bank. They could work with Japanese pioneers directly.

By 1982 many of the projects in China that had been delayed had resumed construction, thanks to Japanese loans, including construction of phase two of the Baoshan Steelworks, the largest of all the joint projects. Plans had originally called for steel production to begin in 1983. Finally, owing to extraordinary efforts on the part of Chinese and Japanese managers and workers, steel production began in 1985. Completion of the Baoshan Steelworks enabled China to accelerate machinery production and construction, and Baoshan became a model for other modern steel plants in China. By 2015, with the addition of other steel plants based on the Baoshan model, China was producing almost one million tons of steel per year, roughly forty times China's steel production in 1977 and more than half of the world's total steel production. Excellent relationships were developed between the Japanese and Chinese officials and engineers working together at Baoshan. Even many years later, Chinese and Japanese officials who had taken part in the technology transfer held reunions to celebrate the success of their joint collaborations, allowing the Chinese to express their appreciation to the Japanese who had assisted in the project.

The Japan-China Economic Association estimated that between 1978 and 1984, China concluded some $11.7 billion in contracts for whole plants and technology from abroad, and Japan won more than $6 billion of those contracts.[5] The Japanese had the lead in China not only in the steel and petrochemical sectors but also in synthetic textiles and chemical fertilizer, which played key roles in producing cloth and raising agricultural output while containing the amount of farmland allocated to cotton production. By 1984 China was beginning to import consumer goods from Japan, including televisions sets, refrigerators, washing machines, and automobiles (mostly for official use); in 1986, however, Chinese officials, worried about inflation and the balance of payments, greatly curtailed imports from Japan, once again leading to the cancellation of orders.

In short, there were frustrations for the Japanese in their efforts to work together with the inexperienced but ambitious Chinese on their path to industrial modernization. However, unlike Russian scientists and technicians who had been advising China and were brought home in 1960, many Chinese and Japanese businessmen found ways to continue working together.

Cultural Exchanges in the 1980s

Deng Xiaoping believed that to maintain robust economic exchanges between China and Japan it was important to strengthen the nations' underlying cultural ties. After the Treaty of Peace and Friendship was signed in 1978, many Japanese religious and cultural groups sent delegations to China to interact with their Chinese counterparts, including Buddhist associations and groups specializing in arts and culture, such as calligraphy, Chinese chess, music, and poetry. Several hundred prefectures, cities, and towns in Japan established sister relations with their Chinese counterparts. Sometimes these cultural groups had an economic impact, as the Japanese groups were hoping for marketing opportunities in China and some Chinese localities were seeking Japanese investments.

Many Japanese books were translated into Chinese. In the 1980s, Japanese movies were widely shown in China, including romantic stories between Chinese and Japanese men and women. Since television was just being introduced in China and China had not yet produced many dramas or historical plays on its own, translations of Japanese television programs were popular. The Japanese family-drama series *O-shin* (*A-xin* in Chinese), about a hard-working, frugal, rural Japanese family in Yamagata, was by far the most popular Japanese series broadcast on Chinese television. The program centered on an impoverished but highly disciplined mother, A-xin, who worked hard, saved, and was completely dedicated to helping her children get a good start in life. A-xin's character displayed the moral qualities that Chinese leaders wished to instill in their people. Many Chinese youths who grew up in the 1980s have fond memories of Japanese stories, songs, movies, and television series.

In October 1984 General Secretary Hu Yaobang and Prime Minister Nakasone Yasuhiro arranged for some 3,000 Japanese young people to visit China, hosted by the Communist Youth League under the direction of Hu Jintao, to help Chinese and Japanese youth build friendships for the future. In January 1987 when Hu Yaobang was criticized and dismissed from office, one of the main criticisms was that he had been too generous in using Chinese resources to entertain the Japanese youths. But the relationships formed during the exchanges were later useful when some of those young people in both countries rose to higher positions and drew on the contacts they had made earlier in dealing with issues between their two countries.

In 1984 Japan and China, under the leadership of Prime Minister Nakasone Yasuhiro and General Secretary Hu Yaobang, established the Commission for Sino-Japanese Friendship in the Twenty-First Century. The commission, consisting of prominent Chinese and Japanese representatives, provided a forum that would continue even after 1992, when relations between the two countries grew tense.

Political Frictions in the 1980s

Compared with the political difficulties between China and Japan that increased after 1992, the years from 1978 to 1992 constituted a golden age of political cooperation, cultural exchange, expanding economic connections, and people-to-people exchanges. However, even during this golden age political frictions arose that foreshadowed problems that would become more serious in the 1990s.

Within Japan, the Japan Teachers' Union after World War II was dominated by leftist intellectuals critical of both Japan's wartime behavior and conservative political officials, such as Kishi Nobusuke and Sato Eisaku. The Japanese Ministry of Education, in contrast, was dominated by conservative educators who sought to teach patriotism to Japanese youth, and it published guidelines for what the textbooks on each subject in each grade should cover. On June 26, 1982, Japanese newspapers criticized the Ministry of Education for attempting to change the guidelines for modern history courses to soften the criticism of Japanese militarism that had led to World War II, suggesting that instead of the word "aggression," the texts should refer to the "advance" of the Japanese troops. (In fact, it was later shown that the newspaper reports were inaccurate.) For almost a month after the newspaper reports were published, the Chinese press hardly paid any attention to this issue.

However, on July 20, 1982, Chinese media launched a full-scale attack on what they said was a Japanese campaign to play down the horrifying behavior of Japanese soldiers during World War II. Graphic pictures of Japanese soldiers decapitating Chinese prisoners and of piles of Chinese corpses appeared in the Chinese press. In articles about the Nanjing Massacre it was reported that 360,000 Chinese were killed, and newspapers showed pictures of chopped-up Chinese corpses. The Japanese wartime experiments in bacteriological warfare on live human subjects were featured in stories and pictures. The Japanese "three alls" policy (kill all, burn all, loot all), carried out in areas where Chinese guerrillas had killed Japanese troops, was also featured. The media campaign reached a peak on August 15, the thirty-seventh anniversary of the Japanese surrender in 1945. Reporting on the campaign was particularly widespread in Chinese youth magazines, and the mid-September 1982 political report presented at the Twelfth National Party Congress by General Secretary Hu Yaobang, who later would play an important role in promoting goodwill between Chinese and Japanese youth, warned against the revival of Japanese militarism. The Chinese media campaign, launched when the Chinese believed the Japanese were beginning to soften their criticism of their own role in the Sino-Japanese War, reflected a deep anger about the Japanese atrocities, but it was also a warning to the Japanese to avoid a return to militarism.

On August 15, 1985, Prime Minister Nakasone Yasuhiro made an official visit to the Yasukuni Shrine to pay respects to the 2.4 million Japanese who had given their lives for their country. He was the first prime minister to pay such a visit while in public office. The Chinese, upset with Nakasone for visiting a place that enshrined the souls of twelve accused class-A war criminals, surprised the prime minister with the strength of their criticism. Nakasone said that he had visited the shrine on the fortieth anniversary of the end of the war to pay respects to those who had given their lives and whose souls were enshrined there. He explained that his own brother was enshrined there and that he went to pay his respects to him as well. However, in the following year Nakasone announced that because of the views of Chinese, Koreans, and others, he would not visit the Yasukuni Shrine again; instead he would find another way to pay his respects to those who had given their lives for the country.

In the summer of 1985, a twenty-eight-part Chinese television drama, *Four Generations under One Roof*, portrayed the suffering of a Chinese family during the Japanese occupation. On September 18, 1985, on the fifty-fourth anniversary of Japan's seizure of Manchuria in 1931, university students in Beijing and other major cities throughout the country demonstrated against the Japanese. The themes of their protests echoed the complaints of earlier generations of Chinese students who had also demonstrated against the Japanese. They opposed Japanese militarism and advocated boycotting Japanese goods. Some students also complained about Chinese leaders who were courting Japanese businessmen. Some gave speeches urging that the Senkaku / Diaoyu Islands be returned to China.

At the same time, the Chinese authorities made efforts to quell the anti-Japanese mood. The official media, including *Zhongguo Qingnian Bao* (China Youth Daily) and *Renmin Ribao* (People's Daily) acknowledged that the Chinese people had suffered at the hands of the Japanese, but they also editorialized that in the new era there were equal relations between China and other countries, and that relations should be based on mutual respect and mutual benefit. At a meeting of the Commission for Sino-Japanese Friendship in the Twenty-First Century, Hu Yaobang said that a revival of militarism in Japan had to be prevented, but that the Chinese had to differentiate between war criminals and the Japanese people.

Disagreements in 1987 about the use of a Kyoto dormitory set off huge anti-Japanese demonstrations by Chinese students. The dormitory (Kokaryo) had been built before World War II, and in 1950 it had been purchased by Taiwan for the use of students studying at Kyoto University. After normalization of relations between China and Japan in 1972, a controversy arose as to whether the property should belong to Taiwan or to the mainland. In 1977, the issue was taken to the Kyoto District Court, and the court ruled that the PRC had acquired ownership in 1978 when Japan broke relations with the Taiwan government and established relations with the mainland. But in 1982, a higher-level court in Osaka ruled on appeal that the dormitory belonged to Taiwan. Finally, when the issue was reviewed by the Osaka High Court on February 26, 1987, the ruling was again in favor of Taiwan. Chinese authorities and Chinese students were furious. The issue about ownership of the dormitory was featured in the Chinese press for months on end, and it was linked to Japanese relations with Taiwan and with the revival of Japanese militarism. A local Taiwanese politician, Lee Teng-hui, whose first language was Japanese and who had attended Kyoto University, became vice president of Taiwan in 1984. After Chiang Ching-kuo died in 1987, some mainlanders tried to stop Lee from becoming president but he gained enough support to become president in 1988. When Lee gained power, mainland Chinese feared that Japan was strengthening its relations with Taiwan.

The ownership of the dormitory was also associated with the idea that Japan was becoming more militaristic and arrogant. In the late 1980s, before the Japanese economic bubble burst in 1989, the value of the yen had increased compared with the U.S. dollar. The Japanese economy was still growing rapidly and Japanese firms were buying up valuable property in the United States as well as elsewhere. Japanese manufacturing was gaining not only in textiles but also in areas that Americans had considered to be their strength—electronics and automobiles. Japanese businesspeople in the late 1980s had so much money to spend abroad that they earned a reputation among Westerners, as well as among the Chinese, of being arrogant. Some Chinese, in observing Japanese businessmen at the time, felt they recalled the behavior of Japanese soldiers during the Sino-Japanese War.

Since the mid-1970s under Prime Minister Miki, there had been an understanding among Japanese political leaders that Japan would spend no more than 1 percent of its GNP on national defense. With Japan's rapid growth in the 1980s, the 1 percent ceiling provided enough money for Japan to expand its defense expenditures. Then in 1987 Prime Minister Nakasone removed the 1 percent ceiling on defense expenditures and allowed the amount to slightly exceed 1 percent. The Chinese press expressed fears that the essential Japanese spirit was the samurai spirit, and that proud Japanese militarism was making a comeback.

Still, throughout the 1980s China was closer to Japan than it was to any other foreign country. In 1986 about 40 percent of the 10,000 foreign experts in China were Japanese. Japanese businesspeople and diplomats had better access to the Chinese than representatives of any other country. Japan played a major role in the transfer of technology and management skills to China, and the Chinese and Japanese involved often developed very good personal relationships.

After Tiananmen, Japan Ends Sanctions Quickly

After the Tiananmen Square tragedy of June 4, 1989, Japanese citizens, like those in Western countries, were deeply upset by the killing of innocent demonstrators on Beijing's streets. In 1988, 69 percent of the Japanese surveyed said they felt close to China, but the next year, following the violent suppression of the Tiananmen Square uprising, only 52 percent reported that they felt close to China.[6]

The Japanese government, along with Western governments, imposed sanctions on China because of its attack on the Chinese protestors. However, Japan's leaders, aware of the suffering Japan had inflicted on the Chinese during the Sino-Japanese War, knew that Japan was not in a strong moral position to criticize others who killed Chinese citizens. They believed that efforts to isolate China, like sanctions, would cause problems for many Chinese people, not just those who were responsible for the crackdown, and would end up strengthening the hard-liners within China who resented foreign interference. They also knew that serious sanctions would hurt Japan's trade with China and ultimately the future of Sino-Japanese relations.

Compared with the Western governments' severe sanctions on China, sanctions imposed by the Japanese government were relatively light. At the Group of Seven (G7) Economic Summit held in mid-July 1989, only weeks after the Tiananmen tragedy, Japan joined the other powers in criticizing China, but it also urged the other countries not to escalate their sanctions. One year later, at the July 1990 G7 Economic Summit, Prime Minister Kaifu Toshiki announced that Japan would resume lending to China, which it had put on hold after June 4, 1989. In 1991 Japan initiated its third batch of loans to China. No Western nation was so quick to remove its sanctions.

In August 1991 Prime Minister Kaifu was the first leader of a major foreign country to visit China after the Tiananmen tragedy. As the only country that had been bombed with nuclear weapons, Japan was then taking the lead in promoting international nuclear nonproliferation. While Kaifu was in Beijing, Chinese officials, appreciative of Japan's leadership in ending the post-Tiananmen sanctions, signed the Nuclear Non-Proliferation Treaty. Kaifu and Chinese leaders also discussed how to make use of 1992, the twentieth anniversary of normalization of relations, to further strengthen relations between the two countries. The boldest idea discussed was the possibility that the Japanese emperor might visit China.

CHAPTER ELEVEN

The Deterioration of Sino-Japanese Relations, 1992–2018

ONLY ONCE IN the 2,000 years of contact between China and Japan has an emperor of Japan or China visited the other country. It was unimaginable that the Chinese would ever have welcomed Emperor Hirohito, the highest symbol of Japanese invaders. After Emperor Hirohito died in January 1989, Japanese political leaders initially tried to play down his responsibility for the war, but China's foreign minister, Qian Qichen, representing China at Emperor Hirohito's funeral ceremonies in Tokyo, rebuked the Japanese for this and told them they should study their history. Not only Chinese spokespersons but also Western and even many Japanese leaders and writers acknowledged that Emperor Hirohito had attended meetings at which war plans were discussed.

In 1989, the succession to the throne of Akihito, who at the end of World War II was only eleven years old, provided an opportunity to highlight the new era of peaceful relations between the two countries. It also gave China, which had been the target of sanctions by Western countries for its crackdown against protesters around Tiananmen Square on June 1989, a chance to showcase its return to the world of international diplomacy.

Emperor Akihito's Visit to China

General Secretary Jiang Zemin visited Japan from April 6 to 10, 1992, to lay the groundwork for Emperor Akihito's visit to China. In Tokyo, Jiang met with Emperor Akihito, high-level Japanese officials, and people from various walks of life. Japanese officials wanted to make sure that a visit by Emperor Akihito to China would not be used by the Chinese to publicize Japanese brutalities during the war, and China provided such assurances.

Because some details of the visit were still unresolved while General Secretary Jiang Zemin was in Tokyo, the emperor's decision to make the trip was not yet publicly announced. Discussions about the visit and Japan's planning for the trip proceeded under the leadership of Prime Minister Miyazawa Kiichi, a well-educated cosmopolitan official who was considered sympathetic to China, and Chief Cabinet Secretary Kato Koichi, a leading Diet member who spoke Chinese and had previously served as a diplomat in the Ministry of Foreign Affairs.[1]

On October 23, 1992, only four days after the close of China's Fourteenth Party Congress, Emperor Akihito and Empress Michiko arrived in China for a five-day visit. In Tiananmen Square, the Japanese emperor was welcomed with a twenty-one-gun salute and a Chinese band playing the Japanese national anthem. Chinese police had cleared the streets of potential protesters, and no incidents occurred. The emperor was warmly welcomed by General Secretary Jiang Zemin and President Yang Shangkun, both of whom were restrained in their criticism of Japan. Beijing's mayor, Chen Xitong, who accompanied Emperor Akihito to the Great Wall, reported that he was "very friendly to China," adding, "we very much welcome him." Chinese television described Emperor Akihito's visit as symbolizing the role that Japan was now playing as a peace-loving country.

Wu Jianmin, then spokesperson for the Ministry of Foreign Affairs, announced, "It is up to the Japanese side to decide what remarks the emperor will make during his visit to China." At the opening banquet in Beijing, Emperor Akihito acknowledged Japanese aggression during World War II and the suffering that had been caused by Japan, saying, "During the long history of Sino-Japanese relations, there was a short period when Japan caused the Chinese people to live in dire misery, about which I feel deep regret." Emperor Akihito visited Xi'an, the site of the Tang dynasty capital that had played such a key role in the formation of Japanese civilization. At the Shaanxi Provincial Museum in Xi'an, the emperor and empress viewed a stone tablet inscribed with the characters 平成 (in Chinese, the characters are read as *pingcheng,* "preserving peace," but in Japanese, they refer to *heisei,* the name Emperor Akihito had chosen as the reign name for his era). This was a testimony to the deep cultural links between the two countries. There were no unpleasant incidents during the entire trip, and the visit was a high point in the history of relations between the two countries.

However, by 1992 new issues were arising that would have an impact on the relationship. That year, China passed a domestic law that for the first time provided a legal basis for its assertion that the Senkaku / Diaoyu Islands were part of Chinese territory. By 1996 China was carrying out oil exploration in the vicinity. China began increasing pressure on the issue of the Senkaku / Diaoyu Islands. As tensions over the islands rose, public opinion in both countries began to change. By 2006 only 27 percent of Japanese surveyed said they had positive views of China, and only 21 percent of Chinese respondents expressed positive attitudes toward Japan. The relationship would continue to deteriorate until 2015.

Sources of Tension after 1992

There were several reasons for the worsening of relations between China and Japan. One was the loss of key "bridge builders" in the two governments, senior members who had worked to normalize relations.

The Exit of Deng, Tanaka, and Other Bridge Builders

A few days before Emperor Akihito traveled to China, Deng Xiaoping was photographed at the 1992 Fourteenth Party Congress as he passed leadership of the party over to Jiang Zemin. Deng had been firmly committed to improving relations with Japan. With his unassailable Communist Party credentials and his seven years spent fighting the Japanese, Deng was not vulnerable to charges of being soft on Japan. In contrast, Jiang Zemin was too young to have fought in the Sino-Japanese War and because Jiang's father, like other Chinese businessmen, had had some contacts with Japanese occupation officials during World War II, Jiang was more vulnerable to criticism if he were judged to be soft on Japan. Some say that Jiang had a scar on his leg from bites by a dog owned by a Japanese official. Whatever the reason, Jiang did not enjoy close relations with Japanese leaders, and unlike Deng, he did not publicly urge that China should maintain good relations with Japan.

After Liao Chengzhi died in 1983, no Chinese leader had comparable knowledge of Japan and such deep friendships. In the course of negotiating normalization, Tanaka Kakuei, Ohira Masayoshi, and Sonoda Sunao had developed personal relationships with their counterparts, but by 1992 they were no longer available. Tanaka was arrested in 1976, Ohira died in 1980, and Sonoda died in 1984. Some of their successors endeavored to continue working with China, but compared with those who built the bridges to normalize relations in 1972 and to negotiate the Treaty of Peace and Friendship in 1978, they lacked the personal connections to Chinese leaders and the determination to maintain the relationship.

The Collapse of the Soviet Union

From 1969, following clashes between China and the Soviet Union along their border, until 1991, when the Soviet Union was dissolved, China, Japan, and the United States had a shared strategic interest in cooperating against the Soviet Union. With the collapse of the Soviet Union in 1991, that shared interest disappeared. Thereafter, the inability of the three countries to count on the cooperation of their former allies created uncertainties, which grew as both China and Japan expanded their military capacity and began to lay claim to the islands between them.

The Reduced Importance of Japanese Assistance

In the early 1980s Japan's financial and technical assistance was critical in launching China's industrial drive. In 1978, China's GDP was $219 billion, and by 1993, as China's growth was spurting forward, it had jumped to $1,712 billion. The second blast furnace at Baoshan Steelworks, built with Japanese assistance, was opened in 1991. China had enough resources by this point that Japanese assistance was no longer crucial. From 1989 to 1992 the Japanese had played a key role in breaking through international sanctions on business and trade with China, but by 1992 the sanctions had greatly eased. Furthermore, by 1993 it was clear that the Japanese economy was not going to recover its rapid growth after the burst of its economic bubble in 1989. Japan was no longer such an attractive model for China.

President Lee Teng-hui and Japan's Links to Taiwanese Localism

When the "locals" took over the leadership of the Taiwan government from the "mainlanders" in 1992, Beijing's leaders worried that local resistance to a reunion with the mainland would grow, and that Japan would support the resistance. Chiang Ching-kuo, who became president of Taiwan after his father, Chiang Kai-shek, died in 1975, believed that long-term stability on Taiwan required giving local people a greater role in governance. He chose a local, Lee Teng-hui, to be vice president, and when Chiang Ching-kuo died of illness in 1992, Lee became president, despite the efforts by some Nationalist Party officials to block his accession. Before Lee's presidency, elections were held in Taiwan as if Taiwan represented all of China and as if the Guomindang had a chance of retaking the mainland. Representatives of the different provinces, nearly all of them mainlanders who had fled to Taiwan after the Nationalists lost the Civil War, selected the members of the legislature. After becoming president, Lee Teng-hui arranged for direct elections of the legislature. The first election was held in 1992, and after that the locals, who made up roughly two-thirds of the population of Taiwan, dominated Taiwan politics.

Chinese leaders in Beijing knew that Japan had earlier supported a two-China policy and that Lee Teng-hui and other locals had close relations with Japan. As a child, Lee Teng-hui had learned Japanese before he had learned Mandarin Chinese. In 1944 and 1945 he had served in the Japanese Army, and his brother died fighting for the Japanese. He had attended Japanese schools in Taiwan and won a scholarship to Kyoto Imperial University, where he studied briefly. As president, he maintained close ties to Japanese leaders, some of whom had worked in Taiwan before 1945. Chinese government officials worried that Japan would support Lee Teng-hui's efforts to remain independent from the mainland.

To maintain pressure on Taiwan to accept mainland rule, Beijing officials sought to restrict the international space in which Taiwan's officials could function. As a condition for normalizing relations, China had required Japan and the United States to agree that their high officials would not visit Taiwan and that top Taiwanese officials not be allowed to visit their countries. Lee Teng-hui sought to break through this constraint. In 1994 he visited several Latin American countries where Taiwan still had formal diplomatic relations, and he requested permission from U.S. officials to stop in Hawaii for refueling on his way home. American officials, trying to balance their agreement with Beijing with Lee's request to stop in Hawaii, decided he could land in Hawaii, but they restricted him to a military base.

Lee Teng-hui publicized his confinement to the Hawaiian military base and this aroused many Americans, who complained that their country had coddled dictators during the Cold War and said it was time to support democratic principles. Why, they asked, should the United States follow the wishes of China, which had shot students protesting near Tiananmen Square, and not allow the visit of a leader of Taiwan, a democratic nation—a leader who had also spent many years in the United States earning a Ph.D. degree from Cornell? The following year, in 1995, Cornell University invited Lee Teng-hui to speak at alumni events. The U.S. House of Representatives voted 398 to 0 and the Senate 97 to 1 that Lee should be allowed to come to the United States to speak at Cornell. Given this popular support, President Bill Clinton felt he had no choice but to suspend the agreement with the mainland that did not allow high-level Taiwan officials to visit the United States. Lee was granted entry and he made full use of the visit that June, attracting a large audience and positive international opinion. Cornell University treated him as a heroic freedom fighter.

Mainland officials were furious with the United States and Canada for granting Lee Teng-hui a visa, and with the Japanese, who were sympathetic to the invitation. In July, shortly after Lee's visit to Cornell, China issued a "warning" to Taiwan about trying to seek independence by conducting missile tests that landed very close to the small Japanese-held island of Yonaguni at the southern end of the Ryukyu chain. In August, Chinese officials conducted a second series of missile tests in the East China Sea, an area 80 to 100 miles north of Taiwan. China also began conducting military exercises in Fujian province, situated opposite Taiwan across the Taiwan Strait. In November, China conducted amphibious assault exercises, and in March 1996, China fired missiles some 25 to 35 miles from Keelung and Kaohsiung, ports on Taiwan's southwest coast, disrupting nearby air and sea traffic. The United States had taken the position that it did not oppose the reunification of Taiwan with the mainland, but it did oppose the use of force to achieve that end. Officials in the United States worried that China was preparing to invade Taiwan. Following the March missile firing, U.S. officials announced that the United States was sending two carrier groups to the vicinity of Taiwan, thus staging the biggest display of U.S. military might in Asia since the Vietnam War. Shortly thereafter, China conducted more amphibious landing exercises and purchased additional military equipment from Russia. Many feared a military confrontation. Jiang Zemin, acutely aware of how weak the Chinese military had become since Deng's 1978 decision to promote economic development instead of investing heavily in military modernization, decided to increase military expenditures. Deng, in contrast, had advocated a policy of *taoguang yanghui* ("avoid the limelight, never take the lead").

In the 1980s Taiwanese locals had begun to develop closer relations with the mainland, but by the early twenty-first century, feeling overwhelmed by the mainland's influence and pressure on Taiwan, many people in Taiwan began to identify themselves as Taiwanese rather than Chinese. In the decades after 1949, because children of mainlanders and children of locals had now grown up and attended schools together, hostilities between the two groups gradually eased, although they did not disappear. And although Taiwanese relations with Japan grew weaker over time, they too did not disappear. Chinese officials continued to worry about the Japanese, who were close to Taiwan locals who wanted to maintain their independence from the mainland.

Growing Chinese Fears of a Japanese Military Revival after the Gulf War

Ever since Japan was defeated in 1945, Chinese leaders had been concerned about the return of Japanese militarism. In the eyes of many Chinese as far back as the Ming dynasty, the true nature of the Japanese people was revealed in the behavior of blood-thirsty Japanese pirates. In the late sixteenth century, violent Japanese troops under Toyotomi Hideyoshi advanced through Korea on their way to China. In 1894–1895, aggressive Japanese troops invaded Korea and China. And many Chinese adults still remembered the cruel Japanese military occupation from 1937 to 1945, while those who had not personally experienced it had heard about it. Following World War II the Chinese public had no contact with the Japanese after they left China, and therefore they had no opportunity to see how firmly the vast majority of Japan's citizens had turned their back on militarism.

In 1969, when U.S. president Richard Nixon announced at a press conference in Guam that while the United States would help, nations should be responsible for their own security, the Chinese began to worry that an independent Japanese military would rise again. In the mid-1980s the Chinese became concerned that Prime Minister Nakasone was reviving the Japanese military, and they saw his visit to the Yasukuni Shrine as a sign that Japan was again honoring its military past. In the late 1980s, as the Japanese economy grew rapidly and tensions between Japan and the United States increased, Chinese leaders worried that Japan might push to increase its independence from the United States. If so, would not Japan use the new military technology it had acquired through the U.S.-Japan Alliance to strengthen its own military? After the Soviet Union collapsed in 1991, China's leaders wondered whether the U.S.-Japan Alliance, the cork that was keeping Japanese militarism under control, could last.

After the Gulf War ended in 1991, the United States was deeply critical of Japan, which imported so much oil from the Middle East, for not contributing more to the war effort. The United States pressed Japan to make a bigger contribution to global peacekeeping by getting "boots on the ground" when troubles appeared around the world. To the Chinese, this increased the danger that the cork was getting out of the bottle.

Over the next several years Japanese officials agreed to take on added international and financial responsibility, not only in covering the expenses for U.S. bases in Japan but also in sharing more military technology and playing a larger role in international peacekeeping activities. By 1996 Japan had agreed to provide logistical support if contingencies should arise in the areas around Japan.

In the 1990s the Japanese media were filled with stories of North Korea's nuclear developments and North Korean abductions of Japanese citizens. When North Korea fired a rocket not far from Japan in 1993, Japan's anxieties increased and Japanese voices calling for strengthening their own military grew stronger. President Jimmy Carter, before coming to office, had proposed that U.S. troops should be pulled out of South Korea. Was the period of U.S dominance over Japan's security policies that had begun with the Allied Occupation now coming to an end? Some in Japan wondered if they could depend on the United States for support against North Korea, and if they could not, why would Japan not expand its military? In short, with the end of the Cold War the Chinese had reason to fear that the U.S.-Japan Alliance would not last and that the United States could no longer keep the "cork in the bottle."

Growing Japanese Concern about China's Military Power

After the Tiananmen Square Incident in 1989, the Japanese grew more worried about the nature of the Chinese political system, and Japanese media were filled with items critical of China. The Japanese also wondered how the Chinese, expressing anti-Japanese rhetoric, would behave as China's economic and military power grew.

China's economy did not yet compare with Japan's, but China was a rising power that could one day challenge Japan for dominance in East Asia. Although foreign sanctions on China following the government's clash with protesters near Tiananmen Square had slowed economic growth, by 1993, following Deng Xiaoping's southern journey in 1992 and the easing of international sanctions, China's economic growth rate suddenly increased to 14 percent that year and was poised to continue. Deng Xiaoping had kept down military expenditures in the 1980s to concentrate on economic growth, but by the 1990s the economic base was much stronger than when he took power in 1978, and his successors were putting a higher percentage of the national budget into the military. In the tensions after Taiwan president Lee Teng-hui's visit to Cornell in 1995, when China fired a missile over Taiwan and the United States sent two carrier groups to the region, Chinese military expenditures grew even faster than the economy, which was continuing to grow at an average of roughly 10 percent a year.

The friction over the Senkaku / Diaoyu Islands that began to intensify in the mid-1990s reflected Japan's increasing concern about China's intentions. For the previous hundred years, Japanese defense officials had been concerned about threats from two fronts: the northern front—that is, the Soviet Union—and the western front, the Korean Peninsula. Now they had to deal with a third front in the southwest: the threat from China over Taiwan and the Senkaku / Diaoyu Islands.

China's Concern about the Weakening of the U.S.-Japan Alliance

Chas Freeman, an American diplomat who was assigned to the Pentagon from 1993 to 1994, observed that after the Soviet Union collapsed, U.S. military planners suffered from what he called an "enemy deficit syndrome."

U.S. military officials, backed by defense industries that sought congressional support for a large military budget, transferred their concern from the Soviet Union to China, and the United States continued advancing its military technology. The Chinese were worried not only that advances in U.S. military weapons would be passed on to the Japanese, but also that Japan, after acquiring those new capacities, might then begin to act more independently.

From 1991 to 1996, following the end of the Gulf War and the collapse of the Soviet Union, uncertainties about the future of the U.S.-Japan Alliance increased Chinese worries about Japan becoming an independent military power. On April 17, 1996, however, when President Clinton and Prime Minister Ryutaro Hashimoto met in Tokyo and signed the Japan-U.S. Joint Declaration on Security Alliance for the Twenty-First Century, China became more confident that the Japanese military would not become independent, at least in the near future. The Joint Declaration stated that both the United States and Japan had an interest "in furthering cooperation with China." But Chinese officials, aware of Western concern about the rise of China, suspected that the declaration was aimed at containing China. During the following year, the United States and Japan revised the guidelines that included Japanese participation in "the areas surrounding Japan," causing the Chinese to worry about Japan's activities around the Senkaku / Diaoyu Islands and Taiwan.

China's Patriotic Education Campaign

After Chinese leaders put down the Tiananmen Square protests, they had reason to worry about whether they could retain the support of Chinese youth. Two years later, observing the collapse of the Soviet Union in 1991 and the end of communism in Eastern Europe, Chinese leaders could not help wondering if China might confront a similar fate. How were China's leaders to respond? Deng Xiaoping decided the answer was to launch a Patriotic Education Campaign aimed at strengthening loyalty to the nation, especially among Chinese youth.

During the Civil War, Mao called for class struggle, stoking the antagonism of peasants and workers toward landlords and capitalists, to win popular support against the Guomindang. As late as 1966–1976 during the Cultural Revolution, Red Guards were mobilized to attack those with "bad class backgrounds"—that is, landlords and the bourgeoisie. But with the reform and opening of 1978, Chinese leaders encouraged independent businesses and sought cooperation with capitalist countries. To proceed with their modernization plans, they also sought the support of the best and the brightest of China's youth, some of whom had come from bad class backgrounds, as well as the support of businesspeople in Taiwan, including followers of Chiang Kai-shek.

The Chinese media did not call attention to the end of class struggle, but by the Thirteenth Party Congress in 1987, publicity about class struggle had faded away and attacks on those from bad class backgrounds had ended. Chiang Kai-shek, who had been criticized for supporting the capitalists and landlords, was praised for his contributions to the nation. Museums that displayed ancient pottery no longer posted signs saying that the artifacts had been made by the working classes who had suffered from oppression. The pottery had been made by Chinese artisans.

In 1992, the way to win broad support for both the government and the Chinese Communist Party was through patriotism—by recalling and celebrating the struggle of all Chinese people, of all classes and of all minority groups, against the foreign imperialists who had invaded China. The media denounced the imperialists who oppressed the Chinese during what China called the "century of humiliation," beginning with the Opium War and continuing through the Japanese invasion and the atrocities committed by the Japanese during the war.

The appeal to patriotism had deep roots among twentieth-century Chinese political leaders seeking broader public support. The Patriotic Education Campaign, first introduced in 1992, made use of not only print media but also TV, the new medium of the day, which had become widespread in the 1980s. The campaign had begun with an announcement in August 1991 and instructions that every school in China was to have a well-developed patriotic curriculum within three years. New middle-school and high-school textbooks began appearing in 1992. In September 1993, when Beijing lost to Sydney in its bid to host the 2000 Summer Olympic Games, students throughout the country were mobilized to stage protests. After denouncing government officials for their actions in 1989, students were now cheering the government officials who complained about the biases of the foreign countries that blocked Beijing's effort to host the 2000 Summer Olympics. Patriotic education was working.

The Patriotic Education Campaign was fully launched in August 1994, with directions for implementing the campaign issued by the Central Committee of the Communist Party. Among the announced goals was the enhancement of cohesion and national pride. After 1994, junior and senior high-school students were required to take courses on patriotism, and all students applying to university had to take entrance examinations that tested their knowledge of the content of the patriotic education courses.

Chinese discussions of Japan's past atrocities and Japan's failure to apologize adequately were central components of the Patriotic Education Campaign. In the 1980s, following Deng Xiaoping's efforts to build a cultural base for better relations with Japan, Chinese audiences had been shown movies that displayed many sides of Japan, but after 1992 the Chinese media paid more attention to subjects such as the Nanjing Massacre, Japan's biochemical warfare, the atrocities committed by Japanese soldiers carrying out the scorched-earth policy known as "kill all, burn all, loot all," and Japan's exploitation of "comfort women" to satisfy the sexual desires of soldiers.

In November 1993 the Publicity (formerly Propaganda) Department of the Chinese Communist Party issued a circular promoting patriotism through movies and television series. By that time, China already had some 230 million television sets. Patriotic television series and movies about the Sino-Japanese War typically depicted Japanese soldiers committing cruelties and Chinese soldiers, Communist guerrilla fighters, and Chinese youths heroically fighting the Japanese enemy. Of all the themes for stirring patriotism, none proved as popular as World War II movies showing the horrible deeds of Japanese soldiers. Some of the movies designed for young audiences showed Chinese children bravely helping to fight the Japanese. In 2000, one such movie, *Devils at the Doorstep*, was banned from circulation because it showed a Japanese soldier being too friendly to Chinese villagers. Many such commercial films were very popular and financially profitable. The 2011 film *Flowers of War*, depicting the Japanese raping Chinese women and slicing up Chinese corpses with swords during the Nanjing Massacre, was the highest grossing film of the year. Nevertheless, some of the commercial movies were ridiculed by Chinese intellectuals for their unrealistic exaggerations. In one film, for instance, a Chinese boy throws a hand grenade that destroys a Japanese plane. Since 1993 Chinese moviegoers and TV viewers have had ample opportunities to view movies depicting the horrible Japanese and the heroic Chinese.

The anniversary of the Japanese invasion of Manchuria on September 18, 1931, and National Humiliation Day, remembering when China was forced to yield to the Twenty-One Demands on May 9, 1915, became occasions for mobilizing anti-Japanese sentiment. On August 15, 2005, the sixtieth anniversary of the end of World War II, China saw very large anti-Japanese demonstrations. The Chinese expressed outrage any time high Japanese political leaders visited the Yasukuni Shrine, where the souls of class-A war criminals were enshrined among the 2.5 million others who died for their country.

In 1994, Chinese local governments were directed to erect monuments and museums commemorating the anti-Japanese struggles of the Chinese people. Museums mounted displays showing heroic Chinese people fighting the Japanese. They built monuments marking the battles that had taken place, and held commemorations at the gravesites of Chinese heroes in the war with Japan. Forty national sites, which also involved foreign countries, were selected in 1995 to promote patriotic education, half of which were sites involving the Japanese. Many people remembered the horror stories about life after the 1931 Japanese invasion and could easily be enlisted to help educate China's young people. According to data collected by the Pew Research Center, by 2006 only 21 percent of Chinese people had favorable impressions of Japan, and by 2016 that number had fallen to 14 percent.[2]

To strengthen patriotic sentiment among China's well-educated readers, one of the most effective means was the publication *Cankao Xiaoxi* (Reference News), which prints Chinese translations of articles from the foreign press. This newspaper was formerly available only to party members, but beginning in the 1980s it was openly sold on the streets. Because the articles were direct translations from foreign media, it became a favorite source of news for the educated public, including students. By selecting the headlines as well as the articles that were published, propaganda officials could shape the messages that they wanted to reach the Chinese public. Officials chose articles by extreme right-wing Japanese who denied historical events, even if those rightists were not well known and considered ridiculous by most people in Japan, *Cankao Xiaoxi* readers in China assumed they represented the general Japanese mood. The Chinese public therefore came to overestimate the extent to which the Japanese public denied certain historical events. Even though Japanese military expenditures did not increase significantly after 1990, the articles selected for reprinting by *Cankao Xiaoxi* conveyed the impression that rising militarism in Japan was a serious problem.

Some of the strongest expressions of anti-Japanese sentiment since the mid-1990s have come not from the elder Chinese generation that had experienced the Japanese occupation but from young people who had received a patriotic education. By 1998, Chinese children could play popular video games online in which heroic Chinese characters fought against Japanese invaders. The Patriotic Education Campaign was quite effective in increasing anti-Japanese attitudes.

China's Patriotic Education Campaign also helped strengthen anti-Japanese public opinion in other countries that had suffered under the Japanese during the war, particularly Korea and Southeast Asia. The campaign found resonance as well in Western countries, where what China criticized as Japan's failure to apologize fully for its actions in World War II was contrasted with the Germans' thorough self-criticism for their nation's wartime atrocities.

In Japan, the Ministry of Education provides guidelines for the material school textbooks should cover, and the requirements for Japanese textbooks give little space to modern history. Thus when Chinese youth, who have received China's patriotic education, meet Japanese youth, they commonly conclude that while Japanese students may know that it was wrong for Japan to invade China and that Japan should apologize, they have little knowledge of Japan's past aggression and have not sufficiently faced their history.

When Japanese visitors to China saw the anti-Japanese movies being shown, and Japanese TV viewers saw dramatic images of Chinese people throwing rocks at Japanese shops in China and the Japanese ambassador's residence in Beijing without police restraint, and Chinese planes and ships buzzing Japanese planes and ships near the Senkaku / Diaoyu Islands, the Japanese became fearful about China. The strong commitment in Japan to pacifism and antimilitarism has not disappeared, but the news from China has strengthened nationalist sentiment in Japan, especially among a minority right-wing fringe. Many Japanese fear a Chinese threat and have a sense that the Japanese living today are the victims of false accusations.

By the mid-1990s the number of Japanese tourists to China began to fall off sharply. Pew data from a survey in 2006 revealed that the number of Japanese who expressed positive feelings toward China had dropped to 27 percent. By 2016 it had fallen further to 11 percent where it remained even in 2017 and 2018, when the number of Chinese respondents reporting positive feelings toward Japan rose to nearly 40 percent from a low of 10 percent. The numbers of Japanese visitors to China did not rise.

The growing tensions between China and Japan after 1992 coincided with the growing confidence in China, and the corresponding fear in Japan, that the size of the Chinese economy would soon surpass that of Japan, and that the size of China's military and its weaponry would also soon surpass Japan's.

China Takes the Dominant Position in Asia

In 1993 China's GNP was still only $443 billion, whereas Japan, with one-tenth of China's population, had a GNP of $4.4 trillion, almost ten times as large. But that same year China's economy grew by 14 percent and seemed poised to continue growing at a rate of more than 10 percent a year, while the Japanese economy was by then stagnating, after the bubble burst in 1989. After 1997, when Japan suffered in the Asian financial crisis and China did not, Chinese officials were confident that their economic and political systems were working better than Japan's. China's entry into the World Trade Organization (WTO) in 2001 further boosted Chinese confidence.

China had acquired nuclear weapons in 1965 and Japan had chosen not to develop them, but in 1993 the Japanese military, though small, was superior to China's in terms of technology and training. Beginning in 1996, however, Chinese military spending began growing even faster than its economy, while Japan's military expenditures remained below 1 percent of its stagnating economy. The Chinese gained confidence that they would soon have more warships and warplanes than Japan. By 2015, although Japanese military specialists believed their military training and technology were still ahead of China's, Chinese naval tonnage was 3.2 times that of Japan, China had 2.7 times the number of aircraft, and it had 260 ballistic missiles whereas Japan had none.[3]

The year 2008 was an important milestone for China's growing confidence, when China was little affected by the global financial crisis that shook Japan and the West. In 2008 the Japanese stock market index fell to less than one-fifth of its peak in 1989. Chinese and Japanese leaders already knew that China's economy would soon surpass that of Japan, and the Western financial crisis further strengthened the belief of the Chinese that their system was as good as the economic systems in the West. Just as the Tokyo Olympics of 1964 had symbolized Japan's debut as a modern industrialized country, and the Olympic Games in Seoul in 1988 represented South Korea's debut on the world stage, so the 2008 Summer Olympic Games in Beijing, presented with a grandeur beyond any previous games, served as China's debut as a major global power that was surpassing Japan and poised to begin challenging the United States. Two years later, in August 2010, Tokyo announced that in the second quarter of 2010, according to World Bank figures, China's GNP was $1.38 trillion and Japan's GNP was $1.28 trillion.

After 2010 China still faced many problems—in completing its modernization throughout the country, in helping residents who had not yet achieved a middle-class standard of living, in creating a social service net for the entire population, in making the transition to a consumer-oriented service economy, and in constructing a world-class high-technology sector. However, the century of humiliation was over and China was no longer daunted by the achievements of the West.

The difficulties between China and Japan in managing the transition in their relationship were exacerbated by the instability of Japan's political leadership from 1994 to 2012. Chinese leadership during this period was relatively stable: President Jiang Zemin was formally selected for two terms, from 1992 to 2002, and President Hu Jintao, from 2002 to 2012. Japan had enjoyed stable government by leaders from the Liberal Democratic Party (LDP) from 1955 through the late 1980s. Then reforms to the electoral system were enacted in 1994, designed to give rise to a strong two-party system that would weaken various factions by replacing the election districts that had each elected several members of the Diet with 180 smaller districts that each elected a single member, and allowing eleven more members to be selected from proportional-representation districts. Because some Diet members from multiple-seat districts lost out when only one member could be selected by their new district, many experienced senior members who had provided a long-term perspective were no longer in government after 1994. Furthermore, during the eighteen years from 1994 to 2012, when Abe Shinzo was elected prime minister, Japan had thirteen prime ministers. Some made an effort to improve relations with China, but the frequent changes of leadership—and especially the period of rule by the inexperienced Democratic Party of Japan from 2009 to 2012—made it difficult for Chinese and Japanese leaders to develop and maintain long-term understandings.

The issue that became the greatest focus of tension during the transition from 1993 to 2010 was the dispute over the Senkaku / Diaoyu Islands in the East China Sea.

The Dispute over the Senkaku / Diaoyu Islands

The eight small islands in question, called the Senkaku Islands by Japan and the Diaoyu Islands by China, are located approximately 100 miles northeast of Taiwan, 100 miles northwest of Ishigaki (in the Ryukyu chain), and 200 miles from mainland China. They have been uninhabited since World War II. In 1971 the U.S. agreement to return Okinawa to Japanese rule and to transfer administration of the Senkaku / Diaoyu Islands to Japan aroused concerns in Taiwan and on the Chinese mainland that Japan was again beginning to expand as a military power. The Taiwan government and Chinese activists from Hong Kong and Taiwan have supported the mainland in claiming that the islands are Chinese territory. The islands became the focus of a dispute over fishing rights when fishermen from China and Japan, having exhausted resources close to their shores, began fishing farther offshore and clashing with each other near the islands. In the 1970s it appeared that significant undersea oil supplies might also be located near the islands, and this heightened interest in controlling the area. But it was the islands' strategic location and the military competition in the area that inflamed the issue.

In 1973, within the framework of the third United Nations Convention on the Law of the Sea (UNCLOS), nations began discussions concerning rights to the use of the oceans. Although UNCLOS did not establish rules about how to determine sovereignty, it did establish rules about exclusive economic zones, low-tide elevations, and rights to maritime resources, including petroleum found beneath the ocean floor. Nations began rushing to make claims on islands in the Western Pacific as well as claims to the disputed Senkaku / Diaoyu Islands. According to the Convention of the Law of the Sea agreed to in 1982, coastal states have sovereignty over the waters within 12 nautical miles of their land at low tide. The agreement also allows for an exclusive economic zone of 200 nautical miles (1 nautical mile is equal to 1.15 statute miles) from a country's coast. The distance between Japan and continental China is 360 nautical miles, so there is no clear agreement on the rights of Japan and China to the seabed. Most countries of the world, including Japan and China, have signed the UNCLOS agreement. Although the United States signed the agreement and has chosen to abide by it, it has not ratified it.

Once the Senkaku / Diaoyu Islands became a focus of attention, both China and Japan pulled out their historical records to strengthen their claims to the islands. China presented documents that reported that Chinese ships had first charted the islands in 1534. China also argued that the Potsdam Agreement of 1945 provided that Taiwan and the affiliated islands would be returned to China. Japan pointed out that the Potsdam Agreement did not specifically mention the Senkaku / Diaoyu Islands as being among the islands near Taiwan that were to be returned to China. It maintained that the islands had traditionally been used as landmarks for all navigators in the region but had not belonged to any one country. Japan announced that it had surveyed the islands in the 1880s and found them uninhabited. Therefore, by a cabinet decision in January 1895, prior to the end of the Sino-Japanese War, it had declared sovereignty over the islands. Japan added that the islands had been returned to Japan by the United States in 1971 as part of the reversion of Okinawa to Japan. China claimed that the islands were assigned to Japan by the 1895 Shimonoseki Treaty at the end of the First Sino-Japanese War, and that with Japan's surrender in 1945, sovereignty over the islands returned to China.

Japan does not acknowledge that there is a dispute over sovereignty of the islands. The United States has taken the position that the question of sovereignty has not been resolved, but that the Japanese have administrative control over the islands. When Chinese ships and planes began operations near the islands, U.S. officials made it clear that if the Japanese were to be attacked on or near the islands, the United States would, according to Article 5 of the U.S.-Japan Security Agreement, come to Japan's defense.

In April 1978, shortly before the Treaty of Peace and Friendship was concluded, nearly 100 small Chinese fishing vessels entered the area, flying banners claiming that the islands were Chinese territory. However, when Deng Xiaoping visited Japan in October 1978 he announced at his press conference that China and Japan "could cooperate in sharing the economic benefits of the islands, and that the question of sovereignty could be resolved by wise leaders in future generations."

Disputes escalated in the 1990s, as Japan began taking more responsibility for defending the waters around the Japanese islands and China began expanding its military capacity over a broader geographical area. China's desire to reunite Taiwan with the mainland and the possibility that it might use force to achieve that goal attracted more attention to the nearby Senkaku / Diaoyu Islands, which would be of strategic importance if conflict were to arise over Taiwan.

In 1994 China began sending scientific research vessels near the territorial waters to explore the seabed. After the tensions in the Taiwan Strait in 1995, the Chinese greatly increased their investment in naval resources to be better prepared in the case of a clash near Taiwan. In July 1996, a right-wing Japanese youth put up a lighthouse on one of the islets, and in August a war memorial stone was erected on Ishigaki, one of the Senkaku / Diaoyu Islands. Following this construction, activists from Hong Kong and Taiwan, in support of China's claims, tried to land on the islands, and ten fishing boats from Taiwan appeared in the vicinity. The Japanese sent in ships to try to prevent Chinese ships from moving into Japanese territorial waters as defined by UNCLOS. The emotions over the Senkaku / Diaoyu Islands reached their peak just when China was replacing Japan as the largest economy in East Asia.

The Transition to China's Dominance, 1993–2012

During the ups and downs as China surpassed Japan as the largest economy in Asia, tensions remained high but both sides tried to prevent the conflict from getting out of control.

The Murayama Declaration, 1995

In 1995, fifty years after the end of the China War, Prime Minister Murayama Tomiichi of Japan made a noble effort to stop the deterioration of relations. After tensions reached a peak when China ignored Japan's request that it end its nuclear testing, Prime Minister Murayama traveled to China in May 1995 to try to improve relations. Murayama, who served from June 30, 1994, to January 11, 1996, was the first non-LDP leader to be prime minister since 1955. A Socialist who led a coalition government, he was a modest and popular leader, the son of a fisherman from Beppu on the northeast coast of Kyushu. He had long believed that Japan should acknowledge the atrocities of World War II. During his visit to China, Murayama went to Xi'an to pay respects to the ancient capital from which Japan had learned so much. He also visited the Marco Polo Bridge, where war had broken out in 1937, to show his empathy for the Chinese suffering during the war and to apologize for Japan's aggression.

On August 15, to mark the fiftieth anniversary of the end of World War II, Prime Minister Murayama gave a speech drafted by Tanino Sakutaro, formerly ambassador to China, expressing his hopes for close cooperation between China and Japan in the twenty-first century. Murayama declared, "Japan, following a mistaken national policy, advanced along the road to war, . . . and through its colonial rule and aggression . . . caused tremendous damage and suffering to the people of many countries. Allow me once again to express my deep remorse and state my heartfelt apology. . . . I would like to reaffirm once more that the Japanese people are firmly determined that Japan will never become a military power." His speech was the fullest apology that a top Japanese leader had ever given for Japanese aggression during World War II. In the future, other Japanese prime ministers would repeat parts of the speech. Murayama was warmly welcomed in China by President Jiang Zemin and Premier Li Peng.

In September 1997, to further reduce tensions, Murayama's successor, Prime Minister Hashimoto Ryutaro, traveled to Beijing to celebrate the twenty-fifth anniversary of the normalization of relations. Prime Minister Hashimoto offered reassurances that the U.S.-Japan Security Treaty was not aimed at China, and he confirmed that Japan did not support Taiwan's independence from mainland rule.

Jiang Zemin's Visit to Japan, 1998

On the twentieth anniversary of the Treaty of Peace and Friendship and Deng Xiaoping's 1978 visit to Japan, President Jiang Zemin made the first formal state visit by a Chinese leader to Japan in the history of the two countries. When Deng had visited Japan in October 1978, he was not officially China's top leader and therefore he had not been received with the protocol of a formal state visit. Jiang Zemin had visited Japan briefly in 1992, before he was president, to help arrange the Japanese emperor's visit to China. This time, during his full six-day state visit, from November 25 to 30, Jiang was welcomed by Prime Minister Obuchi Keizo, treated with formal banquets, welcomed by Emperor Akihito, hosted by political and business leaders, and escorted by Prime Minister Obuchi on trips to Sendai and Hokkaido. The visit was planned to solidify good relations between the two countries, but in the end it led to heightened tensions.

The state visit by Jiang Zemin was originally scheduled to take place before a visit to Japan by South Korean president Kim Dae-jung, but serious flash floods in China caused Jiang to delay his trip until after Kim's visit. President Kim's time in Japan was highly successful, and by comparison, Jiang's visit was judged to be less so. In his speech to the Japanese Diet on October 8, Kim Dae-jung, who, twenty-five year earlier, had been kidnapped in Tokyo by Korean political enemies and had nearly been killed when he was on a small boat headed toward Korea, thanked the Japanese for helping to save his life. He said that when Japan had pursued an imperial path, it had caused great pain to the people of Korea and other nations. But, speaking in Japanese, he acknowledged that Japan had changed after World War II, and he said that he looked forward to future cooperation. Kim's message created a high point of goodwill between Korea and Japan. Prime Minister Obuchi and the Japanese public were moved by Kim's message, and the leaders signed a joint declaration in which Obuchi expressed deep remorse for Japan's behavior during its occupation of Korea.

When Jiang Zemin visited Japan, five years into the period of rapid Chinese growth that had resumed in 1993, he was representing a China that was increasingly confident and had just weathered the Asian financial crisis of 1997 with far less damage than Japan. China was also less worried that the United States might side against it with Japan. In June, President Clinton had made a ten-day visit to China to strengthen Sino-U.S. relations, and despite urging from Japanese officials, he had not stopped in Japan on the way home.

Before Jiang Zemin's visit, Chinese and Japanese officials, engaged in negotiations on the content of the statement the two sides would sign while Jiang was in Tokyo, were close to agreeing on a declaration that would enable Japan to express remorse without making a lengthy apology. But after Japan signed the long written apology with President Kim, Chinese officials requested that Japan sign a similar apology to China.

To Jiang and the overwhelming majority of the Chinese people, Japan had not done enough to apologize for its history. Prime Minister Obuchi did say during Jiang's visit, "The Japanese side is keenly conscious of the responsibility for the serious distress and damage that Japan caused to the Chinese people through its aggression against China during a certain period in the past and expressed deep remorse for this," but Jiang did not regard this as sufficient. What Jiang did not realize was that the Japanese mood had been changing. The Japanese were tiring of China's continued lecturing about Japan's atrocities and its endless requests for apologies, its failure to acknowledge the apologies Japan had made, and its unwillingness to heed Japan's requests, for its part, that China refrain from nuclear tests. Some Japanese were upset that in Japan, Jiang thanked the Japanese for the aid it had given China, but that this expression of appreciation was not reported in the Chinese press.

During his state visit, a portion of Jiang Zemin's evening banquet with Emperor Akihito was televised. In his brief presentation at the banquet, Jiang Zemin gave his opinions on how Japan should view history. To the Chinese, Jiang's comments were appropriate, but to the Japanese it was highly inappropriate to use a banquet, which was meant to be a ceremonial occasion, for what seemed to them like a lecture by a teacher telling a pupil what he should do. Reports by Japanese journalists covering Jiang's visit, reflecting growing irritation, heightened the perception of increasing Chinese arrogance.

When Jiang pressed Prime Minister Obuchi to sign a written statement like the one he had signed with Kim Dae-jung, Jiang expected that, as in the past, Japan would yield. However, Obuchi chose to give an oral apology and not a written one. The prime minister's refusal to sign a written apology reflected his political judgment that the Japanese public was tired of China's lectures, and his judgment turned out to be correct. To the Chinese, it showed that the Japanese were denying history and failing to show proper respect for the Chinese leader.

Despite these tensions, during Jiang's visit Japanese and Chinese officials did discuss ways in which the two countries might work together. They signed a joint declaration for cooperation in thirty-three areas, covering exchanges of officials, economic and scientific collaborations, cultural exchanges, and environmental projects. This declaration paved the way for the implementation of many cooperative efforts. After mainland China was given the China seat in the United Nations in 1971 (taking over the seat previously held by the Republic of China on Taiwan), Japan generally supported China's participation in UN activities and in East Asian regional affairs. Although China opposed Japan's permanent membership on the UN Security Council, it supported meetings with Japan in the Association of Southeast Asian Nations (ASEAN) Plus 3, which was just being launched.[4] After Jiang's visit, Japanese trade and investment in China continued to grow. In 1999, two-way trade between Japan and China totaled $66 billion, four times the amount in 1990.

Prime Minister Obuchi's Visit to China, November 1999

One year after Jiang's visit, in a further effort to improve relations, Prime Minister Obuchi Keizo visited Beijing to join in the celebration of the fiftieth anniversary of the founding of the People's Republic. Chinese diplomats, aware of the negative Japanese reaction to Jiang's pressure on the history issue, were more restrained in asking for Japanese apologies. Prime Minister Obuchi met with Jiang Zemin, who thanked him for his hospitality in Tokyo. In his meeting with Premier Zhu Rongji, Obuchi indicated his support for China's entry into the WTO. He continued to promote the thirty-three areas of cooperation that had been designated during Jiang's visit to Japan, and he offered Japanese assistance for several programs, in particular those in Inner Mongolia, in which he expressed a personal interest. The visit did help lessen somewhat the deterioration in relations.

Premier Zhu's Visit to Japan, 2000

Zhu Rongji, who was highly respected in both China and Japan, was sent to Japan the next year to try to improve relations and solidify Japan's support for China's entry into the WTO. In Japan, Premier Zhu said that the Japanese people, like the Chinese, had suffered during World War II, and he did not request any more apologies. After he took part in a televised dialogue with several Japanese business and political leaders, Japanese viewers, as well as the leaders with whom he met, said they were very impressed with Zhu Rongji's knowledge, frankness, and his desire to develop good business relations. Some even said they wished Japan had such a statesman leading their country. Officials on both sides acknowledged that the visit helped improve relations. Public opinion polls shortly after Zhu's visit reflected a modest improvement in overall Japanese attitudes toward China. Slightly more Japanese respondents had positive opinions of China than had negative opinions.

Prime Minister Koizumi Junichiro and the Yasukuni Issue, 2001–2006

Shortly after he became prime minister in 2001, Koizumi tried to find a balance between resisting Chinese pressures and apologizing for Japan's role in World War II. His political ally, Kato Koichi, consulted with Chinese officials, who advised him that if Koizumi were to visit the Yasukuni Shrine on August 13, 2001, instead of on August 15, the official anniversary of the end of the war, Chinese reaction would be less strong. Still, when Koizumi visited the Yasukuni Shrine on August 13, 2001, the Chinese press was very critical of the visit and demanded that Koizumi not visit the shrine again. The Chinese nonetheless allowed Koizumi to visit China shortly after his visit to the shrine, and on that trip he went to the Marco Polo Bridge Museum, where he acknowledged that Japan was wrong to start the war and apologized to the Chinese people. After that, Koizumi visited the Yasukuni Shrine each year.

In 2006, following attacks on Japanese property and Japanese people in China, Koizumi made his final visit to the Yasukuni Shrine. He knew that within several years China would have an economy larger than Japan's, but he would not bow down. He made his final visit to the Yasukuni Shrine on August 15, the anniversary of the end of the war, a date that would especially annoy the Chinese. He said, "I do not go to justify the past war or to glorify militarism. I go with the feeling that we should not wage war again and that we must not forget the sacrifice of those who went to war and died. I am not going there for the class-A war criminals." The Chinese Ministry of Foreign Affairs announced that Koizumi's visit had "hurt the feelings of the Chinese people" and "undermined the political basis for ties between China and Japan."[5]

To the Japanese, the issue behind whether their prime minister should visit the Yasukuni Shrine was not whether Japan was guilty of crimes during World War II, for the Japanese public accepted that. Rather, as Koizumi told Professor Gerald Curtis, it was that no one, Japanese or foreign, could tell him that he should not pay respect to the Japanese soldiers who had sacrificed their lives for their country. His insistence on visiting the Yasukuni Shrine was popular with the Japanese public. But to the Chinese, Koizumi's visits to the Yasukuni Shrine symbolized what they saw as a Japanese respect for militarists, the Japanese people's unwillingness to face their history, and an unacceptable refusal to respect Chinese requests, especially at a time when China was ascendant and its economy was beginning to pass Japan's. Within Japan, some officials and newspapers were critical of Koizumi for causing tensions with the Chinese and Koreans due to his visits to the Yasukuni Shrine but within Japan he remained popular. While Koizumi was in office, from 2001 to 2006, Sino-Japanese relations reached a new postwar low.

President Hu Jintao's Efforts to Improve Relations, 2003

In China, Hu Jintao, who had become president in 2003, made an effort to improve relations with Japan. In the 1980s he had been one of the Chinese youth welcoming a delegation of 3,000 young people from Japan, and he had maintained contact with some of the Japanese he had met. He did not publicly say that China should improve relations with Japan, but he allowed books and newspaper articles to be published that were more sympathetic to Japan than the prevailing Chinese mood.

In April 2002, even before Hu took office, the Chinese General Administration of Press and Publications gave permission for the publication of a book by Pei Hua titled *ZhongRi waijiao fengyunzhong de Deng Xiaoping* (Deng Xiaoping amid changing Sino-Japanese relations), which, by presenting an accurate account of Deng Xiaoping's trip to Japan in October 1978, was sympathetic to the Japanese who had received him.

Also in 2002, Ma Licheng, a senior writer for *People's Daily*, who had earlier worked at *China Youth Daily*, was dispatched to Japan for more than a month, assigned to write a report on what he observed in Japan. His article, "New Thinking on Relations with Japan," appeared at the end of the year in the Chinese journal *Zhanlüe yu guanli* (Strategy and management), a publication with high-level sponsorship that was noted for fresh thinking on strategic issues. Ma reported that, contrary to conventional Chinese views, in conversations with Japanese people from many different circles, they all said they opposed militarization and they all wanted to pursue peace. He also noted that in 1980, 78 percent of Japanese people said they had favorable impressions of China, but by 2000 the percentage had dropped to 49 percent. Nevertheless, Japanese people from all circles still wanted to have friendly relations with China.

In 2003 *Zhanlüe yu guanli* published an article by Shi Yinhong, a strategist with a military background who was also a professor at People's University, that asserted that better Sino-Japanese relations were in China's interest and that China should support Japan in its bid to become a permanent member of the UN Security Council. For several months following these publications, it appeared as if Sino-Japanese relations might improve.

China also undertook the production of a television series in 2003 on the rise and decline of the great powers. It was a thoughtful, well-researched effort to provide guidance to the public as China was on its way to becoming a great power. The series was aired on Chinese television in 2006. The series presented a balanced and respectful treatment of other countries, including Japan. To be sure, the section on Japan talked of World War II and Japanese aggression, but it also discussed how Japanese industrialization had created better living conditions for its people.

The views on Japan published by Ma Licheng and Shi Yinhong were available in the Chinese media for several years, but they never became part of the mainstream. After 2003 their writings attracted less attention and in 2004, when passions between China and Japan again heated up, some even referred to Ma and Shi as traitors. Ma Licheng never gave up his views, but finding it difficult to work in the mainland, he later moved to Hong Kong; Shi Yinhong, less bold in his praise of Japan, remained a professor at People's University.

Chinese Reaction to Japan's Soccer Victories, 2004

At the time when the UN was beginning to discuss whether to expand the permanent membership of the UN Security Council, the Japanese national soccer team visited various Chinese cities ahead of the 2004 Asian Football Confederation (AFC) Asian Cup, scheduled to be held in Beijing in August, to play the first round of the games. In each city, the Japanese team won the matches, and passionate demonstrations erupted against the Japanese. In the Asian Cup final in Beijing, Japan's victory over China, 3–1, led to boisterous attacks against Japanese people and Japanese products. Chinese police escorted the Japanese team to safety, but the angry crowds continued to demonstrate, jostling the car of a Japanese diplomat and breaking its window. Similar demonstrations took place in several other cities, and scenes of the angry crowds were played and replayed on Japanese television. Emotional expressions of animosity and nationalism in both countries reached a high pitch. Before the emotions died down, the issue of Japan's place in the UN came to a head.

China Blocks Japan in the UN Security Council, 2005

In March 2005, during discussions concerning the upcoming decision on the future permanent membership of the UN Security Council, Secretary General Kofi Annan said that he supported Japan's membership, and it appeared that Japan had the support of more than the two-thirds majority of UN members required for approval. The decision also required the support of all existing permanent members of the Security Council, so China, which had become a permanent member when the UN was first formed immediately after World War II, had the power to prevent Japan from becoming a permanent member. To cast the sole negative vote against Japan would have made China appear vindictive at a time when it was seeking to improve its international stature as a rising power. Chinese diplomats encouraged officials in the Southeast Asian countries, which had also suffered from Japanese aggression during the war, to oppose Japan's membership as well. On April 12, China's premier Wen Jiabao, in registering his opposition to Japan's permanent membership on the UN Security Council, said that only a country that respects history can assume responsibility in the international community. To patriotic Chinese familiar with their history, it was a wonderful reversal of the events of 1920, when Japan became a permanent member of the League of Nations Council and China had to compete to be elected as a nonpermanent member, and of the period prior to 1971, when Japan supported the United States in preventing mainland China from replacing Taiwan in the UN's China seat.

Anti-Japanese demonstrations in China in the spring and summer of 2005 were intended to convey to the world that Japan did not deserve the permanent seat on the Security Council because of its failure to deal properly with its history. In April 2005 China carried out a nationwide online effort to collect signatures from those opposed to granting Japan a permanent seat on the council. In her research, Western scholar Jessica Weiss found evidence of anti-Japanese demonstrations in thirty-eight Chinese cities; in many of the demonstrations Japanese property was damaged. The government, in backing the protests, bused more than 10,000 students to central Beijing to engage in the demonstrations there. Demonstrators broke the windows of Japanese restaurants and shops that sold Japanese goods, smashed Japanese cars, and tore down signs advertising Japanese products. On April 9, crowds threw rocks and tiles at the residence of the Japanese ambassador, breaking windows and terrifying Ambassador Anami Koreshige and his wife, Ginny. Police prevented the demonstrators from scaling the fence to enter the ambassador's property, but for hours they did nothing to stop the demonstrators from throwing rocks. The worst violence occurred in Shanghai, where tens of thousands demonstrated, many Japanese shop windows were broken, and the Japanese consulate was attacked. Chinese officials expressed admiration for the patriotism of Chinese students during the demonstrations, although they then tried to dampen the protests by warning the students against taking illegal actions. After it became clear that Japan would not be admitted as a permanent member of the UN Security Council, the demonstrations died down.

Japanese diplomats felt betrayed by China. Japan had supported China's entry into the WTO and other world organizations, and yet Chinese officials had stirred up popular anti-Japanese sentiment among the Chinese public and in Southeast Asia to block Japan, the second-largest economy in the world and the world's second-highest contributor to the UN, from becoming a permanent member of the Security Council. In December 2005, following the demonstrations in China, a Yomiuri poll showed that 72 percent of Japanese respondents did not trust China. Japanese public opinion did not regain the level of positive feelings toward China that had been expressed before the attacks and China's opposition to making Japan a permanent member of the UN Security Council.

Easing Tensions and Olympic Diplomacy, 2006–2008

Following the demonstrations and destruction of Japanese property in China in 2005, leaders on both sides tried to ease the tensions. None of the several Japanese prime ministers who succeeded Koizumi visited the Yasukuni Shrine while in office, and Chinese officials urged anti-Japanese demonstrators to display restraint. Japan had become China's largest trading partner in 2005 despite the attacks on the Japanese soccer team, and it has remained one of its top three trading partners since then. In 2005, Japanese-owned firms in China, mostly in manufacturing, employed an estimated 10 million Chinese workers.

Chinese leaders, after the impasse with Prime Minister Koizumi over the visit to the Yasukuni Shrine, made efforts to improve relations with Koizumi's successor, Abe Shinzo (who served his first term from September 2006 to September 2007), even though Abe did not promise not to visit the Yasukuni Shrine while he was prime minister. Ordinarily, a newly installed Japanese prime minister would make his first foreign visit to the United States, but on October 8, 2006, only two weeks after becoming prime minister, Abe Shinzo was welcomed in Beijing for a summit meeting. At the meeting Abe apologized to the Chinese for the enormous damage and pain that Japan had caused China during the Sino-Japanese War. President Hu Jintao, aware that Chinese pressure on Japanese leaders not to visit the Yasukuni Shrine had led to a deadlock in relations, avoided publicly pressing Abe on the issue, and Abe chose not to visit the shrine. Hu and Abe agreed to set up a panel of experts, with representatives from both sides, to undertake a joint study on the history problem, a project that was led by Bu Ping and Kitaoka Shinichi.

As the time approached for the 2008 Beijing Olympic Games, Chinese leaders sought to ensure the full cooperation of all countries, including Japan. Abe's successor as prime minister, Fukuda Yasuo, whose father, Prime Minister Fukuda Takeo, had welcomed Deng Xiaoping to Japan in October 1978, also sought good relations with China. In May 2008, two months before the Beijing Olympics, Fukuda welcomed President Hu Jintao to Tokyo. It was the first visit to Japan by a Chinese president since President Jiang Zemin had visited in 1998. Like Jiang, President Hu also met with the Japanese emperor. During the visit the two sides began laying plans to cooperate in a joint natural-gas development project in the East China Sea.

While Fukuda and Hu were working to improve relations in 2008, an issue arose that negatively affected the Japanese public's view of China. The Japanese press reported that several hundred Japanese consumers had suffered severe nausea because of food poisoning after eating Chinese dumplings that had been sold to Japan. It was found that an insecticide had been mixed into dumplings produced by the Tianyang Food Processing Company in Hebei. When the Japanese complained, the Chinese initially played down the incident, saying that since no one had died there was no problem. The Japanese were disturbed by the failure of Chinese officials to take responsibility; explaining that they were acting for reasons of health safety, Japanese officials took several Chinese food products off the market. After some months, just before the Olympics, Chinese officials accepted responsibility, stopped the production of the dumplings, and recalled all dumpling exports.

Eager for cooperation in preparing for the Olympics, the Chinese allowed the Japanese to send in rescue teams in response to the devastating earthquake that struck Wenchuan, in Sichuan province, on May 12, 2008, causing an estimated 69,000 deaths. Japan rushed in 61 workers to offer assistance, and next to Pakistan, it was the largest donor of funds for the victims. The quick dispatch of assistance was welcomed. Although the Chinese did not publicly recognize the Japanese when rescue efforts were ended, they did give positive publicity to Japan for its contributions to aid earthquake survivors. Diet member Nikai Toshihiro, head of the assistance delegation, played a key role in leading other delegations to China to take part in preparations for the Olympics.

Prime Minister Fukuda personally represented Japan at the opening ceremony of the Olympics, and Japan's participation in the Beijing Olympic Games, held August 8–24, 2008, went smoothly. Fukuda was later appointed chairman of the Boao Forum for Asia, China's version of the Davos World Economic Forum, and since then Fukuda has held more meetings with senior Chinese leaders than any other high-level Japanese official.

The Nadir of Sino-Japanese Relations, 2010–2014

When Hatoyama Yukio of the Democratic Party of Japan became prime minister in September 2009, he announced that he wanted to move away from the Liberal Democratic Party's policy of depending on the United States, make Asia the center of his policy, and develop better relations with China. Like Abe, he visited China before he visited the United States, and during his visit he offered a sincere personal apology for Japan's wartime behavior. Later, when he was no longer prime minister, he visited the Memorial Hall of the Victims of the Nanjing Massacre to express sorrow for the atrocities caused by Japanese soldiers. Although the Japanese government had insisted that there was no dispute concerning Japan's sovereignty over the Senkaku / Diaoyu Islands, Hatoyama Yukio said there was a dispute and that it had been caused by Japan rather than China. After less than nine months as prime minister, Hatoyama was replaced by the Democratic Party's Kan Naoto, who also sought to promote good relations with China. For years, Kan had been inviting Chinese students in Japan to his home for friendly visits. Yet despite the stated willingness of the Democratic Party to maintain good relations with China and to take China's side in some key disputes, relations between the two countries reached their nadir in 2010 and 2012 while the party was in power.

Collision at Sea near the Senkaku / Diaoyu Islands, 2010

Within weeks of the World Bank's announcement that the size of China's economy had passed Japan's, an incident occurred that led to a clash between the two countries. The incident was unplanned, and it was not resolved smoothly by officials on the spot, leading to a test of wills at the higher levels of government. As each side tried to force the other side to yield, the raw emotions of an aroused public came to the fore in both countries. Ultimately, China escalated the pressures it brought to bear beyond what was routine to resolve such issues, and Japan yielded. The confrontation ended within three weeks, but the passions it generated brought relations between the two countries to a new low.

On September 7, 2010, a Japanese Coast Guard patrol boat noticed that a Chinese fishing trawler, the *Minjinyu 5179*, was seven and a half miles northeast of the disputed Diaoyu / Senkaku Islands and within the territorial waters administered by Japan. After Japan had taken over administrative control of the islands in 1972, the two countries had reached an understanding that, to avoid incidents, Chinese ships would not enter Japan's territorial waters near the islands. If they were to enter by accident and a Japanese patrol boat asked them to leave, it was agreed that they would do so immediately. In this case, when the patrol boat demanded that the Chinese trawler leave Japan's territorial waters, the trawler did not move. The Japanese Coast Guard boat then demanded that Japanese officials be allowed to board the Chinese trawler to inspect it. The trawler tried to escape, but several Japanese patrol boats, much larger and faster than the trawler, encircled the fishing boat and cut off its exit. The captain of the trawler, Zhan Qixiong, rammed against the side of a patrol boat and then, in trying to escape, ran into the side of another patrol boat. Thereafter, Japanese Coast Guard officials boarded the Chinese trawler and took the captain and the crew. It was later determined that the trawler's presence in the area had not been approved by Chinese officials and, in addition, the trawler captain was drunk.

On the rare occasions when Japanese Coast Guard officials had picked up Chinese crew members near the Diaoyu / Senkaku Islands, they had quickly returned them to China. This time, however, since the Chinese captain had damaged a Japanese boat, the Japanese explained that it was necessary to try the captain in a Japanese court. This news was quickly relayed to Beijing, where Chinese officials called in the Japanese ambassador, Niwa Uichiro, at 3:00 a.m. and demanded that the crew and the trawler be handed over to China immediately. Japan did not yield, and the day after the incident, the Chinese began carrying out demonstrations in front of the Japanese embassy in Beijing, the Japanese consulate in Shanghai, and some Japanese businesses.

Chinese officials continued to demand that the Japanese promptly return the captain and the crew. On September 12, five days after the incident, State Councilor Dai Bingguo again called in Ambassador Niwa in Beijing and told him, "Make a wise political decision and release the Chinese fishermen and trawler immediately." On the next day, fearing further escalation, Japan handed over the crew members and the trawler, but the captain remained in Japan because he had caused damage to Japanese property and was being held for a hearing in a Japanese domestic court.

On September 20, four Japanese construction company employees who had been dispatched to China to remove some of the chemical weapons placed there by Japanese forces during World War II were arrested in Beijing for filming military targets. Demonstrations against the Japanese broke out in various Chinese cities, and many Japanese citizens in China reported that they felt that their lives were in danger. China, which then controlled 97 percent of the world's sources of rare earths, chemical elements necessary for the electronics industry, restricted the export of rare earths to Japan. Japanese electronics companies immediately began discussions with other countries to expand the mining and production of rare-earth metals elsewhere. Chinese officials encouraged Chinese citizens who had been planning to travel to Japan to cancel their trips. On September 19, China announced that all high-level exchanges with Japan would be frozen. On September 22, Premier Wen Jiabao, while in New York attending UN meetings, announced, "I strongly urge Japan to release the ship captain, Zhan Qixiong, immediately and unconditionally." Wen Jiabao stated that China was prepared to take further measures and that Japan would bear "all responsibility for the consequences."

Japan's leaders considered the Chinese response excessive, but they wanted to avoid further escalation of the situation. Two days later Japanese officials, acknowledging that the tense situation was hurting Sino-Japanese relations, released Zhan Qixiong to the Chinese without demanding that he stand trial. In the weeks following the incident, the Chinese and Japanese media were filled with reports of the incident and its outcome. The confrontation increased hostile feelings between Chinese and Japanese officials, as well as between the general populations of the two countries.

The trawler incident occurred just as Ozawa Ichiro was challenging Japan's new prime minister, Kan Naoto, to become head of the Democratic Party, and Japanese political leaders who otherwise might have devoted time to resolving the conflict with China were preoccupied with domestic politics. During the previous decades of LDP-controlled government, when tensions arose between China and Japan, experienced senior China specialists in Japan's Ministry of Foreign Affairs, in cooperation with LDP politicians and through established channels of communication with their Chinese counterparts, had often been able to keep such incidents under control. This time, however, communications between Chinese and Japanese diplomats broke down.

After Zhan Qixiong was returned to China, LDP supporters used the occasion to criticize the inexperienced Democratic Party for its mismanagement of the incident. They criticized the Democratic Party for initially being so firm about holding the crew and insisting that the captain face trial and then caving in completely to China's demands. When Zhan Qixiong was returned to China, he was at first given a hero's welcome. Although there was no public acknowledgment that he had been drunk at the time of the incident, several weeks after his return to China he was unceremoniously sent to the countryside.

After the trawler incident, the Chinese media were filled with more strident anti-Japanese content than usual. The Chinese government increased its patrols in the waters near the Diaoyu / Senkaku Islands, the Japanese government expanded its efforts to defend the Senkaku / Diaoyu Islands, and the U.S. government reaffirmed its commitment to defend Japan if it were to be attacked in territory under Japanese administration.

Between September 2008, before the confrontation over the trawler, and August 2012, China sent several ships into the twelve-nautical-mile territorial zone. Beginning in September 2012 China began sending more than twelve ships each month into the twelve-nautical-mile zone. Although China began decreasing the number of ships sent to this zone in August 2013, it still sent ships to the area each month.[6]

Tensions between the two countries eased slightly following the Tohoku earthquake of March 11, 2011. Just as Japan in 2008 had sent aid to China after the Sichuan earthquake, after the Tohoku earthquake, the Chinese promptly sent aid to Japan. In September 2011, when Noda Yoshihiko became prime minister, he quickly arranged for a two-day visit to Beijing, during which time he expressed his appreciation for China's assistance after the earthquake. But relations between China and Japan remained far more tense than they had been prior to the trawler incident.

Japan's "Nationalization" of the Diaoyu / Senkaku Islands, 2012

Within Japan, the person who ignited the fuse that blew up Sino-Japanese relations in 2012 was a popular, macho writer-turned-politician, Ishihara Shintaro. Ishihara had become a cult figure in 1956 when, as a writer and playwright, he and his brother Yujiro made a famous movie in which they became symbols of a new and assertive young generation. Because Ishihara already had a huge popular following, when he became a politician and was elected governor of Tokyo, he always attracted more attention than other politicians. Aware of Ishihara's vast popularity, other politicians hesitated to criticize him publicly. When the United States was at the peak of its power, Ishihara proclaimed that Japan could say "no" to the United States. In 2010, when the Chinese economy was passing Japan's in size, Ishihara proclaimed that Japan could also say "no" to China. When Ishihara lambasted Democratic Party leaders for their feeble response to China's pressure to release the trawler captain, his views struck a responsive chord among the Japanese public. Since World War II the Senkaku / Diaoyu Islands had been uninhabited, and three of the islands were officially owned by Kurihara Hiroyuki, whose relatives had once used the islands in their business of preparing dried bonito flakes (*katsuobushi*) for the market. In April 2012, in a talk at the Heritage Foundation in Washington, D.C., Ishihara announced his intention to raise money to buy the Kurihara's three islands and build structures on them.

Prime Minister Noda Yoshihiko of the Democratic Party, aware that Ishihara's purchase of the islands would infuriate the Chinese and fearful of how Ishihara might use his possession of the islands, decided it would be better for the Japanese government to buy the islands than to run the risk of problems with China if they were in Ishihara's hands. Noda was more pragmatic than his two Democratic Party predecessors, Hatoyama Yukio and Kan Naoto, but he did not want to appear weak in the face of China's requests. He vastly underestimated China's determination to assert that it was the dominant power in the region.

On July 7, 2012, with limited consultations with other Japanese leaders, Noda decided that the government would buy the islands from the Kurihara family for $25 million, but he wanted to keep his plan secret and then have discussions with the Chinese, hoping this would avoid an escalation of tensions. The next day, however, the *Asahi* newspaper revealed his plan under the headline: "Nationalization." The Chinese were, as Japan's Ministry of Foreign Affairs had predicted, furious and they strongly opposed Japan's "nationalization" of the islands. The issue became a test of political will at a time when China's leaders had gained confidence that they were the dominant country in East Asia. In many Chinese cities, street demonstrations broke out in which Japanese-owned shops and factories were attacked, causing damages totaling $100 million, according to Japanese estimates. Up until this point the Chinese had sent only Chinese Coast Guard ships into the waters near the islands, but on September 14, three days after the Japanese government purchased the three islands, China began sailing government patrol ships near the disputed islands, some even within the twelve-nautical-mile zone that Japan administered. With these actions, the Chinese government made it clear to Japan that it was prepared to go to great lengths to show that it was the dominant power in Asia, and that the Japanese would be in trouble if they did not follow China's requests.

Not until a year later, in October 2013, did relations between China and Japan in the area of the islands began to stabilize. Until that time, China was sending as many as four patrols a week to the islands' territorial waters. Thereafter, it sent only one patrol every several weeks, thus reducing the chance of an incident. The Japanese also worked to avoid any escalation of the dispute by not building on the islands.

To the Japanese, the Chinese reaction to their purchase of the three islands seemed excessive, but by 2012 it was clear to Japan's leaders that China's military and economic power had surpassed Japan's and they had no choice but to accept that reality. However, as in earlier centuries, Japan was determined not to bow down.

For many of the Chinese who had grudgingly recognized since 1895 that Japan was stronger and more modern, China had returned to its proper place in the world and in its relationship with Japan. Now, with a stronger military and a larger economy, as well as the legacy of a great ancient civilization, China could again look down on Japan. But Chinese leaders did not yet have the relaxed confidence that the United States enjoyed between 1945 and 2008 as the world's unquestioned leading power. To them, the demand that Japan must recognize its history meant not only that it must acknowledge past cruelties but also that it must recognize that China had become the leading nation in Asia. At the same time, many Japanese remained determined, as Empress Suiko was in 607, that while Japan would acknowledge the greatness of China, China should treat Japan with respect.

Xi Jinping, Abe Shinzo, and the Stabilization of Relations

After the rapid changes of prime ministers in Japan between 1994 and 2012, the long, stable relationship between Abe Shinzo, who was elected again in 2012 (currently serving until 2021) and China's Xi Jinping (president from 2012 until at least 2022) has enabled the two leaders, after firming up their respective political bases, to move slowly and steadily toward stabilizing the relationship between China and Japan.

When Abe Shinzo first served as prime minister from 2006 to 2007, both Chinese and Japanese leaders wanted to improve relations following the standoff from the Koizumi era, and Abe's relations with Hu Jintao's China went relatively smoothly. But Abe had a conservative political base and he had enjoyed good relations with his grandfather, Kishi Nobusuke, who had been accused of being a class-A war criminal for his role in guiding the economy during World War II. Abe wanted to change Article 9 of the Japanese Constitution to allow Japan to become a normal country with regular armed forces (instead of only "self-defense forces"). In December 2013, a year after he returned to office, Abe displayed his conservative credentials by visiting the Yasukuni Shrine. Not only Chinese but also Koreans and Westerners criticized him for this. Abe was proud and patriotic, but after he made his political statement by visiting the Yasukuni Shrine, he chose to be pragmatic. While in office, he did not again visit the Yasukuni Shrine.

After the years of political instability from 1994 to 2012, the Japanese public longed for a prime minister who could provide steady leadership. During his first year after returning to the position of prime minister in

2012, Abe introduced the economic policy known as "Abenomics," which provided a short-term stimulus for the economy and boosted his popularity. His chief cabinet secretary, Suga Yoshihide, proved skillful in working with other political leaders to manage Abe's agenda. Abe continued to support the defense alliance with the United States, but he avoided being provocative to China. Abe managed to maintain support and to win a third term, which allows him to remain in office until 2021, the year after Tokyo is scheduled to host the Olympics.

Abe came to office within months of the 2012 confrontations over Japan's purchase of three of the Senkaku / Diaoyu Islands. China's ships and planes continued to put pressure on Japan in the area. Japan had already established an Air Defense Identification Zone (ADIZ), which required any airplane flying over the islands to give Japan prior notification, and in 2013 China announced it was establishing its own ADIZ over the islands. Four Japanese airline companies initially made their planes comply, but later, when the Japanese government told them not to notify China, they ceased notification.

Continuing Economic Relations

Just as trade between China and Japan continued during the Qing and Tokugawa periods, when political relations between the two countries were lacking, so trade between China and Japan continued after 1992 despite political problems. In fact, in 2004 when relations between China and Japan were very tense, China's trade with Japan surpassed its trade with the United States.

Although the Japanese worried when the size of China's economy eclipsed Japan's, in many ways Japan is fortunate to be located next to the world's most populous country, particularly now that Chinese per capita incomes have risen to middle-class levels. For 150 years it has been the dream of Japanese business leaders to access the Chinese market. Late in the nineteenth century, the Chinese were so poor that only a few could afford the products that Japan then offered—silk, cotton cloth, laver (a seaweed), and dried squid. Today the Chinese population is ten times that of Japan, and for Japanese companies it means a market of 1.4 billion consumers with increasingly sophisticated taste and considerable disposable income.

For many Japanese companies, the sales and profits from operations outside of Japan are larger than those from their domestic business. Japan's annual repatriation of profits from overseas investments has increased five times since 2000, and by 2014 they amounted to about $200 billion per year. During recent decades, when domestic GDP was growing at 1 percent or less, Japan's overseas operations were growing at an annual rate of 5 percent or more. Japan's balance of trade with China has generally been positive, in stark contrast to the U.S. balance of trade with China.

Japanese investment in China began to grow in the mid-1990s as Chinese economic growth sped up, and it increased again after China joined the WTO in 2001. The amount of new investment declined slightly after 2010, but trade began to grow again in 2014. More companies from Japan have been conducting business in China than companies from any other country. In October 2016, for example, some 32,300 Japanese firms were operating in China. The United States was second, with some 8,400 firms.

Japanese firms have adapted to the changing opportunities in China, moving from producing light industrial goods with low technology to producing heavy industrial goods and goods with higher technology. By the twenty-first century, as Chinese family incomes had risen, Japan increased its sales of consumer goods in China and expanded its investments in the service sector. Between 2006 and 2014, for example, the proportion of Japanese investments in China in the service sector grew from 24 percent to 39 percent.

Japanese companies that invested in China in the 1980s generally took a long-term perspective. As the Chinese economy grew, the Chinese became skilled at using the prospects of its huge market to insist that foreign companies build factories in China and pass on their latest technology. Yet Japanese companies, unlike many Western companies that passed on their latest technology to gain short-term profits, were generally more cautious about sharing their newest technology in their factories in China. They were aware that Chinese employees of foreign companies who became familiar with foreign technology and management would often leave to form their own companies, taking with them the technological knowledge they had gained from their former employer. Japanese companies, in contrast, have been more likely to provide their Chinese employees with long-term incentives, such as supplying housing that employees gradually acquire as their own over many years with the company. They have also integrated their production in China with Chinese companies and sourced high-technology components in Japan, so that it is not easy for Chinese companies to break off from their Japanese partners.

Despite the political tensions, Japan's largest trading companies have administrative offices throughout China that have become as large or larger than their offices in the United States. The largest Japanese trading company in the Chinese market, Itochu, has offices in fourteen cities. Other major trading companies in China—Mitsubishi, Mitsui, and Sumitomo—have offices in all major Chinese cities, with local staff under the leadership of Japanese officials who have learned Mandarin and, in some cases, even local Chinese dialects. They have learned about local politics and markets and have made connections with local officials to learn how to operate in the Chinese environment. By linking up with the large Japanese trading companies in China, small Japanese companies can gain information about the Chinese market and make local connections that are needed to conduct business.

Japanese firms generally keep a low profile in China to avoid anti-Japanese outbursts, and they tend to pay their Chinese employees slightly more than Chinese or Western firms do to compensate for anti-Japanese sentiments. They have continued to benefit from the good reputation of Japanese products, even during periods of anti-Japanese demonstrations when Chinese protesters have boycotted Japanese firms and damaged Japanese property. All these efforts have helped Japanese companies remain in China even during periods of heightened political tensions. Effective working relationships between Japanese and Chinese businesses have provided ballast for the relationship.

At the same time, many Japanese firms have found ways to reduce the risks of depending entirely on their production in China by diversifying their investments to work with other Asian countries. After the 2005 attacks on Japanese goods, a popular expression among Japanese industrialists investing in China was "China plus one." A Japanese company that built a factory in China also built a factory elsewhere, so that if the factory in China were to encounter trouble due to nationalist outbreaks, the company could quickly expand operations elsewhere to meet its production goals. In the years after 2010 the Japanese increased their new investments in industrial plants in Southeast Asia and India more than their new investments in China, both because of concern about boycotts and attacks on Japanese property and because of rising Chinese labor costs. But the Japanese have found ways to deal with risk while remaining active in the Chinese market.

Business leaders in Japanese headquarters consider it an important part of their responsibility to maintain good working relations with Chinese officials, in Beijing and in the regions. When Diet member Nikai Toshihiro, a former economic bureaucrat and former chief cabinet secretary, travels to Beijing, for example, he often takes with him several hundred people with business interests in China. When Prime Minister Abe visited China in October 2018, he was accompanied by more than 500 Japanese businesspeople with interests in China. Since there are direct flights from Tokyo or Osaka to several large Chinese cities, it is now possible for a Japanese businessperson to fly to China in the morning, have one or two meetings, and return the same evening.

Despite government tensions, a program initiated by Deng Xiaoping and Nakasone Yasuhiro in 1983 that enables local Chinese governments to request retired Japanese technical workers (over the age of sixty) to come to China to work in their locality has continued without interruption. By 2018, some 4,700 retired Japanese technicians had been employed by local governments in China, and they have been much appreciated for bringing in new technology.

The Easing of Tensions since 2014

In June 2014 Fukuda Yasuo, who had been head of China's Boao Forum after retiring as prime minister in 2008, traveled to Beijing, where he met with President Xi Jinping and China's leading diplomats, Yang Jiechi and Wang Yi. During his visit, he and his Chinese hosts worked out a four-point mechanism for reducing the risk that an accident near the Senkaku / Diaoyu Islands might lead to a broader conflict. Fukuda and Xi also laid the foundation for a meeting between Abe and Xi in November 2014. Since Fukuda's visit, there has been a very slow but steady improvement in relations.

For two years after Abe returned to the post of prime minister in 2012, China refused Japan's requests for a meeting between Abe and Xi Jinping, but it would have been awkward for them not to meet when Abe attended a meeting of the Asia-Pacific Economic Cooperation (APEC) in Beijing in November 2014. They did meet at the APEC conference, and when the two leaders posed for photographs after their twenty-minute conversation, they each pouted to show their respective home audiences that they had not been too soft on the other country. Aides on the two sides reported, however, that the two leaders were in fact quite cordial during their brief meeting. During his seventeen years working in Fujian, Xi Jinping had often met with Japanese visitors, and the Japanese who spoke with him reported that Xi was businesslike and not personally anti-Japanese.

In April 2015, to celebrate the sixtieth anniversary of the Bandung Conference of Non-Aligned Nations, at which Zhou Enlai played a major role, Abe and Xi met for half an hour and discussed again how the two countries might cooperate to reduce tensions. For the public, they posed displaying cordial smiles, reflecting progress in the relationship but not so much progress as to disturb the left-wing Chinese and right-wing Japanese.

Although high-level Japanese and Chinese political leaders rarely meet, diplomats have met slightly more often. The Chinese have generally assigned as ambassador to Tokyo highly skilled Japanese-language specialists, such as Tang Jiaxuan or Wang Yi, but aside from their diplomatic assignments, they had not lived in Japan. Their Japanese counterparts report that Chinese diplomats sometimes criticize Japan severely, using set phrases, behavior that makes it difficult to sustain friendships with them. However, Cheng Yonghua, who became China's ambassador to Japan in 2010, had gone to Japan in 1975 to attend Soka University (under the Buddhist sect Soka Gakkai), where he had a chance to develop personal relationships with the Japanese before he entered the Chinese Ministry of Foreign Affairs in 1977. As in earlier centuries, the Buddhist connection provided a basis of trust that underpinned business relations between the two countries. Cheng's wife, who received her Ph.D. from Tokyo University, also has Japanese acquaintances from outside diplomatic channels. Cheng has maintained good working relationships with the Japanese and has been allowed by leaders in Beijing to remain as ambassador for a much longer term than usual.

In 2012 Japan appointed a professional diplomat, Nishimiya Shinichi, a China and U.S. specialist, to replace Ambassador Niwa Uichiro, who was not a China specialist but a former president of Itochu, the most successful

Japanese trading company in China. Nishimiya died suddenly before taking up his position. Given the troubled state of Sino-Japanese relations, Japan then chose to send a very senior diplomat, Kitera Masato, a French specialist, to be ambassador in Beijing. During his three and a half years as ambassador, Kitera met Foreign Minister Wang Yi once, and in that meeting in 2013, Wang Yi complained about Abe's visit to the Yasukuni Shrine.[7] When he met with other officials in China, Kitera was presented with carefully worded criticisms of Japan's behavior. Japanese officials were prepared to have more frequent and productive interactions, but China limited the contacts.

In March 2016, Abe named as ambassador to Beijing an experienced China specialist, Yokoi Yutaka, who had served as head of the China section in the Ministry of Foreign Affairs, head of the political section in Japan's embassy in Beijing, consul general in Shanghai, and ambassador to Turkey. His contacts with his Chinese counterparts in Beijing developed slowly but steadily.

Although Japanese visitors to China leveled off after the tensions in 2010, the number of Chinese visitors to Japan has grown rapidly since 2013. By 2013, the rise in the Chinese standard of living and the decline in the value of the yen enabled more Chinese tourists to travel outside the country. According to Japanese government figures, the number of visas granted to Chinese travelers to Japan has undergone a striking increase, as shown in the table.

NUMBER OF CHINESE VISITORS TO JAPAN

2012	1,425,100
2013	2,210,821
2014	2,409,158
2015	4,993,689
2016	6,372,948
2017	7,350,000
2018	8,380,000

Because Japanese products have a good reputation in China, Chinese tourists buy electronic goods, appliances, hi-tech toilet seats, baby formula, and other Japanese products when they visit Japan. Japanese hotels and stores in key tourist cities in Japan have hired Chinese employees who have studied in Japan to help them meet the needs of their Chinese customers. Even large shopping malls in Japan cater to Chinese tourists and have introduced Chinese-language signs. Some have more signs in Chinese than in English.

Given the very negative publicity in China about the Japanese, many first-time tourists have been surprised at how much they have enjoyed Japan. When Chinese tourists began going to Japan in large numbers, they generally traveled in tour groups, but gradually families started visiting Japan on their own. Chinese tourists typically first traveled to the well-known tourist sites in Tokyo, Kyoto, Nara, and Osaka. But on later trips some tourists began visiting various spots in Hokkaido, Kyushu, and Shikoku, and scenic places elsewhere in the country. Just as boorish American tourists in Europe and parts of Asia in the 1950s were known as "ugly Americans" and Japanese tourists going to Southeast Asia in the 1970s were often known as "ugly Japanese," so some of the first groups of nouveau riche tourists from China who traveled abroad were dubbed the "ugly Chinese" for being noisy, careless about property in hotel rooms, and rude to people around them. However, like experienced American and Japanese travelers, Chinese tourists have begun reading guidebooks to learn about expected behavior in other countries, and Japanese complaints about them have declined.

The educated middle-class tourists who have traveled to Japan find that the Japanese people they see and meet personally are courteous, very different from the cruel soldiers depicted in World War II movies. Chinese visitors generally return from Japan convinced that Japan is an orderly and clean country, with little environmental pollution. In questionnaires about whether travelers would like to revisit the country they traveled to, a higher percentage of Chinese tourists report wanting to revisit Japan than any other foreign country. Chinese leaders welcomed the pragmatic attitudes of the Abe administration and its care in avoiding provocative statements against China. Chinese publicity attacking Japan began to decrease. In 2012 fewer than 10 percent of the Chinese surveyed reported having positive impressions of Japan, but surveys from 2017 showed that as many as 40 percent of the Chinese polled had developed positive feelings toward Japan.

Japanese impressions of China have been changing much more slowly. The memories of China putting pressure on Japan in 2010 and 2012, of TV images of Japanese businesses in China being trashed by crowds of protestors, of the buzzing of Japanese ships in the Senkaku / Diaoyu area, of the countless World War II movies showing heroic Chinese soldiers fighting Japanese enemies, and of anti-Japanese Chinese movies and propaganda in general, have been too strong and too recent for the Japanese to feel relaxed about how a strong China will behave.

By 2017 the Chinese had begun to reduce the number of new World War II movies produced for Chinese TV and the numbers of Chinese airplanes flown and ships sailed close to the Senkaku / Diaoyu Islands. It had also begun to cooperate with Japan in exchanging high-level officials.

In May 2018, forty years after China and Japan began preparing for the Treaty of Peace and Friendship that they signed in 1978, Premier Li Keqiang visited Japan, where he met Emperor Akihito and had discussions with Prime Minister Abe on how to improve relations. To symbolize China's receptivity to Japanese companies in China, Li Keqiang visited a Toyota factory in Hokkaido that made parts for Toyota's factories in China. Japan and China agreed on further mechanisms for increasing communication. China made it clear that it welcomed Japan's willingness to cooperate on projects in its Belt and Road Initiative, a plan to strengthen international cooperation and broaden links for infrastructure development, investment, and trade with countries on the Euro-Asian continent. Li Keqiang's visit also reflected his recognition that Japan and China had common interests in responding to President Donald Trump's trade pressures.

In October 2018, Prime Minister Abe made the first visit to China by a Japanese prime minister since 2011, when relations between the two countries were far more tense. Prime Minister Abe and President Xi discussed measures for increasing communications between the two countries and possibilities for cooperation in projects in other countries. During Abe's time in Beijing, October 25 to 27, China and Japan announced a $30 billion currency swap to promote greater stability of their two currencies. Abe said that the two nations could now move from competition to cooperation. By the time of the visit, it was amply clear that China was the dominant economic and military power. After Abe returned to Japan, diplomats from the two sides continued planning to bring Xi Jinping to Japan in 2019, for what would be Xi's first visit to Japan since becoming China's top leader in 2012. It is not expected that the meeting will end the standoff over the Senkaku / Diaoyu Islands, where neither side is prepared to give up its claims, but it could stabilize the situation and further reduce the risk of conflict. As in earlier centuries, particularly in the latter half of the nineteenth century, competition between Japan and China over Korea has intensified again. Japanese efforts to develop a Terminal High Altitude Area Defense (THAAD) missile system, involving cooperation with South Korea and the United States against threats from North Korea, have pulled South Korea toward Japan, but China's publicity about Japan's refusal to face history has exacerbated some cleavages between Korea and Japan that remain strong.

Japan amid Heightened Sino-American Tensions, 2017

The Chinese economy appeared poised to begin surpassing the U.S. economy in overall size in 2017, just as it was poised in 1993 to begin the transition to dominance in Asia as the size of its economy was surpassing that of Japan. And just as relations between China and Japan became very tense during that earlier transition, so relations between China and the United States became more tense over the prospect that China's high-technology, military power, and international influence were beginning to challenge the dominance of the United States in those areas.

The Japanese were in many ways better prepared for the transition to China's gaining the dominant position than Americans are now. The Japanese had historical memories of how the Chinese had treated Japan when Chinese officials presided over a confident civilization that dominated Asia. The Japanese had deeper cultural contacts with the Chinese over the centuries, with an overlap in written language that enabled them to have broader and deeper communications than Americans have with China. Far more Japanese people had lived in China and learned how to work with the Chinese. The Japanese had long been accustomed to tensions with the Chinese, ever since the 1870s when they confronted each other in Korea. Furthermore, Japan had experienced far too many difficulties with China to share the naïve optimism displayed by some Americans in their dealings with China since President Nixon's visit in 1972.

The Japanese also have had a deeper understanding of China's economic nationalism as it has tried to catch up with more modern industrial nations. To be sure, Japan's and China's paths in pursuing their own economic interests were different. After World War II, Japan, which already had a strong industrial base, tried to commercialize its military technology and prepare its infant industries for international market competition while creating nontariff barriers to make it difficult for foreign countries to establish industrial plants in Japan. In 1978, when China suddenly opened up, its industries were so far below international standards that it allowed foreign companies seeking access to its huge market to establish industrial plants in China if they shared their technology. China expected that as their industries caught up, Chinese companies would begin to take the place of the foreign companies. The Japanese were less surprised than the Americans and others when Chinese companies became strong and endeavored to reduce the foreign presence in China. Japanese companies, with deeper roots in local Chinese communities and a broader perspective, were better prepared because they were less interested in short-term profits, more cautious about sharing their most precious technology, and more heavily invested in long-term relationships with the Chinese.

The Japanese cannot expect high levels of military cooperation between their two nations, but they can expand their discussions to further reduce the risk of conflict and extend their cooperation for responding to natural disasters and carrying out peacekeeping projects. The Japanese already have a rich network of relationships with the Chinese in all fields, and that network is likely to expand in the decades ahead.

Yet faced with a strong China, the Japanese have every reason to maintain their ties to the United States, which have grown stronger and deeper in the seven decades since World War II. The Japanese have close relations with the United States in every sphere—military, political, economic, and cultural. There is a high level of comfort between the Americans and the Japanese, and an open exchange of ideas and opinions. Although some in China have an interest in expanding relations with Japan, it is not in China's interest to detach Japan from the U.S.-Japan military alliance, for an independent Japan would develop a stronger military and possibly develop nuclear weapons to defend itself. The Chinese have not erased their image of the Japanese as a militaristic aggressive people, and they believe that the U.S.-Japan Alliance can still help keep the cork in the bottle. Japanese strategists are aware that the Chinese economy will soon be several times larger than their own, that China is putting far more resources into its military than Japan could match, and that Japan's military manpower cannot compare with that of China, which has ten times the population. The Japanese are therefore firmly committed to cooperation with the U.S. military. Though the Japanese are prepared to increase their cooperation with China, their relationship with the U.S. military and the U.S. government since 1945 has made the Japanese feel far more secure working with Americans than with an authoritarian Chinese government that has expressed so much hostility toward Japan.

However, the reduced role of the United States in maintaining global order, the increased role of China in global affairs, and the stabilization of relations between China and Japan provide a new basis for increased cooperation between China and Japan in regional and global affairs. The Chinese and Japanese have already begun discussions about working together in the Mekong Delta, and they have begun cooperating on construction projects in the Belt and Road Initiative. Japan responded to U.S. pressures not to join the Asian Infrastructure Investment Bank (AIIB), but it has begun cooperating with the AIIB for financing various projects in Asia. China and Japan have good channels for working with the AIIB because of Japan's relations with the president of AIIB, Jin Liqun. A cosmopolitan internationalist, Jin was formerly vice president of the Japanese-led Asian Development Bank, and he has for many years enjoyed good relations with Japanese officials as well as officials from the United States and other countries. The nexus of relations between the Chinese and the Japanese, already strong, can be expected to expand in the decades ahead. Yet the history between their countries since the 1870s is so troubled on both sides that Japan's relationship with China cannot undo the deep positive relations between the Japanese and the Americans that have developed since 1945.

CHAPTER TWELVE

Facing the New Era

WHAT IS THE NATURE of the new era that China and Japan face, now that China occupies the dominant position in the relationship? How might the two nations work together in the new era for the benefit of both nations and the rest of the world?

Sino-Japanese Relations after 2014

Until the arrival of Western explorers, merchants, and missionaries, China and Japan were linked in a loose regional order dominated by Chinese civilization. But now the two countries are part of a global order, which, though highly imperfect, operates according to a far more complex structure of rules and procedures that were originally established by Western countries. Even as China surpasses the United States to become the world's largest economy, it remains part of this global structure created by Westerners. As China gains influence and leverage around the world, it is beginning to take on a larger role within existing organizations. It is taking the lead to form new regional and global institutions that, despite being established by China, operate less in the way China has traditionally dealt with the outside and more like the institutions established under the leadership of the United States and other Western countries. Japan, which has been subordinate to the United States since the days of the Allied Occupation, remains a major global economic power and will continue working within the framework of the U.S.-Japan Security Alliance. But since the administration of Donald Trump, which is loosening its links to regional and global institutions, Japan is gaining more independence and beginning slowly to take more initiative in its global political role and in its relations with China.

People in China and Japan now have far more contacts with each other than they had at any time in history. Due to the advances in industrial production and transportation that spread to China in the early decades after reform and opening began in 1978, the scale of goods and people exchanged between the two countries is more than a hundred times what it was in 1972, when they first reestablished formal diplomatic relations. More goods are exchanged, and more people travel between the two countries, in a single day now than in an entire decade during the centuries of the Qing dynasty (1644–1912) and the Tokugawa period (1603–1868). Between World War II and 1972, trade between the two countries never reached $1 billion a year, but by 2017 the countries were trading $300 billion in goods per year.[1] In 1965, the peak year for Japanese visitors to China before normalization, aside from some Japanese visitors to the Guangzhou trade fair, fewer than 5,000 Japanese travelers visited China during the entire year.[2] In 2018, more than 8 million visas were issued to Chinese travelers going to Japan and more than 4 million visas were issued to Japanese individuals going to China. By 2018 an average of more than 20,000 Chinese visitors were arriving in Japan each day, and the number of tourists was continuing to grow.

More than 30,000 Japanese companies now operate in China, far more than companies from any other country. Pragmatic Chinese officials in charge of local economic relations have been willing to work with the Japanese, despite public expressions of anti-Japanese sentiment. Japanese companies are also playing a role in supplying products to Chinese consumers through e-commerce.

However, between the political leaders of Japan and China, the level of trust and empathy and the number of frank discussions is low compared with those between the leaders of other major nations, and the nature of their exchanges tends to be more formal. No high-level political leader on either side has close friendships with or deep knowledge about the people in the other country. Top leaders of the two nations occasionally have their own brief side meetings at gatherings of regional or international organizations, but long discussions between them have not taken place more than once every five years. By Chinese standards for welcoming foreign guests, Japanese officials are often not given honored treatment, and sometimes they are not received at all.

Until the Sino-Japanese War of 1895, most Chinese people living outside of the major east coast cities were hardly aware of Japan's existence. Even during the Sino-Japanese War of 1937–1945, unlike those living near large cities or Japanese military camps, the 80 percent of the Chinese population living in rural areas without access to radio had little awareness of what Japanese soldiers were doing in China. Now, every day, virtually everyone in both Japan and China has access to electronic media presenting news or stories about the other country. In China, state media officials supervise the content of information presented to the public, and between 1992 and 2014, images of Japanese aggressors were widely available to Chinese viewers. Japan did not have an organized propaganda department as it did during World War II, but coverage of China in the Japanese media included televised pictures of Chinese protestors throwing stones at Japanese shops in China, and Chinese ships and planes harassing Japanese ships near the Senkaku / Diaoyu Islands. The result of such media coverage in both countries was a widespread, mutual public antagonism that peaked between 2010 and 2014. Yet as Chinese incomes began to rise, Chinese people acquired a high regard for Japanese industrial products.

The extensive personal contacts and economic relations between China and Japan thus rest on a fragile foundation that is threatened by widespread popular hostility and the changeability of political leaders who lack trust in their counterparts in the other country. Since much of the passion in Sino-Japanese relations is deeply rooted in perceptions of history, it will be difficult for the two countries to place their relations on a more solid, stable base, unless they deal with the volatile emotions stemming from history.

Concerns of Chinese Leaders and Their Use of History

The concerns that Chinese leaders have about Japan are reflected in the issues they raise about history. The three most common issues raised by Chinese leaders are: visits by Japanese political leaders to the Yasukuni Shrine, Japan's failure to acknowledge the horrors of the Nanjing Massacre, and the failure of Japanese textbooks to describe accurately the Sino-Japanese War. What are the concerns underlying China's focus on these issues?

The Yasukuni Shrine

Although many Japanese leaders have expressed goodwill toward China during the past 125 years, ultimately China suffered greatly from attacks by Japanese troops, not only from 1937 to 1945 but also during the Sino-Japanese War of 1894–1895, the Ji'nan Incident of 1928, the Manchurian Incident of 1931, and the Shanghai Incident of 1932. Chinese leaders recall the efforts by Toyotomi Hideyoshi to march through Korea to capture Beijing. They see in Japanese the samurai warrior spirit and the willingness to die for their country. They are concerned that Japan might again become an aggressive militarist power, and they do not believe that Japan's declarations of its peaceful intent are a reliable predictor of its behavior. Therefore, they are alert to any signs that militarists might once again rise to power in Japan. They are sensitive to discussions of increasing military expenditures, to proposals to eliminate Article 9 in the Japanese Constitution forbidding the use of war as a means of settling international disputes, and to the activities and statements by right-wing activists.

For the Chinese, the enshrinement in the Yasukuni Shrine of the souls of Japanese military figures who were tried as class-A war criminals after World War II signals that the Japanese still respect those who took part in attacking China. Japan's failure to separate the war criminals from the place where others who died serving Japan are enshrined is seen by the Chinese as reinforcing the readiness of young Japanese to sacrifice themselves for their country. Knowledgeable Chinese are also aware that the Yushukan Museum at the Yasukuni Shrine glorifies Japanese military achievements.

Having suffered from Japanese military aggression, China's leaders are acutely concerned when they see any sign that Japan might be becoming more militaristic. For them, the return of the souls of Japanese war criminals to the Yasukuni Shrine, and visits made by Japanese political leaders to the Yasukuni Shrine since then, arouse fears that a militaristic spirit is being revived. From the perspective of the Chinese, the actions of Japanese leaders—visiting the place where Japanese war criminals are enshrined—speak louder about Japan's true intentions than their "empty" words about peace.

The Nanjing Massacre

To the Chinese, the Nanjing Massacre represents the vicious nature of Japanese warriors. Many in China are familiar with tales about the cruelties of the Japanese. The reports of the behavior of Japanese soldiers in Nanjing resonate with what the Chinese have long heard about sword-swinging samurai and bloodthirsty Japanese pirates.

When the Chinese hear statements by Japanese scholars arguing that not as many people were killed during the Nanjing Massacre as the Chinese claim, they interpret them as playing down the seriousness of the crimes that Japanese soldiers committed in China. If the Japanese try to soften the horror of the atrocities committed by their troops, it creates doubts about whether they have really turned their backs on the behavior of earlier generations.

The Textbook Issue

The Chinese are concerned that the next generation in Japan, rather than being trained to denounce the militarist past, will be susceptible to becoming aggressors just like earlier generations. If the Japanese are really turning their backs on their militarist past, the Chinese ask, why are they not learning the lessons of history and renouncing their past behavior in what they teach their youth? Textbooks have become a visible, concrete symbol for the Chinese to evaluate how Japanese students are being trained. Knowledgeable Chinese are aware that the textbooks used in high school social-science courses in Japan provide very little background on the two Sino-Japanese Wars. In their view, the youth in Japan today are not sufficiently aware of the horrors that were committed by Japanese soldiers and hence they do not thoroughly reject war making. If Japanese youth were to be drafted into military service by their leaders and called to war, they ask, might they not commit the same cruel acts as their grandfathers and great-grandfathers?

Chinese Leaders' Limited Contacts with Japan

Since World War II, China's leaders, unlike Chinese students who have studied in Japan, have had few contacts with the Japanese, and therefore they have not had opportunities to witness the depth of the Japanese commitment to peace. Their perspectives, like those of the Chinese public in general, are more deeply colored by memories of the Japanese atrocities of World War II.

Chinese Leaders' Use of History

Leaders in China have drawn on their people's historical memories to increase China's leverage over Japan. The Chinese assumption has been that when Japanese leaders show signs of reviving militarism, strong complaints and warnings will eventually deter Japan from pursuing a military course. When they see signs that Japan may be becoming more militaristic, they warn the Japanese of the anger of the Chinese people. China's leaders rallied public opinion to protest Prime Minister Nakasone Yasuhiro's visit to the Yasukuni Shrine on August 15, 1985, for example, on the fortieth anniversary of Japan's surrender to the United States. They set off an anti-Japanese campaign when Japan announced plans in 2010 to try in a domestic court the Chinese fishing-boat captain who had rammed into two Japanese vessels near the Senkaku / Diaoyu Islands. They organized another anti-Japanese publicity campaign in 2012 when Japan announced plans to "nationalize" the islands.

The leaders of China have often called attention to Japan's aggressive history when pursuing specific goals. For example, when it appeared in the 1980s that Japan was hesitating to renew its programs to extend aid to China, Chinese complaints about Japan's handling of history became more pronounced, subsiding only after Japan decided to renew its aid. Many Chinese individuals and Chinese businesses have also criticized Japan for its past aggressions when they have failed to receive payments from Japanese individuals or companies for other offenses.

When the United Nations was considering making Japan a permanent member of the UN Security Council, the Chinese government opposed it, arguing that the position would be unacceptable because of Japan's aggressive

behavior in the past. Chinese leaders mobilized their citizens to sign peti-
tions and to take part in public demonstrations against Japan.

Following the Chinese student demonstrations at Tiananmen Square
in 1989 and the collapse of the Soviet Union in 1991 after its own domestic
protests, Chinese leaders introduced the Patriotic Education Campaign to
encourage patriotism among the next generation. To help build national loyalty, many articles appeared in the Chinese media that were critical of
Japan for its treatment of China. The government also began using new
formats—movies, video games, and other digital media—to display the
brutal behavior of the Japanese and thus build greater support among Chinese youth for their leaders, who sought to protect their country from the
enemy. In 2012, for example, the Chinese government approved the production of 69 anti-Japanese television series and 100 anti-Japanese films. Ever
since 1915, when China opposed Japan's Twenty-One Demands, Chinese
leaders have found anti-Japanese publicity to be a useful tool for building
loyalty to the Chinese government and its leadership.

The Japanese History Problem

The essence of the Japanese history problem is that although the Japanese
overwhelmingly wish to pursue the path of peace, their respect for their own
ancestors and their determination not to bow down to China have prevented
them from satisfying Chinese demands. The Japanese have rejected military pursuits, but they want to respect their fellow countrymen, and especially their relatives, who sacrificed themselves for their nation. They believe
that if their ancestors did bad things, it was not because they were inherently
bad people but because they faced difficult circumstances in which they had
little choice.

Except for members of some right-wing groups in Japan, the Japanese
strongly believe that it was wrong for Japan to invade China, and they deeply
regret that their nation caused so much suffering. But they also feel that
they have paid an enormous price—in the results of the massive aerial
bombing of their cities, the two atomic bombs dropped on Japan, and the
seven years of Allied Occupation. The dominant view among the Japanese
public is that, after the war, the best way to deal with the suffering Japan had
caused in China was to offer assistance for China's modernization program.

They are pleased that their country's pursuit of peace and its generosity toward other countries have earned Japan a positive worldwide reputation, except in China and Korea. In their view, Japan has made great contributions to China, contributions that have been inadequately acknowledged.

The Japanese recognize that the Chinese are becoming stronger, both militarily and economically. In dealings with the Chinese, the Japanese want to be treated as respected equals, not forced to submit to Chinese demands. They also believe that the Chinese use anti-Japanese rhetoric as a way of both maintaining domestic unity and extracting favors from Japan, and they respond negatively when angry Chinese leaders tell them what they must do.

The Japanese believe that the Chinese have used the issue of history to achieve goals not in Japan's interest. They have used it to issue demands for more help and more payments from Japan. They have used it to gain cooperation from other countries that also suffered from Japanese aggression and to pull them closer to China and away from Japan. The Chinese have done this with Korea, in particular, but also with Southeast Asia and the United States. The Japanese have noticed that the Chinese have called attention to the cooperation between the Americans and the Chinese during World War II in confronting their common enemy, Japan. The Japanese were deeply disappointed that China used the history issue to keep Japan from receiving a permanent seat on the United Nations Security Council, in spite of the fact that Japan was the number-two contributor to UN funding and that since 1945 Japan has been pursuing the path of peace.

It has been difficult for Japan to find an effective way to react to accusations of past aggressions. It has responded by saying that many of the complaints about Japanese behavior are exaggerated. The Japanese also feel it is grossly unfair that they are still the focus of such criticism when Americans are no longer constantly criticized for their actions against American Indians, or Belgians for their acts in the Belgian Congo, or the British and other colonial powers for behavior in the colonies that they exploited. Why, Japan's younger generations ask, must they continuously apologize to the Chinese for events that occurred more than seven decades ago, long before they were born? In the Pew polling for 2016, 53 percent of Japanese respondents said that Japan had apologized enough, while only 10 percent of the Chinese polled agreed.

Facing History While Looking Forward

The current dialogue on history between China and Japan has focused on the unfortunate side of the relationship. Less attention has been given to the good relations between the two countries at times of great cultural borrowing, especially in the periods from 600 to 838, when Japan borrowed so heavily from China, and from 1905 to 1937 and 1978 through the 1990s, when China borrowed so much from Japan. The two cultures have changed throughout history, but there remains a broad base of commonality in the written language, literature, Buddhism, Confucianism, art, architecture, and music they share, some of which is even incorporated into popular culture, and this could form the basis for continued cooperation in the future, if permitted by national policies.

Each country has placed more emphasis on its own contributions to the other and its own suffering at the hands of the other. These images have been kept alive to strengthen loyalty to the nation and to the nation's leaders.

The Chinese, especially through popular Sino-Japanese War movies, have emphasized the negative side of Sino-Japanese relations throughout history. Many Chinese people are convinced that the Japanese are aggressive by nature. In China's patriotic narrative, the Sino Japanese War of 1937–1945 is simply the latest chapter revealing the true Japanese character. In this view, the Japanese are polite—on the surface. In the 1920s, for example, the Japanese talked about cooperation, but in the end they initiated incidents and sneak attacks against both China and the United States.

The Chinese people have little awareness of the positive side of their relationship with Japan, of how much they have benefited from the "learn from Japan" programs after 1895 and the "development assistance" programs after 1978. They are not fully aware of the generosity of Japanese aid programs in the 1980s and 1990s. They are also not aware of the extent to which Japan has apologized, or how thoroughly the Japanese have renounced militarism and pursued peace.

Throughout history the Japanese have had a deep sense of the Chinese as a proud and arrogant people who demand subordination by other people. Thus, ever since 607 the Japanese have maintained a reluctance to bow down to the Chinese and a determination to be treated as political equals. For the

Japanese, requests by the Chinese that they grovel in apologies represent the latest version of China's attempts to assert its superiority. The Japanese are willing to apologize, but they are not prepared to bow down and apologize in the way that the Chinese demand.

The Japanese are aware of Japan's positive contributions to China in the modernization of Manchuria and Taiwan and its contributions to China after 1895 and 1978. However, their collective historical memory directs less attention to the harm and suffering Japan caused to China, an issue that is constantly stressed by the Chinese. The Japanese government at times has not allowed textbooks critical of Japan's aggression in China to be used in its schools, and many publications and public discussions in Japan gloss over the atrocities that Japan committed in China.

What Japan and China Can Do to Face History

Both countries could avoid aggravating the problems that arise from history by providing their citizens with a fuller and more accurate account of their history and a more balanced presentation of their current relations. They could help their citizens better understand their long-entangled history in a way that acknowledges how much they have learned from each other and reflects their positive experiences from working together.

The Japanese prime minister and other senior officials could decide that they will not visit the Yasukuni Shrine while they are in office. The Japanese could also provide fuller accounts of the Sino-Japanese War in curriculum guidelines for compulsory high school history courses, in particular by including the word "invasion" (*shinryaku*) in their textbooks. Japan could produce more television programs that give a full accounting of the suffering inflicted on the Chinese people by Japan's invasions. The Japanese people, individually, could make greater efforts to understand the history of Japanese aggression in China, as well as to better understand Chinese society and the attitudes of the Chinese people.

The Chinese could teach their students more about what China learned from Japan between 1905 and 1937 as well as after 1978. They could give the public a fuller account of the Japanese turn to peace after 1945, Japanese contributions to China since 1978, and the apologies already offered by

Japanese officials. They could reduce the number of anti-Japanese movies about World War II produced and shown in China and present more balanced descriptions of Japan in their museums, their classrooms, and the media.

The Chinese could also study the example of Japan's history in the first half of the twentieth century as a warning of what can happen as a country becomes richer and stronger, when support for military expansion becomes so strong that its leaders are unable to restrain superpatriotic passions that can ultimately lead to disaster.

A New Vision: Warm Politics, Hot Economics

It has been customary for the Chinese and Japanese to describe their relationship as "cold politics, hot economics." Despite poor political relations, they have extensive business relations. The question now is whether the two nations can build on their business relations and improve their political relations.

Since 2010 the key leverage for improving relations has been in the hands of the Chinese, because China has suffered more and because China now has the larger economy and more global influence. Chinese leaders will of course consider how much it is in their national interest to work with Japan on regional and international issues. A fundamental question is to what extent Chinese leaders feel confident enough of the loyalty of their own people that they do not need to use anti-Japanese programs to strengthen nationalism among the populace. In the 1990s, war movies depicting Japanese enemies were an effective tool for strengthening patriotism, but their production and use could be reduced as Chinese leaders feel more confident of the patriotism of the public.

It is unrealistic, considering the depth of the historical passions involved, that China and Japan will quickly develop feelings of trust and become close friends. That may be a goal for several decades in the future. A reasonable goal for the next decade would be to manage their relations in a straightforward, frank, and businesslike way so that the two countries can become reliable partners. It is unrealistic to expect that China and Japan in the next decade will enjoy "hot politics." But if they can continue to expand their cooperation in such enterprises as the Belt and Road Initiative, in developing joint projects for solving environmental issues, and in multinational organizations, it is not impossible that they could achieve "warm politics."

A closer businesslike relationship between China and Japan should not be a problem for the United States. Some individual Americans might respond with alarm, but their alarm would be misplaced. A reduction of tensions between China and Japan, increased stability in the Western Pacific, and contributions from both countries toward maintaining world order are all outcomes that accord with the interests of the United States as well as those of other countries.

An Agenda for Sino-Japanese Cooperation

From 2006 to 2008, leaders and representatives of China and Japan held a series of meetings to discuss how their nations could work together for their mutual benefit and laid out an agenda to achieve that goal.

In April 2007 Chinese premier Wen Jiabao visited Japan and gave a key speech—in Chinese, translated for a Japanese audience, and relayed back to China, where it was broadcast to the public in the original Chinese. He publicly stated what Japanese leaders had long hoped a Chinese leader would say. He acknowledged that on many occasions Japan's leaders had expressed their deep remorse and apologies, and he expressed appreciation for Japan's peaceful development. Premier Wen proposed four principles for bringing Sino-Japanese relations to a new stage: mutual trust, a big-picture perspective, common development based on equality and mutual benefit, and strengthening exchanges with an eye toward the future.

The agenda that Chinese and Japanese officials then agreed to pursue includes the following goals:

Expanded exchanges and dialogues among leaders, cabinet ministers, and high-level officials.

Exchanges of young people.

Reciprocal visits by the People's Liberation Navy and the Japan Maritime Self-Defense Force.

Cooperation on issues involving North Korea.

Energy cooperation (including cooperation on energy conservation and environmental protection).

Establishment of a ministerial-level dialogue on energy.

Further cooperation in fields such as agriculture, intellectual property rights, pharmaceutical products, small and medium-size enterprises, information and communications technology, finance, and criminal justice.

This agenda from 2007 has great promise as a starting point not only for the benefit of China and Japan but fot the benefit of global peace and order.

Biographies of Key Figures

Chiang Kai-shek (Jiang Jieshi), 1887–1975

In 1926 Chiang Kai-shek, until then a military officer of modest ability and genuine patriotism, succeeded Sun Yat-sen and became "the Generalissimo" (the supreme commander), the top military and political leader of the Nationalist Party, and from 1928 until his death he was president of the Republic of China, first on the mainland and after 1949 on Taiwan. However, he never acquired the political skills, charisma, or success of Mao Zedong, his Communist rival for four decades. He remained stoic during his failures to unify China in the 1930s, to expel Japan from China (1937–1945), and to win the Civil War (1946–1949). During wartime he was a micromanager, often personally giving directions to local officers. Yet in Nanjing (1927–1937) and Taiwan (1949–1975) while ruling with an aloof grandeur, he brought order and economic progress. He was accused of being a right-wing authoritarian, but in Taiwan he carried out land reform that his base of support did not allow him to implement on the mainland.

Chiang had a complicated history of relations with Japan. He attended a military academy in Japan for three years and admired Japanese soldiers for their military spirit and the Japanese readiness to die for their country. In the early 1920s, for his personal safety, he escaped to Japan for several months. He endured the taunts of patriots for not fighting the Japanese when he realized that they had superior forces. In the Sino-Japanese War, he fought huge battles against the Japanese in Shanghai and Wuhan, and at times he expressed a deep hatred of the Japanese for their cruelties. But after World War II, he did not require the Japanese to pay reparations to China. In Taiwan he welcomed Japanese businesspeople who were a great help to Taiwan's economic growth.

Chiang Kai-shek came from a merchant family in Fenghua county, Zhejiang province, near Ningbo, 150 miles south of Shanghai. The family had enough funds to support his studies under Confucian tutors and his attendance at Confucian schools in Ningbo from 1903 to 1906. Scarcely a year after hearing that Japan had defeated Russia, as it had defeated China in 1895, Chiang signaled his opposition to Manchu rule by cutting off his queue and setting out for Japan to learn the secrets of its military success. He planned to pursue a military career to help unify China and revive its civilization. After several months in Japan studying language, he returned home and passed an exam to enter the Chinese Central Army School in Baoding, where he underwent his first year of military training. He then passed an examination to enter Shimbu Gakko, a school in Japan where Chinese students studied to prepare for entrance into Japanese military schools. Not a brilliant student, at Shimbu Gakko Chiang ranked fifty-fourth among the sixty-two students in his class. He graduated from Shimbu Gakko in November 1909 and was then assigned to the Japanese Nineteenth Field Army Regiment for practical training. Though reserved, he acquired a reputation for being serious, honest, loyal, and dedicated to his country.

In 1908, while in Japan, he joined Sun Yat-sen's Chinese Revolutionary Alliance, the Tongmenghui, at the age of twenty-one. When Chiang got word that the 1911 Revolution had broken out in Wuhan, he joined 120 other Chinese cadets in Japan to immediately return to China. They boarded a Japanese freighter in Nagasaki and landed at a wharf in the Japanese area of Shanghai. Having spent nearly three years in Japan, Chiang spoke and read Japanese fairly well, but he had no close Japanese friends. Chiang regarded the dedication of Japanese soldiers as critical to Japan's military victories in the Sino-Japanese and the Russo-Japanese wars. He was also impressed with Japanese efficiency and Japan's success in building the modern industrial base and transportation system that underpinned its modern military capacity. Chiang hoped to build a similar industrial base and a dedicated military force back in China.

In 1913 when Sun Yat-sen first met Chiang, who was then a midlevel army official, Sun was impressed by his dedication. When Japan announced its Twenty-One Demands in 1915, Sun, still hoping to win Japanese support, wrote a letter in support of the Japanese position. As a result, many of Sun's erstwhile followers abandoned him for being too soft on Japan, but Chiang remained steadfastly loyal to Sun. In early 1916, Chiang, then back in Shanghai, with financial help from Japan, attempted to build a military base to overcome the northern warlords. He began writing letters to Sun offering suggestions for military strategy. Chiang rose to a high position not because of his outstanding military record but because of his personal relationship with Sun Yat-sen, who valued his loyalty, his dedication to the nation, and his military knowledge.

In 1924 Sun Yat-sen founded a national military academy at Huangpu (Whampoa), near Guangzhou, and appointed Chiang Kai-shek, then age thirty-nine, to head it. Although funds for the military academy came from the Soviet Union and the army was modeled after the Soviet military, Chiang attempted to inculcate in the troops the *bushido* spirit—the code of honor and self-sacrifice—that he had observed in Japan. Sun and Chiang both hoped to train dedicated military officers who could work together in a national army to unify the country. Although Chiang had doubts about Sun's policy of including Communists in a united front, he was successful in training excellent officers who would later serve in his Northern Expedition to unify the country.

After Sun died on March 12, 1925, there was a succession struggle between Chiang and Wang Jingwei, whose connections with Japan were deeper than Chiang's. Although Wang initially had a political advantage, Chiang had a military advantage, and one year later Chiang emerged as Sun's successor, while Wang Jingwei was elected head of Sun's Political Council.

In 1922 Chiang Kai-shek proposed marriage to Song (Soong) Meiling, daughter of the rich businessman T. V. Soong, but she refused him. In October 1927, Meiling, her sister Ailing, and their mother were in Japan. Chiang pursued Meiling to Japan, presented her with papers proving he was divorced, and agreed to read the Bible and study Christianity; this time she accepted his marriage proposal. She was twenty-nine years old and he was forty. The Song family gave Chiang access to high-level business circles, and Meiling, who had attended Wellesley College in the United States, provided access to both Chinese and Western Christians. During World War II Meiling would prove to be extraordinarily successful during a U.S. speaking tour in winning American support for China.

For several years before his death in 1925, Sun Yat-sen had managed to maintain the United Front of Communists and Nationalists within the Nationalist Party. However, after Chiang became head of the Nationalist Party in 1927, he split with the Communists because of fears of a coup, and he sought to kill all the Communist leaders. Despite their former alliance, both parties suspected that many in their midst were in fact spies for the other side. By the early 1930s, Chiang became preoccupied with the growth of the Communist base areas in Jiangxi province. Although he regarded the Japanese as a threat from the outside, he regarded the Communists as an immediate threat from the inside, a threat to China's very heart and soul. He therefore led a series of "encirclement campaigns" against the Communist forces. In 1934 the Communists were able to break through Chiang's fifth encirclement campaign and begin their Long March to northwestern China, where they established a base in Yan'an.

From 1927 to 1936 Chiang was generally focused on overcoming the resistance of local leaders, each of whom had his own army, and unifying the country. In 1927 he drew on the core of officers who had trained at Huangpu Military Academy under his leadership and were committed to national unity. He linked up with the Huangpu officers and some warlords to lead the Northern Expedition to overcome resistance by other warlords. With his allies he established a central government that ruled Northern and Central China from the new capital that Chiang established in Nanjing. But warlords still retained power in various regions, and even though Chiang tried to link up with the stronger warlords to unify the country, that goal was beyond his grasp. Nevertheless, during the "Nanjing decade" from 1927 until the outbreak of the Sino-Japanese War in 1937, he was able to attract able bureaucrats to the capital and to make some progress toward improving the economy, expanding education, and stabilizing the provinces in the vicinity of Nanjing, thus maintaining the semblance of a small national government.

During a 1927 armed conflict with the Japanese in Ji'nan, the Japanese captured a Chinese official, cut off his tongue, gouged out his eyes, and then shot him and more than ten of his underlings. That night, writing in his diary, for the first time Chiang used an old Chinese term of abuse for the Japanese—"dwarf pirates." Even though he knew he did not have sufficient military strength to resist the Japanese, he wrote in his diary that every day he would write down another way to kill the Japanese. Chiang remained realistic in assessing his own military weaknesses vis-à-vis the Japanese, and because of this he was criticized over the years by Communists as well as by other patriots for not attacking the Japanese enemies. At several points, he attempted to carry on discussions with the Japanese to avoid clashes, and in Taiwan after 1949 he cooperated with the Japanese to modernize the economy and bring stability to the island.

Chiang proved to be remarkably accurate in his assessment of the overall situation with Japan. In 1934, when he told a group of senior political leaders that the outbreak of war with Japan would occur in less than 1,100 days, the war actually began 1,057 days later. Like Jiang Baili (see his biography in this section), in the case of a Japanese invasion Chiang planned to escape to the southwest and engage in a war of resistance. He believed that the Japanese would be worn down within ten years. At the time, he had no way of anticipating the impacts of the Soviets' entry into the war, the 1945 bombing of Japanese cities by the United States, and finally the dropping of the atomic bombs. But he was prescient: in fact, the war lasted only eight years.

During the first months of World War II, Chiang relied on his well-trained troops to actively fight Japanese troops in Wuhan and Shanghai, but thereafter, together with his troops, he retreated to Chongqing, in Sichuan province, where he braced for a long period of resistance. As the official leader of the Chinese government, he was subjected to criticism by patriots for not doing more to oppose the Japanese occupation. While in Chongqing, with a large national bureaucracy and a military that he was trying to preserve for later use, he had difficulties maintaining discipline and morale. He was criticized by American officials and reporters for not doing more to control the endemic corruption. U.S. general Joseph Stilwell, a strong critic, referred to him derogatorily as "peanut." However, after Chiang's diary became available in 2005, scholars became more positive about his efforts to preserve the Nationalists' strength to fight the Communists after the war.

When Japan surrendered in 1945, Chiang did not want to see Japan side with the Communists, so he did not demand that the Japanese pay war reparations. During the Civil War with the Communists (1946–1949), Chiang failed to develop a program that matched the Communists' appeal to the poor peasants, who hoped to benefit from the Communist land reform policy, and that also satisfied the superpatriots who insisted on stronger actions against the Japanese. As the army's top commander but also a micromanager, Chiang tried to provide advice to his local military leaders.

However, he was not always well-enough informed about the situation on the battlefield to make wise decisions.

After Chiang lost the Civil War and fled to Taiwan, he undertook some progressive measures there, such as land reform, but he also used his Nationalist Army to maintain tight control over the local people, who came to regard him as a military dictator. He persisted, initially with U.S. support, in pursuing the announced goal of retaking the mainland, a goal that became increasingly unlikely, and then, after 1971 when mainland China replaced Taiwan in the UN, impossible.

For further reading, see Jay Taylor, *The Generalissimo: Chiang Kai-shek and the Struggle for Modern China* (Cambridge, Mass.: Belknap Press of Harvard University Press, 2009).

DENG XIAOPING, 1904–1997

As the top leader of China from December 1978 until October 1992, Deng Xiaoping introduced policies of reform and opening that transformed China and, within four decades, enabled its development from a poor backward economy into the largest economy in the world, as measured by purchasing power parity. In 1978 China's per capita income was less than $200 in U.S. dollars. By 2018 it was more than $8,000.

From 1937 to 1945 Deng Xiaoping was a high-level political commissar in the Chinese Army, engaged in fighting Japan during the Sino-Japanese War. However, between 1973 and 1976 he represented China in welcoming Japanese leaders to visit China. A master political strategist, in 1978 he toured Japan, where he won over prominent Japanese financial and technical leaders who would later play crucial roles in launching China's industrialization in the 1980s.

By the time Deng became the de facto top leader of China in December 1978, he had had an incredible range of experiences to prepare him for ruling. He had spent five years in France from 1920 to 1925, observing the operations of a modern Western country while also working as a laborer in a factory and participating in study groups on Marxism-Leninism and the Russian Revolution. While in France he joined the Communist Party and worked in the party office. Thereafter, he was part of the first class established in the Soviet Union to train Chinese leaders for the International Communist Movement. After returning to China, he helped guide the Communist insurrection in Guangxi province, took part in the Communist underground in Shanghai under Zhou Enlai, worked in Guangxi under Mao Zedong, participated in the Long March, and took part in political work in Yan'an. For twelve years he was a leading political commissar in the Chinese Communist Army, sharing responsibilities with one of China's ablest generals, Liu Bocheng. From 1949 to 1952, after the Communists had divided up the country into six large administrative regions, he was appointed party secretary of the Southwest Region, which had a population of more than 100 million, and was responsible for establishing party rule. In 1952 he was recalled to Beijing, where he worked in the party Secretariat. For one year, 1953 to 1954, he was minister of finance. From 1956 to 1966 he served as general secretary of the party, responsible for the administration of nationwide party activities. He was thus in a key position to observe the problems of the Great Leap Forward and its aftermath.

In the 1950s Deng was considered one of Mao's leading choices to be his successor, but in 1966, during the Cultural Revolution, he became Mao's number-two target, after Liu Shaoqi. While "rusticating" in Jiangxi province for more than three years, from October 1969 to February 1973, Deng had ample opportunities to ruminate about the party's errors and to contemplate which policies should be changed and how he could manage to end Mao's policies without splitting the country, should he be given a chance to return to a high position in Beijing. By the time Mao allowed Deng to return to office in 1973, Zhou Enlai was suffering from cancer and Deng became Zhou's understudy in conducting foreign policy and meeting foreign leaders.

Japan normalized relations with China in 1972, and between 1973 and 1976, as the leader responsible for foreign policy, Deng received more than forty Japanese delegations to China, more than he received from any other country. Deng was convinced that, in spite of fifty years of antagonism between China and Japan, the two countries should develop good, peaceful relations that would enable Japan to help China in its modernization efforts. Because he had fought the Japanese during the Sino-Japanese War, he could espouse this new policy without being criticized for being too soft on Japan.

In 1975 Mao chose Vice Premier Hua Guofeng as his successor. Deng was again criticized and removed from his position. But in the summer of

1977, Deng was allowed to return to work under Hua. He volunteered to be responsible for education and culture, areas that were not threatening to Hua's political power. In August 1977 Deng held a meeting of leading educators, and with their support he decided to reinstate the university entrance examinations after a ten-year hiatus. Deng believed China needed high-quality education to train new leaders, and he helped create opportunities for bright Chinese graduates to go abroad to acquire advanced skills that they would later bring back to China.

In the summer of 1978, Deng overcame the obstacles to the signing of the Treaty of Peace and Friendship with Japan by agreeing to include a clause that stated that the treaty was not being formed against any third party (i.e., the Soviet Union). In October 1978 Deng set out for the treaty signing in Japan, where he was very well received. The trip paved the way for important Japanese assistance to China in the 1980s.

In December 1978, at the Third Plenum of the Eleventh Central Committee, senior Communist Party leaders, who believed that Deng had the authority, respect, and wisdom to manage a dramatic change in party policy, chose him as the top party leader. By quoting Mao's saying, "Seek truth from facts," Deng was able to show respect for Mao while at the same time putting an end to some of his most disastrous policies that had plagued the country. To avoid social unrest among the unemployed urban youth who had just returned from the countryside, Deng allowed them to start their own enterprises. Conservatives found this method of opening markets acceptable, even though in years past such activities would have been vilified as pursuing the capitalist path. He told Wan Li, party secretary of Anhui province, to find ways to end the starvation in his province. When some villages discovered that allowing the local brigade or production team to contract work down to the family unit led to increased production, thus ending the starvation, Deng allowed Wan Li and others to publicize their success. When other areas found that this method worked, Deng said that where local conditions were appropriate and villagers were amenable, the government would not oppose contracting down to the household to solve China's production problems. Even conservatives found it difficult to oppose this new policy, and before long most areas had eliminated the communes that Mao had promoted and were permitting household farming.

Deng greatly expanded freedom of public expression, but when student movements in December 1986 threatened stability, he tightened controls. On May 20, 1989, when traffic in Beijing was blocked by huge demonstrations of students and local civilians, Deng brought in unarmed troops to restore order. However, organized groups of protesters blocked them as they began to move through the city, so the troops withdrew to the suburbs and the demonstrators continued to occupy Tiananmen Square. On June 3, Deng directed radio and television broadcasts to announce that everyone should clear the streets. That night, Deng gave orders that the troops should do whatever was necessary to end the demonstrations. The implication was that they had permission to use weapons against the demonstrators. Estimates of the numbers killed on the streets during the night of June 3 and the early morning of June 4 range from several hundred to three thousand. Although many leaders in China felt that there had been no other way to restore order, Deng was strongly denounced both in China and abroad.

Deng resigned from all his formal government positions in 1989, but in January–February 1992, when he felt that conservative leaders had stalled China's progress, he took a "family vacation," that is, his "southern tour" that relit the fire for continuing the nation's reform and opening policies. Deng retired completely after the Fourteenth Party Congress in October 1992 and remained removed from politics until his death in 1997.

For further reading, see Ezra F. Vogel, *Deng Xiaoping and the Transformation of China* (Cambridge, Mass.: Belknap Press of Harvard University Press, 2011).

ISHIBASHI TANZAN, 1884–1973

A brilliant and influential essayist on political and economic issues, Ishibashi Tanzan opposed Japanese colonial ambitions and attacks on China in the 1920s and the 1930s because he could foresee the consequences. But his warnings fell on deaf ears as Japan's aggressive military leaders and compliant political leaders moved ahead with the Manchurian invasion of 1931 and then an invasion of China in 1937. After World War II, Ishibashi served as finance minister in 1946 in Prime Minister Yoshida's first cabinet, as minister of trade and industry under Prime Minister Hatoyama Ichiro in 1953, and briefly as prime minister, from December 1956 to February 1957. At that time, his rival for the post of prime minister was Kishi Nobusuke, who supported very different policies. Kishi ran on a platform of allying with the United States during the Cold War, whereas Ishibashi ran on a platform of neutrality and supporting the reestablishment of relations with China. Ishibashi was particularly popular among students, pacifists, and the left wing of the Liberal Democratic Party.

Ishibashi's father had been a priest in the Buddhist Nichiren sect, and at the age of ten Ishibashi served as an apprentice in a Yamanashi-prefecture temple, where he studied Buddhism and attended a school run by disciples of William Clark, a well-known American educator who inspired a generation of Japanese youths with the phrase, "Boys, be ambitious." In 1907 Ishibashi graduated from Waseda University, the leading center of independent liberal thinking in Japan, with a degree in philosophy.

In 1911 Ishibashi joined Toyo Keizai, a company that published several periodicals focusing on economics and business, including *Toyo Keizai Shimpo* (Oriental economist). He was first assigned to work for *Toyo Jiron*, a publication specializing in political and social commentary, where he applied his philosophy training to adopt a set of basic principles that would become the framework for his future essays. One such principle was the concept of "absolute individualism," by which he meant that economic, political, and social systems exist for the well-being of the individual, not the other way around. In keeping with absolute individualism, he was an avid advocate of gender equality and birth control.

Ishibashi constantly criticized Japanese prejudices against the Chinese and Koreans as well as pronouncements supporting Japanese exceptionalism. He had deep respect for the Meiji emperor, but he was a constant critic of what he called the "mystical spell of the imperial system."

Though committed to certain ideals and principles, Ishibashi was a well-informed realist whose readers were business leaders, bankers, bureaucrats, and politicians. His arguments against Japan's expansionist colonial policy were based on his calculation that colonies would be a net drain on the economy and that the colonized, deprived of their basic rights to self-determination, would inevitably resent the colonizers and create problems for Japan that would be difficult to manage.

Ishibashi vehemently opposed Japan's invasion of China. He thought Japan's military had underestimated the ability of the Chinese to resist and that the China venture would end with Japan in a meaningless quagmire. Influenced by the Japanese media, he felt that Japanese people in general and Japanese soldiers in particular had no respect for the Chinese, and therefore the Chinese would later remain anti-Japanese.

In 1920, when Ishibashi was sent a warning by the army because of his criticism of the intervention in Siberia, he bravely published the army's warning verbatim and continued to criticize the military's actions. After the war, Ishibashi was purged by the Allied Occupation in 1947, and as he had done previously, he published the purge notice verbatim in *Toyo Keizai*.

By the 1940s Ishibashi was not only the editor but also the president of the Toyo Keizai publishing company, with a staff of 250 employees. The government censored various articles in *Toyo Keizai* and reduced its quotas for ink and paper in order to limit its reach. Eventually Ishibashi was faced with deciding whether to close the paper and divide the remaining cash among his employees or submit to government censorship. Ishibashi found a middle way. Along with many Japanese, he felt that Japan was nearing defeat in the war in China and the Pacific and that it was important to plan for a post-defeat future. He and his staff devised an editorial policy that would circumvent government censorship by carefully following government directives while continuing to make clear the meaning of the articles as they continued to publish. For example, in referring to policies in Korea and Taiwan, they stopped using the term "colony" and instead referred to those areas as "Japan's economic region."

When Germany surrendered to the Allies in Europe, the headline in *Toyo Keizai* read: "We can no longer expect miracles in the current war," and when the emperor finally surrendered on August 15, 1945, the lead sentence in Ishibashi's editorial was: "We are now at the door of Japan's rebirth; in fact, the potential is without limit." Ishibashi surely was tempted to cheer the defeat, but that would have been an insult to his readers, many of whom had lost loved ones during the war. In fact, Ishibashi himself had lost a son. So rather than dwelling on Japan's defeat, he began to plan for Japan's future.

As finance minister in the Yoshida cabinet, he battled against the policy of the Allied Occupation General Headquarters, which required that Japan pay a significant portion of the expenses for the Occupation officials, including housing, staff, and luxuries such as hotel stays, golf courses, and chauffeured vehicles. This burden amounted to one-third of Japan's entire government budget, making it difficult to fund the rebuilding of Japan's devastated infrastructure.

During his two months as prime minister Ishibashi sought to promote better relations with China. He intended to visit China as a first step toward normalization, but he fell sick before he could make the trip. After he left office and recovered from his illness, he did visit China twice, in 1959 and 1961, and he met with Zhou Enlai. In 1972, before Tanaka Kakuei made his historic trip to China, Tanaka called on Ishibashi, who was then near death, and vowed to fulfill Ishibashi's dream of normalizing Sino-Japanese relations. Ishibashi had lived to see Japan reject its colonial empire, and just before he died, he could take comfort in seeing Japan take the first steps toward normalizing relations with China.

For further reading, see Sharon H. Nolte, *Liberalism in Modern Japan: Ishibashi Tanzan and his Teachers, 1905–1960* (Berkeley: University of California Press, 1987); Matsuo Takayoshi 松尾尊兊, ed., *Ishibashi Tanzan hyoronshu*石橋湛山評論集 (The critical works of Ishibashi Tanzan) (Tokyo: Iwanami Shoten, 1984); Shumpei Okamoto, "Ishibashi Tanzan and the Twenty-One Demands," in *The Chinese and the Japanese: Essays in Political and Cultural Interactions*, ed. Akira Iriye, 148–198 (Princeton, N.J.: Princeton University Press, 1980).

ISHIWARA KANJI, 1889–1949

A Nichiren zealot, Ishiwara Kanji was a brilliant military analyst and strategist who in 1931 defied higher military authorities and led the plot that resulted in the Manchurian Incident. Yet in 1936 he played a key role in putting down those who took part in the February 26 failed coup d'état by Japanese government leaders, and in 1937 he opposed the war against China.

Ishiwara was born on January 18, 1889, the son of a policeman whose forefathers had been low-level samurai on the Shonai Plain in Yamagata prefecture, a poor farming area in the northwestern part of Japan's main island. The Shonai Plain had been under direct rule of the Tokugawa, and the area sided with the Tokugawa shogun in resisting the Meiji Restoration. Ishiwara and Okawa Shumei, also from that area, became superpatriots, proving to Meiji leaders that they had no lingering loyalty to the Tokugawa family. Ishiwara was intensely patriotic, strong-willed, independent, and outspoken.

At the age of thirteen Ishiwara entered a military preparatory school, and at eighteen he enrolled in the Central Military Academy. In 1910, as a second lieutenant, he was sent to Korea just after its annexation. In 1915, after passing highly competitive exams, he entered the Army Staff College, from which he graduated second in his class in 1918. He applied for service in China, and in 1920 he was assigned to spend a year in the Central China Garrison in Wuhan. While in China, he often took trips to the countryside to get a sense of the country. He expressed disgust with the rude way some Japanese visitors treated the Chinese; after riding a rickshaw, for example, they would pay the rickshaw puller by throwing the coins on the ground. Ishiwara had hoped that China and Japan, Asian brethren, could unite against the West. As he traveled in China, he was bitterly disappointed to find widespread disorder and poverty. He concluded that China could not build a modern state on its own and it would need assistance from Japan to achieve the leadership's goals.

Ishiwara was also disgusted by the behavior he saw in Japan, especially the selfish capitalism. He first took an interest in Shinto, but concluded that it did not provide sufficient dynamism. He then turned to Nichiren Buddhism, founded in the thirteenth century by Nichiren, a militant patriot, and in 1919 Ishihara, then age thirty, became a dedicated Nichiren follower who believed that Japan had a mission to propagate to the rest of the world: after a final war of unprecedented turmoil, the world would usher in a lasting golden age of peace and harmony. Each day, Ishiwara read Nichiren texts and observed Nichiren daily rituals.

In 1922 Ishiwara was dispatched to Germany for three years to study the German language and then military history. He learned about the weapons first used in World War I—tanks, machine guns, and airplanes—that drew on new technology and were far more advanced than those Japan had used in its wars against China and Russia. Ishiwara concluded that whereas earlier wars had been fought by military specialists, after the arousal of national passions and democratic ideologies, World War I became a total war, involving not only professional soldiers but all able-bodied males and the civilian population. He understood that in the future, new technologies, especially planes, would be critical, and entire cities could be wiped out at once. Total wars of long duration would be decided not only by military factors but also by economic and social factors. Because Japan lacked the resources and economic depth to win such a total war, Ishiwara believed Japan should engage in short wars that it could win by striking a quick, decisive, overwhelming blow (*kessenteki senso*) immediately after hostilities began. His analysis was remarkably prescient.

In 1925 Ishiwara left Germany and traveled on the Trans-Siberian Railway to Harbin. After returning home, Ishiwara lectured for three years on military history at the Army Staff College. His broad strategic analysis and the depth of his convictions, reflecting his Nichiren commitments, made him the most influential strategist among a generation of Japan's leading young military officers.

On October 20, 1928, Ishiwara arrived in Manchuria on an assignment as an operations officer for the Kwantung Army. His powerful influence on the Japanese Army in Manchuria stemmed not from his position but from his reputation as Japan's leading strategist.

By 1930 Ishiwara had concluded that Japan and the United States, because of their conflicting interests, spheres of power, and ideologies, were destined for a showdown. Should that come about, he believed the United States would try to blockade Japan, and therefore Japan should build up a substantial navy. The war with the United States would likely be a protracted one, and Manchuria was necessary to provide a broad economic base for such a military effort. Ishiwara believed that by building up a strong industrial base in Manchuria, Japan could win a total war with the United States, a mistaken judgment that would have grave consequences.

With the support of the Mantetsu research staff, Ishiwara compiled information on the military and economic situations in Manchuria. He believed that Manchuria was not originally Chinese but had belonged to local tribes, and so Japan had as much right to Manchuria as China. Unlike the Chinese military cliques that had oppressed the people of Manchuria, he and his Japanese colleagues were working for the good of the Manchurians.

On September 18, 1931, under the leadership of Ishiwara and his colleague Colonel Itagaki Seishiro, Japanese troops planted a bomb that exploded on the railway tracks near Shenyang. They initially claimed that the bomb had been planted by the Chinese, but within weeks it became clear that it had been planted by the Japanese. During the next two weeks, Japanese troops overwhelmed Chinese forces in the nearby areas of Manchuria. Japan's Central Army Headquarters in Tokyo directed Ishiwara and Itagaki to return the railway to China. But by this time Ishiwara and Itagaki had stirred up civilian chaos, and they explained that military action was necessary to protect the Japanese in Manchuria. Japanese troops used the railway explosion as an excuse to move with lightning speed to take over nearby cities. By January 1932 Japanese troops occupied Shanhaiguan, the pass between Manchuria and North China, and by the next spring Japanese troops occupied Harbin. There is no record that Tokyo was notified in advance of these actions by the Japanese military in Manchuria.

Ishiwara and others in the Kwantung Army planned to create a Manchu state, led by their puppet, Pu Yi, the Manchu child emperor who had been deposed during the 1911 Revolution. At the formal installation of Pu Yi six months after the Japanese Army took over, it was announced that the independent Kingdom of Manchuria (Manshukoku, in Japanese) was being established to promote racial harmony. In fact, the kingdom was controlled by the Kwantung Army and Japan retained control of defense, foreign relations, transportation, and communications. Not only did non-Japanese have no power in the administration but even Japanese residents in Manchuria had little power. Furthermore, the Japanese government in Tokyo had little leverage over the government, which was dominated by the Kwantung Army.

Japanese civilians in Manchuria, concerned about their safety owing to personal attacks being carried out by the Chinese, felt safer because of Ishiwara's bold actions, and Japanese merchants applauded the strong actions by Japanese troops to resist Chinese boycotts of Japanese goods. Ishiwara, viewed as brilliant and dedicated, enjoyed the support of younger officers in Manchuria.

By early 1932, Ishiwara had come to envision Manchuria as a place for harmonious cooperation among all races in China, including Manchus, Chinese, Mongolians, Koreans, and Japanese. During the previous year he had grown more optimistic that the Chinese people might play a leading role in the Manchurian government and the government of Japan would have no control over activities in Manchuria. The Kwantung Army would help maintain peace, but it too would have no role in the government. The Japanese in Manchuria would not receive any special privileges and the wages of Japanese officials would be reduced so that they were the same as those of Manchu and Chinese officials who held comparable jobs. Manchuria would be led by the Concordia Association (Kyoowakai in Japanese; Xiehehui in Chinese) that would promote harmony among all ethnic groups.

Westerners and the Chinese did not support Ishiwara's efforts to create a harmonious Manchurian government that in fact would be controlled by the Japanese, who were criticized by the West and hated by the Chinese. Higher military and political leaders in Tokyo were unhappy that Ishiwara would not listen to them. The hard reality was that the Japanese Army in Manchuria controlled the government and Ishiwara's vision of Manchuria's future role heightened tensions with the United States that ultimately resulted in World War II.

When Ishiwara returned to Japan in August 1932, he was pleased with his success in making Manchuria a part of Japan. He became part of the Army General Staff and was stationed in Japan's northeast. As a member of the General Staff, he took part in the discussions in the League of Nations on the Manchurian question. He also played a key role in persuading Ayukawa Yoshisuke to develop the Manchurian economy. Convinced of the importance of planes in a future war, he focused particularly on aircraft production.

When radicals in the Japanese Army killed several members of the Japanese cabinet in an attempted coup on February 26, 1936, Ishiwara, who was immediately notified, rushed to the military police headquarters, where he played a major role in organizing the government response and mobilizing the troops to put down the rebellion. At a meeting at the headquarters, when many officials were reluctant to send in troops to crush the rebellion, Ishiwara said: "The army will wait until noon of February 28. Then it will begin its assault to crush the rebellion." Ishiwara gave specific orders regarding what should be done, and by force of his personality, not his position, his orders were followed. Yet many of those who took part in the attempted coup earlier had been among his followers.

Though Ishiwara played a central role in the Manchurian Incident in 1931, by 1937 he was vehemently opposed to expanding the war south of Manchuria into China. He believed that Japan should focus on building up its economy to prepare for a possible war with either the Soviet Union or the United States. In 1937 Ishiwara felt that Chinese nationalism was much stronger than it had been in 1931, and hence he was prepared to cooperate with Chiang Kai-shek.

After the July 7 Marco Polo Bridge Incident in 1937 that set off the China War, Ishiwara, who at the time was stationed at the military headquarters in Ichigaya, urged restraint. In August, when Chiang sent his troops to Shanghai, Ishiwara felt that Japan should withdraw both its troops and its civilians to avoid an all-out clash with China.

To refrain from becoming involved in a major confrontation with China, Ishiwara said that Prime Minister Konoe Fumimaro should go to China to negotiate with Chiang Kai-shek, but after some consideration, Konoe decided against it. Nevertheless, Ishiwara continued to speak out against the China War, even though he had already lost the support of his former colleagues, whom he publicly criticized for their moral corruption. In September 1937 he was removed from the General Staff. That fall Ishiwara returned to Manchuria as vice chief of staff of the Kwantung Army. Critical of the prerogatives enjoyed by Kwantung Army officials, he promoted racial equality. But by late 1938, his acerbic personality and his criticism of his colleagues had alienated him from other leaders in Manchuria, so he arranged to return to Japan.

Back in Tokyo in 1938, Ishiwara advocated forming a federation of equal Asian nations. On March 1, 1941, he officially retired, whereupon he became a lecturer at Ritsumeikan University. He regarded the Pacific War as a disastrous error and even criticized himself for not having done more to stop its escalation. He also privately criticized the attack on Pearl Harbor, and he predicted Japan would lose the war because it had not done enough to strengthen its economic base to match that of the United States. After leaving the military, Ishiwara had serious doubts about the path Japan was pursuing, but his accounts were not always consistent. He lacked his former confidence and became dispirited. In September 1942 he resigned from Ritsumeikan University and returned to his home area in Yamagata. After the war he was called before the International Military Tribunal. Because he was ill, the tribunal allowed him to be tried in Yamagata, where he was purged but not punished. Ishiwara Kanji died on August 18, 1949.

For further reading, see Mark R. Peattie, *Ishiwara Kanji and Japan's Confrontation with the West* (Princeton, N.J.: Princeton University Press, 1975).

ITO HIROBUMI, 1841–1909

As head of the Privy Council that drafted Japan's 1888–1889 Constitution, the first prime minister under the new Constitution, and the leading adviser to Emperor Meiji, Ito Hirobumi was the single most important architect of the Meiji reforms. He not only helped shape Japan's political structure but also served as prime minister four times, from 1885 to 1888, 1892 to 1896, for six months in 1898, and from 1900 to 1901. Fluent in English even before the Meiji Restoration, Ito played a key role in Meiji-period negotiations with Western, Chinese, Korean, and Russian representatives. In Japan he was known for his wise strategic judgment about the nation's long-term interests and his moderate views about foreign policy, but in China he was regarded as a symbol of the harsh measures imposed on China at the end of the Sino-Japanese War. In Korea he was hated for imposing Japanese rule, and the Korean assassin An Chung-gun who ultimately shot him in Harbin in 1909 has been celebrated as a great national hero. Ito's father was born on a farm but he was adopted by a samurai. Like other samurai of the Choshu domain who played key roles during the Meiji period, Ito attended the informal village school of Yoshida Shoin, a dedicated teacher who was obsessed with any and all military threats to Japan and was ready to go anywhere to learn more about military issues.

In 1863, even before the Meiji Restoration, Ito was selected as a promising youth to go to England to study English and naval science. In 1870, he was sent to the United States to study currency systems, and on his return he became director of the Japanese government's Tax Division. He took part in the Iwakura Mission, 1871–1873, after which he was appointed minister of public works. In 1881 he became a leading advocate of developing a constitution in Japan. In preparation, he spent eighteen months in Germany studying under leading constitutional scholars. While working on the new constitution, Ito also wrote a draft of the Imperial Household Law, which provided land and funding to the imperial household so that it could maintain its economic independence from the government. In 1885, when a modern cabinet system was introduced in the national government, Ito became Japan's first prime minister. The Japanese Constitution entered into effect in 1889, and in the following year Japan elected members to its first Diet.

In 1893 the Japanese Diet, Asia's first parliament, opened debate on an issue that Japan considered of great importance—revocation of the unequal treaties. As prime minister in 1894, Ito, with Foreign Minister Mutsu Munemitsu, succeeded in convincing England to abolish extraterritoriality in Japan. On several occasions Ito was Japan's key negotiator with China's Li Hongzhang on Sino-Japanese issues, including the Treaty of Shimonoseki in 1895 at the end of the Sino-Japanese War.

Ito believed that many party politicians were motivated by mere selfish interests and were incapable of dealing objectively with the overall needs of the country. He believed in a parliamentary system that allowed politicians to express different views, but he was unwilling to grant them power to make decisions. He had more respect for bureaucrats, whom he considered to be more committed than politicians to overall national interests. But he believed in political parties as a way to express different views, and from 1900 to 1903 he attempted to establish his own political party to support the government. But he soon abandoned party politics to focus on issues that he considered to be in the interest of the country over the long run.

In 1901 Ito went to Russia, where he proposed the idea of giving Russia a dominant role in influencing policies in Manchuria; in exchange, Russia would grant Japan dominance over policies in Korea. The Russians did not agree, however, and three years later the Russo-Japanese War broke out. Japan's victory in that war gave it the control over Korean foreign policy that Ito had sought.

From 1906 to 1909 Ito was Japan's resident-general in Korea, where he negotiated the details of Korea's status as a Japanese protectorate. In Japan he was regarded as a moderate who hoped to compromise with China and Korea to retain their goodwill. However, as a government spokesman, he represented Japan's expanding ambitions. When he was killed in Harbin in 1909, the Chinese as well as the Koreans cheered his assassination. In Japan, the assassination strengthened support for strict Japanese rule after Korea was annexed in 1910.

For further reading, see Albert M. Craig, *Choshu in the Meiji Restoration* (Cambridge, Mass.: Harvard University Press, 1961); Okazaki Hisahiko, *From Uraga to San Francisco: A Century of Japanese Diplomacy, 1853–1952* (Tokyo: Japan Echo, 2007); Takii Kazuhiro, *Ito Hirobumi: Japan's First Prime Minister and Father of the Meiji Constitution*, trans. Takechi Manabu (Abingdon, U.K.: Routledge, 2014).

JIANG BAILI, 1882–1938

A Chinese military strategist, educator, and essayist, Jiang Baili had a deep understanding of Japan. One of the first Chinese students to study in Japan, Jiang graduated first in his class from Japan's Military Officers Academy in 1906. After additional studies in Germany, he returned to China to become president of the Baoding Military Academy during the presidency of Yuan Shikai. As early as 1923 Jiang could foresee a coming Chinese conflict with Japan, and he proposed a strategy of "long resistance," which he believed would enable China to prevail after a Japanese invasion.

Jiang was born in a town near Hangzhou in Zhejiang province as part of an extended family of prosperous landlords and scholars. His father was one of nineteen children, but because he had been born deformed, he was sent away from the family to be raised in a local temple. Jiang's mother, a self-educated orphan, devoted her life to the education of her precocious son. Jiang had read the four classical Confucian texts by the age of four, and he had particularly enjoyed reading heroic classics, such as *Water Margin* and *Romance of the Three Kingdoms*. He lived a cultured life in a large family, enjoying music, poetry, calligraphy, and the traditional arts.

At the time of the Sino-Japanese War, when Jiang was twelve years old, he had already begun to take an interest in current events. He and his friends read all the newspapers they could find, even though the papers would arrive in his village one or two months late. He attended a school that later became Hangzhou University and then, in 1901, he joined one of the first groups of Chinese students to study in Japan. Several months after his arrival in Japan, he met Liang Qichao and became a part-time editor for one of Liang's journals.

Like Liang Qichao and many other Chinese students, Jiang read Japanese writers such as Fukuzawa Yukichi. Jiang was a prolific essayist, and he wrote many essays on the evolution of nationalism in Europe and Japan.

For Jiang, Japan was the only country in Asia where nationalism had taken root. But he also noted that the nationalism described by Fukuzawa and other Japanese writers was influenced by Herbert Spencer, who wrote about the survival of the fittest and was prone to support national expansionism against weaker countries.

At the military academy in Japan, Jiang's fellow students included many who would become senior officers in the Japanese Army, including Doihara Kenji, a famous mastermind of Japan's strategy in northern China; Oka-mura Yasuji, general of the Northern China Expeditionary Army at the time of Japan's surrender in 1945; Itagaki Seijiro, a partner of Ishiwara Kanji in planning the invasion of Manchuria in 1931; and Nagata Tetsuzan, who graduated first in his class one year before Jiang. Jiang made frequent trips back and forth to Japan in the 1920s and 1930s, and he usually met with his former fellow students. In an essay about the 1935 assassination of a respected friend, General Nagata Tetsuzan, Jiang warned his Japanese colleagues that junior officers in Japan had become so disobedient that Japan was no longer capable of developing a coherent military strategy.

When Jiang was head of the Baoding Military Academy under Yuan Shikai, he grew extremely frustrated with the spread of corruption, particularly in the appointment of military officers and the selection of students at the academy, and also with the lack of higher-level support for his school, and he attempted suicide in front of an assembly of cadets. Luckily, the bullet he fired missed his heart and he was nursed back to health in a Japanese hospital near Beijing. The Japanese nurse who cared for him, Sato Yato, told him that he should study *gaman* (forbearance). He and the nurse fell in love and married, and they became an especially devoted couple.

Like many Chinese students who studied in Japan, Jiang admired the Japanese, but at the same time he felt that Japan and China would clash at some point in the future. After a trip with Liang Qichao to Europe, where he analyzed the battles between Germany and France during World War I, he returned to China to focus on analyzing Japan's military capabilities and devising strategies in case war should break out between China and Japan. In 1929 Chiang Kai-shek had Jiang arrested because one of Jiang's former students had rebelled against Chiang. Jiang spent two years in prison, unsure if he would even survive. His wife and daughters visited him daily. In prison, Jiang spent his time listening to recordings of Beethoven and

Wagner, copying Buddhist sutras, and reading classical Chinese stories to his daughters. He was released in 1931 in time to return to Japan before the invasion of Manchuria.

Late in 1937, after the Japanese had invaded China, Jiang wrote a book entitled *The Japanese: A Foreigner's Analysis*, which describes Japan's strengths and weaknesses. In it, he spells out his views on how the Chinese could defeat the Japanese through patient, long-term resistance. His book became a bestseller and it is still available in Chinese. Jiang was called on to give speeches that described his strategy of resisting the Japanese. On a speaking tour in November 1938, he died of a heart attack.

For further reading, see Lu Yan, *Re-understanding Japan: Chinese Perspectives, 1895–1945* (Honolulu: Association for Asian Studies and University of Hawai'i Press, 2004).

LI HONGZHANG, 1823–1901

An extraordinarily talented official who enjoyed striking success, Li Hongzhang was a scholar, general, political leader, and manager of foreign relations. Standing over six feet tall, brimming with confidence, Li had the broad perspective to realize how far behind China was, and he also had support from the higher levels of government, enabling him to introduce the Self-Strengthening Movement to promote China's industrialization and military development. At a time when many top Chinese leaders had no clear vision for how to guide foreign policy, Li Hongzhang continued to study foreign policy and to dominate foreign-policy decision making from 1870 to 1895, when he was branded as a traitor.

Li Hongzhang passed the *jinshi* degree, the highest-level imperial exam, at the unusually young age of twenty-four, earning the third highest score among 4,000 exam takers. Although he was a well-trained Confucian scholar, a skilled calligrapher and poet, and was welcomed by scholars, by the time he passed the examinations Li had decided that he wanted to accomplish something in the real world so he gave up his scholarly pursuits.

Even before completing his examinations, Li became an apprentice to Zeng Guofan, the most respected political and military leader of the era, renowned for fighting and defeating the Taiping. Li's father had passed the examinations in the same group as Zeng. Zeng assigned Li to return to his native province of Anhui to organize and lead the local militia to fight the Taiping. Zeng was impressed with reports of Li's successes and invited Li to serve on his personal staff. Within months, Zeng made Li his chief secretary. Beginning in 1859 and for more than three years, Li was responsible for drafting the documents and letters that Zeng Guofan sent to Beijing. Li was then assigned to expand local militias in the fight against the Taiping, so he returned to Anhui where he built up the Huai Army, considered one of the most modern and successful military forces in China.

Li had once tutored Prince Gong and he remained loyal to both the prince and the empress dowager, but as a Han serving Manchu leaders he was aware that he had to behave respectfully and cautiously. Because of Li's success, Zeng Guofan, with the approval of the imperial court, arranged for Li to be appointed acting governor of Jiangsu at the age of thirty-nine. In Shanghai, Zeng became acutely aware of the challenge of the West, as he saw that foreign military forces, with their modern armaments, were far superior to those of his "ever victorious army." Li believed that China had to train its troops, but first it had to have the technology to make up-to-date armaments, and to do that it had to have funding.

In Li's time, China did not have a Ministry of Foreign Affairs. After 1870 and for the following twenty-five years, Li held key positions as Zhili governor (China's most important governorship, of an area that includes present-day Hebei, Beijing, and Tianjin), superintendent of trade of the north (with an office in Tianjin, so he could greet foreign visitors before they went to Beijing), and head of the Beiyang Fleet (China's northern fleet). He thus became the dominant voice in China's foreign affairs. But it was his grasp of foreign issues, his confidence in accepting responsibility in areas where the lines of authority were unclear, and his awareness of how far the imperial court would go to support him that led others to turn over foreign-policy issues to him.

Li knew that China could not become strong simply by buying foreign ships and foreign military equipment or by relying on foreign forces as allies. For this reason he took the initiative to promote China's Self-Strengthening Movement (1861–1895), which sought to create a military and industrial base to support the military. He led the establishment of the Jiangnan Arsenal and the Tianjin Arsenal to enable China to produce more modern ships as well as weapons such as rifles. In 1872–1873 he established the Merchant Steamship Navigation Company to help Chinese merchants compete with foreign steamship companies, and by the late 1870s the company had surpassed the British trading firms in terms of size. Li knew that China had to send people abroad to learn foreign languages, not only to serve as interpreters but also to study foreign developments. Additionally, he set up institutions to train people in modern engineering and he tried to expand iron and coal mining to avoid the financial drain due to purchasing foreign resources. Unlike many of his peers who were overconfident about the superiority of all things Chinese, Li was acutely aware of China's organizational weaknesses compared with those of the Western powers and Japan, and he sought to avoid conflicts with foreign countries while China's strength was still in its infancy.

Having seen Japan's strengths as well as those of the Western powers when he served in Shanghai, as early as 1863 Li expressed admiration for Japan for its advances in military armaments and technological training and as a model for military self-strengthening. In 1871 he was the Chinese negotiator supporting the first treaty between Japan and Qing China, which fixed trade tariffs between the two countries. However, Japan's initiatives in Korea and its handling of the issue of the Rykuyu fishermen convinced him that the Japanese, while polite on the surface, were crafty in pursuing their own ambitions. He remained wary of Japan's intentions, but he was also dedicated to finding ways to maintain a stable, peaceful relationship with Japan.

Despite his talent and his ability to analyze problems, Li did not have the depth of foreign training and contacts with foreign leaders, or the deep understanding of foreign strategies, that his main Japanese negotiating partner, Ito Hirobumi, had acquired during his time abroad and from the Japanese bureaucracy's systematic collection and analysis of foreign intelligence. Operating within the range of what was possible in his day, Li accepted China's examination system, administrative structure, and educational system; thus the results of his Self-Strengthening Movement, focusing mainly on military and technology, were far narrower than the results of Japan's institutional changes.

It is China's tragedy that the Self-Strengthening Movement was weakened in 1885, when Prince Gong lost power, and again in 1894–1895, when China became involved in the Sino-Japanese War. After the war, Li accepted responsibility for negotiating the treaty that ended the war, knowing that he would be criticized by Chinese conservatives for making too many concessions, even though China was not in a position to refuse. While in Japan for the negotiations, Li was shot by a radical Japanese would-be assassin. He chose not to have the bullet, lodged near his eye, removed, and within several days he had generally recovered. He is remembered in Chinese history as a traitor who signed a humiliating treaty that Japan was able to force on China because of its weaknesses—weaknesses that Li had dedicated himself to correcting against strong domestic opposition.

For further reading, see Samuel C. Chu and Kwang-Ching Liu, eds., *Li Hung-chang and China's Early Modernization* (Armonk, N.Y.: M. E. Sharpe, 1994).

Liao Chengzhi, 1908–1983

The Chinese politician Liao Chengzhi was the only Politburo member who had deep and warm personal relations with the Japanese. His grandfather, a Hakka from Huizhou, the prefectural capital east of Guangzhou, had been a representative of the Hong Kong–Shanghai Bank in San Francisco, where Liao's father, Liao Zhongkai, was born.

Liao Chengzhi's father returned to Hong Kong in 1893, but in 1902 Liao Zhongkai went to study in Japan at Waseda University and Chuo University. While in Japan he met Sun Yat-sen, a fellow Cantonese, and he became a founding member of Sun's Revolutionary Alliance (Tongmenghui). He was close to Sun and played a key role in publicizing Sun's thinking, as well as serving as Sun's frequent traveling partner. On his return to China Liao Zhongkai became governor of Guangdong and a member of the Executive Committee of the Guomindang.

Liao Chengzhi was born in Japan in 1908. He and his family returned to Hong Kong for several years and then, in 1915, went back to Japan, where he entered the second grade at Gyosei, an elite Catholic school that taught its students in Japanese, English, and French. At Gyosei, Chengzhi was the only non-Japanese student in his class of thirty. He made many friends among the Japanese children with whom he played. His Japanese friends defended him when other classmates criticized him because he was Chinese. Because his family was well-to-do, while they were in Japan they could afford to live in an upper-middle-class neighborhood and to employ a series of nursemaids to take care of Chengzhi.

Immediately after Sun's death, Chengzhi's father, Liao Zhongkai, was one of the three leading candidates, along with Wang Jingwei and Hu Hanmin, to be Sun's successor. But Liao Zhongkai was shot in 1925, presumably by assassins hired by Hu Hanmin, a member of the right wing of the Guomindang. Liao's only sibling, Cynthia Liao, who was five years older and had also studied in Japan, became personal secretary to Sun Yat-sen's widow.

After his father was killed by a right-wing party member, Liao Chengzhi turned firmly to the left, and in 1927, when Chiang Kai-shek began killing the Communists in the Guomindang, Liao escaped to Japan, where he attended Waseda University from 1927 to 1928. It was during that year he joined the Chinese Communist Party. In May 1928, after the Ji'nan Incident of May 3, he took part in activities criticizing the Japanese government. He retained his friendships with Japanese, but he was expelled from Japan. He did not return to Japan until 1954, when he was part of an official Chinese delegation.

In 1928 Liao Chengzhi returned to China briefly, but he then went to Germany and then to Moscow to attend Sun Yat-sen University, where he was a classmate of Chiang Ching-kuo, son of Chiang Kai-shek, whom he had known when their fathers were both serving under Sun Yat-sen. Liao returned to China to take part in the Shanghai underground and then, because of the danger in the city, he moved to rural Sichuan. When the Long Marchers passed through Sichuan, he joined them on their trek to Yan'an.

During World War II Liao was dispatched from Yan'an to Hong Kong, not far from his home in Huizhou, to take part in underground Communist Party work. In 1942 he was captured by the Guomindang and he remained in custody until 1946, when he was rescued from prison. During the Chinese Civil War he was involved in propaganda work and served for a time as head of the Xinhua News Agency, where he was a liaison with foreign countries.

In 1952 Zhou Enlai, who first knew Liao Chengzhi in Guangzhou in 1924 when Zhou was a political commissar at the Huangpu Military Academy, assigned Liao to take charge of relations with Japan. For three decades, beginning in 1952, Liao was the key official in Beijing responsible for meeting Japanese guests. He also had responsibility for managing United Front activities with overseas Chinese, Africans, and Russians. When high-level Japanese officials met with Mao, Liao usually served as interpreter. Japanese visitors to China regarded Liao as an icon and a friend of Japan. They were eager to meet him and to have their pictures taken with him because of his fame, because he spoke Japanese like a native and could banter with them like an insider about events in Japan, and because they believed he was influential in the Chinese Communist hierarchy. His Japanese visitors included Socialist and Communist Party members and also mainstream politicians. A 1954 delegation included Nakasone Yasuhiro, a future prime minister, and Sonoda Sunao, who later, as foreign minister, would play a key role in the normalization of Sino-Japanese relations.

On his 1954 visit to Japan, his first trip there since being expelled in 1928, Liao was part of a Red Cross delegation, but he used the occasion to renew contacts with Japanese friends involved in various Sino-Japanese friendship associations.

Despite the fact that he had been arrested twelve times, in Japan, Germany, the Soviet Union, and China, and had been imprisoned by the Guomindang from 1942 to 1946, Liao remained a warm, effusive, and confident person with a good sense of humor, and he played a key role in maintaining relations with the Japanese. Prior to normalization, he worked with Takasaki Tatsunosuke to expand Sino-Japanese trade relations. In October 1978, after the Treaty of Peace and Friendship was signed, when Deng Xiaoping traveled to Japan to seek help with China's new opening and reform policy, he had Liao Chengzhi at his side. Liao died in 1983.

For further reading, see Mayumi Itoh, *Pioneers of Sino-Japanese Relations: Liao and Takasaki* (New York: Palgrave Macmillan, 2012); Donald W. Klein and Anne B. Clark, "Liao Ch'eng-chih," in *Biographic Dictionary of Chinese Communism, 1921–1965*, 2 vols. (Cambridge, Mass.: Harvard University Press, 1971).

SUN YAT-SEN (SUN ZHONGSHAN, SON BUN), 1866–1925

Sun Yat-sen, an English-speaking Cantonese, played a key role traveling abroad to gather support for overthrowing the Qing dynasty. After the 1911 Revolution he was named the first provisional president of the Republic of China, and he is therefore celebrated as the founding father of the Republic. However, just six weeks after becoming president Sun yielded his position to General Yuan Shikai, who had the military support that Sun Yat-sen lacked. Between 1912 and 1920 Sun did not play a major role in the Chinese government, but in 1920, when the warlords held power in Beijing, he used the Nationalist Party (Guomindang) that he had established shortly after the 1911 Revolution to establish a base in Guangzhou. There, with Soviet help, he set up the Huangpu Military Academy led by Chiang Kai-shek, to train military officers who could play a leading role in building a national army to unify the country. Sun attracted to Guangzhou Zhou Enlai, who was a political commissar at the academy; Mao Zedong, who founded the Peasant Training Institute there; and other progressive young leaders. Sun managed to keep the Communists within the Guomindang, but two years after his death, in 1927, the Nationalists who had welcomed the Communists began attacking them, and the two parties have been split ever since.

Sun Yat-sen had a very close relationship with Japan and lived there for many years. In 1905, when his life was in danger in China for promoting revolution, he escaped to Japan and disguised himself by taking the Japanese name Nakayama (in Chinese, Zhongshan). After the revolution, when he split with Yuan Shikai, he once again sought refuge in Japan. He had many supporters there, including Miyazaki Torazo (also known as Miyazaki Toten), who remained a dedicated right-hand man to Sun throughout his last two decades.

Sun Yat-sen was born into a Hakka family in the village of Cuiheng just north of Macao, on the western side of the Pearl River Delta, in a county that has since been named after him (Zhongshan). After attending local schools, in 1878, at the age of thirteen, he moved to Hawaii where he lived with an elder brother and attended school until 1883, when he returned to China. For the next three years he studied in Hong Kong schools, and during this time he also was baptized as a Christian. From 1886 to 1892 he studied Western medicine in Hong Kong, graduating in 1892. He came to believe that science in China was far behind Western science and thus China had to undertake great changes. In 1894 Sun and a group of his friends founded the Revive China Society. Upset about China's failure to modernize and disappointed with China's loss in the war with Japan in 1895, the Revive China Society planned to attack the Guangdong government, but word leaked out and the attack was completely foiled. Leading officials in Beijing, who had studied the Confucian classics, looked down on Sun Yat-sen as someone not properly educated, and they did not consider his 1895 attack in Guangdong to have been a major threat.

After 1895 Sun escaped to Japan and then traveled to the United States and Europe. While in London in 1896, he was picked up by the Chinese legation, which planned to execute him. British acquaintances publicized his case in an attempt to free him, and after twelve days he was released. His case received such great publicity in England that Sun became a well-known public figure in Chinese communities throughout the world. As Marie-Claire Bergère writes, Sun was an able publicist, skilled at telling his audiences what they wanted to hear in order to achieve his political goals. The content of his speeches varied from country to country, but he was consistent in doing what he thought would be most useful to make China a strong modern nation.

In 1900 Sun helped organize an uprising in Huizhou, the prefectural capital east of Guangzhou, but it too ended in failure. When he returned to Japan again in 1905, most Chinese students were associating with people from the same province. Along with others, he formed the Revolutionary Alliance (Tongmenghui) to build a China-wide organization of students from Hunan, Hubei, Shanghai, Guangdong, and elsewhere. He continued traveling abroad to raise funds, and when he heard about the 1911 Revolution, he was raising funds in Colorado.

On November 29, 1911, while Sun was still traveling abroad, a number of representatives from different localities who had supported the revolution met in Nanjing and selected Sun as leader of the new Republic of China. He was officially inaugurated as provisional president on January 1, 1912. Because Sun was an effective publicist and fundraiser and had traveled widely, he was well known in overseas Chinese communities. His Three Principles, which he publicly enunciated in 1905—nationalism, democracy, livelihood—did not represent a well-developed philosophy, and their content was modified over the years, but they became an effective banner for mobilizing support for the revolution among the Chinese living overseas.

Sun's skills as a practical political organizer, as Marie-Claire Bergère makes clear, did not match his skills as a publicist. After Yuan Shikai and his troops took over the government on February 12, 1912, Sun sought refuge in Japan. At this time, he was not a promising revolutionary and a potential president of China but a refugee without a clear future. His former allies in Japan were seeking to do business with the one in power, Yuan Shikai. But Sun was secretly courting Song Qingling, the daughter of a rich businessman, Charlie Soong, even though she was a generation younger than he. In 1915, against her father's orders, she left home and went to Tokyo, where she married Sun. (She was the second of four daughters; the youngest, Song Meiling, would later wed Chiang Kai-shek, in a marriage also consummated in Japan.) When Song Qingling ran away to marry him, Sun lost the support of her father, of other Chinese who valued filial piety, and of Christians, both in China and abroad, who objected to Sun's marriage without first divorcing his previous wife. From 1918 to 1920 Sun and his new wife lived in the French Concession in Shanghai and rarely took part in public activities.

In 1920, in an effort to regain national political power and become the leader of all of China, Sun tried to establish a base in Guangzhou, but he had difficulty with the local warlord Chen Jiongming, who wanted to maintain a strong base in Guangdong and did not want to waste resources on attempts to retake the whole country. In early 1923 Sun, his base in Guangzhou precarious, turned to the Soviet Union, with whose help he was able to make use of mercenaries who defeated Chen Jiongming.

With Soviet help, Sun also attracted some political talent to Guangdong, including a number of leftists who would later become key founders of the Chinese Communist Party in 1921. In January 1924 Sun put Chiang Kai-shek in charge of planning for the new Huangpu Military Academy, which was to train officers for a national army that would unify the country, and by May 1924 500 cadets had arrived for the first class. Political training at the academy was conducted under Liao Zhongkai, father of Liao Chengzhi, and Zhou Enlai who served in the Political Department. In 1923, Sun invited Mao Zedong to launch a Peasant Training Institute in Guangzhou to train cadres who would then go to the countryside and mobilize peasants for the Communist cause.

On November 1, 1924, Sun received a formal invitation from the warlord Feng Yuxiang to attend a conference in Beijing on national unification, and Sun, thinking that he might play an important role, accepted. On November 13 Sun boarded a ship to travel from Hong Kong to Shanghai, then to Kobe, and then to Tianjin. While in Kobe from November 24 to 30, Sun delivered a speech entitled "Doctrine of Greater Asia," in which he praised Japan for freeing itself from domination by Western civilization, and he argued for cooperation among the East Asian countries to abolish the unequal treaties. Sun was seriously ill by the time he arrived in Tianjin, and the next day he was hospitalized. Guomindang officials assembled in the hospital to discuss the future of their party, and Sun there approved the testament written for him by Wang Jingwei. Sun never left the hospital. He died on March 12, 1925.

Western scholars studying Sun Yat-sen have acknowledged his role as a publicist and his historical importance, but they do not regard him as one who possessed great leadership skills or theoretical insights. However, he has been elevated to a grand position in official Chinese writings. Although the Guomindang and the Communist Party split two years after his death, each claimed to be Sun's rightful heir. In writings about Sun, both the Communists and the Guomindang glorify him as the father of the 1911 Revolution and a great patriotic leader who courageously and wisely worked to unify the country. Chiang Kai-shek presented himself as Sun's ever-loyal follower, dedicated to carrying out his mission. In 1929 Chiang brought Sun's coffin to Purple Mountain in Nanjing, where it was placed in a large tomb that can only be approached by climbing a long flight of stairs. During World War II, in writings about Sun's career, neither the Guomindang nor the Communists discussed Sun's close relations with the Japanese.

For further reading, see Marie-Claire Bergère, *Sun Yat-sen* (Stanford, Calif.: Stanford University Press, 1998); Marius B. Jansen, *The Japanese and Sun Yat-sen* (Stanford, Calif.: Stanford University Press, 1970).

TAKASAKI TATSUNOSUKE, 1885–1964

Businessman Takasaki Tatsunosuke was the head of Manchurian Heavy Industry from 1942 to 1945, a group that included all the factories in Manchuria. In this position, he tried to promote industrial efficiency while at the same time coping with Japanese military commanders who did not understand business. In 1944–1945, he also had to deal with factory damage caused by U.S. air raids. After World War II, from 1945 to 1948 he served as president of the association of Japanese who stayed in Manchuria, negotiating in turn with the Russians, the Guomindang, and the Communists for the livelihood and repatriation of the Japanese in Manchuria and for the maintenance of production in the factories that were still operating. After returning to Japan, Takasaki promoted trade with China, and in 1962 he represented Japan in negotiations with Liao Chengzhi to create the Liao-Takasaki agreements that increased trade between the two countries.

Takasaki grew up in a farm family in a village located between Kyoto and Osaka, where he had the reputation of being mischievous and adventuresome. In school, he was influenced by a teacher who told students that because Japan had such a small amount of arable land, it could not grow all the food it needed. The teacher said that fish from the waters in the vicinity of Japan should be canned and exported to other countries, earning income that could then be used to purchase grain to feed the local population. At the time, Japan had only one fishery training program, the Imperial Fisheries Institute, a three-year technical high school in Tokyo that had been established in 1889 by the Ministry of Agriculture and Commerce. After completing junior middle school, Takasaki enrolled in the Imperial Fisheries Institute in September 1902, with a major in manufacturing. During his time there, the Russo-Japanese War broke out, and to meet the huge increase in demand for canned fish to feed the Japanese soldiers, students from the school were sent to areas along Japan's coast to assist at the local canneries. Thus Takasaki acquired early practical experience in manufacturing. After he graduated, he worked for several years in fish canning at Oriental Fisheries (Toyo Suisan) in Japan. In an effort to help build a better market for Japanese canned fish abroad, Takasaki traveled to the United States, where he found a job in a small cannery in San Diego. After various ventures with American fish canning in California and along the coast of Mexico, he helped Californians improve their tuna canning process.

While in California Takasaki met a mining engineer, Herbert Hoover, who was interested in developing mines in Tangshan, China and who later would become president of the United States. Like Hoover, who became a lifelong friend, Takasaki believed the goal of business should be to bring happiness to humankind, provide social services, and make employees into stockholders.

After several years in North America, Takasaki returned to Japan, and in 1915 he founded his own company, Toyo Seikan, that made cans for the fishing industry. He hired two U.S. canning engineers and imported U.S. can-making machinery, which was far superior to what his competitors in

Japan were using. He standardized products, expanded the production of cans for other products, and within several years he had the largest can-making company in Japan.

When the United States, concerned about Japan's aggression in China, began restricting sales of steel and tin to Japan, Takasaki traveled to Manchuria on several occasions in search of new supplies. Ayukawa Gisuke, head of Nissan in Manchuria, was impressed with Takasaki and invited him to join his company in Manchuria. For several years Takasaki refused the offer, but finally, in February 1941, he accepted the position of vice president of Manchuria Industries. Takasaki and Ayukawa had both opposed Japan's pact with Germany and Italy and its declaration of war on the United States, but they accepted responsibility for trying to improve their country's industrial capacity.

Japanese factories in Manchuria had originally been organized by the military, which treated the workers like slave labor and was only concerned with output, not efficiency. Ayukawa and Takasaki both found it difficult to work with the military, but they sought to improve efficiency and working conditions. When Ayukawa's term in Manchuria ended in 1942, he returned to Japan, leaving Takasaki as president of Manchuria Industries. Takasaki, although still under pressure from the military, tried to clean up the plants, make production more efficient, and develop better relationships with the industrial workers, who were mostly Japanese, as well as with the service personnel, who were mostly Chinese. After July 1944, when U.S. forces conquered Saipan, from which American B-29 bombers could reach Manchuria, the factories were frequently bombed and it was Takasaki's responsibility to oversee repairs and maintain production.

Takasaki's family returned to Japan before the end of the war, but he remained in Manchuria. Japanese soldiers began returning home soon after the war ended, but many civilians were left behind. Several leading Japanese civilians in Manchuria began organizing to provide food, shelter, and eventually repatriation for fellow Japanese citizens stranded there, and they asked Takasaki to be president of their association. By March 1946 some 25,000 of the Japanese stranded in Changchun had died. As the head of the industrial sector in Manchuria, Takasaki was useful to the Soviets and later to the Chinese, who wanted to see production continue. He thus had leverage as a negotiator with the Soviets in the association's efforts to find food and shelter for the Japanese. In April 1946, after the start of the Civil War, Changchun was occupied by the Communists, whom Takasaki found to be very disciplined, and they in turn found Takasaki to be reasonable to work with.

In May 1946 the Guomindang retook Changchun and Takasaki proceeded to work with them. The Guomindang wanted the factories to resume production and Takasaki was useful to them in managing the factories. Takasaki wanted to restore the industry that he had worked so hard to build and he also wanted to be useful to the Chinese. In July 1946 the Guomindang reorganized their offices for dealing with the Japanese in Manchuria, but they retained Takasaki as president of the association for stranded Japanese civilians. Although most of the Japanese wanted to be repatriated, they were willing to work in Manchurian factories until they could return. More than one million Japanese in Manchuria were repatriated between May and October 1946, but in December 1946 more than 9,000 Japanese engineers and 21,000 family members were still in Manchuria, employed by the Guomindang government. With diminished resources for manufacturing, the need for Japanese engineers declined, and by September 1947 fewer than 1,400 Japanese engineers, with fewer than 5,000 family members, remained in the factories. Takasaki, realizing that some would still have to remain, decided that he personally would stay until all Japanese wishing to return to Japan could do so. In October 1947 the Guomindang sent Takasaki to Japan to negotiate with Japanese steel factories for war reparations. He tried to convince the Occupation forces that Japan should pay reparations, but shortly thereafter the Allied Occupation officials decided not to force the Japanese to pay such reparations. In November 1947 he was purged by the Occupation for cooperating with Japan's wartime efforts, but in August 1951 the purge was lifted.

In 1952 Prime Minister Yoshida appointed Takasaki president of J-Power, where he proceeded to help rebuild Japan's electric power industry. In 1955 Takasaki became a cabinet member as head of the Ministry of Trade and Industry and also head of the newly established Economic Planning Agency.

Takasaki retained a desire to help rebuild Chinese industry and to improve relations between the two countries. In 1955 he attended the Bandung Conference in Jakarta that China was using to expand its relations with other countries. At the conference, Zhou Enlai invited Takasaki, through his interpreter Liao Chengzhi, to visit the factories that had been established in Manchuria. Zhou explained that the Soviets had taken much of the equipment but the factories had been revived by the Chinese. Takasaki was personally ready to accept Zhou's invitation to begin talks about expanding trade with Japan, but he did not have his government's permission to move ahead. Their 1955 meeting, however, paved the way for the future establishment of formal Sino-Japanese trade relations through what became known as the Liao-Takasaki agreement. In the spring of 1960 when Takasaki visited the United States, he told an American senator that "Japan should help China in an effort to atone for its acts of aggression." At the time, Takasaki was receiving threatening letters from right-wing groups in Japan, and in October 1960 two young men were sent to assassinate him, but they were unsuccessful. Takasaki believed that it was in Japan's interest to improve relations with China, so he kept working to rebuild ties and to expand trade with China. In 1962 Liao Chengzhi and Takasaki Tatsunosuke signed an agreement on long-term comprehensive trade, establishing semiformal arrangements to expand trade between the two countries. The Liao-Takasaki agreement was updated in 1964, shortly before Takasaki's death. In October 1978, when Deng Xiaoping visited Osaka, he met with Takasaki's daughter, whom he had asked to see, to express his appreciation for her father's contribution to Sino-Japanese relations.

For further reading, see Mayumi Itoh, *Pioneers of Sino-Japanese Relations: Liao and Takasaki* (New York: Palgrave Macmillan, 2012).

TANAKA KAKUEI, 1918–1993

Unlike the elite, well-educated former bureaucrats who dominated Japanese politics after World War II, Tanaka Kakuei, prime minister from July 1972 to December 1974, had little formal education and was a rough commoner from rural Niigata. Nevertheless, he is considered one of the most brilliant and effective political deal makers, or "fixers," in Japanese history. Known as a "computerized bulldozer" for his ability to remember massive amounts of information and to charge ahead, in 1972, within three months after becoming prime minister, he was already in Beijing normalizing Sino-Japanese relations. For the first time since World War II the Japanese flag was flying in Beijing. Tanaka and Zhou Enlai signed their agreement not with Western pens but with Asian brushes.

Tanaka had assisted Japan's elite-track prime ministers manage politics, much as Lyndon Johnson had done for President John Kennedy. Unlike the former bureaucrats who were cautious, methodical, and somewhat aloof, Tanaka was bold, irreverent, and charmingly direct. He also did not hesitate to use cash to solve problems, an approach that brought him many friends, but later exposure of this led to his resignation and, still later, to his house arrest.

Tanaka grew up in a small village in the poor "snow country" of Niigata. His father, unlike his hard-working mother and most Japanese farmers, tried various schemes to avoid physical labor. Unlike the many frugal (*kinken chochiku*) Japanese famers, Tanaka's father invested the family's meager savings to import Holstein cows from Holland, to trade horses, to bet on horse races, and to build a large carp pond. His father had more failures than successes, and Kakuei, like his father, was bold in trying new ventures. Kakuei, as the only boy, was exempt from doing any housework, unlike his six sisters. In 1934, when Japan was still suffering from the worldwide depression and Kakuei was fifteen, he quit school and set out for Tokyo. He stayed with a friend's relative and found various odd jobs, doing construction work, delivering newspapers, and working as a handyman. He then found a job in a firm engaged in construction, attended some architecture classes in the evening, and at age nineteen started his own construction company, without any partners or employees.

Tanaka was drafted into the army in March 1939 and was sent with the cavalry to Manchuria, where he was assigned a clerical job. One year later he came down with such a serious case of pneumonia and pleurisy that he was sent back to Tokyo. He remained in critical condition for some time and was discharged from the army. Physically unable to serve in the armed forces, he found work in construction for Riken, an industrial group created to make use of advanced science and technology. As wartime shortages increased, Tanaka was imaginative about acquiring necessary materials and accomplishing his work. For the time, he had quite a high income. At twenty-four, he married a thirty-one-year-old woman whose father, a successful construction businessman, had died a few months earlier. Tanaka took over and expanded the business. As bombing destroyed much of Tokyo, Tanaka moved some Riken factories to southern Korea. The war ended before Riken was firmly established in Korea, but Tanaka had already reaped large profits for managing the move. In the immediate aftermath of the war, when many people were considering entering politics, one of Tanaka's friends asked him, with his then plentiful amount of money, to contribute funds to a political campaign. He also encouraged Tanaka to enter politics himself, and Tanaka agreed to give it a try. Using some of his personal funds for campaigning and relying on support from the workers in his construction company, Tanaka was soon elected as a member of the Diet.

Tanaka proposed construction projects in his home district that included building tunnels and roads through the mountains to link the snow country with western Japan. He knew where construction would make a difference in his election district and he was able to make it happen, quickly. He was not a sophisticated diplomat, but with foreigners his directness and creativity enabled him to solve problems. In 1971 he helped Prime Minister Sato deal with his promise to limit textile exports, an issue that had enraged President Nixon. Within three months he had found a solution, paying off Japanese textile companies to limit their exports.

Within the Liberal Democratic Party, the former elite bureaucrats found Tanaka to be an enormous asset for raising money and managing the selection of local candidates to run for the Diet. His prodigious memory helped him understand the conditions in each election district and select appealing candidates and appropriate messages. Tanaka could work with the elites, but he never pretended to be one of them. Local people happily called him by his nickname, Kaku-san, while they referred to the elite bureaucrats by more formal names. He was a crowd-pleaser, with stories, humor, nostalgia, and an irreverence that moved his audiences. To the common people, Tanaka was one of them. In 1972 he became the youngest prime minister since World War II and the only one without a college degree.

Tanaka became prime minister shortly after the United States had embarrassed Japanese leaders by rushing ahead of Japan to open contacts with China. Within months Tanaka not only opened Japan's channel for expanding contacts with China, but rushed ahead of the United States in normalizing relations. For making this breakthrough, he won praise from Chinese leaders.

Niigata is on the western side of the main Japanese island, the "back side" (*ura Nippon*), and was relatively neglected compared with the east coast, which had prospered when trade with the United States increased after World War II. As a Diet member looking out for his home district, Tanaka drew on his construction-company experience to win national support for building projects—roads, tunnels, mountain passes, power generators, train routes, and train stations—to help develop his more backward district.

Later, as prime minister, Tanaka's main domestic effort was a plan to extend economic construction to areas that had not yet benefited from Japan's expanding industrialization, a plan known as *Nihon Retto Kaizoron* (Building a New Japan: A Plan for Remodeling the Japanese Archipelago). This plan was a natural for Japan at the time. Like the takeoff in China's growth two decades later, Japan's growth began in the big urban areas along the east coast, near Tokyo and Osaka, and points in between, while the rest of the country lagged behind. The idea of new construction was always dear to Tanaka's heart, and his efforts to win national support by spreading modernization to more backward areas was an extension of what he had been trying to do in his own home prefecture. Initially, his plan brought some success to the backward areas, but over time the plan reached a point of diminishing returns. The first bridge between Honshu and the smaller island of Shikoku brought great economic benefits, but the third bridge produced marginal results at best. Within years, some people were blaming Tanaka for wasting money on construction without thinking about the environment and quality of life.

Although Tanaka was welcomed when he visited the United States and Europe in 1973–1974, when he visited Indonesia and Malaysia in 1974 the local people, harboring anger at the Japanese as a result of Japan's invasion in World War II, rioted. Tanaka and other Japanese leaders quickly got the message. When Ohira Masayoshi and Fukuda Takeo later visited Southeast Asia and brought promises of aid, their reception was much more favorable.

Tanaka was vulnerable to charges of corruption. He had acquired a bus company and a lot of real estate by working with another tycoon, Osamu Kenji. In 1974 the popular magazine *Bungei shunju* revealed that several of

Tanaka's friends had been permitted to buy property just before new public developments in a locality were announced, thus allowing them to reap great profits as the value of the property rose rapidly. The article also exposed the fact that Tanaka's girlfriend had profited in this way as well. Rather than testify, Tanaka resigned from the Diet in 1974.

In 1976 the vice president of the American aerospace company Lockheed told a court investigating the company's payments that Tanaka Kakuei had been paid off in 1972 for arranging for All Nippon Airways' purchase of twenty-one Lockheed aircraft. Tanaka was arrested, and for seven years, from 1977 to 1983, he was summoned to the Tokyo District Courthouse each week. It was found that he had received $2 million in bribes, and he was sentenced to four years in prison. Despite the payoff accusations, Tanaka's popularity increased. His faction had fewer than 80 members before the Lockheed scandal broke in 1976, but by 1981 the number had increased to more than 150 members. In the election of 1983, shortly after the court's decision was announced, Tanaka won more votes than any other candidate in the country. He continued to be politically influential until 1985, when he suffered a stroke and withdrew from politics. He died in 1993. Throughout Japan Tanaka has his admirers as well as critics, but in Niigata he is a beloved and revered hero.

For further reading, see Jacob M. Schlesinger, *Shadow Shoguns: The Rise and Fall of Japan's Postwar Political Machine* (New York: Simon & Schuster, 1997).

WANG JINGWEI, 1883–1944

While studying in Japan from 1903 to 1905, Wang Jingwei met Sun Yat-sen, a fellow Cantonese student. Like Sun, Wang was thoroughly convinced that the Manchu leaders could not solve China's problems. He joined Sun's Revolutionary Alliance and was Sun's close personal aide for the rest of Sun's life. After Sun Yat-sen died in 1925, Wang was considered a leading candidate to succeed him; however, within a year Chiang Kai-shek had become Sun's successor. But Wang never accepted Chiang as a rightful successor. Wang had been an excellent student in Japan and spoke far better Japanese than Chiang Kai-shek. Although Wang briefly joined Chiang in Chongqing after the Japanese invasion of China, for years the two remained political rivals. In March 1940, the Japanese who led the occupation of China desired a Chinese face to administer the government. Wang Jingwei, as a high-level leader who spoke excellent Japanese, was a logical choice, and they offered him the presidency of the government. After lengthy negotiations, the Japanese made the position attractive enough for Wang to accept. Wang claimed that while he was president he remained a patriot and tried to use his position to help the Chinese. However, the Japanese tightly controlled his pronouncements and his actions, and he had little room to maneuver.

Wang was born in Sanshui in the northwest outskirts of Guangzhou. In 1903 he went to Japan to study on a provincial government scholarship, and in 1905 he graduated from Hosei University (Tokyo Institute of Law and Public Administration). On his return to China, Wang continued to read widely in legal theory and Western philosophy. In contrast to Liang Qichao, who believed that China needed an emperor, Wang believed that China needed more laws that expressed the general will. In 1910 Wang was arrested for plotting against the Manchu prince regent, and he remained in prison until the 1911 Revolution. Shortly after his release, he became well known as a hero to the revolutionary cause. An articulate orator, he became a popular public speaker and attracted large audiences. He was also recognized as an essayist and poet.

During World War I Wang went to France, where he studied French literature. He returned to China in 1917 to become Sun's personal assistant, writing many of the papers issued in Sun's name and accompanying Sun on his travels. He taught Guomindang Party history at the Huangpu Military Academy, and in 1925 he became a member of the Guomindang Central Executive Committee. He was at Sun's bedside when Sun died on March 12, 1925, and he was the lead author of Sun's political testament.

After Sun's death, Wang was elected head of the Central Standing Committee. At the time, Chiang Kai-shek was not a member of the committee and was not yet considered a candidate to become Sun's successor. But Chiang was respected by the corps commanders of the Guomindang Army, and on June 5, 1925, while preparing for the Northern Expedition, Chiang was named commander in chief of the National Revolutionary Army. One month later, Chiang became the Generalissimo (supreme commander). On August 20, 1925, Liao Zhongkai, another possible candidate to succeed Sun, was shot, and Chiang became a member of the Central Standing Committee. Russian adviser Mikhail Borodin and Li Zongren, a Guangxi military leader, believed that Wang Jingwei's ambitions made him unpredictable and unreliable. Wang was surprised when the military declared its support for Chiang. Just as Yuan Shikai, the soldier, had become president rather than Sun Yat-sen, the politician, so Chiang, the soldier who knew little about politics, became president rather than Wang. It seemed to Wang that his rightful place as Sun's successor had been stolen from him. Fearing for his life, Wang Jingwei fled to Shanghai and then to France.

In 1927 when Chiang established his national government in Nanjing, Wang set up what he hoped would be the national government headquarters in Wuhan, but Wang's Wuhan headquarters gained little support and was soon abandoned. In 1930 Wang Jingwei cooperated with the warlords Yan Xishan and Feng Yuxiang to set up a government in opposition to Chiang's.

In 1935, when the Guomindang Central Executive Committee was posing for a group photo, a photographer pulled out a gun and took several shots at Wang Jingwei, one of which caused a serious wound. Since Chiang Kai-shek was not at the photo session, some speculated that Chiang had ordered the assassination attempt. For medical treatment, Wang Jingwei and his wife went to Europe, where Wang spent some months recuperating and studying. After the Japanese invasion of China and Chiang's withdrawal to Chongqing, Wang Jingwei followed him there and briefly served under Chiang as head of the National Defense Council.

In November 1937 the German ambassador to China, Oskar Trautmann, was entrusted by Japan to negotiate with Chiang. Discussions were held, but they failed to lead to an agreement to end the fighting. Wang Jingwei, hoping to stop the war and save lives, continued to meet with prominent Japanese officials in an attempt to reach an agreement, even after he left Chongqing for Hanoi. At times it appeared there might be some hope for an agreement, but in the end Chiang Kai-shek was determined to fight on and Wang Jingwei's efforts were called an unpatriotic "peace conspiracy." In Hanoi, Wang was wounded for a second time by an assassin, apparently sent by the Guomindang.

In March 1940 the Japanese offered Wang Jingwei the position of president of the Republic of China. Wang hesitated for some weeks but then, announcing that he was working with Japan to fight communism and Western imperialism, he finally accepted. After Wang accepted, Japan established its own government in Nanjing and publicized it as the return of a true Guomindang government. Since Wang had no troops, he was in a weak position to resist the Japanese. He was reported to be depressed because he had so little success in convincing the Japanese to be less repressive. He became sick in 1944 and was sent to a Japanese hospital in Nagoya, where he died shortly thereafter.

Those who regard Wang as a traitor point to a speech he gave in support of Japan's Greater East Asia Co-Prosperity Sphere, and to his November 1940 signing of the Japan-China Basic Relations Treaty, which, they claim, was similar to accepting the Twenty-One Demands. After Wang's death, both the Guomindang and the Communists denounced him as a collaborator and led huge public campaigns attacking him as a traitor. His tomb in Nanjing was destroyed by Chiang's troops. Today, both Guomindang and Communist history books attack Wang Jingwei as one of the most notorious traitors in Chinese history and downplay his close relationship with Sun Yat-sen.

For further reading, see Gerald Bunker, *The Peace Conspiracy: Wang Ching-wei and the China War, 1937–1941* (Cambridge, Mass.: Harvard University Press, 1972).

Yoshida Shigeru, 1878–1967

Yoshida Shigeru, the preeminent Japanese leader from 1946 to 1952, during and immediately after the Allied Occupation, set Japan on its new political course after World War II. As elected prime minister for most of the time from 1946 to 1954, Yoshida, a former elite-track diplomat, made an effort to represent Japan's national interests to the Allied Occupation officials. Yet he knew the Occupation officials had ultimate power and he willingly accepted and implemented most of their policies. Concerned that many political leaders voted in under the new system of democratic elections might not have the knowledge or perspective to govern wisely, Yoshida helped recruit former senior bureaucrats who were knowledgeable about governmental affairs to become politicians. These ex-bureaucrats, a group known as the "Yoshida school," sought to maintain Japan's alliance with the United States. They supported economic growth through a government-guided market economy and they managed affairs with sufficient success that within two decades after the war, the vast majority of Japanese citizens had become members of the middle class. For four decades after the war, most of Japan's prime ministers were members of the Yoshida School, including Ikeda Hayato, Sato Eisaku, Fukuda Takeo, Ohira Masayoshi, and Miyazawa Kiichi.

Yoshida was born in Yokohama and at a young age was adopted by a rich childless merchant, Yoshida Kenzo. He lived a privileged aristocratic life and was educated at elite schools and Tokyo Imperial University. He married the daughter of Count Makino Nobuaki, the adopted son of Okubo Toshimichi, the leading statesman during the first decade of the Meiji period, which gave him a very high status within the bureaucracy.

When he was a Foreign Ministry official, Yoshida was considered a member of the Anglo-American school and he had great respect for the British political system. But he spent more years serving in China than serving in English-speaking countries. His first overseas assignment was in the Japanese consulate in Shenyang, from 1907 to 1908. He served as consul in Dandong (then called Andong) on the border with Korea from 1912 to 1915, and then he was assigned to Ji'nan, in Shandong province, in 1918. He was consul general in the port city of Tianjin from 1922 to 1925 and in Shenyang from 1925 to 1928.

During his first assignment in Dandong, he wrote reports expressing his opposition to the Twenty-One Demands that Japan had presented to China in 1915. He wrote that it was necessary to build China's trust and cooperation and that the "*Shina ronin*" (China drifters), who were then engaged in intrigue and espionage in China, made it difficult for the Japanese to develop friendly trade relations with China. After Yoshida voiced his opposition to the Twenty-One Demands, he was criticized within the ministry and assigned to work in records instead of receiving a plum assignment in Washington. Yoshida attended the 1919 peace conference at Versailles, where he was persuaded that national power was more influential than idealism. He also became cynical about U.S. expressions of idealism when there was so much discrimination against the Japanese in California.

In the 1920s Yoshida quickly grew pessimistic, believing that no Chinese leader would be able to unify China and provide effective leadership. Late in the decade he expressed frustration with Zhang Zuolin because Zhang did not manage things well and his statements could not be trusted. Having concluded that China's leaders did not respond to expressions of friendship unless backed by force, he favored a firm policy toward China.

As Japan's ambassador in England from 1936 to 1938, Yoshida persisted in seeking ways to restore good relations with England. But once Japanese troops moved into North China on July 7, 1937, any chance of success disappeared. Yoshida returned to Tokyo in 1938.

In 1942 Yoshida concluded that Japan could not win the war, and he began working with others to try to negotiate a settlement. The group was known to Japanese police as *Yohansen* (Yoshida Anti-War). He worked with Prince Konoe Fumimaro, who was briefly prime minister in 1940–1941, to prepare the "Konoe Memorial," which Konoe was finally allowed to present to the emperor on February 14, 1945, urging the emperor to surrender. At the time, the emperor did not agree to end the war, and on April 15, 1945, Yoshida was arrested for supporting Konoe's attempt to bring about Japan's surrender.

On April 10, 1946, in the first postwar election for the Diet, Hatoyama Ichiro's Liberal Party won a substantial plurality and it was expected that he would become the first postwar prime minister. However, Occupation officials had already processed the papers for the purge of Hatoyama, who in the 1930s had praised Hitler and Mussolini. After receiving the purge order, Hatoyama, who knew Yoshida well, asked Yoshida to form the new government. In May 1946 Yoshida became prime minister. General Douglas MacArthur, head of the Allied Occupation, and Yoshida found that they could work well with each other. Yoshida was prime minister between 1946 and 1954, except for the period from April 1947 through November 1948 when he was out of office because of losing the election.

In the view of the Allied Occupation officials in 1946, Yoshida was the best possible choice to be prime minister. He had a good command of English and he was considered to be pro–Anglo-American. He had been imprisoned by the militarists for his efforts to end the war, and he had unusually good relations with Joseph Grew, the respected U.S. ambassador to Japan from 1932 to 1941. Grew's wife had been good friends with Yoshida's wife, and the Grews were a great help to Yoshida's wife in her last months, when she was suffering from a terminal illness. After Pearl Harbor, when Grew was confined in Japan before being repatriated, Yoshida, at some personal risk, sent food and other items to Grew. With this background, Yoshida was a natural choice for the Americans, who were looking for a prime minister with whom they could communicate and in whom they had confidence.

On September 20, 1945, Yoshida, as foreign minister, had his first meeting with MacArthur. At scarcely five feet tall, Yoshida was a head shorter than MacArthur, but when meeting him he displayed the natural poise and dignity of a member of the meritocratic elite from an aristocratic family. During this first meeting with MacArthur, as the American general paced the room giving Yoshida what the Japanese called a "sermon," Yoshida broke into a slight laugh. When MacArthur inquired why, Yoshida said he felt as if he was Daniel listening to a lecture inside a lion's cage. MacArthur reportedly first glared and then laughed.

During the meeting, Yoshida made a point that he would later repeat many times in many different ways—to have democracy, one first had to improve economic conditions. It was not until 1947 that U.S. policy in Japan began to emphasize economic growth. Also at this meeting, Yoshida suggested that MacArthur should meet the emperor, and a meeting with the emperor took place one week later.

As an outspoken aristocrat, Yoshida was not a populist and was not even popular with the elected Diet members who came from humbler backgrounds. In March 1953 he lost an election after he yelled at a Socialist Diet member, "Bakayaro!" (You idiot!). Yet Yoshida was respected by much of the Japanese public for speaking to the Occupation authorities frankly and with dignity, even when Japan was in a weak position.

In his years as prime minister during the Occupation, Yoshida accepted the reality that foreign and domestic policy were to be determined by the Allied forces, but he continued to make the case that Japan should be allowed to rebuild its economy. He argued in favor of allowing Japan to increase its trade with China, against punishing so many "war criminals," and against breaking up Japanese companies because it would prevent economic growth—all with little success. However, what is known as the "Yoshida doctrine" allowed the United States to provide for Japan's military security so Japan could reduce its military expenses and focus on economic recovery. Yoshida was a smart, persistent negotiator who managed to end the Occupation without making a commitment to build a large military.

Early in his career Yoshida had been a firm believer in the Anglo-Japanese alliance that lasted until 1922. The alliance was based on Britain and Japan's common fear of Russia, even long before the Russian Revolution. To Yoshida, the U.S.-Japan alliance also made sense, for he believed the greatest danger to Japan was still Russia, even though it was now Soviet Russia instead of Imperial Russia.

Yoshida argued that allowing Japan to develop trade with China would help pull China away from the Soviet Union, but U.S. officials would not yield. Yoshida retained his deep interest in China and wanted to develop peaceful relations. He believed that more trade between China and Japan would be good for both countries, and that Great Britain's decision to establish diplomatic relations with Communist China in January 1950, within months after the establishment of Communist rule, was wise, and the failure of the United States to do likewise was unwise. He did not have the power to force the U.S.-led Occupation to allow Japan to expand trade with China, but he wanted as much trade as the United States would allow and to pave the way for a time in the future when more trade would be possible. In the meantime, he sought to continue trade with Taiwan, making use of Japan-Taiwan ties that had been built in the half-century of Japanese occupation.

After the Allied Occupation ended on April 28, 1952, Yoshida remained in office for another two and a half years. During that time, he lived up to the letter he had written to U.S. Secretary of State John Foster Dulles in December 1951, promising that he would maintain relations with Taiwan and not move closer to mainland China.

While in office after the Occupation, Yoshida made no great policy changes except when, in 1954, the "police reserves" that had been earlier established were converted into a new Self-Defense Force, with an authorized 152,115 troops. After retiring, Yoshida retained his informal role as statesman, welcoming to his home both politicians and foreign visitors. When MacArthur died in April 1964, Yoshida, at age eighty-six, traveled to the United States for the funeral, signifying the persistence of a close relationship between the two men and between the two countries. Yoshida died three years later.

For further reading, see John Dower, *Empire and Aftermath: Yoshida Shigeru and the Japanese Experience, 1878–1954* (Cambridge, Mass.: Council on East Asian Studies, Harvard University, 1979); Richard B. Finn, *Win-*

ners in Peace: MacArthur, Yoshida, and Postwar Japan (Berkeley: University of California Press, 1992).

ZHOU ENLAI, 1898–1976

Henry Kissinger described Zhou Enlai, the legendary Chinese premier and foreign minister, as "one of the two or three most impressive men" he ever met, "infinitely patient, extraordinarily intelligent, subtle." Zhou studied in Japan for nineteen months from 1917 to 1919, just when Chinese nationalism was growing. He was in France from 1920 to 1924, as it was recovering from World War I and evaluating the significance of the Russian Revolution. Zhou joined the Chinese Communist Party in 1921, the year it was founded. After the establishment of the People's Republic of China in 1949, he served as premier, with responsibility for foreign affairs, from 1949 until his death in 1976. Zhou had a remarkable capacity to remember and manage details while devising national strategy and finding ways to work with other nations.

Zhou Enlai grew up in a middle-class, well-educated family, with four brothers. His parents allowed him to be adopted by his father's younger brother, who was dying of tuberculosis, so his uncle would have an heir. Zhou's stepmother, Madame Chen, doted on him and provided him with an excellent Confucian education in which he excelled, but she died when he was ten years old, a year after Zhou's natural mother died. Zhou's natural father moved away, but another of his father's brothers, who had no children, took an interest in Zhou's education and brought him along when he moved to Shenyang, where Zhou attended the city's best primary school. The uncle then brought Zhou with him to Tianjin, where Zhou passed the entrance examination for Nankai Middle School—one of China's best middle schools, modeled after Phillips Academy in the United States—which Zhou attended from age fifteen to nineteen. The school was a highly structured boarding school. Students lived in dormitories, rose early, took classes in modern subjects, ate together, and developed strong feelings of camaraderie. Zhou thrived there, wrote for the school newspaper, had a lead role in a school play, was covaledictorian of his class, and won a graduation prize for an outstanding Chinese essay. He was much beloved and respected by the faculty and his fellow students.

Before Zhou went to Japan in 1917 he was already familiar with Japanese life, since some 200,000 Japanese lived in Shenyang when he was in school there. In Tokyo, Zhou soon moved from a Chinese inn to a Japanese inn because it was quieter, and then he moved to a dormitory for Chinese students, where they could do their own cooking. He entered a Japanese-language program at East Asian Higher Preparatory School, a school with nearly 1,000 Chinese students who were preparing for admission into regular Japanese institutions. Most of his friends in Tokyo were from a group of thirty graduates from his middle school. His uncle sent him some money to cover his expenses in Tokyo, but Zhou was constantly short of funds, and several former schoolmates from Nankai Middle School chipped in to help him out financially.

After some months of studying Japanese and English, Zhou took an examination to enter Tokyo Education School, but he failed. He later took another entrance examination, for Number One High School, which he also failed. In his diary he blames himself for his failures. He also records his sadness about the deaths in his family, the untended graves of his mother and stepmother, the death of his uncle who had helped him out, and his inability to help his family. Friends reported that while in Japan Zhou became depressed. The fact that he failed the examinations was a terrible embarrassment because he had been an outstanding student at Nankai, because many of his former schoolmates did pass their entrance examinations in Japan, and because his friends in Japan had to help him out financially.

Zhou did not have any close Japanese friends but he had friendly acquaintances. He expressed appreciation to the president of his preparatory school, Master Matsumoto Kamejiro, who had formerly taught at Kano Jigoro's Kobun Institute. (When Zhou's widow, Deng Yingchao, visited Japan in April 1979, she paid her respects to Matsumoto's grandsons.) Yasuda Ryumon, an art student in the same rooming house where Zhou lived, painted Zhou's picture, and in 2000 the painter's son presented the portrait to the Zhou Enlai and Deng Yingchao Memorial Museum in Tianjin. Later, in his writings, Zhou was critical of Japanese politicians and militarists who had imperialist designs on China, and he was also critical of the Chinese who called other Chinese "traitors" if they had Japanese friends. Although he later took part in anti-Japanese demonstrations, he did not express antipathy toward the Japanese people. He was quite comfortable in dealing with Japanese visitors later in his career, and he reminisced fondly about his time in Japan, especially remembering his visits to the Kanda bookstores and to Kyoto.

In his diary Zhou commented on how well organized and disciplined the Japanese were. He lamented that the Chinese were so poorly organized and were not making rapid progress toward modernization. He read newspapers about the Russian Revolution and books in Japanese about Marxism. The Japanese author he found most interesting was Kawakami Hajime, whose book *The Tale of Poverty* analyzes the causes and distribution of poverty and what nations might do to deal with it. Even rich nations had poor people, Zhou learned. Zhou, like Kawakami, had come from a comfortable family and was becoming concerned about moral issues, including the need to help the poor. Zhou made an effort to enter Kyoto University to study under Kawakami, but it did not work out. Like Kawakami, Zhou was not yet a Marxist, but also like Kawakami, such concerns paved the way for his later commitment to Marxism.

In the summer of 1918 Zhou was troubled by Japan's rice riots. A group of farm housewives had blocked people from taking rice from the villagers to sell in urban markets. Inflation was high and rice merchants were making a great deal of money, but the rice farmers were receiving a very low price for their crop. An estimated 700,000 people, including some urban residents upset by the spiraling costs owing to inflation, joined in the riots. For Zhou, the riots raised questions about justice for the poor farmers, who were being squeezed out by a capitalist system that brought profits only to the merchants. While a student at Nankai, Zhou had written essays praising Japan's economic progress, but the rice riots raised questions about whether China should be copying the Japanese economic system, and if so, how its policies should be modified. In December 1918 Zhou also observed the demonstrations of Korean students at the Korean YMCA in Kanda as the Korean Independence Movement was growing. In 1921 Zhou joined the Chinese Communist Party.

In March 1919, after he failed the examinations for a second time, Zhou, who had relied on friends for funding, decided it would be better to return home than to continue burdening his Chinese friends. But before he returned to China, he stayed with a Nankai friend for a month in Kyoto, where he took some last looks at the gardens and wrote poems about their beauty. "Cherry blossoms, delicately pink, tenderly sweet," he wrote. "All soul-enchanting. Beauty of nature, untouched by artfulness."

In late April Zhou boarded a ship in Kobe for Pusan, and from there he went on to Beijing. Fortuitously, Zhou arrived home just before May 4, and he immediately threw himself into the demonstrations for a national awakening. Zhou formed the Awakening Society, a secret organization to help raise national awareness. The society included some who had been his friends in Japan and several who later became Communists. His two years in Japan, when he was wrestling with the issues of poverty, capitalism, and imperialism, had helped prepare him for his role as an intellectual leader in the aftermath of May 4, 1919.

In January 1920 Zhou and some other members of his Awakening Society were arrested in Tianjin for participating in demonstrations. After his release some six months later, Zhou and others set sail for France for further study, where they would gain a greater understanding of European social conditions and a clearer picture of what needed to be done in China. Unlike most young Chinese students then in France who were on work-study programs, Zhou had received funding to write for a Tianjin newspaper and he could devote himself full-time to writing and organizing. Chinese youths who were selected to go to France on the work-study programs were among the most able elite students, but the depression in France at the time made it impossible for them to earn enough money working, mostly in factories, to pay for their tuition. Therefore they studied not in the classrooms but outside them, through observation and reading, and sifting through new ideas in their discussion groups. Zhou remained in touch with friends in China, and in 1921, just months after the Chinese Communist Party was formed, Zhou and others organized a Chinese Communist Party cell in France. Zhou became a full-time party organizer, traveling to England, Belgium, and Germany to help expand the Chinese Communist Party among Chinese students in Europe. In 1923, he also joined the Nationalist Party. By this time, having already been imprisoned and with many friends living under fear of arrest, Zhou had been hardened.

In the fall of 1924 Zhou returned to China and was assigned by the party to serve as political commissar at the Huangpu Military Academy, working under Chiang Kai-shek as part of the United Front. In the next year he married Deng Yingchao, who had been a member of his Awakening Society in Tianjin. Throughout his life, she remained his partner in marriage and in the Communist cause.

In 1926 Zhou left the Huangpu Military Academy to engage in organizing work in Shanghai. Following the split between the Communists and Nationalists in April 1927, Zhou and the other Communists became engaged in life-and-death battles with the Nationalists. It was Zhou's responsibility to obtain intelligence from the Nationalists. In 1934 he received secret intelligence that helped the Communists break through the Nationalist encirclement and start on the Long March. Even after the two sides restored the United Front in December 1936, each remained suspicious of the other side and what it would do after the Anti-Japanese War ended. Zhou Enlai carried on negotiations with the Nationalists while also looking for informants who would reveal to him the Nationalists' secrets. During the Anti-Japanese War Zhou spent some time in Chongqing, the Nationalist headquarters, where he negotiated with the Nationalists and met with Westerners, and he also spent some time in Yan'an with Mao and other Communist leaders. When the Marshall Mission, led by U.S. Army general George Marshall, was dispatched to Chongqing in 1946–1947 to try to avert a civil war, Zhou joined with Mao in the negotiations.

From the time the Communists took power in 1949 until his death in 1976, Zhou was a central pillar in all Chinese policies, domestic and foreign, and all major negotiations, owing to his broad strategic perspective, extraordinary command of detail, capacity for incredibly long hours of work, and good relations with the major Communist leaders. Mao had the power to make all important decisions, such as entering the Korean War, allying with the Soviet Union, later breaking with the Soviets, and opening to the West. But Zhou carried out the detailed negotiations. He negotiated the Treaty of Friendship with the Soviet Union in 1950, and he managed the negotiations surrounding the Korean War. In 1955, when permitted by Mao, Zhou attended the Geneva Conference to expand China's diplomatic arena and improve relations with Japan and the Western countries. His negotiations with Henry Kissinger over resuming diplomatic relations between China and the United States, beginning in 1971 when they represented their respective countries, have become legendary.

Mao purged many leading party officials, especially in 1942–1943, 1957–1959, and 1966–1967. He often disparaged Zhou Enlai and expressed great displeasure that many officials seemed at times to respect Zhou more than they respected Mao himself. Zhou was always self-effacing, however, he always deferred to Mao, and he wisely anticipated Mao's moods. Mao also realized that no one could compare with Zhou in his knowledge of foreign affairs and the respect he enjoyed among foreign leaders.

As Japan began its programs for economic growth in the 1950s, Zhou was deeply worried about the danger that Japan would use its newfound economic strength to return to militarism. Yet after 1949 Zhou welcomed Japanese "friends of China" to Beijing, and after 1972 he welcomed mainstream Japanese visitors from across the political spectrum, all of whom regarded Zhou as an icon.

During the weeks when Zhou Enlai was on his hospital deathbed in late 1975, Mao never visited him. After Zhou died on January 8, 1976, Mao chose not to attend his funeral, and he forbade foreign countries from sending delegations to pay their respects. On April 3, two days before the annual grave-sweeping festival, Beijing officials, knowing that many people were unhappy that Zhou had not been given appropriate funeral services and anticipating that large crowds might use the occasion to remember Zhou, issued an order from Mao: Do not go to Tiananmen Square to lay wreaths. Nevertheless, on April 5, 1976, an estimated two million people, touched by Zhou's contributions to China for more than five decades, especially his tireless efforts to curb the excesses of the Great Leap Forward and the Cultural Revolution, went to the square to honor Zhou. Mao, ailing himself, but well enough to understand that Zhou's popularity exceeded his own, died five months later.

For further reading, see Gao Wenqian, *Zhou Enlai: The Last Perfect Revolutionary: A Biography* (New York: Public Affairs, 2007); Miyumi Itoh, *The Origins of Contemporary Sino-Japanese Relations: Zhou Enlai and Japan* (New York: Palgrave Macmillan, 2016); Henry Kissinger, *White House Years* (Boston: Little, Brown, 1979).

Notes

CHAPTER 1. CHINESE CONTRIBUTIONS TO JAPANESE CIVILIZATION, 600–838

I profited from the guidance of Yukio Lippit and Robert Borgen for scholarship on this period, especially concerning architecture. For the overall history of the period, I drew especially on the first two volumes of *The Cambridge History of Japan* and *East Asia: Tradition and Transformation* by Fairbank, Reischauer, and Craig. For the account of the clans and use of the *kabane* system, I relied on research by Richard Miller. I am indebted to Mark Byington for helping me understand the Korean influence. For information about the development of the Japanese language, I relied on work by David Lurie. For the Japanese military, I relied especially on work by William Wayne Farris. I also benefited from the advice of Richard Dyck, Andrew Gordon, Li Tingjiang, Benjamin Ng, and Wang Yong.

1. For convenience, I use the names "China," "Japan," and "Korea" to describe the political units of the time, even though they did not then have the well-developed political structure of a modern nation-state and did not cover as broad a geographical area as they do today.
2. I use "clan" for the Japanese word *uji*. The *uji* was basically a patrilineal descent group, but it could also include those who married in or others who were added in. There is insufficient recorded information to be precise about who was added to the basic descent groups.
3. There is disagreement among specialists about the historical authenticity of Prince Shotoku. He was not called Prince Shotoku until after his death. Some Buddhists believed he was the reincarnation of a Chinese monk. The legend of Shotoku that developed after his death is traced in Michael I. Como, *Shotoku: Ethnicity, Ritual, and Violence in the Japanese Buddhist Tradition* (Oxford: Oxford University Press, 2008). For my account of Shotoku, I have relied on the view of most historians.
4. Gina L. Barnes, *Archaeology of East Asia: The Rise of Civilization in China, Korea and Japan* (Philadelphia: Oxbow Books, 2015), 270–271.
5. Some scholars have assumed that the term *wo* in *woren* implied that the Japanese were dwarfs, but more recent scholarship casts doubts on this conjecture.
6. Inoue Mitsusada, with Delmer M. Brown, "The Century of Reform," in *The Cambridge History of Japan: Volume 1, Ancient Japan*, ed. Delmer Brown (Cambridge: Cambridge University Press, 1993), 182.

7. William Wayne Farris, *Heavenly Warriors: Evolution of Japan's Military, 500–1300* (Cambridge, Mass.: Council on East Asian Studies, Harvard University Press, 1992), 38–39.

CHAPTER 2. TRADE WITHOUT TRANSFORMATIVE LEARNING, 838–1862

I have benefited from detailed advice from Paula Harrell and Robert Innes on all parts of this chapter. I have also benefited from the advice of Robert Borgen, Richard Von Glahn, and Peter Bol on the Song period, Michael Szonyi on the Ming period, and Ronald Toby on trade between China and Japan. On the role of the monks, I have profited especially from the thesis by Li Yiwen, in which Li traces the role of monks during the six centuries when there were no tribute missions. For an account of the views of Xu Guangqi, I have drawn on Timothy Brook, in Fogel, ed., *Sagacious Monks and Bloodthirsty Warriors*. For the lasting image of Japanese pirates, I have drawn on the article by Wang Yong in the same volume. I am indebted to Wang Yong for his help on the earlier centuries.

1. The discovery in the 1970s of two Chinese shipwrecks still filled with Chinese goods added to our knowledge about trade between China and Japan. In 1976 a sunken ship, now called the *Sinan*, which had been headed from Ningbo to Hakata, was discovered off the coast of South Korea. It was built and owned by Chinese merchants. Many records were found on the ship. When the *Sinan* sank on its 1323 voyage from China to Japan, its cargo included some 28,000 tons of copper coins and 20,000 pieces of Chinese ceramics. More than 350 wooden slips were attached to the goods, indicating to whom they belonged. Apparently most of the people on board the *Sinan* were Japanese, and the goods were all connected to the Jotenji Monastery in Hakata. Another sunken ship was discovered in 1974 in the bay off Quanzhou (in Fujian province). Many of the goods on that ship were owned by the Japanese Tokufuji Monastery, but some were owned by merchants. In another find in the 1970s, when a subway was being built in Hakata thousands of Chinese coins and fragments of ceramics were discovered.

    For some decades, Japanese Buddhists believed that to prevent the deterioration of the world until the arrival of the next Buddha, it was necessary to bury sutras in mounds whenever someone died. Thousands of such mounds were built in Japan between the eleventh and nineteenth centuries, and they were discovered throughout Japan in the twentieth century. Most were found in Kyushu and in the area around Kyoto, but many were also found on the island of Shikoku, on the Inland Sea route for Chinese goods traveling from Kyushu to the area near Kyoto. Thousands of Chinese goods, especially Chinese sutra containers, were found in the sutra mounds in Japan, but no such sutra mounds have been found in China. Coins, knives, and images of Buddha were also found with the sutras in mounds dating from the eleventh to the thirteenth century. The presence of so many goods from China in these sutra mounds reflects the high prestige of Chinese goods in Japan during that time.

2. It has been estimated that some 50 Chinese ships visited Japan in the ninth century, approximately 100 ships in the tenth century, 100 ships in the eleventh century, 120 ships in the twelfth century, approximately 50 in the thirteenth century, very few in the fourteenth and fifteenth centuries, and nearly 100 in the sixteenth century. Few Japanese ships ventured abroad in the tenth to the twelfth centuries, but an estimated 200 Japanese ships sailed to China in the thirteenth century. Fewer ships went abroad in the fourteenth century, but after learning about Ming shipbuilding advances, the Japanese built better ships and sent more than 1,000 to China every year during the fifteenth and sixteenth centuries. Richard Von Glahn, "The Ningbo-Hakata Merchant Network and the Reorientation of East Asian Maritime Trade, 1150–1350," *Harvard Journal of Asiatic Studies* 74, no. 2 (2014): 249–279.

3. Reported by Von Glahn, in "The Ningbo-Hakata Merchant Network."

4. Jurgis Elisonas [George Elison], "The Inseparable Trinity: Japan's Relations with China and Korea," in *The Cambridge History of Japan: Volume 4, Early Modern Japan*, ed. John Whitney Hall and James L. McClain (Cambridge: Cambridge University Press, 1991), 235–300. Here, see p. 278, where Elisonas cites Frois, a Jesuit in Japan at the time.

5. Xing Hang, "The Shogun's Chinese Partners: The Alliance between Tokugawa Japan and the Zheng Family in Seventeenth-Century Maritime East Asia," *Journal of Asian Studies* 75, no. 1 (2016): 111–136.

6. Marius B. Jansen, *China in the Tokugawa World* (Cambridge, Mass.: Harvard University Press, 1992), 13.

7. Ibid., 29.

CHAPTER 3. RESPONDING TO WESTERN CHALLENGES AND
REOPENING RELATIONS, 1839–1882

1. Masao Miyoshi, *As We Saw Them: The First Japanese Embassy to the United States* (Philadelphia: Paul Dry Books, 2005), 2.

2. Foo Ah Fong, "The Seven Lamps of a Sustainable City," in *Sustainable Cities of the 21st Century*, ed. A. F. Foo and Belinda Yuen, 118 (Singapore: National University of Singapore Press and World Scientific, 1999).

CHAPTER 4. RIVALRY IN KOREA AND THE
SINO-JAPANESE WAR, 1882–1895

I am indebted to Carter Eckert, Sheila Jager, and Alex Dudden for their reading of this chapter and for their advice, and to Jenny Huangfu Day for sharing her research. For the situation in Korea prior to the war period and for the role of Japan in Korea, I have relied on works by Conroy, Deuchler, Dudden, Eckert, Fogel, Kallander, Larsen, Okazaki, Palais, and Reynolds. Frederick Foo Chien wrote his Ph.D. thesis as a young scholar at Yale, but he later became a leading Taiwan diplomat and headed the Taiwan mission in Washington, D.C. For the immediate background of the Sino-Japanese War, the war itself, and its impact, I have drawn especially on works by Elleman, Paine, and Evans and Peattie. The studies by Duus, Iriye, Jansen, and Schmid follow the impact of the war. The work in Chinese (also available in Japanese) edited by Bu Ping and Kitaoka Shin-ichi, based on efforts by the two countries to work toward achieving a common perspective on their history, provides a summary of Chinese and Japanese scholarly views.

1. Ki-Baik Lee, *A New History of Korea* (Cambridge, Mass.: Published for the Harvard-Yenching Institute by Harvard University Press, 1984), 282.
2. Bruce A. Elleman, *Modern Chinese Warfare, 1795–1989* (London: Routledge, 2001), 101.

CHAPTER 5. JAPANESE LESSONS FOR A
MODERNIZING CHINA, 1895–1937

This chapter draws on the research and analysis in Paula S. Harrell, *Asia for the Asians: China in the Lives of Five Meiji Japanese*, and Paula Harrell, *Sowing the Seeds of Change: Chinese Students, Japanese Teachers, 1895–1905*, and in particular on the following sources cited therein: Aida Tsutomu and Kawashima Naniwa, *Kawashima Naniwa Ō*; Fang Zhaoying, *Qingmo minchu yangxue xuesheng timinglu chuqi* (Preliminary listing of students abroad in the late Qing–early Republican period; *Gaikō jihō* (*Revue diplomatique*), for articles by Ariga Nagao, 1898–1920; Hattori Unokichi, *Pekin rōjō nikki* (Diary of the siege of Beijing); Konoe Atsumaro, *Konoe Atsumaro nikki* (Diary of Konoe Atsumaro); *Sanetō Bunko Mokuroku* (Catalogue of the Sanetō Collection), Hibiya Library, for trip reports by official Chinese visitors to Japan, 1898–1906; and all of Sanetō Keishū's monumental works, including *Chūgokujin Nihon ryūgaku shi* (A history of Chinese students in Japan).

Archival sources consulted include Gaimushō Gaikō Shiryōkan 外務省外交史料館 (Diplomatic Archives of the Ministry of Foreign Affairs of Japan), Tokyo, for documents on Japanese advisers in China, 1902–1915; also *Hubei xuesheng jie* 湖北學生界 (Hubei students circle), *Jiangsu* 江蘇, *Zhejiang chao* 浙江潮 (Tide of Zhejiang), and other Chinese student magazines, republished by Zhongguo guomindang dangshi shiliao bianzuan weiyuanhui 中國國民黨 黨史史料編纂委員會 (Guomindang Party Historical Materials Compilation Committee), Taipei (1968).

Douglas R. Reynolds, *China, 1898–1912*, is an excellent authoritative source, as is his work on Toa Dobun Shoin. See "Training Young China Hands: Tōa Dōbun Shoin and Its Precursors, 1886–1945," in Peter Duus, Ramon H. Myers, and Mark R. Peattie, eds., *The Japanese Informal Empire in China, 1895–1937* (Princeton, N.J.: Princeton University Press, 1989). See also Paul A. Cohen, *History in Three Keys*; Marius B. Jansen's unsurpassed *The Japanese and Sun Yat-sen*; Luke S. K. Kwong, *A Mosaic of the Hundred Days*; and Edward J. M. Rhoads, *Manchus and Han*. For the discussion of Shimoda Utako and Kano Jigoro, see Paula Harrell, "The Meiji 'New Woman' and China," in Joshua A. Fogel, ed., *Late Qing China and Meiji Japan*. I also appreciate the advice of Nagatomi Hirayama.

1. Quoted in Paula S. Harrell, *Asia for the Asians: China in the Lives of Five Meiji Japanese* (Portland, Maine: MerwinAsia, 2012), 43.
2. Ibid., 21.
3. Ibid., 51.
4. Ibid., 59.
5. Paula Harrell, *Sowing the Seeds of Change: Chinese Students, Japanese Teachers, 1895–1905* (Stanford, Calif.: Stanford University Press, 1992), 66.
6. Quoted in ibid., 45.
7. Ibid., 46.
8. Ibid., 50.
9. Ibid., 53
10. Quoted in Harrell, *Asia for the Asians*, 111.
11. Ibid., 331.
12. Quoted in Harrell, *Sowing the Seeds*, 34.

CHAPTER 6. THE COLONIZATION OF TAIWAN AND MANCHURIA, 1895–1945

1. Thomas R. Gottschang and Diana Lary, *Swallows and Settlers: The Great Migration from North China to Manchuria* (Ann Arbor: Center for Chinese Studies, University of Michigan, 2000), 2.

CHAPTER 7. POLITICAL DISORDER AND THE ROAD TO WAR, 1911–1937

1. Lu Yan, *Re-understanding Japan: Chinese Perspectives, 1895–1945* (Honolulu: Association for Asian Studies and University of Hawai'i Press, 2004), 204–205.

CHAPTER 8. THE SINO-JAPANESE WAR, 1937–1945

In this chapter I rely heavily on the work of scholars who took part in a series of conferences on the Second Sino-Japanese War held, over several years, at Harvard, on the Hawaiian island of Maui, in Hakone, and in Chongqing. I hosted the first conference in cooperation with Yang Tianshi, Yamada Tatsuo, Stephen MacKinnon, Diana Lary, Mark Peattie, Hirano Kenichi, and Hans van de Ven. Peattie played the major role in organizing the second conference, Yamada and Hirano the third conference, Yang Tianshi the fourth conference. Hans van de Ven has become the key leader in continuing the research following the conferences. These meetings brought Chinese, Japanese, and Western scholars together with the goal of achieving a comprehensive picture of the war. In analyzing the military campaigns, I have drawn particularly on the volume edited by Peattie, Drea, and Van de Ven, which is based on papers that they and other scholars, Western, Chinese, and Japanese, prepared for the second conference in our series. For the account of the Nanjing Incident, I relied heavily on the diary by Rabe, the documents collected by Timothy Brook, the work of Yang Daqing, and the volume edited by Joshua Fogel.

1. As mentioned in the preface, I use the name Beiping here, rather than Beijing, because the city was not then the capital. Many historians, including many Japanese historians, now refer to 1931, when the Japanese took over Manchuria, as the date when the Sino-Japanese War began. (The Chinese generally refer to the conflict as the War of Resistance.) I use the term "Sino-Japanese War" and identify 1937 as the year the war started because these are the designations commonly used by Western scholars.

2. Mark R. Peattie, Edward J. Drea, and Hans J. van de Ven, eds., *The Battle for China: Essays on the Military History of the Sino-Japanese War of 1937–1945* (Stanford, Calif.: Stanford University Press, 2011), 115.

3. David Askew, "Part of the Numbers Issue: Demography and Civilian Victims," in *The Nanking Atrocity, 1937–1938: Complicating the Picture*, ed. Bob Tadashi Wakabayashi, 86–114 (New York: Berghahn Books, 2007).

4. Ibid.

5. Frederic E. Wakeman Jr., *Spymaster: Dai Li and the Chinese Secret Service* (Berkeley: University of California Press, 2003).

6. Lyman Van Slyke, "The Chinese Communist Movement during the Sino-Japanese War 1937–1945," in *The Cambridge History of China*, vol. 13: *Republican China 1912–1949, Part 2*, ed. John K. Fairbank and Albert Feuerwerker (Cambridge: Cambridge University Press, 1986), 629.

7. Ibid., 620–621.

8. Parks M. Coble, *Chinese Capitalists in Japan's New Order: The Occupied Lower Yangzi, 1937–1945* (Berkeley: University of California Press, 2003), 1. There are no reliable figures, and other estimates run higher and lower.

CHAPTER 9. THE COLLAPSE OF THE JAPANESE EMPIRE AND THE COLD WAR, 1945–1972

For a chronology and summary of events during the period covered in this chapter, see the work by Kokubun, Soeya, Takahara, and Kawashima. The role of Emperor Hirohito is spelled out in the book by Herbert Bix. For an account of the Sino-Japanese Friendship Association, see Franziska Seraphim. For work on the broad context of war guilt and its management, see Barak Kushner. For the experience of Japanese repatriates, I have drawn on the work by Watt. For the Korean War, I have relied especially on the works by Chen, Cumings, Jager, Oberdorfer, and Tsui. I first visited Taiwan in 1958 and heard stories from Taiwanese acquaintances, including Dr. Lin Tsung-yi, about their experiences living under the Japanese and readjusting after the Japanese left Taiwan. When I did fieldwork on Japanese families in 1958–1960 I also heard stories from Japanese friends who had been repatriated. I have had Japanese friends, including Nakasone Yasuhiro and Okita Saburo, who played a role in this history, and I have had opportunities to talk with many of the Japanese, Chinese, and Western scholars who have worked on these topics.

1. Franziska Seraphim, *War Memory and Social Politics in Japan, 1945–2005* (Cambridge, Mass.: Harvard University Asia Center, 2006), 124–125.

2. Lori Watt, *When Empire Comes Home: Repatriation and Reintegration in Postwar Japan* (Cambridge, Mass.: Harvard University Asia Center, 2009), 1–2.

3. Amy King, *China-Japan Relations after World War II: Empire, Industry and War, 1949–1971* (Cambridge: Cambridge University Press, 2016), 61–63.

4. James P. Harrison, *The Long March to Power: A History of the Chinese Communist Party, 1921–1972* (New York: Praeger, 1972).

5. Tsukasa Takamine, *Japan's Development Aid to China: The Long-Running Foreign Policy of Engagement* (London: Routledge, 2006), 27.

6. Barak Kushner, *Men to Devils, Devils to Men: Japanese War Crimes and Chinese Justice* (Cambridge, Mass.: Harvard University Press, 2015), 8.

7. Chak Wing David Tsui, *China's Military Intervention in Korea: Its Origin and Objectives* (Bloomington, Ind.: Trafford Publishing, 2015).

8. Don Oberdorfer, *Two Koreas: A Contemporary History* (Reading, Mass.: Addison-Wesley, 1997), 9.

9. John W. Dower, *Empire and Aftermath: Yoshida Shigeru and the Japanese Experience, 1878–1954* (Cambridge, Mass.: Council on East Asian Studies, Harvard University, 1979), 407.

10. Ibid., 403.

11. Chae-Jin Lee, *Japan Faces China: Political and Economic Relations in the Postwar Era* (Baltimore: Johns Hopkins University Press, 1976), 79.

12. Mayumi Itoh, *Pioneers of Sino-Japanese Relations: Liao and Takasaki* (New York: Palgrave Macmillan, 2012), 101–103.

CHAPTER 10. WORKING TOGETHER, 1972–1992

1. Pei Hua 裴华, *ZhongRi waijiao fengyunzhong de Deng Xiaoping* 中日外交风云中的邓小平 (Deng Xiaoping in the whirlwind of Sino-Japanese relations) (Beijing: Zhongyang wenxian chubanshe, 2002), 125.

2. Chae-Jin Lee, *China and Japan: New Economic Diplomacy* (Stanford, Calif.: Hoover Institution Press, 1984), 19.

3. Ibid., 140–141.

4. Tsukasa Takamine, *Japan's Development Aid to China: The Long-Running Foreign Policy of Engagement* (London: Routledge, 2006), 5–6.

5. Ryosei Kokubun, "The Politics of Foreign Economic Policy-Making in China: The Case of Plant Cancellations with Japan," *China Quarterly*, no. 105 (March 1986): 19–44; here, 34.

6. Japanese government polling, reported by Takahara Akio, in Ezra F. Vogel, Yuan Ming, and Akihiko Tanaka, eds., *The Age of Uncertainty: The U.S.-China-Japan Triangle from Tiananmen (1989) to 9/11 (2001)* (Cambridge, Mass.: Harvard University Asia Center, 2004), 256.

CHAPTER 11. THE DETERIORATION OF SINO-JAPANESE RELATIONS, 1992–2018

I am indebted to many scholars for their histories of Sino-Japanese relations since 1972, including Tom Berger, Richard Bush, June Dreyer, Peter Dutton, Taylor Fravel, Iriye Akira, Lam Peng Er, Richard McGregor, Giulio Pugliese and Aurelio Insisa, James Reilly, Caroline Rose, Franziska Seraphim, Sheila Smith, Ming Wan, Jessica Weiss, Yang Daqing, and the scholars who contributed to the conferences and volumes edited by Yuan Ming, Tanaka Akihiko, and myself. I am also indebted to many individuals with whom I have spoken about these issues. Among the Japanese are the late Kato Koichi, the late Eto Shinkichi, and Akimoto Satohiro, Anami Ginny, Anami Koreshige, Fukuda Yasuo, Hirano Kenichiro, Iokibe Makoto, Isobe Koichi, Katayama Kazuyuki, Kato Yoshikazu, Kawashima Shin, Kitaoka Shinichi, Kojima Kazuko, Kokubun Ryosei, Michii Rokuichiro, Minemura Kenji, Miyamoto Yuji, Mori Kazuko, Niwa Uichiro, Ouchi Hiroshi, Seguchi Kiyoyuki, Soeya Yoshihide, Suzuki Michihiko, Takahara Akio, Tanino Sakutaro, Togo Kazuhiko, Yamada Tatsuo, and Yokoi Yutaka. I am indebted to Masuo Chisako for her advice and for her continuing help in guiding all aspects of my work in Japan.

I have had many conversations with Li Tingjiang, professor at Chuo University, who also helped me arrange many interviews with both Japanese and Chinese scholars. Wu Huaizhong, of the Japan Research Center, Chinese Academy of Social Sciences, spent several months helping me understand Chinese perspectives. Among the Chinese who helped increase my understanding about these issues are Cheng Yonghua, Cheng Zhongyuan, Bob Ching, Chung Yen-lin, Cui Tiankai, the late He Fang, Li Rui, Li Wei, Ma Licheng, Ren Yi, Wang Jisi, Wang Yi, Wu Xinbo, Yuan Ming, Zhang Baijia, Zhang Tuosheng, Zhang Yunling, and Zhu Jiamu. Until he died suddenly in late 2018, I was greatly assisted in my work by my long-time research assistant, Dou Xinyuan. Among the Americans with whom I have discussed Sino-Japanese relations are Thomas Berger, Richard Bush, Gerald Curtis, Andrew Gordon, Robert Hoppins, Mike Mochizuki, Greg Noble, William Overholt, Douglas Paal, Susan Pharr, Richard Samuels, Joseph Schmelzeis, Franziska Seraphim, Michael Swaine, and Daqing Yang. I appreciate the advice of Todd Hall on both this chapter and Chapter 12.

1. I had the privilege of being Kato Koichi's master's thesis adviser when he was studying at Harvard University and meeting with him from time to time after he became a member of the Diet.
2. Bruce Stokes, "Hostile Neighbors: China vs. Japan," Pew Research Center: Global Attitudes and Trends, September 13, 2016, www.pewglobal.org/2016/09 /13/hostile-neighbors-china-vs-japan/.
3. Yukio Okamoto, "Journey through U.S.-Japan Relations," unpublished manuscript, 2018.
4. The three additional countries in ASEAN Plus 3 are China, Japan, and the Republic of Korea.
5. Justin McCurry, "Koizumi's Final Shrine Trip Draws Protests," *Guardian*, August 15, 2006, www.theguardian.com/world/2006/aug/15/japan.justinmccurry.
6. Sheila A. Smith, *Intimate Rivals: Japanese Domestic Politics and a Rising China* (New York: Columbia University Press, 2014), 229.
7. Tanino Sakutaro 谷野作太郎, *Chukoku Gaiko Hiwa: Aru China Hando no kaisou* 中国外交秘話: 實藤惠秀回想 (The secrets of China policy: Recollections of a China hand) (Tokyo: Toyo Keizai Shinbunsha, 2017), 315.

CHAPTER 12. FACING THE NEW ERA

1. Chae-Jin Lee, *Japan Faces China: Political and Economic Relations in the Postwar Era* (Baltimore: Johns Hopkins University Press, 1976), 144.
2. Ibid., 79.

Sources and Further Reading

CHAPTER I. CHINESE CONTRIBUTIONS TO
JAPANESE CIVILIZATION, 600–838

Asakawa, Kan'ichi. *The Early Institutional Life of Japan: A Study in the Reform of 645 A.D.* 2nd ed. New York: Paragon Book Reprint, 1963.

Barnes, Gina L. *Archaeology of East Asia: The Rise of Civilization in China, Korea and Japan.* Philadelphia: Oxbow Books, 2015.

Batten, Bruce L. *Gateway to Japan: Hakata in War and Peace, 500–1300.* Honolulu: University of Hawai'i Press, 2006.

Best, Jonathan W. "The Transition and Transformation of Early Buddhist Culture in Korea and Japan." In *Transmitting the Forms of Divinity: Early Buddhist Art from Korea and Japan,* by Washizuka Hiromitsu, Park Youngbok, and Kang Woo-bang. Edited by Naomi Noble Richard, 18–45. New York: Japan Society, 2003.

Borgen, Robert. *Sugawara no Michizane and the Early Heian Court.* Cambridge, Mass.: Council on East Asian Studies, Harvard University, 1986.

Brown, Delmar M., ed. *The Cambridge History of Japan: Volume 1, Ancient Japan.* Cambridge: Cambridge University Press, 1993.

Como, Michael I. *Shotoku: Ethnicity, Ritual, and Violence in the Japanese Buddhist Tradition.* Oxford: Oxford University Press, 2008.

Deal, William E., and Brian Rupert. *A Cultural History of Japanese Buddhism.* Chichester, West Sussex: Wiley Blackwell, 2015.

Duthie, Torquil. *Man'yoshū and the Imperial Imagination in Early Japan.* Leiden: Brill, 2014.

Fairbank, John K., Edwin O. Reischauer, and Albert M. Craig. *East Asia: Tradition and Transformation.* Rev. ed. Boston: Houghton Mifflin, 1989.

Farris, William Wayne. *Heavenly Warriors: Evolution of Japan's Military, 500–1300.* Cambridge, Mass.: Council on East Asian Studies, Harvard University Press, 1992.

Hall, John W., and Jeffrey P. Maas, eds. *Medieval Japan: Essays in Institutional History.* New Haven, Conn.: Yale University Press, 1974.

Hardacre, Helen. *Shinto: A History.* Oxford: Oxford University Press, 2016.

Holcombe, Charles. *The Genesis of East Asia, 221 B.C.–A.D. 907.* Honolulu: Association for Asian Studies and University of Hawai'i Press, 2001.

Liu, Lydia H. *Translingual Practice: Literature, National Culture, and Translated Modernity—China, 1900–1937*. Stanford, Calif.: Stanford University Press, 1995.

Lurie, David B. *Realms of Literacy: Early Japan and the History of Writing*. Cambridge, Mass.: Harvard University Asia Center, 2011.

Miller, Richard J. *Ancient Japanese Nobility: The Kabane Ranking System*. Berkeley: University of California Press, 1974.

Mitsusada, Inoue, with Delmer M. Brown. "The Century of Reform." In *The Cambridge History of Japan: Volume 1, Ancient Japan*, edited by Delmer M. Brown, 163–220. Cambridge: Cambridge University Press, 1993.

Piggott, Joan R. *The Emergence of Japanese Kingship*. Stanford, Calif.: Stanford University Press, 1997.

Reischauer, Edwin O., trans. *Ennin's Diary: The Record of a Pilgrimage to China in Search of the Law*. New York: Ronald Press, 1955.

———. *Ennin's Travels in T'ang China*. New York: Ronald Press, 1955.

Rosenfeld, John M. *Portraits of Chogen: The Transformation of Buddhist Art in Early Medieval Japan*. Leiden: Brill, 2011.

Rossabi, Morris, ed. *China among Equals: The Middle Kingdom and Its Neighbors, 10th–14th Centuries*. Berkeley: University of California Press, 1983.

Saeki, Arikiyo. *Treatise on the People of Wa in the Chronicle of the Kingdom of Wei: The World's Earliest Written Text on Japan*. Translated by Joshua A. Fogel. Portland, Maine: MerwinAsia, 2018.

Sansom, George. *A History of Japan to 1334*. 3 vols. Stanford, Calif.: Stanford University Press, 1958–1963.

Shively, Donald H., and William H. McCullough. *The Cambridge History of Japan: Volume 2, Heian Japan*. Cambridge: Cambridge University Press, 1999.

Tsunoda, Ryūsaku, and L. Carrington Goodrich. *Japan in the Chinese Dynastic Histories: Later Han through Ming Dynasties*. South Pasadena, Calif.: P. D. and Ione Perkins, 1951.

Twitchett, Denis C., ed. *The Cambridge History of China: Volume 3, Sui and T'ang China, 589–906 AD, Part 1*. Cambridge: Cambridge University Press, 1979.

Verschuer, Charlotte von. *Across the Perilous Sea: Japanese Trade with China and Korea from the Seventh to the Sixteenth Centuries*. Translated by Kristen Lee Hunter. Ithaca, N.Y.: East Asia Program, Cornell University, 2006.

Wang Yong 王勇, ch. ed. *Lidai zhengshi Riben zhuan kaozhu, di er juan, Sui Tang juan* 历代正史日本传考注：第二卷，隋唐卷 (Japanese historical biographies, vol. 2: Sui and Tang dynasties). Shanghai: Shanghai jiaotong daxue chubanshe, 2016.

Wang Zhenping. *Ambassadors from the Islands of Immortals: China-Japan Relations in the Han-Tang Period*. Honolulu: University of Hawai'i Press, 2005.

CHAPTER 2. TRADE WITHOUT TRANSFORMATIVE
LEARNING, 838–1862

Batten, Bruce L. *To the Ends of Japan: Premodern Frontiers, Boundaries, and Interactions.* Honolulu: University of Hawai'i Press, 2003.

Berry, Mary Elizabeth. *Hideyoshi.* Cambridge, Mass.: Council on East Asian Studies, Harvard University, 1989.

Borgen, Robert. *Sugawara Michizane and the Early Heian Court.* Cambridge, Mass.: Council on East Asian Studies, Harvard University, 1986.

Dore, R. P. *Education in Tokugawa Japan.* Berkeley: University of California Press, 1965.

Eikenberry, Karl W. "The Imjin War." *Military Review* 68, no. 2 (February 1988): 74–82.

Elisonas, Jurgis [George Elison]. "The Inseparable Trinity: Japan's Relations with China and Korea." In *The Cambridge History of Japan: Volume 4, Early Modern Japan,* edited by John Whitney Hall and James L. McClain, 235–300. Cambridge: Cambridge University Press, 1991.

Fairbank, John King, ed. *The Chinese World Order: Traditional China's Foreign Relations.* Cambridge, Mass.: Harvard University Press, 1968.

Fogel, Joshua A., ed. *Crossing the Yellow Sea: Sino-Japanese Cultural Contacts, 1600–1950.* Norwalk, Conn.: Eastbridge, 2007.

———. *The Literature of Travel in the Japanese Rediscovery of China, 1862–1945.* Stanford, Calif.: Stanford University Press, 1996.

———. *Sagacious Monks and Bloodthirsty Warriors: Chinese Views of Japan in the Ming-Qing Period.* Norwalk, Conn.: Eastbridge, 2002.

Hang, Xing. "The Shogun's Chinese Partners: The Alliance between Tokugawa Japan and the Zheng Family in Seventeenth Century Maritime East Asia." *Journal of Asian Studies* 75, no. 1 (February 2016): 111–136.

Hansen, Valerie. *The Open Empire: A History of China to 1800.* 2nd ed. New York: Norton, 2015.

Ikegami, Eiko. *The Taming of the Samurai: Honorific Individualism and the Making of Modern Japan.* Cambridge, Mass.: Harvard University Press, 1995.

Innes, Robert LeRoy. "The Door Ajar: Japan's Foreign Trade in the Seventeenth Century." Ph.D. diss., University of Michigan, 1980.

Jansen, Marius B. *China in the Tokugawa World.* Cambridge, Mass.: Harvard University Press, 1992.

Kang, David C. *East Asia before the West: Five Centuries of Trade and Tribute.* New York: Columbia University Press, 2010.

Ledyard, Gari. "Confucianism and War: The Korean Security Crisis of 1598." *Journal of Korean Studies* 6 (1988–1989): 81–119.

Li, Yiwen. "Networks of Profit and Faith: Spanning the Sea of Japan and the East China Sea, 838–1403." Ph.D. diss., Yale University, 2017.

Nakai, Kate Wildman. "Naturalization of Confucianism in Tokugawa Japan: The Problem of Sinocentrism." *Harvard Journal of Asiatic Studies* 40, no. 1 (June 1980): 157–199.

Ōba, Osamu. *Books and Boats: Sino-Japanese Relations in the Seventeenth and Eighteenth Centuries.* Translated by Joshua A. Fogel. Portland, Maine: MerwinAsia, 2012.

Rawski, Evelyn S. *Early Modern China and Northeast Asia: Cross-Border Perspectives.* Cambridge: Cambridge University Press, 2015.

Reischauer, Edwin O., and John King Fairbank. *East Asia: The Great Tradition.* Boston: Houghton Mifflin, 1960.

Rossabi, Morris, ed. *China among Equals: The Middle Kingdom and Its Neighbors, 10th–14th Centuries.* Berkeley: University of California Press, 1983.

Satō Saburō 佐藤三郎. *Kindai Nitchū kōshōshi no kenkyū* 近代日中交渉史研究 (Research on the history of Sino-Japanese negotiations in the modern era). Tokyo: Yoshikawa Kōbunkan, 1984.

Segal, Ethan Isaac. *Coins, Trade, and the State: Economic Growth in Early Medieval Japan.* Cambridge, Mass.: Harvard University Asia Center, 2111.

Swope, Kenneth. "Crouching Tigers, Secret Weapons: Military Technology Employed during the Sino-Japanese-Korean War, 1592–1598." *Journal of Military History* 69, no. 1 (January 2005): 11–41.

Szonyi, Michael. *The Art of Being Governed: Everyday Politics in Late Imperial China.* Princeton, N.J.: Princeton University Press, 2017.

Toby, Ronald P. *State and Diplomacy in Early Modern Japan: Asia in the Development of the Tokugawa Bakufu.* Princeton, N.J.: Princeton University Press, 1984.

Turnbull, Stephen. *Samurai Invasion: Japan's Korea War, 1592–98.* London: Cassell & Co., 2002.

Verschuer, Charlotte von. *Across the Perilous Sea: Japanese Trade with China and Korea from the Seventh to the Sixteenth Centuries.* Translated by Kristen Lee Hunter. Ithaca, N.Y.: East Asia Program, Cornell University, 2006.

Von Glahn, Richard. *The Economic History of China: From Antiquity to the Nineteenth Century.* Cambridge: Cambridge University Press, 2016.

———. "The Ningbo-Hakata Merchant Network and the Reorientation of East Asian Maritime Trade, 1150–1350." *Harvard Journal of Asiatic Studies* 74, no. 2 (2014): 249–279.

Wu, Jiang. *Leaving for the Rising Sun: Zen Master Yinyuan and the Authenticity Crisis in Early Modern East Asia.* Oxford: Oxford University Press, 2014.

CHAPTER 3. RESPONDING TO WESTERN CHALLENGES AND
REOPENING RELATIONS, 1839–1882

Bu Ping 步平 and Kitaoka Shinichi 北冈伸一, eds. *ZhongRi gongtong lishi yanjiu baogao* 中日共同历史研究报告 (Sino-Japanese joint history research report). Beijing: Shehui kexue wenxian chubanshe, 2014.

Chen, Frederick Foo. *The Opening of Korea, 1876–1885*. N.p.: Kaun Tang International Publications, 2008.

Chu, Samuel C., and Kwang-Ching Liu, eds. *Li Hung-chang and China's Early Modernization*. Armonk, N.Y.: M. E. Sharpe, 1994.

Conroy, Hilary. *The Japanese Seizure of Korea, 1868–1910: A Study of Realism and Idealism in International Relations*. Philadelphia: University of Pennsylvania Press, 1960.

Day, Jenny Huangfu. *Qing Travelers to the Far West: Diplomacy and Information Order in Late Imperial China*. Cambridge: Cambridge University Press, 2018.

Fairbank, John K., ed. *The Cambridge History of China: Volume 10, Late Ch'ing, 1800–1911, Part 1*. Cambridge: Cambridge University Press, 1978.

Fogel, Joshua A. *Between China and Japan: The Writings of Joshua Fogel*. Leiden: Brill, 2015.

———. *The Cultural Dimension of Sino-Japanese Relations: Essays on the Nineteenth and Twentieth Centuries*. Armonk, N.Y.: M. E. Sharpe, 1995.

———, ed. *Late Qing China and Meiji Japan: Political and Cultural Aspects*. Norwalk, Conn.: Eastbridge, 2004.

———. *The Literature of Travel in the Japanese Rediscovery of China, 1862–1945*. Stanford, Calif.: Stanford University Press, 1996.

———. *Maiden Voyage: The Senzaimaru and the Creation of Modern Sino-Japanese Relations*. Berkeley: University of California Press, 2014.

———. *Politics and Sinology: The Case of Naito Konan, 1866–1934*. Cambridge, Mass.: Harvard University Press, 1984.

Iriye, Akira, ed. *The Chinese and the Japanese: Essays in Political and Cultural Interactions*. Princeton, N.J.: Princeton University Press, 1980.

Jansen, Marius B. *China in the Tokugawa World*. Cambridge, Mass.: Harvard University Press, 1992.

———. *Japan and China: From War to Peace, 1894–1972*. Chicago: Rand McNally College Publishing, 1975.

———. *The Japanese and Sun Yat-sen*. Stanford, Calif.: Stanford University Press, 1970.

Kamachi, Noriko. *Reform in China: Huang Tsun-hsien and the Japanese Model*. Cambridge, Mass.: Council on East Asian Studies, Harvard University, 1981.

Keene, Donald. *Emperor of Japan: Meiji and His World, 1852–1912*. New York: Columbia University Press, 2002.

Kindai Nitchū kenkeishi nenpyō: 1799–1949 近代日中関係史年表：1799–1949 (Chronology on the history of modern Sino-Japanese relations: 1799–1949). Edited by the Editorial Committee for the Chronology on the History of Modern Sino-Japanese Relations. Tokyo: Iwanami Shoten, 2006.

Kume, Kunitake. *Japan Rising: The Iwakura Embassy to the USA and Europe, 1871–1873*. Cambridge: Cambridge University Press, 2009.

Kuo Ting-yee, comp., and James W. Morley, ed. *Sino-Japanese Relations, 1862–1927: A Checklist of the Chinese Foreign Ministry Archives*. New York: East Asian Institute, Columbia University, 1965.

Larsen, Kirk W. *Tradition, Treaties, and Trade: Qing Imperialism and Choson Korea, 1850–1910*. Cambridge, Mass.: Harvard University Asia Center, 2008.

Miyoshi, Masao. *As We Saw Them: The First Japanese Embassy to the United States (1860)*. Berkeley: University of California Press, 1979.

Morley, James William, ed. *Japan's Foreign Policy, 1868–1941: A Research Guide*. New York: Columbia University Press, 1974. [See especially chapter 5 by Eto Shinkichi, "Japan's Policies toward China."]

Okazaki, Hisahiko. *From Uraga to San Francisco: A Century of Japanese Diplomacy, 1853–1952*. Tokyo: Japan Echo, 2007.

Reynolds, Douglas, with Carol T. Reynolds. *East Meets East: Chinese Discover the Modern World in Japan, 1854–1898: A Window on the Intellectual and Social Transformation of Modern China*. Ann Arbor, Mich.: Association for Asian Studies, 2014.

Rudolph, Jennifer. *Negotiated Power in Late Imperial China: The Zongli Yamen and the Politics of Reform*. Ithaca, N.Y.: East Asia Program, Cornell University, 2008.

Van de Ven, Hans J. *Breaking with the Past: The Maritime Customs Service and the Global Origins of Modernity in China*. New York: Columbia University Press, 2014.

Wright, Mary C. *The Last Stand of Chinese Conservatism: The T'ung Chih Restoration, 1862–1874*. Stanford, Calif.: Stanford University Press, 1957.

Yang, Daqing et al., eds. *Toward a History beyond Borders: Contentious Issues in Sino-Japanese Relations*. Cambridge, Mass.: Harvard University Asia Center, 2012.

CHAPTER 4. RIVALRY IN KOREA AND THE
SINO-JAPANESE WAR, 1882–1895

Bu Ping 步平 and Kitaoka Shinichi 北冈伸一, eds. *ZhongRi gongtong lishi yanjiu baogao* 中日共同历史研究报告 (Sino-Japanese joint history research report). Beijing: Shehui kexue wenxian chubanshe, 2014.

Chandra, Vipan. *Imperialism, Resistance, and Reform in Late Nineteenth-Century Korea: Enlightenment and the Independence Club*. Berkeley: Institute of East Asian Studies, University of California, 1988.

Chien, Frederick Foo. *The Opening of Korea: A Study of Chinese Diplomacy, 1876–1885.* N.p.: Kaun Tang International Publications, 2008.

Ch'oe, Yŏng-ho. "The Kapsin Coup of 1884: A Reassessment." *Korean Studies* 6 (1982): 105–124.

Chu, Samuel C., and Kwang-Ching Liu. *Li Hung-chang and China's Early Modernization.* Armonk, N.Y.: M. E. Sharpe, 1994.

Conroy, Hilary. *The Japanese Seizure of Korea, 1868–1910: A Study of Realism and Idealism in International Relations.* Philadelphia: University of Pennsylvania Press, 1960.

Cumings, Bruce. *Korea's Place in the Sun: A Modern History.* New York: W. W. Norton, 1997.

Day, Jenny Huangfu. *Qing Travelers to the Far West: Diplomacy and Information Order in Late Imperial China.* Cambridge: Cambridge University Press, 2018.

Deuchler, Martina. *Confucian Gentlemen and Barbarian Envoys: The Opening of Korea, 1875–1885.* Seattle: University of Washington Press, 1977.

Dudden, Alexis. *Japan's Colonization of Korea: Discourse and Power.* Honolulu: University of Hawai'i Press, 2005.

Duus, Peter. *The Abacus and the Sword: The Japanese Penetration of Korea, 1895–1910.* Berkeley: University of California Press, 1995.

Duus, Peter, Ramon H. Myers, and Mark R. Peattie, eds. *The Japanese Informal Empire in China, 1895–1937.* Princeton, N.J.: Princeton University Press, 1989.

Eckert, Carter J., et al. *Korea Old and New: A History.* Cambridge, Mass.: Korea Institute, Harvard University, 1990.

Elleman, Bruce A. *Modern Chinese Warfare, 1795–1989.* London: Routledge, 2001.

Evans, David C., and Mark R. Peattie. *Kaigun: Strategy, Tactics, and Technology in the Imperial Japanese Navy, 1887–1941.* Annapolis, Md.: Naval Institute Press, 1997.

Fogel, Joshua A. *The Literature of Travel in the Japanese Rediscovery of China, 1862–1945.* Stanford, Calif.: Stanford University Press, 1996.

Fukuzawa, Yukichi. *The Autobiography of Fukuzawa Yukichi.* New York: Columbia University Press, 2007.

Hackett, Roger F. *Yamagata Aritomo in the Rise of Modern Japan, 1838–1922.* Cambridge, Mass.: Harvard University Press, 1971.

Iriye, Akira. *China and Japan in the Global Setting.* Cambridge, Mass.: Harvard University Press, 1992.

———, ed. *The Chinese and the Japanese: Essays in Political and Cultural Interactions.* Princeton, N.J.: Princeton University Press, 1980.

Jansen, Marius B., ed. *The Cambridge History of Japan: Volume 5, The Nineteenth Century.* Cambridge: Cambridge University Press, 1989.

———. *Japan and China: From War to Peace, 1894–1972.* Chicago: Rand McNally College Publishing, 1975.

Jaundrill, D. Colin. *Samurai to Soldier: Remaking Military Service in Nineteenth-Century Japan.* Ithaca, N.Y.: Cornell University Press, 2016.

Kallander, George L. *Salvation through Dissent: Tonghak Heterodoxy and Early Modern Korea.* Honolulu: University of Hawai'i Press, 2013.

Kim, Key-Hiuk. *The Last Phase of the East Asian World Order: Korea, Japan, and the Chinese Empire, 1860–1882.* Berkeley: University of California Press, 1980.

Larsen, Kirk W. *Tradition, Treaties, and Trade: Qing Imperialism and Choson Korea, 1850–1910.* Cambridge, Mass.: Harvard University Asia Center, 2008.

Mutsu, Munemitsu. *Kenkenroku: A Diplomatic Record of the Sino-Japanese War, 1894–95.* Edited and translated by Gordon Mark Berger. Princeton, N.J.: Princeton University Press, 1982.

Nakae, Chomin. *Discourse by Three Drunkards on Government.* New York: Weatherhill, 1984.

Okazaki, Hisahiko. *From Uraga to San Francisco: A Century of Japanese Diplomacy, 1853–1952.* Tokyo: Japan Echo, 2007.

Paine, S. C. M. *The Sino-Japanese War of 1894–1895: Perceptions, Power, and Primacy.* Cambridge: Cambridge University Press, 2003.

Palais, James B. *Politics and Policy in Traditional Korea.* Cambridge, Mass.: Harvard University Press, 1975.

Reynolds, Douglas R., with Carol T. Reynolds. *East Meets East: Chinese Discover the Modern World in Japan, 1854–1898: A Window on the Intellectual and Social Transformation of Modern China.* Ann Arbor, Mich.: Association for Asian Studies, 2014.

Samuels, Richard J. *"Rich Nation, Strong Army": National Security and the Technological Transformation of Japan.* Ithaca, N.Y.: Cornell University Press, 1994.

Schmid, Andre. *Korea between Empires, 1895–1919.* New York: Columbia University Press, 2002.

Stephan, John J. *The Russian Far East: A History.* Stanford, Calif.: Stanford University Press, 1994.

CHAPTER 5. JAPANESE LESSONS FOR A MODERNIZING CHINA, 1895–1937

Aida Tsutomu 會田勉 and Kawashima Naniwa 川島浪速. *Kawashima Naniwa Ō* 川島浪速翁 (The elderly Mr. Kawashima Naniwa). Tokyo: Bunsuikaku, 1936.

Akimoto, Satohiro. "The Development Corporation in Japan's Early Modernization," Ph.D. thesis, Harvard University, 1994.

Cohen, Paul A. *History in Three Keys: The Boxers as Event, Experience, and Myth.* New York: Columbia University Press, 1997.

Fang Zhaoying 房兆楹. *Qingmo minchu yangxue xuesheng timinglu chuji* 清末民初洋學學生題名錄初輯 (Preliminary listing of students abroad in the late Qing–early Republican period). Taipei: Academia Sinica, 1962.

Gaikō jihō (Revue diplomatique) 外交時報. Tokyo: Gaikōjihōsha, 1898–1986. [Published irregularly 1898–1906; semimonthly 1912–March 1944.]

Harrell, Paula S. *Asia for the Asians: China in the Lives of Five Meiji Japanese*. Portland, Maine: MerwinAsia, 2012.

———. "The Meiji 'New Woman' and China." In *Late Qing China and Meiji Japan: Political and Cultural Aspects*, edited by Joshua A. Fogel. Norwalk, Conn.: Eastbridge, 2004.

———. *Sowing the Seeds of Change: Chinese Students, Japanese Teachers, 1895–1905*. Stanford, Calif.: Stanford University Press, 1992.

Hattori Unokichi 服部宇之吉. *Pekin rōjō nikki* 北京籠城日記 (Diary of the siege of Beijing). Tokyo: Heibonsha, 1965.

Jansen, Marius B. *The Japanese and Sun Yat-sen*. Stanford, Calif.: Stanford University Press, 1970.

Konoe Atsumaro 近衛篤麿. *Konoe Atsumaro nikki* 近衛篤麿日記 (Diary of Konoe Atsumaro). 5 vols. plus supplement. Tokyo: Kajima kenkyujo shuppankai, 1968.

Kwong, Luke S. K. *A Mosaic of the Hundred Days: Personalities, Politics, and Ideas of 1898*. Cambridge, Mass.: Council on East Asian Studies, Harvard University, 1984.

Reynolds, Douglas R. *China, 1898–1912: The Xinzheng Revolution and Japan*. Cambridge, Mass.: Council on East Asian Studies, Harvard University, 1993.

Rhoads, Edward J. M. *Manchus and Han: Ethnic Relations and Political Power in Late Qing and Early Republican China, 1861–1928*. Seattle: University of Washington Press, 2000.

Sanetō Bunko Mokuroku 実藤文庫目録 (Catalogue of the Sanetō Collection [in Chinese]), Hibiya Library. Tokyo: Hibiya Library, 1966.

Sanetō Keishū 實藤惠秀. *Chūgokujin Nihon ryūgaku shi* 中國人日本留学史 (A history of Chinese students in Japan). Tokyo: Kuroshio shuppan, 1960.

CHAPTER 6. THE COLONIZATION OF TAIWAN AND MANCHURIA, 1895–1945

Coble, Parks M. *Facing Japan: Chinese Politics and Japanese Imperialism, 1931–1937*. Cambridge, Mass.: Council on East Asian Studies, Harvard University, 1991.

Croizier, Ralph C. *Koxinga and Chinese Nationalism: History, Myth, and the Hero*. Cambridge, Mass.: East Asian Research Center, Harvard University, 1977.

Culver, Annika A. *Glorify the Empire: Japanese Avant-Garde Propaganda in Manchuria*. Vancouver: University of British Columbia Press, 2013.

Duara, Prasenjit. *Sovereignty and Authenticity: Manchukuo and the East Asian Modern*. Lanham, Md.: Rowman & Littlefield, 2003.

Duus, Peter, Ramon Hawley Myers, and Mark R. Peattie, eds. *The Japanese Informal Empire in China, 1895–1937*. Princeton, N.J.: Princeton University Press, 1989.

————. *The Japanese Wartime Empire, 1931–1945*. Princeton, N.J.: Princeton University Press, 1996.

Fairbank, John K., and Kwang-Ching Liu, eds. *The Cambridge History of China: Volume 11, Late Ch'ing, 1800–1911, Part 2*. Cambridge: Cambridge University Press, 1980.

Gottschang, Thomas R., and Diana Lary. *Swallows and Settlers: The Great Migration from North China to Manchuria*. Ann Arbor: Center for Chinese Studies, University of Michigan, 2000.

Iguchi, Haruo. *Unfinished Business: Ayukawa Yoshisuke and U.S.-Japan Relations, 1937–1953*. Cambridge, Mass.: Harvard University Asia Center, 2003.

Ito, Takeo. *Life along the South Manchurian Railway: The Memoirs of Ito Takeo*. Translated by Joshua A. Fogel. Armonk, N.Y.: M. E. Sharpe, 1988.

Jiang Yaohui 蒋耀挥. *Dalian kaibu jianshi* 大连开埠建市 (Dalian's Kailuan city). Dalian: Dalian chubanshe, 2013.

Jukes, Geoffrey. *The Russo-Japanese War, 1904–1905*. Oxford: Osprey Publishing, 2002.

Lin, Tsung-Yi. *An Introduction to 2-28 Tragedy in Taiwan: For World Citizens*. Taipei: Taiwan Renaissance Foundation Press, 1998.

Matsusaka, Yoshihisa Tak. *The Making of Japanese Manchuria, 1904–1932*. Cambridge, Mass.: Harvard University Asia Center, 2001.

Mitter, Rana. *The Manchurian Myth: Nationalism, Resistance, and Collaboration in Modern China*. Berkeley: University of California Press, 2000.

Myers, Ramon Hawley, and Mark R. Peattie, eds. *The Japanese Colonial Empire, 1895–1945*. Princeton, N.J.: Princeton University Press, 1984.

O'Dwyer, Emer. *Significant Soil: Settler Colonialism and Japan's Urban Empire in Manchuria*. Cambridge, Mass.: Harvard University Asia Center, 2015.

Ogata, Sadako N. *Defiance in Manchuria: The Making of Japanese Foreign Policy, 1931–32*. Berkeley: University of California Press, 1964.

Roberts, John G. *Mitsui: Three Centuries of Japanese Business*. New York: Weatherhill, 1973.

Smith, Norman. *Intoxicating Manchuria: Alcohol, Opium, and Culture in China's Northeast*. Vancouver: University of British Columbia Press, 2012.

Tsurumi, E. Patricia. *Japanese Colonial Education in Taiwan, 1895–1945*. Cambridge, Mass.: Harvard University Press, 1977.

Watt, Lori. *When Empire Comes Home: Repatriation and Reintegration in Postwar Japan*. Cambridge, Mass.: Harvard University Asia Center, 2009.

Wu, Bohao. "Beyond Thanotourism and *Lieu de Memoire*: A Critical Review of the Commemoration of Japanese Immigrants at Different Memorial Sites." Unpublished paper, 2018.

Yang, Daqing. *Technology of Empire: Telecommunications and Japanese Expansion in Asia, 1883–1945*. Cambridge, Mass.: Harvard University Asia Center, 2010.

Young, Louise. *Japan's Total Empire: Manchuria and the Culture of Wartime Imperialism*. Berkeley: University of California Press, 1998.

CHAPTER 7. POLITICAL DISORDER AND THE
ROAD TO WAR, 1911–1937

Akita, George. *Foundations of Constitutional Government in Modern Japan, 1868–1900*. Cambridge, Mass.: Harvard University Press, 1967.

Asada, Sadao. *From Mahan to Pearl Harbor: The Imperial Japanese Navy and the United States*. Annapolis, Md.: Naval Institute Press, 2006.

Bamba, Nobuya. *Japanese Diplomacy in a Dilemma: New Light on Japan's China Policy, 1924–1929*. Vancouver: University of British Columbia Press, 1971.

Benedict, Ruth. *The Chrysanthemum and the Sword: Patterns of Japanese Culture*. With a foreword by Ezra F. Vogel. Boston: Houghton Mifflin, 1989.

Coble, Parks M. *Facing Japan: Chinese Politics and Japanese Imperialism, 1931–1937*. Cambridge, Mass.: Council on East Asian Studies, Harvard University, 1991.

Crowley, James. *Japan's Thrust for Autonomy*. Princeton, N.J.: Princeton University Press, 1966.

Drea, Edward J. *Japan's Imperial Army: Its Rise and Fall, 1853–1945*. Lawrence: University Press of Kansas, 2009.

Duus, Peter. *Party Rivalry and Political Change in Taishō Japan*. Cambridge, Mass.: Harvard University Press, 1968.

Embree, John. *Suye Mura: A Japanese Village*. Chicago: University of Chicago Press, 1939.

Fairbank, John K., ed. *The Cambridge History of China: Volume 12, Republican China, 1912–1949*. Cambridge: Cambridge University Press, 1983.

Fogel, Joshua A. "'Shanghai-Japan': The Japanese Residents' Association of Shanghai." *Journal of Asian Studies* 59, no. 4 (November 2000): 927–950.

Gifford, Sydney. *Japan among the Powers, 1890–1990*. New Haven, Conn.: Yale University Press, 1994.

Gluck, Carol. *Japan's Modern Myths: Ideology in the Late Meiji Period*. Princeton, N.J.: Princeton University Press, 1985.

Goto-Shibata, Harumi. *Japan and Britain in Shanghai, 1925–31*. New York: St. Martin's Press, 1995.

Havens, Thomas R. H. *Farm and Nation in Modern Japan: Agrarian Nationalism, 1870–1940*. Princeton, N.J.: Princeton University Press, 1940.

Humphreys, Leonard. *The Way of the Heavenly Sword: The Japanese Army in the 1920's*. Stanford, Calif.: Stanford University Press, 1995.

Hunsberger, Warren S., ed. *Japan's Quest: The Search for International Role, Recognition, and Respect*. Armonk, N.Y.: M. E. Sharpe, 1997.

Iriye, Akira. *After Imperialism: The Search for a New Order in the Far East, 1921–1931.* Cambridge, Mass.: Harvard University Press, 1965.

———, ed. *The Chinese and the Japanese: Essays in Political and Cultural Interactions.* Princeton, N.J.: Princeton University Press, 1980.

Jansen, Marius B. *Japan and China: From War to Peace, 1894–1972.* Chicago: Rand McNally College Publishing, 1975.

———. *The Japanese and Sun Yat-sen.* Stanford, Calif.: Stanford University Press, 1970.

Jordan, Donald A. *China's Trial by Fire: The Shanghai War of 1932.* Ann Arbor: University of Michigan Press, 2001.

———. *Chinese Boycotts versus Japanese Bombs: The Failure of China's "Revolutionary Diplomacy," 1931–32.* Ann Arbor: University of Michigan Press, 1991.

Keene, Donald. *Emperor of Japan: Meiji and His World, 1852–1912.* New York: Columbia University Press, 2002.

Lary, Diana. *Warlord Soldiers: Chinese Common Soldiers, 1911–1937.* Cambridge: Cambridge University Press, 2010.

Maruyama, Masao. *Thought and Behaviour in Modern Japanese Politics.* London: Oxford University Press, 1963.

Morris, Ivan. *The Nobility of Failure: Tragic Heroes in the History of Japan.* New York: Holt, Rinehart and Winston, 1975.

Najita, Tetsuo. *Hara Kei in the Politics of Compromise: 1905–1915.* Cambridge, Mass.: Harvard University Press, 1967.

Orbach, Danny. *Curse on This Country: The Rebellious Army of Imperial Japan.* Ithaca, N.Y.: Cornell University Press, 2017.

Pollard, Robert T. *China's Foreign Relations, 1917–1931.* New York: Macmillan, 1933.

Scalapino, Robert. *Democracy and the Party Movement in Prewar Japan.* Berkeley: University of California Press, 1953.

Sheridan, James E. *China in Disintegration: The Republican Era in Chinese History, 1912–1949.* New York: Free Press, 1975.

Smethurst, Richard J. *A Social Basis for Prewar Japanese Militarism: The Army and the Rural Community.* Berkeley: University of California Press, 1974.

Takii, Kazuhiro. *The Meiji Constitution: The Japanese Experience of the West and the Shaping of the Modern State.* Tokyo: International House of Japan, 2007.

Tawney, R. H. *A Memorandum on Agriculture and Industry in China.* Honolulu: Institute of Pacific Relations, 1931. [Report commissioned by the Institute of Pacific Relations for the Shanghai Conference in 1931.]

Taylor, Jay. *The Generalissimo: Chiang Kai-shek and the Struggle for Modern China.* Cambridge, Mass.: Belknap Press of Harvard University Press, 2009.

Utsumi Aiko 内海愛子. *Nihongun no horyo seisaku* 日本軍の捕虜政策 (The Japanese military policy toward prisoners). Tokyo: Aoki Shoten, 2005.

Wang Yuan 王元. *Chūka Minkoku no kenryoku kōzō ni okeru kikoku ryūgakusei no ichizuke: Nankin Seifu (1928–1949-nen) o chūshin to shite* 中華民国の権力構造における帰国留学生の位置づけ (The position of returnee students in the power structure of the Republic of China). Tokyo: Hakuteisha, 2010.

White, James W., Michio Umegaki, and Thomas R. H. Havens, eds. *The Ambivalence of Nationalism: Modern Japan between East and West.* Lanham, Md.: University Press of America, 1990.

Wray, William D. *Mitsubishi and the N.Y.K., 1870–1914.* Cambridge, Mass.: Council on East Asian Studies, Harvard University, 1984.

Yamaguchi Ichiro 山口一郎. *Kindai Chugoku tainichikan no Kenkyū* 近代中国対日観の研究、アジア経済研究所 (Research on Chinese attitudes toward the Japanese during the modern period). Tokyo: Ajia Keizai Kenkyūjo shuppan butsu, 1970.

Young, Earnest. "Politics in the Aftermath of Revolution: The Era of Yuan Shih-k'ai, 1912–16." In *The Cambridge History of China: Volume 12, Republican China, 1912–1949, Part I,* edited by John K. Fairbank, 208–255. Cambridge: Cambridge University Press, 1983.

CHAPTER 8. THE SINO-JAPANESE WAR, 1937–1945

Benton, Gregor. *New Fourth Army: Communist Resistance along the Yangtze and the Huai, 1938–1841.* Berkeley: University of California Press, 1999.

Bianco, Lucien. *Origins of the Chinese Revolution, 1915–1949.* Stanford, Calif.: Stanford University Press, 1971.

Brook, Timothy. *Collaboration: Japanese Agents and Local Elites in Wartime China.* Cambridge, Mass.: Harvard University Press, 2005.

———. *Documents on the Rape of Nanking.* Ann Arbor: University of Michigan Press, 1999.

Coble, Parks M. *Chinese Capitalists in Japan's New Order: The Occupied Lower Yangzi, 1937–1945.* Berkeley: University of California Press, 2003.

Dower, John W. *War without Mercy: Race and Power in the Pacific War.* New York: Pantheon Books, 1986.

Embree, John F. *The Japanese Nation: A Social Survey.* New York: Farrar & Rinehart, 1945.

———. *Suye Mura: A Japanese Village.* Chicago: University of Chicago Press, 1939.

Fairbank, John K., and Albert Feuerworker, eds. *The Cambridge History of China: Volume 13, Republican China 1912–1949, Part 2.* Cambridge: Cambridge University Press, 1986. [See especially chapters 10–12.]

Feng Chongyi, and David S. G. Goodman, eds. *North China at War: The Social Ecology of Revolution, 1937–1945.* Lanham, Md.: Rowman & Littlefield, 2000.

Fogel, Joshua A. *Nakae Ushikichi in China: The Mourning of Spirit*. Cambridge, Mass.: Council on East Asian Studies, Harvard University, 1989.

———, ed. *The Nanjing Massacre in History and Historiography*. Berkeley: University of California Press, 2000.

Hata Ikuhiko. 秦郁彦 著. *Nankin Jihen* 南京事件 (The Nanjing Incident). Tokyo: Chuo Koron, 1986.

Henriot, Christian, and Wen-Hsin Yeh, eds. *In the Shadow of the Rising Sun: Shanghai under Japanese Occupation*. Cambridge: Cambridge University Press, 2004.

Honda, Katsuichi. *The Nanjing Massacre: A Japanese Journalist Confronts Japan's National Shame*. Translated by Karen Sandness. Armonk, N.Y.: M. E. Sharpe, 1999.

Hotta, Eri. *Pan-Asianism and Japan's War, 1931–1945*. New York: Palgrave Macmillan, 2005.

Iriye, Akira. *Power and Culture: The Japanese-American War, 1941–1945*. Cambridge, Mass.: Harvard University Press, 1981.

Lary, Diana, and Stephen MacKinnon, eds. *Scars of War: The Impact of Warfare on Modern China*. Vancouver: University of British Columbia Press, 2001.

McKinnon, Stephen R., Diana Lary, and Ezra F. Vogel, eds. *China at War: Regions of China, 1937–45*. Stanford, Calif.: Stanford University Press, 2007.

Mitter, Rana. *Forgotten Ally: China's World War II, 1937–1945*. Boston: Houghton Mifflin, 2013.

Morley, James W., ed. *The China Quagmire: Japan's Expansion on the Asian Continent, 1933–1941: Selected Translations*. New York: East Asian Institute, Columbia University, 1983.

Okita, Saburo. *Japan's Challenging Years: Reflections on My Lifetime*. Canberra: Australia-Japan Research Centre, Australian National University, 1983.

Peattie, Mark R., Edward J. Drea, and Hans J. van de Ven, eds. *The Battle for China: Essays on the Military History of the Sino-Japanese War of 1937–1945*. Stanford, Calif.: Stanford University Press, 2011.

Pomfret, John. *The Beautiful Country and the Middle Kingdom: America and China, 1776 to the Present*. New York: Henry Holt, 2016.

Qiu, Peipei. *Chinese Comfort Women: Testimonies from Imperial Japan's Sex Slaves*. Vancouver: University of British Columbia Press, 2013.

Rabe, John. *The Good Man of Nanking: The Diaries of John Rabe*. Edited by Erwin Wickert. New York: Knopf, 1998.

Taylor, Jay. *The Generalissimo: Chiang Kai-shek and the Struggle for Modern China*. Cambridge, Mass.: Belknap Press of Harvard University Press, 2009.

Van de Ven, Hans J., Diana Lary, and Stephen R. MacKinnon, eds. *Negotiating China's Destiny in World War II*. Stanford, Calif.: Stanford University Press, 2015.

Wakabayashi, Bob Tadashi, ed. *The Nanking Atrocity, 1937–38: Complicating the Picture*. New York: Berghahn Books, 2007.

Wakeman, Frederic E., Jr. *Spymaster: Dai Li and the Chinese Secret Service.* Berkeley: University of California Press, 2003.

CHAPTER 9. THE COLLAPSE OF THE JAPANESE
EMPIRE AND THE COLD WAR, 1945–1972

Barnett, A. Doak. *China and the Major Powers in East Asia.* Washington, D.C.: Brookings Institution, 1977. [See especially part 2, "China and Japan."]

Bix, Herbert P. *Hirohito and the Making of Modern Japan.* New York: HarperCollins, 2000.

Braddock, C. W. *Japan and the Sino-Soviet Alliance, 1950–1964: In the Shadow of the Monolith.* New York: Palgrave Macmillan, 2004.

Chen, Jian. *China's Road to the Korean War: The Making of the Sino-American Confrontation.* New York: Columbia University Press, 1994.

Cumings, Bruce. *Korea's Place in the Sun: A Modern History.* New York: W. W. Norton, 1997.

Curtis, Gerald L. *The Japanese Way of Politics.* New York: Columbia University Press, 1988.

———. *The Logic of Japanese Politics: Leaders, Institutions, and the Limits of Change.* New York: Columbia University Press, 1999.

Dower, John W. *Empire and Aftermath: Yoshida Shigeru and the Japanese Experience, 1878–1954.* Cambridge, Mass.: Council on East Asian Studies, Harvard University, 1979.

Dreyer, June Teufel. *Middle Kingdom and Empire of the Rising Sun: Sino-Japanese Relations, Past and Present.* Oxford: Oxford University Press, 2016.

Finn, Richard B. *Winners in Peace: MacArthur, Yoshida, and Postwar Japan.* Berkeley: University of California Press, 1992.

Fogel, Joshua A. *Nakae Ushikichi in China: The Mourning of Spirit.* Cambridge, Mass.: Council on East Asian Studies, Harvard University, 1989.

Fuess, Harald, ed. *The Japanese Empire in East Asia and Its Postwar Legacy.* Munich: Iudicium, 1998.

Fukui, Haruhiko. *Party in Power: The Japanese Liberal-Democrats and Policy-Making.* Berkeley: University of California Press, 1970.

Harrison, James P. *The Long March to Power: A History of the Chinese Communist Party, 1921–72.* New York: Praeger, 1972.

Heer, Paul J. *Mr. X and the Pacific: George F. Kennan and American Policy in East Asia.* Ithaca, N.Y.: Cornell University Press, 2018.

Hoppens, Robert. *The China Problem in Postwar Japan: Japanese National Identity and Sino-Japanese Relations.* London: Bloomsbury Academic, 2015.

Itoh, Mayumi. *Pioneers of Sino-Japanese Relations: Liao and Takasaki.* New York: Palgrave Macmillan, 2012.

Jager, Sheila Miyoshi. *Brothers at War: The Unending Conflict in Korea.* New York: W. W. Norton, 2013.

Kawai, Kazuo. *Japan's American Interlude.* Chicago: University of Chicago Press, 1960.

King, Amy. *China-Japan Relations after World War Two: Empire, Industry and War, 1949–1971.* Cambridge: Cambridge University Press, 2016.

Kokubun, Ryosei, Soeya Yoshihide, Takahara Akio, and Kawashima Shin. *Japan-China Relations in the Modern Era.* Edited by Keith Krulak. London: Routledge, 2017.

Kushner, Barak. *Men to Devils, Devils to Men: Japanese War Crimes and Chinese Justice.* Cambridge, Mass.: Harvard University Press, 2015.

Lee, Chae-Jin. *China and Japan: New Economic Diplomacy.* Stanford, Calif.: Hoover Institution Press, 1984.

———. *Japan Faces China: Political and Economic Relations in the Postwar Era.* Baltimore: Johns Hopkins University Press, 1976.

Levine, Steven I. *Anvil of Victory: The Communist Revolution in Manchuria, 1945–1948.* New York: Columbia University Press, 1987.

Minear, Richard. *Victor's Justice: The Tokyo War Crimes Trial.* Princeton, N.J.: Princeton University Press, 1971.

Oberdorfer, Don. *Senator Mansfield: The Extraordinary Life of a Great American Statesman and Diplomat.* Washington, D.C.: Smithsonian Books, 2003.

———. *Two Koreas: A Contemporary History.* Reading, Mass.: Addison-Wesley, 1997.

Ogata, Sadako. "The Business Community and Japanese Foreign Policy: Normalization of Relations with the People's Republic of China." In *The Foreign Policy of Modern Japan,* edited by Robert A. Scalapino. Berkeley: University of California Press, 1977.

Okita, Saburo. *Japan's Challenging Years: Reflections on My Lifetime.* Canberra: Australia-Japan Research Centre, Australian National University, 1983.

Pomfret, John. *The Beautiful Country and the Middle Kingdom: America and China, 1776 to the Present.* New York: Henry Holt, 2016.

Pyle, Kenneth B. *Japan in the American Century.* Cambridge, Mass.: Belknap Press of Harvard University Press, 2018.

Samuels, Richard J. *"Rich Nation, Strong Army": National Security and the Technological Transformation of Japan.* Ithaca, N.Y.: Cornell University Press, 1994.

Schaller, Michael. *The American Occupation of Japan: The Origins of the Cold War in Asia.* Oxford: Oxford University Press, 1985.

Seraphim, Franziska. *War Memory and Social Politics in Japan, 1945–2005.* Cambridge, Mass.: Harvard University Asia Center, 2006.

Shiroyama, Saburo. *War Criminal: The Life and Death of Hirota Koki.* Tokyo: Ko-dansha, 1974.

Soeya, Yoshihide. *Japan's Economic Diplomacy with China, 1945–1978.* Oxford: Clarendon Press, 1998.

Takamine, Tsukasa. *Japan's Development Aid to China: The Long-Running Foreign Policy of Engagement.* London: Routledge, 2006.

Thayer, Nathaniel B. *How the Conservatives Rule Japan.* Princeton, N.J.: Princeton University Press, 1969.

Togo, Kazuhiko. *Japan's Foreign Policy, 1954–2003: The Quest for a Proactive Policy.* Leiden: Brill, 2005.

Tsui, Chak Wing David. *China's Military Intervention in Korea: Its Origin and Objectives.* Bloomington, Ind.: Trafford Publishing, 2015.

Wakabayashi, Bob Tadashi, ed. *The Nanking Atrocity, 1937–38: Complicating the Picture.* New York: Berghahn Books, 2007.

Walder, Andrew G. *China under Mao: A Revolution Derailed.* Cambridge, Mass.: Harvard University Press, 2015.

Watt, Lori. *When Empire Comes Home: Repatriation and Reintegration in Postwar Japan.* Cambridge, Mass.: Harvard University Asia Center, 2009.

Whiting, Allen S. *China Eyes Japan.* Berkeley: University of California Press, 1989.

CHAPTER 10. WORKING TOGETHER, 1972–1992

Armstrong, Shiro Patrick. "The Japan-China Relationship: Distance, Institutions, and Politics." Ph.D. diss., Australian National University, 2009.

Barnett, A. Doak. *China and the Major Powers in East Asia.* Washington, D.C.: Brookings Institution, 1977.

Berger, Thomas U. *Cultures of Antimilitarism: National Security in Germany and Japan.* Baltimore: Johns Hopkins University Press, 1998.

———. *War, Guilt, and World Politics after World War II.* Cambridge: Cambridge University Press, 2012.

Destler, I. M., Haruhiko Fukui, and Hideo Sato. *The Textile Wrangle: Conflict in Japanese-American Relations, 1969–1979.* Ithaca, N.Y.: Cornell University Press, 1979.

Finger, Thomas, ed. *Uneasy Partnerships: China's Engagement with Japan, the Koreas, and Russia in the Era of Reform.* Stanford, Calif.: Stanford University Press, 2017.

Fuess, Harald, ed. *The Japanese Empire in East Asia and Its Postwar Legacy.* Munich: Iudicium, 1998.

Funabashi, Yoichi, ed. *Reconciliation in the Asia-Pacific.* Washington, D.C.: United States Institute of Peace Press, 2003.

Hoppens, Robert. *The China Problem in Postwar Japan: Japanese National Identity and Sino-Japanese Relations*. London: Bloomsbury Academic, 2015.

Kokubun, Ryosei. "The Politics of Foreign Economic Policy-Making in China: The Case of Plant Cancellations with Japan." *China Quarterly*, no. 105 (March 1986): 19–44.

Lee, Chae-Jin. *China and Japan: New Economic Diplomacy*. Stanford, Calif.: Hoover Institution Press, 1984.

———. *Japan Faces China: Political and Economic Relations in the Postwar Era*. Baltimore: Johns Hopkins University Press, 1976.

Pei Hua 裴华. *ZhongRi waijiao fengyunzhong de Deng Xiaoping* 中日外交风云中的邓小平 (Deng Xiaoping in the whirlwind of Sino-Japanese relations). Beijing: Zhongyang wenxian chubanshe, 2002.

Okita, Saburo. *A Life in Economic Diplomacy*. Canberra: Australia-Japan Research Centre, Australian National University, 1993.

Qian Qichen. *Ten Episodes in China's Diplomacy*. With a foreword by Ezra F. Vogel. New York: HarperCollins, 2005.

Rose, Caroline. *Interpreting History in Sino-Japanese Relations: A Case Study in Political Decision-Making*. London: Routledge, 1998.

Sato, Seizaburo, Ken'ichi Koyama, and Shumpei Kumon. *Postwar Politician: The Life of Former Prime Minister Masayoshi Ohira*. Translated by William R. Carter. Tokyo: Kodansha, 1990.

Schaller, Michael. *Altered States: The United States and Japan since the Occupation*. Oxford: Oxford University Press, 1997.

Soeya, Yoshihide. *Japan's Economic Diplomacy with China, 1945–1978*. Oxford: Clarendon Press, 1998.

Sugimoto Nobuyuki 杉本信行. *Daichi no hōkō: Moto Shanhai sōryoji ga mita Chūgoku* 大地の咆哮: 元上海総領事が見た中国 (The roar of the earth: China as seen by a former consul general in Shanghai). Tokyo: PHP Kenkyujyo, 2006.

Takamine, Tsukasa. *Japan's Development Aid to China: The Long-Running Foreign Policy of Engagement*. London: Routledge, 2006.

Vogel, Ezra F. *Deng Xiaoping and the Transformation of China*. Cambridge, Mass.: Belknap Press of Harvard University Press, 2011.

Vogel, Ezra F., Yuan Ming, and Tanaka Akihiko, eds. *The Age of Uncertainty: The U.S.-China-Japan Triangle from Tiananmen (1989) to 9/11 (2001)*. Harvard East Asian monographs online. Cambridge, Mass.: Harvard University Asia Center, 2004.

———. *The Golden Age of the U.S.-China-Japan Triangle, 1972–1989*. Cambridge, Mass.: Harvard University Asia Center, 2002.

Whiting, Allen. *China Eyes Japan*. Berkeley: University of California Press, 1989.

Zhao, Quansheng. *Japanese Policymaking: The Politics behind Politics: Informal Mechanisms and the Making of China Policy*. Westport, Conn.: Praeger, 1993.

CHAPTER 11. THE DETERIORATION OF SINO-JAPANESE
RELATIONS, 1992–2018

Berger, Thomas U. *War, Guilt, and World Politics after World War II*. Cambridge: Cambridge University Press, 2012.

Bush, Richard C. *The Perils of Proximity: China-Japan Security Relations*. Washington, D.C.: Brookings Institution Press, 2010.

Curtis, Gerald, Ryosei Kokubun, and Wang Jisi, eds. *Getting the Triangle Straight: Managing China-Japan-US Relations*. Tokyo: Japan Center for International Exchange, 2010.

Dreyer, June Teufel. *Middle Kingdom and Empire of the Rising Sun: Sino-Japanese Relations, Past and Present*. Oxford: Oxford University Press, 2016.

Drysdale, Peter, and Dong Zhang, eds. *Japan and China: Rivalry or Cooperation in East Asia?* Canberra: Asia-Pacific Press of Australian National University, 2000.

Emmott, Bill. *Rivals: How the Power Struggle between China, India, and Japan Will Shape Our Next Decade*. Orlando, Fla.: Harcourt, 2008.

Fogel, Joshua A., ed. *The Nanjing Massacre in History and Historiography*. Berkeley: University of California Press, 2000.

Fravel, M. Taylor. *Active Defense: China's Military Strategy since 1949*. Princeton, N.J.: Princeton University Press, 2019.

———. "Explaining China's Escalation over the Senkaku (Diaoyu) Islands." *Global Summitry* 2, no. 1 (June 2016): 24–37.

———. *Strong Borders, Secure Nation: Cooperation and Conflict in China's Territorial Disputes*. Princeton, N.J.: Princeton University Press, 2008.

French, Howard W. *Everything under the Heavens: How the Past Helps Shape China's Push for Global Power*. New York: Knopf, 2017.

Green, Michael J., and Patrick M. Cronin, eds. *The U.S.-Japan Alliance: Past, Present, and Future*. New York: Council on Foreign Relations Press, 1999.

Gries, Peter Hays. *China's New Nationalism: Pride, Politics, and Diplomacy*. Berkeley: University of California Press, 2004.

Hayton, Bill. *The South China Sea: The Struggle for Power in Asia*. New Haven, Conn.: Yale University Press, 2014.

He, Yinan. *The Search for Reconciliation: Sino-Japanese and German-Polish Relations since World War II*. Cambridge: Cambridge University Press, 2009.

Jager, Sheila Miyoshi, and Rana Mitter, eds. *Ruptured Histories: War, Memory, and the Post-Cold War in Asia*. Cambridge, Mass.: Harvard University Press, 2007.

King, Ambrose Yeo-chi. *China's Great Transformation: Selected Essays on Confucianism, Modernization, and Democracy*. Hong Kong: Chinese University Press, 2018.

Kokubun, Ryosei, Yoshihide Soeya, Akio Takahara, and Shin Kawashima. *Japan-China Relations in the Modern Era*. Translated by Keith Krulak. London: Routledge, 2017.

Lam, Peng Er. *China-Japan Relations in the 21st Century: Antagonism Despite Interdependency*. London: Palgrave Macmillan, 2017.

Ma Licheng马立诚. *Chouhen meiyou weilai: ZhongRi guanxi xin siwei* 仇恨没有未来: 中日关系新思维 (Hatred has no future: China's new thinking on Japan). Hong Kong: Zhonghe chuban youxian gongsi, 2013.

Okamoto, Yukio. "Journey through U.S.-Japan Relations." Unpublished manuscript, 2018.

Pugliese, Giulio, and Aurelio Insasa. *Sino-Japanese Power Politics: Might, Money and Minds*. London: Palgrave Macmillan, 2017.

Reilly, James. *Strong Society, Smart State: The Rise of Public Opinion in China's Japan Policy*. New York: Columbia University Press, 2012.

Rose, Caroline. *Interpreting History in Sino-Japanese Relations: A Case Study in Political Decision-Making*. London: Routledge, 1998.

Seraphim, Franziska. *War Memory and Social Politics in Japan, 1945–2005*. Cambridge, Mass.: Harvard University Asia Center, 2006.

Shambaugh, David, ed. *Power Shift: China and Asia's New Dynamics*. Berkeley: University of California Press, 2006.

Smith, Sheila A. *Intimate Rivals: Japanese Domestic Politics and a Rising China*. New York: Columbia University Press, 2014.

Soeya, Yoshihide. *Japan's Economic Diplomacy with China, 1945–1978*. Oxford: Clarendon Press, 1998.

Suganuma, Unryu. *Sovereign Rights and Territorial Space in Sino-Japanese Relations: Irredentism and the Diaoyu / Senkaku Islands*. Honolulu: University of Hawai'i Press, 2000.

Takamine, Tsukasa. *Japan's Development Aid to China: The Long-Running Foreign Policy of Engagement*. London: Routledge, 2006.

Tam, King-fai, Timothy Y. Tsu, and Sandra Wilson, eds. *Chinese and Japanese Films on the Second World War*. London: Routledge, 2014.

Tanaka, Yuki. *Hidden Horrors: Japanese War Crimes in World War II*. Boulder, Colo.: Westview Press, 1996.

Togo, Kazuhiko. *Japan's Foreign Policy, 1945–2003*. 3rd ed. Boston: Brill, 2010.

Vogel, Ezra F., Yuan Ming, and Tanaka Akihiko, eds. *The Age of Uncertainty: The U.S.-China-Japan Triangle from Tiananmen (1989) to 9/11 (2001)*. Harvard East Asian monographs online. Cambridge, Mass.: Harvard University Asia Center, 2004.

Wan, Ming. *Sino-Japanese Relations: Interaction, Logic, and Transformation*. Washington, D.C.: Woodrow Wilson Center Press; Stanford, Calif.: Stanford University Press, 2006.

Wang, Gungwu. *Ideas Won't Keep: The Struggle for China's Future.* Singapore: Eastern Universities Press, 2003.

Wang, Zheng. "National Humiliation, History Education, and the Politics of Historical Memory: Patriotic Education Campaign in China." *International Studies Quarterly* 52, no. 4 (December 2008): 783–806.

Weiss, Jessica Chen. *Powerful Patriots: National Protest in China's Foreign Relations.* Oxford: Oxford University Press, 2014.

Yang, Daqing, et al., eds. *Toward a History beyond Borders: Contentious Issues in Sino-Japanese Relations.* Cambridge, Mass.: Harvard University Asia Center, 2012.

ACKNOWLEDGMENTS

My two collaborators in this project are Paula Harrell and Richard Dyck. Paula is the main author of Chapter 5, which is based on her research. She read every chapter of the book in early draft form and offered detailed, informed suggestions. As the manuscript neared completion, she reread every chapter and again offered wise comments on both content and organization. Rick is the main author of Chapter 7, which is based on his research, and the author of the biography of Jiang Baili in this volume. He did an amazing amount of reading while working as a businessman, and he offered many helpful suggestions for other chapters. Both Paula and Rick are an inspiration and a joy to work with.

For acknowledgments to those who gave me help with specific chapters, please see the headnote to each chapter in the Notes section.

I owe special thanks to Joshua Fogel for reading the entire manuscript and advising me on revisions. Fogel, the world's leading specialist on Sino-Japanese history, for four decades has worked in the trenches, reading Japanese and Chinese sources, and raising the level of our understanding through his research, writings, translations, and editing.

Paul Cohen, an eminent Chinese historian, provided detailed comments on the entire manuscript that helped me correct many errors. Andrew Gordon, an outstanding scholar of Japan, kindly read through relevant parts of the manuscript and broadened my perspective. Gerald Curtis, the West's preeminent specialist on modern Japanese politics, was kind enough to read the postwar chapters and offer advice. Paul Evans, Yen-lin Chung, Kato Yoshikazu, and Joseph Schmelzeis graciously helped me broaden my vision in the final chapters. Colleagues at Harvard's Fairbank Center, Reischauer Institute, Asia Center, and the Program on U.S.-Japan Relations provided a wonderful intellectual atmosphere in which to conduct the work, and the staff members went out of their way to be helpful. I owe special thanks to Bill Overholt, Bill Hsiao, Holly Angell, Jorge Espada, and Shinju Fujihira.

Dou Xinyuan, who was my friend, my assistant, and my teacher during all of my research on China for more than three decades, was extraordinarily helpful in improving my understanding of Chinese perspectives from the time he served as my guide in Guangdong in the 1980s. He passed away suddenly, several months before the completion of this book. I benefited from the knowledge and advice of Dr. Wu Huaizhong of the Japan Research Center of the Chinese Academy of Social Sciences, Professor Li Tingjiang of Tsinghua University and Chuo University, and Professor Masuo Chisako of Kyushu University, who gave me detailed advice on content and helped me find other people and sources to further my research. Osawa Hajime and Iwatani Nobu, Ye Minlei and the staff of The Chinese University Press, Hong Kong, and its anonymous readers, kindly helped correct many errors. In some cases, my conclusions differ from those of my advisers; none of them should be held responsible for my conclusions. Nancy Hearst, the outstanding librarian of the Fairbank Collection in the Fung Library at Harvard, was my adviser, my research assistant in finding sources, my proofreader, and my copyeditor.

My wife, Charlotte Ikels, made every effort to be patient with a workaholic for the long years it took to complete this volume. She was a wonderful sounding board as I began to get an overview of the various time periods. She read the entire manuscript and gave professional as well as editorial advice.

Index